Standard & Poor's
100 Best Dividend-Paying Stocks

Standard & Poor's 100 Best Dividend-Paying Stocks

Standard & Poor's

McGraw-Hill
New York   San Francisco   Washington, D.C.   Auckland   Bogotá
Caracas   Lisbon   London   Madrid   Mexico City   Milan
Montreal   New Delhi   San Juan   Singapore
Sydney   Tokyo   Toronto

FOR STANDARD & POOR'S
Vice President, Publications, S&P Equity Services: Ron Oliver.
Managing Editor: Joseph Spiers
Associate Publisher: Frank LoVaglio.

McGraw-Hill

A Division of The McGraw·Hill Companies

1 2 3 4 5 6 7 8 9 0   DOC/DOC   9 0 2 1 0 9 8 7

ISBN 0-07-052556-0

The sponsoring editor for this book was Allyson Arias, the editing supervisor was Jim Halston, and the production supervisor was Claire B. Stanley. The front matter and section opening materials were set by Priscilla Beer of McGraw-Hill's Professional Book Group composition unit.

Printed and bound by R. R. Donnelley & Sons Company.

McGraw-Hill books are available at special quantity discounts to use as premiums and sales promotions, or for use in corporate training programs. For more information, please write to the Director of Special Sales, McGraw-Hill, 11 West 19th Street, New York, NY 10011. Or contact your local bookstore.

This publication is designed to provide accurate and authoritative information in regard to the subject matter covered. It is sold with the understanding that the publisher is not engaged in rendering legal, accounting or other professional service. If legal advice or other expert assistance is required, the services of a competent professional person should be sought.
—From a declaration of principles jointly adopted by a committee of the American Bar Association and a committee of publishers

---

This book is printed on recycled, acid-free paper containing a minimum of 50% recycled, de-inked fiber.

Contents

ABOUT THE AUTHORS

Standard & Poor's, a division of The McGraw-Hill Companies, Inc., is the nation's leading securities information company. It provides a broad range of financial services, including the respected debt ratings and stock rankings, advisory services, data guides, and the most closely watched and widely reported gauges of stock market activity—the S&P 500, S&P MidCap 400, S&P Small Cap 600, and the S&P SuperComposite 1500 stock price indexes. S&P products are marketed around the world and used extensively by financial professionals and individual investors.

Joseph Tigue and Joseph Lisanti, who authored this book's introduction, are Managing Editor and Senior Editor, respectively, of *The Outlook*, Standard & Poor's investment advisory newsletter. They are also the authors of *The Dividend Rich Investor,* published in 1997 by McGraw-Hill.

Introduction

Investors looking for income stocks have had a tough row to hoe over the past few years. Thanks to a roaring bull market, dividend yields have been paltry. The yield on the S&P 500 index, a proxy for the market as a whole, has been below 3% for four years. In fact, this year, it has pretty much stayed below 2%. Nevertheless, we believe the 100 stocks profiled on the following pages fit the bill for income investors. We have culled them from Standard & Poor's vast database and believe they are, as this book is entitled, the best dividend-paying stocks.

We have chosen the issues not on dividend yield alone, of course. As we point out in *The Dividend Rich Investor* (McGraw-Hill, 1997), which lays out the rationale for dividend investing, *never* buy a stock solely because its dividend yield is a juicy one. A well-above-average yield could mean that the stock price is depressed either because the company's earnings have been poor or some adverse news is expected. (Remember, the price of a stock and its yield move in the opposite direction.) A lofty yield, therefore, could presage either a dividend cut or dividend omission in the not too distant future.

We've split the best 100 dividend-paying stocks into two categories. The first 50 are stocks that don't offer very high current yields, *but* have boosted their dividends rapidly and regularly over the years. We expect them to continue to increase payments to shareholders. The vast majority carry a high S&P quality ranking (see page xv for definitions). The second category comprises 50 issues that have above-average yields and, in our opinion, safe dividends.

If you're looking for income from stocks, we believe it is impor-
tant that you own both high-yielding stocks where the dividend is
considered safe, as well as issues whose yields may be below average
but where dividends likely will be hiked regularly. The dividend
growers help you to keep ahead of inflation.

When dividend payments are hiked regularly, the yield on your
original investment can increase dramatically over time. Take
Campbell Soup, which is profiled in this book. If you had bought
the stock of the well-known food company in 1986 at a median
price of 16 (adjusted for stock splits), you would have received a
dividend of $0.33 for a 2.1% yield. Based on the current indicated
annual dividend rate of $1.54, however, you would be getting a
return of 9.6% on your 1986 cost. In other words, long-term hold-
ers of Campbell Soup now almost match the market's roughly 10%
historical annual total return with dividends alone. Campbell's dividend has increased at an annual rate of 17% over the past ten
years; the annual total return (appreciation plus dividends) is
21.4%. Stocks whose dividends have been raised steadily, as is the
case with Campbell and others in this book's first category, tend to
appreciate strongly in price. In addition to food companies, the
first group also contains pharmaceutical companies, makers of
household products, manufacturers, and a large number of financial services companies, including banks.

The second category—high yielders—includes the usual
income-type stocks such as electric and gas utilities, certain banks,
real estate investment trusts, and telephone companies.

Years ago, it was a simple matter to pick stocks in these industry groups, especially the electric utilities, which generally were the
highest yielders and were considered safe enough for widows and
orphans. Deregulation has changed all that. Whereas markets for
electricity were strictly delineated by geographic lines in the past,
utilities are now facing an increasingly competitive environment.
Companies have been given the freedom to cross into each other's
territories for wholesale transactions, while retail competition will
soon be seen.

A utility's ability to cut costs has become one of the most

important factors in its efforts to remain viable. Location is another factor: A successful utility will likely be located in a service area with a growing population and a healthy economy. Other considerations include ample access to a low-cost source of fuel, a low percentage of industrial customers (where competition will be most intense), and limited exposure to high-cost nuclear assets.

Telephone stocks are similar to utilities in that they were once regarded as good investments for conservative income investors. Like the utilities, telephone companies were highly regulated and could be depended on for steady dividend increases and rising stock prices. Now, the market is more competitive.

For example, Bell regionals such as Ameritech, Bell Atlantic, BellSouth, SBC Communications, and US West, as well as the long distance carriers (AT&T, MCI Communications, and Sprint) are investing in growth opportunities, such as cellular telephones, cable, and international ventures, and have cut back on dividend increases. But some of the stocks still offer above-average yields and are well-situated to compete in the new environment. Four of them—Alltel, Ameritech, Bell Atlantic, and GTE—are included in this book.

Four high-yielding banks are also profiled. Banks generally have paid dividends for many years and are among the most consistent dividend boosters. The stocks, however, have enjoyed a spectacular price run-up in recent years, thanks to low interest rates, good loan and fee growth, and merger activity. Thus, yields are relatively low. The stocks we've picked to be included in this section of the book—American Bank of Connecticut, Bankers Trust, CoreStates Financial, and Merchants New York Bancorp—enjoy both above-average yields and favorable growth prospects.

Real estate investment trusts (REITs) currently carry the highest yields. REITs, which are enjoying stable interest rates and a healthy real estate environment, are tax-advantaged corporations that permit small investors to share in the benefits of commercial property ownership or mortgage lending. REITs pay no taxes, providing they pay out at least 95% of their income in dividends. We believe Capstead Mortgage, CRIMI Mae, Federal Realty Investment Trust, Health & Retirement Properties, Meditrust,

Merry Land & Investment, and Weingarten are among the better-situated REITs.

Several companies in this book could have easily fit into either the first or second group. Meditrust, Merchants New York Bancorp, Philip Morris, and UST all have strong dividend growth histories as well as relatively high current yields. We've included all of these stocks in the second group—above-average yielders—because, with the market so strong, it is more difficult to find good higher-yielding issues.

WHY NOW?

The strong stock market (the S&P 500 was up 34% in 1995 and more than 20% in 1996) may lead many investors to ask, "Who needs dividends?" Why concern yourself with a modest quarterly cash payment when stock prices climb higher almost daily? Many companies agree, which is why the market's yield is at an historic low. So why a book about the 100 best dividend-paying stocks now?

An old Wall Street adage is "Trees don't grow to the sky." Returns such as we have seen recently are unsustainable over the long run. That doesn't mean that the stock market necessarily will crash any time soon, but over the next decade, you probably won't see gains of the magnitude that we have had so far in the 1990s.

History supports us: Over the last seven decades, the market's annual total return has averaged a little more than 10%. That time frame encompasses the bull market of the late 1920s, the 1929 crash and the Great Depression, the steady gains of the 1950s, the go-go 1960s, the secular bear market of the 1970s, and the current huge advance that began in 1982.

Many people argue that the market will continue to rise because things are different now. And it's true. Things are different. We now have near-perfect conditions—low inflation paired with good growth in corporate profits, while the U.S. is again the world's leading economy with our goods in demand around the globe. But are these conditions permanent? Just a few years ago, U.S. companies feared that Japan would dominate the world's economy. Today, the Japanese economy is mired in difficulties.

What could derail the current U.S. stock market euphoria? A step-up in inflation, higher interest rates, a stronger dollar that makes U.S. goods less competitive overseas, war, political scandal, or simply the fear of any of these could give investors the jitters. "Yes, but," you may be saying, "what about Baby Boomers saving for retirement in their 401(k) plans? They won't take money out of stocks." Maybe not, but if they stop putting as much into stocks, the market advance could come to a halt. When a 6% return from a guaranteed investment contract begins to look better than no return (or even a loss) in the stock market, many people will redirect retirement assets. For a large number of retirement plan participants, that can be accomplished in a day with just one phone call.

So why a book about the best dividend-paying stocks now? Consider dividends as insurance against the day when the market enters a period of underperformance. And just as you don't wait for your house to burn down to buy homeowners insurance, you shouldn't wait for the market to stall or even skid before investing in dividend-paying stocks.

We believe you should include dividend-paying stocks in your portfolio for several reasons:

- They produce a real return now. When you invest in stocks that pay no dividends, your returns are potential until you sell.
- Dividend-paying stocks give you a leg up on your goal of making money in the market. A stock with a secure dividend that yields 5% will take you almost halfway to matching the average annual total return of the market over the last 70 years.
- Dividend-paying stocks cut down the volatility of your portfolio. In the 1987 crash, stocks that paid the highest dividends fell considerably less than those that paid no dividends.
- Stocks with regularly growing dividends provide an ongoing hedge against inflation and steadily increase the return on your original investment.

TIPS ON USING THIS BOOK

When you choose stocks from this book for your portfolio, be certain to diversify by industry group. Select a mix rather than putting all of your eggs in one industry basket. Invest for the long term. If you are ten or more years from retirement, growing dividend stocks should make up a larger portion of your portfolio.

What follows are detailed descriptions of what we believe are the 100 best dividend-paying stocks now. Some words of explanation are in order before you proceed. "Best" is necessarily a subjective term. We have selected these issues primarily on the basis of strong dividend growth or solid current yield. In doing so, we have given less weight to other valuation methods, including Standard & Poor's Stock Appreciation Ranking System (STARS), which uses fundamental analysis to predict a stock's near-term appreciation potential. Description of STARS and other ranking instruments are in the Notes section.

The stocks in this book are our choices for the best dividend-paying issues as of mid-February 1997. Many will continue to be among the best dividend stocks a year or two from now. But some will fall off the list. Remember, the only constant in life is change. Companies can raise or cut their dividends, change management or lines of business, develop major innovative products, or face potent new competitors. In the months and years ahead, you can receive updated information on any stock in this book by ordering the latest version of the company's S&P Stock Report. Touch-tone phone users may obtain reports by fax or mail. A basic two-page Stock Report is $6 and quantity discounts are available. For a free sample, call 800-292-0808. Stock Reports are also sold via S&P's website: http://www.stockinfo.standardpoor.com.

Joseph Tigue
Joseph Lisanti

NOTES

STARS RANKINGS:

*****Buy—Expected to be among the best performers over the next 12 months.

****Accumulate—Expected to be an above-average performer.

***Hold—Expected to be an average performer.

**Avoid—Likely to be a below-average performer.

*Sell—Expected to be a well-below-average performer and fall in price.

QUANTITATIVE EVALUATIONS:

Outlook—Using S&Ps exclusive prorietary quantitative model, stocks are ranked in one of five groups—ranging from Group 5, listing the most undervalued stocks, to Group 1, the most overvalued issues. Group 5 stocks are expected to generally outperform all others. To identify a stock that is in a strengthening or weakening position, a positive (+) or negative (-) Timing Index is placed next to the ranking.

Fair Value—The price at which a stock should sell today as calculated by S&P's computers using our quantitative model based on the company's earnings, growth potential, return on equity relative to the S&P 500 and its industry group, price to book ratio history, current yield relative to the S&P 500, and other factors. The current fair price is shown given today's S&P 500 level. Each stock's Fair Value is calculated weekly.

Risk—Rates the volatility of the stock's price over the past year.

Earnings and Dividend Ranking (Quality ranking)—S&P's appraisal of a stock's growth and stability of earnings and dividends over the past 10 years. The highest letter ranking is A+ and the lowest is C. Stocks of companies with less than 10 years of earnings history and those in industries not included in the ranking system are not ranked (NR). Quality rankings are not intended to predict stock price movements.

Technical Evaluation—In researching the past market history of prices and trading volume for each company, S&P's computer models apply special technical methods and formulas to identify and project price trends for the stock. They analyze how the price of the stock is moving and evaluate the interrelationships between the moving averages to ultimately determine buy or sell signals—and to decide whether they're bullish, neutral, or bearish for the stock. The date the signals were initiated is also provided so you can take advantage of a recent or ongoing uptrend in price, or see how a stock has performed over time since our last technical signal was generated.

Relative Strength Rank—Shows, on a scale of 1 to 99, how the stock has performed compared with all other companies in S&P's universe of companies on a rolling 13-week basis.

Insider Activity—Gives an insight as to insider sentiment by showing whether directors, officers, and key employees—who may have proprietary information not available to the general public—are buying or selling the company's stock during the most recent six months.

Standard & Poor's 100 Best Dividend-Paying Stocks

STOCKS WITH STRONG DIVIDEND GROWTH

18-FEB-97 Industry:
Drugs

Summary: This company is a leading maker of pharmaceutical, nutritional, and hospital and laboratory products.

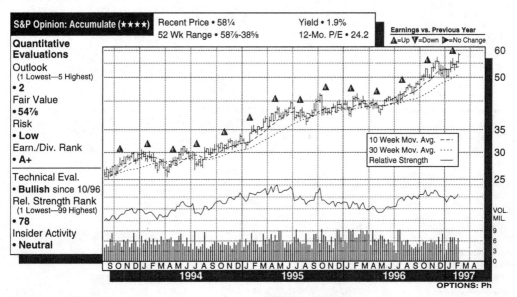

S&P Opinion: Accumulate (★★★★)

Recent Price • 58¼	Yield • 1.9%
52 Wk Range • 58⅞-38⅝	12-Mo. P/E • 24.2

Quantitative Evaluations

Outlook
(1 Lowest—5 Highest)
• 2

Fair Value
• 54⅞

Risk
• **Low**

Earn./Div. Rank
• **A+**

Technical Eval.
• **Bullish** since 10/96

Rel. Strength Rank
(1 Lowest—99 Highest)
• 78

Insider Activity
• **Neutral**

Earnings vs. Previous Year
▲=Up ▼=Down ▶=No Change

10 Week Mov. Avg. - - -
30 Week Mov. Avg. ·····
Relative Strength —

OPTIONS: Ph

Overview - 18-FEB-97

Sales growth in 1997 is expected to approximate 8%-10%. Despite anticipated generic erosion in the Hytrin line by about midyear, drug sales should benefit from continued strong gains in established lines such as Biaxin antibiotic, Depakote anticonvulsant and newer drugs such as Prevacid antiulcer agent, Norvir for HIV and Serlect for schizophrenia (presently under FDA review). Further gains are also seen for adult nutritionals, while a new improved formula of Similac should bolster the infant nutritionals business. The new CD 4000 diagnostic system, recently approved contrast agents, and new DNA probe tests should help the diagnostics business. Although MediSense (glucose monitoring products) is expected to remain slightly dilutive, overall margins should widen on the better volume and productivity enhancements. Per share comparisons should also benefit from ongoing common share repurchases.

Valuation - 18-FEB-97

The stock performed well in recent months, buoyed by solid earnings momentum and new product approvals. Near term sales should be augmented by the recent launch of Zyflo asthma treatment and anticipated FDA marketing clearance for other new drugs such as Serlect for schizophrenia and Gabitril for epilepsy. Abbott should maintain double-digit profit growth in the years ahead, fortified by dominant positions in niche pharmaceutical, adult nutritionals and diagnostic products markets; good control over costs; and a proven ability to generate lucrative new cost-saving medical products. The 1996 purchase of MediSense has given ABT entry into the rapidly growing glucose monitoring field and strategic alliances with others have expanded Abbott's position in diagnostic imaging. The shares are recommended for long-term capital appreciation.

Key Stock Statistics

S&P EPS Est. 1997	2.70	Tang. Bk. Value/Share	6.06
P/E on S&P Est. 1997	21.6	Beta	0.90
Dividend Rate/Share	1.08	Shareholders	89,800
Shs. outstg. (M)	776.8	Market cap. (B)	$ 45.3
Avg. daily vol. (M)	1.261	Inst. holdings	48%

Value of $10,000 invested 5 years ago: $ 18,875

Fiscal Year Ending Dec. 31

	1996	1995	1994	1993	1992	1991
Revenues (Million $)						
1Q	2,672	2,524	2,215	2,046	1,878	1,654
2Q	2,699	2,500	2,204	2,074	1,909	1,683
3Q	2,646	2,391	2,255	2,060	1,969	1,654
4Q	2,996	2,597	2,482	2,228	2,096	1,886
Yr.	11,013	10,012	9,156	8,408	7,852	6,877
Earnings Per Share ($)						
1Q	0.61	0.52	0.45	0.41	0.35	0.30
2Q	0.60	0.53	0.46	0.42	0.37	0.32
3Q	0.54	0.48	0.43	0.38	0.33	0.30
4Q	0.66	0.59	0.53	0.48	0.42	0.37
Yr.	2.41	2.12	1.87	1.69	1.47	1.28

Next earnings report expected: early April

Dividend Data (Dividends have been paid since 1926.)

Amount ($)	Date Decl.	Ex-Div. Date	Stock of Record	Payment Date
0.240	Jun. 14	Jul. 11	Jul. 15	Aug. 15 '96
0.240	Sep. 13	Oct. 10	Oct. 15	Nov. 15 '96
0.240	Dec. 13	Jan. 13	Jan. 15	Feb. 15 '97
0.270	Feb. 14	Apr. 11	Apr. 15	May. 15 '97

Business Summary - 18-FEB-97

Abbott Laboratories is a leading player in several growing health care markets, with an outstanding record of long-term sales and earnings growth. The company was founded in the late 19th century by Dr. Wallace C. Abbott, a pioneer of pharmaceutical medicine. Through highly successful acquisition, diversification and R&D programs, Abbott now offers a wide range of prescription pharmaceuticals, infant and adult nutritionals, and hospital and laboratory products. Foreign operations accounted for 34% of sales and 33% of profits in 1995. Sales and earnings in 1995 by product segment were divided:

	Sales	Profits
Pharmaceutical & nutritional	56%	65%
Hospital & laboratory	44%	35%

Accounting for about 30% of total sales, Abbott's pharmaceutical division represents the principal driver of future earnings growth. Key products include Biaxin (sales of $1 billion in 1996), the largest selling broad-spectrum antibiotic, which is used for a wide variety of infections including h-pylori (associated with duodenol ulcers); Hytrin ($550 million), a treatment for hypertension and enlarged prostates; and Depakote ($400 million), a leading anti-epileptic agent that is also indicated for the treatment of manic-depressive disorder. Other pharmaceutical products include Norvir protease inhibitor for AIDS, Abbokinase anti-thrombotic agent, Ogen oral estrogen, Survanta lung surfactant and Zyflo asthma treatment. Equity earnings are derived from a 50% interest in TAP Holdings, a joint venture with Takeda Chemical Industries of Japan. Major TAP drugs include Prevacid gastrointestinal agent and Lupron treatment for prostate cancer.

Nutritional businesses (about one quarter of total sales) include leading positions in infant formulas, medical nutritionals for patients with special dietary needs and enteral feeding items. Leading brands are Similac and Isomil infant formulas, Ensure medical nutritionals and the Flexiflo enteral feeding device.

Abbott is also a major producer of immunodiagnostics, offering a wide range of tests and diagnostic systems for blood banks, hospitals and laboratories. Products include intravenous and irrigation fluids and related administration equipment. The May 1996 acquisition of MediSense provided Abbott entry into the fast growing field home glucose monitoring for diabetics. Hospital items consist of anesthesia products, specialized electronic drug delivery systems, diagnostic imaging agents and other products.

Capitalization

Long Term Debt: $682,166,000 (9/96).

Per Share Data ($) (Year Ended Dec. 31)	1996	1995	1994	1993	1992	1991	1990	1989	1988	1987
Tangible Bk. Val.	NA	5.58	5.04	4.48	4.00	3.77	3.30	3.08	2.74	2.31
Cash Flow	NA	2.80	2.50	2.27	1.97	1.72	1.52	1.31	1.14	0.96
Earnings	2.41	2.12	1.87	1.69	1.47	1.28	1.11	0.97	0.84	0.70
Dividends	0.93	0.82	0.74	0.66	0.58	0.48	0.40	0.34	0.29	0.24
Payout Ratio	39%	39%	39%	39%	39%	38%	36%	35%	34%	34%
Prices - High	57 3/8	44 3/4	34	30 7/8	34 1/4	34 7/8	23 1/4	17 5/8	13 1/8	16 3/4
- Low	38 1/8	30 5/8	25 3/8	22 5/8	26 1/8	19 5/8	15 5/8	11 5/8	10 3/4	10
P/E Ratio - High	24	21	18	18	23	27	21	18	16	24
- Low	16	14	14	13	18	15	14	12	13	14
Income Statement Analysis (Million $)										
Revs.	NA	10,012	9,156	8,408	7,852	6,877	6,159	5,380	4,937	4,388
Oper. Inc.	NA	2,949	2,655	2,442	2,169	1,936	1,762	1,528	1,373	1,249
Depr.	NA	566	511	484	428	379	356	307	271	244
Int. Exp.	NA	69.0	50.0	54.0	53.0	64.0	91.0	74.0	85.0	78.0
Pretax Inc.	NA	2,396	2,167	1,943	1,739	1,544	1,351	1,194	1,055	937
Eff. Tax Rate	NA	30%	30%	28%	29%	30%	29%	28%	29%	33%
Net Inc.	NA	1,689	1,517	1,399	1,239	1,089	966	860	752	633
Balance Sheet & Other Fin. Data (Million $)										
Cash	NA	316	315	379	258	146	53.0	49.0	583	520
Curr. Assets	NA	4,227	3,876	3,586	3,232	2,891	2,461	2,103	2,353	2,156
Total Assets	NA	9,413	8,524	7,689	6,941	6,255	5,563	4,852	4,825	4,386
Curr. Liab.	NA	3,790	3,476	3,095	2,783	2,229	2,001	1,384	1,440	1,487
LT Debt	NA	435	287	307	110	125	135	147	349	271
Common Eqty.	NA	4,397	4,049	3,675	3,348	3,203	2,834	2,726	2,465	2,093
Total Cap.	NA	4,900	4,392	4,033	3,779	3,675	3,378	3,312	3,213	2,730
Cap. Exp.	NA	947	929	953	1,007	771	641	573	521	402
Cash Flow	NA	2,255	2,027	1,883	1,667	1,468	1,322	1,167	1,023	876
Curr. Ratio	NA	1.1	1.1	1.2	1.2	1.3	1.2	1.5	1.6	1.4
% LT Debt of Cap.	NA	8.9	6.5	7.6	2.9	3.4	4.0	4.4	10.9	9.9
% Net Inc.of Revs.	NA	16.9	16.6	16.6	15.8	15.8	15.7	16.0	15.2	14.4
% Ret. on Assets	NA	18.8	18.9	19.3	18.9	18.5	18.8	17.9	16.4	15.4
% Ret. on Equity	NA	40.0	39.7	40.2	38.1	36.2	35.3	33.4	33.1	32.8

Data as orig. reptd.; bef. results of disc. opers. and/or spec. items. Per share data adj. for stk. divs. as of ex-div. date. E-estimated. NA-Not Available. NM-Not Meaningful. NR-Not Ranked.

Office—100 Abbott Park Road, IL 60064.**Tel**—(708) 937-6100 **Website**—http://www.abbott.com **Chrmn & CEO**—D. L. Burnham **Pres & COO**—T. R. Hodgson. **SVP & Secy**—J. M. de Lasa. **SVP-Fin & CFO**—G. P. Coughlan. **VP & Treas**—T. C. Freyman. **Investor Contact**—Patricia Bergeron. **Dirs**—F. K. Austen, D. L. Burnham, H. L. Fuller, The Lord Hayhoe PC, T. R. Hodgson, A. F. Jacobson, D. A. Jones, B. Powell, Jr., A. B. Rand, W.A. Reynolds, W. D. Smithburg, J. R. Walter, W. L. Weiss. **Transfer Agent & Registrar**—First National Bank of Boston. **Incorporated**—in Ilinois in 1900. **Empl**—52,000 **S&P Analyst:** H. B. Saftlas

15-FEB-97

Industry:
Retail Stores

Summary: This operator of supermarkets and combination food-drug stores, the fourth largest U.S. food retailer, operates more than 815 stores in 19 states.

S&P Opinion: Hold (★★★)	Recent Price • 35½	Yield • 1.7%
	52 Wk Range • 43¾-33¾	12-Mo. P/E • 18.1

Quantitative Evaluations

Outlook
(1 Lowest—5 Highest)
• **2**

Fair Value
• **34%**

Risk
• **Low**

Earn./Div. Rank
• **A+**

Technical Eval.
• **Bearish** since 11/96

Rel. Strength Rank
(1 Lowest—99 Highest)
• **33**

Insider Activity
• **Neutral**

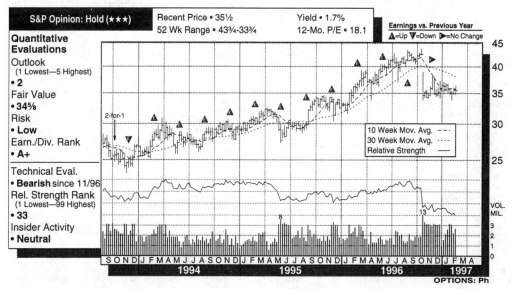

Earnings vs. Previous Year
▲=Up ▼=Down ▶=No Change

10 Week Mov. Avg.
30 Week Mov. Avg.
Relative Strength

OPTIONS: Ph

Overview - 27-JAN-97

We expect revenues to advance about 10% in FY 98 (Jan.), reflecting contributions from 60 to 70 new stores in operation, and same-store sales gains in excess of 2%. Same-store sales increases will reflect the renovation of more than 40 stores, and ABS's commitment to several new initiatives. These include company-wide investments in customer service, home meal replacement, and training at both the division and store levels. Other programs in certain markets to combat competitive store openings will include the introduction of quick meal ideas, the addition of front-end managers in all retail stores, and special services, including pharmacies and in-store banks. We expect gross margins to widen modestly on the higher volume. SG&A expense ratios should decline somewhat, on more controlled investment expenses. Strong management and a presence in areas with expanding populations continue to bode well for future earnings gains.

Valuation - 27-JAN-97

The shares have underperformed the market thus far in 1997, declining 1.1% through mid-January, versus a 6.1% rise for the S&P 500 and a 0.7% increase for the S&P Retail (Food Chains) Index. EPS gains have recently slowed from the enviable annual pace of 18% over the past decade. This reflects higher SG&A expense as a percentage of sales, as a result of rapid expansion and various investments aimed at improving ABS's competitive position. We expect EPS to rise to $2.15 in FY 98, up 10% from the $1.95 we see for FY 97. However, strong cash flows continue to provide ample funds for a substantial capital spending program and common share repurchases. With the shares recently trading at about 17X our FY 98 EPS estimate, we recommend holding the stock for now.

Key Stock Statistics

S&P EPS Est. 1997	1.95	Tang. Bk. Value/Share	8.59
P/E on S&P Est. 1997	18.2	Beta	0.11
S&P EPS Est. 1998	2.15	Shareholders	18,000
Dividend Rate/Share	0.60	Market cap. (B)	$ 8.9
Shs. outstg. (M)	251.0	Inst. holdings	43%
Avg. daily vol. (M)	0.628		

Value of $10,000 invested 5 years ago: $ 19,635

Fiscal Year Ending Jan. 31

	1997	1996	1995	1994	1993	1992
Revenues (Million $)						
1Q	3,344	3,083	2,910	2,720	2,297	2,160
2Q	3,481	3,119	2,988	2,768	2,604	2,192
3Q	3,376	3,104	2,928	2,734	2,585	2,130
4Q	—	3,279	3,069	3,062	2,687	2,199
Yr.	—	12,585	11,895	11,284	10,174	8,680
Earnings Per Share ($)						
1Q	0.45	0.39	0.34	0.29	0.13	0.22
2Q	0.48	0.42	0.37	0.30	0.25	0.22
3Q	0.42	0.42	0.37	0.25	0.27	0.22
4Q	E0.60	0.61	0.57	0.50	0.40	0.31
Yr.	E1.95	1.84	1.65	1.34	1.04	0.97

Next earnings report expected: early March

Dividend Data (Dividends have been paid since 1960.)

Amount ($)	Date Decl.	Ex-Div. Date	Stock of Record	Payment Date
0.150	Mar. 04	May. 01	May. 03	May. 25 '96
0.150	May. 24	Jul. 31	Aug. 02	Aug. 25 '96
0.150	Sep. 03	Oct. 30	Nov. 01	Nov. 25 '96
0.150	Dec. 02	Jan. 29	Jan. 31	Feb. 25 '97

A Division of The McGraw-Hill Companies

Business Summary - 27-JAN-97

At May 2, 1996, Albertson's operated 777 stores in 19 western, midwestern and southern states. The stores consisted of 646 combination food and drug units, 78 conventional units and 40 warehouse stores. As of May 2, 1996, ABS operated 37.1 million sq. ft. of retail space, 95% of which has been opened or remodeled in the last 10 years.

Combination food and drug stores range in size from 35,000 sq. ft. to 75,000 sq. ft. Selling space is divided between prescription and proprietary drugs and general merchandise, and regular supermarket products.

Conventional supermarkets range from 15,000 sq. ft. to 35,000 sq. ft. in size and offer a full line of grocery items and, in many locations, feature in-store bakeries and delicatessens.

Warehouse stores vary in size from 17,000 sq. ft. to 73,000 sq. ft. The no-frills units offer significant savings on meat and produce and from large, bulk packaging.

Retail operations are supported by 12 company-owned distribution centers. About 77% of all products purchased by company stores are supplied from facilities operated by Albertson's.

A $3.8 billion capital spending plan for the five years from 1995 through 2000 includes building 388 new stores and making 265 remodels. Square footage would rise about 8% annually. The balance of the program is earmarked for retail replacement equipment, distribution and new information systems. The company aims for a 12% return on average assets and a 15% annual gain in share earnings. During FY 97 (Jan.), ABS planned to open 68 new stores and remodel 43 existing stores. Capital expenditures for FY 97 were slated to approximate $660 million.

Important Developments

Nov. '96—During the 39 weeks ended October 31, 1996, the company repurchased 666,800 common shares, under a March 1996 authorization to buy back up to seven million shares through March 31, 1997.

Nov. '96—During the first nine months of FY 97, ABS opened 53 new stores and completed 33 remodels. Plans called for 17 additional new stores and nine remodels during the fourth quarter. In October, the company purchased a 26,200 sq. ft. food-drug store in Riverton, UT, from Gorman Foods, Inc.

Capitalization

Long Term Debt: $1,003,592,000, incl. $126,355,000 of lease obligs. (10/31/96).

Per Share Data ($)

(Year Ended Jan. 31)	1996	1995	1994	1993	1992	1991	1990	1989	1988	1987
Tangible Bk. Val.	7.75	6.65	5.48	5.24	4.54	4.06	3.47	2.99	2.51	2.22
Cash Flow	2.83	2.54	2.11	1.70	1.47	1.33	1.14	0.94	0.74	0.63
Earnings	1.84	1.65	1.34	1.05	0.97	0.88	0.74	0.61	0.47	0.38
Dividends	0.52	0.53	0.35	0.31	0.27	0.23	0.19	0.13	0.12	0.10
Payout Ratio	28%	32%	26%	30%	28%	26%	25%	22%	25%	27%
Cal. Yrs.	1995	1994	1993	1992	1991	1990	1989	1988	1987	1986
Prices - High	34⅝	30⅞	29⅝	26¾	25¾	18⅞	15⅛	9¾	8½	6¼
- Low	27¼	25⅛	23⅜	18⅜	16⅜	12¼	9⅛	6	5⅛	3⅞
P/E Ratio - High	19	19	22	26	26	22	21	16	18	17
- Low	15	15	19	18	17	14	13	10	11	10

Income Statement Analysis (Million $)

	1996	1995	1994	1993	1992	1991	1990	1989	1988	1987
Revs.	12,585	11,895	11,284	10,174	8,680	8,219	7,423	6,773	5,869	5,380
Oper. Inc.	1,059	961	826	695	548	498	428	349	290	255
Depr.	251	226	197	172	134	122	108	88.0	73.0	66.0
Int. Exp.	63.1	66.1	55.2	47.7	28.1	29.0	25.8	22.6	22.4	21.3
Pretax Inc.	759	679	552	444	406	366	310	257	212	185
Eff. Tax Rate	39%	39%	39%	38%	37%	36%	37%	37%	41%	46%
Net Inc.	465	417	340	276	258	234	197	163	125	100

Balance Sheet & Other Fin. Data (Million $)

	1996	1995	1994	1993	1992	1991	1990	1989	1988	1987
Cash	69.1	50.0	62.0	40.0	34.0	23.0	44.0	82.0	201	246
Curr. Assets	1,283	1,190	1,122	1,013	751	677	668	592	635	625
Total Assets	4,136	3,622	3,295	2,946	2,216	2,014	1,863	1,591	1,402	1,265
Curr. Liab.	1,088	1,095	990	816	652	586	555	488	440	380
LT Debt	732	512	665	508	152	159	218	177	183	187
Common Eqty.	1,953	1,688	1,389	1,388	1,199	1,088	929	800	665	594
Total Cap.	2,686	2,202	2,083	1,917	1,360	1,259	1,170	990	860	796
Cap. Exp.	656	473	456	331	273	255	303	327	194	139
Cash Flow	716	644	536	448	392	356	305	251	198	167
Curr. Ratio	1.2	1.1	1.1	1.2	1.2	1.2	1.2	1.2	1.4	1.6
% LT Debt of Cap.	27.3	23.3	31.9	26.5	11.1	12.6	18.7	17.9	21.3	23.5
% Net Inc.of Revs.	3.7	3.5	3.0	2.7	3.0	2.8	2.6	2.4	2.1	1.9
% Ret. on Assets	12.0	12.1	11.1	10.7	12.3	12.1	11.4	10.8	9.4	8.4
% Ret. on Equity	25.5	27.1	25.0	21.3	22.7	23.2	22.7	22.1	20.0	18.0

Data as orig. reptd.; bef. results of disc. opers. and/or spec. items. Per share data adj. for stk. divs. as of ex-div. date. E-Estimated. NA-Not Available. NM-Not Meaningful. NR-Not Ranked.

Office—250 Parkcenter Blvd., P.O. Box 20, Boise, ID 83726. **Tel**—(208) 385-6200. **Chrmn & CEO**—G. G. Michael. **Pres & COO**—R. L. King. **SVP-Fin & CFO**—A. C. Olson. **VP & Treas**—John Danielson. **Secy**—Kaye L. O'Riordan. **Investor Contact**—Renee Bergquist. **Dirs**—K. Albertson, A. G. Ames, C. D. Andrus, J. B. Carley, P. I. Corddry, J. B. Fery, C. A. Johnson, C. D. Lein, W. E. McCain, G. G. Michael, B. Rivera, J. B. Scott, T. L. Stevens, Jr., W. M. Storey, S. D. Symms. **Transfer Agents & Registrars**—ChaseMellon Shareholder Services, L.L.C., NYC; West One Bank, Idaho, Boise. **Incorporated**—in Idaho in 1945; reincorporated in Delaware in 1969. **Empl**— 80,000. **S&P Analyst:** Maureen C. Carini

STANDARD &POOR'S
STOCK REPORTS

ALLIED Group

64G

NYSE Symbol **GRP**

In S&P SmallCap 600

15-FEB-97

Industry: Insurance

Summary: This regional property-casualty insurance holding company specializes in personal lines, marketing its products throughout the central and western United States.

Quantitative Evaluations

Outlook (1 Lowest—5 Highest)
• 1⁻

Fair Value
• 29¼

Risk
• **Low**

Earn./Div. Rank
• **A**

Technical Eval.
• **NA**

Rel. Strength Rank (1 Lowest—99 Highest)
• 63

Insider Activity
• **Neutral**

Recent Price • 32⅝

52 Wk Range • 34¼-22⅜

Yield • 1.8%

12-Mo. P/E • 13.5

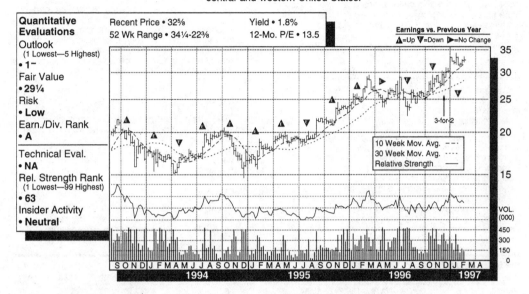

Earnings vs. Previous Year
▲=Up ▼=Down ▶=No Change

10 Week Mov. Avg. – – –
30 Week Mov. Avg. ·····
Relative Strength —

3-for-2

VOL. (000)

Business Profile - 12-FEB-97

GRP's largest operating segment includes three property and casualty insurance companies that write personal lines and small commercial lines of insurance. This segment accounts for approximately 87% of the company's total revenues. Management's stated goal is to maintain a 15% ROE by pursuing more transfer business, increasing the independent agency force, expanding the distribution system and building new territories. At December 31, 1996, GRP's invested assets totaled $819.6 million and consisted almost entirely of investment-grade fixed-income securities. Through an ESOP, employees control a significant number of voting shares. Split-adjusted dividends were raised 2.3% in December 1996.

Operational Review - 12-FEB-97

Based on a preliminary report, total revenues for 1996 rose 7.9% from those of the prior year, reflecting an 8.3% increase in premiums earned, 4.2% higher investment income and an 8.2% rise in other income. Losses and expenses climbed 9.6%, principally due to losses and loss adjusting expenses that were fueled by widespread winter storms and arctic temperatures. Pretax income declined 3.4%. After taxes at 28.4%, versus 29.1%, net income fell 2.5%, to $51,084,213 ($2.42 a share, based on 41% more shares), from $52,376,829 ($3.25).

Stock Performance - 14-FEB-97

In the past 30 trading days, GRP's shares have increased 0.77%, compared to a 8% rise in the S&P 500. Average trading volume for the past five days was 25,700 shares, compared with the 40-day moving average of 44,433 shares.

Key Stock Statistics

Dividend Rate/Share	0.60	Shareholders	1,000
Shs. outstg. (M)	20.3	Market cap. (B)	$0.663
Avg. daily vol. (M)	0.031	Inst. holdings	78%
Tang. Bk. Value/Share	15.48		
Beta	0.80		

Value of $10,000 invested 5 years ago: $ 47,528

Fiscal Year Ending Dec. 31

	1996	1995	1994	1993	1992	1991
Revenues (Million $)						
1Q	143.3	132.3	119.7	114.8	106.8	—
2Q	146.6	134.7	127.3	119.8	108.2	—
3Q	150.7	140.2	127.1	126.0	114.9	—
4Q	155.7	145.6	133.2	121.8	116.7	—
Yr.	596.3	552.8	507.4	482.4	446.6	—
Earnings Per Share ($)						
1Q	0.78	0.78	0.71	0.71	0.56	0.47
2Q	0.32	0.79	0.89	0.61	0.38	0.07
3Q	0.67	0.83	0.67	0.53	0.40	0.39
4Q	0.70	0.86	0.71	0.61	0.48	0.25
Yr.	2.42	3.27	2.99	2.45	1.80	1.28

Next earnings report expected: mid April

Dividend Data (Dividends have been paid since 1985.)

Amount ($)	Date Decl.	Ex-Div. Date	Stock of Record	Payment Date
0.220	May. 01	Jun. 07	Jun. 11	Jun. 25 '96
0.220	Jul. 25	Sep. 11	Sep. 13	Sep. 27 '96
3-for-2	Oct. 21	Dec. 02	Nov. 15	Nov. 29 '96
0.150	Oct. 21	Dec. 10	Dec. 12	Dec. 26 '96

A Division of The McGraw·Hill Companies

Business Summary - 12-FEB-97

ALLIED Group, Inc. is a regional holding company that writes, through subsidiaries, primarily personal automobile and homeowners lines of insurance. The company's subsidiaries also write commercial lines of insurance for small businesses, provide excess and surplus lines insurance and offer investment and data processing services.

Contributions to pretax income by business segment in recent years were:

	1995	1994
Property-casualty	87%	81%
Excess & surplus lines	7%	7%
Investment services	6%	6%
Data processing	Loss	6%

Property-casualty insurance accounted for 85.4% of consolidated revenues in 1995. Products in this segment are marketed through three distribution systems: independent agencies, exclusive agencies, and direct mail and telemarketing.

The company's excess and surplus lines subsidiary, Western Heritage Insurance Co., primarily underwrites commercial property and casualty coverage that standard insurers are unable or unwilling to provide.

In 1995, the property-casualty segment had a statutory combined ratio of 95.7% (97.1% in 1994), which was divided by lines of business as follows: personal automobile 96.5% (97.4%), homeowners 99.2% (107.4%) and excess and surplus lines 102.2% (99.9%).

GRP's investment services subsidiary originates, purchases and services single-family residential mortgages and acquires servicing rights from savings and loan associations, banks and other mortgage companies. Through its ALLIED Group Information Systems and The Freedom Group units, GRP markets data processing services and a complete line of software products to affiliated and nonaffiliated insurance companies.

Important Developments

Feb. '97—Trading in the company's common shares moved to the New York Stock Exchange from the Nasdaq Stock Market.
Dec. '96—The company raised its quarterly cash dividend by 2.3% (adjusted for the November 3-for-2 split), to $0.15 a share.

Capitalization

Notes Payable: $34,094,468 (12/96).
6.75% Series Pfd. Stk.: 1,827,222 shs. (no par); owned by ALLIED Mutual; represents 15% ownership.

Per Share Data ($)

(Year Ended Dec. 31)	1996	1995	1994	1993	1992	1991	1990	1989	1988	1987
Tangible Bk. Val.	NA	18.91	14.54	12.69	9.56	8.79	8.44	7.37	6.75	6.31
Oper. Earnings	NA	NA	2.03	2.27	1.70	1.14	0.72	0.64	0.65	0.78
Earnings	2.42	3.27	2.99	2.45	1.80	1.28	0.75	0.65	0.67	0.79
Dividends	0.59	0.45	0.40	0.34	0.29	0.25	0.21	0.20	0.18	0.16
Payout Ratio	24%	14%	13%	14%	16%	19%	28%	30%	26%	20%
Prices - High	33¼	24½	20⅝	21⅞	14⅞	9½	6	6	5⅜	6¾
- Low	22⅜	15½	14⅝	13⅛	7½	5½	5½	4¼	4	3¾
P/E Ratio - High	14	7	7	9	8	7	8	9	8	9
- Low	9	5	5	5	4	4	7	7	6	5

Income Statement Analysis (Million $)

	1996	1995	1994	1993	1992	1991	1990	1989	1988	1987
Premium Income	NA	455	413	368	320	248	219	163	159	146
Net Invest. Inc.	NA	47.2	41.0	39.0	32.7	28.0	23.2	14.5	21.2	16.0
Oth. Revs.	NA	50.0	53.8	75.1	93.7	78.2	62.6	35.0	17.3	11.1
Total Revs.	NA	553	507	482	447	354	305	212	198	159
Pretax Inc.	NA	73.8	66.7	56.8	39.0	22.1	13.2	14.0	14.5	15.6
Net Oper. Inc.	NA	NA	27.5	36.8	27.4	15.6	10.0	9.9	10.1	11.6
Net Inc.	NA	52.4	47.6	39.9	28.7	17.0	10.7	10.0	10.2	11.7

Balance Sheet & Other Fin. Data (Million $)

	1996	1995	1994	1993	1992	1991	1990	1989	1988	1987
Cash & Equiv.	NA	11.9	11.9	12.2	10.2	8.8	7.3	7.4	7.0	8.5
Premiums Due	NA	76.1	68.5	61.8	63.5	61.8	41.9	38.9	27.4	24.8
Inv Assets Bonds	NA	755	645	589	452	351	299	204	282	231
Inv. Assets Stock	NA	7.9	5.0	10.3	7.9	6.3	4.4	3.4	2.0	5.9
Inv. Assets Loans	NA	Nil	Nil	Nil	Nil	Nil	Nil	Nil	14.2	8.4
Inv. Assets Total	NA	772	656	607	460	357	303	207	298	246
Deferred Policy Cost	NA	41.7	38.3	34.4	28.6	23.3	19.8	13.6	40.1	35.6
Total Assets	NA	1,011	893	856	688	558	458	373	389	324
Debt	NA	65.7	72.0	112	97.1	112	83.1	56.4	10.4	6.2
Common Eqty.	NA	268	196	173	88.0	69.8	53.2	113	103	94.0
Prop&Cas Loss	NA	69.4	69.6	59.4	59.8	64.7	63.2	76.2	72.8	66.0
Prop&Cas Expense	NA	26.0	27.0	39.9	42.7	43.2	43.1	30.1	31.0	32.0
Prop&Cas Comb.	NA	95.7	97.1	99.3	102.5	107.9	106.3	102.7	103.8	97.9
% Ret. on Revs.	NA	9.5	9.4	8.3	6.4	4.8	3.5	4.7	5.2	6.5
% Return on Equity	NA	19.5	21.9	25.0	27.4	21.3	11.2	9.2	10.4	12.7

Data as orig. reptd.; bef. results of disc. opers. and/or spec. items. Per share data adj. for stk. divs. as of ex-div. date. E-Estimated. NA-Not Available. NM-Not Meaningful. NR-Not Ranked.

Office—701 Fifth Ave., Des Moines, IA 50391-2000. **Tel**—(515) 280-4611. **Chrmn**—J. E. Evans. **Pres (P-C)**—D. L. Andersen. **Pres (Fin), Treas & Investor Contact**—Jim H. Shaffer. **Secy**—G. T. Oleson. **Dirs**—J. W. Callison, H. S. Carpenter, C. I. Colby, H. S. Evans, J. E. Evans, R. O. Jacobson, J. P. Taylor, W. E. Timmons, D. S. Willis. **Transfer Agent**—Harris Trust & Savings Bank, Chicago. **Incorporated**—in Iowa in 1971. **Empl**— 2,243.
S&P Analyst: Thomas C. Ferguson

Anheuser-Busch   201B

NYSE Symbol **BUD**

In S&P 500

14-FEB-97 Industry: Beverages

Summary: Parent company of the world's largest brewer, Anheuser-Busch also has interests in entertainment operations.

S&P Opinion: Accumulate (★★★★)	Recent Price • 43½	Yield • 2.2%
	52 Wk Range • 45-32⅜	12-Mo. P/E • 18.5

Quantitative Evaluations

Outlook
(1 Lowest—5 Highest)
• **3+**

Fair Value
• **43¼**

Risk
• **Low**

Earn./Div. Rank
• **A**

Technical Eval.
• **Bearish** since 12/96

Rel. Strength Rank
(1 Lowest—99 Highest)
• **68**

Insider Activity
• **Neutral**

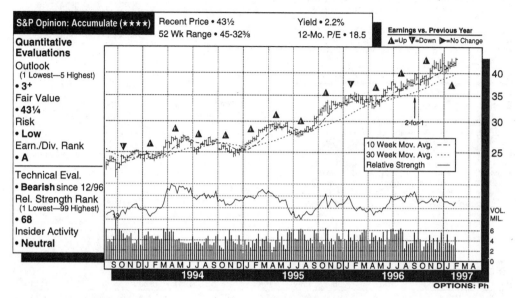

Earnings vs. Previous Year
▲=Up ▼=Down ▶=No Change

10 Week Mov. Avg. - - -
30 Week Mov. Avg. - - -
Relative Strength —

2-for-1

OPTIONS: Ph

Overview - 14-FEB-97

Net sales (after excise taxes) from ongoing operations should rise at a middle single-digit pace in 1997, primarily reflecting 2% to 3% greater beer shipments and higher selling prices. Operating margins are expected to widen, aided by easing packaging costs and cost savings accruing from the recent realignment of production facilities. The early-1996 shedding of various non-beer assets should continue to enable heavy marketing support behind BUD's core brewing operations. Excess cash generated from operations should continue to be used primarily for international expansion and for share repurchases. We estimate earnings per share to reach $2.45 in 1997, up 11% from 1996's $2.21 before special items.

Valuation - 14-FEB-97

The shares have performed well since BUD's October 1995 announcement that it would sell various of its underperforming assets in order to help streamline its brewing production system. The moves, completed by March 1996, have allowed BUD to become an even more focused and efficient brewer than before. Also, the business disposals freed up a significant amount of funds which have been used to better support the company's core brands and accelerate BUD's push abroad. Although the highly mature U.S. beer market (growing at about 1% annually) will still pose formidable challenges to BUD's sales growth prospects, we view this dominant market leader as capable of generating steady, reliable 10%-plus annual EPS growth over the longer-term. Trading at about the P/E multiple of the S&P 500, we expect the shares to modestly outperform over the next 12 months.

Key Stock Statistics

S&P EPS Est. 1997	2.45	Tang. Bk. Value/Share	8.14
P/E on S&P Est. 1997	17.8	Beta	0.70
Dividend Rate/Share	0.96	Shareholders	66,000
Shs. outstg. (M)	499.3	Market cap. (B)	$ 22.1
Avg. daily vol. (M)	0.742	Inst. holdings	57%

Value of $10,000 invested 5 years ago: NA

Fiscal Year Ending Dec. 31

	1996	1995	1994	1993	1992	1991
Revenues (Million $)						
1Q	2,372	2,318	2,628	2,503	2,620	2,540
2Q	2,961	2,823	3,169	2,991	2,950	2,850
3Q	3,064	2,967	3,298	3,157	3,090	2,940
4Q	2,487	2,233	2,959	2,854	2,730	2,670
Yr.	10,884	10,341	12,054	11,505	11,390	11,000
Earnings Per Share ($)						
1Q	0.54	0.42	0.38	0.35	0.37	0.35
2Q	0.71	0.63	0.60	0.56	0.54	0.50
3Q	0.75	0.66	0.63	-0.14	0.54	0.51
4Q	0.30	-0.47	0.34	0.31	0.29	0.28
Yr.	2.28	1.24	1.95	1.08	1.74	1.63

Next earnings report expected: mid May

Dividend Data (Dividends have been paid since 1932.)

Amount ($)	Date Decl.	Ex-Div. Date	Stock of Record	Payment Date
0.480	Jul. 24	Aug. 07	Aug. 09	Sep. 09 '96
2-for-1	Jul. 24	Sep. 13	Aug. 15	Sep. 12 '96
0.240	Oct. 23	Nov. 06	Nov. 08	Dec. 09 '96
0.240	Dec. 18	Feb. 06	Feb. 10	Mar. 10 '97

STANDARD
&POOR'S
STOCK REPORTS

Anheuser-Busch Companies, Inc.

201B

14-FEB-97

Business Summary - 14-FEB-97

Anheuser-Busch is the largest U.S. brewer. The company is also one of the largest theme park operators in the U.S., and the second-largest U.S. manufacturer of aluminum beverage containers. In late 1995, BUD disposed of its food-related businesses; in early 1996, BUD sold its St. Louis National Baseball Club (Cardinals). Sales and operating profit (excluding special charges and disposed businesses) in 1995 (latest available) were:

	Sales	Profits
Beer	93%	$1,718
Entertainment	7%	75

Beer brands include Budweiser, Bud Light, Bud Dry Bud Ice, Michelob, Michelob Light, Michelob Dry, Michelob Golden Draft, Busch, Busch Light, Natural Light, Natural Pilsner, King Cobra, Elk Mountain, Red Wolf, and non-alcoholic malt beverages O'Doul's and Busch NA. The company operates 12 breweries, strategically located across the country, to economically serve its distribution system. Sales in 1996 totaled 91.1 million barrels (up 4.1% from 87.5 million barrels in 1995), or approximately 45% of U.S. industry sales. Vertically integrated operations include can manufacturing, metalized paper printing and barley malting.

Entertainment operations include nine theme parks, including Busch Gardens in Florida and Virginia; Sea World parks in Florida, Texas, Ohio and California; and water parks in Florida and Virginia. In early 1996, BUD sold its St. Louis National Baseball Club (Cardinals).

Important Developments

Feb. '97—BUD reported beer sales volume of 91.1 million barrels in 1996, an increase of 3,600,000 barrels, or 4.1%, over the prior year. The increased sales volume resulted in BUD's market share rising 1.1% to 45.2% of U.S. industry shipments. Separately, BUD continued to discuss the possible purchase of an additional 25% equity stake in Grupo Modelo, Mexico's leading brewer. That would bring BUD's total direct and indirect holdings in the company and its subsidiaries to 37%.

Capitalization

Long Term Debt: $3,235,300,000 (9/96).

Per Share Data ($)

(Year Ended Dec. 31)	1996	1995	1994	1993	1992	1991	1990	1989	1988	1987
Tangible Bk. Val.	NA	7.85	7.64	7.04	7.39	6.88	5.57	4.53	5.29	4.73
Cash Flow	NA	2.82	3.14	2.18	2.73	2.56	2.35	2.05	1.83	1.50
Earnings	2.28	1.24	1.95	1.08	1.74	1.63	1.48	1.34	1.23	1.02
Dividends	0.92	0.84	0.76	0.68	0.60	0.53	0.47	0.40	0.33	0.27
Payout Ratio	40%	67%	39%	63%	34%	32%	32%	30%	26%	27%
Prices - High	45	34	27³/₄	30¹/₈	30³/₈	31	22⁵/₈	23	17¹/₄	20¹/₈
- Low	32³/₈	25³/₈	23⁵/₈	21¹/₂	25⁷/₈	19⁵/₈	17	15³/₈	14¹/₂	12⁷/₈
P/E Ratio - High	20	27	14	28	17	19	15	17	14	20
- Low	14	20	12	20	15	12	11	11	12	13

Income Statement Analysis (Million $)

	1996	1995	1994	1993	1992	1991	1990	1989	1988	1987
Revs.	NA	10,341	12,054	11,505	11,394	10,996	10,744	9,481	8,924	8,258
Oper. Inc.	NA	2,359	2,527	2,385	2,343	2,256	2,080	1,735	1,620	1,441
Depr.	NA	566	628	608	567	534	482	406	356	312
Int. Exp.	NA	226	221	208	200	239	283	178	142	124
Pretax Inc.	NA	1,462	1,707	1,050	1,615	1,521	1,352	1,227	1,160	1,056
Eff. Tax Rate	NA	39%	40%	43%	38%	38%	38%	38%	38%	42%
Net Inc.	NA	887	1,032	595	994	940	842	767	716	615

Balance Sheet & Other Fin. Data (Million $)

	1996	1995	1994	1993	1992	1991	1990	1989	1988	1987
Cash	NA	94.0	156	127	215	97.0	95.0	36.0	64.0	111
Curr. Assets	NA	1,511	1,862	1,795	1,816	1,628	1,426	1,277	1,194	1,125
Total Assets	NA	10,591	11,045	10,880	10,538	9,987	9,634	9,026	7,110	6,492
Curr. Liab.	NA	1,242	1,669	1,816	1,460	1,403	1,412	1,303	1,179	1,042
LT Debt	NA	3,270	3,078	3,032	2,643	2,645	3,147	3,307	1,615	1,397
Common Eqty.	NA	4,434	4,415	4,255	4,620	4,438	3,679	3,100	3,103	2,892
Total Cap.	NA	8,837	8,752	8,458	8,540	8,584	8,222	7,723	5,931	5,449
Cap. Exp.	NA	953	785	777	737	703	899	1,646	951	823
Cash Flow	NA	1,453	1,660	1,203	1,561	1,474	1,324	1,174	1,072	906
Curr. Ratio	NA	1.2	1.1	1.0	1.2	1.2	1.0	1.0	1.0	1.1
% LT Debt of Cap.	NA	37.0	35.2	35.8	30.9	30.8	38.3	42.8	27.2	25.6
% Net Inc.of Revs.	NA	8.6	8.6	5.2	8.7	8.5	7.8	8.1	8.0	7.4
% Ret. on Assets	NA	8.4	9.6	5.7	9.8	9.5	9.0	9.5	10.7	9.6
% Ret. on Equity	NA	20.0	24.2	13.7	22.2	23.1	24.9	24.8	24.3	22.0

Data as orig. reptd.; bef. results of disc. opers. and/or spec. items. Per share data adj. for stk. divs. as of ex-div. date. E-Estimated. NA-Not Available. NM-Not Meaningful. NR-Not Ranked.

Office—1 Busch Place, St. Louis, MO 63118. **Tel**—(314) 577-2000. **Chrmn & Pres**—A. A. Busch III. **EVP & CFO**—R. Baker. **Secy**—JoBeth G. Brown. **Investor Contact**—David Sauerhoff. **Dirs**—R. T. Baker, A. A. Busch III, A. B. Craig III, B. A. Edison, A. Fernandez R., C. Fernandez G., P. M. Flanigan, J. E. Jacob, C. F. Knight, V. R. Loucks, Jr., V. S. Martinez, S. C. Mobley, J. B. Orthwein, A. C. Taylor, D. A. Warner III, W. H.— Webster, E. E. Whitacre, Jr. **Transfer Agent & Registrar**—Boatmen's Trust Co., St. Louis. **Incorporated**—in Missouri in 1925; reincorporated in Delaware in 1979. **Empl**— 42,529. **S&P Analyst:** Kenneth A. Shea

Associated Banc-Corp   3170K

NASDAQ Symbol **ASBC**

15-FEB-97 | Industry: Banking

Summary: This multibank holding company, with $4.4 billion in assets, is the third largest in Wisconsin, with more than 95 banking locations in Wisconsin and Illinois.

Quantitative Evaluations

Outlook
(1 Lowest—5 Highest)
• **3⁻**

Fair Value
• **44⅛**

Risk
• **Low**

Earn./Div. Rank
• **A+**

Technical Eval.
• **Bearish** since 1/96

Rel. Strength Rank
(1 Lowest—99 Highest)
• **56**

Insider Activity
• **Neutral**

Recent Price • 43½
52 Wk Range • 43¾-35¼
Yield • 2.7%
12-Mo. P/E • 13.9

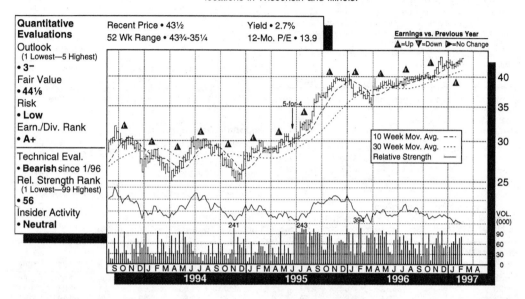

Earnings vs. Previous Year
▲=Up ▼=Down ▶=No Change

10 Week Mov. Avg. ---
30 Week Mov. Avg. ⋯⋯
Relative Strength ——

Business Profile - 29-JAN-97

Associated's strategy for remaining a competitive supercommunity bank in its Upper Midwest target region includes adding technology/systems to enhance productivity and customer service, new sources of noninterest income, a larger customer base, and franchise growth through acquisitions and marketplace expansion. The bank's five-year financial goals are based on earnings and dividend growth, return on equity and the level of nonperforming loans. During 1996, ASBC completed several acquisitions that boosted assets by approximately $450 million, to $4.4 billion. The company expects to complete another acquisition in early 1997 that will increase assets by an additional $79 million.

Operational Review - 29-JAN-97

Net interest income rose 9.7% in 1996, as a 15% increase in loans outweighed a narrower net interest margin (4.53% vs. 4.64%). The provision for loan losses increased 8.7%, to $4.7 million. Following 18% greater noninterest income and 8.0% higher noninterest expense, net income was up 19%, to $57,244,000 ($3.12 a share, on 5% more shares), from $48,028,000 ($2.75), as restated for a pooled acquisition.

Stock Performance - 14-FEB-97

In the past 30 trading days, ASBC's shares have increased 3%, compared to a 8% rise in the S&P 500. Average trading volume for the past five days was 16,120 shares, compared with the 40-day moving average of 13,487 shares.

Key Stock Statistics

Dividend Rate/Share	1.16	Shareholders	5,000
Shs. outstg. (M)	18.4	Market cap. (B)	$0.799
Avg. daily vol. (M)	0.017	Inst. holdings	28%
Tang. Bk. Value/Share	20.77		
Beta	0.51		

Value of $10,000 invested 5 years ago: $ 26,892

Fiscal Year Ending Dec. 31

	1996	1995	1994	1993	1992	1991
Revenues (Million $)						
1Q	84.00	72.91	60.71	60.06	48.33	48.34
2Q	89.85	75.66	62.63	62.61	63.75	48.90
3Q	94.24	81.32	65.22	62.20	63.18	48.73
4Q	97.98	82.62	70.20	64.20	79.92	49.01
Yr.	376.8	317.4	258.8	249.1	255.2	195.0
Earnings Per Share ($)						
1Q	0.73	0.65	0.60	0.54	0.46	0.43
2Q	0.77	0.68	0.63	0.57	0.48	0.45
3Q	0.80	0.74	0.66	0.59	0.52	0.49
4Q	0.82	0.76	0.68	0.61	0.54	0.49
Yr.	3.12	2.83	2.57	2.31	2.00	1.86

Next earnings report expected: late April

Dividend Data (Dividends have been paid since 1970.)

Amount ($)	Date Decl.	Ex-Div. Date	Stock of Record	Payment Date
0.290	Jul. 25	Aug. 01	Aug. 05	Aug. 15 '96
0.290	Oct. 23	Oct. 31	Nov. 04	Nov. 15 '96
0.290	Jan. 22	Jan. 31	Feb. 04	Feb. 14 '97
6-for-5	Jan. 22	Mar. 03	Mar. 05	Mar. 17 '97

A Division of The McGraw·Hill Companies

STANDARD
&POOR'S
STOCK REPORTS

Associated Banc-Corp

3170K
15-FEB-97

Business Summary - 29-JAN-97

Associated Banc-Corp is a bank holding company headquartered in Green Bay, Wis., and is the third largest in the state. The company operates more than 95 banking locations in Wisconsin and Illinois. Through its subsidiaries, Associated provides a complete range of retail banking services to individuals and small to medium-size businesses. The company also has mortgage banking and brokerage subsidiaries.

Loans outstanding totaled $2.61 billion at the end of 1995 and were divided:

	1995
Commercial, financial & agricultural	30%
Real estate--mortgage	54%
Real estate--construction	5%
Instalment loans to individuals	11%

Net loan chargeoffs were $2,052,000 (0.08% of average loans) in 1995, versus $1,470,000 (0.07%) the year before. As of December 31, 1995, nonperforming loans (including nonaccrual loans, accruing loans past due 90 days or more, and restructured loans) aggregated $17,442,000 (0.67% of total loans), compared with $17,753,000 (0.76%) a year earlier.

Average deposits totaling $2.8 billion in 1995 were apportioned: 45% time, 13% money market, 14% savings, 18% noninterest-bearing demand, and 10% interest-bearing demand.

Interest and fees on loans contributed 69% of total income for 1995, interest and fees on investment securities 14%, other interest income 1%, trust service fees 7%, service charges on deposit accounts 3%, and other noninterest income 6%.

During 1995, ASBC acquired one mortgage company and a bank holding company, expanding its presence in the Chicago marketplace. Acquisitions completed in 1996 include the March acquisition of SBL Capital Bank Shares ($65 million of assets), the April acquisition of Greater Columbia Bancshares ($211 million), and the July acquisitions of F&M Bankshares of Reedsburg Inc. ($139 million) and Mid-America National Bancorp Inc. ($39 million).

Important Developments

Jan. '97—Associated Banc-Corp declared its regular quarterly cash dividend and announced a 6-for-5 stock split to be effected as a 20% stock dividend.
Nov. '96—ASBC announced that it reached a definitive agreement to acquire Centra Financial Inc. (assets of $79 million) in a stock-for-stock merger transaction.

Capitalization

Long Term Debt: $21,863,000 (9/96).

Per Share Data ($)

(Year Ended Dec. 31)	1996	1995	1994	1993	1992	1991	1990	1989	1988	1987
Tangible Bk. Val.	NA	19.72	21.78	16.33	14.38	13.54	12.17	10.99	9.89	8.84
Earnings	3.12	2.83	2.57	2.31	2.00	1.86	1.68	1.51	1.35	1.21
Dividends	1.14	0.97	0.85	0.75	0.61	0.57	0.50	0.42	0.36	0.30
Payout Ratio	37%	34%	33%	32%	31%	30%	30%	28%	27%	25%
Prices - High	43¾	41	30⅝	32	24½	21½	16⅛	16	13⅛	14⅞
- Low	35¼	27⅜	25	23½	18	12	11⅝	11⅛	10¼	8⅞
P/E Ratio - High	14	14	12	14	12	12	10	11	10	12
- Low	11	10	10	10	9	6	7	7	8	7

Income Statement Analysis (Million $)

	1996	1995	1994	1993	1992	1991	1990	1989	1988	1987
Net Int. Inc.	NA	147	131	124	115	74.7	65.9	61.2	56.2	49.5
Tax Equiv. Adj.	NA	3.9	4.0	4.5	5.4	4.8	4.8	5.4	6.0	8.1
Non Int. Inc.	NA	52.7	47.6	48.2	44.9	32.2	28.0	25.3	23.4	20.2
Loan Loss Prov.	NA	3.2	2.8	5.5	6.2	5.0	3.2	3.1	3.4	2.5
% Exp/Op Revs.	NA	61	62	63	66	65	65	66	68	67
Pretax Inc.	NA	73.4	62.4	54.9	44.8	29.5	26.5	23.0	19.4	16.1
Eff. Tax Rate	NA	36%	35%	34%	32%	28%	28%	25%	22%	17%
Net Inc.	NA	46.7	40.4	36.3	30.6	21.3	19.2	17.3	15.1	13.3
% Net Int. Marg.	NA	4.67	4.79	4.71	4.60	4.50	4.40	4.40	4.30	4.40

Balance Sheet & Other Fin. Data (Million $)

	1996	1995	1994	1993	1992	1991	1990	1989	1988	1987
Earning Assets:										
Money Mkt	NA	43.7	57.9	93.0	177	101	58.0	133	112	132
Inv. Securities	NA	1,041	667	634	537	436	413	402	422	405
Com'l Loans	NA	781	676	709	714	566	558	471	431	433
Other Loans	NA	1,831	1,601	1,328	1,198	802	666	585	549	446
Total Assets	NA	3,698	3,010	2,982	2,882	2,097	1,870	1,751	1,674	1,548
Demand Deposits	NA	595	589	510	475	340	281	277	264	278
Time Deposits	NA	2,378	2,074	1,922	1,904	1,325	1,172	1,096	1,072	982
LT Debt	NA	18.1	3.9	16.4	17.9	14.8	26.6	30.4	33.1	33.1
Common Eqty.	NA	326	275	257	222	158	139	126	113	98.0
% Ret. on Assets	NA	1.4	1.3	1.2	1.1	1.1	1.1	1.0	0.9	0.9
% Ret. on Equity	NA	15.3	15.3	15.3	14.8	14.6	14.6	14.6	14.4	14.5
% Loan Loss Resv.	NA	1.5	1.6	1.7	1.6	1.3	1.1	1.2	1.1	1.1
% Loans/Deposits	NA	86.0	83.7	83.8	80.4	82.2	84.2	76.9	73.3	69.5
% Equity to Assets	NA	8.8	8.7	8.1	7.7	7.7	7.4	7.1	6.6	6.4

Data as orig. reptd.; bef. results of disc. opers. and/or spec. items. Per share data adj. for stk. divs. as of ex-div. date. E-Estimated. NA-Not Available. NM-Not Meaningful. NR-Not Ranked.

Office—112 N. Adams St., P.O. Box 13307, Green Bay, WI 54307-3307. **Tel**—(414) 433-3166. **Chrmn & CEO**—H. B. Conlon. **Vice Chrmn**—R. C. Gallagher. **SVP, CFO & Investor Contact**—Joseph B. Selner (414-433-3203). **Secy**—B. R. Bodager. **Dirs**—H. B. Conlon, R. Feitler, R. C. Gallagher, R. R. Harder, J. S. Holbrook, W. R. Hutchinson, J. F. Janz, W. J. Lawson, J. C. Meng, J. D. Quick. **Transfer Agent & Registrar**—Harris Trust & Savings Bank, Chicago. **Incorporated**—in Wisconsin in 1964. **Empl**—1,763. **S&P Analyst:** E. Fitzpatrick.

15-FEB-97

Industry:
Office Equipment

Summary: This company is a leading worldwide manufacturer of pressure sensitive adhesives and materials, office products, labels, retail systems and specialty chemicals.

S&P Opinion: Accumulate (★★★★)	Recent Price • 40½	Yield • 1.7%
	52 Wk Range • 41-24¾	12-Mo. P/E • 24.1

Quantitative Evaluations

Outlook
(1 Lowest—5 Highest)
• **3+**

Fair Value
• **38**

Risk
• **Low**

Earn./Div. Rank
• **A-**

Technical Eval.
• **Bearish** since 12/96

Rel. Strength Rank
(1 Lowest—99 Highest)
• **90**

Insider Activity
• **Favorable**

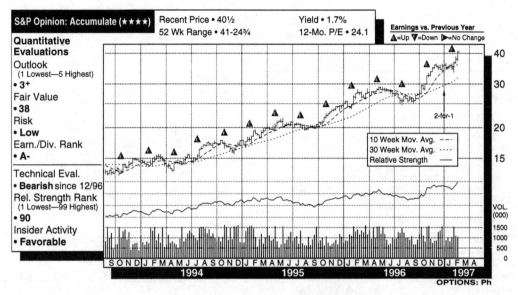

Earnings vs. Previous Year
▲=Up ▼=Down ▶=No Change

10 Week Mov. Avg. – – –
30 Week Mov. Avg. ·····
Relative Strength ——

2-for-1

VOL. (000)

OPTIONS: Ph

Overview - 13-FEB-97

Sales for this manufacturer of pressure sensitive adhesives and materials are expected to advance 5%-10% in 1997, as all business segments continue to benefit from growing global economies and strong packaging, durable goods, office and retail markets. Growth of newer products, such as battery labels and postal stamps, will also aid sales, boosted by capacity expansions in Germany, China, and Latin America. Currency exchange rates will remain unfavorable through the first half of 1997. Profitability should continue to improve on the higher volumes and ongoing productivity gains, while raw material costs are expected to be remain relatively stable. AVY will see the full impact of restructuring actions taken in late 1995. The pace of stock buybacks may be slower than 1996 levels, which were aided by the use of the proceeds from the sale of assets near the end of 1995. Capital spending is expected to be nearly $200 million, versus $188 million in 1996.

Valuation - 13-FEB-97

The company intends to focus on its core adhesives and office products businesses and grow through internal as well as geographic expansion. Long-term growth is being driven by the widening use of non-impact printing systems for computers and for product tracking and information needs. The proliferation of high quality graphics on packaging and consumer products is also spurring sales of pressure sensitive labels. The shares performed well since 1995, reflecting continued good gains in sales and earnings. A 2-for-1 split was paid at the end of 1996, and dividends have been increased for 21 consecutive years. The shares are still attractive in view of the positive earnings outlook for the company.

Key Stock Statistics

S&P EPS Est. 1997	1.90	Tang. Bk. Value/Share	6.63
P/E on S&P Est. 1997	21.3	Beta	0.87
Dividend Rate/Share	0.68	Shareholders	9,600
Shs. outstg. (M)	104.2	Market cap. (B)	$ 4.2
Avg. daily vol. (M)	0.238	Inst. holdings	61%

Value of $10,000 invested 5 years ago: $ 33,981

Fiscal Year Ending Dec. 31

	1996	1995	1994	1993	1992	1991
Revenues (Million $)						
1Q	796.6	773.2	667.7	666.5	670.0	660.0
2Q	797.7	780.5	718.6	662.2	668.0	627.0
3Q	819.3	783.5	733.7	638.1	656.0	609.0
4Q	808.9	776.7	736.7	641.9	630.0	649.0
Yr.	3,223	3,134	2,857	2,609	2,623	2,545
Earnings Per Share ($)						
1Q	0.38	0.32	0.22	0.19	0.17	0.14
2Q	0.39	0.33	0.25	0.19	0.19	0.13
3Q	0.44	0.33	0.25	0.17	0.15	0.10
4Q	0.46	0.36	0.26	0.17	0.16	0.15
Yr.	1.68	1.35	0.99	0.72	0.66	0.51

Next earnings report expected: early May

Dividend Data (Dividends have been paid since 1964.)

Amount ($)	Date Decl.	Ex-Div. Date	Stock of Record	Payment Date
0.300	Jul. 25	Aug. 30	Sep. 04	Sep. 18 '96
0.170	Oct. 24	Dec. 04	Dec. 06	Dec. 20 '96
2-for-1	Oct. 24	Dec. 23	Dec. 06	Dec. 20 '96
0.170	Jan. 31	Mar. 03	Mar. 05	Mar. 19 '97

Business Summary - 13-FEB-97

Avery Dennison Corp. is a leading global manufacturer of pressure sensitive technology and self-adhesive solutions for consumer products and label systems, including office products, product identification and control systems, and specialty tapes and chemicals. The company was formed through the October 1990 merger of Avery International Corp. and Dennison Manufacturing Corp. Industry segment contributions in 1996:

	Sales	Profits
Adhesives and materials	50%	50%
Consumer and converted products	50%	50%

Foreign operations, primarily in Europe, accounted for 36% of sales and 27% of profits in 1995.

The adhesives and materials group includes pressure sensitive, self-adhesive coated papers, plastic films and metal foils in roll and sheet form, graphic and decoration films and labels, specialty fastening and bonding tapes, and adhesives, protective coatings and electroconductive resins for industrial, automotive, aerospace, appliance, electronic, medical and consumer markets.

Consumer products consist of pressure sensitive labels, laser and ink-jet print labels and software, notebooks, binders, presentation and organizing systems, marking devices and numerous other products for office, home and school uses.

Converted products include custom labels and application and imprinting machines for the industrial, durable goods, cosmetic, battery, consumer packaged goods and electronic data processing markets; self-adhesive postal stamps; and tags, labels, printers, marking and coding systems, application devices, plastic fasteners and cable ties for apparel, retail and industrial markets for use in identification, tracking and control applications.

Important Developments

Jan. '97—AVY reported record sales and earnings in 1996, despite investments in new businesses and products. Earnings included a net gain of $0.03 a share in the third quarter from the divestiture of a joint venture in Japan. AVY noted that it achieved a 21.4% return on equity. Excluding divested units and currency, sales increased 6.4%. Some 3.8 million common shares were repurchased during 1996, for a total cost of $109 million. AVY has repurchased about 20% of its common stock since 1991 for a total of $430 million. About 5 million shares were remaining in a stock buyback authorization.

Capitalization

Long Term Debt: $370,700,000 (12/96).

Per Share Data ($) (Year Ended Dec. 31)	**1996**	**1995**	**1994**	**1993**	**1992**	**1991**	**1990**	**1989**	**1988**	**1987**
Tangible Bk. Val.	NA	6.52	5.54	5.17	5.65	5.54	5.60	4.55	4.22	3.95
Cash Flow	NA	2.36	1.90	1.54	1.44	1.26	0.77	1.55	1.39	0.84
Earnings	1.68	1.35	0.99	0.72	0.66	0.51	0.05	0.98	0.88	0.40
Dividends	0.62	0.55	0.50	0.45	0.41	0.38	0.32	0.27	0.23	0.21
Payout Ratio	37%	41%	50%	62%	60%	74%	672%	28%	26%	52%
Prices - High	36½	25⅛	18	15¾	14⅝	12⅞	16½	16⅝	13	14⅝
- Low	23¾	16⅝	13¼	12⅝	11⅝	9½	7¾	10½	9⅝	7⅝
P/E Ratio - High	22	19	18	22	22	25	NM	17	15	36
- Low	14	12	13	17	17	19	NM	11	11	19
Income Statement Analysis (Million $)										
Revs.	NA	3,114	2,857	2,609	2,623	2,545	2,590	1,732	1,582	1,466
Oper. Inc.	NA	375	318	271	266	235	245	195	197	161
Depr.	NA	108	103	95.4	93.9	92.3	90.1	50.3	45.1	36.3
Int. Exp.	NA	47.5	45.7	45.5	44.9	42.6	43.3	24.3	26.3	23.9
Pretax Inc.	NA	225	173	132	130	105	16.0	139	128	78.0
Eff. Tax Rate	NA	36%	37%	37%	39%	40%	62%	38%	39%	55%
Net Inc.	NA	144	109	83.3	80.1	63.0	5.9	86.5	77.7	34.7
Balance Sheet & Other Fin. Data (Million $)										
Cash	NA	27.0	3.1	5.8	3.9	5.3	6.5	3.1	5.9	8.0
Curr. Assets	NA	800	677	615	661	701	847	506	503	489
Total Assets	NA	1,964	1,763	1,639	1,684	1,740	1,890	1,142	1,119	1,051
Curr. Liab.	NA	673	554	473	439	475	548	324	330	324
LT Debt	NA	334	347	311	335	330	376	213	215	204
Common Eqty.	NA	816	729	719	803	825	846	539	509	466
Total Cap.	NA	1,191	1,116	1,075	1,205	1,235	1,310	818	790	727
Cap. Exp.	NA	190	163	101	88.0	123	149	83.0	90.0	103
Cash Flow	NA	252	212	179	174	155	96.0	137	123	71.0
Curr. Ratio	NA	1.2	1.2	1.3	1.5	1.5	1.5	1.6	1.5	1.5
% LT Debt of Cap.	NA	28.0	31.1	28.9	27.8	26.7	28.7	26.1	27.2	28.0
% Net Inc.of Revs.	NA	4.6	3.8	3.2	3.1	2.5	0.2	5.0	4.9	2.4
% Ret. on Assets	NA	7.7	6.6	5.1	4.8	3.5	0.3	7.6	7.1	3.5
% Ret. on Equity	NA	18.2	15.5	11.2	10.0	7.6	0.7	16.5	15.9	8.2

Data as orig. reptd.; bef. results of disc. opers. and/or spec. items. Per share data adj. for stk. divs. as of ex-div. date. E-Estimated. NA-Not Available. NM-Not Meaningful. NR-Not Ranked.

Office—150 North Orange Grove Blvd., Pasadena, CA 91103. **Tel**—(818) 304-2000. **E-mail**—investorcom@averydennison.com **Website**—http://www.averydennison.com**Chrmn & CEO**—C. D. Miller. **Pres & COO**—P. M. Neal. **SVP-Fin & CFO**—R. G. Jenkins. **VP-Secy**—R. G. van Schoonenberg. **VP-Treas & Investor Contact**—Wayne H. Smith. **Dirs**—D. L. Allison Jr., J. C. Argue, J. T. Bok, F. V. Cahouet, R. M. Ferry, C. D. Miller, P. W. Mullin, P. M. Neal, S. R. Petersen, J. B. Slaughter. **Transfer Agent & Registrar**—First Interstate Bank, Los Angeles. **Incorporated**—in California in 1946; reincorporated in Delaware in 1977. **Empl**— 15,850. **S&P Analyst:** Richard O'Reilly, CFA

14-FEB-97   Industry:
Food

Summary: Campbell Soup is a major producer of branded soups and other grocery food products. The Dorrance family controls more than 50% of the common stock.

| **S&P Opinion: Accumulate (★★★★)** | Recent Price • 83¼ | Yield • 1.8% |
| | 52 Wk Range • 84⅞-56 | 12-Mo. P/E • 29.5 |

Quantitative Evaluations

Outlook
(1 Lowest—5 Highest)
• **1+**

Fair Value
• **70⅝**

Risk
• **Low**

Earn./Div. Rank
• **B+**

Technical Eval.
• **Bullish** since 4/96

Rel. Strength Rank
(1 Lowest—99 Highest)
• **62**

Insider Activity
• **Neutral**

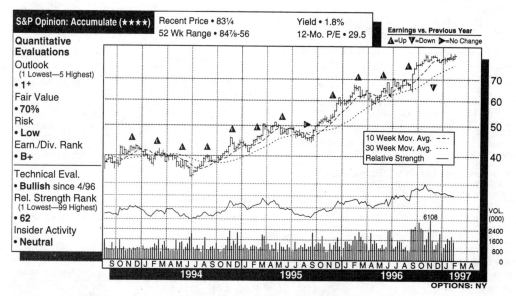

Earnings vs. Previous Year
▲=Up ▼=Down ▶=No Change

10 Week Mov. Avg. – – –
30 Week Mov. Avg. · · · · ·
Relative Strength ──

VOL. (000)

OPTIONS: NY

Overview - 14-FEB-97

Net sales are projected to rise at a middle single-digit rate in FY 97 (Jul.), as unit volume gains for core soup and grocery products, contributions from acquisitions, and higher average selling prices more than offset the impact of recent business divestments. The company's relatively high operating profitability is expected to be further enhanced by the increased volumes, improvements in product mix, and productivity gains derived from the organizational and strategic actions announced in September 1996. Net interest expense in FY 97 may nearly double from prior year levels, reflecting an increased amount of debt to aggressively repurchase shares, holding net income growth in FY 97 to approximately 10%. However, assuming a 3% to 5% reduction in outstanding shares, EPS should advance by 15% in FY 97, to $3.70 (before charges).

Valuation - 14-FEB-97

Given the company's reliable double-digit EPS gains and high relative returns on shareholder equity, we view Campbell Soup Co. as among the premier U.S. consumer growth companies. As such, we believe that this equity warrants its current premium valuation relative to its peers and to the S&P 500, and is attractive for purchase. In the near-term, earnings growth should be driven by steady volume growth, additional synergistic contributions from the integration of Pace Foods (acquired in January 1995), and aggressive cost cutting measures, which will allow for healthy EPS comparisons in FY 97 and beyond. In addition, the company's current aggressive stock repurchase stance should help support the stock's ascent over the next 12 months. Future earnings growth should also benefit from a more aggressive push abroad.

Key Stock Statistics

S&P EPS Est. 1997	3.05	Tang. Bk. Value/Share	3.78
P/E on S&P Est. 1997	27.3	Beta	0.92
Dividend Rate/Share	1.54	Shareholders	43,000
Shs. outstg. (M)	233.6	Market cap. (B)	$ 20.2
Avg. daily vol. (M)	0.384	Inst. holdings	27%

Value of $10,000 invested 5 years ago: $ 21,833

Fiscal Year Ending Jul. 31

	1997	1996	1995	1994	1993	1992
Revenues (Million $)						
1Q	2,052	1,990	1,864	1,763	1,696	1,547
2Q	2,317	2,217	2,040	1,894	1,789	1,746
3Q	—	1,831	1,744	1,568	1,632	1,536
4Q	—	1,640	1,630	1,465	1,470	1,433
Yr.	—	7,678	7,278	6,690	6,586	6,263
Earnings Per Share ($)						
1Q	0.36	0.88	0.79	0.66	0.62	0.51
2Q	1.18	1.03	0.93	0.81	-0.46	0.64
3Q	E0.68	0.58	0.51	0.47	0.43	0.36
4Q	E0.83	0.73	0.57	0.57	0.48	0.44
Yr.	E3.05	3.22	2.80	2.51	1.02	1.95

Next earnings report expected: mid May

Dividend Data (Dividends have been paid since 1902.)

Amount ($)	Date Decl.	Ex-Div. Date	Stock of Record	Payment Date
0.345	Mar. 28	Apr. 08	Apr. 10	Apr. 30 '96
0.345	Jun. 27	Jul. 08	Jul. 10	Jul. 31 '96
0.345	Sep. 26	Oct. 07	Oct. 09	Oct. 31 '96
0.385	Nov. 20	Jan. 06	Jan. 08	Jan. 31 '97

A Division of The McGraw-Hill Companies

STANDARD
&POOR'S
STOCK REPORTS

Campbell Soup Company

428

14-FEB-97

Business Summary - 14-FEB-97

Campbell Soup Co., through its subsidiaries, manufactures and markets branded convenience food products worldwide. Operations outside the United States accounted for 31% of net sales and 18% of pretax earnings in FY 96 (Jul.), mostly in Europe (14% and 5%) and Australia (8% and 6%). Contributions to sales and operating profits by division in FY 96 were:

	Sales	Profits
U.S.A.	59%	76%
Bakery & Confectionery	22%	14%
International Grocery	19%	10%

Major U.S. products include both condensed and ready to serve soups (Campbell's, Home Cookin', Chunky, Healthy Request); convenience meals (Swanson, Hungry Man); beans (Homestyle Pork and Beans); juices (Campbell's Tomato, V8); canned spaghetti and gravies (Franco-American); spaghetti sauce (Prego); pickles (Vlasic); refrigerated salad dressings (Marie's); and Mexican sauces (Pace). Foodservice operations serve the away-from-home eating market.

Bakery and Confectionery division products include Pepperidge Farm, Inc. in the U.S., a producer of bread, cakes and related products; Belgium-based Biscuits Delacre, a maker of biscuit and chocolate products; and Arnotts Biscuits Ltd. of Australia, a maker of biscuit and bakery products. Godiva Chocolatier (worldwide) and Lamy-Lutti (Europe) serve the candy market.

The International Grocery division consists of soup, grocery and frozen foods businesses in Canada, Mexico, Argentina, Europe, Australia and Asia. Major brands include Fray Bentos, Betis, Pleybin, Freshbake and Groko.

Important Developments

Nov. '96—Excluding restructuring charges amounting to $216.3 million ($160 million after-tax, or $0.65 per share) incurred during the first quarter of FY 96 (Jul.), operating earnings during the first half rose 12%, to $868 million, from $777 million. Earnings growth in the U.S.A. division (+16%) and Bakery & Confectionery (+9%) more than offset a decline for International Grocery (-9%). During the first half of FY 97, the company purchased 15.4 million of its common shares pursuant to an existing three-year share repurchase program of $2.5 billion.

Capitalization

Long Term Debt: $938,000,000 (1/97).

Per Share Data ($)

(Year Ended Jul. 31)	1996	1995	1994	1993	1992	1991	1990	1989	1988	1987
Tangible Bk. Val.	3.78	3.02	5.67	4.40	6.31	5.35	5.06	5.06	5.42	6.17
Cash Flow	4.53	3.98	3.60	1.91	2.74	2.35	0.73	0.73	1.56	1.49
Earnings	3.22	2.80	2.51	1.02	1.95	1.58	0.02	0.05	0.94	0.96
Dividends	1.35	1.21	1.09	0.91	0.71	0.56	0.49	0.45	0.40	0.35
Payout Ratio	42%	43%	43%	90%	36%	35%	879%	890%	43%	37%
Prices - High	70¾	61¼	46	45⅜	45¼	43⅞	31	30⅜	17⅝	17¾
- Low	56	41	34¼	35¼	31½	27	21⅞	15¼	12	11⅜
P/E Ratio - High	22	22	18	44	23	28	NM	NM	19	19
- Low	17	15	14	35	16	17	NM	NM	13	12

Income Statement Analysis (Million $)

	1996	1995	1994	1993	1992	1991	1990	1989	1988	1987
Revs.	7,678	7,278	6,690	6,586	6,263	6,204	6,206	5,672	4,869	4,490
Oper. Inc.	1,715	1,504	1,323	1,178	1,093	970	790	711	616	558
Depr.	326	294	273	223	200	195	184	176	162	139
Int. Exp.	137	123	85.0	96.0	120	137	122	98.0	61.0	59.0
Pretax Inc.	1,197	1,042	963	529	799	675	185	112	395	423
Eff. Tax Rate	33%	33%	36%	50%	39%	39%	95%	84%	37%	40%
Net Inc.	802	698	630	257	491	402	4.0	13.0	242	247

Balance Sheet & Other Fin. Data (Million $)

	1996	1995	1994	1993	1992	1991	1990	1989	1988	1987
Cash	34.0	53.0	96.0	70.0	118	192	103	147	121	425
Curr. Assets	1,618	1,581	1,601	1,686	1,502	1,519	1,666	1,602	1,363	1,431
Total Assets	6,632	6,315	4,992	4,898	4,354	4,149	4,116	3,932	3,610	3,090
Curr. Liab.	2,229	2,164	1,665	1,851	1,300	1,278	1,298	1,232	863	686
LT Debt	744	857	560	462	693	773	806	629	526	380
Common Eqty.	2,742	2,468	1,989	1,704	2,028	1,793	1,692	1,778	1,895	1,736
Total Cap.	4,028	3,865	2,951	2,435	3,032	2,848	2,789	2,680	2,731	2,388
Cap. Exp.	416	391	421	644	374	361	422	284	387	334
Cash Flow	1,128	992	903	480	691	596	189	189	404	386
Curr. Ratio	0.7	0.7	1.0	0.9	1.2	1.2	1.3	1.3	1.6	2.1
% LT Debt of Cap.	18.5	22.2	19.0	19.0	22.9	27.1	28.9	23.5	19.3	15.9
% Net Inc.of Revs.	10.5	9.6	9.4	3.9	7.8	6.5	0.1	0.2	5.0	5.5
% Ret. on Assets	12.4	11.1	12.7	5.6	11.6	9.8	0.1	0.3	7.2	8.4
% Ret. on Equity	30.8	31.3	34.1	13.8	25.8	23.2	0.3	0.7	13.4	15.1

Data as orig. reptd.; bef. results of disc. opers. and/or spec. items. Per share data adj. for stk. divs. as of ex-div. date. E-Estimated. NA-Not Available. NM-Not Meaningful. NR-Not Ranked.

Office—Campbell Place, Camden, NJ 08103-1799. Tel—(609) 342-4800. Website—http://www.campbellsoups.com Chrmn, Pres & CEO—D. W. Johnson. CFO & Treas—B. L. Anderson. Secy—J. J. Furey. Investor Contact—Leonard F. Griehs. Dirs—A. A. App, E. M. Carpenter, B. Dorrance, T. W. Field Jr., K. B. Foster, H. Golub, D. W. Johnson, D. K. P. Li, P. E. Lippincott, M. A. Malone, C. H. Mott, G. M. Sherman, D. M. Stewart, G. Strawbridge Jr., C. C. Weber. Transfer Agent & Registrar—First Chicago Trust Co. of New York, Jersey City, NJ. Incorporated—in New Jersey in 1922. Empl— 40,650. S&P Analyst: Kenneth A. Shea

STANDARD &POOR'S
STOCK REPORTS

Clorox Co.

556

NYSE Symbol **CLX**

In S&P 500

15-FEB-97

Industry:
Household Products

Summary: This company is a diversified producer of household cleaning, grocery and specialty food products.

S&P Opinion: Accumulate (★★★★)	Recent Price • 122	Yield • 1.9%
	52 Wk Range • 123½-78⅜	12-Mo. P/E • 26.8

Quantitative Evaluations

Outlook
(1 Lowest—5 Highest)
• **1+**

Fair Value
• **97⅛**

Risk
• **Low**

Earn./Div. Rank
• **A**

Technical Eval.
• **Bullish** since 10/96
Rel. Strength Rank
(1 Lowest—99 Highest)
• **87**
Insider Activity
• **Neutral**

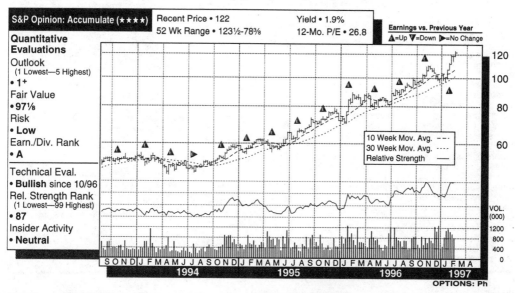

Earnings vs. Previous Year
▲=Up ▼=Down ▶=No Change

10 Week Mov. Avg. - - -
30 Week Mov. Avg. ....
Relative Strength ——

VOL. (000)

OPTIONS: Ph

Overview - 10-FEB-97

Sales of this diversified producer of household cleaning, grocery and specialty food products should continue in a solid uptrend for the second half of FY 97 (Jun.), spurred by higher sales of existing products, contributions from new products (especially in overseas markets), line extensions of existing products, and an aggressive acquisition strategy. Sales should be enhanced by ongoing expansion overseas, particularly in Latin America, the Asia/Pacific region, Russia and Eastern Europe. The company expects 20% of revenues to be derived from overseas markets by 2000, up from 14% FY 96. CLX is pursuing overseas growth mainly through acquisitions of strong businesses in core categories, as well as joint ventures. Margins could widen, as efforts to control overhead and operating costs (estimated at $25 million in the next two years) should offset aggressive new product spending, continued competitive pricing, and costs of overseas expansion. EPS comparisons will also benefit from fewer shares outstanding.

Valuation - 10-FEB-97

CLX shares have climbed nearly 20% so far this year, on top of a 40% gain in 1996, outpacing both its peers and the broader market. We attribute the stock's strong performance to CLX's aggressive overseas expansion strategy, numerous innovative new product introductions, and strong efforts by management to control costs and improve fundamentals. We expect these measures will keep annual earnings growth in the range of 12% to 15% in the foreseeable future. The stock, recently trading at about 25 times estimated FY 97 EPS of $4.80, is priced slightly higher than that of comparable companies in the household products industry. However, we feel that this premium is warranted, given CLX's prospects, and recommend that investors accumulate the stock for capital gains.

Key Stock Statistics

S&P EPS Est. 1997	4.80	Tang. Bk. Value/Share	4.45
P/E on S&P Est. 1997	25.4	Beta	0.67
Dividend Rate/Share	2.32	Shareholders	13,000
Shs. outstg. (M)	51.6	Market cap. (B)	$ 6.3
Avg. daily vol. (M)	0.196	Inst. holdings	47%

Value of $10,000 invested 5 years ago: $ 32,610

Fiscal Year Ending Jun. 30

	1997	1996	1995	1994	1993	1992
Revenues (Million $)						
1Q	590.8	518.5	476.4	449.7	394.7	418.0
2Q	530.2	466.8	414.5	370.8	327.4	352.0
3Q	—	560.1	499.1	481.9	435.6	455.0
4Q	—	672.8	594.3	534.4	476.6	492.0
Yr.	—	2,218	1,984	1,837	1,634	1,717
Earnings Per Share ($)						
1Q	1.27	1.12	1.00	0.85	0.82	0.79
2Q	0.85	0.73	0.64	0.57	0.50	0.45
3Q	E1.30	1.15	1.02	0.93	0.83	0.71
4Q	E1.38	1.28	1.13	1.00	1.00	0.22
Yr.	E4.80	4.28	3.78	3.35	3.07	2.17

Next earnings report expected: mid April

Dividend Data (Dividends have been paid since 1968.)

Amount ($)	Date Decl.	Ex-Div. Date	Stock of Record	Payment Date
0.530	Mar. 20	Apr. 24	Apr. 26	May. 15 '96
0.580	Jul. 17	Jul. 24	Jul. 26	Aug. 15 '96
0.580	Sep. 18	Oct. 23	Oct. 25	Nov. 15 '96
0.580	Jan. 15	Jan. 29	Jan. 31	Feb. 14 '97

A Division of The McGraw-Hill Companies

STANDARD
&POOR'S
STOCK REPORTS

The Clorox Company

556

15-FEB-97

Business Summary - 10-FEB-97

Clorox Co. is an international company whose principal products include non-durable household consumer products sold primarily to grocery stores and other retail stores. In FY 93 (Jun.), the company implemented a new strategy for its domestic operations, and sold two non-strategic businesses, including the frozen food and bottled water divisions. In its continuing operations, CLX is now focused on developing new products and line extensions of existing products, as well as making strategic acquisitions. During FY 96, acquisitions totaled $165.2 million, and included Black Flag insecticides, Lestoil cleaner, and two companies in South America. The two offshore acquisitions were part of CLX's international expansion into developing countries, mainly through joint ventures and acquisitions. Wal-Mart was CLX's largest customer in FY 96, accounting for 14% of total sales.

Clorox's business is divided into three areas, including domestic retail products, international, and institutional. The domestic retail products includes laundry additives, home cleaning products, cat litters, insecticides, charcoal briquets, salad dressings, sauces and water filter systems. Major brand names and products include various laundry and cleaning products using the Clorox name; Liquid-plumr drain unclogger; Formula 409, Lestoil and Pine Sol cleaning solutions; Soft Scrub abrasive liquid cleanser; Tilex mildew cleaner; Kingsford and Match Light charcoals; Scoop Fresh, Control and Fresh Step cat litters; Combat and Black Flag insecticides; Hidden Valley salad dressings; K. C. Masterpiece barbeque sauce; Kitchen Bouquet browning and seasoning sauce; Salad Crispins mini-croutons; Brita water filter systems; and S.O.S steel wool soap pads and home cleaning products.

The international division includes household products, consisting of laundry additives, home cleaning products and insecticides. Products are sold in more than 70 countries, and are manufactured in over 35 plants in the U.S., Puerto Rico and abroad. The institutional division includes institutional cleaning products and food products.

On January 2, 1997, CLX completed its acquisition of Armor All Products Corp. (NASDAQ: ARMR), a producer of auto cleaning products, for about $360 million. Armor All will be operated as a wholly-owned subsidiary of Clorox.

Important Developments

Jan. '97—The company announced that starting March 31, 1997, it will begin to consolidate Armor All Products' operations at its Oakland headquarters and Pleasanton, CA, technical center into like functions at Clorox's general offices. Approximately 106 employees will be affected.

Capitalization

Long Term Debt: $355,575,000 (9/96).

Per Share Data ($)

(Year Ended Jun. 30)	1996	1995	1994	1993	1992	1991	1990	1989	1988	1987
Tangible Bk. Val.	4.45	6.70	7.30	7.57	6.13	5.36	13.12	12.39	9.50	8.43
Cash Flow	6.52	5.73	5.69	4.42	3.65	2.48	3.67	3.38	3.14	2.55
Earnings	4.28	3.78	3.35	3.07	2.17	0.98	2.80	2.63	2.46	1.96
Dividends	2.12	1.92	1.80	1.71	1.59	1.47	1.29	1.09	0.92	0.79
Payout Ratio	50%	51%	54%	56%	74%	151%	45%	41%	38%	40%
Prices - High	96½	79¼	59½	55⅜	52	42⅜	45⅜	44½	33¾	36
- Low	70	55¼	47	44	39½	35	32⅛	30⅛	26⅛	23½
P/E Ratio - High	23	21	18	18	24	43	16	17	14	18
- Low	16	15	14	14	18	36	11	11	11	12

Income Statement Analysis (Million $)

	1996	1995	1994	1993	1992	1991	1990	1989	1988	1987
Revs.	2,218	1,984	1,837	1,634	1,717	1,646	1,484	1,356	1,260	1,126
Oper. Inc.	532	463	420	348	311	295	260	243	237	200
Depr.	117	104	94.1	73.6	80.5	81.4	47.8	41.3	36.6	31.4
Int. Exp.	38.3	25.1	18.4	18.9	24.7	28.2	3.9	7.2	4.1	5.4
Pretax Inc.	370	338	307	275	211	86.0	244	230	212	187
Eff. Tax Rate	40%	41%	41%	39%	44%	39%	37%	37%	37%	44%
Net Inc.	222	201	180	168	118	53.0	154	146	133	105

Balance Sheet & Other Fin. Data (Million $)

	1996	1995	1994	1993	1992	1991	1990	1989	1988	1987
Cash	90.8	137	NA	116	69.0	114	125	233	259	246
Curr. Assets	574	600	504	532	418	467	418	615	504	452
Total Assets	2,179	1,907	1,698	1,649	1,615	1,603	1,138	1,213	1,156	933
Curr. Liab.	624	479	376	372	421	348	226	331	314	194
LT Debt	356	253	216	204	257	400	8.0	7.0	29.0	27.0
Common Eqty.	933	944	909	879	814	784	811	786	713	616
Total Cap.	1,438	1,342	1,258	1,227	1,188	1,247	912	882	842	739
Cap. Exp.	84.8	62.9	36.6	78.0	125	132	157	92.0	170	56.0
Cash Flow	339	305	306	242	198	134	201	187	169	136
Curr. Ratio	0.9	1.3	1.3	1.4	1.0	1.3	1.9	1.9	1.6	2.3
% LT Debt of Cap.	24.8	18.9	17.1	16.6	21.6	32.1	0.8	0.8	3.5	3.6
% Net Inc.of Revs.	10.0	10.1	9.7	10.3	6.9	3.2	10.4	10.7	10.5	9.3
% Ret. on Assets	10.9	11.1	10.7	10.3	7.3	3.8	13.2	12.1	12.6	11.7
% Ret. on Equity	23.7	21.7	20.1	19.8	14.7	6.6	19.5	19.2	19.9	18.0

Data as orig. reptd.; bef. results of disc. opers. and/or spec. items. Per share data adj. for stk. divs. as of ex-div. date. E-Estimated. NA-Not Available. NM-Not Meaningful. NR-Not Ranked.

Office—1221 Broadway, Oakland, CA 94612. **Tel**—(510) 271-7000. **Chrmn & CEO**—G. C. Sullivan. **VP & CFO**—W. F. Ausfahl.**VP & Secy**—E. A. Cutter. **VP, Treas & Investor Contact**—K. M. Rose. **Dirs**—W. F. Ausfahl, D. Boggan Jr., J. W. Collins, U. Fairchild, J. Manchot, D. O. Morton, K. Morwind, E. L. Scarff, L. R. Scott, F. N. Shumway, G. C. Sullivan, J. A. Vohs, C. A. Wolfe. **Transfer Agent & Registrar**—First Chicago Trust Co. of New York, Jersey City, NJ.**Incorporated**—in Ohio in 1957; reincorporated in Delaware in 1986. **Empl**— 5,300. **S&P Analyst:** Maureen C. Carini

15-FEB-97 Industry: Food

Summary: ConAgra is the largest independent U.S. food processor, with interests in branded dry grocery and frozen food products, processed meats, flour milling, and grain merchandising.

S&P Opinion: Accumulate (★★★★)	

Recent Price • 53¼
52 Wk Range • 54¾-37⅝

Yield • 2.0%
12-Mo. P/E • 56.1

Quantitative Evaluations

Outlook
(1 Lowest—5 Highest)
• **2**

Fair Value
• **49⅜**

Risk
• **Low**

Earn./Div. Rank
• **A+**

Technical Eval.
• **Bearish** since 11/95

Rel. Strength Rank
(1 Lowest—99 Highest)
• **65**

Insider Activity
• **NA**

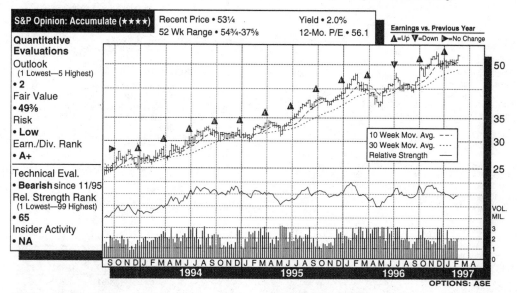

Earnings vs. Previous Year
▲=Up ▼=Down ▶=No Change

10 Week Mov. Avg. ---
30 Week Mov. Avg. ·····
Relative Strength ——

OPTIONS: ASE

Overview - 20-DEC-96

Sales are expected to trend modestly upward in FY 97 (May), as internal growth and acquisition contributions help offset soft beef product selling prices. Grocery/Diversified profits should climb by about 15% in FY 97, driven by continued strength for Hunt-Wesson and frozen foods divisions, and from contributions from acquisitions. Refrigerated product profits should rise only modestly, helped by a strong recovery in FY 97's second half for beef and chicken processing businesses. Inputs & Ingredients profits should record strong mid-teen profit growth, aided by an improved business mix and favorable grain merchandising conditions. The elimination of preferred dividend requirements should also contribute to earnings per share growth of 15% in FY 97, to $2.70, from FY 96's $2.34 (excluding $1.55 of nonrecurring charges).

Valuation - 20-DEC-96

The shares of this well diversified food company have only tracked the overall market in 1996, but have outperformed most other food issues. Although market conditions for meat and chicken processors have been very difficult in recent quarters, ConAgra has been able to offset such operating pressures due to its broad base of businesses, which involve virtually all segments of the food processing industry. We believe that such insulation from changing market conditions should allow the company to extend its targeted long-term EPS growth of 14% well into the future, a goal that exceeds the ability of most of its peers. Trading at only about the P/E level of the S&P 500 index, the shares of this dependable earnings grower are attractive for above average long-term capital gains.

Key Stock Statistics

S&P EPS Est. 1997	2.70	Tang. Bk. Value/Share	NM
P/E on S&P Est. 1997	19.7	Beta	0.83
S&P EPS Est. 1998	3.10	Shareholders	31,000
Dividend Rate/Share	1.09	Market cap. (B)	$ 12.8
Shs. outstg. (M)	240.1	Inst. holdings	49%
Avg. daily vol. (M)	0.374		

Value of $10,000 invested 5 years ago: $ 16,273

Fiscal Year Ending May 31

	1997	1996	1995	1994	1993	1992
Revenues (Million $)						
1Q	6,404	6,436	6,246	5,687	5,520	5,330
2Q	6,765	6,630	6,289	6,355	5,560	5,470
3Q	—	5,773	5,758	5,581	5,060	4,850
4Q	—	5,983	5,817	5,888	5,378	5,570
Yr.	—	24,822	24,109	23,512	21,519	21,220
Earnings Per Share ($)						
1Q	0.42	0.36	0.31	0.27	0.27	0.27
2Q	0.82	0.72	0.63	0.56	0.52	0.46
3Q	E0.65	0.55	0.49	0.43	0.37	0.33
4Q	E0.81	-0.84	0.63	0.55	0.42	0.43
Yr.	E2.70	0.79	2.06	1.81	1.58	1.50

Next earnings report expected: late March

Dividend Data (Dividends have been paid since 1976.)

Amount ($)	Date Decl.	Ex-Div. Date	Stock of Record	Payment Date
0.237	Apr. 05	May. 01	May. 03	Jun. 01 '96
0.237	Jul. 12	Jul. 31	Aug. 02	Sep. 01 '96
0.272	Sep. 26	Oct. 30	Nov. 01	Dec. 02 '96
0.272	Dec. 05	Jan. 29	Jan. 31	Mar. 01 '97

A Division of The McGraw-Hill Companies

STANDARD
&POOR'S
STOCK REPORTS

ConAgra, Inc.

601

15-FEB-97

Business Summary - 20-DEC-96

ConAgra is a diversified producer of processed foods, agricultural commodities and other related products. Sales and operating profit contributions by business segment in FY 96 (May) were:

	Sales	Profits
Grocery/Diversified Products	21%	50%
Refrigerated Foods	52%	27%
Food Inputs & Ingredients	27%	23%

The Grocery/Diversified Products segment consists of those companies that produce branded shelf-stable and frozen food products. Major shelf-stable grocery brands include Hunt's and Healthy Choice tomato products; Wesson oils; Healthy Choice soups; Orville Redenbacher's and Act II popcorn; Peter Pan peanut butter; and Van Camp's canned beans. Major frozen grocery brands include Healthy Choice, Banquet, Marie Callender's, Kid Cuisine, Morton, Chun King and La Choy. Diversified products companies include Lamb-Weston (frozen potatoes); Arrow Industries (maker of private label products); and business interests in seafood, pet products, and frozen microwave products in the U.K.

Refrigerated Foods consists of beef, pork and lamb products (Monfort, Armour); branded processed meats (Armour, Swift Premium, Eckrich, Healthy Choice); poultry (Butterball, Country Pride); cheeses (County Line); and refrigerated dessert toppings (Reddi-Wip);

Food Inputs & Ingredients businesses include crop protection chemicals and fertilizers; grain processing (flour, oat and dry corn milling; barley processing); and worldwide commodity trading (grains, oilseeds, edible beans and peas, and other commodities).

Important Developments

Dec. '96—The company attributed a nearly 15% rise in earnings per share in FY 97 (May)'s first half to strong operating profit growth for the company's Grocery/Diversified (26%) and Food Input & Ingredients (19%) segments, which outweighed a 20% decline at Refrigerated Foods. Management continues to expect double-digit earnings per share growth in FY 97, which would represent the company's 17th consecutive year of record earnings, excluding non-recurring charges.

Capitalization

Long Term Debt: $2,252,300,000 (8/96).

Per Share Data ($)

(Year Ended May 31)	1996	1995	1994	1993	1992	1991	1990	1989	1988	1987
Tangible Bk. Val.	NM	0.30	-1.61	-2.45	-2.12	-4.26	4.59	4.61	4.22	3.71
Cash Flow	2.60	3.70	3.42	3.07	2.88	2.33	1.90	1.61	1.34	1.23
Earnings	0.79	2.06	1.81	1.58	1.50	1.42	1.25	1.09	0.86	0.82
Dividends	0.92	0.78	0.70	0.60	0.52	0.44	0.39	0.33	0.29	0.25
Payout Ratio	116%	38%	38%	41%	35%	32%	31%	30%	33%	30%
Cal. Yrs.	1995	1994	1993	1992	1991	1990	1989	1988	1987	1986
Prices - High	41¾	33⅛	33⅝	35¾	36½	25½	20⅛	15⅛	16⅞	14¼
- Low	29¾	25½	22¾	24½	22⅜	15⅛	12⅞	10½	9¼	8⅝
P/E Ratio - High	53	16	19	23	24	18	16	14	20	17
- Low	38	12	13	16	15	11	10	10	11	10

Income Statement Analysis (Million $)

	1996	1995	1994	1993	1992	1991	1990	1989	1988	1987
Revs.	24,822	24,109	23,512	21,519	21,219	19,505	15,501	11,340	9,475	9,002
Oper. Inc.	1,629	1,476	1,337	1,213	1,207	1,040	623	538	382	395
Depr.	408	376	368	349	319	251	120	94.0	85.0	73.0
Int. Exp.	352	311	289	283	356	329	192	149	76.0	60.0
Pretax Inc.	409	826	720	631	588	515	357	312	240	272
Eff. Tax Rate	54%	40%	39%	38%	37%	40%	35%	37%	36%	45%
Net Inc.	189	496	437	392	372	311	232	198	155	149

Balance Sheet & Other Fin. Data (Million $)

	1996	1995	1994	1993	1992	1991	1990	1989	1988	1987
Cash	114	60.0	452	447	536	967	333	607	168	195
Curr. Assets	5,567	5,140	5,143	4,487	4,371	4,343	3,348	3,160	2,076	1,707
Total Assets	11,197	10,801	10,722	9,989	9,759	9,420	4,804	4,278	3,043	2,483
Curr. Liab.	5,194	3,965	4,753	4,273	4,081	4,087	2,968	2,651	1,636	1,237
LT Debt	2,263	2,520	2,207	2,159	2,124	2,093	635	560	490	429
Common Eqty.	2,256	2,495	2,227	2,055	2,232	1,817	1,096	950	814	723
Total Cap.	5,044	5,895	4,889	4,570	4,713	4,266	1,837	1,627	1,407	1,246
Cap. Exp.	669	428	395	341	370	332	349	253	196	202
Cash Flow	597	847	782	716	667	543	350	291	238	221
Curr. Ratio	1.1	1.3	1.1	1.1	1.1	1.1	1.1	1.2	1.3	1.4
% LT Debt of Cap.	44.9	42.7	45.1	47.3	45.1	49.1	34.6	34.4	34.8	34.4
% Net Inc.of Revs.	0.8	2.1	1.9	1.8	1.8	1.6	1.5	1.7	1.6	1.7
% Ret. on Assets	1.7	4.6	4.2	3.8	3.7	4.2	5.1	5.3	5.6	6.4
% Ret. on Equity	7.6	20.0	19.4	16.4	16.4	19.0	22.3	22.0	20.0	22.3

Data as orig. reptd.; bef. results of disc. opers. and/or spec. items. Per share data adj. for stk. divs. as of ex-div. date. E-Estimated. NA-Not Available. NM-Not Meaningful. NR-Not Ranked.

Office—One ConAgra Dr., Omaha, NE 68102-5001. **Tel**—(402) 595-4000. **Chrmn & CEO**—P. B. Fletcher. **Vice-Chrmn & Pres**—B. Rohde. **VP & Investor Contact**—Walter H. Casey. **Dirs**—P. B. Fletcher, C. M. Harper, R. A. Krane, G. Rauenhorst, C. E. Reichardt, B. Rohde, R. W. Roskens, M. R. Scardino, W. Scott, Jr., W. G. Stocks, J. J. Thompson, F. B. Wells, T. R. Williams, C. K. Yeutter. **Transfer Agent & Registrar**—Chase Bank, NYC. **Incorporated**—in Nebraska in 1919; reincorporated in Delaware in 1975. **Empl**— 90,871. **S&P Analyst:** Kenneth A. Shea

Eaton Vance

804G

NYSE Symbol **EV**

In S&P SmallCap 600

15-FEB-97 Industry:
Securities

Summary: This Boston-based holding company's primary business is investment management. In August 1996, trading moved to the NYSE from the Nasdaq Stock Market.

S&P Opinion: Accumulate (★★★★)

| Recent Price • 46 | Yield • 1.7% |
| 52 Wk Range • 49¾-30 | 12-Mo. P/E • 12.3 |

Quantitative Evaluations

Outlook
(1 Lowest—5 Highest)
• 1⁻

Fair Value
• 35¼

Risk
• NA

Earn./Div. Rank
• A-

Technical Eval.
• NA

Rel. Strength Rank
(1 Lowest—99 Highest)
• 59

Insider Activity
• Favorable

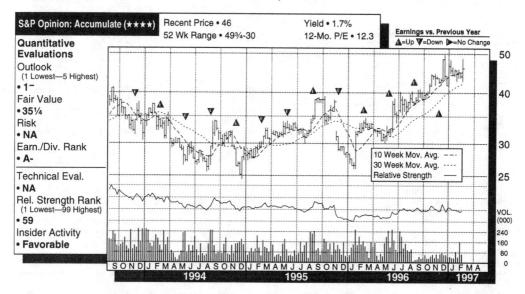

Earnings vs. Previous Year
▲=Up ▼=Down ▷=No Change

10 Week Mov. Avg. - - -
30 Week Mov. Avg. · · · ·
Relative Strength ——

Overview - 10-FEB-97

Operating earnings per share are expected to increase 15% in FY 97, as lower expenses and steady growth in assets under management should help profits grow at a faster rate than investment advisory revenue and distribution fees. Despite strong performance records, Eaton Vance's equity funds, which account for 20% of managed assets, have been slow growers relative to the rapidly expanding mutual fund industry. The company has targeted this area for improvement and will pursue strategic acquisitions of funds and fund managers to quicken the pace of growth. Expansion is also planned for EV's Medallion series of offshore funds and international funds managed by Eaton's Lloyd George Management affiliate, based in Hong Kong. EV's strong balance sheet includes $116.4 million ($12.15 per share) in cash, cash equivalents and short-term investments, providing the company with flexibility to make acquisitions and repurchase shares. We also expect the dividend to be increased by at least 10% in 1997.

Valuation - 10-FEB-97

The shares of this investment management firm surged 69% in 1996, more than triple the gain in the S&P SmallCap 600 Index. Despite the rapid ascent, the shares of Eaton Vance remain undervalued relative to its peers in the mutual fund industry and the market as a whole. The stock was recently trading at just 10.5 times our 1997 EPS estimate of $4.30 and at two times the company's book value. The rapid pace of growth in the mutual fund industry is expected to continue in 1997 and with new management taking a proactive role in expanding market share, we continue to recommend Eaton Vance for above-average appreciation.

Key Stock Statistics

S&P EPS Est. 1997	4.30	Tang. Bk. Value/Share	22.14
P/E on S&P Est. 1997	10.7	Beta	0.36
Dividend Rate/Share	0.80	Shareholders	1,000
Shs. outstg. (M)	9.5	Market cap. (B)	$0.435
Avg. daily vol. (M)	0.017	Inst. holdings	31%

Value of $10,000 invested 5 years ago: NA

Fiscal Year Ending Oct. 31

	1997	1996	1995	1994	1993	1992
Revenues (Million $)						
1Q	47.59	44.50	41.54	53.89	42.88	—
2Q	—	45.46	40.73	54.25	46.25	—
3Q	—	45.06	42.69	54.81	49.38	—
4Q	—	46.34	42.96	55.83	50.65	41.08
Yr.	—	181.4	167.9	218.0	189.1	153.0
Earnings Per Share ($)						
1Q	1.03	1.04	0.61	0.67	0.62	0.64
2Q	E1.05	0.93	0.65	0.80	0.86	0.53
3Q	E1.15	0.98	0.92	0.65	1.19	0.78
4Q	E1.05	0.79	0.72	0.89	0.41	0.59
Yr.	E4.30	3.74	2.90	3.00	3.09	2.49

Next earnings report expected: mid February

Dividend Data (Dividends have been paid since 1976.)

Amount ($)	Date Decl.	Ex-Div. Date	Stock of Record	Payment Date
0.170	Apr. 10	Apr. 26	Apr. 30	May. 13 '96
0.170	Jul. 17	Jul. 29	Jul. 31	Aug. 12 '96
0.200	Oct. 09	Oct. 29	Oct. 31	Nov. 11 '96
0.200	Jan. 08	Jan. 29	Jan. 31	Feb. 10 '97

A Division of The McGraw-Hill Companies

Business Summary - 10-FEB-97

Eaton Vance Corp. is a Boston, MA-based investment advisory firm that manages over 160 mutual funds as well as investments for over 800 individual and institutional clients. Historically, the company has focused its energies on offering products in the fixed-income sector, with a particular emphasis on tax-free municipal bonds. However, with industry dynamics pushing an increasing number of investors to the stock market for superior investment returns, Eaton Vance has targeted its equity business as a growth area. At fiscal year-end 1996 (October), EV's $17.4 billion in assets under management were divided as follows:

	FY 96 (Oct)
Non-taxable fixed income	53%
Equities	20%
Bank loans	18%
Taxable fixed income	8%
Money market	1%

Eaton Vance derives the vast majority of its revenue from investment advisor and administration fees and distribution income received from the Eaton Vance funds and separately managed accounts. These fees are calculated as a percentage of assets under management, and as such, the company's operating results are largely dependent upon its ability to attract and retain funds, and on the overall health of the securities markets. In fiscal 1996, assets under management rose 8%, reflecting a strong rise in mutual fund sales, the

introduction of three new equity funds and better off-shore fund sales.

Net fund sales rose $0.5 billion in FY 96, due in large part to a successful sales campaign. Eaton Vance employs two separate mutual fund sales teams that operate through different distribution channels. The company uses targeted marketing to push its funds through a wide variety of national and regional broker/dealers, independent broker/dealers and banks. To further improve distribution, EV has recently begun marketing its products through independent fee-based advisors.

Eaton Vance has placed particular emphasis on growing its equity fund business, which despite strong performance in recent years, has not attracted a strong influx of investor funds. The company has introduced new equity funds, and it will continue to seek top-performing managers to help the cause. EV's strong balance sheet gives the company the ability to seek acquisitions to fuel growth in its equity business.

Also targeted for expansion is the Eaton Vance Medallion family of offshore funds. These international equity funds are managed by 24%-owned Lloyd George Management, based in Hong Kong.

Eaton Vance also operates Northeast Properties, a real estate subsidiary with 670,000 square feet of property in Massachusetts, New Hampshire and New York. EV expects to complete the termination of its gold mining operations at the end of calendar 1997.

Capitalization

Long Term Debt: $54,549,000 (10/96).

Per Share Data ($)

(Year Ended Oct. 31)	1996	1995	1994	1993	1992	1991	1990	1989	1988	1987
Tangible Bk. Val.	22.14	20.67	17.97	15.57	10.05	7.74	6.25	5.62	4.73	4.54
Cash Flow	3.99	3.16	8.97	8.11	6.59	5.25	3.80	2.52	1.45	1.42
Earnings	3.74	2.90	3.00	3.09	2.49	1.75	1.03	0.99	1.37	1.35
Dividends	0.71	0.65	0.60	0.49	0.36	0.29	0.24	0.21	0.19	0.15
Payout Ratio	19%	22%	20%	16%	14%	17%	23%	21%	14%	11%
Prices - High	44¾	39¼	37½	41¼	30½	16½	14	14⅛	11¾	16⅜
- Low	26	27¼	24½	29	15½	7⅞	7⅜	11	7½	6½
P/E Ratio - High	12	14	13	13	12	9	14	14	9	12
- Low	7	9	8	9	6	5	7	11	5	5

Income Statement Analysis (Million $)

	1996	1995	1994	1993	1992	1991	1990	1989	1988	1987
Commissions	100	85.4	85.8	75.2	69.5	61.5	55.1	NA	NA	NA
Int. Inc.	NA	NA	4.9	4.6	3.7	3.7	2.7	3.3	2.0	1.5
Total Revs.	181	168	218	189	153	120	94.0	64.0	47.0	52.0
Int. Exp.	3.7	4.7	5.3	4.9	3.3	3.1	3.6	NA	NA	NA
Pretax Inc.	59.9	46.1	47.7	47.0	33.1	21.1	16.4	13.5	17.0	20.3
Eff. Tax Rate	40%	38%	40%	42%	42%	40%	53%	46%	39%	47%
Net Inc.	35.8	30.4	28.5	27.3	19.3	12.7	7.7	7.3	10.7	11.6

Balance Sheet & Other Fin. Data (Million $)

	1996	1995	1994	1993	1992	1991	1990	1989	1988	1987
Total Assets	360	358	456	426	318	278	224	242	77.0	81.0
Cash Items	116	79.0	34.0	28.7	25.5	17.1	15.7	91.0	11.0	6.0
Receivables	7.7	1.6	13.1	11.6	10.5	7.2	4.1	3.5	1.9	3.7
Secs. Owned	NA	NA	88.3	80.2	64.0	50.8	36.1	NA	NA	NA
Sec. Borrowed	NA	Nil	Nil	Nil	Nil	Nil	Nil	NA	NA	NA
Due Brokers & Cust.	NA	Nil	Nil	Nil	Nil	Nil	Nil	NA	NA	NA
Other Liabs.	125	138	226	205	162	153	124	NA	NA	NA
Capitalization:										
Debt	54.5	56.1	60.3	73.2	78.4	64.0	50.6	14.2	14.2	7.5
Equity	211	195	166	145	77.5	59.6	47.9	43.9	37.4	41.8
Total	336	333	229	221	156	125	100	58.0	52.0	49.0
% Ret. on Revs.	19.8	16.1	13.1	14.5	12.6	10.6	8.2	11.4	23.1	22.3
% Ret. on Assets	10.0	6.6	6.5	7.4	6.4	5.1	3.3	3.6	13.6	8.1
% Ret. on Equity	17.7	15.0	18.3	24.7	28.0	23.5	16.9	17.9	29.1	31.2

Data as orig. reptd.; bef. results of disc opers. and/or spec. items. Per share data adj. for stk. divs. as of ex-div. date. E-Estimated. NA-Not Available. NM-Not Meaningful. NR-Not Ranked.

Office—24 Federal St., Boston, MA 02110. **Tel**—(617) 482-8260. **Chrmn**—L. T. Clay. **Vice Chrmn**—M. D. Gardner. **Pres & CEO**—J. B. Hawkes. **VP & Secy**—T. Otis. **CFO & Investor Contact**—William M. Steul. **Dirs**—J. G. L. Cabot, L. T. Clay, M. D. Gardner, J. B. Hawkes, B. A. Rowland, Jr., R. Z. Sorenson. **Transfer Agent & Registrar**—BostonEquiserve. **Incorporated**—in Maryland in 1959. **Empl**— 369. **S&P Analyst:** M.B., B.M.

15-FEB-97

Industry:
Retail Stores

Summary: Family Dollar operates a chain of more than 2,610 retail discount stores in 38 states, located mostly in communities with populations under 50,000.

Quantitative Evaluations

Outlook
(1 Lowest—5 Highest)
• **2**

Fair Value
• **21⅞**

Risk
• **Average**

Earn./Div. Rank
• **A-**

Technical Eval.
• **Bearish** since 12/96

Rel. Strength Rank
(1 Lowest—99 Highest)
• **87**

Insider Activity
• **Neutral**

Recent Price • 22⅞	Yield • 2.1%
52 Wk Range • 23¼-12¼	12-Mo. P/E • 20.4

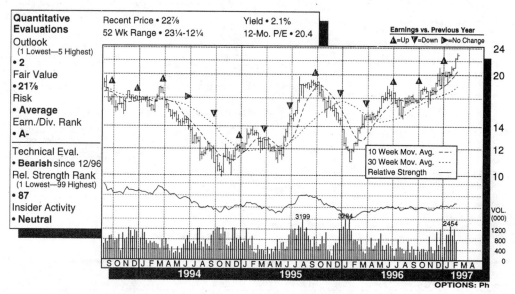

Earnings vs. Previous Year
▲=Up ▼=Down ▶=No Change

10 Week Mov. Avg. ---
30 Week Mov. Avg. ....
Relative Strength ——

VOL. (000)

OPTIONS: Ph

Business Profile - 14-JAN-97

The company's aggressive expansion program continued in FY 96 (Aug.) with the opening of 223 new stores (58 stores were closed). FDO currently operates 2,612 stores and plans a net addition of 185 stores for FY 97. A move to everyday low pricing has helped increase traffic at its stores. The company has also adopted a new interior store layout which presents a more customer-friendly environment. FDO noted that 250 stores operated under this new format by the end of FY 96 and that more than 100 other locations will be remodeled or refurbished in FY 97.

Operational Review - 14-JAN-97

Net sales in the first quarter of FY 97 (Aug.) advanced 15%, year to year, reflecting more stores in operation, and a move to everyday low pricing; same-store sales rose 8.2%. Gross margins narrowed, and SG&A expenses were 15% higher; pretax income was up 20%. After taxes at 38.8% in both periods, net income increased to $17,359,822 ($0.31 a share) from $14,507,769 ($0.26). Comparable store sales of hardline and softline (primarily apparel and shoes) goods rose 13% and 1.0%, respectively, during the period.

Stock Performance - 14-FEB-97

In the past 30 trading days, FDO's shares have increased 15%, compared to a 8% rise in the S&P 500. Average trading volume for the past five days was 148,160 shares, compared with the 40-day moving average of 209,928 shares.

Key Stock Statistics

Dividend Rate/Share	0.48	Shareholders	2,500
Shs. outstg. (M)	57.0	Market cap. (B)	$ 1.3
Avg. daily vol. (M)	0.276	Inst. holdings	58%
Tang. Bk. Value/Share	7.83		
Beta	0.85		

Value of $10,000 invested 5 years ago: $ 14,565

Fiscal Year Ending Aug. 31

	1997	1996	1995	1994	1993	1992
Revenues (Million $)						
1Q	454.9	396.2	356.3	335.1	305.0	264.0
2Q	—	448.3	420.9	398.8	356.5	318.0
3Q	—	427.9	379.8	349.2	310.1	280.0
4Q	—	442.3	389.8	345.4	326.3	297.0
Yr.	—	1,715	1,547	1,428	1,297	1,159
Earnings Per Share ($)						
1Q	0.31	0.26	0.28	0.27	0.25	0.21
2Q	—	0.28	0.30	0.39	0.37	0.32
3Q	—	0.33	0.29	0.31	0.31	0.27
4Q	—	0.20	0.16	0.13	0.22	0.20
Yr.	—	1.07	1.03	1.10	1.15	1.00

Next earnings report expected: early April

Dividend Data (Dividends have been paid since 1976.)

Amount ($)	Date Decl.	Ex-Div. Date	Stock of Record	Payment Date
0.110	May. 15	Jun. 12	Jun. 14	Jul. 15 '96
0.110	Aug. 15	Sep. 12	Sep. 16	Oct. 15 '96
0.110	Nov. 08	Dec. 11	Dec. 13	Jan. 15 '97
0.120	Jan. 16	Mar. 12	Mar. 14	Apr. 15 '97

A Division of The **McGraw-Hill** *Companies*

Business Summary - 14-JAN-97

This company operates a chain of self-service retail discount stores under the Family Dollar name. As of January 7, 1997, there were 2,612 stores operating in 38 states, ranging as far northwest as South Dakota, northeast to Maine, southeast to Florida and southwest to New Mexico. States with significant concentrations of stores include Texas, North Carolina, Georgia, Ohio, Florida, Virginia, Tennessee, South Carolina, Pennsylvania and Alabama.

The number of stores in operation at the end of recent fiscal years were:

	1996
1996	2,581
1995	2,416
1994	2,215
1993	2,035
1992	1,885
1991	1,759

Each Family Dollar store sells a wide variety of mostly first-quality merchandise, with 37% of sales in FY 96 (Aug.) (down from 39% in FY 95) derived from soft goods, such as apparel, shoes, linen, blankets, bedspreads and curtains; the stores also carry hard goods, including automotive supplies, paints, toys, housewares, school supplies, candy and health and beauty aids.

Merchandise, the majority of which is priced at $17.99 or less, is purchased from about 1,500 suppliers. About 63% of the items carried are manufactured in the U.S.

Stores are located in both rural and urban areas, and more than 50% of the stores operate in communities with populations under 15,000. The units are freestanding or located in shopping centers, with the typical store averaging 6,000 to 8,000 sq. ft. of total area. Most of the stores are leased.

During FY 96, the company opened 223 new stores and closed 58 outlets, ending the year with 2,518 stores in operation in 38 states. FDO expects to open approximately 235 new stores in FY 97, close 50 stores and expand or relocate an additional 100 locations.

Important Developments

Jan. '97—FDO reported that net sales in the first quarter of FY 97 (Aug.) rose 15%, year to year, reflecting more stores in operation and higher sales in existing stores; same-store sales increased 8.2%. Also, Family Dollar announced that December total sales also advanced 15% and that comparable same-store sales climbed 8.0%.

Capitalization

Long Term Debt: None (11/96).

Per Share Data ($)

(Year Ended Aug. 31)	1996	1995	1994	1993	1992	1991	1990	1989	1988	1987
Tangible Bk. Val.	7.83	7.19	6.54	5.74	4.85	4.08	3.55	3.23	3.02	2.75
Cash Flow	1.50	1.42	1.44	1.45	1.26	0.96	0.75	0.61	0.67	0.58
Earnings	1.07	1.03	1.10	1.15	1.00	0.72	22.00	0.39	0.49	0.43
Dividends	0.42	0.37	0.32	0.28	0.24	0.21	0.19	0.17	0.15	0.13
Payout Ratio	39%	36%	29%	24%	24%	29%	37%	44%	30%	30%
Prices - High	18½	19¾	18⅜	23⅝	24⅝	17⅛	7⅝	7⅛	8	9⅞
- Low	11	10⅞	10⅛	15⅛	13⅛	5¾	4½	4⅞	4¼	3½
P/E Ratio - High	17	19	17	21	25	23	15	18	16	23
- Low	10	11	9	13	13	8	9	13	9	8

Income Statement Analysis (Million $)

	1996	1995	1994	1993	1992	1991	1990	1989	1988	1987
Revs.	1,715	1,547	1,428	1,297	1,159	989	874	757	669	560
Oper. Inc.	123	117	120	120	103	76.0	54.0	43.0	50.0	50.0
Depr.	24.6	22.2	19.5	17.2	14.7	13.1	12.7	12.0	10.1	8.5
Int. Exp.	Nil	Nil	0.4	0.2	Nil	0.4	1.1	1.7	0.9	Nil
Pretax Inc.	99	94.0	100	103	88.9	63.7	47.6	35.1	44.2	46.8
Eff. Tax Rate	39%	39%	38%	37%	37%	37%	40%	39%	38%	47%
Net Inc.	60.6	58.0	62.0	64.4	55.7	40.2	28.7	21.5	27.3	24.8

Balance Sheet & Other Fin. Data (Million $)

	1996	1995	1994	1993	1992	1991	1990	1989	1988	1987
Cash	18.8	8.9	9.9	5.7	1.7	25.0	4.6	0.7	7.0	13.3
Curr. Assets	508	475	436	402	359	294	252	219	192	159
Total Assets	697	636	593	537	478	399	355	324	291	242
Curr. Liab.	234	210	206	197	188	158	144	132	113	75.0
LT Debt	Nil	Nil	Nil	Nil	Nil	Nil	Nil	Nil	Nil	Nil
Common Eqty.	445	408	370	323	272	227	197	179	167	160
Total Cap.	463	426	387	339	287	242	211	192	177	167
Cap. Exp.	54.3	27.7	42.6	32.5	30.1	14.8	12.5	18.3	25.8	26.0
Cash Flow	85.2	80.3	81.4	81.6	70.4	53.3	41.4	33.5	37.5	33.3
Curr. Ratio	2.2	2.3	2.1	2.0	1.9	1.9	1.8	1.7	1.7	2.1
% LT Debt of Cap.	Nil	Nil	Nil	Nil	Nil	Nil	Nil	Nil	Nil	Nil
% Net Inc.of Revs.	3.6	3.8	4.5	5.0	4.8	4.1	3.3	2.8	4.1	4.4
% Ret. on Assets	9.1	9.5	10.9	12.7	12.7	10.6	8.5	7.0	10.5	10.8
% Ret. on Equity	14.3	15.0	17.8	21.6	22.3	18.9	15.3	12.4	17.1	16.5

Data as orig. reptd.; bef. results of disc. opers. and/or spec. items. Per share data adj. for stk. divs. as of ex-div. date. E-Estimated. NA-Not Available. NM-Not Meaningful. NR-Not Ranked.

Office—10401 Old Monroe Rd., Matthews, NC, 28105. **Tel**—(704) 847-6961. **Chrmn, CEO & Treas**—L. Levine.**Pres & COO**—J. D. Reier.**Exec VP-Secy & Investor Contact**—George R. Mahoney Jr. **Sr VP-Fin**—C. M. Sowers. **Dirs**—M. R. Bernstein, J. H. Hance, L. Levine, G. R. Mahoney Jr., J. G. Martin, J. D. Reier. **Transfer Agent & Registrar**—ChaseMellon Shareholder Services, L.L.C., NYC. **Incorporated**—in Delaware in 1969. **Empl**— 20,700. **S&P Analyst:** Philip D. Wohl

15-FEB-97

Industry: Finance

Summary: "Fannie Mae," a U.S. Government-sponsored company, uses mostly borrowed funds to buy a variety of mortgages, thereby creating a secondary market for mortgage lenders.

S&P Opinion: Accumulate (★★★★)	Recent Price • 42⅝	Yield • 2.0%
	52 Wk Range • 43¾–27½	12-Mo. P/E • 17.0

Quantitative Evaluations

Outlook (1 Lowest—5 Highest)
• **3**

Fair Value
• **40%**

Risk
• **Low**

Earn./Div. Rank
• **A**

Technical Eval.
• **Bullish** since 3/96

Rel. Strength Rank (1 Lowest—99 Highest)
• **79**

Insider Activity
• **NA**

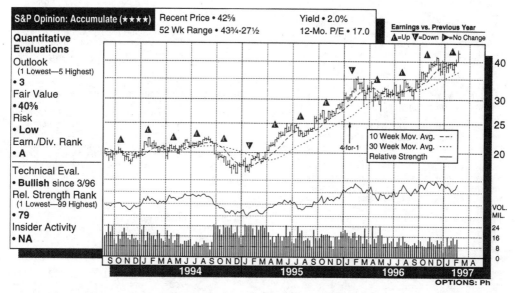

Earnings vs. Previous Year
▲=Up ▼=Down ▶=No Change

10 Week Mov. Avg. ----
30 Week Mov. Avg. ····
Relative Strength —

4-for-1

VOL. MIL.

OPTIONS: Ph

Overview - 06-FEB-97

Fannie Mae should increase its earnings per share 10% to 15% a year for the foreseeable future (excluding nonrecurring expenses such as a charitable contribution in 1995). This outlook reflects projected growth in the mortgage portfolio Fannie Mae holds for its own account (about two-thirds of profits). FNM should expand this portfolio about 10%-13% in 1997, based on projected growth of 7% to 9% in mortgage debt, home price inflation and FNM's plans to increase its purchases of mortgage-backed securities. The mortgage-backed securities segment (about one-third of net income) is growing more slowly, partly reflecting the fact that a high percentage of mortgages has already been securitized and reduced demand for MBS on the part of certain financial institutions. No major increase in credit provisioning is likely, given the company's strong reserve position. Long-term prospects are further enhanced by share repurchases.

Valuation - 06-FEB-97

Fannie Mae, which we regard as a solid core holding, carries an accumulate recommendation. The company enjoys favorable long-term growth prospects, a result of projected increases in mortgage debt outstanding, new housing initiatives and its access to low-cost financing by virtue of its quasi-agency status. Another positive is the fact that Fannie Mae faces only one competitor in its major markets. The company typically generates a high return on shareholders' equity. The stock is selling at a P/E ratio of about 14 on projected 1997 earnings per share of $2.80, below the market's P/E. Given the company's strengths, we believe the shares deserve a richer P/E multiple.

Key Stock Statistics

S&P EPS Est. 1997	2.80	Tang. Bk. Value/Share	10.04
P/E on S&P Est. 1997	15.2	Beta	1.37
Dividend Rate/Share	0.84	Shareholders	11,000
Shs. outstg. (M)	1092.0	Market cap. (B)	$ 46.5
Avg. daily vol. (M)	2.625	Inst. holdings	76%

Value of $10,000 invested 5 years ago: $ 26,156

Fiscal Year Ending Dec. 31

	1996	1995	1994	1993	1992	1991
Revenues (Million $)						
1Q	6,065	5,290	4,304	2,863	3,470	3,315
2Q	6,146	5,452	4,496	3,897	3,642	3,265
3Q	6,317	5,631	4,735	4,071	3,670	3,364
4Q	—	5,866	5,038	4,222	3,777	3,402
Yr.	—	22,250	18,573	16,053	14,559	13,346
Earnings Per Share ($)						
1Q	0.61	0.51	0.50	0.44	0.35	0.30
2Q	0.61	0.52	0.50	0.45	0.38	0.38
3Q	0.63	0.55	0.49	0.48	0.39	0.32
4Q	0.65	0.37	0.47	0.49	0.39	0.33
Yr.	2.50	1.96	1.95	1.86	1.50	1.33

Next earnings report expected: mid April

Dividend Data (Dividends have been paid since 1956.)

Amount ($)	Date Decl.	Ex-Div. Date	Stock of Record	Payment Date
0.190	Apr. 16	Apr. 26	Apr. 30	May. 25 '96
0.190	Jul. 16	Jul. 29	Jul. 31	Aug. 25 '96
0.190	Oct. 15	Oct. 29	Oct. 31	Nov. 25 '96
0.210	Jan. 21	Jan. 29	Jan. 31	Feb. 25 '97

A Division of The McGraw·Hill Companies

Business Summary - 06-FEB-97

The Federal National Mortgage Association, more commonly known as "Fannie Mae," is a government-sponsored enterprise, chartered by Congress to increase the availability of mortgage credit for homebuyers. Its mission, in essence, is to increase the rate of home ownership--which in turn makes American society more stable. The company's predecessor was formed during the Great Depression to make home ownership possible during a time when it was nearly impossible for people in certain parts of the country to obtain a mortgage. The company basically operates in two business segments.

In its retained portfolio business, which accounts for about two-thirds of profits, the company buys a variety of mortgages from banks, thrifts, mortgage bankers and others for its own account. The term "retained" is intended to indicate that Fannie Mae holds these mortgages for investment just as an S & L, which originates mortgages, holds mortgages in its own portfolio. The company finances its mortgage purchases by debt offerings of various maturities. This business activity is especially profitable because FNM enjoys access to low-cost funds by virtue of its quasi-agency status, that is, investors believe there is a very low risk of default on the company's bonds because, in the event of trouble, the government would probably step in and make good on the obligation. Fannie Mae is an ex-

tremely large company. As an indication of the company's size, at the end of 1995, Fannie Mae owned $253.5 billion of mortgages, equal to some 6.5% of the total mortgages outstanding nationwide.

In its securitization operations, which account for much of the remaining profits, the company swaps mortgage-backed securities for mortgages with various lending institutions and in the process earns a fee of about one-fifth of 1% or 0.20%. One reason lenders would swap loans for MBS is that the latter add to its liquidity. Fannie Mae essentially functions as a "mortgage insurer" to the extent that it accepts the risk of default on the mortgage in exchange for a fee or a premium.

Finally, the company earns a small amount for guaranteeing complex mortgage-backed securities that are put together by Wall Street firms.

Although FNM is highly profitable in a variety of interest rate environments, Congress is constantly concerned about its risk exposure on the $800 billion of mortgages and mortgage-backed securities outstanding--since the U. S. government ultimately would have to make good on large scale defaults. Therefore, Congress has established capital standards, which the company meets.

Capitalization

Short Term Debt: $151,549,000,000 (9/96).
Long Term Debt: $167,604,000,000 (9/96).
Preferred Stock: $1,000,000,000.

Per Share Data ($)

(Year Ended Dec. 31)	1996	1995	1994	1993	1992	1991	1990	1989	1988	1987
Tangible Bk. Val.	NA	10.04	8.74	7.39	6.20	5.08	4.14	3.13	2.39	1.92
Earnings	2.50	1.94	1.95	1.86	1.50	1.33	1.13	0.79	0.54	0.39
Dividends	0.76	0.68	0.60	0.46	0.35	0.26	0.18	0.11	0.06	0.03
Payout Ratio	30%	35%	31%	25%	23%	20%	16%	14%	11%	8%
Prices - High	41⅝	31½	22⅝	21½	19⅜	17⅜	11⅛	11⅝	4⅜	4
- Low	27½	17¼	17	18¼	13¾	8⅛	6¼	4¼	2⁷⁄₁₆	2⅛
P/E Ratio - High	17	16	12	12	13	13	10	15	8	10
- Low	11	9	9	10	9	6	6	5	5	5

Income Statement Analysis (Million $)

	1996	1995	1994	1993	1992	1991	1990	1989	1988	1987
Int. Mtgs.	NA	18,154	15,851	13,957	12,651	11,603	10,958	10,103	9,629	9,586
Int. Invest.	NA	2,917	1,496	876	884	990	1,111	977	597	257
Int. Exp.	NA	18,024	14,524	12,300	11,476	10,815	10,476	9,889	9,389	8,953
Guaranty Fees	NA	0.0	1,083	961	834	675	536	408	328	263
Loan Loss Prov.	NA	140	155	175	320	370	310	310	365	360
Admin. Exp.	NA	546	525	443	381	319	286	254	218	197
Pretax Inc.	NA	2,995	3,146	3,005	2,382	2,081	1,647	1,104	663	568
Eff. Tax Rate	NA	28%	32%	32%	31%	30%	29%	27%	24%	34%
Net Inc.	NA	2,155	2,141	2,042	1,649	1,455	1,173	807	507	376

Balance Sheet & Other Fin. Data (Million $)

	1996	1995	1994	1993	1992	1991	1990	1989	1988	1987
Mtges.	NA	252,588	220,525	189,892	156,021	126,486	113,875	107,756	99,867	93,470
Inv.	NA	57,273	46,335	21,396	14,786	10,999	9,868	6,656	5,289	3,468
Cash & Equiv.	NA	318	231	977	5,193	3,194	4,178	5,214	2,859	2,457
Total Assets	NA	316,550	272,508	216,979	180,978	147,072	133,113	124,315	112,258	103,459
ST Debt	NA	146,153	112,602	71,950	56,404	34,608	38,453	36,346	36,599	29,718
LT Debt	NA	153,021	144,628	129,162	109,896	99,329	84,950	79,718	68,860	67,339
Equity	NA	10,959	9,541	8,052	6,774	5,547	3,941	2,991	2,260	1,811
% Ret. on Assets	NA	0.7	0.9	1.0	1.0	1.0	0.9	0.7	0.5	0.4
% Ret. on Equity	NA	21.0	24.3	27.5	26.8	30.7	33.8	30.7	24.9	25.1
Equity/Assets Ratio	NA	3.5	3.6	3.7	3.8	3.4	2.7	2.2	1.9	NA
Price Times Book Value:										
Hi	NA	3.1	2.6	2.9	3.1	3.4	2.7	3.7	1.8	2.1
Low	NA	1.7	1.9	2.5	2.2	1.6	1.5	1.3	1.0	1.1

Data as orig. reptd.; bef. results of disc. opers. and/or spec. items. Per share data adj. for stk. divs. as of ex-div. date. E-Estimated. NA-Not Available. NM-Not Meaningful. NR-Not Ranked.

Office—3900 Wisconsin Ave. N.W., Washington, DC 20016. **Tel**—(202) 752-7000. **Website**—http://www.fanniemae.com **Chrmn & CEO**—J. A. Johnson. **Pres**—L. M. Small. **Exec VP-CFO**—J. T. Howard. **Exec VP-Secy**—C. S. Bernstein. **Investor Contact**—Jayne Shontell (202) 752-7115. **Dirs**—F. M. Beck, R. E. Birk, E. Broad, W. M. Daley, T. P. Gerrity, J. A. Johnson, T. A. Leonard, V. A. Mai, A. McLaughlin, R. D. Parsons, F. D. Raines, J. R. Sasso, A. Shusta, L. M. Small, C. J. Sumner, J. H. Villarreal, K. H. Williams. **Incorporated**—under the laws of the United States in 1938. **Empl**— 3,400. **S&P Analyst:** Paul L. Huberman, CFA

15-FEB-97 | Industry: Banking

Summary: This regional bank holding company, with about $20.5 billion in assets, operates 414 offices in Ohio, Indiana, Kentucky and Florida.

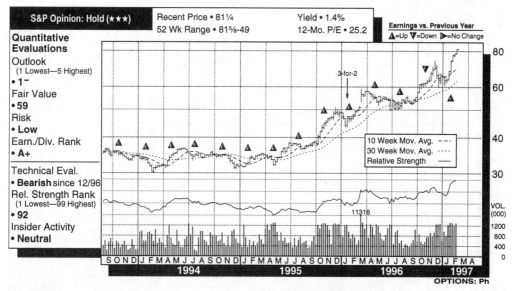

S&P Opinion: Hold (★★★)	Recent Price • 81¼	Yield • 1.4%
	52 Wk Range • 81⅝-49	12-Mo. P/E • 25.2

Quantitative Evaluations

Outlook (1 Lowest—5 Highest)
• **1⁻**

Fair Value
• **59**

Risk
• **Low**

Earn./Div. Rank
• **A+**

Technical Eval.
• **Bearish** since 12/96

Rel. Strength Rank (1 Lowest—99 Highest)
• **92**

Insider Activity
• **Neutral**

Earnings vs. Previous Year
▲=Up ▼=Down ▶=No Change

3-for-2

10 Week Mov. Avg. ---
30 Week Mov. Avg. ·····
Relative Strength —

1131B

VOL. (000)

1994 1995 1996 1997

OPTIONS: Ph

Overview - 21-JAN-97

Operating earnings grew 20% in 1996, paced by strong growth in net interest and fee income. Average earning assets were up 20%, and the net interest margin increased nine basis points, to 3.99%. We expect loan and lease volume to increase at a 10% to 12% annual pace in coming periods, driven by sustained growth in the commercial lease and consumer installment loan portfolios. FITB continues to benefit from an aggressive promotional campaign, with rapid growth in core deposits helping to improve the funding mix and generating fee income. We expect noninterest revenue to grow in excess of 20% into 1997, on higher transaction account charges, trust fees and data processing income. Fifth Third is one of the most efficient U.S. banking organizations. Despite faster than normal expense growth related to acquisitions, the company's overhead ratio improved to a low 43.5% in 1996, as revenues expanded faster than costs. Credit quality remains strong, with nonperforming assets accounting for just 0.28% of loans and leases at year-end.

Valuation - 21-JAN-97

Fifth Third continues to be one of the industry's top performers in key measures of profitability, generating a return on assets of 1.78% and a return on equity of 17.8% in 1996. The bank holding company's shares outperformed the broader market in 1996, posting a 29% gain. With this price appreciation, the stock was recently trading at over 17X our 1997 EPS estimate of $3.75, and at over 3X the company's book value. Both measures are at the high-end of FITB's historical valuation, and significantly higher than valuations given to other regional banks. While fundamentals remain strong, we believe that the shares are fully valued at present.

Key Stock Statistics

S&P EPS Est. 1997	3.75	Tang. Bk. Value/Share	19.18
P/E on S&P Est. 1997	21.7	Beta	0.95
Dividend Rate/Share	1.16	Shareholders	13,800
Shs. outstg. (M)	105.9	Market cap. (B)	$ 8.6
Avg. daily vol. (M)	0.402	Inst. holdings	35%

Value of $10,000 invested 5 years ago: $ 28,591

Fiscal Year Ending Dec. 31

	1996	1995	1994	1993	1992	1991
Revenues (Million $)						
1Q	406.7	339.5	273.4	231.4	215.1	217.2
2Q	435.4	360.5	280.2	237.6	224.0	220.5
3Q	454.4	383.1	290.4	241.5	224.0	224.0
4Q	456.8	395.9	334.2	243.4	231.4	223.8
Yr.	1,773	1,479	1,178	953.9	894.5	885.4
Earnings Per Share ($)						
1Q	0.79	0.68	0.59	0.50	0.41	0.35
2Q	0.80	0.70	0.62	0.53	0.45	0.39
3Q	0.75	0.75	0.65	0.57	0.48	0.41
4Q	0.88	0.78	0.67	0.58	0.49	0.41
Yr.	3.22	2.91	2.53	2.19	1.83	1.55

Next earnings report expected: mid April

Dividend Data (Dividends have been paid since 1952.)

Amount ($)	Date Decl.	Ex-Div. Date	Stock of Record	Payment Date
0.260	Mar. 19	Mar. 27	Mar. 29	Apr. 15 '96
0.260	Jun. 18	Jun. 26	Jun. 28	Jul. 15 '96
0.290	Sep. 16	Sep. 26	Sep. 30	Oct. 15 '96
0.290	Dec. 17	Dec. 27	Dec. 31	Jan. 15 '97

A Division of The **McGraw·Hill** Companies

Business Summary - 21-JAN-97

Fifth Third Bancorp is a regional bank holding company operating through affiliate banks in Ohio, Kentucky, Indiana, and Naples, FL. The company also owns subsidiaries engaged in payment services, discount brokerage, travel and leasing. At December 31, 1996, there were 414 banking offices, including 95 grocery store locations.

The company has pursued an active acquisition policy, acquiring Cumberland Federal Bancorp (assets of $1.1 billion) in 1994, Falls Financial, Inc. (assets of $573 million) and the Dayton division of PNC Bank ($256 million in deposits and $215 million in assets) in 1995, and Kentucky Enterprise Bancorp. (assets of $276 million) in March 1996.

Gross loans and leases outstanding, which amounted to $12.51 billion at the end of 1996, versus $11.69 billion a year earlier, were divided:

	1996	1995
Commercial	32%	31%
Real estate--construction	3%	3%
Real estate--mortgage loans	24%	24%
Consumer loans	21%	26%
Lease financing	21%	17%

The reserve for loan losses was $187,278,000 (1.50% of loans and leases outstanding) at the end of 1996, versus $177,378,000 (1.52%) a year earlier. Net chargeoffs in 1996 totaled $18,196,000 (0.58% of average loans), versus $10,772,000 (0.37%) in 1995. Nonperforming assets at 1996 year end amounted to $35,237,000 (0.28% of loans, leases and other real estate owned), down from $40,680,000 (0.35%) a year earlier.

Deposits of $12.5 billion at December 31, 1996, were divided: demand deposits 17%, interest checking 14%, savings 14%, money market 10%, other time 39%, CDs over $100,000 5%, and foreign office 1%.

Important Developments

Dec. '96—Fifth Third said it had begun a share repurchase program to fund its stock option, dividend reinvestment and employee stock repurchase plans. The company expects to repurchase 3% of the approximately 105.9 million total shares outstanding. Purchases will take place at various times throughout the year, with annual buybacks expected to total between 350,000 and 400,000 shares.

Capitalization

Long Term Debt: $278,000,000 (12/96).

Per Share Data ($) (Year Ended Dec. 31)	1996	1995	1994	1993	1992	1991	1990	1989	1988	1987
Tangible Bk. Val.	NA	16.17	14.10	13.00	10.57	9.47	8.83	7.87	6.91	6.03
Earnings	3.22	2.91	2.53	2.19	1.83	1.55	1.37	1.24	1.17	0.90
Dividends	1.10	0.96	0.80	0.68	0.60	0.52	0.45	0.40	0.35	0.30
Payout Ratio	34%	33%	32%	31%	33%	33%	33%	32%	30%	33%
Prices - High	74¼	51	36⅝	39⅜	36	30⅜	16⅜	17⅝	13½	12⅜
- Low	43½	31⅜	30	33	26½	13⅛	10⅜	13⅛	9⅜	9
P/E Ratio - High	23	18	14	18	20	20	12	14	12	14
- Low	14	11	12	15	14	8	8	11	8	10
Income Statement Analysis (Million $)										
Net Int. Inc.	NA	563	517	436	394	332	293	275	189	143
Tax Equiv. Adj.	NA	32.5	24.6	20.4	17.2	19.1	14.4	15.1	14.8	18.9
Non Int. Inc.	NA	301	256	227	199	168	138	118	91.0	73.0
Loan Loss Prov.	NA	43.0	35.8	44.5	65.3	55.7	39.9	36.5	26.1	18.9
% Exp/Op Revs.	NA	44	47	48	47	48	50	51	48	49
Pretax Inc.	NA	431	365	295	240	199	168	150	112	83.0
Eff. Tax Rate	NA	33%	33%	33%	32%	30%	29%	28%	25%	28%
Net Inc.	NA	288	244	196	164	138	120	108	84.0	60.0
% Net Int. Marg.	NA	3.90	4.16	4.51	4.73	4.58	4.56	4.74	4.80	4.83
Balance Sheet & Other Fin. Data (Million $)										
Earning Assets:										
Money Mkt	NA	4,151	1,129	3.0	1.0	192	336	274	226	246
Inv. Securities	NA	194	2,531	1,487	1,933	2,064	1,355	1,059	767	628
Com'l Loans	NA	5,209	4,345	3,933	3,223	2,684	2,696	2,547	2,004	1,509
Other Loans	NA	6,808	5,586	4,878	4,371	3,228	2,912	2,736	1,845	1,319
Total Assets	NA	17,053	14,957	11,966	10,213	8,826	7,956	7,143	5,246	4,051
Demand Deposits	NA	1,828	1,680	1,463	1,307	1,151	989	961	784	646
Time Deposits	NA	10,658	8,951	7,165	6,225	5,536	5,396	4,822	3,310	2,538
LT Debt	NA	425	179	283	254	13.0	14.0	13.0	12.0	13.0
Common Eqty.	NA	1,725	1,399	1,198	1,005	879	783	699	509	402
% Ret. on Assets	NA	1.8	1.8	1.8	1.7	1.7	1.6	1.6	1.8	1.6
% Ret. on Equity	NA	18.4	18.6	18.2	17.3	16.6	16.2	16.5	18.0	16.3
% Loan Loss Resv.	NA	1.5	1.5	1.5	1.5	1.6	1.5	1.5	1.6	1.6
% Loans/Deposits	NA	93.6	95.3	100.5	99.2	86.8	86.1	89.3	91.7	86.7
% Equity to Assets	NA	7.5	9.5	9.9	10.1	10.1	10.1	9.8	10.0	9.9

Data as orig. reptd.; bef. results of disc. opers. and/or spec. items. Per share data adj. for stk. divs. as of ex-div. date. E-Estimated. NA-Not Available. NM-Not Meaningful. NR-Not Ranked.

Office—Fifth Third Center, Cincinnati, OH 45263. **Tel**—(513) 579-5300. **Website**—http://www.fifththird.com **Pres & CEO**—G. A. Schaefer Jr. **SVP, CFO & Investor Contact**—P. Michael Brumm (513-579-4216). **SVP & Secy**—M. K. Keating. **SVP & Treas**—N. E. Arnold. **Dirs**—J. F. Barrett, M. C. Boesel Jr., C. L. Buenger, G. V. Dirvin, T. B. Donnell, R. T. Farmer, J. D. Geary, I. W. Gorr, J. H. Head Jr., J. R. Herschede, W. G. Kagler, W. J. Keating, J. D. Kiggen, R. B. Morgan, M. H. Norris, B. H. Rowe, J. J. Schiff, Jr., D. J. Sullivan, Jr., D. S. Taft. **Transfer Agent & Registrar**—Fifth Third Bank. **Incorporated**—in Ohio in 1975. **Empl**— 6,549. **S&P Analyst:** Brendan McGovern

STANDARD &POOR'S
STOCK REPORTS

First Commercial Corp.

3875X

NASDAQ Symbol **FCLR**

In S&P SmallCap 600

15-FEB-97

Industry: Banking

Summary: First Commercial Corp. owns 24 affiliate banks in Arkansas, Texas, Tennessee and Louisiana, and a 50% interest in an Oklahoma bank.

Quantitative Evaluations

Outlook (1 Lowest—5 Highest)
• **2⁻**

Fair Value
• **36⅞**

Risk
• **Low**

Earn./Div. Rank
• **A+**

Technical Eval.
• **Bearish** since 1/97

Rel. Strength Rank (1 Lowest—99 Highest)
• **64**

Insider Activity
• **Neutral**

Recent Price • 38¾

52 Wk Range • 39-27⅞

Yield • 2.5%

12-Mo. P/E • 16.4

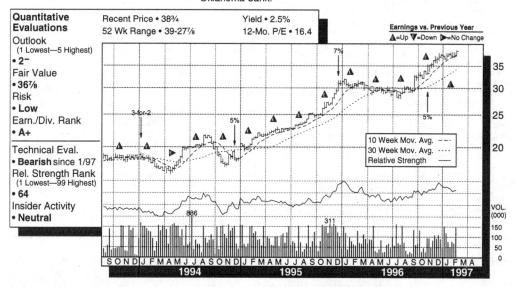

Earnings vs. Previous Year
▲=Up ▼=Down ▶=No Change

10 Week Mov. Avg. ---
30 Week Mov. Avg. ····
Relative Strength —

Business Profile - 10-FEB-97

This $5.4 billion asset multi-bank holding company operates 24 affiliate banks in Arkansas, Texas, Tennessee and Louisiana, and it owns a 50% interest in a 25th bank in Oklahoma. First Commercial has employed an aggressive acquisition policy to grow its asset base and expand its mortgage financing operations. In January 1997, FCLR entered into an agreement to acquire First Central Corporation, the parent company of $260 million asset First National Bank of Searcy, AR, for 1.65 million FCLR common shares (valued at around $62 million). The transaction is expected to be completed in the second quarter of 1997. FCLR plans to continue to expand in its existing markets, through new products and expanded delivery systems, and to enter additional markets by adding new affiliates.

Operational Review - 10-FEB-97

Based on a preliminary report, net interest income rose 18% in 1996, on a 14% increase in average earning asset levels, and a wider net interest margin (4.66%, versus 4.53%). The loan loss provision more than doubled, to $7,452,000. Noninterest income advanced 40%, reflecting much higher mortgage servicing fee income, and noninterest expense expanded 22%; pretax income climbed 24%. After taxes at 34.9%, versus 33.2%, net income was up 21%, to $68,562,000 ($2.37 a share, on 4.9% more shares), from $56,910,000 ($2.07).

Stock Performance - 14-FEB-97

In the past 30 trading days, FCLR's shares have increased 5%, compared to a 8% rise in the S&P 500. Average trading volume for the past five days was 29,140 shares, compared with the 40-day moving average of 18,995 shares.

Key Stock Statistics

Dividend Rate/Share	0.96	Shareholders	3,300
Shs. outstg. (M)	28.5	Market cap. (B)	$ 1.1
Avg. daily vol. (M)	0.017	Inst. holdings	17%
Tang. Bk. Value/Share	16.00		
Beta	0.57		

Value of $10,000 invested 5 years ago: $ 24,741

Fiscal Year Ending Dec. 31

	1996	1995	1994	1993	1992	1991
Revenues (Million $)						
1Q	117.2	86.39	78.35	54.99	58.46	55.72
2Q	118.5	91.54	79.63	59.62	57.73	56.00
3Q	119.1	96.44	81.87	59.98	56.00	58.95
4Q	122.7	121.8	86.55	62.77	53.64	60.25
Yr.	479.9	396.2	326.4	237.4	228.9	230.9
Earnings Per Share ($)						
1Q	0.55	0.46	0.44	0.44	0.38	0.33
2Q	0.58	0.50	0.47	0.42	0.40	0.36
3Q	0.60	0.53	0.47	0.44	0.41	0.37
4Q	0.64	0.56	0.49	0.45	0.41	0.37
Yr.	2.37	2.07	1.87	1.75	1.59	1.42

Next earnings report expected: mid April

Dividend Data (Dividends have been paid since 1981.)

Amount ($)	Date Decl.	Ex-Div. Date	Stock of Record	Payment Date
0.210	May. 21	Jun. 13	Jun. 17	Jul. 01 '96
0.210	Aug. 20	Sep. 12	Sep. 16	Oct. 01 '96
5%	Oct. 15	Oct. 29	Oct. 31	Nov. 15 '96
0.240	Oct. 15	Dec. 12	Dec. 16	Jan. 02 '97

Business Summary - 10-FEB-97

First Commercial Corporation has employed an aggressive acquisition campaign in an effort to combat growing competition from non-bank entities. The company is expanding its traditional banking services, focusing on becoming a complete "financial services provider", offering a one stop shop for all of its customers' financial needs. To that end, this Little Rock, AR-based bank holding company has stepped up its mortgage financing, investment advisory and personal trust services. FCLR notes, however, that it intends to retain its customer orientation and community bank approach, which it feels sets the bank apart from regional bank and non-bank competitors.

In recent years, First Commercial has experienced steady, consistent earnings growth. This success can be attributed to strong net interest margins, improved credit quality (and therefore lower loan loss provisioning), growth in non-interest income and diligent expense control.

In 1996, FCLR experienced fast growth in net interest income (interest income received on loans and other investments less interest expense paid to fund these assets), as loans grew rapidly and repriced at higher rates. Also during the year, non-interest income grew 40% over the 1995 level, reflecting the impact of higher mortgage servicing revenue generated by acquisitions made in late 1995. Contributions to earnings from this income were tempered by amortization and other expenses associated with rapid expansion.

At First Commercial, the acquisition front remains busy. Consistent with its goal to boost other revenue sources, FCLR acquired Ahart & Bryan Inc. in the third quarter of 1996. The firm specializes in institutional sales of government and municipal bonds. Most recently, in January 1997, First Commercial reached an agreement to purchase First Central Corporation for approximately $62 million in stock. First Central is the parent of First National Bank of Searcy, AR, a $260 million asset bank, with loans of $140 million and deposits of $230 million.

The banking industry has been characterized by rapid consolidation in recent years, with participants searching for ways to improve efficiency and broaden the scope of their operations. With this in mind, FCLR plans to continue to make acquisitions in strategic markets, enabling it to offer a comprehensive array of financial products and services.

Capitalization

Long Term Debt: $6,097,000 (12/96).

Per Share Data ($)

(Year Ended Dec. 31)	1996	1995	1994	1993	1992	1991	1990	1989	1988	1987
Tangible Bk. Val.	NA	13.26	11.96	11.99	10.72	9.55	8.15	7.29	6.54	5.94
Earnings	2.37	2.07	1.87	1.75	1.59	1.42	1.21	1.05	0.85	0.73
Dividends	0.84	0.73	0.66	0.54	0.44	0.38	0.33	0.29	0.24	0.22
Payout Ratio	35%	35%	35%	31%	28%	26%	27%	27%	29%	30%
Prices - High	38¼	31⅝	21¾	19½	18⅝	17½	9⅝	10⅛	7¾	7¼
- Low	27⅞	19⅜	16½	16½	14¼	7½	7⅜	7⅜	5⅝	5¼
P/E Ratio - High	16	15	12	11	12	12	8	10	9	10
- Low	12	9	9	9	9	5	6	7	7	7

Income Statement Analysis (Million $)

	1996	1995	1994	1993	1992	1991	1990	1989	1988	1987
Net Int. Inc.	NA	185	159	115	106	93.3	80.6	60.0	52.7	48.8
Tax Equiv. Adj.	NA	3.5	3.6	1.9	2.4	3.3	3.3	3.5	3.0	NA
Non Int. Inc.	NA	74.0	68.5	53.1	46.5	41.3	33.2	23.9	21.3	NA
Loan Loss Prov.	NA	3.1	3.1	3.3	6.6	7.9	7.5	4.8	6.8	9.5
% Exp/Op Revs.	NA	65	68	66	63	64	65	65	65	NA
Pretax Inc.	NA	85.2	74.3	53.2	48.4	38.8	30.3	22.0	17.0	15.0
Eff. Tax Rate	NA	33%	32%	30%	31%	28%	27%	22%	22%	23%
Net Inc.	NA	56.9	50.3	37.5	33.4	27.9	22.2	17.1	13.3	11.5
% Net Int. Marg.	NA	4.53	4.30	4.30	4.60	4.70	4.70	4.90	4.90	5.20

Balance Sheet & Other Fin. Data (Million $)

	1996	1995	1994	1993	1992	1991	1990	1989	1988	1987
Earning Assets:										
Money Mkt	NA	108	72.0	126	40.5	80.0	71.1	86.3	85.1	NA
Inv. Securities	NA	1,325	1,309	1,147	823	856	565	385	397	NA
Com'l Loans	NA	545	519	337	264	274	302	384	273	NA
Other Loans	NA	2,723	2,062	1,469	1,206	1,150	964	594	558	NA
Total Assets	NA	5,361	4,374	3,401	2,619	2,615	2,122	1,583	1,493	1,299
Demand Deposits	NA	1,018	768	644	504	472	353	371	334	NA
Time Deposits	NA	3,613	3,058	2,398	1,821	1,866	1,539	1,024	992	NA
LT Debt	NA	7.2	8.2	19.2	32.3	37.3	30.2	31.8	33.3	34.7
Common Eqty.	NA	432	343	249	217	192	150	119	103	94.0
% Ret. on Assets	NA	1.2	1.2	1.2	1.3	1.2	1.1	1.2	1.0	1.0
% Ret. on Equity	NA	15.0	15.0	15.4	15.7	16.0	15.6	15.2	13.5	12.8
% Loan Loss Resv.	NA	1.6	1.8	2.2	2.2	2.4	2.2	2.3	1.9	NA
% Loans/Deposits	NA	69.5	66.3	59.4	62.0	59.7	65.7	62.0	62.0	NA
% Equity to Assets	NA	8.1	7.8	7.8	7.9	7.2	7.1	7.6	7.5	7.6

Data as orig. reptd.; bef. results of disc opers. and/or spec. items. Per share data adj. for stk. divs. as of ex-div. date. E-Estimated. NA-Not Available. NM-Not Meaningful. NR-Not Ranked.

Office—400 W. Capitol Ave., Little Rock, AR 72201. **Tel**—(501) 371-7000. **Website**—http://www.firstcommercial.com **Chrmn, Pres & CEO**—B. Grace. **Vice Chrmn**—J. R. Cobb. **CFO & Investor Contact**—J. Lynn Wright. **Dirs**—J. W. Allison, T. Arnold, W. H. Bowen, J. R. Cobb, R. G. Cress, C. W. Cupp Jr., B. Grace, F. D. Hickingbotham, W. E. Hussman Jr., F. E. Joyce, J. G. Justus, W. M. Lemley, C. H. Murphy Jr., M. W. Murphy, W. C. Nolan Jr., S. C. Sowell, P. D. Tilley. **Transfer Agent & Registrar**—First Commercial Bank, Little Rock. **Incorporated**—in Arkansas in 1980. **Empl**—2,724. **S&P Analyst:** Brendan McGovern

15-FEB-97

Industry: Banking

Summary: FMBC is a $3.5 billion diversified financial services company with 14 affiliate banks and offices throughout Michigan.

Quantitative Evaluations

Outlook
(1 Lowest—5 Highest)
• 1⁻

Fair Value
• 23¼

Risk
• **Low**

Earn./Div. Rank
• **A+**

Technical Eval.
• **Bullish** since 12/94

Rel. Strength Rank
(1 Lowest—99 Highest)
• 62

Insider Activity
• **NA**

Recent Price • 29¾
52 Wk Range • 31¼-20⅜

Yield • 2.4%
12-Mo. P/E • 18.9

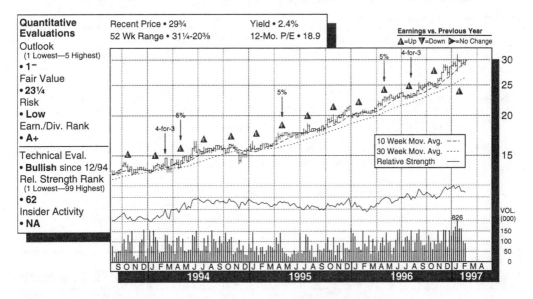

Business Profile - 11-FEB-97

FMBC's earnings and dividends have grown consistently, culminating in 1996, when it attained its 15th consecutive year of record annual net income. The company's results have been driven by an expanded loan portfolio, higher levels of fee income and careful cost control. Profitability indicators have been favorable, with ROA and ROE at 1.27% and 16.01% respectively, for 1996. Asset quality remains strong, as nonperforming assets were only 0.69% of total loans for the period. During the year, in addition to cash dividends, the company paid a 5% stock dividend and effected a four-for-three stock split. The stock split was FMBC's third in the past six and a half years. With the January 1997 payment, the company increased its quarterly cash dividend by 12.5%.

Operational Review - 11-FEB-97

Based on a preliminary report, net interest income in 1996 rose 8.8% from that of the prior year, fueled by a higher level of earning assets. The provision for loan losses advanced 42%, to $11.3 million, from $8.0 million. Noninterest income grew 21%, and noninterest expenses advanced 6.7%. Pretax income was up 15%. Following taxes at 27.8%, versus 26.3%, net income rose 13%, to $42,168,000 ($1.57), from $13,312,000 ($1.40).

Stock Performance - 14-FEB-97

In the past 30 trading days, FMBC's shares have increased 2%, compared to a 8% rise in the S&P 500. Average trading volume for the past five days was 17,540 shares, compared with the 40-day moving average of 57,641 shares.

Key Stock Statistics

Dividend Rate/Share	0.72	Shareholders	5,000
Shs. outstg. (M)	26.3	Market cap. (B)	$0.782
Avg. daily vol. (M)	0.036	Inst. holdings	10%
Tang. Bk. Value/Share	10.11		
Beta	0.38		

Value of $10,000 invested 5 years ago: $ 43,256

Fiscal Year Ending Dec. 31

	1996	1995	1994	1993	1992	1991
Revenues (Million $)						
1Q	70.96	63.23	50.95	44.83	46.75	44.87
2Q	74.41	66.94	53.53	46.73	46.59	46.08
3Q	77.49	69.02	54.83	47.62	46.44	48.63
4Q	—	71.46	57.36	47.70	46.40	48.74
Yr.	—	270.6	211.0	186.9	186.2	188.3
Earnings Per Share ($)						
1Q	0.36	0.31	0.29	0.25	0.23	0.19
2Q	0.38	0.34	0.31	0.29	0.24	0.21
3Q	0.41	0.36	0.33	0.29	0.24	0.22
4Q	0.42	0.38	0.33	0.30	0.26	0.23
Yr.	1.57	1.40	1.25	1.12	0.97	0.86

Next earnings report expected: mid April

Dividend Data (Dividends have been paid since 1977.)

Amount ($)	Date Decl.	Ex-Div. Date	Stock of Record	Payment Date
0.210	Jun. 13	Jun. 26	Jun. 28	Jul. 31 '96
4-for-3	Jun. 13	Jul. 29	Jul. 01	Jul. 26 '96
0.160	Aug. 15	Sep. 26	Sep. 30	Oct. 31 '96
0.180	Dec. 12	Dec. 27	Dec. 31	Jan. 31 '97

A Division of The **McGraw·Hill** Companies

Business Summary - 11-FEB-97

FMBC owns 13 subsidiary community banks engaged in commercial and retail banking and one engaged primarily in trust services. The banks operate 86 branch offices throughout Michigan. The company has two nonbank subsidiaries, providing credit life, health and accident insurance to customers of the banks and also offering brokerage services. The three largest subsidiary banks are FMB-First Michigan Bank, FMB-Lumberman's Bank and FMB-First Michigan Bank--Grand Rapids. Since the end of 1987, FMBC has acquired FMB-Reed City Bank, FMB-Commercial Bank, FMB-Security Bank, FMB-Maynard Allen Bank, FMB-Trust, FMB-Northwestern Bank, FMB-Old State Bank, Superior Financial Corp. and Arcadia Financial Corp.

The allowance for loan losses was $26,824,000 at 1995 year-end (equal to 1.26% of gross loans outstanding), versus $23,758,000 (1.26%) a year earlier. Net chargeoffs during 1995 totaled $4,602,000 (0.23% of average loans), up from $3,224,000 (0.18%) in 1994. As of December 31, 1995, nonperforming assets (including real estate acquired through foreclosure) amounted to $10,215,000 (0.48% of total loans), down from $11,471,000 (0.61%) a year earlier.

Gross loans outstanding totaled $2.13 billion at December 31, 1995, and were divided:

	1995	1994
Commercial, financial & agricultural	27%	28%
Real estate--residential	25%	25%
Real estate--commercial	21%	21%
Consumer	20%	20%
Real estate--construction	7%	6%

Average deposits of $2.55 billion in 1995 were apportioned: 55% time, 34% savings and NOW accounts and 11% noninterest-bearing.

Interest and fees on loans provided 72% of total income for 1995.

On a tax-equivalent basis, the net interest margin declined to 4.78% in 1995, from 4.88% in 1994.

Capitalization

Long Term Debt: $29,714,000 (9/96).

Per Share Data ($)

(Year Ended Dec. 31)	1996	1995	1994	1993	1992	1991	1990	1989	1988	1987
Tangible Bk. Val.	NA	9.66	8.56	8.01	7.24	6.54	5.87	5.29	4.71	4.23
Earnings	1.57	1.39	1.25	1.12	0.98	0.86	0.81	0.75	0.66	0.57
Dividends	0.61	0.55	0.48	0.35	0.28	0.26	0.23	0.21	0.18	0.17
Payout Ratio	39%	39%	38%	31%	29%	31%	29%	28%	27%	29%
Prices - High	29⅝	21⅜	16⅝	14⅜	11¾	9	7½	7⅞	6¾	6
- Low	19⅝	15½	13¼	10⅞	7¾	5¾	4⅝	5¾	4⅜	4¼
P/E Ratio - High	19	15	13	13	12	11	9	11	10	10
- Low	13	11	11	10	8	7	6	8	7	7

Income Statement Analysis (Million $)

	1996	1995	1994	1993	1992	1991	1990	1989	1988	1987
Net Int. Inc.	NA	125	108	91.6	86.3	76.4	65.2	59.1	47.0	39.5
Tax Equiv. Adj.	NA	16.9	7.2	6.9	6.3	5.9	5.4	5.0	3.8	4.3
Non Int. Inc.	NA	30.1	27.6	29.4	25.6	19.1	13.1	11.6	9.5	8.5
Loan Loss Prov.	NA	7.7	6.3	5.0	6.2	5.4	4.8	4.5	3.2	2.2
% Exp/Op Revs.	NA	61	62	63	64	65	63	61	62	62
Pretax Inc.	NA	48.5	41.0	35.4	29.9	24.8	21.4	20.0	15.9	13.7
Eff. Tax Rate	NA	26%	24%	23%	21%	19%	18%	19%	20%	22%
Net Inc.	NA	35.9	31.2	27.3	23.7	20.0	17.6	16.3	12.8	10.8
% Net Int. Marg.	NA	4.78	4.91	4.80	4.80	4.70	4.70	4.70	4.70	4.70

Balance Sheet & Other Fin. Data (Million $)

	1996	1995	1994	1993	1992	1991	1990	1989	1988	1987
Earning Assets:										
Money Mkt	NA	118	4.3	12.3	38.3	15.9	42.9	37.5	19.2	32.0
Inv. Securities	NA	167	684	677	623	566	451	380	351	291
Com'l Loans	NA	574	503	411	401	503	451	398	305	259
Other Loans	NA	1,561	1,289	1,071	914	732	677	620	510	400
Total Assets	NA	3,136	2,689	2,327	2,161	1,966	1,748	1,558	1,288	1,055
Demand Deposits	NA	326	289	231	234	188	176	172	146	123
Time Deposits	NA	2,103	1,995	1,764	1,619	1,505	1,330	1,164	941	769
LT Debt	NA	5.2	4.9	7.0	7.7	9.0	5.1	5.9	6.6	6.5
Common Eqty.	NA	247	209	192	175	156	131	114	92.0	80.0
% Ret. on Assets	NA	1.2	1.2	1.2	1.2	1.1	1.1	1.1	1.1	1.1
% Ret. on Equity	NA	15.5	15.2	14.9	14.2	13.8	14.5	15.0	14.5	13.6
% Loan Loss Resv.	NA	1.3	1.3	1.3	1.3	1.3	1.3	1.3	1.3	1.2
% Loans/Deposits	NA	78.6	78.4	74.3	70.9	72.8	74.9	76.3	75.0	73.9
% Equity to Assets	NA	7.8	8.1	8.2	8.1	7.8	7.5	7.3	7.4	7.2

Data as orig. reptd.; bef. results of disc opers. and/or spec. items. Per share data adj. for stk. divs. as of ex-div. date. E-Estimated. NA-Not Available. NM-Not Meaningful. NR-Not Ranked.

Office—One Financial Plaza, 10717 Adams St., Holland, MI 49423. **Tel**—(616) 355-9200. **Chrmn & CEO**—D. M. Ondersma. **Pres, COO & Secy**—S. A. Stream. **Exec VP, CFO & Investor Contact**—Larry D. Fredricks (616) 355-9389.**Dirs**—R. A. Andersen, J. H. Bloem, D. M. Cassard, D. A. Hayes, R. J. Kapenga, M. B. Leeke, D. W. Maine, J. H. Miller, D. M. Ondersma, M. J. Prins, J. W. Spoelhof, S. A. Stream. **Transfer Agent & Registrar**—FMB Shareholder Services. **Incorporated**—in Michigan in 1973. **Empl**— 1,700. **S&P Analyst:** Thomas C. Ferguson

15-FEB-97   Industry:
Banking

Summary: This holding company, whose principal subsidiary is First Tennessee Bank, operates more than 235 offices and is the state's largest banking organization.

S&P Opinion: Accumulate (★★★★)	Recent Price • 44⅜ Yield • 2.7% 52 Wk Range • 44¾-28½ 12-Mo. P/E • 16.6

Quantitative Evaluations

Outlook
(1 Lowest—5 Highest)
• **1**

Fair Value
• **29¾**

Risk
• **Low**

Earn./Div. Rank
• **A**

Technical Eval.
• **Bullish** since 8/96

Rel. Strength Rank
(1 Lowest—99 Highest)
• **90**

Insider Activity
• **Neutral**

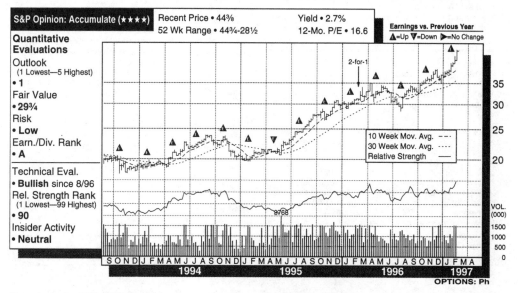

Earnings vs. Previous Year
▲=Up ▼=Down ▶=No Change

2-for-1

10 Week Mov. Avg. — —
30 Week Mov. Avg. - - - -
Relative Strength ——

VOL. (000)
1500
1000
500
0

S O N D J F M A M J J A S O N D J F M A M J J A S O N D J F M A M J J A S O N D J F M A
1994   1995   1996   1997
OPTIONS: Ph

Overview - 29-JAN-97

First Tennessee, with total assets of $13.1 billion at December 31, 1996, provides banking and other financial services. Earnings should advance in 1997, as FTEN's well-diversified business mix softens the impact of interest rate swings and changes in the economic climate. The bank currently derives about 55% of its net revenues (net interest income + noninterest income) from fee-based products -- an unusually high percentage for a bank its size. Noninterest income was up 16% in 1996, largely due to increases in mortgage operations, which have been greatly expanded through acquisitions. Total noninterest expenses were up 16%, primarily reflecting higher activity levels in the commission-based mortgage banking line. At December 31, 1996, nonperforming loans were 0.24% of total loans, down slightly from 0.26% a year earlier. Despite a one-time $3.8 million SAIF assessment charge, net income rose 9.1% to $179.9 million ($2.68 a share), from $164.9 million ($2.42). ROE for the year was 20.05%.

Valuation - 29-JAN-97

Following renewed merger activity in regional banking, and increased profitability for FTEN, the shares of this service-oriented regional bank holding company recently hit new highs, and are now trading at a relatively pricey 3.1X tangible book value. However, growth of interest-earning assets and noninterest income should continue to fuel earnings. The bond business continues to add customers and should benefit as interest rates stabilize. With the stock currently yielding more than 3% and trading at about 12X our 1997 EPS estimate of $3.20, the shares are recommended for conservative growth investors.

Key Stock Statistics

S&P EPS Est. 1997	3.20	Tang. Bk. Value/Share	11.96
P/E on S&P Est. 1997	13.9	Beta	0.66
Dividend Rate/Share	1.20	Shareholders	7,800
Shs. outstg. (M)	67.2	Market cap. (B)	$ 3.0
Avg. daily vol. (M)	0.279	Inst. holdings	35%

Value of $10,000 invested 5 years ago: $ 35,964

Fiscal Year Ending Dec. 31

	1996	1995	1994	1993	1992	1991
Revenues (Million $)						
1Q	354.2	305.6	269.6	206.9	207.5	181.3
2Q	355.7	317.5	256.9	204.5	210.1	183.2
3Q	368.2	337.9	261.7	210.7	205.4	190.8
4Q	389.5	357.9	267.5	234.8	201.2	200.5
Yr.	1,468	1,319	1,056	857.0	824.3	755.8
Earnings Per Share ($)						
1Q	0.56	0.51	0.57	0.54	0.44	0.29
2Q	0.63	0.59	0.56	0.54	0.46	0.33
3Q	0.69	0.66	0.57	0.52	0.47	0.35
4Q	0.80	0.67	0.58	0.53	0.21	0.37
Yr.	2.68	2.42	2.28	2.13	1.60	1.35

Next earnings report expected: mid April

Dividend Data (Dividends have been paid since 1895.)

Amount ($)	Date Decl.	Ex-Div. Date	Stock of Record	Payment Date
0.265	Apr. 16	Jun. 19	Jun. 21	Jul. 01 '96
0.265	Jul. 16	Sep. 18	Sep. 20	Oct. 01 '96
0.300	Oct. 23	Dec. 11	Dec. 13	Jan. 01 '97
0.300	Jan. 21	Mar. 12	Mar. 14	Apr. 01 '97

A Division of The McGraw·Hill Companies

Business Summary - 29-JAN-97

First Tennessee National Corp., which owns First Tennessee Bank, is the largest bank holding company in that state, operating through 236 locations in Tennessee's major metropolitan areas and 16 locations in Mississippi and Arkansas.

Consolidated gross loans totaling $8.12 billion at the end of 1995 were divided:

	1995
Commercial	41%
Consumer	31%
Mortgage for sale	10%
Permanent mortgage	9%
Credit card receivables	6%
Other	3%

The allowance for loan losses at December 31, 1995, was $112,567,000 (1.39% of loans, net of unearned income), compared with $109,859,000 (1.57%) a year earlier. Net chargeoffs in 1995 were $20,516,000 (0.27% of average loans, net), versus $18,043,000 (0.27%) in 1994. Nonperforming assets at 1995 year-end amounted to $31,856,000 (0.39% of total loans--net, plus foreclosed real estate and other assets), compared with $38,281,000 (0.54%).

Interest and fees on loans contributed 51% of total income for 1995, interest on investment securities 10%, other interest income 2%, mortgage banking 16%, the bond division 6%, and other noninterest income 15%.

Consolidated deposits of $8.58 billion at year-end 1995 were divided: demand 23%, checking/interest 1%, savings 7%, money market 29%, certificates of deposit (CDs) of $100,000 or more 6%, and other CDs and time 34%.

On a tax-equivalent basis, the average yield on total earning assets in 1995 was 8.20% (7.50% in 1994), while the average rate paid on interest-bearing liabilities was 5.09% (3.93%), for a net spread of 3.11% (3.57%).

In October 1995, FTEN acquired Financial Investment Corp., parent of First National Bank of Springdale (deposits of $286 million), of Springdale, Ark., for $70 million in stock.

Important Developments

Dec. '96—Directors approved the repurchase of up to $130 million of FTEN common stock over a two-year period. Two new members, Ken Glass, president of FTEN's Tennessee banking group, and John Kelley, president of the Memphis banking group, were elected to the board of directors.

Capitalization

Long Term Debt: $255,998,000 (9/96).

Per Share Data ($)

(Year Ended Dec. 31)	1996	1995	1994	1993	1992	1991	1990	1989	1988	1987
Tangible Bk. Val.	NA	11.08	9.21	9.67	10.63	7.82	7.92	7.32	7.07	6.28
Earnings	2.68	2.42	2.28	2.13	1.60	1.35	1.01	0.60	1.11	0.73
Dividends	1.10	0.97	0.87	0.75	0.63	0.57	0.54	0.48	0.43	0.39
Payout Ratio	41%	40%	38%	35%	39%	42%	54%	80%	38%	54%
Prices - High	38⁷/₈	30⁷/₈	23⁷/₈	23⁵/₈	19	13⁷/₈	9¹/₈	10	9³/₄	12¹/₈
- Low	28¹/₂	19⁵/₈	18¹/₂	17⁷/₈	13¹/₈	7¹/₄	6	7⁷/₈	7¹/₄	6⁵/₈
P/E Ratio - High	15	13	10	11	12	10	9	16	9	16
- Low	11	8	8	8	8	5	6	13	6	9

Income Statement Analysis (Million $)

	1996	1995	1994	1993	1992	1991	1990	1989	1988	1987
Net Int. Inc.	NA	391	381	347	323	265	243	225	214	192
Tax Equiv. Adj.	NA	5.0	4.9	5.3	7.7	9.8	13.3	17.4	20.0	29.1
Non Int. Inc.	NA	494	369	270	227	177	142	125	110	120
Loan Loss Prov.	NA	20.6	16.7	34.5	43.2	53.7	63.6	63.9	25.4	52.3
% Exp/Op Revs.	NA	69	72	64	65	67	64	68	67	66
Pretax Inc.	NA	253	207	184	144	84.6	63.3	36.3	67.5	34.7
Eff. Tax Rate	NA	35%	29%	35%	38%	25%	24%	21%	22%	5.30%
Net Inc.	NA	165	146	121	89.2	63.8	47.9	28.8	52.3	32.9
% Net Int. Marg.	NA	3.92	4.28	4.35	4.37	4.43	4.40	4.48	4.66	4.62

Balance Sheet & Other Fin. Data (Million $)

	1996	1995	1994	1993	1992	1991	1990	1989	1988	1987
Earning Assets:										
Money Mkt	NA	67.0	440	324	475	586	710	526	399	243
Inv. Securities	NA	2,111	2,094	2,170	2,912	2,241	1,417	1,342	1,106	1,057
Com'l Loans	NA	3,331	2,889	2,519	2,200	2,231	2,107	2,031	2,071	2,161
Other Loans	NA	4,792	3,829	3,480	2,342	1,739	1,787	1,707	1,606	1,537
Total Assets	NA	12,077	10,522	9,609	8,926	7,904	6,708	6,398	5,972	5,762
Demand Deposits	NA	1,984	1,702	1,888	1,468	1,403	1,117	1,051	1,187	1,229
Time Deposits	NA	6,598	5,987	5,258	5,449	4,638	4,227	3,899	3,470	3,248
LT Debt	NA	260	92.4	90.0	127	127	127	128	131	133
Common Eqty.	NA	873	749	679	598	438	398	381	372	327
% Ret. on Assets	NA	1.4	1.5	1.4	1.1	0.9	0.7	0.5	0.9	0.6
% Ret. on Equity	NA	20.0	20.0	19.0	15.4	15.3	12.3	7.7	14.8	10.3
% Loan Loss Resv.	NA	1.4	1.6	1.7	2.1	2.2	2.2	1.7	1.3	1.8
% Loans/Deposits	NA	94.6	87.4	83.8	65.4	65.2	71.7	74.0	76.9	80.3
% Equity to Assets	NA	7.2	7.2	7.1	7.0	6.1	6.0	6.1	6.1	5.7

Data as orig. reptd.; bef. results of disc. opers. and/or spec. items. Per share data adj. for stk. divs. as of ex-div. date. E-Estimated. NA-Not Available. NM-Not Meaningful. NR-Not Ranked.

Office—165 Madison Ave., Memphis, TN 38103. **Tel**—(901) 523-4027. **Website**—http://www.ftb.com **Chrmn, Pres & CEO**—R. Horn. **EVP & CFO**—E. L. Thomas Jr. **VP, Treas & Investor Contact**—Teresa A. Fehrman. **Dirs**—R. C. Blattberg, C. H. Cantu, G. E. Cates, K. Glass, R. Horn, J. A. Haslam III, J. Kelley, R. B. Martin, J. Orgill III, V. G. Roman, M. D. Rose, W. B. Sansom, G. P. Street Jr. **Transfer Agent**—Norwest Bank Minnesota, South St. Paul. **Incorporated**—in Tennessee in 1968; bank chartered in 1864. **Empl**— 7,476. **S&P Analyst:** E. Fitzpatrick

First Union Corp.

901K

NYSE Symbol **FTU**

In S&P 500

15-FEB-97 **Industry:** Banking

Summary: North Carolina-based First Union merged with New Jersey-based First Fidelity Bancorp. in early 1996, creating the sixth largest bank holding company in the U.S.

S&P Opinion: Buy (★★★★)	Recent Price • 91½	Yield • 2.5%
	52 Wk Range • 91⅝-56½	12-Mo. P/E • 17.1

Earnings vs. Previous Year
▲=Up ▼=Down ▶=No Change

Quantitative Evaluations

Outlook (1 Lowest—5 Highest)
• **2⁻**

Fair Value
• **82%**

Risk
• **Low**

Earn./Div. Rank
• **A-**

Technical Eval.
• **Bullish** since 10/95

Rel. Strength Rank (1 Lowest—99 Highest)
• **92**

Insider Activity
• **Favorable**

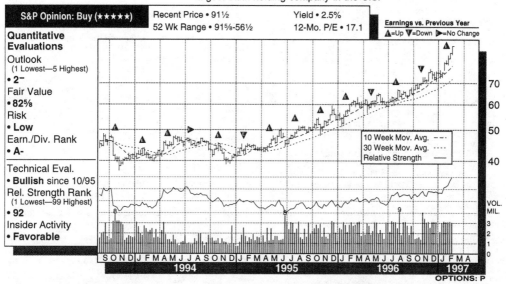

10 Week Mov. Avg. - - -
30 Week Mov. Avg. ·····
Relative Strength ——

VOL. MIL.

OPTIONS: P

Overview - 30-JAN-97

Net interest income is expected to rise in the mid to high single-digits in 1997, aided by an increase in earning assets due to acquisitions and strong internal loan growth. Margins should benefit from the recent sale of $8 billion in securities as part of a balance sheet management initiative. Increased contributions from noninterest income sources, particularly capital management (mutual funds, trust and brokerage services), due to a higher level of assets under management, and capital markets (merchant banking, loan syndication and asset securitization), are expected. This follows significant investments made in these areas over the past three years as part of a corporate-wide strategy of having fee-based businesses account for at least 40% of the total revenue base by the year 2000, from 22% currently. Internal financial goals include a return on equity of 18%-20%, earnings growth of 10%-13% and return on assets of 1.3%-1.5%, as well as an efficiency ratio of 53%-57%.

Valuation - 30-JAN-97

Acquisitions and an economically robust Southeast regional service territory should provide above-average earnings growth in the year ahead. In addition to recently raising return on equity and assets and earnings per share goals, efforts are under way to significantly increase the proportion of revenues coming from fee-based businesses. We see this as an opportunity to diversify risk and provide a larger base for future revenue growth, since these areas are expanding at a faster pace than traditional lending activities. The stability that such revenues bring should also allow the shares to command a higher price/earnings multiple in the market. Trading at a modest valuation of less than 12 times our 1997 earnings estimate of $6.95 a share, the shares are recommended for purchase.

Key Stock Statistics

S&P EPS Est. 1997	6.95	Tang. Bk. Value/Share	31.94
P/E on S&P Est. 1997	13.2	Beta	0.91
Dividend Rate/Share	2.32	Shareholders	89,300
Shs. outstg. (M)	283.7	Market cap. (B)	$ 26.0
Avg. daily vol. (M)	0.716	Inst. holdings	41%

Value of $10,000 invested 5 years ago: $ 34,349

Fiscal Year Ending Dec. 31

	1996	1995	1994	1993	1992	1991
Revenues (Million $)						
1Q	2,866	1,753	1,443	1,371	1,399	1,041
2Q	2,977	1,882	1,509	1,424	1,406	997.3
3Q	3,021	2,044	1,610	1,465	1,381	1,103
4Q	3,120	2,146	1,691	1,495	1,358	1,180
Yr.	11,985	7,825	6,254	5,755	5,544	4,321
Earnings Per Share ($)						
1Q	0.85	1.32	1.27	1.17	0.81	0.67
2Q	1.55	1.45	1.32	1.32	0.90	0.61
3Q	1.29	1.50	1.35	1.12	1.06	0.61
4Q	1.66	1.58	1.04	1.12	0.95	0.60
Yr.	5.35	5.85	4.98	4.73	3.72	2.55

Next earnings report expected: mid April

Dividend Data (Dividends have been paid since 1914.)

Amount ($)	Date Decl.	Ex-Div. Date	Stock of Record	Payment Date
0.520	Feb. 21	Feb. 27	Feb. 29	Mar. 15 '96
0.520	Apr. 16	May. 29	May. 31	Jun. 15 '96
0.580	Jun. 18	Aug. 28	Aug. 30	Sep. 16 '96
0.580	Oct. 15	Nov. 26	Nov. 29	Dec. 16 '96

Business Summary - 30-JAN-97

First Union Corp., following its January 1996 merger with New Jersey-based First Fidelity Bancorp., is now the sixth largest bank holding company in the U.S., with approximately $140 billion in assets. It operates full-service branch offices in Connecticut, Delaware, Florida, Georgia, Maryland, New Jersey, New York, North Carolina, Pennsylvania, Virginia, South Carolina, Tennessee and Washington, D.C.

Average earning assets of $75.8 billion in 1995 (up from $65.5 billion in 1994) were divided: commercial loans 35%, residential real estate loans 22%, consumer loans 21%, investment securities 5%, securities available for sale 11% and other assets 6%. Average sources of funds were: interest-free deposits 13%, savings and money-market accounts 28%, time deposits 27%, foreign deposits 3%, short-term borrowings 14%, long-term debt 6%, equity 7% and other 2%.

At year-end 1995, nonperforming assets were $602 million (0.92% of loans and related assets), versus $558 million (1.03%) a year earlier. The reserve for loan losses was $967 million (161% of nonperforming assets) at December 31, 1995, compared with $979 million (175%) a year earlier.

Important Developments

Jan. '97—Directors authorized the repurchase of up to 25 million FTU common shares.

Dec. '96—The company said it acquired Keystone Investments, Inc., a Boston-based investment management firm with $11.7 billion in assets under management, for 2.6 million FTU common shares.

Nov. '96—FTU said it completed the acquisition of Home Financial Corp. (Nasdaq: HOFL), parent of Home Savings Bank (assets of $1.2 billion), in a transaction whereby each HOFL shares was exchanged for 0.2257 common shares of FTU. Home Savings operates eight offices in Florida's Broward, Dade and Highlands Counties. Separately, the company acquired Center Financial Corp. (Nasdaq; CFCX; assets of $3.7 billion), which operates 46 branch offices in Connecticut through its Centerbank subsidiary, for about $379 million in FTU common stock.

Capitalization

Long Term Debt: $7,660,000,000 (12/96).
Preferred Beneficial Interests: $495,000,000.

Per Share Data ($)

(Year Ended Dec. 31)	1996	1995	1994	1993	1992	1991	1990	1989	1988	1987
Tangible Bk. Val.	NA	26.28	23.04	23.69	20.62	16.08	14.54	15.51	14.20	13.46
Earnings	5.35	5.85	4.98	4.73	3.72	2.55	2.52	2.40	2.76	2.55
Dividends	2.20	1.96	1.72	1.50	1.28	1.12	1.08	1.00	0.86	0.77
Payout Ratio	41%	34%	35%	32%	34%	44%	43%	42%	31%	30%
Prices - High	77¾	59½	48	53⅛	44⅞	31	22	27	23⅞	29½
- Low	51⅛	41⅜	39	37¼	29⅛	13½	13¾	19⅝	19¼	16¼
P/E Ratio - High	15	10	10	11	12	12	9	11	9	12
- Low	10	7	8	8	8	5	5	8	7	6

Income Statement Analysis (Million $)

	1996	1995	1994	1993	1992	1991	1990	1989	1988	1987
Net Int. Inc.	NA	3,263	3,034	2,766	2,008	1,476	1,278	1,030	1,038	989
Tax Equiv. Adj.	NA	82.3	92.7	101	91.0	107	120	129	135	173
Non Int. Inc.	NA	1,429	1,166	1,165	843	746	542	394	410	416
Loan Loss Prov.	NA	180	100	222	250	482	178	81.0	61.0	82.0
% Exp/Op Revs.	NA	62	62	63	64	63	65	68	67	64
Pretax Inc.	NA	1,559	1,415	1,221	722	396	400	308	362	347
Eff. Tax Rate	NA	35%	35%	33%	29%	20%	24%	17%	18%	19%
Net Inc.	NA	1,013	925	818	515	319	304	256	297	283
% Net Int. Marg.	NA	4.41	4.78	4.78	4.98	4.27	4.06	4.23	4.72	5.07

Balance Sheet & Other Fin. Data (Million $)

	1996	1995	1994	1993	1992	1991	1990	1989	1988	1987
Earning Assets:										
Money Mkt	NA	5,971	3,523	1,716	1,945	1,357	1,683	452	522	1,679
Inv. Securities	NA	15,171	11,482	14,437	9,934	6,595	8,055	6,120	5,509	7,170
Com'l Loans	NA	21,289	17,521	14,196	10,120	10,260	9,220	7,347	7,099	6,465
Other Loans	NA	45,513	37,181	33,014	23,529	22,160	17,316	14,668	11,974	9,053
Total Assets	NA	96,740	77,314	70,787	51,327	46,085	40,781	32,131	28,978	27,630
Demand Deposits	NA	11,788	10,524	10,861	8,053	6,662	5,140	3,964	4,231	4,008
Time Deposits	NA	53,212	48,435	42,881	31,337	29,936	22,540	17,535	15,802	13,417
LT Debt	NA	6,444	3,429	3,062	2,522	2,039	1,191	872	634	654
Common Eqty.	NA	6,152	5,398	5,176	3,800	2,981	2,532	2,076	1,923	1,794
% Ret. on Assets	NA	1.2	1.3	1.2	1.1	0.8	0.8	0.8	1.1	1.1
% Ret. on Equity	NA	17.4	16.5	16.5	14.2	10.8	11.1	12.8	16.2	16.5
% Loan Loss Resv.	NA	1.5	1.8	2.2	2.1	2.0	1.7	1.2	1.3	1.7
% Loans/Deposits	NA	101.0	91.6	87.2	84.7	87.7	94.8	101.6	94.5	88.3
% Equity to Assets	NA	6.6	7.5	7.1	7.1	6.4	6.3	6.6	6.6	6.7

Data as orig. reptd.; bef. results of disc. opers. and/or spec. items. Per share data adj. for stk. divs. as of ex-div. date. E-Estimated. NA-Not Available. NM-Not Meaningful. NR-Not Ranked.

Office—Two First Union Center, Charlotte, NC 28288-0570. **Tel**—(704) 374-6565. **Website**—http://www.firstunion.com **Chrmn & CEO**—E. E. Crutchfield Jr. **Vice Chrmn**—J. R. Georgius. **Pres**—A. P. Terracciano. **Exec VP-CFO**—R. T. Atwood. **Exec VP-Secy**—M. A. Cowell Jr. **Investor Contact**—Alice Lehman. **Dirs**—E. E. Barr, G. A. Bernhardt, W. W. Bradley, R. J. Brown, E. E. Crutchfield Jr., R. D. Davis, R. S. Dickson, B. F. Dolan, R. Dowd Sr., J. R. Georgius, A. M. Goldberg, W. H. Goodwin Jr., B. S. Halsey, H. H. Haworth, T. E. Hemby Jr., F. M. Henry, L. G. Herring,— J. R. Inciarte, J. A. Laughery, M. Lennon, R. D. Lovett, J. Neubauer, H. D. Perry Jr., R. N. Reynolds, R. G. Shaw, L. L. Smith, A. P. Terracciano, D. L. Trogdon, J. D. Uible, B. J. Walker, K. G. Younger. **Transfer Agent & Registrar**—First Union National Bank of North Carolina, Charlotte. **Incorporated**—in North Carolina in 1967; bank chartered in 1908. **Empl**— 44,536. **S&P Analyst:** Stephen R. Biggar

STANDARD &POOR'S
STOCK REPORTS

Firstar Corp.

902G

NYSE Symbol **FSR**

In S&P MidCap 400

14-FEB-97 Industry: Banking

Summary: FSR, with more than 240 offices in Wisconsin, Iowa, Illinois, Minnesota, Arizona and Florida, owns Firstar Bank Milwaukee, Wisconsin's largest commercial bank.

Quantitative Evaluations		
Recent Price • 58⅞	Yield • 2.5%	
52 Wk Range • 59¼-42⅛	12-Mo. P/E • 17.5	

Outlook (1 Lowest—5 Highest)
• **2+**

Fair Value
• **53%**

Risk
• **Low**

Earn./Div. Rank
• **A-**

Technical Eval.
• **Bullish** since 5/95

Rel. Strength Rank (1 Lowest—99 Highest)
• **86**

Insider Activity
• **Neutral**

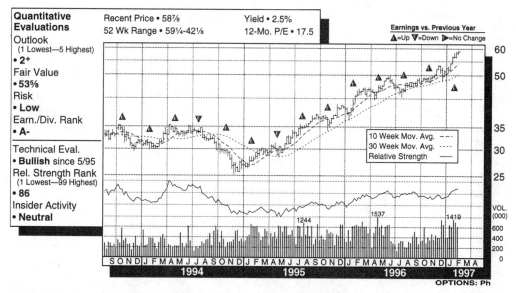

Earnings vs. Previous Year
▲=Up ▼=Down ▷=No Change

10 Week Mov. Avg. ----
30 Week Mov. Avg. ·····
Relative Strength ——

1244 1537 1419

OPTIONS: Ph

Business Profile - 14-FEB-97

This Wisconsin-based multi-bank holding company is in the midst of an aggressive acquisition program to expand its geographic marketplace, as well as its presence in Wisconsin. FSR is also actively consolidating bank subsidiaries to streamline operations, reduce overhead, and improve customer service. A restructuring plan focusing on continued process improvements and new investments in technology should be completed this year. A 2-for-1 stock split and an 8% stock buyback were recently announced.

Operational Review - 14-FEB-97

Net interest revenue rose 3.4% in 1996, to $750 million, as higher average loan balances outweighed a narrower net interest margin (4.51% versus 4.55%). Results benefited from an 11% increase in other operating revenue, mostly trust and investment management fees, and despite non-recurring charges of $0.45 a share (restructuring charges of $0.43 plus a one-time SAIF charge of $0.06, less a tax settlement of $0.04) versus acquisition-related charges of $0.36 a share, net income rose 9.3%, to $250.2 million ($3.37 a share), from $228.9 million ($3.00).

Stock Performance - 07-FEB-97

In the past 30 trading days, FSR's shares have increased 12%, compared to a 4% rise in the S&P 500. Average trading volume for the past five days was 115,183 shares, compared with the 40-day moving average of 180,833 shares.

Key Stock Statistics

Dividend Rate/Share	1.52	Shareholders	11,700
Shs. outstg. (M)	75.2	Market cap. (B)	$ 4.6
Avg. daily vol. (M)	0.207	Inst. holdings	38%
Tang. Bk. Value/Share	21.79		
Beta	0.82		

Value of $10,000 invested 5 years ago: $ 28,820

Fiscal Year Ending Dec. 31

	1996	1995	1994	1993	1992	1991
Revenues (Million $)						
1Q	447.2	410.5	297.8	297.2	300.0	312.5
2Q	447.1	435.6	309.6	300.5	296.9	311.8
3Q	464.4	440.5	320.1	304.6	298.3	314.6
4Q	—	453.3	345.8	306.9	303.7	315.3
Yr.	—	1,740	1,273	1,209	1,199	1,254
Earnings Per Share ($)						
1Q	0.50	0.48	0.83	0.78	0.59	0.49
2Q	0.96	0.70	0.66	0.78	0.65	0.53
3Q	0.93	0.88	0.87	0.79	0.68	0.55
4Q	0.98	0.95	0.86	0.80	0.70	0.57
Yr.	3.37	3.00	3.22	3.15	2.62	2.14

Next earnings report expected: mid April

Dividend Data (Dividends have been paid since 1940.)

Amount ($)	Date Decl.	Ex-Div. Date	Stock of Record	Payment Date
0.380	Jul. 18	Jul. 25	Jul. 29	Aug. 15 '96
0.380	Oct. 17	Oct. 24	Oct. 28	Nov. 15 '96
0.190	Jan. 16	Jan. 23	Jan. 27	Feb. 15 '97
2-for-1	Jan. 16	Feb. 18	Jan. 27	Feb. 14 '97

Business Summary - 14-FEB-97

Firstar Corporation (formerly First Wisconsin) is the largest bank holding company in Wisconsin. At December 31, 1995, Firstar operated, through subsidiaries, 244 branches, including 125 offices in Wisconsin, 44 in Iowa, 41 in Illinois, 31 in Minnesota and three in Arizona. The lead bank is Firstar Bank Milwaukee, which is the largest commercial bank in Wisconsin, with approximately $7.1 billion in assets. It also provides correspondent and international banking services, retail brokerage, trust and investment services, residential mortgage banking, title insurance, business insurance, consumer and credit-related insurance and operational services.

Total loans at year-end 1995 were $12.6 billion ($11.9 billion a year earlier), divided as follows:

	1995	1994
Commercial & industrial	24%	25%
Commercial real estate	23%	24%
Other commercial	8%	8%
Real estate mortgage	22%	20%
Credit card	5%	5%
Home equity	7%	6%
Other consumer	11%	12%

In 1995, loans accounted for 74% of average earning assets, securities and deposits with banks for 25%, and federal funds sold and resale agreements for 1%.

Average sources of funds in 1995 were interest-bearing demand accounts 9%, money market accounts 12%, passbook accounts 9%, CDs 29%, noninterest bearing demand deposits 15%, borrowed funds and other liabilities 18% and shareholders' equity 8%.

In 1995, the average yield on interest-earning assets was 8.28% (7.69% in 1994).

The loan loss reserve was 1.55% of total loans at 1995 year end. Nonperforming assets were $97.9 million (0.77% of total loans and foreclosed assets).

Important Developments

Jan. '97—FSR said it expects to complete a major corporate restructuring in 1997, putting it in an excellent competitive position operationally, technologically and strategically.
Jul. '96—Firstar acquired American Bancorporation (assets of $1.2 billion), a bank holding company with four banks in Minnesota, for $218 million in cash and stock.

Capitalization

Long Term Debt: $602,000,000 (9/96).

Per Share Data ($)

(Year Ended Dec. 31)	1996	1995	1994	1993	1992	1991	1990	1989	1988	1987
Tangible Bk. Val.	NA	18.81	18.42	17.95	14.02	12.31	10.63	9.57	8.35	8.25
Earnings	3.37	3.00	3.22	3.15	2.62	2.14	2.05	1.87	2.44	-1.38
Dividends	1.48	1.32	1.16	1.00	0.80	0.71	0.63	0.54	0.49	0.45
Payout Ratio	44%	44%	36%	32%	31%	33%	31%	29%	20%	NM
Prices - High	53¾	41	35⅜	37¼	31⅞	24½	17	17½	13½	16
- Low	36⅝	26¼	25⅛	29⅜	23⅛	12¾	11	12⅞	10⅜	8⅞
P/E Ratio - High	16	14	11	12	12	11	8	9	6	NM
- Low	11	9	8	9	9	6	5	7	4	NM

Income Statement Analysis (Million $)

	1996	1995	1994	1993	1992	1991	1990	1989	1988	1987
Net Int. Inc.	NA	726	598	568	539	481	335	321	294	245
Tax Equiv. Adj.	NA	33.4	29.0	29.4	31.7	35.6	31.7	26.6	22.7	28.1
Non Int. Inc.	NA	398	335	342	300	271	212	195	231	159
Loan Loss Prov.	NA	36.8	17.1	25.0	45.0	50.0	37.0	44.0	34.0	167
% Exp/Op Revs.	NA	63	63	63	64	66	65	64	60	67
Pretax Inc.	NA	347	311	298	238	187	136	123	164	-50.0
Eff. Tax Rate	NA	34%	33%	31%	30%	28%	28%	29%	33%	NM
Net Inc.	NA	229	208	204	166	134	98.0	87.0	110	-49.0
% Net Int. Marg.	NA	4.55	5.03	5.21	5.27	5.00	4.89	5.06	5.01	4.57

Balance Sheet & Other Fin. Data (Million $)

	1996	1995	1994	1993	1992	1991	1990	1989	1988	1987
Earning Assets:										
Money Mkt	NA	125	376	299	432	332	233	290	431	370
Inv. Securities	NA	4,475	3,391	2,834	2,864	2,870	1,997	1,723	1,256	1,159
Com'l Loans	NA	6,966	2,753	2,470	2,086	1,988	1,619	1,505	1,451	1,298
Other Loans	NA	5,666	7,082	6,514	6,025	5,557	4,173	3,845	3,537	3,390
Total Assets	NA	19,168	15,104	13,794	13,169	12,310	9,383	8,608	7,842	7,257
Demand Deposits	NA	5,064	2,778	3,064	2,782	2,396	1,901	1,700	1,586	1,628
Time Deposits	NA	9,248	8,457	8,100	8,103	7,667	5,621	5,136	4,708	4,323
LT Debt	NA	734	60.1	125	137	142	160	162	167	67.0
Common Eqty.	NA	1,525	1,307	1,156	998	866	609	530	457	338
% Ret. on Assets	NA	1.2	1.5	1.6	1.4	1.2	1.1	1.1	1.5	NM
% Ret. on Equity	NA	15.2	17.0	18.6	17.4	15.9	16.4	16.6	24.3	NM
% Loan Loss Resv.	NA	1.5	1.8	2.0	2.1	2.0	1.9	1.8	1.7	3.6
% Loans/Deposits	NA	88.3	87.5	80.5	74.5	75.0	77.0	78.3	79.3	78.8
% Equity to Assets	NA	8.1	8.9	8.8	7.7	7.1	6.7	6.3	6.0	5.7

Data as orig. reptd.; bef. results of disc. opers. and/or spec. items. Per share data adj. for stk. divs. as of ex-div. date. E-Estimated. NA-Not Available. NM-Not Meaningful. NR-Not Ranked.

Office—777 East Wisconsin Ave., Milwaukee, WI 53202.**Tel**—(414) 765-5748. **Chrmn & CEO**—R. L. Fitzsimonds. **COO & Pres**—J. A. Becker. **SVP-Fin & Treas**—J. B. Weeden. **SVP & Secy**—W. J. Schulz. **Investor Contact**—Joe Messinger (414-765-5235). **Dirs**—M. E. Batten, J. A. Becker, R. C. Buchanan, G. M. Chester Jr., R. H. Derusha, R. L. Fitzsimonds, J. L. Forbes, H. Foster, J. H. Hendee Jr., J. M. Hiegel, J. F. Hladky III, C. P. Johnson, J. H. Keyes, S. B. Lubar, D. F. McKeithan Jr., — G. W. Mead II, G. A. Osborn, J. D. Pyle, C. V. Smith Jr., W. W. Wirtz. **Transfer Agent & Registrar**—Firstar Trust Co., Milwaukee. **Incorporated**—in Wisconsin in 1929. **Empl**— 17,034. **S&P Analyst:** C.F.B.

15-FEB-97 | **Industry:** Electronics/Electric | **Summary:** GE's major businesses include aircraft engines, medical systems, power systems, broadcasting, appliances, lighting and financial services.

S&P Opinion: Buy (★★★★)	Recent Price • 106⅝	Yield • 2.0%
	52 Wk Range • 107⅞-73⅝	12-Mo. P/E • 24.2

Quantitative Evaluations

Outlook
(1 Lowest—5 Highest)
• **1+**

Fair Value
• **82**

Risk
• **Low**

Earn./Div. Rank
• **A+**

Technical Eval.
• **Bullish** since 10/96

Rel. Strength Rank
(1 Lowest—99 Highest)
• **64**

Insider Activity
• **NA**

Earnings vs. Previous Year
▲=Up ▼=Down ▶=No Change

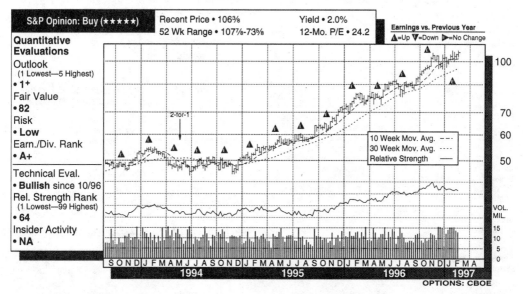

10 Week Mov. Avg. – – –
30 Week Mov. Avg. ·······
Relative Strength ———

VOL. MIL.

OPTIONS: CBOE

Overview - 28-JAN-97

Revenues are expected to rise about 10% in 1997 from those of 1996, reflecting favorable trends in key businesses, emphasis on international expansion, acquisitions, and a concerted effort to boost aftermarket repair and services revenues from GE's traditional manufacturing businesses. The focus on service will be most visible in the aircraft engine, medical equipment and power generation businesses. At the original equipment end of the business, aircraft engines should benefit from a sharp increase in market share. NBC will continue to be aided by strong ratings and special event broadcasts. Financial services should continue to expand at a 20% annual rate, aided by aggressive marketing and acquisitions. GE's consolidated earnings should benefit from improved margins on greater volume, improved manufacturing efficiencies and strong cost control programs.

Valuation - 28-JAN-97

We continue to recommend purchase of the shares of this diversified powerhouse. GE has long established itself as a well managed company that delivers consistent earnings growth. As a result, the shares have been awarded an above-average P/E multiple. Despite this premium valuation, we think that the shares remain attractive. The company actively manages its portfolio of businesses, retaining leaders and divesting those lacking promise. This has enabled GE to achieve consistently robust growth, which should continue. The primary risk facing the company is a broad deterioration in economic conditions; however, given its focus on rapid international expansion, we see the downside risk as minimal. Substantial share repurchases and a rising dividend enhance the appeal of the shares.

Key Stock Statistics

S&P EPS Est. 1997	4.85	Tang. Bk. Value/Share	9.77
P/E on S&P Est. 1997	21.9	Beta	1.09
Dividend Rate/Share	2.08	Shareholders	459,000
Shs. outstg. (M)	1646.4	Market cap. (B)	$175.1
Avg. daily vol. (M)	2.964	Inst. holdings	50%

Value of $10,000 invested 5 years ago: $ 31,207

Fiscal Year Ending Dec. 31

	1996	1995	1994	1993	1992	1991
Revenues (Million $)						
1Q	17,098	15,126	12,657	12,900	12,430	13,330
2Q	19,066	17,809	14,768	14,761	14,200	14,770
3Q	20,021	17,341	14,481	14,858	14,210	14,580
4Q	22,994	19,752	17,791	18,087	16,230	17,550
Yr.	79,179	70,028	60,108	60,562	57,073	60,240
Earnings Per Share ($)						
1Q	0.91	0.81	0.71	0.63	0.56	0.57
2Q	1.15	1.02	0.91	0.39	0.66	0.65
3Q	1.08	0.96	0.85	0.71	0.59	0.60
4Q	1.26	1.12	0.99	0.87	0.71	0.73
Yr.	4.40	3.90	3.46	2.59	2.51	2.55

Next earnings report expected: mid April

Dividend Data (Dividends have been paid since 1899.)

Amount ($)	Date Decl.	Ex-Div. Date	Stock of Record	Payment Date
0.460	Jun. 21	Jul. 01	Jul. 03	Jul. 25 '96
0.460	Sep. 13	Sep. 26	Sep. 30	Oct. 25 '96
0.520	Dec. 19	Dec. 27	Dec. 31	Jan. 27 '97
0.520	Feb. 07	Mar. 04	Mar. 06	Apr. 25 '97

Business Summary - 28-JAN-97

General Electric is a diversified company with interests in services, technology and manufacturing. Industry segment contributions in 1995 were:

	Revs.	Profits
Aircraft engines	9%	11%
Appliances	8%	6%
Broadcasting	6%	7%
Industrial products & systems	14%	14%
Materials	9%	13%
Power generation	9%	7%
Technical products/services	6%	7%
Financial services	38%	32%
Other	1%	3%

International operations, including exports, accounted for 38% of sales and 27% of operating income in 1995.

Aircraft engines and related replacement parts are produced for military and commercial aircraft, for naval ships for propulsion and as industrial power sources.

Appliances include refrigerators, ranges, microwave ovens, freezers, dishwashers, clothes washers and dryers and room air conditioners.

Broadcasting consists primarily of the National Broadcasting Co. (NBC).

Industrial products and systems encompasses lighting products, electrical distribution and control equipment, transportation systems, motors, industrial automation products and GE Supply.

Materials include high-performance engineered plastics, silicones, superabrasives and laminates.

Power generation and related services are provided mainly for the generation of electricity.

Technical products consists of medical systems and information services. Other revenues are derived from licensing the use of GE technology to others.

Financial services primarily consist of GE Capital Services (including General Electric Capital Corp. and Employers Reinsurance Corp.).

Important Developments

Jan. '97—GE noted the results of its major 1996 initiatives in globalization, service, quality and new products. Foreign revenues rose to $33 billion, more than 40% of 1996 revenues. Servicing of GE equipment increased at a double digit rate to $8.4 billion. Some $200 million was spent in 1996 and $300 million will be spent in 1997 to train employees in Six Sigma practices which aim to improve product and process quality. GE expects savings of between $400 and $500 million in 1997 from this investment. New products included launch of MSNBC, a 24-hour news service, expansion into the insurance, annuity and computer servicing markets by acquisition and extended range approval for the GE90 engine on Boeing 777s.

Capitalization

Long Term Debt: $48,799,000,000 (9/96).
Minority Interest: $2,947,000,000.

Per Share Data ($)

(Year Ended Dec. 31)	1996	1995	1994	1993	1992	1991	1990	1989	1988	1987
Tangible Bk. Val.	NA	9.76	8.80	9.05	8.16	6.87	7.07	6.67	5.49	6.68
Cash Flow	NA	6.04	5.34	4.50	4.16	4.18	3.84	3.42	3.14	2.01
Earnings	4.40	3.90	3.46	2.59	2.51	2.55	2.42	2.18	1.88	1.17
Dividends	1.90	1.69	1.49	1.26	1.16	1.04	0.96	0.85	0.73	0.66
Payout Ratio	43%	43%	43%	38%	46%	41%	39%	39%	39%	56%
Prices - High	106⅛	73⅛	54⅞	53½	43¾	39⅛	37¾	32⅜	24	33¼
- Low	69½	49⅞	45	40½	36⅜	26½	25	21¾	19¼	19½
P/E Ratio - High	24	19	16	21	17	15	16	15	13	28
- Low	16	13	13	16	14	10	10	10	10	17

Income Statement Analysis (Million $)

	1996	1995	1994	1993	1992	1991	1990	1989	1988	1987
Revs.	NA	70,028	59,316	59,827	56,274	59,379	57,662	53,884	49,414	39,315
Oper. Inc.	NA	20,821	16,194	16,241	15,205	15,887	15,377	13,944	11,190	5,223
Depr.	NA	3,594	3,207	3,261	2,818	2,832	2,508	2,256	2,266	1,544
Int. Exp.	NA	7,327	5,024	7,057	6,943	7,504	7,544	6,812	5,129	668
Pretax Inc.	NA	9,737	8,831	6,726	6,326	6,508	6,229	5,787	4,782	3,207
Eff. Tax Rate	NA	33%	31%	32%	31%	31%	30%	31%	28%	34%
Net Inc.	NA	6,573	5,915	4,424	4,305	4,435	4,303	3,939	3,386	2,119

Balance Sheet & Other Fin. Data (Million $)

	1996	1995	1994	1993	1992	1991	1990	1989	1988	1987
Cash	NA	43,890	33,556	3,218	3,129	1,971	1,975	2,258	2,187	2,692
Curr. Assets	NA	NA	NA	NA	NA	NA	NA	NA	NA	15,739
Total Assets	NA	228,035	194,484	251,506	192,876	168,259	153,884	128,344	110,865	38,920
Curr. Liab.	NA	82,001	72,854	155,729	120,475	102,611	93,022	73,902	61,800	12,671
LT Debt	NA	51,027	36,979	28,270	25,376	22,682	21,043	16,110	15,082	4,491
Common Eqty.	NA	29,609	26,387	25,824	23,459	21,683	21,680	20,890	18,466	16,480
Total Cap.	NA	90,972	70,418	60,859	54,719	49,392	47,746	41,544	37,902	21,352
Cap. Exp.	NA	6,447	7,492	4,739	4,824	5,000	4,523	5,474	3,681	1,778
Cash Flow	NA	10,162	9,122	7,685	7,123	7,267	6,811	6,195	5,652	3,663
Curr. Ratio	NA	NA	NA	NA	NA	NA	NA	NA	NA	1.2
% LT Debt of Cap.	NA	56.1	52.5	46.5	46.4	45.9	44.1	38.8	39.8	21.0
% Net Inc.of Revs.	NA	9.4	10.0	7.4	7.7	7.5	7.5	7.3	6.9	5.4
% Ret. on Assets	NA	3.2	2.7	2.0	2.4	2.8	3.1	3.3	4.5	5.8
% Ret. on Equity	NA	23.5	22.7	18.0	19.2	20.6	20.6	20.0	19.4	13.5

Data as orig. reptd.; bef. results of disc. opers. and/or spec. items. Per share data adj. for stk. divs. as of ex-div. date. E-Estimated. NA-Not Available. NM-Not Meaningful. NR-Not Ranked.

Office—3135 Easton Turnpike, Fairfield, CT 06431. **Tel**—(203) 373-2211. **Website**—http://www.ge.com **Chrmn & CEO**—J. F. Welch Jr. **VP & Secy**—B. W. Heineman Jr. **SVP-Fin & CFO**—D. D. Dammerman. **Investor Contact**—Mark Begor (203-373-2816). **Dirs**—D. W. Calloway, S. S. Cathcart, D. D. Dammerman, P. Fresco, C. X. Gonzalez, R. E. Mercer, G. G. Michelson, S. Nunn, J. D. Opie, R. S. Penske, B. S. Preiskel, F. H. T. Rhodes, A. C. Sigler, D. A. Warner III, J. F. Welch Jr. **Transfer Agent & Registrar**—Bank of New York, NYC. **Incorporated**—in New York in 1892. **Empl**— 239,000. **S&P Analyst:** Joshua M. Harari, CFA.

Glacier Bancorp   3999
NASDAQ Symbol GBCI

15-FEB-97 | **Industry:** Banking | **Summary:** This multibank thrift holding company operates 16 banking offices primarily in northwestern Montana.

Quantitative Evaluations

Outlook (1 Lowest—5 Highest)
- **NA**

Fair Value
- **NA**

Risk
- **Low**

Earn./Div. Rank
- **A+**

Technical Eval.
- **Bullish** since 8/96

Rel. Strength Rank (1 Lowest—99 Highest)
- **52**

Insider Activity
- **Favorable**

Recent Price • 24½
52 Wk Range • 25¼-18⅜
Yield • 2.6%
12-Mo. P/E • 14.8

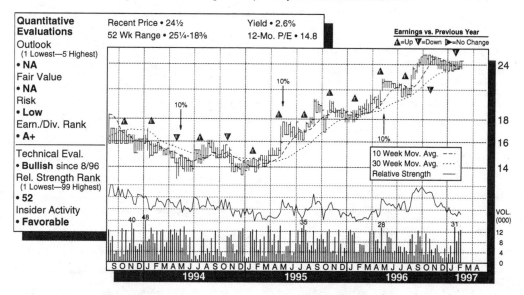

Earnings vs. Previous Year
▲=Up ▼=Down ▶=No Change

10 Week Mov. Avg. – – –
30 Week Mov. Avg. ·······
Relative Strength ——

Business Profile - 12-FEB-97

This bank holding company, with over $540 million in assets, operates 16 banking offices in 10 western Montana communities. In December 1996, the company completed the acquisition of Missoula Bancshares, Inc., parent company of First Security Bank of Missoula. The company said that the acquisition would allow it to expand its strong western Montana franchise by gaining significant presence in the Missoula market area, which is forecast to be one of the two fastest growing markets in Montana through 1998.

Operational Review - 12-FEB-97

Based on a preliminary report, net interest income for 1996 rose 8.7%, year to year, as strong consumer and real estate loan growth outweighed a narrower net interest margin. Noninterest income increased 9.8%, but noninterest expense increased at a more rapid 21%, penalized by a one-time SAIF assessment ($0.13 par share, after tax) and merger-related expenses ($0.12). As a result of these charges, net income declined 6.9%, to $7,425,000 ($1.65 a share), from $7,975,000 ($1.77, restated and adjusted).

Stock Performance - 14-FEB-97

In the past 30 trading days, GBCI's shares have increased 3%, compared to a 8% rise in the S&P 500. Average trading volume for the past five days was 4,020 shares, compared with the 40-day moving average of 2,262 shares.

Key Stock Statistics

Dividend Rate/Share	0.64	Shareholders	700
Shs. outstg. (M)	4.5	Market cap. (B)	$0.110
Avg. daily vol. (M)	0.004	Inst. holdings	13%
Tang. Bk. Value/Share	11.54		
Beta	-0.03		

Value of $10,000 invested 5 years ago: $ 35,835

Fiscal Year Ending Dec. 31

	1996	1995	1994	1993	1992	1991
Revenues (Million $)						
1Q	8.93	7.78	6.24	6.39	4.96	4.70
2Q	9.24	8.20	6.65	6.67	5.23	4.77
3Q	9.44	8.77	7.10	7.02	5.81	4.77
4Q	—	8.88	7.51	6.56	6.24	4.92
Yr.	—	33.63	27.50	26.64	22.24	19.16
Earnings Per Share ($)						
1Q	0.49	0.37	0.31	0.36	0.26	0.19
2Q	0.47	0.41	0.39	0.38	0.32	0.24
3Q	0.25	0.45	0.43	0.44	0.35	0.24
4Q	0.44	0.45	0.40	0.38	0.35	0.24
Yr.	1.65	1.69	1.53	1.55	1.28	0.92

Next earnings report expected: late April

Dividend Data (Dividends have been paid since 1985.)

Amount ($)	Date Decl.	Ex-Div. Date	Stock of Record	Payment Date
10%	Apr. 24	May. 07	May. 09	May. 23 '96
0.160	Jun. 26	Jul. 09	Jul. 11	Jul. 25 '96
0.160	Sep. 25	Oct. 10	Oct. 15	Oct. 24 '96
0.160	Dec. 23	Jan. 09	Jan. 13	Jan. 23 '97

Business Summary - 12-FEB-97

Glacier Bancorp, Inc. is a multibank thrift holding company operating in northwestern Montana through the following subsidiaries: Glacier Bank with 10 banking offices in northwest Montana, two offices in Billings in south central Montana, and an office in Hamilton in western Montana; First National Bank of Whitefish, and First National Bank of Eureka, both located in northwest Montana; and First Security Bank of Missoula in western Montana. The banks operate a total of 16 full-service offices in 10 northwestern Montana communities. Glacier Bank, Inc. operates Community First, Inc., a wholly owned subsidiary that runs an independent full-service brokerage program, INVEST.

At December 31, 1995, gross loans outstanding totaled $283.1 million, and were divided as follows:

	1995
First mortgage and trust deed loans	50%
Instalment and other loans	20%
Commercial loans	18%
FHA and VA loans	8%
Construction loans /Loans held for sale	4%

The allowance for losses on loans totaled $2,061,000 (0.73% of gross loans outstanding) at December 31, 1995, versus $1,863,000 (0.72%) a year earlier. Net chargeoffs came to $83,000 in 1995, versus $28,000 in 1994. Total nonperforming assets, consisting of nonaccrual loans, loans past due 90 days and other real estate owned, were $314,000 (0.08% of total assets) at 1995 year end, up from $293,000 (0.09%) at the end of 1994.

Total deposits amounted to $197.8 million as of December 31, 1995, and were apportioned: 13% demand accounts, 24% NOW accounts, 18% statement savings accounts, 7% money-market accounts, and 38% certificate accounts.

Interest on real estate loans accounted for 43% of total income in 1995, interest on mortgage-backed securities 7%, interest on instalment and other loans 27%, interest on investment securities 8%, service charges and other fees 12%, and other noninterest income 3%.

Important Developments

Dec. '96—GBCI completed the acquisition of Missoula Bancshares, Inc. of Missoula, Montana, for approximately 1.1 million common shares, valued at $26.6 million. Missoula Bancshares is the parent company of First Security Bank of Missoula, a state chartered commercial bank with $110 million of assets. Following the acquisition, the company operates 16 offices in 10 western Montana communities and has over $540 million in assets. First Security will continue to operate under its own name, retaining local management and decision making.

Capitalization

FHLB Advances and Other Borrowed Funds: $158,282,000 (12/96).

Per Share Data ($)

(Year Ended Dec. 31)	1996	1995	1994	1993	1992	1991	1990	1989	1988	1987
Tangible Bk. Val.	NA	11.44	9.86	8.99	8.06	7.06	6.45	5.63	5.21	4.75
Earnings	1.65	1.69	1.53	1.55	1.28	0.92	0.83	0.78	0.61	0.58
Dividends	0.61	0.60	0.47	0.42	0.36	0.30	0.27	0.21	0.13	0.12
Payout Ratio	37%	35%	31%	27%	28%	33%	33%	27%	22%	20%
Prices - High	25¼	20	17⅛	19⅛	13⅜	8	6	3¾	4⅛	4¼
- Low	17¾	13⅝	13⅛	11⅝	7¼	4⅝	3⅞	2½	2½	2⅞
P/E Ratio - High	15	12	11	12	10	9	7	6	7	7
- Low	11	8	9	8	6	5	5	4	4	5

Income Statement Analysis (Million $)

	1996	1995	1994	1993	1992	1991	1990	1989	1988	1987
Net Int. Inc.	NA	15.6	13.6	12.5	10.1	7.8	7.1	5.7	5.3	4.9
Loan Loss Prov.	NA	0.3	0.2	0.2	0.2	0.2	0.2	0.7	0.2	0.2
Non Int. Inc.	NA	4.8	4.4	5.0	3.1	1.9	NA	3.3	2.0	NA
Non Int. Exp.	NA	10.8	9.4	8.9	6.4	4.9	NA	4.3	4.1	NA
Pretax Inc.	NA	9.3	8.4	8.4	6.6	4.7	4.4	4.1	3.0	2.8
Eff. Tax Rate	NA	39%	39%	39%	38%	38%	38%	40%	38%	38%
Net Inc.	NA	5.7	5.1	5.1	4.1	2.9	2.6	2.4	1.9	1.8
% Net Int. Marg.	NA	4.52	4.71	4.48	4.38	4.26	4.30	4.10	3.60	3.80

Balance Sheet & Other Fin. Data (Million $)

	1996	1995	1994	1993	1992	1991	1990	1989	1988	1987
Total Assets	NA	388	340	288	268	197	179	165	148	142
Loans	NA	281	258	240	223	177	162	142	126	NA
Deposits	NA	198	183	181	183	120	119	100	93.0	NA
Capitalization:										
Debt	NA	55.2	41.3	54.7	36.8	25.4	17.7	11.4	14.9	NA
Equity	NA	37.8	33.2	30.0	25.9	22.4	20.4	17.8	15.9	NA
Total	NA	93.4	75.0	84.7	62.7	47.8	38.1	29.2	30.8	NA
% Ret. on Assets	NA	1.6	1.6	1.8	1.8	1.6	1.5	1.5	1.3	1.3
% Ret. on Equity	NA	16.0	17.1	19.8	18.3	14.2	13.6	14.3	12.3	12.9
% Loan Loss Resv.	NA	0.7	0.7	0.8	0.8	0.7	0.8	0.9	NA	NA
% Risk Based Capital	NA	18.1	11.5	20.5	20.8	NA	20.8	NA	NA	NA
Price Times Book Value:										
Hi	NA	1.7	1.7	2.1	1.6	1.1	0.9	0.7	0.8	NA
Low	NA	1.2	1.3	1.3	0.9	0.7	0.6	0.4	0.5	NA

Data as orig. reptd.; bef. results of disc opers. and/or spec. items. Per share data adj. for stk. divs. as of ex-div. date. E-Estimated. NA-Not Available. NM-Not Meaningful. NR-Not Ranked.

Office—202 Main St., P.O. Box 27, Kalispell, MT 59903-0027. **Organized**—in Montana in 1955; incorporated in Delaware in 1990. **Tel**—(406) 756-4200. **Website**—http://www.glacierbank.com**Chrmn, Pres & CEO**—J. S. MacMillan. **SVP, COO & Secy**—M. J. Blodnick. **SVP & Treas**—S. J. Van Helden. **VP & CFO**—J. H. Strosahl. **Dirs**—M. J. Blodnick, L. P. Larson, J. S. MacMillan, D. R. Martin, F. C. Mercord, E. A. Sliter, H. A. Tutvedt. **Transfer Agent & Registrar**—TrustCorp, Great Falls, Mont. **Empl**— 165. **S&P Analyst:** E. Fitzpatrick.

Hanna (M. A.) 1095K

NYSE Symbol **MAH**

In S&P MidCap 400

15-FEB-97

Industry:
Plastic/Products

Summary: This specialty chemical company's primary businesses are plastics and rubber compounding, color and additive concentrates, resin distribution and polymer products.

S&P Opinion: Accumulate (★★★★)	Recent Price • 20¾	Yield • 2.0%
	52 Wk Range • 24⅛-18⅜	12-Mo. P/E • 16.1

Quantitative Evaluations

Outlook
(1 Lowest—5 Highest)
• **3⁺**

Fair Value
• **20⅝**

Risk
• **Low**

Earn./Div. Rank
• **B**

Technical Eval.
• **Bearish** since 8/96

Rel. Strength Rank
(1 Lowest—99 Highest)
• **28**

Insider Activity
• **Neutral**

Earnings vs. Previous Year
▲=Up ▼=Down ▶=No Change

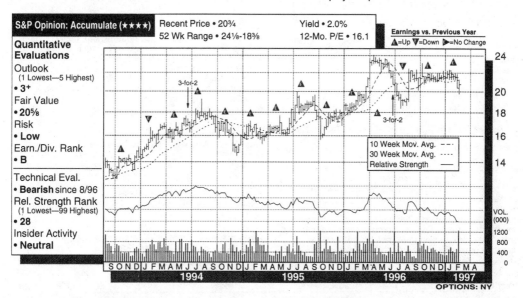

10 Week Mov. Avg. − − −
30 Week Mov. Avg. · · · ·
Relative Strength ——

OPTIONS: NY

Overview - 06-FEB-97

Revenues should continue high single-digit growth in 1997, as MAH's end markets should remain solid for at least the next several quarters. Although results for rubber compounds are being hurt by the loss of toll mixing for the tire market, the processing segment will benefit from increased demand for plastic compounds and colorants. The distribution business is also expected to remain strong. The acquisition of CTi (which established MAH's presence in Asia) and Victor International has lifted the international business to one-fifth of total sales. However, margins will narrow a bit, as the less favorable product mix of the acquisitions slightly outweighs the higher volume, stable raw material costs, effective expense controls and the consolidation in the coloring business. The balance sheet remains solid, with debt below 30% of total capital.

Valuation - 06-FEB-97

We continue to recommend accumulation of the shares, which gained 17% in 1996, versus 20% for the S&P 500 and 7% for the specialty chemicals index. With an improved end market outlook lifting 1997's projected top line growth at least into the high single-digits, a reduction in interest expense, and the continuing enhancement of MAH's operational and administrative efficiencies, the company should be able to achieve mid-teen bottom line growth. Based on their recent price, and our EPS estimate of $1.50 for 1997, the shares remain attractive from both a near- and long-term perspective.

Key Stock Statistics

S&P EPS Est. 1997	1.50	Tang. Bk. Value/Share	3.21
P/E on S&P Est. 1997	13.8	Beta	1.16
Dividend Rate/Share	0.42	Shareholders	4,200
Shs. outstg. (M)	51.8	Market cap. (B)	$ 1.1
Avg. daily vol. (M)	0.149	Inst. holdings	62%

Value of $10,000 invested 5 years ago: $ 26,011

Fiscal Year Ending Dec. 31

	1996	1995	1994	1993	1992	1991
Revenues (Million $)						
1Q	497.5	492.8	388.5	362.0	297.0	258.0
2Q	537.3	483.3	422.5	385.0	333.0	278.0
3Q	531.9	464.1	448.6	388.0	356.0	308.0
4Q	499.5	461.8	459.7	384.5	348.5	303.0
Yr.	2,066	1,902	1,719	1,520	1,334	1,148
Earnings Per Share ($)						
1Q	0.29	0.26	0.13	0.10	0.05	0.06
2Q	0.34	0.41	0.20	0.17	0.15	0.10
3Q	0.34	0.29	0.24	0.19	0.16	-0.54
4Q	0.32	0.26	0.22	0.19	0.24	0.02
Yr.	1.29	1.22	0.80	0.65	0.61	-0.33

Next earnings report expected: early April

Dividend Data (Dividends have been paid since 1944.)

Amount ($)	Date Decl.	Ex-Div. Date	Stock of Record	Payment Date
3-for-2	May. 01	Jun. 18	May. 24	Jun. 17 '96
0.100	Aug. 07	Aug. 14	Aug. 16	Sep. 12 '96
0.105	Nov. 06	Nov. 25	Nov. 27	Dec. 12 '96
0.105	Jan. 27	Feb. 13	Feb. 18	Mar. 12 '97

A Division of The **McGraw·Hill** *Companies*

STANDARD
&POOR'S
STOCK REPORTS

M.A. Hanna Company

1095K
15-FEB-97

Business Summary - 06-FEB-97

M.A. Hanna Co. is a leading international producer of plastic and rubber compounds and a major producer of color and additive concentrates for plastics. It is also an international distributor of engineered plastic shapes and resins, and manufactured polymer products. Contributions by segment in 1996 were:

	Sales	Profits
Processing	54%	66%
Distribution	44%	27%
Other	2%	7%

In 1995 (latest available), foreign operations provided 17% of sales (compared to 14% in 1994) and 18% (14%) of profits.

The processing segment is engaged in the custom compounding of plastic and rubber materials, mixing plastic resins or rubber with additives to achieve a desired physical and/or aesthetic quality. The segment also produces custom formulated colorants for plastics. In January 1996, the company acquired CIMCO Inc., and entered into a plastics compounding joint venture in China. MAH intended to sell CIMCO's plastics components business, and to retain its plastics compounding business, Compounding Technology, Inc. (CTi), which has plants in Singapore, California, North Carolina and one under construction in France. In 1994, MAH acquired Theodor Bergmann GmbH & Co. Kunststoffwerk

KG, one of Germany's largest producers of specialty and reinforced thermoplastic compounds.

The company's resin distribution group links the major thermoplastics producers with thousands of processors and manufacturers, while Cadillac Plastic engages in worldwide distribution of plastic shapes, including sheet, rod, tube and steel. In October 1995, MAH combined Burton Rubber Processing and Colonial Rubber Works into M.A. Hanna Rubber Compounding. Other segments include MAH's diversified polymer products business and its marine and insurance operations.

In 1991, the company divested its natural resources businesses. In May 1995, MAH sold its remaining interest in Iron Ore Co. of Canada, and, in June 1995, it sold Day International, a producer of highly engineered printing blankets.

Important Developments

Jan. '97—MAH noted that the inclusion of acquisitions Compounding Technology, Inc. (CTi), Victor International Plastics, Ltd., and Chase Elastomer, contributed 7% of the total 8% sales growth in the fourth quarter of 1996. Earlier, in November 1996, the company said it would continue to pursue strategic acquisitions to achieve its target of doubling sales to $4 billion in the next five years.

Capitalization

Long Term Debt: $207,705,000 (12/96).

Per Share Data ($)

(Year Ended Dec. 31)	1996	1995	1994	1993	1992	1991	1990	1989	1988	1987
Tangible Bk. Val.	NA	3.14	1.57	-0.32	-0.04	-0.13	2.77	2.13	0.05	-1.00
Cash Flow	NA	2.23	1.71	1.69	1.73	0.48	1.57	2.18	2.24	1.11
Earnings	1.29	1.22	0.80	0.65	0.61	-0.33	0.90	1.48	1.55	0.73
Dividends	0.40	0.37	0.34	0.32	0.29	0.28	0.24	0.20	0.15	0.12
Payout Ratio	31%	30%	43%	49%	59%	NM	26%	15%	10%	19%
Prices - High	24⅛	20	19¼	15⅛	13⅜	11½	12⅛	13¼	10	8⅝
- Low	17¾	15⅜	14¼	11½	8¾	7⅞	6½	8½	5⅝	5
P/E Ratio - High	19	16	24	23	19	NM	13	9	6	12
- Low	14	13	18	18	12	NM	7	6	4	7

Income Statement Analysis (Million $)

	1996	1995	1994	1993	1992	1991	1990	1989	1988	1987
Revs.	NA	1,902	1,719	1,515	1,330	1,146	1,116	1,110	1,019	459
Oper. Inc.	NA	164	142	134	121	107	118	112	99	31.0
Depr.	NA	47.2	41.9	48.1	47.9	43.2	41.7	39.4	33.4	15.3
Int. Exp.	NA	26.3	28.5	32.3	32.5	23.2	18.3	21.3	23.9	15.4
Pretax Inc.	NA	99	66.0	53.0	42.0	-1.0	74.0	100	90.0	37.0
Eff. Tax Rate	NA	43%	44%	44%	37%	NM	25%	13%	8.00%	3.20%
Net Inc.	NA	56.7	37.0	30.0	26.0	-17.0	56.0	87.0	83.0	36.0

Balance Sheet & Other Fin. Data (Million $)

	1996	1995	1994	1993	1992	1991	1990	1989	1988	1987
Cash	NA	111	23.1	42.7	80.0	24.5	25.5	18.3	21.6	16.1
Curr. Assets	NA	575	566	420	439	296	292	280	258	287
Total Assets	NA	1,232	1,215	1,141	1,178	1,033	1,065	1,036	964	1,001
Curr. Liab.	NA	335	337	274	252	202	197	182	184	212
LT Debt	NA	232	289	322	351	331	138	135	138	232
Common Eqty.	NA	485	415	365	398	380	568	543	369	299
Total Cap.	NA	717	704	688	749	711	705	677	607	630
Cap. Exp.	NA	55.9	47.0	23.4	19.2	26.8	28.3	25.6	38.5	14.0
Cash Flow	NA	104	79.0	78.0	74.0	25.0	98.0	124	108	45.0
Curr. Ratio	NA	1.7	1.7	1.5	1.7	1.5	1.5	1.5	1.4	1.4
% LT Debt of Cap.	NA	32.4	41.0	46.8	46.9	46.5	19.5	19.9	22.7	36.7
% Net Inc.of Revs.	NA	3.0	2.2	2.0	2.0	NM	5.0	7.8	8.2	7.9
% Ret. on Assets	NA	4.6	3.1	2.6	2.3	NM	5.4	7.6	8.5	4.7
% Ret. on Equity	NA	12.6	9.5	7.8	6.7	NM	10.3	16.7	22.3	10.6

Data as orig. reptd.; bef. results of disc. opers. and/or spec. items. Per share data adj. for stk. divs. as of ex-div. date. E-Estimated. NA-Not Available. NM-Not Meaningful. NR-Not Ranked.

Office—Suite 36-5000, 200 Public Square, Cleveland, OH 44114-2304. **Tel**—(216) 589-4000. **Chrmn & CEO**—M. D. Walker. **Pres & COO**—D. J. McGregor. **VP & CFO**—M. S. Duffey. **Treas**—C. R. Sachs. **VP & Secy**—J. S. Pyke, Jr. **Investor Contact**—Barbara Gould (800-688-4259). **Dirs**—B. C. Ames, C. A. Cartwright, W. R. Embry, J. T. Eyton, G. D. Kirkham, M. L. Mann, D. J. McGregor, R. W. Pogue, M. D. Walker. **Transfer Agent & Registrar**—Society National Bank, Cleveland. **Incorporated**—in Delaware in 1927. **Empl**— 5,695. **S&P Analyst:** Justin McCann

Heinz (H.J.)

1126M

NYSE Symbol **HNZ**

In S&P 500

15-FEB-97

Industry: Food

Summary: H.J. Heinz Co. produces a wide variety of food products worldwide, with major presence in the U.S. in condiments, canned tuna, pet food and frozen potatoes and meals.

S&P Opinion: Accumulate (★★★★)	Recent Price • 42 / 52 Wk Range • 42-29¾ Yield • 2.8% / 12-Mo. P/E • 23.1

Quantitative Evaluations

Outlook (1 Lowest—5 Highest)
• 2

Fair Value
• 39⅜

Risk
• **Low**

Earn./Div. Rank
• **A+**

Technical Eval.
• **Bearish** since 1/97

Rel. Strength Rank (1 Lowest—99 Highest)
• **78**

Insider Activity
• **Neutral**

Earnings vs. Previous Year
▲=Up ▼=Down ▶=No Change

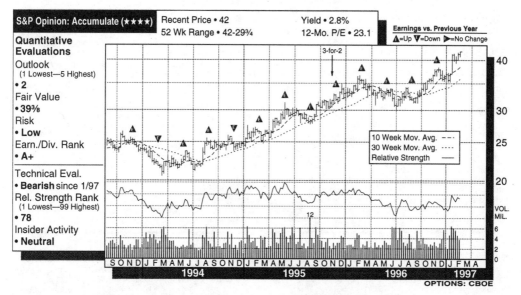

10 Week Mov. Avg. – – –
30 Week Mov. Avg. ·····
Relative Strength —

OPTIONS: CBOE

Overview - 17-DEC-96

Sales are expected to rise at a high single-digit rate in FY 97 (Apr.), driven primarily by broad-based unit volume growth, and, to a lesser extent, by higher selling prices. Near-term gross margins should be supported by the increased volumes, and by continuing productivity enhancement actions. Operating profit margins should also benefit from these factors, as well as from an easing in marketing outlays as compared to high FY 96 levels. Net interest expense comparisons will ease, as acquisition-related debt is paid down. The effective tax rate is likely to rebound to about 37% from FY 96's unusually low level of 35.6%. Overall, we anticipate that earnings per share from continuing operations should advance by approximately 10% in FY 97.

Valuation - 17-DEC-96

Based on our forecast of positive earnings per share growth in FY 97, we view the relatively low-risk shares as attractive for accumulation at current levels. Recent management actions aimed at streamlining HNZ's business portfolio to better focus on core businesses position it well for approximate 10%-plus sales and earnings growth in coming periods. Although the shares have risen sharply from early-1994 levels, we anticipate that the company's reliable earnings growth momentum will push the shares higher at an above-average rate in 1997. HNZ's strong financial condition, historical high returns on common equity, and dependable dividend increases should continue to make the shares attractive for long-term investors as well.

Key Stock Statistics

S&P EPS Est. 1997	1.93	Tang. Bk. Value/Share	0.87
P/E on S&P Est. 1997	21.8	Beta	0.84
Dividend Rate/Share	1.16	Shareholders	59,400
Shs. outstg. (M)	368.2	Market cap. (B)	$ 15.5
Avg. daily vol. (M)	0.986	Inst. holdings	54%

Value of $10,000 invested 5 years ago: $ 19,031

Fiscal Year Ending Apr. 30

	1997	1996	1995	1994	1993	1992
Revenues (Million $)						
1Q	2,209	2,094	1,736	1,583	1,564	1,500
2Q	2,394	2,288	1,975	1,808	1,739	1,592
3Q	—	2,193	1,954	1,710	1,767	1,622
4Q	—	2,537	2,421	1,945	2,034	1,867
Yr.	—	9,112	8,087	7,047	7,103	6,582
Earnings Per Share ($)						
1Q	0.48	0.46	0.41	0.39	0.37	0.63
2Q	0.47	0.42	0.37	0.50	0.40	0.31
3Q	E0.46	0.42	0.37	0.33	0.41	0.29
4Q	E0.52	0.45	0.43	0.34	0.18	0.37
Yr.	E1.93	1.75	1.59	1.57	1.36	1.60

Next earnings report expected: mid March

Dividend Data (Dividends have been paid since 1911.)

Amount ($)	Date Decl.	Ex-Div. Date	Stock of Record	Payment Date
0.265	Mar. 13	Mar. 21	Mar. 25	Apr. 10 '96
0.265	Jun. 12	Jun. 21	Jun. 25	Jul. 10 '96
0.290	Sep. 10	Sep. 19	Sep. 23	Oct. 10 '96
0.290	Dec. 05	Dec. 18	Dec. 20	Jan. 10 '97

A Division of The McGraw-Hill Companies

Business Summary - 17-DEC-96

Although largely known for its familiar ketchup, H.J. Heinz boasts many other branded food products--ranging from StarKist tuna to Weight Watchers frozen dinners--which are consumed by millions of consumers every day. The company's current operating strategy rests upon three pillars: renewed focus on core competencies, acquisitions, and cost control. Sales are geographically broadly based, with contributions by major region derived in FY 96 (Apr.) as follows:

	Sales	Profits
North America	61%	62%
Europe	24%	26%
Asia/Pacific	12%	9%
Other	3%	3%

The company is looking to increase it's leadership--through both internal growth and acquisitions--in six core businesses around the world: foodservice, baby foods, ketchup and condiments, pet food, tuna and weight control. In particular, developing international markets should provide significant opportunities for Heinz's portfolio of consumer products. Its stable of products already include 26 global brands with annual sales of $100 million or more. Also, the company recently signaled that it would rid itself of non-core operations that did not fit well with this strategy.

The company's expansive product line includes Heinz-brand ketchup, sauces and other condiments (19% of FY 96 sales); pet food (12%), with products such as 9Lives cat food, Kibbles N' Bits and Ken-L-Ration dog food, Jerky Treats and Meat Bones dog snacks; StarKist tuna and other seafood products (9%); lower-calorie products (Weight Watchers frozen entrees and desserts); soup (Chef Francisco); sauces/pastes, condiments and pickles, beans full-calorie frozen entrees, and many other related food products.

HNZ also operates and franchises weight control classes, and operates other related programs and activities through its Weight Watchers International subsidiary. Although the entire domestic weight-loss industry continues to exhibit weakness, the U.S. market share for the Weight Watchers meetings program exceeds 50%. As a result of an improved cost structure and an established infrastructure, Weight Watchers meeting operations would benefit if the percentage of dieters using weight-loss services increases.

Capitalization

Long Term Debt: $3,165,082,000 (7/31/96).
$1.70 Third Cum. Conv. Preferred Stk.: 27,100 shs. ($10 par); ea. conv. into nine com. shs.

Per Share Data ($)

(Year Ended Apr. 30)	1996	1995	1994	1993	1992	1991	1990	1989	1988	1987
Tangible Bk. Val.	0.87	0.34	2.67	2.49	3.11	3.92	3.26	3.04	3.26	3.07
Cash Flow	2.66	2.43	2.21	1.95	2.13	1.91	1.69	1.48	1.31	1.10
Earnings	1.75	1.59	1.57	1.36	1.57	1.42	1.27	1.11	0.97	0.83
Dividends	1.04	0.94	0.86	0.78	0.70	0.62	0.54	0.46	0.40	0.34
Payout Ratio	59%	59%	55%	56%	42%	42%	41%	41%	40%	38%
Cal. Yrs.	1995	1994	1993	1992	1991	1990	1989	1988	1987	1986
Prices - High	34⁷/₈	26	30¹/₈	30³/₈	32³/₈	24⁵/₈	23⁷/₈	16⁵/₈	17¹/₄	16¹/₈
- Low	24¹/₄	20¹/₂	22³/₄	23³/₈	21	18³/₈	15	12¹/₂	11¹/₈	9³/₄
P/E Ratio - High	20	16	19	22	20	17	19	15	18	20
- Low	14	13	15	17	13	13	12	11	12	12

Income Statement Analysis (Million $)

	1996	1995	1994	1993	1992	1991	1990	1989	1988	1987
Revs.	9,112	8,087	7,047	7,103	6,582	6,647	6,086	5,801	5,244	4,639
Oper. Inc.	1,631	1,471	1,189	1,285	1,097	1,230	1,087	949	819	707
Depr.	344	315	248	232	212	193	165	146	135	114
Int. Exp.	278	211	149	146	144	146	120	78.0	74.0	51.0
Pretax Inc.	1,024	938	922	716	984	903	811	725	623	565
Eff. Tax Rate	36%	37%	35%	26%	35%	37%	38%	39%	38%	40%
Net Inc.	659	591	603	530	638	568	504	440	386	339

Balance Sheet & Other Fin. Data (Million $)

	1996	1995	1994	1993	1992	1991	1990	1989	1988	1987
Cash	108	207	142	224	273	314	241	238	253	565
Curr. Assets	3,047	2,823	2,292	2,623	2,280	2,120	2,014	1,775	1,664	1,857
Total Assets	8,624	8,247	6,381	6,821	5,932	4,935	4,487	4,002	3,605	3,364
Curr. Liab.	2,715	2,564	2,564	2,866	2,844	1,430	1,280	1,116	1,075	1,035
LT Debt	2,282	2,327	1,727	1,009	178	717	875	693	524	586
Common Eqty.	2,707	2,472	2,338	2,321	2,367	2,274	1,886	1,776	1,593	1,392
Total Cap.	5,308	5,148	4,314	3,526	2,881	3,337	3,072	2,752	2,381	2,221
Cap. Exp.	335	342	275	431	331	345	355	323	238	185
Cash Flow	1,003	906	850	762	850	761	669	586	520	452
Curr. Ratio	1.1	1.1	1.4	0.9	0.8	1.5	1.6	1.6	1.5	1.8
% LT Debt of Cap.	43.0	45.2	40.0	28.6	6.2	21.5	28.5	25.2	22.0	26.4
% Net Inc.of Revs.	7.2	7.3	8.6	7.5	9.7	8.5	8.3	7.6	7.4	7.3
% Ret. on Assets	7.8	8.1	9.2	8.3	11.9	11.9	12.0	11.5	11.1	11.1
% Ret. on Equity	25.4	24.6	26.2	22.6	27.8	27.0	27.7	26.0	25.9	25.0

Data as orig. reptd.; bef. results of disc. opers. and/or spec. items. Per share data adj. for stk. divs. as of ex-div. date. E-Estimated. NA-Not Available. NM-Not Meaningful. NR-Not Ranked.

Office—600 Grant St., Pittsburgh, PA 15219. **Tel**—(412) 456-5700. **Chrmn, Pres & CEO**—A. J. F. O'Reilly. **Vice Chrmn**—J. J. Bogdanovich. **Treas**—P. F. Renne. **Secy**—B. E. Thomas, Jr. **Investor Contact**—John Mazur (412-456-6014). **Dirs**—J. J. Bogdanovich, N. F. Brady, R. M. Cyert, T. S. Foley, E. E. Holiday, S. C. Johnson, W. R. Johnson, D. R. Keough, A. Lippert, L. J. McCabe, A. J. F. O'Reilly, L. Ribolla, H. J. Schmidt, D. W. Sculley, E. B. Sheldon, W. P. Snyder III, W.— C. Springer, S. D. Wiley, D. R. Williams. **Transfer Agent & Registrar**—Mellon Bank, Pittsburgh. **Incorporated**—in Pennsylvania in 1900. **Empl**— 43,300. **S&P Analyst:** Kenneth A. Shea

15-FEB-97 Industry: Banking

Summary: This Illinois bank holding company operates 15 banking offices in the southwest metropolitan Chicago market and a trust company that serves all branches.

Quantitative Evaluations		
	Recent Price • 24¼	Yield • 2.5%
	52 Wk Range • 24½-18¼	12-Mo. P/E • 13.6

Outlook (1 Lowest—5 Highest)
• **NA**

Fair Value
• **NA**

Risk
• **Low**

Earn./Div. Rank
• **A**

Technical Eval.
• **Bullish** since 4/96

Rel. Strength Rank (1 Lowest—99 Highest)
• **73**

Insider Activity
• **Neutral**

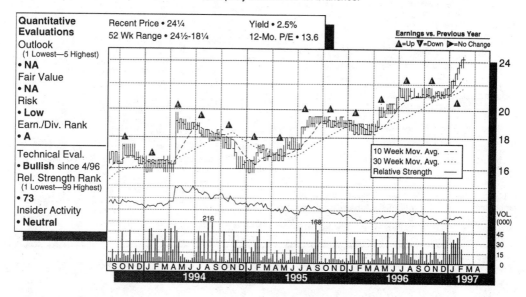

Earnings vs. Previous Year
▲=Up ▼=Down ▶=No Change

10 Week Mov. Avg. ----
30 Week Mov. Avg. ----
Relative Strength ——

Business Profile - 28-JAN-97

Heritage's primary organizational emphasis is commercial lending. In recent years, competition and slower economic conditions have reduced demand for short-term commercial credit. Much of that decline has been offset by real estate and home equity lending. HERS is sufficiently well capitalized to continue its strategy of expanding through acquisitions, and management anticipates internal growth driven by the bank's location in one of the fastest growing areas of metropolitan Chicago.

Operational Review - 28-JAN-97

Based on a preliminary report, for the year ended December 31, 1996, net interest income was up 12% from that of the prior year, principally reflecting a 17% increase in average earning assets, which was fueled by the acquisition of First National Bank of Lockport during the first quarter. The provision for loan losses rose to $400,000, from $200,000. Noninterest income and noninterest expense both advanced 11%. After taxes at 31.7%, versus 32.2%, net income increased 12%, to $14,838,000 ($1.78 a share), from $13,294,000 ($1.60).

Stock Performance - 14-FEB-97

In the past 30 trading days, HERS's shares have increased 8%, compared to a 8% rise in the S&P 500. Average trading volume for the past five days was 4,320 shares, compared with the 40-day moving average of 6,603 shares.

Key Stock Statistics

Dividend Rate/Share	0.60	Shareholders	800
Shs. outstg. (M)	7.9	Market cap. (B)	$0.192
Avg. daily vol. (M)	0.008	Inst. holdings	19%
Tang. Bk. Value/Share	10.39		
Beta	0.47		

Value of $10,000 invested 5 years ago: $ 26,587

Fiscal Year Ending Dec. 31

	1996	1995	1994	1993	1992	1991
Revenues (Million $)						
1Q	21.77	18.87	14.70	15.25	15.45	15.00
2Q	22.95	20.19	15.56	15.54	15.48	15.10
3Q	23.27	20.81	17.97	15.51	15.14	15.47
4Q	—	20.97	18.42	15.06	14.63	15.11
Yr.	—	80.83	66.65	61.36	60.70	60.69
Earnings Per Share ($)						
1Q	0.42	0.37	0.34	0.29	0.27	0.22
2Q	0.45	0.39	0.38	0.35	0.30	0.23
3Q	0.46	0.41	0.39	0.35	0.31	0.26
4Q	0.45	0.43	0.39	0.35	0.30	0.25
Yr.	1.78	1.60	1.50	1.34	1.18	0.97

Next earnings report expected: late April

Dividend Data (Dividends have been paid since 1987.)

Amount ($)	Date Decl.	Ex-Div. Date	Stock of Record	Payment Date
0.130	Apr. 16	Apr. 25	Apr. 29	May. 14 '96
0.130	Jul. 24	Aug. 01	Aug. 05	Aug. 20 '96
0.130	Oct. 23	Oct. 31	Nov. 04	Nov. 19 '96
0.150	Jan. 15	Jan. 28	Jan. 30	Feb. 11 '97

Business Summary - 28-JAN-97

Heritage Financial Services, Inc. is an Illinois bank holding company that has as its primary subsidiaries Heritage Bank and Heritage Trust Co. As of December 31, 1995, Heritage Bank operated 15 offices in the southwestern suburbs of Chicago, with $1.07 billion in total assets. The bank conducts substantially all of its lending activities in southwestern Chicago and, to a lesser extent, the metropolitan Chicago area. A majority of the commercial loan portfolio represents loans to small and mid-size companies in businesses such as light manufacturing, wholesale, distribution and other service operations.

Loans outstanding totaled $571.9 million as of December 31, 1995, and were divided:

	1995
Commercial real estate	25%
Residential real estate	35%
Commercial & industrial	23%
Consumer	15%
Construction	2%

The allowance for loan losses at the end of 1995 amounted to $8,477,000 (1.49% of loans outstanding), compared with $8,720,000 (1.66%) a year earlier. Net chargeoffs of $443,000 (0.08% of average loans) in 1995 contrasted with net recoveries of $125,000

(0.03%) in 1994. As of December 31, 1995, nonperforming assets amounted to $5,617,000 (0.98% of total loans and other real estate owned), compared with $6,036,000 (1.15%) a year earlier.

Total deposits of $915.3 million at December 31, 1995, were divided: 18% demand deposits, 9% NOW, 11% money-market accounts, 22% regular savings and 41% time deposits.

Interest and fees on loans contributed 60% of total income for 1995, interest on investment securities 29%, interest on federal funds sold and other interest income 3%, service charges on deposit accounts 5% and income for trust services and other noninterest income 3%.

The average yield on total interest-earning assets was 8.10% in 1995 (7.56% in 1994), while the average rate paid on interest-bearing liabilities was 4.29% (3.28%), for a net spread of 3.81% (4.28%).

Important Developments

Jan. '97—Heritage said that asset quality continued to improve during 1996. At December 31, 1996, nonperforming loans as a percentage of total loans were 0.66%, compared to 0.85% at December 31, 1995; the allowance for loan losses as a percentage of nonperforming loans was 224%, versus 175%.

Capitalization

Notes Payable: $9,000,000 (9/96).

Per Share Data ($)

(Year Ended Dec. 31)	1996	1995	1994	1993	1992	1991	1990	1989	1988	1987
Tangible Bk. Val.	NA	10.48	8.59	8.35	7.09	7.55	6.85	6.33	5.65	5.01
Earnings	1.78	1.60	1.50	1.34	1.18	0.97	0.77	0.88	0.81	0.73
Dividends	0.52	0.44	0.36	0.32	0.30	0.28	0.25	0.20	0.16	0.13
Payout Ratio	29%	28%	24%	24%	25%	29%	32%	23%	20%	17%
Prices - High	22	19½	19¾	17½	14	11¾	10¾	10⅜	7⅛	6⅞
- Low	18¼	15¾	15¾	12¾	10¼	6¾	5¾	6¾	5½	4⅞
P/E Ratio - High	12	12	13	13	12	12	14	12	9	9
- Low	10	10	10	10	9	7	7	8	7	7

Income Statement Analysis (Million $)

	1996	1995	1994	1993	1992	1991	1990	1989	1988	1987
Net Int. Inc.	NA	40.5	38.0	34.1	30.3	26.8	25.1	22.5	20.6	18.6
Tax Equiv. Adj.	NA	2.8	2.7	2.8	3.0	3.0	3.3	3.3	3.3	NA
Non Int. Inc.	NA	6.8	6.5	6.1	5.4	4.5	4.2	3.6	3.1	NA
Loan Loss Prov.	NA	0.2	0.1	0.5	0.6	1.5	3.5	1.1	1.3	0.9
% Exp/Op Revs.	NA	55	56	56	56	58	58	57	56	NA
Pretax Inc.	NA	19.6	18.2	15.5	13.0	9.9	7.0	8.2	7.2	6.8
Eff. Tax Rate	NA	32%	32%	29%	26%	21%	12%	14%	10%	9.00%
Net Inc.	NA	13.3	12.4	11.0	9.6	7.8	6.2	7.1	6.5	6.1
% Net Int. Marg.	NA	4.58	4.90	4.80	4.80	5.00	5.00	4.90	4.90	5.20

Balance Sheet & Other Fin. Data (Million $)

	1996	1995	1994	1993	1992	1991	1990	1989	1988	1987
Earning Assets:										
Money Mkt	NA	56.0	49.3	30.4	39.5	1.6	16.6	26.8	26.5	NA
Inv. Securities	NA	416	308	289	271	220	171	172	152	NA
Com'l Loans	NA	131	124	127	133	137	152	155	159	NA
Other Loans	NA	441	404	330	323	248	242	214	164	NA
Total Assets	NA	1,066	953	834	824	653	622	609	543	514
Demand Deposits	NA	233	222	193	190	126	93.0	97.0	89.0	NA
Time Deposits	NA	682	602	534	539	442	447	438	386	NA
LT Debt	NA	Nil	6.5	Nil	5.0	Nil	Nil	Nil	2.6	4.4
Common Eqty.	NA	96.8	83.1	75.0	66.4	59.2	53.8	50.8	45.3	40.2
% Ret. on Assets	NA	1.3	1.4	1.3	1.3	1.2	1.0	1.2	1.2	1.2
% Ret. on Equity	NA	14.8	15.8	15.6	15.5	13.9	11.8	14.9	15.1	15.9
% Loan Loss Resv.	NA	1.5	1.7	1.7	1.7	1.3	1.1	1.1	1.1	NA
% Loans/Deposits	NA	62.2	63.7	62.4	62.2	67.6	72.4	68.4	67.6	NA
% Equity to Assets	NA	8.9	8.8	8.5	8.4	8.6	8.6	8.3	8.1	7.9

Data as orig. reptd.; bef. results of disc opers. and/or spec. items. Per share data adj. for stk. divs. as of ex-div. date. E-Estimated. NA-Not Available. NM-Not Meaningful. NR-Not Ranked.

Office—17500 S. Oak Park Ave., Tinley Park, IL 60477. **Tel**—(708) 532-8000. **Chrmn & CEO**—R. T. Wojcik. **Pres**—F. J. Sampias. **Exec VP, Treas & Investor Contact**—Paul A. Eckroth (708) 636-3200. **Exec VP-Secy**—R. P. Groebe. **Dirs**—J. J. Gallagher, R. P. Groebe, L. W. Mathis, J. Payan, F. J. Sampias, A. E. Sieloff, J. L. Sterling, C. Stranczek, A. G. Tichenor, D. J. Velo, R. T. Wojcik. **Transfer Agent & Registrar**—Harris Bank & Trust, Chicago. **Incorporated**—in Illinois in 1984. **Empl**—434. **S&P Analyst:** Thomas C. Ferguson

15-FEB-97

Industry:
Medical equipment/
supply

Summary: This company manufactures hospital equipment, burial caskets, and high security locks. It also offers insurance to cover the cost of funerals.

| S&P Opinion: Hold (★★★) | Recent Price • 37⅝ | Yield • 1.8% |
| | 52 Wk Range • 40¼-32 | 12-Mo. P/E • 18.6 |

Quantitative Evaluations

Outlook
(1 Lowest—5 Highest)
• **4+**

Fair Value
• **43¼**

Risk
• **Low**

Earn./Div. Rank
• **A**

Technical Eval.
• **Bullish** since 10/96

Rel. Strength Rank
(1 Lowest—99 Highest)
• **41**

Insider Activity
• **Favorable**

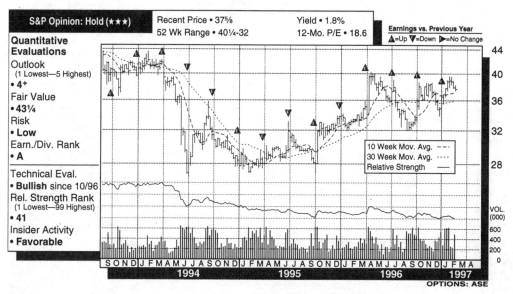

Earnings vs. Previous Year
▲=Up ▼=Down ▶=No Change

10 Week Mov. Avg. ---
30 Week Mov. Avg. ····
Relative Strength —

OPTIONS: ASE

Overview - 21-JAN-97

We expect revenues to advance at a low single-digit pace in FY 97 (Nov.), reflecting relatively flat top-line growth in the healthcare and funeral service segments, as well as prolonged weakness in European operations. However, the funeral insurance segment, which accounted for 13% of total revenues in FY 96, should continue to grow at a near 18% rate. Operating margins are expected to widen slightly on a more favorable product mix and continued cost cutting efforts in the healthcare segments. Following lower interest expense and continued share repurchases, EPS from continuing operations are projected to rise 16% to $2.20 in FY 97, from $1.90 in FY 96. HB recorded a gain of $0.12 a share in FY 96 from the sale of its Block Medical unit.

Valuation - 21-JAN-97

HB is currently selling at 17 times our FY 97 (Nov.) estimate of $2.20, which is in line with market averages and the company's anticipated EPS growth rate. Although the shares are trading at the low end of their historical P/E range, we are maintaining our hold recommendation due to uncertainties surrounding a number of the company's operating segments. Profitability in the funeral services segment continues to hampered by a slowing death rate and a shift in product mix towards lower margin caskets. Sluggish European sales and changes in Medicare reimbursement policies continue to adversely impact results in the healthcare segments. However, we still believe HB is a solid long term holding given its market leading position, conservative capital structure, on-going share repurchases and our anticipation of a turnaround in European operations by the end of FY 97.

Key Stock Statistics

S&P EPS Est. 1997	2.20	Tang. Bk. Value/Share	8.19
P/E on S&P Est. 1997	17.1	Beta	1.01
Dividend Rate/Share	0.66	Shareholders	30,000
Shs. outstg. (M)	68.8	Market cap. (B)	$ 2.6
Avg. daily vol. (M)	0.089	Inst. holdings	32%

Value of $10,000 invested 5 years ago: $ 11,548

Fiscal Year Ending Nov. 30

	1996	1995	1994	1993	1992	1991
Revenues (Million $)						
1Q	433.9	396.3	377.4	348.0	348.0	283.0
2Q	424.2	404.9	382.7	365.0	352.0	301.0
3Q	404.1	398.7	377.8	340.6	346.0	283.0
4Q	422.0	425.0	439.1	393.5	385.0	331.0
Yr.	1,684	1,625	1,577	1,448	1,430	1,199
Earnings Per Share ($)						
1Q	0.48	0.39	0.53	0.48	0.37	0.27
2Q	0.48	0.39	0.46	0.50	0.41	0.31
3Q	0.50	0.37	-0.30	0.41	0.35	0.29
4Q	0.56	0.12	0.57	0.47	0.34	0.35
Yr.	2.02	1.27	1.26	1.86	1.47	1.22

Next earnings report expected: early April

Dividend Data (Dividends have been paid since 1948.)

Amount ($)	Date Decl.	Ex-Div. Date	Stock of Record	Payment Date
0.155	Apr. 09	Apr. 24	Apr. 26	May. 31 '96
0.155	Jul. 09	Jul. 24	Jul. 26	Aug. 30 '96
0.155	Oct. 10	Oct. 23	Oct. 25	Nov. 29 '96
0.165	Jan. 20	Feb. 12	Feb. 14	Feb. 28 '97

A Division of The McGraw-Hill Companies

Hillenbrand Industries, Inc.

Business Summary - 21-JAN-97

Hillenbrand Industries, through subsidiaries, is a leading manufacturer of metal and hardwood burial caskets and electrically operated hospital beds, provides wound therapy treatment systems, makes security locks, and sells life insurance. Segment contributions in FY 95 (Nov.) were:

	Revs.	Profits
Health care	57%	34%
Funeral services	43%	77%
Other	Nil	-9%

In the health care segment, Hill-Rom Co. and SSI Medical Services were combined to form Hill-Rom Inc. in FY 94. The division manufactures hospital beds and hospital patient furniture for acute and long-term care health facilities worldwide. It also provides rental therapy units to health care facilities for wound therapy, the management of pulmonary complications in critically ill patients, and incontinence management. Medeco Security Locks, Inc. manufactures high security lock cylinders made of brass and steel sold internationally to locksmith supply distributors, original equipment manufacturers and various government agencies.

In the funeral services segment, Batesville Casket Co. manufactures burial caskets of steel, copper, bronze and hardwood, including caskets for the cremation market. Caskets are marketed by the company's sales organization to funeral director customers in the U.S., Australia, Puerto Rico and Canada. An inventory of caskets is maintained at 68 service centers in North America. Batesville owns a fleet of trucks to transport the inventory.

The Forethought Group provides life insurance products designed to cover the cost of funerals. This specialized funeral planning product is offered through licensed funeral homes. Customers choose the funeral home, merchandise and type of service they want. The program offers inflation protection, allowing the funeral home to guarantee that the planned funeral will be available as specified.

In July 1996, HB completed the sale of substantially all of the assets of its Block Medical Inc. subsidiary to I-Flow Corp. (Nasdaq: IFLO). In exchange for the assets, HB received $15 million in cash, $2 million of I-Flow common stock, and five-year, non-callable warrants to acquire an additional 250,000 shares of I-Flow stock.

Important Developments

Jan. '97—The company said that losses in certain European countries will continue to impact results in FY 97 (Nov). However, restructuring efforts, which are already well underway, are expected to reduce those losses. HB projects that European operations will be at a breakeven run rate by the end of FY 97.

Capitalization

Long Term Debt: $204,837,000 (11/96).

Per Share Data ($) (Year Ended Nov. 30)	1996	1995	1994	1993	1992	1991	1990	1989	1988	1987
Tangible Bk. Val.	NA	8.30	7.12	7.04	5.37	4.26	4.59	4.14	3.59	3.12
Cash Flow	NA	3.07	2.62	3.21	3.07	2.53	2.30	2.10	1.85	1.47
Earnings	2.02	1.27	1.26	1.86	1.47	1.22	1.03	1.01	0.93	0.76
Dividends	0.62	0.60	0.57	0.45	0.35	0.29	0.28	0.25	0.20	0.17
Payout Ratio	31%	47%	45%	24%	24%	24%	27%	25%	21%	23%
Prices - High	40¼	34⅛	43⅝	48⅝	43⅝	35¼	24	22⅝	17⅞	15⅝
- Low	31⅞	27	26⅝	36½	33½	18¾	15⅛	13¼	11⅜	9⅝
P/E Ratio - High	20	27	35	26	30	29	23	22	19	21
- Low	16	21	21	20	23	15	15	13	12	13
Income Statement Analysis (Million $)										
Revs.	NA	1,625	1,577	1,448	1,430	1,199	1,107	1,138	884	725
Oper. Inc.	NA	333	341	345	319	253	231	221	204	180
Depr.	NA	128	98.0	97.0	115	95.0	94.0	81.0	69.0	54.0
Int. Exp.	NA	20.3	23.5	21.3	21.2	13.2	15.9	17.6	17.8	17.3
Pretax Inc.	NA	170	145	222	171	146	126	127	120	110
Eff. Tax Rate	NA	47%	38%	40%	38%	39%	40%	41%	42%	48%
Net Inc.	NA	90.0	89.0	132	106	89.0	76.0	75.0	70.0	57.0
Balance Sheet & Other Fin. Data (Million $)										
Cash	NA	171	120	210	150	55.0	87.0	49.0	28.0	51.0
Curr. Assets	NA	640	NA	NA	NA	NA	NA	NA	306	284
Total Assets	NA	3,070	2,694	2,271	1,935	1,532	1,268	1,010	735	660
Curr. Liab.	NA	301	NA	NA	NA	NA	NA	NA	154	139
LT Debt	NA	207	209	108	185	104	108	113	118	124
Common Eqty.	NA	746	693	640	548	491	436	405	353	312
Total Cap.	NA	953	922	768	758	645	609	576	516	471
Cap. Exp.	NA	103	100	114	106	67.0	61.0	95.0	93.0	70.0
Cash Flow	NA	217	187	229	221	184	170	156	139	112
Curr. Ratio	NA	2.1	NA	NA	NA	NA	NA	NA	2.0	2.0
% LT Debt of Cap.	NA	21.7	22.6	14.0	24.4	16.1	17.8	19.7	22.9	26.3
% Net Inc.of Revs.	NA	5.5	5.7	9.2	7.4	7.4	6.8	6.6	7.9	7.9
% Ret. on Assets	NA	3.1	3.6	6.3	6.1	6.4	6.7	8.6	10.1	9.3
% Ret. on Equity	NA	12.5	13.4	22.4	20.5	19.3	18.1	19.8	21.1	19.2

Data as orig. reptd.; bef. results of disc. opers. and/or spec. items. Per share data adj. for stk. divs. as of ex-div. date. E-Estimated. NA-Not Available. NM-Not Meaningful. NR-Not Ranked.

Office—700 State Route 46 East, Batesville, IN 47006. **Tel**—(812) 934-7000. **Website**—http://www.hillenbrand.com**Chrmn**—D. A. Hillenbrand. **Pres & CEO**—W. A. Hillenbrand. **VP & Secy**—M. R. Lindenmeyer. **VP, Treas & Investor Contact**—Mark R. Lanning. **Dirs**—L. R. Burtschy, P. F. Coffaro, E. S. Davis, L. Granoff, J. C. Hancock, D. A. Hillenbrand, G. M. Hillenbrand II, J. A. Hillenbrand II, R. J. Hillenbrand, W. A. Hillenbrand, L. M. Smith. **Transfer Agent & Registrar**—Harris Trust & Savings Bank, Chicago. **Incorporated**—in Indiana in 1969. **Empl**— 10,000. **S&P Analyst:** Ronald M. Mushock

15-FEB-97 **Industry:** Office Equipment

Summary: This major manufacturer of wood and metal office furniture also makes fireplaces, woodburning stoves and accessories.

Quantitative Evaluations

Recent Price • 37¾
52 Wk Range • 42¾-21½

Yield • 1.5%
12-Mo. P/E • 16.7

Outlook
(1 Lowest—5 Highest)
• **2**

Fair Value
• **31½**

Risk
• **Average**

Earn./Div. Rank
• **A-**

Technical Eval.
• **Bullish** since 10/96

Rel. Strength Rank
(1 Lowest—99 Highest)
• **76**

Insider Activity
• **Neutral**

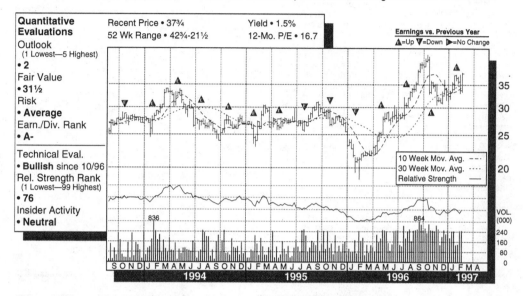

Earnings vs. Previous Year
▲=Up ▼=Down ▶=No Change

10 Week Mov. Avg. ----
30 Week Mov. Avg. ----
Relative Strength ——

Business Profile - 02-DEC-96

This maker of office furniture seeks to accelerate growth by acquisitions in its basic market segments for office furniture. Its long-term goal of doubling earnings every five years requires a 15% average annual growth rate. In October 1996, HONI acquired Heat-N-Glo Fireplace Products, Inc. for $76 million in cash and debt. In August, directors authorized an additional share repurchase program of $20 million. The company repurchased 65,665 shares in the third quarter of 1996 and 398,631 shares in the first nine months of the year.

Operational Review - 02-DEC-96

Net sales in the nine months ended September 28, 1996, rose 8.7%, year to year, reflecting a gain in market share. Gross margin expanded on the higher volume and productivity improvements. Results were also helped by a $3.2 million gain on the sale of a subsidiary. After higher net interest income and taxes at 34.3%, versus 37.3%, net income grew 45%, to $47,028,000 ($1.56 a share), from $32,542,000 ($1.07).

Stock Performance - 14-FEB-97

In the past 30 trading days, HONI's shares have increased 14%, compared to a 8% rise in the S&P 500. Average trading volume for the past five days was 60,620 shares, compared with the 40-day moving average of 47,890 shares.

Key Stock Statistics

Dividend Rate/Share	0.56	Shareholders	5,500
Shs. outstg. (M)	30.1	Market cap. (B)	$ 1.1
Avg. daily vol. (M)	0.043	Inst. holdings	27%
Tang. Bk. Value/Share	8.11		
Beta	-0.35		

Value of $10,000 invested 5 years ago: $ 21,356

Fiscal Year Ending Dec. 31

	1996	1995	1994	1993	1992	1991
Revenues (Million $)						
1Q	233.5	216.5	200.7	186.1	159.0	142.0
2Q	219.3	206.6	193.1	177.5	164.0	135.0
3Q	255.3	228.2	222.1	203.1	196.0	161.0
4Q	290.0	241.8	230.1	213.6	188.2	170.0
Yr.	998.1	893.1	846.0	780.3	706.5	608.0
Earnings Per Share ($)						
1Q	0.55	0.41	0.37	0.25	0.22	0.18
2Q	0.41	0.25	0.30	0.25	0.26	0.16
3Q	0.60	0.41	0.49	0.36	0.38	0.32
4Q	0.70	0.28	0.58	0.53	0.32	0.36
Yr.	2.26	1.35	1.74	1.39	1.18	1.02

Next earnings report expected: early May

Dividend Data (Dividends have been paid since 1955.)

Amount ($)	Date Decl.	Ex-Div. Date	Stock of Record	Payment Date
0.120	May. 13	May. 21	May. 23	May. 31 '96
0.120	Aug. 12	Aug. 20	Aug. 22	Aug. 30 '96
0.140	Nov. 11	Nov. 19	Nov. 21	Nov. 29 '96
0.140	Feb. 12	Feb. 20	Feb. 24	Feb. 28 '97

A Division of The McGraw-Hill Companies

STANDARD
&POOR'S
STOCK REPORTS

HON INDUSTRIES Inc.

4169

15-FEB-97

Business Summary - 02-DEC-96

HON INDUSTRIES primarily makes office furniture and products. The company also manufactures prefabricated fireplaces, woodburning stoves and accessories.

In the area of office furniture and products, the company manufactures, through its HON Co. division and its BPI Inc., Holga Inc., Gunlocke Co. and Chandler Attwood Ltd. subsidiaries, a broad line of metal and wood office furniture. Products include file cabinets, desks, chairs, storage cabinets, combination cabinets, tables, bookcases, machine stands, credenzas, reception area furniture, freestanding office partitions, panel systems, wall systems, office coordinates and stools. These products are available in both contemporary and conventional styles and are priced to sell in all price ranges. HON Co. also makes commercial file cabinets and a limited line of file cabinets designed principally for the home market. During 1993, HON formed a new operation to manufacture new assembly hardware and casegoods furniture for the growing used systems furniture market.

Heatilator Inc. makes factory-built fireplaces, fireplace inserts, freestanding stoves and accessories serving the homebuilding products industry. Heatilator was expanded in 1993 through the $1.2 million acquisition of the Dovre brand of cast-iron fireplaces and wood stoves (for North and South America) from Dovre Industries, NV. Heatilator's products accounted for less than 10% of total revenues in the past three years.

HON Export Ltd. markets selected products from all company operating units. Its selling efforts are conducted outside of the U.S. and Canada.

Office furniture is marketed throughout the U.S. through more than 5,000 stationery and office furniture retailers and 30 wholesalers/distributors. HON also makes products for sale by mass-market retailers and office product specialists, and several operating companies sell directly to the U.S. Government. Fireplace and stove products are sold through 1,600 dealers and 200 distributors. HON Export Ltd. sales are made through more than 90 office furniture dealers and 200 distributors.

In January 1996, HON sold its Ring King Visibles, Inc. unit, which sells personal computer accessories, to Esselte Corp. for $8 million in cash.

Important Developments

Oct. '96—HONI acquired Heat-N-Glo Fireplace Products, Inc., for approximately $76 million in cash and debt. The merger took place through the company's Heatilator Inc. subsidiary, which was then renamed Hearth Technologies Inc.

Capitalization

Long Term Liabs.: $46,965,000 (9/96), incl. $7,207,000 of lease obligs.

Per Share Data ($)

(Year Ended Dec. 31)	1996	1995	1994	1993	1992	1991	1990	1989	1988	1987
Tangible Bk. Val.	NA	7.11	6.35	5.67	5.04	4.64	4.06	3.76	3.95	3.33
Cash Flow	NA	2.05	2.35	1.89	1.62	1.43	1.69	1.14	0.99	0.89
Earnings	2.26	1.35	1.74	1.39	1.18	1.02	1.30	0.79	0.69	0.62
Dividends	0.50	0.48	0.44	0.40	0.37	0.36	0.30	0.24	0.21	0.20
Payout Ratio	22%	36%	25%	29%	31%	35%	23%	30%	31%	32%
Prices - High	42¾	31¼	34	29¼	23½	20½	23	19⅞	10¼	11½
- Low	18½	23	24	21½	16½	13¼	13½	8¾	7⅞	8⅛
P/E Ratio - High	19	23	20	21	20	20	18	25	15	19
- Low	8	17	14	15	14	13	10	11	11	13

Income Statement Analysis (Million $)

	1996	1995	1994	1993	1992	1991	1990	1989	1988	1987
Revs.	NA	893	846	780	707	608	664	602	532	555
Oper. Inc.	NA	88.1	106	87.3	76.8	67.8	81.0	76.5	54.8	55.9
Depr.	NA	21.4	19.0	15.9	14.5	13.3	12.8	12.2	11.3	10.6
Int. Exp.	NA	3.6	3.3	3.1	3.4	3.5	3.7	3.2	4.2	3.5
Pretax Inc.	NA	65.5	86.3	70.9	61.9	52.7	69.1	44.8	41.5	43.9
Eff. Tax Rate	NA	37%	37%	37%	38%	38%	38%	38%	39%	44%
Net Inc.	NA	41.1	54.4	44.6	38.7	32.9	43.2	27.5	25.8	24.8

Balance Sheet & Other Fin. Data (Million $)

	1996	1995	1994	1993	1992	1991	1990	1989	1988	1987
Cash	NA	46.9	30.7	44.4	45.9	34.6	32.4	37.0	68.1	28.3
Curr. Assets	NA	194	189	188	171	151	147	163	175	142
Total Assets	NA	410	373	352	323	281	277	284	276	248
Curr. Liab.	NA	129	111	111	92.0	82.0	93.0	106	79.0	68.0
LT Debt	NA	53.6	54.7	51.1	54.2	35.7	39.6	38.3	38.7	42.3
Common Eqty.	NA	216	195	180	163	150	132	128	148	126
Total Cap.	NA	280	261	242	231	199	184	178	197	180
Cap. Exp.	NA	53.9	35.0	28.9	36.1	15.2	25.6	32.2	11.2	21.6
Cash Flow	NA	62.5	73.4	60.5	53.2	46.2	55.9	39.6	37.1	35.4
Curr. Ratio	NA	1.5	1.7	1.7	1.9	1.8	1.6	1.5	2.2	2.1
% LT Debt of Cap.	NA	19.1	20.9	21.2	23.5	18.0	21.6	21.5	19.6	23.6
% Net Inc.of Revs.	NA	4.6	6.4	5.7	5.5	5.4	6.5	4.6	4.8	4.5
% Ret. on Assets	NA	10.5	15.2	13.4	12.8	11.8	15.8	10.2	9.9	10.2
% Ret. on Equity	NA	20.0	29.5	26.3	24.7	23.5	34.1	20.9	19.0	19.5

Data as orig. reptd.; bef. results of disc. opers. and/or spec. items. Per share data adj. for stk. divs. as of ex-div. date. E-Estimated. NA-Not Available. NM-Not Meaningful. NR-Not Ranked.

Office—414 E. Third St., P.O. Box 1109, Muscatine, IA 52761-7109. **Tel**—(319) 264-7400. **Chrmn**—S. M. Howe. **Vice Chrmn**—R. H. Stanley. **Pres & CEO**—J. D. Michaels. **VP & CFO**—D. C. Stuebe. **Treas**—W. F. Snydacker. **VP & Secy**—A. M. Harvey Jr. **Dirs**—R. C. Cox, W. J. Farrell, S. M. Howe, R. L. Katz, L. Liu, J. D. Michaels, C. C. Michalski, M. S. Plunkett, H. J. Schmidt, R. H. Stanley, J. K. Ver Hagen, L. R. Waxlax. **Transfer Agent**—Co.'s office. **Incorporated**—in Iowa in 1944. **Empl**—6,131. **S&P Analyst:** Brian Goodstadt

STANDARD &POOR'S
STOCK REPORTS

Hormel Foods

1157E

NYSE Symbol **HRL**

In S&P MidCap 400

15-FEB-97 **Industry:** Food

Summary: This company is a leading processor of branded, convenience meat products (primarily pork) for the consumer market.

| S&P Opinion: Hold (★★★) | Recent Price • 24⅞ | Yield • 2.5% |
| | 52 Wk Range • 28-19⅜ | 12-Mo. P/E • 23.9 |

Quantitative Evaluations

Outlook (1 Lowest—5 Highest)
• **3⁻**

Fair Value
• **24⅞**

Risk
• **Low**

Earn./Div. Rank
• **A**

Technical Eval.
• **Bearish** since 11/96

Rel. Strength Rank (1 Lowest—99 Highest)
• **31**

Insider Activity
• **Neutral**

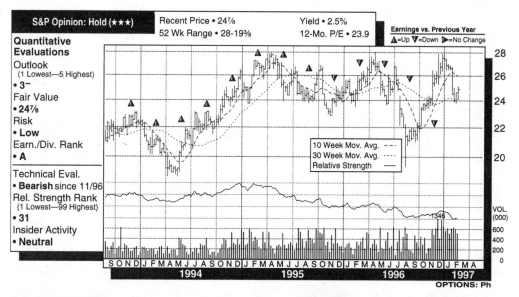

Earnings vs. Previous Year
▲=Up ▼=Down ▶=No Change

10 Week Mov. Avg. – – –
30 Week Mov. Avg. ·······
Relative Strength ——

VOL. (000)

OPTIONS: Ph

Overview - 03-DEC-96

Sales are expected to advance modestly in FY 97 (Oct.), aided mainly by selling price increases taken during FY 96 to help pass on the sharp rise in live hogs, the company's most significant input cost. In recent months, these costs have eased, thanks in large part to a reduction in corn prices, which is the main feed ingredient farmers use to raise hogs. Assuming a continued reduction in hog prices in the months ahead, we look for operating margins to make substantial recovery from FY 96's depressed levels. Meanwhile, continued healthy demand for the company's growing base of branded prepared foods should also provide margin support. Non-operating expenses are relatively minor items for this virtually debt-free company, thus positioning it well for a possible sharp rebound in FY 97 EPS from FY 96's depressed $1.04.

Valuation - 03-DEC-96

The shares have recovered sharply from their mid-1996 low, reflecting investor expectations of easing in live hog prices, which could bolster the company's operating margins, and hence, EPS comparisons throughout the year. Although we anticipate a gradual decline in live hog prices as well, we view the shares as amply valued at current levels. The stock's P/E multiple (approximately 18 times anticipated FY 97 EPS of $1.50), is at about the same level as that of the S&P 500, in line with their recent past relative valuation. Therefore, we anticipate only market performance over the next 12 months. Despite the above-average volatility of earnings, the shares are suitable for low-risk accounts due to the company's low debt levels and conservative acquisition program.

Key Stock Statistics

S&P EPS Est. 1997	1.50	Tang. Bk. Value/Share	8.53
P/E on S&P Est. 1997	16.6	Beta	0.75
Dividend Rate/Share	0.62	Shareholders	11,200
Shs. outstg. (M)	77.4	Market cap. (B)	$ 1.9
Avg. daily vol. (M)	0.136	Inst. holdings	21%

Value of $10,000 invested 5 years ago: $ 12,944

Fiscal Year Ending Oct. 31

	1997	1996	1995	1994	1993	1992
Revenues (Million $)						
1Q	810.3	724.4	730.7	716.2	682.0	628.0
2Q	—	746.7	748.0	767.0	676.7	672.0
3Q	—	749.9	732.4	741.1	677.8	671.0
4Q	—	877.8	835.1	840.5	817.4	842.0
Yr.	—	3,099	3,046	3,065	2,854	2,814
Earnings Per Share ($)						
1Q	0.27	0.27	0.46	0.27	0.24	0.22
2Q	—	0.32	0.33	0.30	0.27	0.26
3Q	—	0.05	0.28	0.26	0.23	0.21
4Q	—	0.40	0.50	0.71	0.57	0.55
Yr.	E1.50	1.04	1.57	1.54	1.31	1.24

Next earnings report expected: late February

Dividend Data (Dividends have been paid since 1928.)

Amount ($)	Date Decl.	Ex-Div. Date	Stock of Record	Payment Date
0.150	Mar. 25	Apr. 17	Apr. 20	May. 15 '96
0.150	May. 20	Jul. 17	Jul. 20	Aug. 15 '96
0.150	Sep. 30	Oct. 16	Oct. 19	Nov. 15 '96
0.155	Nov. 25	Jan. 15	Jan. 18	Feb. 14 '97

STANDARD
&POOR'S
STOCK REPORTS

Hormel Foods Corporation

1157E

15-FEB-97

Business Summary - 03-DEC-96

Hormel Foods is a leading processor of convenience meat products (primarily pork), which accounted for 54% of FY 95 (Oct.) sales. It also makes prepared foods (28%) and processes poultry, fish and other products (18%).

Meat products include fresh meats, sausages, hams, wieners and bacon. Prepared foods include canned luncheon meats, shelf-stable microwaveable entrees, stews, chilis, hash, meat spreads and frozen processed products. Other items include turkey and catfish products. Important brand names are Hormel, Black Label, By George, Cure 81, Curemaster, Di Lusso, Dinty Moore, Frank 'N Stuff, Homeland, Layout Pack, Light & Lean, Light & Lean 97, Little Sizzlers, Mary Kitchen, Range Brand, Rosa Grande, Sandwich Maker, Spam, Wranglers, Top Shelf, Jennie-O, Farm Fresh, Kid's Kitchen, Fast 'N Easy, Dubuque, Quick Meal, Old Smokehouse and House of Tseng. HRL holds 17 foreign and 24 U.S. patents.

In recent years, the company has concentrated on processed, consumer branded products with year-round demand to minimize the seasonal impact of commodity-type products. Pork continues to be the primary raw material for HRL products, and, although live-pork producers are moving toward larger and year-round confinement operations, there is still a seasonal variation in the supply of fresh pork materials.

HRL's larger subsidiaries include Jennie-O Foods, Inc., a major turkey processor, and Farm Fresh Catfish, a breeder, grower and processor of catfish.

Important Developments

Nov. '96—Management attributed the company's 34% decline in net earnings during FY 96 principally to the high costs of feed grains and hogs, and the company's inability to increase prices quickly enough to pass through raw materials cost increases. Sales tonnage during FY 96 fell 12% from the prior year's level, primarily reflecting the termination of fresh pork purchases by Dubuque Foods from HRL's subsidiary FDL Foods, Inc. Management said it remains focused on its proven strategic initiatives, and looked optimistically to FY 97.

Capitalization

Long Term Debt: $15,213,000 (7/96).

Per Share Data ($)

(Year Ended Oct. 31)	1996	1995	1994	1993	1992	1991	1990	1989	1988	1987
Tangible Bk. Val.	8.53	8.48	7.59	6.50	7.85	7.02	5.96	5.57	4.87	4.26
Cash Flow	Nil	2.05	2.02	1.73	1.75	1.60	1.47	1.40	1.25	1.04
Earnings	1.04	1.57	1.54	1.31	1.24	1.13	1.01	0.92	0.79	0.60
Dividends	0.60	0.58	0.50	0.44	0.36	0.30	0.26	0.22	0.18	0.15
Payout Ratio	58%	37%	32%	34%	29%	27%	26%	24%	23%	25%
Prices - High	28	28	26¾	25½	24¾	23⅛	19¾	16⅞	13¾	14¾
- Low	19⅜	22⅞	18¾	20¼	16¾	16	14	10⅛	8¾	8⅛
P/E Ratio - High	27	18	17	19	20	20	20	19	17	24
- Low	19	15	12	15	14	14	14	11	11	14

Income Statement Analysis (Million $)

	1996	1995	1994	1993	1992	1991	1990	1989	1988	1987
Revs.	3,099	3,046	3,065	2,854	2,814	2,836	2,681	2,341	2,293	2,314
Oper. Inc.	164	221	224	187	185	170	156	147	134	121
Depr.	42.8	37.2	36.6	32.2	39.0	36.3	35.6	36.9	35.5	33.5
Int. Exp.	1.6	1.5	2.5	1.4	3.9	2.9	3.3	3.8	8.7	9.5
Pretax Inc.	125	195	191	161	151	138	121	111	95.0	80.0
Eff. Tax Rate	37%	38%	38%	38%	37%	37%	36%	37%	37%	43%
Net Inc.	70.4	120	118	101	95.2	86.4	77.1	70.1	60.2	45.9

Balance Sheet & Other Fin. Data (Million $)

	1996	1995	1994	1993	1992	1991	1990	1989	1988	1987
Cash	203	197	260	172	226	172	102	78.0	69.0	64.0
Curr. Assets	723	659	708	620	609	546	487	417	376	366
Total Assets	1,436	1,224	1,197	1,094	913	857	799	727	707	698
Curr. Liab.	266	218	265	227	208	200	193	188	220	218
LT Debt	127	17.0	10.3	5.7	7.6	22.8	24.5	19.2	20.4	48.8
Common Eqty.	786	732	661	571	644	583	514	471	419	373
Total Cap.	913	749	671	577	668	634	565	530	481	477
Cap. Exp.	123	97.2	65.4	59.7	22.9	33.7	35.0	23.7	34.4	42.8
Cash Flow	113	158	155	133	134	123	113	107	96.0	79.0
Curr. Ratio	2.7	3.0	2.7	2.7	2.9	2.7	2.5	2.2	1.7	1.7
% LT Debt of Cap.	13.9	2.3	1.5	1.0	1.1	3.6	4.3	3.6	4.2	10.2
% Net Inc.of Revs.	2.3	4.0	3.8	3.5	3.4	3.0	2.9	3.0	2.6	2.0
% Ret. on Assets	5.3	10.0	10.3	10.0	10.7	10.4	10.1	9.8	8.6	7.2
% Ret. on Equity	9.2	17.3	19.2	16.6	15.5	15.7	15.7	15.8	15.2	12.9

Data as orig. reptd.; bef. results of disc. opers. and/or spec. items. Per share data adj. for stk. divs. as ex-div. date. E-Estimated. NA-Not Available. NM-Not Meaningful. NR-Not Ranked.

Office—1 Hormel Place, Austin, MN 55912-3680. **Tel**—(507) 437-5737. **Chrmn & CEO**—J. W. Johnson. **EVP & CFO**—D. J. Hodapp. **Treas & Investor Contact**—Michael J. McCoy. **Secy**—T. J. Leake. **Dirs**—J. W. Allen, J. W. Cole, W. S. Davila, D. N. Dickson, L. G. Goldberg, D. J. Hodapp, J. W. Johnson, G. M. Joseph, S. E. Kerber, E. B. Olson, R. F. Patterson, G. J. Ray, R. V. Rose, R. R. Waller. **Transfer Agent & Registrar**—Norwest Bank Minnesota, South St. Paul. **Incorporated**—in Delaware in 1928. **Empl**— 10,600. **S&P Analyst:** Kenneth A. Shea

Hubbell Inc.   1167

NYSE Symbol **HUB.B**

In S&P MidCap 400

15-FEB-97   **Industry:** Electronics/Electric

Summary: Hubbell produces a broad range of electrical and electronic products for commercial, industrial, telecommunications and utility applications.

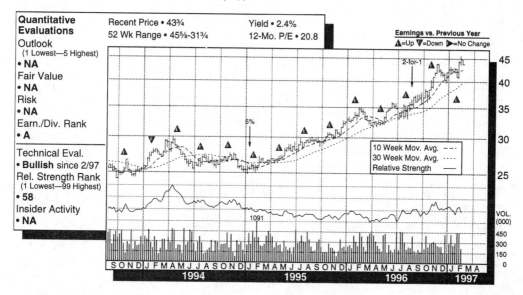

Quantitative Evaluations		
Outlook (1 Lowest—5 Highest)		
• **NA**		
Fair Value		
• **NA**		
Risk		
• **NA**		
Earn./Div. Rank		
• **A**		

Recent Price • 43¾
52 Wk Range • 45⅝-31¾

Yield • 2.4%
12-Mo. P/E • 20.8

Earnings vs. Previous Year
▲=Up ▼=Down ▶=No Change

2-for-1

5%

1091

10 Week Mov. Avg. ---
30 Week Mov. Avg. ···
Relative Strength —

Technical Eval.
• **Bullish** since 2/97

Rel. Strength Rank (1 Lowest—99 Highest)
• **58**

Insider Activity
• **NA**

VOL. (000)

S O N D J F M A M J J A S O N D J F M A M J J A S O N D J F M A M J J A S O N D J F M A
1994   1995   1996   1997

Business Profile - 12-FEB-97

With more than $1.3 billion in annual revenue, this company manufactures electrical and electronic products in North America, Puerto Rico, Mexico, Singapore and the U.K., participates in joint ventures in Brazil and Taiwan, and has sales offices in Malaysia, Hong Kong, South Korea and the Middle East. Earnings have increased consistently since 1961, with the exception of 1993 (when profits were penalized by a restructuring charge). In recent periods, Hubbell has achieved record results and accelerated its pace of strategic acquisitions. Margins have improved, aided by its leading position in many markets and the benefits of its restructuring program, which the company anticipates will continue. Hubbell and Roche family trusts control 32% of the voting power.

Operational Review - 12-FEB-97

Based on a preliminary report, sales rose 13% in 1996, reflecting strength in all areas and contributions from Anderson Electrical Connector and Gleason Reel Corp., acquired in January 1996. Results benefited from the increased volume and improved operating efficiencies due to the company's restructuring program, and net income was up 16%, to $141,532,000 ($2.10 a share), from $121,934,000 ($1.83, as adjusted).

Stock Performance - 14-FEB-97

In the past 30 trading days, HUB.B's shares have increased 3%, compared to a 8% rise in the S&P 500. Average trading volume for the past five days was 42,400 shares, compared with the 40-day moving average of 64,274 shares.

Key Stock Statistics

Dividend Rate/Share	1.04	Shareholders	6,800
Shs. outstg. (M)	66.0	Market cap. (B)	$ 2.9
Avg. daily vol. (M)	0.070	Inst. holdings	55%
Tang. Bk. Value/Share	8.52		
Beta	0.67		

Value of $10,000 invested 5 years ago: $ 19,708

Fiscal Year Ending Dec. 31

	1996	1995	1994	1993	1992	1991
Revenues (Million $)						
1Q	304.6	278.4	207.0	198.0	188.0	182.0
2Q	328.9	295.0	261.9	211.3	195.0	197.0
3Q	332.8	287.0	267.5	211.5	202.0	192.0
4Q	331.1	282.7	277.2	211.7	201.0	185.0
Yr.	1,297	1,143	1,014	832.4	786.0	756.0
Earnings Per Share ($)						
1Q	0.47	0.43	0.37	0.36	0.35	0.34
2Q	0.53	0.45	0.40	0.38	0.37	0.36
3Q	0.55	0.47	0.41	0.35	0.34	0.33
4Q	0.55	0.47	0.43	-0.09	0.35	0.34
Yr.	2.10	1.82	1.60	1.00	1.41	1.37

Next earnings report expected: mid April

Dividend Data (Dividends have been paid since 1934.)

Amount ($)	Date Decl.	Ex-Div. Date	Stock of Record	Payment Date
0.520	Jun. 13	Jun. 20	Jun. 24	Jul. 11 '96
2-for-1	Jun. 13	Aug. 12	Jul. 17	Aug. 09 '96
0.260	Sep. 12	Sep. 19	Sep. 23	Oct. 11 '96
0.260	Dec. 11	Dec. 19	Dec. 23	Jan. 10 '97

A Division of The *McGraw-Hill* Companies

Business Summary - 12-FEB-97

Hubbell Incorporated manufactures a wide variety of electrical products used in low-voltage applications (wiring devices, industrial controls and lighting products) and high-voltage applications (insulated electric wire and cable and power distribution equipment). Other products include outlet boxes and fittings, a line of telecommunications equipment and holding devices. Industry segment contributions in 1995 were:

	Sales	Profits
Low voltage	44%	54%
High voltage	20%	14%
Other	36%	32%

International sales (largely in Canada) accounted for about 6.0% of total sales in 1995.

Low-voltage products (600 volts and less) are made by the Wiring Device division, which specializes in the manufacture and sale of highly durable and reliable wiring devices primarily for industrial and commercial customers; the Lighting subsidiary, which sells lighting fixtures for both outdoor and indoor applications; the Industrial Controls subsidiary, which makes and sells a variety of heavy-duty electrical and radio control products with broad application in the control of industrial equipment and processes; and the Killark Electric subsidiary, which manufactures and sells weatherproof and hazardous-location products for explosion-proof and other hostile-area applications.

In the high-voltage area (over 600 volts), the Kerite unit makes and sells high-performance insulated electric power cable and accessories for application in vital circuits of electric utilities and major industries; and Ohio Brass makes polymer insulators and surge arrestors used in electrical transmission and distribution lines and substations. A.B. Chance Industries makes electrical distribution switches, cutouts, sectionalizers, fuses, insulators and insulator systems. Hipotronics, Inc. makes high-voltage test and measurement systems.

Other products include outlet boxes and fittings; fabricated steel enclosures such as rainproof and dust-tight panels, consoles and cabinets, and wireway. The company also makes voice and data signal processing equipment and components, holding devices (grips) and cord connectors.

Important Developments

Jan. '97—Hubbell said it had agreed to acquire Fargo Mfg. Co. Inc., which supplies a variety of products, principally to the utility industry, that will expand its power systems platform.

Capitalization

Long Term Debt: $99,442,000 (9/96).
Class A Stock: 11,447,000 shs. ($0.01 par); 20 votes each. Hubbell and Roche family trusts control 40%.
Class B Stock: 54,541,000 shs. ($0.01 par); one vote each.
Options: To buy 4,503,884 Cl. A and Cl. B shs. at $10.95 to $32.07 ea. (12/95).

Per Share Data ($)

(Year Ended Dec. 31)	1996	1995	1994	1993	1992	1991	1990	1989	1988	1987
Tangible Bk. Val.	NA	8.04	7.09	7.48	7.35	7.40	6.98	6.42	5.83	5.26
Cash Flow	NA	2.37	2.11	1.39	1.82	1.67	1.56	1.44	1.29	1.14
Earnings	2.10	1.83	1.60	1.00	1.41	1.37	1.30	1.20	1.07	0.94
Dividends	1.02	0.92	0.81	0.78	0.76	0.70	0.63	0.53	0.42	0.38
Payout Ratio	48%	50%	51%	78%	53%	50%	47%	44%	39%	40%
Prices - High	43⅞	33⅛	30	28	28⅝	25⅝	21½	19⅞	15⅛	16⅜
- Low	31¾	24⅞	25	24⅛	21⅜	19⅛	15⅛	13¾	11⅞	10
P/E Ratio - High	21	18	19	28	20	19	16	17	14	18
- Low	15	14	16	24	15	14	12	11	11	11

Income Statement Analysis (Million $)

	1996	1995	1994	1993	1992	1991	1990	1989	1988	1987
Revs.	NA	1,143	1,014	832	786	756	720	669	614	581
Oper. Inc.	NA	201	175	146	145	139	128	121	112	103
Depr.	NA	36.2	34.0	25.9	26.8	20.2	16.6	15.8	14.3	13.5
Int. Exp.	NA	8.5	6.1	3.4	0.7	0.6	0.7	0.7	0.8	0.6
Pretax Inc.	NA	167	146	81.0	131	129	125	117	106	99
Eff. Tax Rate	NA	27%	27%	19%	28%	30%	31%	32%	33%	37%
Net Inc.	NA	122	107	66.3	94.1	90.6	86.0	79.4	71.3	62.5

Balance Sheet & Other Fin. Data (Million $)

	1996	1995	1994	1993	1992	1991	1990	1989	1988	1987
Cash	NA	87.9	39.0	44.0	28.0	92.0	103	101	67.0	61.0
Curr. Assets	NA	500	445	362	330	344	354	341	279	261
Total Assets	NA	1,057	1,042	874	807	685	625	576	523	469
Curr. Liab.	NA	195	332	230	200	111	105	101	88.0	81.0
LT Debt	NA	102	2.7	2.7	2.7	8.1	8.1	8.1	8.1	8.3
Common Eqty.	NA	667	609	558	541	519	469	428	393	354
Total Cap.	NA	785	625	565	559	556	505	463	426	379
Cap. Exp.	NA	38.2	53.2	25.1	22.9	38.9	40.9	21.5	17.2	18.7
Cash Flow	NA	158	141	92.0	121	111	103	95.0	85.0	76.0
Curr. Ratio	NA	2.6	1.3	1.6	1.6	3.1	3.4	3.4	3.2	3.2
% LT Debt of Cap.	NA	13.0	0.4	0.5	0.5	1.5	1.6	1.8	1.9	2.2
% Net Inc.of Revs.	NA	10.7	10.5	8.0	12.0	12.0	12.0	11.9	11.6	10.8
% Ret. on Assets	NA	11.6	11.1	7.9	12.6	13.8	14.3	14.5	14.3	13.8
% Ret. on Equity	NA	19.1	18.2	12.1	17.7	18.3	19.2	19.4	19.0	18.3

Data as orig. reptd.; bef. results of disc. opers. and/or spec. items. Per share data adj. for stk. divs. as of ex-div. date. E-Estimated. NA-Not Available. NM-Not Meaningful. NR-Not Ranked.

Office—584 Derby Milford Rd., Orange, CT 06477. Tel—(203) 799-4100. Fax—(203) 799-4223. Chrmn & Pres—G. J. Ratcliffe. Treas—J. H. Biggart Jr. Secy—R. W. Davies. Dirs—E. R. Brooks, G. W. Edwards Jr., J. S. Hoffman, H. G. McDonell, A. McNally IV, D. J. Meyer, G. J. Ratcliffe, J. A. Urquhart, M. Wallop. Transfer Agent & Registrar—ChaseMellon Shareholder Services, Ridgefield Park, NJ. Incorporated—in Connecticut in 1905. Empl— 7,410. S&P Analyst: C.F.B.

15-FEB-97 | Industry: Banking | **Summary:** This $21 billion regional bank holding company has a network of branches throughout the Midwest and in Florida.

S&P Opinion: Hold (★★★)	Recent Price • 31⅜	Yield • 2.5%
	52 Wk Range • 31¾-21	12-Mo. P/E • 17.4

Quantitative Evaluations

Outlook (1 Lowest—5 Highest)
• **1+**

Fair Value
• **20⅛**

Risk
• **Low**

Earn./Div. Rank
• **A**

Technical Eval.
• **Bullish** since 10/96

Rel. Strength Rank (1 Lowest—99 Highest)
• **94**

Insider Activity
• **Favorable**

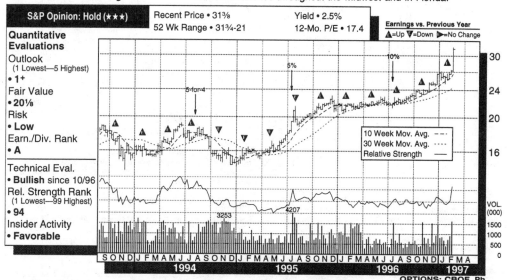

Earnings vs. Previous Year
▲=Up ▼=Down ▶=No Change

10 Week Mov. Avg. – – –
30 Week Mov. Avg. ·······
Relative Strength ——

OPTIONS: CBOE, Ph

Overview - 13-FEB-97

Net income for 1996 was up 7.2%, from that of the prior year, and EPS, which were in line with expectations, rose to $1.80, from $1.62. EPS should continue to grow at a higher rate than net earnings, as HBAN has board authorization for an ongoing common share repurchase program. HBAN's competitive advantages derive from its position as a community bank that relies heavily on technology to enhance its distribution capabilities, and to maximize efficiencies in the face of geographical expansion, product differentiation and escalating competition. In recent periods, the bank has expanded its presence in Florida and, through marketing arrangements with large convenience store retailers, has become one of the largest ATM operators in Ohio. We expect that, given its community banking niche, consumer lending will continue to lead HBAN's growth, and margins should widen as higher levels of relatively low-cost deposits replace higher-cost borrowed funds. In 1997, we anticipate moderate economic growth in the Midwest and Southeast, and forecast EPS of $2.00. HBAN increased provisions for loan losses during 1996, and additional provisioning is not expected to constrain earnings in 1997.

Valuation - 13-FEB-97

Much of HBAN's recent growth has been fueled by acquisitons, which we see continuing, as core growth within the company's geographic region is expected to be moderate through 1997. On fundamentals, HBAN remains an attractive long-term investment, but near-term, trading at more than 13X estimated 1997 earnings, with expected growth of about 11% and a 2.8% yield, shares appear fairly valued. The company's rich price to tangible book valuation of 2.8X, suggests a premium valuation, which is warranted given the quality of HBAN's franchise, the stability of its earnings, and its consistent dividend increases.

Key Stock Statistics

S&P EPS Est. 1997	2.00	Tang. Bk. Value/Share	10.40
P/E on S&P Est. 1997	15.7	Beta	0.24
S&P EPS Est. 1998	2.20	Shareholders	31,800
Dividend Rate/Share	0.80	Market cap. (B)	$ 4.5
Shs. outstg. (M)	144.7	Inst. holdings	17%
Avg. daily vol. (M)	0.245		

Value of $10,000 invested 5 years ago: $ 37,615

Fiscal Year Ending Dec. 31

	1996	1995	1994	1993	1992	1991
Revenues (Million $)						
1Q	442.5	401.4	362.9	314.9	298.3	302.7
2Q	442.3	420.1	359.5	348.8	331.5	308.7
3Q	449.5	439.1	359.1	388.7	310.8	303.5
4Q	419.3	449.8	373.6	489.7	318.4	304.6
Yr.	1,783	1,710	1,455	1,542	1,259	1,219
Earnings Per Share ($)						
1Q	0.43	0.36	0.44	0.37	0.26	0.21
2Q	0.45	0.38	0.45	0.39	0.28	0.24
3Q	0.46	0.44	0.37	0.41	0.28	0.24
4Q	0.47	0.45	0.36	0.42	0.31	0.26
Yr.	1.80	1.62	1.62	1.60	1.14	0.96

Next earnings report expected: early April

Dividend Data (Dividends have been paid since 1912.)

Amount ($)	Date Decl.	Ex-Div. Date	Stock of Record	Payment Date
0.200	May. 15	Jun. 12	Jun. 14	Jul. 01 '96
10%	May. 15	Jul. 12	Jul. 16	Jul. 31 '96
0.200	Aug. 21	Sep. 12	Sep. 16	Oct. 01 '96
0.200	Nov. 20	Dec. 12	Dec. 16	Jan. 02 '97

Business Summary - 13-FEB-97

Huntington Bancshares is a $20 billion regional bank holding company headquartered in Columbus, OH. At April 10, 1996, the company's banking subsidiaries operated 339 offices in six states: Ohio, Kentucky, Indiana, Michigan, West Virginia and Florida. In addition, its mortgage, trust, investment banking and automobile finance subsidiaries operated through 80 offices in these states and in Georgia, Illinois, Maryland, New Jersey, North Carolina, Pennsylvania, Texas and Virginia as well. HBAN's principal subsidiary is The Huntington National Bank. Gross loans and leases of $13.26 billion at December 31, 1995, were divided:

	1995
Consumer	38%
Commercial	32%
Real estate-mortgage	21%
Lease financing	6%
Real estate-construction	3%

The reserve for loan and lease losses at the end of 1995 was $194.5 million (equal to 1.47% of total loans and leases outstanding), versus $200.5 million (1.63%) a year earlier. Net chargeoffs in 1995 amounted to

$41.6 million (0.32% of average loans), versus $28.0 million (0.24%) in 1994. Nonperforming assets totaled $77.0 million (0.58% of total loans and other real estate) at December 31, 1995, versus $96.4 million (0.78%) a year earlier.

Average deposits of $12.2 billion in 1995 were apportioned: 18% noninterest-bearing demand, 21% interest-bearing demand, 16% savings, 7% time CDs of $100,000 or more, and 38% other time deposits. On a tax-equivalent basis, the average yield on interest-earning assets in 1995 was 8.34% (7.97% in 1994), while the average rate paid on interest-bearing liabilities was 4.93% (3.58%) for a net spread of 3.41% (4.39%).

Important Developments

Jan. '97—HBAN reported that, at December 31, 1996, non-performing assets as a percentage of total loans and other real estate were 0.47% and the coverage ratio was 394.3%, representing improvements over each of the three preceding quarters and indicating that asset quality remains strong.

Capitalization

Long Term Debt: $1,556,326,000 (12/96).

Per Share Data ($)

(Year Ended Dec. 31)	1996	1995	1994	1993	1992	1991	1990	1989	1988	1987
Tangible Bk. Val.	NA	10.38	9.39	8.79	7.68	6.99	6.43	6.14	5.74	5.17
Earnings	1.80	1.62	1.62	1.60	1.14	0.96	0.69	0.92	0.89	0.48
Dividends	0.76	0.71	0.62	0.52	0.43	0.39	0.35	0.30	0.27	0.24
Payout Ratio	42%	44%	39%	32%	38%	41%	51%	33%	30%	51%
Prices - High	28⁷⁄₈	23¹⁄₈	19¹⁄₄	19	14³⁄₄	10³⁄₄	8⁷⁄₈	9⁷⁄₈	7³⁄₄	8¹⁄₈
- Low	20¹⁄₂	14⁵⁄₈	14³⁄₈	13¹⁄₂	9⁵⁄₈	5³⁄₈	4³⁄₈	6¹⁄₂	5³⁄₄	5³⁄₄
P/E Ratio - High	16	14	12	12	13	10	13	11	9	17
- Low	11	9	9	8	9	6	6	7	7	12

Income Statement Analysis (Million $)

	1996	1995	1994	1993	1992	1991	1990	1989	1988	1987
Net Int. Inc.	NA	725	756	796	610	478	424	389	328	308
Tax Equiv. Adj.	NA	6.8	9.5	11.7	11.6	14.5	17.7	20.9	20.8	32.0
Non Int. Inc.	NA	248	233	279	201	167	153	139	107	101
Loan Loss Prov.	NA	28.7	15.3	79.3	75.7	56.7	71.0	39.9	26.3	76.0
% Exp/Op Revs.	NA	58	61	61	69	67	66	63	65	64
Pretax Inc.	NA	378	366	364	200	166	115	144	112	50.0
Eff. Tax Rate	NA	35%	34%	35%	31%	30%	26%	25%	22%	5.00%
Net Inc.	NA	244	243	237	139	117	85.0	108	88.0	48.0
% Net Int. Marg.	NA	4.15	4.96	5.20	5.27	4.63	4.17	4.31	4.48	4.76

Balance Sheet & Other Fin. Data (Million $)

	1996	1995	1994	1993	1992	1991	1990	1989	1988	1987
Earning Assets:										
Money Mkt	NA	495	18.0	76.0	265	84.0	84.0	141	417	603
Inv. Securities	NA	4,789	3,780	4,199	3,564	2,756	2,606	2,918	1,916	1,780
Com'l Loans	NA	4,190	4,257	3,916	3,188	2,903	3,010	3,073	2,608	2,354
Other Loans	NA	9,072	8,146	8,070	5,724	5,390	4,880	4,239	3,322	2,977
Total Assets	NA	20,255	17,771	17,619	13,895	12,333	11,809	11,680	9,506	8,836
Demand Deposits	NA	4,861	4,816	2,069	1,729	1,531	1,470	1,412	1,349	1,151
Time Deposits	NA	7,776	7,149	9,976	8,223	7,980	7,645	7,177	5,758	5,451
LT Debt	NA	2,103	1,023	684	270	137	141	153	153	154
Common Eqty.	NA	1,519	1,412	1,325	941	853	786	721	570	512
% Ret. on Assets	NA	1.3	1.5	1.4	1.1	1.0	0.7	1.0	1.0	0.6
% Ret. on Equity	NA	16.7	17.3	19.5	15.5	14.3	11.1	15.8	16.2	9.3
% Loan Loss Resv.	NA	1.5	1.6	1.8	1.6	1.5	1.5	1.1	1.1	1.7
% Loans/Deposits	NA	104.9	103.7	99.5	89.6	87.2	86.6	85.1	83.4	80.4
% Equity to Assets	NA	7.7	8.4	7.2	7.0	7.0	6.6	6.5	6.2	6.3

Data as orig. reptd.; bef. results of disc opers. and/or spec. items. Per share data adj. for stk. divs. as of ex-div. date. E-Estimated. NA-Not Available. NM-Not Meaningful. NR-Not Ranked.

Office—41 S. High St., Columbus, OH 43287.**Tel**—(614) 480-8300. **Website**—http://www.huntington.com   **Chrmn & CEO**—F. Wobst. **Vice Chrmn**—P. E. Geier, W. L. Hoskins, R. J. Seiffert. **Pres, Treas & COO**—Z. Sofia. **EVP & CFO**—G. R. Williams. **Secy**—R. K. Frasier. **Investor Contact**—Jacqueline Thurston (614-480-3878). **Dirs**—D. M. Casto III, D. Conrad, J. B. Gerlach, W. L. Hoskins, W. J. Lhota, G. E. Mayo, T. P. Smucker, Z. Sofia, M. E. White, W. J. Williams, F. Wobst, M. A. Wolf. **Transfer Agent**—Huntington National Bank, Columbus. **Incorporated**—in Maryland in 1966. **Empl**—8,152. **S&P Analyst:** Thomas C. Ferguson

15-FEB-97

Industry:
Cosmetics/Toiletries

Summary: This leading producer of flavors and fragrances, used in a wide variety of consumer goods, derives over two-thirds of sales and earnings from operations outside the U.S.

S&P Opinion: Hold (★★★)

Recent Price • 46⅛	Yield • 3.1%
52 Wk Range • 51¾-40¾	12-Mo. P/E • 27.0

Quantitative Evaluations

Outlook
(1 Lowest—5 Highest)
• 1

Fair Value
• 40⅝

Risk
• Low

Earn./Div. Rank
• A

Technical Eval.
• **Bullish** since 10/96

Rel. Strength Rank
(1 Lowest—99 Highest)
• 54

Insider Activity
• Neutral

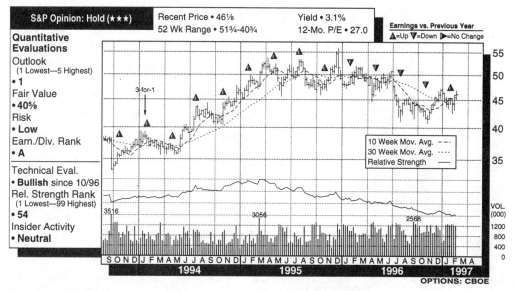

Earnings vs. Previous Year
▲=Up ▼=Down ▶=No Change

10 Week Mov. Avg. – – –
30 Week Mov. Avg. · · · ·
Relative Strength ——

OPTIONS: CBOE

Overview - 14-FEB-97

We expect sales to rebound in 1997. There will be rising volumes of flavors, fragrances and aromas in most parts of the world, especially in less developed countries, reflecting growing consumer demand for personal care, detergent, household, food and beverage products. A continued high level of new product introductions by customers will be beneficial. The North American and European fine fragrance sales should begin to pick up, on the resumption of normal ordering patterns. Assuming more normal summer weather, better sales of flavors are expected to the beverage, ice cream and yogurt industries. Price softness for certain flavors and aroma chemicals will likely continue to restrict results. A stronger U.S. dollar should also modestly restrict sales growth. Initial cost savings from the streamlining of worldwide aroma chemical production facilities will be seen in the second half. EPS comparisons will benefit from a continuing stock repurchase program. Second quarter 1996 results included a nonrecurring charge of $0.29 a share for plant consolidation.

Valuation - 14-FEB-97

The stock was an excellent performer until 1995, reflecting steady growth in sales and net income over the past decade. Weakness since 1995 has been caused by lower than expected earnings resulting from sluggish retail sales of fine fragrances, as well as slower flavor sales to the food and beverage markets. In late June 1996, we downgraded our opinion of IFF to hold, from accumulate, in view of lower than expected EPS. The shares remain an attractive long term holding, as business remains fundamentally sound, with high levels of new product development projects. The dividend was recently raised, for the 36th consecutive year, and increases should continue in the future.

Key Stock Statistics

S&P EPS Est. 1997	2.20	Tang. Bk. Value/Share	9.97
P/E on S&P Est. 1997	21.0	Beta	0.85
Dividend Rate/Share	1.44	Shareholders	5,500
Shs. outstg. (M)	110.3	Market cap. (B)	$ 5.1
Avg. daily vol. (M)	0.297	Inst. holdings	53%

Value of $10,000 invested 5 years ago: $ 15,581

Fiscal Year Ending Dec. 31

	1996	1995	1994	1993	1992	1991
Revenues (Million $)						
1Q	382.8	373.6	323.5	309.0	284.0	270.0
2Q	374.4	394.3	345.2	321.3	296.0	266.0
3Q	354.9	360.1	341.7	298.6	292.0	255.0
4Q	324.0	311.5	304.8	259.6	254.0	226.0
Yr.	1,436	1,439	1,315	1,189	1,126	1,017
Earnings Per Share ($)						
1Q	0.60	0.63	0.53	0.49	0.44	0.41
2Q	0.26	0.68	0.58	0.53	0.48	0.43
3Q	0.48	0.57	0.53	0.44	0.43	0.37
4Q	0.37	0.36	0.39	0.32	0.19	0.26
Yr.	1.71	2.24	2.03	1.78	1.53	1.47

Next earnings report expected: early May

Dividend Data (Dividends have been paid since 1956.)

Amount ($)	Date Decl.	Ex-Div. Date	Stock of Record	Payment Date
0.340	May. 09	Jun. 02	Jun. 27	Jul. 11 '96
0.340	Sep. 10	Sep. 25	Sep. 27	Oct. 11 '96
0.360	Dec. 10	Dec. 24	Dec. 27	Jan. 10 '97
0.360	Feb. 11	Mar. 21	Mar. 25	Apr. 11 '97

A Division of The McGraw-Hill Companies

STANDARD
&POOR'S
STOCK REPORTS

International Flavors & Fragrances Inc.

1211

15-FEB-97

Business Summary - 14-FEB-97

Dollars and scents are nothing new to the major specialty chemicals company. Founded in 1909, International Flavors & Fragrances is the leading maker of products used by other manufacturers which enhance the aromas and taste of consumers' everyday life.

IFF already receives about two-thirds of its sales from outside the U.S. IFF's future opportunities for growth include markets in Asia, Latin America and Eastern Europe, where rising consumer income are likely to boost demand for manufactured products which used the types of ingredients provided by IFF. The company's sales and profits in 1995 derived by geographic areas were:

	Sales	Profits
U.S.	31%	27%
Western Europe	42%	52%
Other	27%	21%

Fragrance products account for about 60% of IFF's sales. Fragrances are used in the manufacture of soaps, detergents, cosmetic creams, lotions and powders, lipsticks, aftershave lotions, deodorants, hair preparations, air fresheners, perfumes and colognes and other consumer products. Most of the major U.S. companies in the industries are customers of IFF. Cosmetics (including perfumes and toiletries) and household products (soaps and detergents) are the company's two largest customer groups.

Flavor products account for IFF's remaining sales. Flavors are sold principally to the food, beverage and other industries for use in such consumer products as soft drinks, candies, cake mixes, desserts, prepared foods, dietary foods, dairy products, drink powders, pharmaceuticals, oral care products, alcoholic beverages and tobacco. Two of the company's largest customers for flavors products are major producers of prepared foods and beverages in the U.S.

IFF uses both synthetic and natural ingredients in its compounds. IFF has had a consistent commitment to R&D, spending 6% to 7% of total sales on R&D for over the past three decades. Research and development is conducted in 28 laboratories in 22 countries.

IFF has achieved steady sales and earnings growth over the past decade. However, the company was hurt during 1996 by slow customer reordering of fine fragrances. Meanwhile, flavor sales were limited by the impact of consolidation and downsizing among food customers, while unusual cool weather resulted in lower sales to beverage and ice cream industries. A streamlining of IFF's aroma chemicals production should generate pretax cost savings of $20 million per year.

IFF is financially strong with almost no long term debt. The cash dividend was recently increased for the 36th consecutive year, one of the few companies on the NYSE that can claim such an impressive record.

Capitalization

Long Term Debt: $8,830,000 (9/96).

Per Share Data ($)

(Year Ended Dec. 31)	1996	1995	1994	1993	1992	1991	1990	1989	1988	1987
Tangible Bk. Val.	NA	10.06	9.04	7.96	8.48	8.39	7.84	6.70	6.11	5.82
Cash Flow	NA	2.61	2.35	2.09	1.83	1.73	1.62	1.43	1.33	1.13
Earnings	1.71	2.24	2.03	1.78	1.53	1.47	1.37	1.22	1.13	0.94
Dividends	1.38	1.27	1.12	1.02	0.93	0.83	0.73	0.66	0.56	0.44
Payout Ratio	81%	57%	55%	57%	61%	56%	54%	54%	50%	47%
Prices - High	51⅞	55⅞	47⅞	39⅞	38¾	35	25	25⅞	18⅛	19⅜
- Low	40¾	45⅛	35⅝	33	31½	22⅞	18¼	16⅛	14⅜	12⅜
P/E Ratio - High	30	25	24	22	25	24	18	21	16	20
- Low	24	20	18	19	20	16	13	13	13	13

Income Statement Analysis (Million $)

	1996	1995	1994	1993	1992	1991	1990	1989	1988	1987
Revs.	NA	1,439	1,315	1,189	1,126	1,017	963	870	840	746
Oper. Inc.	NA	425	385	341	318	284	268	238	234	200
Depr.	NA	40.7	36.4	35.1	34.0	29.4	28.2	24.3	22.7	20.7
Int. Exp.	NA	3.2	13.5	17.4	12.4	9.5	22.1	7.5	8.2	9.6
Pretax Inc.	NA	394	360	324	282	269	252	223	209	175
Eff. Tax Rate	NA	35%	37%	38%	37%	37%	38%	38%	39%	39%
Net Inc.	NA	249	226	202	177	169	157	139	129	107

Balance Sheet & Other Fin. Data (Million $)

	1996	1995	1994	1993	1992	1991	1990	1989	1988	1987
Cash	NA	297	302	311	430	410	376	289	236	253
Curr. Assets	NA	1,036	964	879	965	918	853	724	646	646
Total Assets	NA	1,534	1,400	1,225	1,268	1,217	1,129	970	882	875
Curr. Liab.	NA	276	260	227	195	181	158	140	126	151
LT Debt	NA	11.6	14.3	Nil	Nil	Nil	Nil	Nil	Nil	Nil
Common Eqty.	NA	1,117	1,008	892	977	960	898	765	695	660
Total Cap.	NA	1,142	1,037	903	984	982	919	782	714	678
Cap. Exp.	NA	94.4	101	82.3	51.1	53.3	41.2	33.4	40.2	36.9
Cash Flow	NA	290	262	238	211	198	185	163	151	128
Curr. Ratio	NA	3.8	3.7	3.9	5.0	5.1	5.4	5.2	5.1	4.3
% LT Debt of Cap.	NA	1.0	1.4	Nil	Nil	Nil	Nil	Nil	Nil	Nil
% Net Inc.of Revs.	NA	17.3	17.2	17.0	15.7	16.6	16.3	15.9	15.3	14.3
% Ret. on Assets	NA	17.0	17.3	16.5	14.2	14.4	14.9	14.9	14.6	13.8
% Ret. on Equity	NA	23.4	23.9	22.0	18.2	18.2	18.8	18.9	19.0	18.1

Data as orig. reptd.; bef. results of disc. opers. and/or spec. items. Per share data adj. for stk. divs. as of ex-div. date. E-Estimated. NA-Not Available. NM-Not Meaningful. NR-Not Ranked.

Office—521 W. 57th St., New York, NY 10019-2960. **Tel**—(212) 765-5500. **Chrmn & Pres**—E. P. Grisanti. **VP & Secy**—S. A. Block. **VP-Fin, Treas & Investor Contact**—Thomas H. Hoppel. **Dirs**—M. Hayes Adame, R. Chandler Duke, R. M. Furlaud, E. P. Grisanti, T. H. Hoppel, H. R. Kirkpatrick, H. G. Reid, G. Rowe Jr., S. M. Rumbough Jr., H. P. van Ameringen, H. C. van Baaren, W. D. Van Dyke III. **Transfer Agent & Registrar**—Bank of New York, NYC. **Incorporated**—in New York in 1909. **Empl**—4,650. **S&P Analyst:** Richard O'Reilly, CFA

STANDARD &POOR'S
STOCK REPORTS

Jefferson-Pilot

1260

NYSE Symbol **JP**

In S&P 500

14-FEB-97

Industry:
Insurance

Summary: Jefferson-Pilot provides an array of insurance and communications products and services. The bulk of revenues and income is derived from life insurance and annuity operations.

S&P Opinion: Hold (★★★)	Recent Price • 58⅞	Yield • 2.4%
	52 Wk Range • 60-49⅞	12-Mo. P/E • 14.4

Quantitative Evaluations

Outlook
(1 Lowest—5 Highest)
• 3

Fair Value
• 59¼

Risk
• **Low**

Earn./Div. Rank
• **A+**

Technical Eval.
• **Bullish** since 5/94

Rel. Strength Rank
(1 Lowest—99 Highest)
• 57

Insider Activity
• **NA**

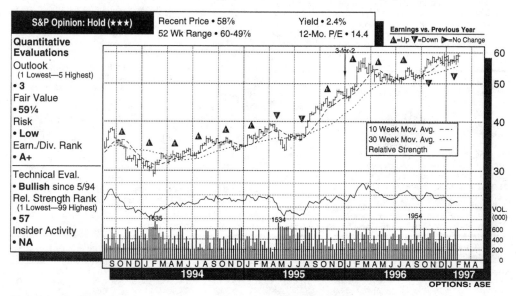

Earnings vs. Previous Year
▲=Up ▼=Down ▶=No Change

10 Week Mov. Avg. - - -
30 Week Mov. Avg. ·····
Relative Strength ——

VOL. (000)

OPTIONS: ASE

Overview - 14-FEB-97

The forecast of higher operating earnings (from continuing businesses) in coming periods is predicated on continued strong individual life insurance premium growth. JP's recent growth here has been the result of an acquisition and robust sales of individual annuities and interest-sensitive life insurance products. Although many of these products increase JP's risk to interest rate changes, this risk is manageable. Steps taken to increase agent productivity and reduce expenses are also aiding profit margins. Margins in the group insurance area may come under continued pressure from adverse disability claim trends and increased price competition in traditional medical coverages. An improved advertising market augurs well for the communications group. Investment income growth will be modest amid a relatively lower interest rate environment, but asset writedowns to the portfolio are unlikely.

Valuation - 14-FEB-97

After trending upward during much of 1995, thanks to a favorable interest rate environment for financial stocks, the shares of this life and health insurer corrected in early 1996 amid fears of higher interest rates. While those fears have eased somewhat, the shares remain in a narrow trading range, and will likely continue to do so. Trading at almost 14 times our aggressive 1997 operating earnings estimate of $4.25 a share (before realized investment gains or losses), the shares are at the upper end of their historical P/E range, and are fairly valued near term.

Key Stock Statistics

S&P EPS Est. 1997	4.25	Tang. Bk. Value/Share	29.02
P/E on S&P Est. 1997	13.9	Beta	0.46
Dividend Rate/Share	1.60	Shareholders	10,000
Shs. outstg. (M)	70.7	Market cap. (B)	$ 4.2
Avg. daily vol. (M)	0.122	Inst. holdings	40%

Value of $10,000 invested 5 years ago: $ 27,164

Fiscal Year Ending Dec. 31

	1996	1995	1994	1993	1992	1991
Revenues (Million $)						
1Q	534.2	315.2	307.3	306.7	300.0	—
2Q	528.5	328.9	314.5	308.1	296.1	—
3Q	515.0	381.6	312.5	302.7	299.6	—
4Q	—	543.7	334.6	329.2	306.6	—
Yr.	—	1,569	1,269	1,247	1,202	—
Earnings Per Share ($)						
1Q	0.98	0.71	0.72	0.66	0.64	0.54
2Q	1.02	0.71	0.77	0.69	0.63	0.57
3Q	0.90	0.92	0.78	0.69	0.64	0.55
4Q	1.05	1.21	0.89	0.87	0.75	0.63
Yr.	4.09	3.55	3.15	2.91	2.66	2.29

Next earnings report expected: mid May

Dividend Data (Dividends have been paid since 1913.)

Amount ($)	Date Decl.	Ex-Div. Date	Stock of Record	Payment Date
0.360	May. 07	Aug. 14	Aug. 16	Sep. 06 '96
0.360	Aug. 12	Nov. 13	Nov. 15	Dec. 06 '96
0.360	Nov. 04	Feb. 12	Feb. 14	Mar. 05 '97
0.400	Feb. 10	May. 14	May. 16	Jun. 05 '97

STANDARD
&POOR'S
STOCK REPORTS

Jefferson-Pilot Corporation

1260

14-FEB-97

Business Summary - 14-FEB-97

Jefferson-Pilot Corp. is a holding company whose principal insurance subsidiary is Jefferson-Pilot Life Insurance Co.. In early 1995, the company sold Jefferson-Pilot Title Insurance Co. and Jefferson-Pilot Fire & Casualty Co. JP also owns and operates radio and television stations, and produces televised sports programs. Jefferson-Pilot Communications Co., a provider of electronic data services, was also sold in early 1995. Segment contributions from continuing operations in 1996:

	Revs.	Net Income
Individual life insurance	44%	53%
Annuities & investment products	21%	22%
Group insurance	24%	8%
Communications & other (incl. inv. gains)	11%	17%

Jefferson Pilot Life Insurance Co. underwrites an array of life insurance products, including whole life, term life, annuity and endowment policies, on an individual and group basis. Products are marketed through a general agency system that utilizes the services of career agents, home service agents, and independent marketing organizations. Accident and health insurance is also offered, mostly on a group basis.

Jefferson-Pilot Communication Co. owns and operates three television and 15 radio stations (as of June 30, 1996) in North Carolina, South Carolina, Virginia, Georgia, Florida, Colorado and California. Other operations include a sports production and syndication business and a co-op advertising business.

In May 1995, JP acquired the life insurance and annuity business of Kentucky Central Life and Health Insurance Co. (KC). JP assumed assets of $869 million and recorded a liability of $1.1 billion in connection with the acquisition of KC, which was seized by state regulators in 1993.

Important Developments

Feb. '97—JP's operating earnings from continuing operations for the year ended December 31, 1996 rose to $3.66 a share, up from $3.09 a share reported in 1995. Commenting on results for 1996, management noted that results were driven by strength in the core individual life insurance and annuity lines of business. Results here were aided by internal growth, and by contributions from the acquisition of Alexander Hamilton Life Insurance Co. of America. JP acquired Alexander Hamilton Life in October 1995 from Household International for $575 million. Also, the company noted that its group accident and health insurance business continued to be affected by "significant competitive pressure". But, JP said it was taking steps to address this issue.

Capitalization

Debt: $370,150,000 (12/96).

Per Share Data ($)

(Year Ended Dec. 31)	1996	1995	1994	1993	1992	1991	1990	1989	1988	1987
Tangible Bk. Val.	NA	29.30	23.09	22.83	21.92	19.89	16.98	17.11	15.01	14.05
Oper. Earnings	NA	3.09	2.62	2.41	2.24	1.99	1.73	1.49	1.11	1.02
Earnings	4.09	3.55	3.15	2.91	2.66	2.29	1.96	1.62	1.15	1.65
Dividends	1.40	1.25	1.12	1.01	0.87	0.73	0.66	0.60	0.56	0.52
Relative Payout	34%	35%	36%	35%	33%	32%	34%	37%	49%	32%
Prices - High	59⅝	48¼	36¾	38⅝	33	26⅛	19⅞	20¼	16⅝	18⅞
- Low	45⅛	33⅝	28⅞	30⅜	22¼	15¼	14⅜	13¼	11⅜	10¼
P/E Ratio - High	15	14	12	13	12	11	10	12	15	18
- Low	11	9	9	10	8	7	7	8	10	10

Income Statement Analysis (Million $)

	1996	1995	1994	1993	1992	1991	1990	1989	1988	1987
Life Ins. In Force	NA	111,383	45,049	41,591	40,843	38,460	38,465	36,977	36,291	40,078
Prem.Inc Life A&H	NA	810	655	627	NA	NA	NA	NA	NA	NA
Prem.Inc Cas/Prop	NA	Nil	Nil	Nil	NA	NA	NA	NA	NA	NA
Net Invest. Inc.	NA	541	375	370	361	353	342	333	314	298
Oth. Revs.	NA	218	238	250	NA	NA	NA	NA	NA	NA
Total Revs.	NA	1,569	1,269	1,247	1,202	1,173	1,163	1,140	1,223	1,052
Pretax Inc.	NA	381	348	322	286	245	222	198	139	130
Net Oper. Inc.	NA	222	190	158	171	153	139	126	98.0	91.0
Net Inc.	NA	255	230	219	206	176	158	138	101	148

Balance Sheet & Other Fin. Data (Million $)

	1996	1995	1994	1993	1992	1991	1990	1989	1988	1987
Cash & Equiv.	NA	279	90.0	101	223	226	185	232	211	83.0
Premiums Due	NA	134	64.2	60.5	42.6	40.1	39.3	44.4	38.5	16.1
Inv Assets Bonds	NA	9,986	3,547	3,222	2,816	2,580	2,341	2,243	2,101	2,049
Inv. Assets Stock	NA	863	718	833	838	784	610	780	618	526
Inv. Assets Loans	NA	2,201	887	798	782	769	767	743	747	774
Inv. Assets Total	NA	13,168	5,220	4,917	4,493	4,189	3,774	3,818	3,518	3,396
Deferred Policy Cost	NA	835	329	278	260	249	236	221	215	206
Total Assets	NA	16,478	6,140	5,641	5,236	4,925	4,455	4,530	4,174	3,890
Debt	NA	137	Nil	Nil	Nil	Nil	Nil	Nil	Nil	Nil
Common Eqty.	NA	2,156	1,733	1,733	1,687	1,563	1,353	1,475	1,336	1,243
Comb. Loss-Exp.Ratio	NA	NA	95.4	96.5	NA	NA	NA	NA	NA	NA
% Ret. on Revs.	NA	16.3	18.1	17.6	16.9	15.0	13.6	12.1	8.0	8.7
% Ret. on Equity	NA	13.1	13.3	12.9	12.5	12.1	11.1	9.9	7.6	7.3
% Invest. Yield	NA	3.4	7.4	7.9	NA	NA	NA	NA	NA	NA

Data as orig. reptd.; bef. results of disc. opers. and/or spec. items. Per share data adj. for stk. divs. as of ex-div. date. E-Estimate. NA-Not Available. NM-Not Meaningful. NR-Not Ranked.

Office—100 North Greene St., Greensboro, NC 27401. **Tel**—(910) 691-3000. **Pres & CEO**—D. A. Stonecipher. **VP-CFO & Treas**—D. R. Glass.**VP-Secy**—J. D. Hopkins. **Dirs**— T. M. Belk, W. E. Blackwell, E. B. Borden, W. H. Cunningham, C. R. Ferguson, R. G. Greer, G. W. Henderson, III, A. L. Holton Jr., H. L. McColl Jr., C. W. McCoy, E. S. Melvin, W. P. Payne, D. S. Russell Jr., R. H. Spilman. —D. A. Stonecipher, M. A. Walls. **Transfer Agent & Registrar**—First Union National Bank, Charlotte. **Incorporated**—in North Carolina in 1968. **Empl**— 12,650. **S&P Analyst:** Catherine A. Seifert

STANDARD &POOR'S
STOCK REPORTS

Kimberly-Clark

1298

NYSE Symbol **KMB**

In S&P 500

14-FEB-97

Industry: Household Products

Summary: KMB makes consumer and personal care products, including Huggies diapers and Kleenex tissues, with operations substantially expanded by the late 1995 purchase of Scott Paper.

S&P Opinion: Accumulate (★★★★)	Recent Price • 97⅞	Yield • 1.9%
	52 Wk Range • 103⅜-68⅝	12-Mo. P/E • 19.7

Quantitative Evaluations

Outlook
(1 Lowest—5 Highest)
• 3⁻

Fair Value
• 98⅜

Risk
• Low

Earn./Div. Rank
• A

Technical Eval.
• **Bearish** since 1/97

Rel. Strength Rank
(1 Lowest—99 Highest)
• 50

Insider Activity
• **Favorable**

Earnings vs. Previous Year
▲=Up ▼=Down ▷=No Change

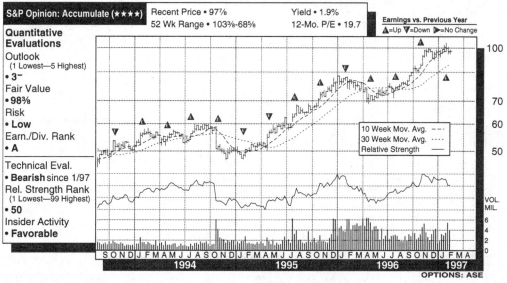

10 Week Mov. Avg. ---
30 Week Mov. Avg. ····
Relative Strength ——

OPTIONS: ASE

Overview - 14-FEB-97

Modest sales growth from comparable operations is expected in 1997, boosted by KMB's broader consumer and personal care products mixture and stronger European organization following its late 1995 takeover of Scott Paper. Those gains are likely to be offset a bit by lower average consumer tissue prices, following spring 1996 price cuts. Sales might also fall slightly in the commodities paper area, where average prices are also likely to be somewhat lower, although moderate economic growth and the end of inventory workdowns should firm many grades after the steep pricing downturn of the past year. Margins should widen on the integration of Scott, as KMB eliminates redundant overhead costs, consolidates work forces, and streamlines production; annual savings are slated to exceed $500 million by 1998, with $400 million to be seen in 1997 (up from over $250 million in 1996). Comparisons will be distorted by $0.23 a share of one-time gains in 1996.

Valuation - 14-FEB-97

Outside of a modest pullback in the first half of 1996 that was generated by price cuts on tissue products, KMB's shares have moved much higher since the start of 1995. The upturn in 1995 was related to better conditions in consumer tissue markets and investor excitement over the late 1995 takeover of Scott Paper, while the resumption of the uptrend since mid-1996 was generated by a firming of pulp markets, which made additional consumer tissue price cuts unlikely. A part of KMB's recent stock price surge was also related to periods of investor nervousness about an economic slowdown, which brought consumer products firms into favor. Given our forecast of ongoing profit gains, and the belief that economic factors will continue to make consumer growth firms popular, KMB shares should extend their outperformance.

Key Stock Statistics

S&P EPS Est. 1997	5.50	Tang. Bk. Value/Share	13.00
P/E on S&P Est. 1997	17.8	Beta	0.95
Dividend Rate/Share	1.84	Shareholders	58,000
Shs. outstg. (M)	282.5	Market cap. (B)	$ 29.0
Avg. daily vol. (M)	0.811	Inst. holdings	66%

Value of $10,000 invested 5 years ago: NA

Fiscal Year Ending Dec. 31

	1996	1995	1994	1993	1992	1991
Revenues (Million $)						
1Q	3,202	3,255	1,777	1,702	1,740	1,668
2Q	3,348	3,484	1,830	1,726	1,749	1,688
3Q	3,276	3,607	1,837	1,781	1,794	1,695
4Q	3,324	3,443	1,921	1,764	1,809	1,727
Yr.	13,149	13,789	7,364	6,973	7,091	6,777
Earnings Per Share ($)						
1Q	1.11	0.71	0.85	0.78	0.82	0.75
2Q	1.30	1.10	0.94	0.83	0.84	0.77
3Q	1.34	1.32	0.88	0.69	0.84	0.79
4Q	1.23	-3.01	0.66	0.88	-0.35	0.87
Yr.	4.98	0.12	3.33	3.18	2.14	3.18

Next earnings report expected: early May

Dividend Data (Dividends have been paid since 1935.)

Amount ($)	Date Decl.	Ex-Div. Date	Stock of Record	Payment Date
0.460	Feb. 13	Mar. 06	Mar. 08	Apr. 02 '96
0.460	Apr. 18	Jun. 05	Jun. 07	Jul. 02 '96
0.460	Aug. 01	Sep. 04	Sep. 06	Oct. 02 '96
0.460	Nov. 22	Dec. 04	Dec. 06	Jan. 03 '97

A Division of The McGraw·Hill Companies

Business Summary - 14-FEB-97

Kimberly-Clark produces a wide variety of household and personal care products, with operations in those areas substantially expanded by the December 1995 acquisition of Scott Paper. KMB also makes newsprint and other commodities paper. Kimberly spun off its tobacco-related businesses in late 1995, and sold its air transportation services unit in two separate public offerings (80% in September 1995 and the rest in May 1996). Contributions in 1995 (profits exclude restructuring and other unusual charges):

	Sales	Profits
Personal Care Products	31%	32%
Tissue-Based Products	57%	53%
Newsprint, Paper & Other	12%	15%

Operations outside of North America accounted for about 30% of sales and 20% of operating profits in 1995. The company has extensive operations in Europe, the Far East, Latin America and Africa.

Personal care products include disposable diapers, training and youth pants; feminine and adult incontinence care products; wet wipes; health care products; and related products. Brand names in this area include Huggies, Pull-Ups, GoodNites, Kotex, New Freedom, Lightdays, Depend and Poise.

Tissue-based products include facial and bathroom tissue, paper towels and wipers for household and away-from-home use; pulp; and related products. The products are sold under the Kleenex, Scott, Cottonelle, Viva, Kimwipes and Wypall brand names.

The newsprint, paper and other category includes newsprint, printing papers, premium business and correspondence papers, specialty papers, technical papers and other products and services.

Important Developments

Dec. '96—KMB signed a letter of intent to sell its Alabama pulp and newsprint mill, plus inventories and related woodlands, to Montreal-based Alliance Forest Products, for about $600 million in cash.
Oct. '96—The company recorded gains totaling $0.10 a share in the third quarter of 1996, on the sale of certain European tissue businesses and a tissue mill in Prudhoe, England, and an agreement reached in August 1996 to sell its Lakeview tissue mill in Neenah, WI. The transactions were undertaken to satisfy U.S. and European regulatory requirements for KMB's December 1995 takeover of Scott Paper (for 119 million KMB shares); upon consummation of the Lakeview transaction, KMB will have made all disposals required in connection with the merger. Other divestitures completed in 1996 to satisfy merger requirements were the July 1996 sale of the Scotties facial tissue business and Scott's Fort Edward, NY, tissue mill to Irving Tissue; and the June 1996 sale of Scott's domestic baby wipes business to Procter & Gamble (for $200 million).

Capitalization

Long Term Debt: $1,744,200,000 (9/96).

Per Share Data ($)

(Year Ended Dec. 31)	1996	1995	1994	1993	1992	1991	1990	1989	1988	1987
Tangible Bk. Val.	NA	13.00	16.20	15.27	13.63	15.74	14.14	12.93	11.59	9.81
Cash Flow	NA	2.20	5.37	5.01	3.95	4.84	4.21	3.94	3.52	2.93
Earnings	4.98	0.12	3.33	3.18	2.15	3.18	2.70	2.63	2.36	1.87
Dividends	1.84	1.80	1.76	1.72	1.64	1.52	1.36	1.30	0.80	0.72
Payout Ratio	37%	NM	53%	54%	76%	48%	50%	49%	34%	39%
Prices - High	99⅝	83	60	62	63¼	52¼	42⅞	37¾	32⅞	31⅝
- Low	68⅝	47¼	47	44⅝	46¼	38	30¾	28¾	23⅛	19¾
P/E Ratio - High	20	NM	18	19	29	16	16	14	14	17
- Low	14	NM	14	14	22	12	11	11	10	11

Income Statement Analysis (Million $)

Revs.	NA	13,789	7,364	6,973	7,091	6,777	6,407	5,734	5,393	4,885
Oper. Inc.	NA	2,235	1,149	1,096	1,082	1,007	994	884	828	772
Depr.	NA	582	330	296	289	266	240	211	188	186
Int. Exp.	NA	254	139	132	118	117	108	88.0	88.0	67.0
Pretax Inc.	NA	186	828	811	545	757	719	680	630	569
Eff. Tax Rate	NA	18%	33%	35%	34%	31%	39%	36%	37%	41%
Net Inc.	NA	33.0	535	511	345	508	432	424	379	325

Balance Sheet & Other Fin. Data (Million $)

Cash	NA	222	24.0	35.0	41.0	43.0	60.0	164	84.0	90.0
Curr. Assets	NA	3,814	1,810	1,675	1,683	1,475	1,397	1,443	1,236	1,135
Total Assets	NA	11,439	6,716	6,381	6,029	5,650	5,284	4,923	4,268	3,886
Curr. Liab.	NA	3,870	2,059	1,909	1,823	1,433	1,466	1,293	979	996
LT Debt	NA	1,985	930	933	995	875	729	745	743	687
Common Eqty.	NA	3,650	2,596	2,457	2,191	2,520	2,260	2,086	1,866	1,572
Total Cap.	NA	6,594	4,218	4,042	3,797	4,128	3,711	3,580	3,288	2,890
Cap. Exp.	NA	818	485	655	691	537	659	696	438	247
Cash Flow	NA	615	865	807	634	774	672	635	566	511
Curr. Ratio	NA	1.0	0.9	0.9	0.9	1.0	1.0	1.1	1.3	1.1
% LT Debt of Cap.	NA	30.1	22.0	23.1	26.2	21.2	19.6	20.8	22.6	23.8
% Net Inc.of Revs.	NA	1.0	7.3	7.3	4.9	7.5	6.7	7.4	7.0	6.7
% Ret. on Assets	NA	1.0	8.2	8.2	5.9	9.3	8.5	9.2	9.3	9.2
% Ret. on Equity	NA	1.0	21.2	22.0	14.6	21.3	20.0	21.4	22.0	20.0

Data as orig. reptd.; bef. results of disc. opers. and/or spec. items. Per share data adj. for stk. divs. as of ex-div. date. E-Estimated. NA-Not Available. NM-Not Meaningful. NR-Not Ranked.

Office—P.O. Box 619100, D/FW Airport Station, Dallas, TX 75261-9100. **Tel**—(214) 830-1200. **Chrmn & CEO**—W. R. Sanders. **SVP & CFO**—J. W. Donehower. **Investor Contact**—Mike Masseth. **Dirs**—J. F. Bergstrom, P. S. J. Cafferty, P. J. Collins, R. W. Decherd, W. O. Fifield, C. X. Gonzalez, L. E. Levy, F. A. McPherson, L. Johnson Rice, W. R. Sanders, W. R. Schmitt, R. L. Tobias. **Transfer Agent & Registrar**—First National Bank of Boston. **Incorporated**—in Delaware in 1928. **Empl**—55,341. **S&P Analyst:** Michael W. Jaffe

McCormick & Co. 4560

Nasdaq Symbol **MCCRK**

In S&P MidCap 400

15-FEB-97

Industry: Food

Summary: This company primarily produces spices, seasonings and flavorings for the retail food, foodservice and industrial markets. Trademarks include McCormick and Schilling.

| S&P Opinion: Hold (★★★) | Recent Price • 25⅛ | Yield • 2.4% |
| | 52 Wk Range • 25⅜-18⅞ | 12-Mo. P/E • 40.6 |

Quantitative Evaluations

Outlook (1 Lowest—5 Highest)
• **3+**

Fair Value
• **24⅞**

Risk
• **Low**

Earn./Div. Rank
• **A-**

Technical Eval.
• **Bullish** since 10/96

Rel. Strength Rank (1 Lowest—99 Highest)
• **61**

Insider Activity
• **NA**

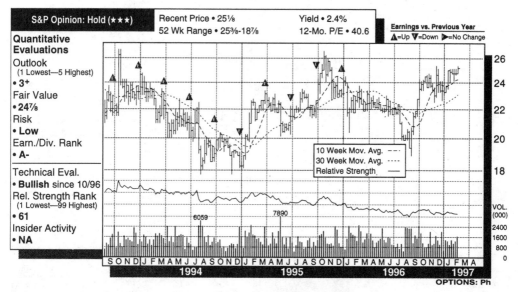

Earnings vs. Previous Year
▲=Up ▼=Down ▶=No Change

10 Week Mov. Avg. - - -
30 Week Mov. Avg. ·······
Relative Strength ——

OPTIONS: Ph

Overview - 20-JAN-97

Sales for FY 97 (Nov.) are projected to grow at a single-digit rate versus comparable year earlier levels (adjusted for recent asset disposals), led by an even mix of unit volume growth and higher selling prices. Operating profit margins are expected to widen modestly, aided by improved U.S. consumer spice (and related products) market conditions, and benefits accruing from recent reorganizational actions. However, extended competitive market conditions facing international operations could be somewhat offsetting. A more aggressive share repurchase stance (McCormick recently announced a new 10 million share repurchase program) should allow earnings per share to trend upward in FY 97.

Valuation - 20-JAN-97

Poor earnings trends have kept these shares in a narrow trading range over the past two years. In response, management has undertaken a series of reorganization actions over the past two years in an effort to better focus on the company's most promising business opportunities, namely its U.S. consumer and industrial product divisions. The recent disposal of non-strategic assets, together with an expected improvement in the U.S. consumer spice business, should allow for a good earnings recovery in FY 97. However, we believe that the stock's current valuation (about 10 times cash flow per share) is ample. The stock, which is down about 15% from its early 1993 level, is a worthwhile holding for long-term accounts. Long-term growth prospects remain bright, given the company's leading U.S. spice market share (about 45%) and growing presence abroad.

Key Stock Statistics

S&P EPS Est. 1997	1.30	Tang. Bk. Value/Share	3.82
P/E on S&P Est. 1997	19.4	Beta	0.90
Dividend Rate/Share	0.60	Shareholders	12,500
Shs. outstg. (M)	79.5	Market cap. (B)	$ 2.0
Avg. daily vol. (M)	0.262	Inst. holdings	46%

Value of $10,000 invested 5 years ago: $ 10,627

Fiscal Year Ending Nov. 30

	1996	1995	1994	1993	1992	1991
Revenues (Million $)						
1Q	—	425.4	367.7	339.6	322.0	324.0
2Q	—	445.0	396.3	361.3	337.0	333.0
3Q	1,195	432.0	422.1	394.9	360.0	341.8
4Q	537.4	556.3	508.6	460.8	452.0	430.0
Yr.	1,733	1,859	1,695	1,557	1,471	1,428
Earnings Per Share ($)						
1Q	--	0.24	0.23	0.21	0.21	0.18
2Q	--	0.20	0.23	0.21	0.23	0.18
3Q	-0.04	0.25	0.32	0.30	0.29	0.25
4Q	0.58	0.52	-0.03	0.50	0.43	0.37
Yr.	0.54	1.20	0.75	1.22	1.16	0.98

Next earnings report expected: mid March

Dividend Data (Dividends have been paid since 1929.)

Amount ($)	Date Decl.	Ex-Div. Date	Stock of Record	Payment Date
0.140	Mar. 20	Mar. 28	Apr. 01	Apr. 10 '96
0.140	Jun. 18	Jun. 26	Jun. 28	Jul. 10 '96
0.140	Sep. 16	Sep. 26	Sep. 30	Oct. 10 '96
0.150	Dec. 16	Dec. 27	Dec. 31	Jan. 20 '97

Business Summary - 20-JAN-97

Founded in 1889, McCormick & Company is the largest spice company world, with operations engaged in the manufacture, marketing and distribution of spices, seasonings, flavorings and other specialty food products, which are sold to the retail food, foodservice and industrial markets under the McCormick and Schilling names. The company also makes plastic bottles and tubes for various industries. Sales in recent fiscal years (ended Nov.) were derived as follows:

	1995	1994	1993
Americas	39%	42%	45%
Europe	17%	14%	13%
Asia/Pacific	3%	2%	2%
Industrial	31%	31%	29%
Packaging	8%	8%	8%
Gilroy Energy	2%	3%	3%

The Americas segment includes the U.S. consumer products business, the Food Service Division and wholly owned subsidiaries in Canada, El Salvador and Venezuela. New product development continues to be an important factor in generating sales growth for this division.

The European segment includes the company's operations in the United Kingdom, Switzerland and Finland. The Asia/Pacific segment operations participate in consumer, foodservice and industrial businesses.

The McCormick industrial division serves food processors and major restaurant chains with spices, seasonings and flavorings. International markets served include Mexico and India.

Plastic bottles and tubes are produced in the packaging division for the pharmaceutical, cosmetics and food industries.

During the third quarter of FY 96 (Nov.), the company incurred a restructutung charge amounting to $57.5 million, which reduced net income during the year by $39.2 million, or $0.49 per share. The company purchased 2.5 million of its common shares outstanding during its FY 96 (Nov.) fourth quarter as part of its stock buyback program.

Capitalization

Long Term Debt: $291,194,000 (11/30/96).

Per Share Data ($) (Year Ended Nov. 30)	1996	1995	1994	1993	1992	1991	1990	1989	1988	1987
Tangible Bk. Val.	NA	4.17	3.62	4.15	4.36	4.00	3.61	3.48	2.54	2.36
Cash Flow	NA	1.98	1.45	1.79	1.65	1.43	1.23	0.96	0.72	0.59
Earnings	0.54	1.20	0.75	1.22	1.16	0.98	0.83	0.60	0.39	0.33
Dividends	0.56	0.52	0.48	0.44	0.38	0.28	0.23	0.17	0.13	0.13
Payout Ratio	104%	43%	64%	36%	33%	28%	28%	27%	35%	38%
Prices - High	25⅜	26⅝	24¾	29¾	30¼	26½	13¼	13½	7¼	6½
- Low	18⅞	18⅛	17¾	20	20½	12¼	9	6⅜	4½	3¾
P/E Ratio - High	47	22	33	24	26	27	16	22	19	20
- Low	35	15	24	16	18	13	11	11	12	11

Income Statement Analysis (Million $)

	1996	1995	1994	1993	1992	1991	1990	1989	1988	1987
Revs.	NA	1,859	1,695	1,557	1,471	1,428	1,323	1,246	1,184	1,078
Oper. Inc.	NA	264	256	227	207	183	160	134	110	88.0
Depr.	NA	63.4	56.8	46.7	40.0	37.0	33.3	31.9	31.6	24.5
Int. Exp.	NA	55.3	38.7	31.1	30.9	27.5	29.3	32.9	30.2	30.9
Pretax Inc.	NA	151	95.0	160	148	124	108	82.0	58.0	49.0
Eff. Tax Rate	NA	36%	36%	38%	36%	35%	36%	36%	39%	37%
Net Inc.	NA	97.5	61.2	100	95.2	80.9	69.4	52.5	35.6	30.6

Balance Sheet & Other Fin. Data (Million $)

	1996	1995	1994	1993	1992	1991	1990	1989	1988	1987
Cash	NA	12.5	15.6	12.8	1.8	6.0	5.3	51.6	11.3	7.4
Curr. Assets	NA	671	658	540	468	445	409	427	387	367
Total Assets	NA	1,614	1,569	1,313	1,131	1,032	947	865	770	718
Curr. Liab.	NA	647	601	393	420	360	306	245	277	272
LT Debt	NA	349	374	346	201	208	211	211	166	139
Common Eqty.	NA	519	490	467	438	389	364	346	294	280
Total Cap.	NA	894	883	852	697	652	623	606	483	439
Cap. Exp.	NA	82.1	87.7	97.0	92.0	75.9	60.6	56.6	67.2	47.0
Cash Flow	NA	161	118	146	135	118	103	84.0	67.0	55.0
Curr. Ratio	NA	1.0	1.1	1.4	1.1	1.2	1.3	1.7	1.4	1.3
% LT Debt of Cap.	NA	39.0	42.4	40.6	28.8	31.8	34.0	34.7	34.3	31.7
% Net Inc.of Revs.	NA	5.2	3.6	6.4	6.5	5.7	5.2	4.2	3.0	2.8
% Ret. on Assets	NA	6.1	4.2	8.1	8.8	8.2	7.8	6.7	4.9	4.6
% Ret. on Equity	NA	19.3	12.8	21.9	22.9	21.5	19.9	17.0	12.6	11.2

Data as orig. reptd.; bef. results of disc. opers. and/or spec. items. Per share data adj. for stk. divs. as of ex-div. date. E-Estimated. NA-Not Available. NM-Not Meaningful. NR-Not Ranked.

Office—18 Loveton Circle, Sparks, MD 21152-6000. **Tel**—(410) 771-7301. **Fax**—(410) 527-8289. **Website**—http://www.mccormick.com **Chrmn**—C. P. McCormick Jr. **Pres & CEO**—R. J. Lawless. **EVP & CFO**—R. G. Davey. **VP-Treas & Investor Contact**—C. J. Kurtzman. **Dirs**—J. J. Albrecht, J. S. Cook, R. G. Davey, H. J. Handley, G. W. Koch, R. J. Lawless, C. P. McCormick Jr., G. V. McGowan, C. D. Nordhoff, R. W. Schroeder, R. W. Single Sr., W. E. Stevens, K. D. Weatherholtz. **Transfer Agent & Registrar**—Co.'s office. **Co-Transfer Agent**—Security Trust Co., Baltimore. **Incorporated**—in Maryland in 1915. **Empl**— 8,900. **S&P Analyst:** Kenneth A. Shea

STANDARD &POOR'S
STOCK REPORTS

Merck & Co.

1476

NYSE Symbol **MRK**

In S&P 500

15-FEB-97

Industry: Drugs

Summary: Merck is one of the world's largest prescription pharmaceuticals concerns. Its Medco Containment unit is the leading U.S. pharmacy benefits management company.

S&P Opinion: Buy (★★★★)	Recent Price • 97⅜	Yield • 1.6%
	52 Wk Range • 99⅞-56½	12-Mo. P/E • 30.4

Quantitative Evaluations

Outlook
(1 Lowest—5 Highest)
• **1+**

Fair Value
• **74⅛**

Risk
• **Low**

Earn./Div. Rank
• **A+**

Technical Eval.
• **Bullish** since 6/96

Rel. Strength Rank
(1 Lowest—99 Highest)
• **90**

Insider Activity
• **Neutral**

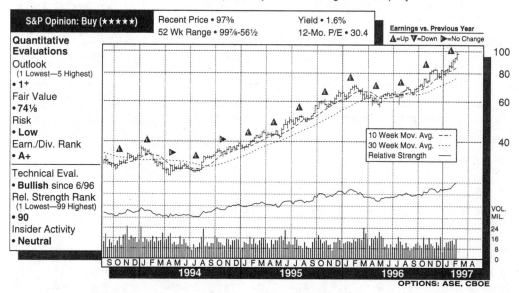

Earnings vs. Previous Year
▲=Up ▼=Down ▶=No Change

10 Week Mov. Avg. - - -
30 Week Mov. Avg. ·······
Relative Strength ——

OPTIONS: ASE, CBOE

Overview - 29-JAN-97

Fueled by strength in established lines and contributions from new drugs, another strong double-digit sales gain is indicated for 1997. Volume growth should be paced by robust gains in the new Cozaar/Hyzaar angiotensin II blocker anti-hypertensives, Prinivil/Prinzide ACE inhibitor heart drugs, Proscar for enlarged prostates, and Zocor cholesterol lowering agent. Merck's Zocor and Mevacor cholesterol drugs represent about 40% of the total worldwide cholesterol-reduction market. Recent results from a Scandinavian study showed Zocor was able to save lives and prevent heart attacks in people with heart disease and high cholesterol. Good gains are also seen for new drugs such as Fosamax for osteoporosis, Crixivan for AIDS, and Varivax chicken pox vaccine. The Medco managed care unit should also chalk up strong growth, aided by continued expansion of the membership base. Margins should benefit from the greater volume and productivity improvements.

Valuation - 29-JAN-97

Together with those of most other leading drug companies, the shares moved higher in recent months, aided by investor attraction to proven growth companies in defensive industries and Merck's impressive ongoing earning performance. Merck's net earnings in 1996 increased 22% (EPS rose 24%), with cost controls and productivity improvements more than offsetting the effects of inflationary cost increases and negative foreign exchange. Merck is expected to retain its premier status in the U.S. drug industry, aided by an unmatched broad-based portfolio of high-quality drugs in important therapeutic classes, a strong lineup of new products, and continuing benefits and synergies from Medco. The stock remains a choice selection for superior long-term capital appreciation.

Key Stock Statistics

S&P EPS Est. 1997	3.75	Tang. Bk. Value/Share	3.82
P/E on S&P Est. 1997	26.0	Beta	1.45
Dividend Rate/Share	1.60	Shareholders	82,300
Shs. outstg. (M)	1205.4	Market cap. (B)	$117.4
Avg. daily vol. (M)	2.742	Inst. holdings	50%

Value of $10,000 invested 5 years ago: $ 19,791

Fiscal Year Ending Dec. 31

	1996	1995	1994	1993	1992	1991
Revenues (Million $)						
1Q	4,530	3,817	3,514	2,380	2,223	2,049
2Q	4,909	4,136	3,792	2,574	2,374	2,122
3Q	4,983	4,171	3,792	2,544	2,464	2,117
4Q	5,406	4,557	3,872	3,001	2,601	2,314
Yr.	19,829	16,681	14,970	10,498	9,663	8,603
Earnings Per Share ($)						
1Q	0.70	0.61	0.54	0.54	0.48	0.42
2Q	0.80	0.69	0.61	0.15	0.56	0.48
3Q	0.83	0.70	0.62	0.62	0.55	0.48
4Q	0.87	0.70	0.61	0.56	0.53	0.46
Yr.	3.20	2.70	2.38	1.87	2.12	1.83

Next earnings report expected: mid April

Dividend Data (Dividends have been paid since 1935.)

Amount ($)	Date Decl.	Ex-Div. Date	Stock of Record	Payment Date
0.340	Feb. 27	Mar. 06	Mar. 08	Apr. 01 '96
0.340	May. 29	Jun. 06	Jun. 10	Jul. 01 '96
0.400	Jul. 23	Sep. 04	Sep. 06	Oct. 01 '96
0.400	Nov. 26	Dec. 05	Dec. 09	Jan. 02 '97

A Division of The McGraw-Hill Companies

Business Summary - 29-JAN-97

Merck is the premier U.S.-based pharmaceutical company, manufacturing and marketing a wide range of prescription drugs in many therapeutic classes both in the U.S.and abroad. Foreign operations are significant, representing 30% of sales and 26% of pretax profits in 1995. The company was originally founded in 1887 as a U.S. branch of E. Merck of Germany and grew significantly in subsequent years through aggressive new drug development and acquisition programs.

The company is the undisputed leader in vast market for high-margin cardiovascular drugs, with five drugs generating sales of over $7.4 billion in 1996. Principal products include cholesterol-lowering agents such as Zocor (sales of $2.8 billion) and Mevacor ($1.3 billion); and treatments for high blood pressure and congestive heart failure like Vasotec/Vaseretic ($2.5 billion) and Prinivil/Prinzide ($485 million). Merck has an estimated 40% share of the rapidly expanding worldwide cholesterol reduction market and about one third of the moderately growing hypertension-angina market. Cozaar/Hyzaar, the first of a new class of antihypertensives, is exhibiting vigorous growth aided by an improved side effect profile over conventional blood pressure agents.

Other drugs exhibiting notable strength include Fosamax for osteoporosis, whose sales are being helped by a study showing its effectiveness in the prevention of bone loss and restoration of bone mass in postmenopausal women; and Crixivan, a protease inhibitor AIDS drug, which in combination of other agents has been able to decrease HIV in the bloodstream to undetectable levels. Other key drugs include Pepcid antiulcer agent and Proscar for enlarged prostates.

The huge success of Merck's drugs has enabled it support a $1.5 billion R&D program, which promises to spawn an ongoing stream of blockbuster drugs in the years ahead. Key products in late stage clinical trials include treatments for migraine, asthma, male pattern baldness, and angina. Merck recently discovered a new class of anti-infectives aimed at drug resistant bacteria which could revolutionize the antibiotics market.

Through a joint venture with Astra AB of Sweden, Merck sells Prilosec, the world's second largest antiulcer drug. Over-the-counter medications such as Pepcid AC and others are offered through a venture with Johnson & Johnson. Merck plans to combine its animal health business with those of Rhone-Poulenc. Medco Containment, acquired in 1993, is one of the nation's leading mail order drug marketers.

Capitalization

Long Term Debt: $1,328,000,000 (9/96).
Minority Interest: $2,319,400,000 (9/96).

Per Share Data ($) (Year Ended Dec. 31)	1996	1995	1994	1993	1992	1991	1990	1989	1988	1987
Tangible Bk. Val.	NA	4.00	3.15	2.69	4.24	4.06	3.12	2.78	2.23	1.61
Cash Flow	NA	3.24	2.92	2.20	2.37	2.04	1.72	1.43	1.18	0.90
Earnings	3.20	2.70	2.38	1.87	2.12	1.83	1.52	1.26	1.02	0.74
Dividends	1.48	1.28	1.16	1.06	0.96	0.79	0.67	0.57	0.46	0.30
Payout Ratio	46%	47%	49%	57%	45%	43%	44%	45%	45%	40%
Prices - High	84¼	67¼	39½	44⅛	56⅝	55¾	30⅜	27	19⅞	24⅞
- Low	56½	36⅜	28⅛	28⅝	40½	27⅜	22⅜	18¾	16	13⅝
P/E Ratio - High	26	25	17	24	27	30	20	21	20	33
- Low	18	13	12	15	19	15	15	15	16	18

Income Statement Analysis (Million $)

	1996	1995	1994	1993	1992	1991	1990	1989	1988	1987
Revs.	NA	16,681	14,970	10,498	9,663	8,603	7,672	6,550	5,939	5,061
Oper. Inc.	NA	5,262	5,075	4,262	3,782	3,352	2,883	2,443	2,056	1,558
Depr.	NA	667	670	377	290	243	231	206	189	189
Int. Exp.	NA	99	124	84.7	72.7	68.7	69.8	53.2	76.5	56.4
Pretax Inc.	NA	4,889	4,509	3,153	3,596	3,192	2,730	2,321	1,915	1,434
Eff. Tax Rate	NA	30%	32%	30%	31%	33%	34%	34%	35%	35%
Net Inc.	NA	3,335	2,997	2,166	2,447	2,122	1,781	1,495	1,207	906

Balance Sheet & Other Fin. Data (Million $)

	1996	1995	1994	1993	1992	1991	1990	1989	1988	1987
Cash	NA	3,349	2,270	1,542	1,094	1,412	1,197	1,144	1,550	1,148
Curr. Assets	NA	8,618	6,922	5,735	4,400	4,311	3,766	3,410	3,389	3,007
Total Assets	NA	23,832	21,857	19,928	11,086	9,499	8,030	6,757	6,127	5,680
Curr. Liab.	NA	5,690	5,449	5,896	3,617	2,814	2,827	1,907	1,909	2,209
LT Debt	NA	1,373	1,146	1,121	496	494	124	118	143	167
Common Eqty.	NA	11,736	11,139	10,022	5,003	4,916	3,834	3,521	2,856	2,117
Total Cap.	NA	13,109	14,735	12,650	6,215	6,296	4,764	4,459	3,878	3,248
Cap. Exp.	NA	1,006	1,009	1,013	1,067	1,042	671	433	373	254
Cash Flow	NA	4,002	3,667	2,543	2,737	2,364	2,013	1,702	1,396	1,095
Curr. Ratio	NA	1.5	1.3	1.0	1.2	1.5	1.3	1.8	1.8	1.4
% LT Debt of Cap.	NA	10.5	7.8	8.9	8.0	7.8	2.6	2.6	3.7	5.2
% Net Inc.of Revs.	NA	20.0	20.0	20.6	25.3	24.7	23.2	22.8	20.3	17.9
% Ret. on Assets	NA	14.6	14.4	13.5	23.9	24.2	24.3	23.3	20.4	17.1
% Ret. on Equity	NA	29.2	28.4	27.9	49.6	48.5	48.9	47.0	48.4	39.5

Data as orig. reptd.; bef. results of disc. opers. and/or spec. items. Per share data adj. for stk. divs. as of ex-div. date. E-Estimated. NA-Not Available. NM-Not Meaningful. NR-Not Ranked.

Office—One Merck Drive, P.O. Box 100, Whitehouse Station, NJ 08889. **Tel**—(908) 423-1000. **Website**—http://www.merck.com **Chrmn, Pres & CEO**—R. V. Gilmartin. **Secy**—C. A. Colbert. **VP & CFO**—J. C. Lewent. **Treas**—C. Dorsa. **Investor Contact**—James Hinrichs (908-423-6883). **Dirs**—H. B. Atwater, Jr., Sir Derek Birkin, L. A. Bossidy, W. G. Bowen, J. B. Cole, C. K. Davis, L. C. Elam, C. E. Exley, Jr., R. V. Gilmartin, W. N. Kelley, E. M. Scolnick, S. O. Thier, D. Weatherstone. **Transfer Agent & Registrar**—Norwest Bank Minnesota. **Incorporated**—in New Jersey in 1934. **Empl**— 45,200. **S&P Analyst:** H. B. Saftlas

15-FEB-97 | Industry: Auto parts/equipment

Summary: Modine makes heat-transfer products for original equipment manufacturers, the automotive aftermarket and nonresidential building market.

S&P Opinion: Hold (★★★)	Recent Price • 28⅝	Yield • 2.4%
	52 Wk Range • 29¾-22½	12-Mo. P/E • 14.2

Quantitative Evaluations

Outlook
(1 Lowest—5 Highest)
• **2**

Fair Value
• **27**

Risk
• **Average**

Earn./Div. Rank
• **A**

Technical Eval.
• **Bullish** since 1/97

Rel. Strength Rank
(1 Lowest—99 Highest)
• **73**

Insider Activity
• **Neutral**

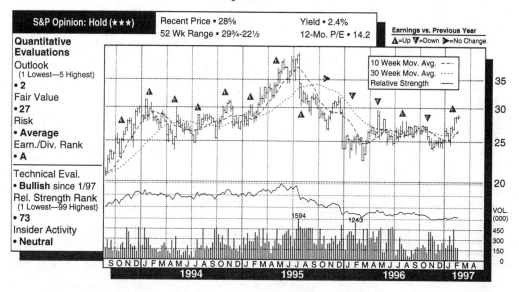

Earnings vs. Previous Year
▲=Up ▼=Down ▶=No Change

10 Week Mov. Avg. – – –
30 Week Mov. Avg. ......
Relative Strength ——

Overview - 15-JAN-97

Earnings should grow approximately 4% in FY 97 (Mar.), on higher overseas sales and contributions by acquisitions, though margins could remain under pressure from high raw material costs. Sales of original equipment components in North America may remain flat, as the sharp decline in the North American heavy-duty truck market is offset by a small rise in production of cars and light trucks. Domestic aftermarket sales may also be soft as a long-term consolidation in the replacement parts continues; this consolidation is being driven by the improved durability of new parts. But European aftermarket sales continue to be strong. New applications for MODI's proprietary parallel-flow heat exchangers in automotive air conditioning, and the possible development of new products from a recently licensed cool-storage technology that may allow quick cooling of a vehicle's passenger compartment, should provide solid growth opportunities over the long term.

Valuation - 15-JAN-97

We are maintaining our hold recommendation on Modine. MODI's long-term fundamentals remain strong, and we expect it to continue to exploit its proprietary technology and develop new product lines. Still, given the softness of its domestic markets, we think the stock will be only an average performer over the near term. Trading toward the low end of its recent P/E range, the stock might be held by long-term investors as we expect MODI to resume its strong growth record as it obtains contracts for new applications and develops new products.

Key Stock Statistics

S&P EPS Est. 1997	2.08	Tang. Bk. Value/Share	10.56
P/E on S&P Est. 1997	13.8	Beta	0.71
S&P EPS Est. 1998	2.50	Shareholders	4,700
Dividend Rate/Share	0.68	Market cap. (B)	$0.855
Shs. outstg. (M)	29.9	Inst. holdings	35%
Avg. daily vol. (M)	0.055		

Value of $10,000 invested 5 years ago: $ 26,320

Fiscal Year Ending Mar. 31

	1997	1996	1995	1994	1993	1992
Revenues (Million $)						
1Q	248.5	239.2	208.4	147.2	134.0	126.0
2Q	254.2	254.3	221.8	157.0	144.0	133.0
3Q	253.0	252.8	240.5	172.4	147.0	131.0
4Q	—	244.2	242.3	193.1	145.8	137.0
Yr.	—	990.5	913.0	669.5	570.8	527.0
Earnings Per Share ($)						
1Q	0.54	0.52	0.49	0.32	0.28	0.22
2Q	0.51	0.55	0.55	0.39	0.28	0.25
3Q	0.51	0.49	0.57	0.35	0.25	0.22
4Q	E0.53	0.46	0.63	0.35	0.31	0.26
Yr.	E2.08	2.02	2.24	1.41	1.12	0.94

Next earnings report expected: mid April

Dividend Data (Dividends have been paid since 1959.)

Amount ($)	Date Decl.	Ex-Div. Date	Stock of Record	Payment Date
0.170	May. 15	May. 22	May. 28	Jun. 06 '96
0.170	Jul. 17	Aug. 22	Aug. 26	Sep. 05 '96
0.170	Oct. 16	Nov. 21	Nov. 25	Dec. 05 '96
0.170	Jan. 15	Feb. 20	Feb. 24	Mar. 06 '97

Business Summary - 15-JAN-97

Modine Manufacturing Company is a maker of heat-transfer equipment, serving vehicular, industrial, commercial and building HVAC (heating, ventilating, air-conditioning) and refrigeration equipment markets. The company makes heat exchangers for various original equipment manufacturer applications and for sale to the automotive aftermarket (as replacement parts) and to a wide variety of building markets.

Sales in recent fiscal years were derived as follows:

	1995	1994
Radiators/radiator cores	41%	42%
Air conditioning	17%	14%
Oil coolers	16%	16%
Charge air coolers	12%	12%
Building HVAC	8%	9%
Miscellaneous	6%	7%

Heat exchangers are supplied for cooling all types of engines, transmissions, auxiliary hydraulic equipment, air-conditioning components used in cars, trucks, farm and construction machinery and equipment, and heating and cooling equipment for residential and commercial building HVAC.

Shipment of original equipment for cars and light trucks has grown in recent years and became the largest single market in fiscal 1996, at 24% of sales (22% in fiscal 1995). Aftermarket sales constituted the second largest market in fiscal 1996 with 23% of the total (24%).

In July 1995, Modine acquired Signet Systems, Inc., a supplier of climate control systems and components to the automotive, truck and off-highway markets in both North America and Europe. In May 1995, the company acuired its joint venture partner's majority interest in Mexican-based Radinam S.A., as well as Spain-based Radiadores Montana S.A. In August 1995, MODI acquired an exclusive worldwide license for cool-storage technology for use in on-road and off-road vehicles. In October 1995, Modine sold its copper tubing manufacturing business.

Export sales from the U.S. accounted for 13% of sales in fiscal 1995, down from 14% in fiscal 1995 and fiscal 1994. In addition, foreign operations accounted for 31% of sales in fiscal 1996, up from 27% in fiscal 1995 and 14% in fiscal 1994.

Important Developments

Jan. '97—Net income rose 3.7% in the third quarter of fiscal 1997 on flat sales; Sales growth was constrained by lower-than-anticipated revenues from some domestic markets, and the translation effect of a stronger dollar on foreign-currency-denominated sales.

Capitalization

Long Term Debt: $86,161,000 (1/97).

Per Share Data ($)

(Year Ended Mar. 31)	1996	1995	1994	1993	1992	1991	1990	1989	1988	1987
Tangible Bk. Val.	9.37	9.23	7.42	7.31	7.05	6.64	6.05	5.69	5.10	4.44
Cash Flow	3.32	3.34	2.25	1.96	1.77	1.74	1.37	1.32	1.30	1.03
Earnings	2.02	2.24	1.41	1.12	0.94	1.02	0.84	0.87	0.84	0.66
Dividends	0.60	0.52	0.46	0.42	0.38	0.34	0.30	0.26	0.22	0.19
Payout Ratio	30%	23%	33%	38%	40%	33%	35%	30%	26%	28%
Cal. Yrs.	1995	1994	1993	1992	1991	1990	1989	1988	1987	1986
Prices - High	40½	31¼	30¼	18⅞	14⅜	11½	11	9½	11⅜	7¼
- Low	23¾	23¾	17½	11¾	7⅞	8⅝	7¾	6⅞	6½	5⅝
P/E Ratio - High	20	14	21	17	15	11	13	11	14	11
- Low	12	11	12	10	8	8	9	8	8	9

Income Statement Analysis (Million $)

	1996	1995	1994	1993	1992	1991	1990	1989	1988	1987
Revs.	990	913	670	571	527	482	436	424	395	349
Oper. Inc.	134	146	102	83.1	69.2	54.8	58.4	58.2	57.5	50.1
Depr.	39.6	33.5	25.4	25.5	25.1	21.3	17.0	14.6	13.9	11.2
Int. Exp.	6.8	6.4	6.0	5.9	7.1	7.2	5.4	4.0	4.2	3.5
Pretax Inc.	99	109	73.0	54.1	43.4	48.3	39.7	41.4	41.5	37.5
Eff. Tax Rate	38%	37%	41%	38%	36%	37%	37%	37%	40%	48%
Net Inc.	61.4	68.4	43.1	33.7	28.0	30.5	25.2	26.2	25.0	19.6

Balance Sheet & Other Fin. Data (Million $)

	1996	1995	1994	1993	1992	1991	1990	1989	1988	1987
Cash	18.0	32.7	38.5	33.6	18.8	27.0	27.0	24.0	15.6	4.7
Curr. Assets	351	340	272	221	202	212	189	170	156	129
Total Assets	672	590	510	405	383	398	328	289	271	237
Curr. Liab.	181	170	140	94.7	75.7	88.1	73.8	71.9	61.7	62.6
LT Debt	87.8	62.2	77.6	52.4	74.3	88.1	55.4	33.1	43.9	33.6
Common Eqty.	349	308	252	223	215	205	184	171	154	131
Total Cap.	449	383	339	287	308	310	254	217	209	174
Cap. Exp.	55.7	34.1	28.0	23.6	16.9	28.8	20.5	14.2	14.6	14.4
Cash Flow	101	102	68.5	59.2	53.1	51.8	41.2	39.9	38.9	30.8
Curr. Ratio	1.9	2.0	1.9	2.3	2.7	2.4	2.6	2.4	2.5	2.1
% LT Debt of Cap.	19.6	16.2	22.9	18.3	24.1	28.4	21.8	15.2	21.0	19.3
% Net Inc.of Revs.	6.2	7.5	6.4	5.9	5.3	6.3	5.8	6.2	6.3	5.6
% Ret. on Assets	9.7	12.4	9.4	8.5	7.2	8.4	8.2	9.4	9.8	8.7
% Ret. on Equity	18.7	24.4	18.1	15.3	13.4	15.7	14.3	16.1	17.3	15.6

Data as orig. reptd.; bef. results of disc. opers. and/or spec. items. Per share data adj. for stk. divs. as of ex-div. date. E-Estimated. NA-Not Available. NM-Not Meaningful. NR-Not Ranked.

Office—1500 DeKoven Ave., Racine, WI 53403-2552. **Tel**—(414) 636-1200. **Chrmn & CEO**—R. T. Savage. **Pres**—D. R Johnson**SVP & Secy**—W. E. Pavlick. **VP-Fin & CFO**—A. D. Reid. **Treas**—R. M. Gunnerson. **Investor Contact**—Gerald J. Sweda (414) 636-1361. **Dirs**—R. J. Doyle, T. J. Guendel, F. W. Jones, D. J. Kuester, V. L. Martin, G. L. Neale, R. T. Savage, S. W. Tisdale, M. T. Yonker. **Transfer Agent & Registrar**—American Stock Transfer & Trust Co., NYC. **Incorporated**—in Wisconsin in 1916. **Empl**— 7,561. **S&P Analyst:** Robert Schpoont

15-FEB-97

Industry:
Banking

Summary: This bank holding company emphasizes asset management and servicing, portfolio management, finance and advisory services, asset and liability management, and sales and trading.

S&P Opinion: Hold (★★★)	Recent Price • 106¾ Yield • 3.3% 52 Wk Range • 107¼-75½ 12-Mo. P/E • 14.0

Quantitative Evaluations

Outlook
(1 Lowest—5 Highest)
• **2+**

Fair Value
• **100⅛**

Risk
• **Low**

Earn./Div. Rank
• **B+**

Technical Eval.
• **Bullish** since 2/95

Rel. Strength Rank
(1 Lowest—99 Highest)
• **76**

Insider Activity
• **Neutral**

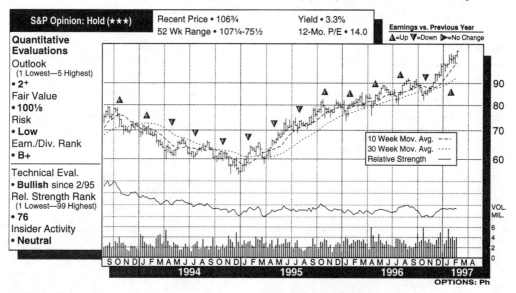

Earnings vs. Previous Year
▲=Up ▼=Down ▷=No Change

10 Week Mov. Avg. ----
30 Week Mov. Avg. ····
Relative Strength ——

OPTIONS: Ph

Overview - 05-FEB-97

Following an earnings rebound in 1996, which mainly reflected strong revenues from trading activities, relatively modest year-to-year comparisons are expected in 1997. Net interest revenues have been affected by the maturing of higher-yielding assets and liability management positions. Trading and investment banking revenues should contribute much of the projected earnings growth for 1997, as efforts to earn a growing portion of its clients' business succeed. Overall, investment banking, market making and investment management operations are providing growth opportunities. Limiting earnings growth will be higher employee compensation and benefits expense due to a greater proportion of revenues from client-based businesses and competitive market conditions. Credit quality remains strong, with the allowance for loan losses at 9.3X the level of nonperforming assets at December 31, 1996.

Valuation - 05-FEB-97

The shares were up about 22% in 1996, keeping pace with the S&P 500, but well below the money center bank index. Concerns of sluggish overall revenue growth and rising compensation expense tied to an increasing proportion of revenues derived from client-based business and competitive market conditions appear to be holding back share gains. On the plus side, JPM continues to attract a growing share of its clients' business in the areas of equity and debt underwriting, corporate finance, market making and investment management. With more than half of revenues derived from volatile trading/investment activities, earnings are inherently difficult to predict, but strong year-to-year comparisons in 1997 will be difficult. With strong credit quality and a good yield, the shares remain a worthwhile long-term holding.

Key Stock Statistics

S&P EPS Est. 1997	8.00	Tang. Bk. Value/Share	55.85
P/E on S&P Est. 1997	13.3	Beta	0.89
Dividend Rate/Share	3.52	Shareholders	29,400
Shs. outstg. (M)	185.2	Market cap. (B)	$ 19.8
Avg. daily vol. (M)	0.758	Inst. holdings	60%

Value of $10,000 invested 5 years ago: $ 18,839

Fiscal Year Ending Dec. 31

	1996	1995	1994	1993	1992	1991
Revenues (Million $)						
1Q	3,898	3,358	2,831	2,884	2,442	2,697
2Q	3,923	3,346	2,957	2,945	2,668	2,463
3Q	3,799	3,346	3,048	3,124	2,711	2,655
4Q	4,246	3,639	3,079	2,988	2,410	2,499
Yr.	15,866	13,838	11,915	11,941	10,231	10,314
Earnings Per Share ($)						
1Q	2.13	1.27	1.69	2.16	1.50	1.40
2Q	2.14	1.56	1.73	2.12	1.94	1.17
3Q	1.32	1.78	1.63	2.30	2.01	1.72
4Q	2.04	1.80	0.96	1.92	1.48	1.35
Yr.	7.63	6.42	6.02	8.48	6.92	5.63

Next earnings report expected: mid April

Dividend Data (Dividends have been paid since 1892.)

Amount ($)	Date Decl.	Ex-Div. Date	Stock of Record	Payment Date
0.810	Mar. 13	Mar. 21	Mar. 25	Apr. 15 '96
0.810	Jun. 12	Jun. 20	Jun. 24	Jul. 15 '96
0.810	Sep. 11	Sep. 19	Sep. 23	Oct. 15 '96
0.880	Dec. 11	Dec. 19	Dec. 23	Jan. 15 '97

A Division of The McGraw·Hill Companies

J.P. Morgan & Co. Incorporated

Business Summary - 05-FEB-97

This holding company owns Morgan Guaranty Trust, the fourth largest bank in the U.S. JPM's global business activities are divided into five major sectors: Asset Management and Servicing (investment management, private banking, exchange-traded product brokerage, securities and cash services, and Euroclear operations); Equity Investments; Finance and Advisory; Asset and Liability Management; and Sales and Trading. Revenues and pretax income in 1995 were derived:

	Revs.	Pretax Inc.
Asset management/servicing	21%	13%
Finance & advisory	25%	14%
Sales & trading	28%	17%
Equity investments	9%	20%
Asset/liability management	17%	36%

During 1995, average earning assets of $136.1 billion (up from $134.4 billion in 1994) were divided: domestic loans 5%, foreign loans 13%, investment securities 16%, trading account assets 28%, other temporary investments 35% and other 3%. Average sources of funds were: noninterest-bearing liabilities 22%, interest-bearing deposits 25%, trading account liabilities 10%, short-term borrowings 33%, long-term debt 5% and equity 5%.

At December 31, 1995, nonperforming assets totaled $118 million (0.50% of loans and related assets), down from $220 million (1.00%). The reserve for loan losses was 4.82% of loans, versus 5.12%. Net chargeoffs were 0.01% of average loans in 1995, versus 0.11% in 1994.

At December 31, 1996, the Tier 1 capital ratio (estimated) was 8.7%, versus 8.8% at December 31, 1995. The total capital ratio (estimated) was 12.2%, versus 13.0%.

Important Developments

Jan. '97—Directors authorized the repurchase of up to 7 million JPM common shares through 1997 year end in the open market or through privately negotiated transactions. The company repurchased 7 million shares in 1996.

Dec. '96—JPM sold its institutional U.S. cash processing business to HSBC Financial Institutions, a division of Marine Midland Bank, for an undisclosed amount. The sale is not expected to have a material effect on the company's ongoing financial results.

Capitalization

Long Term Debt: $13,103,000,000 (12/96).
Variable Cum. Pfd. Stock: $250,000,000.
Fixed Cum. Pfd. Stock: $200,000,000.
Adj.-Rate Cum. Pfd. Stock: $244,000,000.
Redeem. Pfd. Stock: $750,000,000.

Per Share Data ($) (Year Ended Dec. 31)	1996	1995	1994	1993	1992	1991	1990	1989	1988	1987
Tangible Bk. Val.	NA	53.21	46.73	48.50	34.30	29.41	25.29	21.78	30.52	26.57
Earnings	7.63	6.42	6.02	8.48	6.92	5.63	3.99	-7.04	5.38	0.39
Dividends	3.31	3.06	2.79	2.48	2.23	2.03	1.86	1.70	1.54	1.39
Payout Ratio	43%	48%	46%	29%	32%	36%	47%	NM	29%	358%
Prices - High	100 1/8	82 1/2	72	79 3/8	70 1/2	70 1/2	47 1/4	48 1/8	40 1/4	53 5/8
- Low	73 1/2	56 1/8	55 1/8	59 3/8	51 1/2	40 1/2	29 5/8	34	30 3/4	27
P/E Ratio - High	13	13	12	9	10	13	12	NM	7	NM
- Low	10	9	9	7	7	7	7	NM	6	NM
Income Statement Analysis (Million $)										
Net Int. Inc.	NA	2,003	1,981	1,772	1,708	1,484	1,158	1,144	1,508	1,596
Tax Equiv. Adj.	NA	106	120	138	161	173	197	244	271	366
Non Int. Inc.	NA	3,880	3,536	4,176	2,562	2,531	2,033	1,671	1,748	1,217
Loan Loss Prov.	NA	Nil	Nil	Nil	55.0	40.0	50.0	2,045	200	960
% Exp/Op Revs.	NA	67	66	59	64	59	62	63	51	51
Pretax Inc.	NA	1,906	1,825	2,691	1,749	1,485	1,054	-1,099	1,315	360
Eff. Tax Rate	NA	32%	33%	36%	21%	25%	27%	NM	24%	77%
Net Inc.	NA	1,296	1,215	1,723	1,382	1,114	775	-1,274	1,002	83.0
% Net Int. Marg.	NA	1.55	1.56	1.51	1.78	1.77	1.48	1.53	2.75	2.74
Balance Sheet & Other Fin. Data (Million $)										
Earning Assets:										
Money Mkt	NA	123,381	90,542	76,094	44,827	35,939	32,740	33,964	28,811	20,451
Inv. Securities	NA	24,638	22,657	19,547	21,511	22,180	18,541	16,294	16,297	14,795
Com'l Loans	NA	12,035	4,243	5,694	4,990	4,639	5,266	7,000	7,864	9,070
Other Loans	NA	11,418	17,837	18,686	21,448	23,158	22,296	21,650	20,460	21,581
Total Assets	NA	184,879	154,917	133,888	102,941	103,468	93,103	88,964	83,923	75,414
Demand Deposits	NA	4,031	4,460	5,520	3,983	4,313	6,642	5,491	5,765	6,919
Time Deposits	NA	42,407	38,625	34,882	28,536	32,663	30,915	33,667	36,704	37,068
LT Debt	NA	9,327	6,802	5,276	5,443	5,395	4,723	4,690	4,052	2,754
Common Eqty.	NA	9,957	9,074	9,365	6,572	5,574	4,695	4,001	5,534	4,786
% Ret. on Assets	NA	0.8	0.7	1.5	1.1	1.0	0.8	NM	1.2	0.1
% Ret. on Equity	NA	13.4	12.9	21.3	22.5	21.3	16.7	NM	19.1	1.5
% Loan Loss Resv.	NA	4.8	4.8	4.8	4.8	5.1	6.7	9.1	5.2	5.6
% Loans/Deposits	NA	50.5	51.3	60.3	81.3	75.2	73.4	73.2	66.7	69.6
% Equity to Assets	NA	5.6	5.3	6.8	5.1	4.7	4.4	5.2	6.3	6.0

Data as orig. reptd.; bef. results of disc. opers. and/or spec. items. Per share data adj. for stk. divs. as of ex-div. date. E-Estimated. NA-Not Available. NM-Not Meaningful. NR-Not Ranked.

Formed—in 1969; bank incorporated in New York in 1864. **Office**—60 Wall St., New York, NY 10260-0060. **Tel**—(212) 483-2323. **Website**—http://www.jpmorgan.com **Chrmn, Pres & CEO**—D. A. Warner III. **CFO**—J. T. Flynn. **Secy**—B. S. Stokes. **Investor Contact**—Ann B. Patton (212) 648-9446. **Dirs**—R. P. Bechtel, M. Feldstein, H. H. Gray, J. R. Houghton, J. L. Ketelsen, K. A. Krol, W. S. Lee, R. G. Mendoza, M. E. Patterson, L. R. Raymond, R. D. Simmons, K. F. Viermetz, D. A. Warner III, D. Weatherstone, D. C. Yearley. **Transfer Agent & Registrar**—First Chicago Trust Co. of New York, Jersey City, NJ. **Empl**— 15,527. **S&P Analyst:** Stephen R. Biggar

NationsBank Corp.   1626M

NYSE Symbol **NB**

In S&P 500

15-FEB-97

Industry:
Banking

Summary: This bank holding company, following its January 1997 merger with Boatmen's Bancshares, operates offices in 16 states and the District of Columbia.

S&P Opinion: Buy (★★★★★)	Recent Price • 119¾	Yield • 2.2%
	52 Wk Range • 120½-71	12-Mo. P/E • 15.0

Quantitative Evaluations

Outlook
(1 Lowest—5 Highest)
• **4⁻**

Fair Value
• **129%**

Risk
• **Low**

Earn./Div. Rank
• **A-**

Technical Eval.
• **Bearish** since 10/96

Rel. Strength Rank
(1 Lowest—99 Highest)
• **91**

Insider Activity
• **NA**

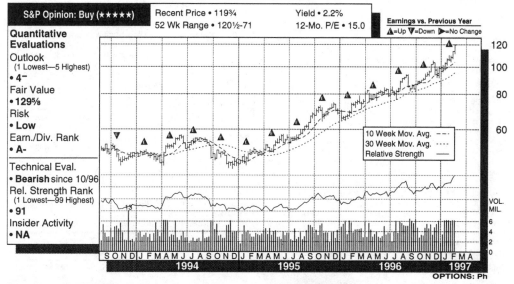

Earnings vs. Previous Year
▲=Up ▼=Down ▶=No Change

10 Week Mov. Avg. ---
30 Week Mov. Avg. ····
Relative Strength ——

VOL.
MIL.

OPTIONS: Ph

Overview - 07-FEB-97

Loan growth is expected in the high single-digits in 1997, absent the effect of securitizations, reflecting a reasonably healthy service territory. Net interest margins should show further improvement, on balance sheet initiatives that have included sales of investment securities. Double-digit gains in noninterest income are expected on increased contributions from mortgage servicing and investment banking income. Noninterest expense is projected to increase only 3%, mainly for spending on technology and infrastructure, allowing NB to achieve its annual target of 12% to 15% earnings growth, an efficiency ratio of under 60%, and an ROE of 15% to 18%. Encouraged by its strong results over the past few quarters, the company recently raised its internal financial goals to 17% to 20% ROE and an efficiency ratio under 50% by 1999. The allowance for loan losses now stands at 1.89% of loans, and modestly higher provisions will be necessary to maintain this level, given expected loan portfolio growth.

Valuation - 07-FEB-97

The expectation of above average earnings gains in 1997, resulting from healthy loan growth in the company's service territory, acquisitions and rising fee-based income, should continue to propel the shares higher. We view the recent acquisition of Boatmen's Bancshares as beneficial for several reasons, including an increase in geographic coverage from nine to 16 states, enhanced trust and asset management capabilities, and substantial cost savings opportunities. NB's shares typically trade at a slight discount to the regional bank group, at least in part reflecting the low multiple afforded its capital markets group and its perceived acquisitive nature. Nevertheless, at 12X our 1997 EPS estimate of $8.80, the shares appear poised for superior appreciation in the year ahead.

Key Stock Statistics

S&P EPS Est. 1997	8.80	Tang. Bk. Value/Share	40.10
P/E on S&P Est. 1997	13.6	Beta	1.26
Dividend Rate/Share	2.64	Shareholders	105,800
Shs. outstg. (M)	385.4	Market cap. (B)	$ 46.2
Avg. daily vol. (M)	1.443	Inst. holdings	41%

Value of $10,000 invested 5 years ago: $ 34,657

Fiscal Year Ending Dec. 31

	1996	1995	1994	1993	1992	1991
Revenues (Million $)						
1Q	4,472	3,799	3,092	2,375	2,731	2,983
2Q	4,353	4,126	3,146	2,408	2,459	2,891
3Q	4,335	4,184	3,346	2,641	2,576	2,833
4Q	4,349	4,236	3,529	2,968	2,176	2,887
Yr.	17,509	16,345	13,113	10,392	9,942	11,594
Earnings Per Share ($)						
1Q	1.70	1.60	1.52	1.11	1.28	0.70
2Q	2.00	1.71	1.58	1.20	1.00	0.88
3Q	2.12	1.95	1.55	1.33	1.40	0.31
4Q	2.19	1.87	1.46	1.37	0.92	-1.08
Yr.	8.00	7.13	6.12	5.00	4.60	0.76

Next earnings report expected: mid April

Dividend Data (Dividends have been paid since 1903.)

Amount ($)	Date Decl.	Ex-Div. Date	Stock of Record	Payment Date
0.580	Jul. 16	Sep. 04	Sep. 06	Sep. 27 '96
0.660	Oct. 23	Dec. 04	Dec. 06	Dec. 27 '96
2-for-1	Jan. 22	Feb. 28	Feb. 07	Feb. 27 '97
0.330	Jan. 22	Mar. 05	Mar. 07	Mar. 28 '97

A Division of The McGraw·Hill Companies

Business Summary - 07-FEB-97

A common sight in recent years has been a work crew pulling down the sign outside the neighborhood bank and erecting in its place a shiny new sign bearing the name NationsBank. Led by its hard-driving chairman Hugh McColl, Jr., this super-regional bank holding company has grown its asset base to $186 billion (at December 31, 1996) through a dizzying series of acquisitions in the past several years. Following the January 1997 acquisition of St.-Louis based Boatmen's Bancshares, NB expanded its service territory from nine to 16 states and its assets to $227 billion, making it the fourth largest bank holding company in the U.S.

NB has looked to increase profits through acquisitions and expansion of banking products and services to a wider variety of customers. While NB's traditional branch banking, or General Bank, segment still accounts for the lion's share (about 72%) of revenues, other non-traditional segments make up an increasing portion of the business. The Global Finance segment (21%) offers corporate and investment banking services such as treasury management, loan syndication, underwriting and trading. The Financial Services segment (7%) includes mainly consumer finance and commercial finance units.

NB derives the greatest proportion of its revenues from net interest income, defined as the interest income it receives on loans and other investments less the interest expense it pays for the use of funds. The chief factor affecting net interest income is the level of earnings assets (i.e., loans and investments), since more earning assets will produce greater interest income. At the end of 1996, NationsBank had average earning assets of $177 billion, up from $167 billion the year before. Net interest margin, an important measure of the profitability of the lending business, was 3.62% in 1996, up from 3.33% in 1995.

Like most other banks, NationsBank has experienced higher credit costs over the past year, mostly due to weakness in the consumer lending segment. In 1996, the company made a $605 million provision for potential loan losses, up from $382 million a year earlier. The provision is added to a reserve for loan losses and held in anticipation of actual losses. The reserve totaled $2.3 billion at December 31, 1996, up from $2.2 billion a year earlier. Net charge-offs, or the amount of loans actually written off as uncollectible, were $598 million (0.48% of average loans) during that period, versus 0.38% the year before.

Capitalization

Long Term Debt: $22,985,000,000 (12/96).
Preferred Stock: $171,000,000.
Pfd. Beneficial Interests: $965,000,000.

Per Share Data ($)

(Year Ended Dec. 31)	1996	1995	1994	1993	1992	1991	1990	1989	1988	1987
Tangible Bk. Val.	NA	38.19	33.24	31.02	26.86	21.88	20.79	20.95	14.88	12.65
Earnings	8.00	7.13	6.12	5.00	4.60	0.76	3.40	4.62	2.90	2.03
Dividends	2.40	2.08	1.88	1.64	1.51	1.48	1.42	1.10	0.94	0.86
Payout Ratio	30%	29%	31%	33%	33%	195%	42%	24%	32%	42%
Prices - High	105¼	74¾	57⅜	58	53⅜	42¾	47¼	55	29¼	29⅞
- Low	64⅜	44⅝	43⅜	44½	39⅝	21½	16⅞	27	17½	15½
P/E Ratio - High	13	10	9	12	12	56	14	12	10	14
- Low	8	6	7	9	9	28	5	6	6	8

Income Statement Analysis (Million $)

	1996	1995	1994	1993	1992	1991	1990	1989	1988	1987
Net Int. Inc.	NA	5,447	5,211	4,673	4,098	3,799	1,816	1,703	898	821
Tax Equiv. Adj.	NA	113	94.0	86.0	92.0	141	39.0	76.0	82.0	94.0
Non Int. Inc.	NA	3,078	2,597	2,101	1,913	1,742	912	623	353	298
Loan Loss Prov.	NA	382	310	430	715	1,582	505	239	122	195
% Exp/Op Revs.	NA	60	62	65	68	76	68	70	61	63
Pretax Inc.	NA	2,991	2,555	1,991	1,396	109	378	516	330	201
Eff. Tax Rate	NA	35%	34%	35%	18%	NM	3.20%	13%	24%	17%
Net Inc.	NA	1,950	1,690	1,301	1,145	202	366	447	252	167
% Net Int. Marg.	NA	3.33	3.58	4.00	4.10	3.82	3.25	3.61	3.83	3.91

Balance Sheet & Other Fin. Data (Million $)

	1996	1995	1994	1993	1992	1991	1990	1989	1988	1987
Earning Assets:										
Money Mkt	NA	26,393	23,212	19,133	6,110	2,436	1,052	3,580	2,467	1,578
Inv. Securities	NA	23,847	25,825	29,054	24,729	24,879	15,894	16,170	4,727	6,826
Com'l Loans	NA	52,101	48,109	43,538	34,478	31,164	18,937	17,735	11,154	9,877
Other Loans	NA	66,919	55,580	50,166	38,236	37,944	18,540	16,984	7,870	7,338
Total Assets	NA	187,298	169,604	157,686	118,059	110,319	65,285	66,191	29,848	28,915
Demand Deposits	NA	23,414	21,380	20,719	17,701	16,270	8,939	8,439	3,914	3,862
Time Deposits	NA	77,277	79,090	70,394	65,026	71,805	41,283	40,137	16,756	15,688
LT Debt	NA	17,775	8,488	7,648	3,066	2,876	1,697	1,466	493	568
Common Eqty.	NA	12,699	10,900	9,771	7,695	6,145	2,958	2,712	1,692	1,510
% Ret. on Assets	NA	1.1	1.0	0.9	1.0	0.2	0.6	0.8	0.9	0.6
% Ret. on Equity	NA	16.5	16.3	14.8	15.9	2.7	12.0	20.5	16.2	11.7
% Loan Loss Resv.	NA	1.9	2.1	2.3	2.0	2.3	1.8	1.4	1.2	1.5
% Loans/Deposits	NA	116.2	103.2	102.8	87.9	78.5	73.9	70.8	91.5	87.4
% Equity to Assets	NA	6.6	6.2	6.3	6.1	5.4	4.5	3.8	5.3	5.3

Data as orig. reptd.; bef. results of disc opers. and/or spec. items. Per share data adj. for stk. divs. as of ex-div. date. E-Estimated. NA-Not Available. NM-Not Meaningful. NR-Not Ranked.

Office—NationsBank Corporate Center, Charlotte, NC 28255. **Tel**—(704) 386-5000.**Website**—http://www.nationsbank.com **Chrmn & CEO**—H. L. McColl, Jr. **Pres**—K. D. Lewis. **Vice Chrmn & CFO**—J. H. Hance, Jr. **Investor Contacts**—Kevin Stitt, Jenny Repass. **Dirs**—R. W. Allen, R. C. Anderson, W. M. Barnhardt, T. E. Capps, C. W. Coker, T. G. Cousins, A. T. Dickson, W. F. Dowd, Jr., P. Fulton, L. L. Gellerstedt, Jr., T. L. Guzzle, W. W. Johnson, H. L. McColl, Jr., B. Mickel, J. J. Murphy, J. C. Slane, J. W. Snow, M.— R. Spangler, R. H. Spilman, R. Townsend, E. C. Wall Jr., J. M. Ward. **Transfer Agent**—Chase Bank, NYC. **Incorporated**—in North Carolina in 1968. **Empl**— 62,971. **S&P Analyst:** Stephen R. Biggar

Northern Trust Corp. 4828

Nasdaq Symbol **NTRS**

In S&P MidCap 400

15-FEB-97 | **Industry:** Banking | **Summary:** This Chicago-based interstate bank holding company's lead subsidiary is Northern Trust Co., the third largest commercial bank in Illinois.

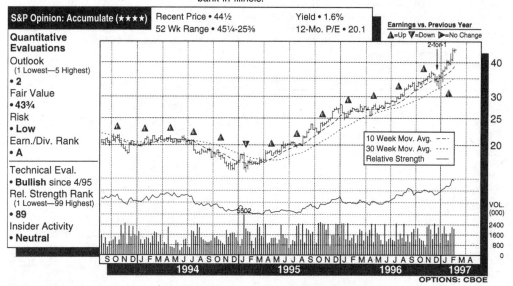

S&P Opinion: Accumulate (★★★★)	Recent Price • 44½	Yield • 1.6%
	52 Wk Range • 45¼-25⅜	12-Mo. P/E • 20.1

Earnings vs. Previous Year
▲=Up ▼=Down ▶=No Change

Quantitative Evaluations

Outlook
(1 Lowest—5 Highest)
• **2**

Fair Value
• **43¾**

Risk
• **Low**

Earn./Div. Rank
• **A**

Technical Eval.
• **Bullish** since 4/95

Rel. Strength Rank
(1 Lowest—99 Highest)
• **89**

Insider Activity
• **Neutral**

- 10 Week Mov. Avg. ---
- 30 Week Mov. Avg. ····
- Relative Strength ——

OPTIONS: CBOE

Overview - 24-JAN-97

Earnings per share rose 18% in 1996, to $2.21, reflecting strong revenue growth and well controlled expenses. Trust fees, which accounted for 76% of total noninterest income and 49% of total revenue during the year, increased 17%, on balanced growth in personal and corporate services. The strong increase in fee revenue reflected rapid growth in assets under management and administration. This growth should continue in 1997, aided by continued geographic expansion, as well as market share gains resulting from First Chicago NBD's decision to exit master trust and domestic institutional custody services businesses. We expect low double-digit loan growth, led by the residential mortgage and commercial and industrial loan segments, to fuel net interest income in 1997, with margins remaining stable at around 2.25%. Credit quality remains exceptionally strong, with net chargeoffs totaling just .02% of average loans during the fourth quarter. Although the fourth quarter provision for loan losses was cut in half from that of the 1995 quarter, the reserve for loan losses was essentially unchanged.

Valuation - 24-JAN-97

The shares of this diversified bank holding company rose 30% in 1996, easily outpacing the broader market. We expect the stock to continue to outperform in 1997, driven by continued rapid growth in assets under management, which will fuel trust revenues. Despite an uptick in the fourth quarter of 1996, expenses should moderate in the coming year, as initiatives undertaken in 1995 to contol costs take hold. Given the consistent, low risk earnings stream produced by this blended investment management, transactions processing, and bank holding company, the shares deserve a premium valuation. At less than 16X our 1997 EPS estimate of $2.53, the shares are an attractive investment.

Key Stock Statistics

S&P EPS Est. 1997	2.53	Tang. Bk. Value/Share	10.56
P/E on S&P Est. 1997	17.6	Beta	0.78
Dividend Rate/Share	0.72	Shareholders	3,300
Shs. outstg. (M)	111.8	Market cap. (B)	$ 5.0
Avg. daily vol. (M)	0.354	Inst. holdings	66%

Value of $10,000 invested 5 years ago: $ 29,518

Fiscal Year Ending Dec. 31

	1996	1995	1994	1993	1992	1991
Revenues (Million $)						
1Q	472.6	422.8	333.4	308.3	310.2	327.6
2Q	481.3	439.6	378.2	312.7	311.7	314.6
3Q	484.2	459.2	373.4	320.2	303.7	310.6
4Q	—	460.5	393.5	317.6	305.7	307.4
Yr.	—	1,782	1,479	1,259	1,231	1,260
Earnings Per Share ($)						
1Q	0.52	0.43	0.40	0.36	0.32	0.42
2Q	0.54	0.45	0.43	0.36	0.32	0.43
3Q	0.57	0.50	0.42	0.38	0.33	0.42
4Q	0.58	0.51	0.35	0.38	0.34	0.44
Yr.	2.21	1.87	1.58	1.48	1.32	1.71

Next earnings report expected: mid April

Dividend Data (Dividends have been paid since 1896.)

Amount ($)	Date Decl.	Ex-Div. Date	Stock of Record	Payment Date
0.310	May. 21	Jun. 06	Jun. 10	Jul. 01 '96
0.310	Jul. 17	Sep. 06	Sep. 10	Oct. 01 '96
0.180	Nov. 19	Dec. 06	Dec. 10	Jan. 02 '97
2-for-1	Nov. 19	Dec. 10	Dec. 02	Dec. 09 '96

A Division of The McGraw·Hill Companies

Business Summary - 24-JAN-97

Northern Trust Corporation is an interstate bank holding company whose lead bank is Northern Trust Co. of Chicago, the third largest bank in Illinois. It also owns a growing network of smaller banks and nonbanking subsidiaries in Illinois, Florida, Arizona, California, New York and Texas, providing banking, stock brokerage and other services. At December 31, 1995, total assets came to $19.9 billion, and trust assets under administration totaled $613.9 billion. Gross loans of $9.9 billion at December 31, 1995, were divided:

	1995
Real estate--residential	39%
Commercial	32%
Leasing	2%
Consumer	8%
Real estate--commercial	5%
International	4%
Brokerage	3%
Other	6%

The allowance for loan losses at 1995 year-end was $147.1 million (1.49% of loans and leases outstanding), up from $144.8 million (1.69%) a year earlier. Net chargeoffs during 1995 amounted to $5.9 million (equal to 0.06% of average loans), down from $6.7 million (0.08%) in 1994. Nonperforming assets at December 31, 1995, totaled $33.7 million (0.17% of total assets), versus $30.0 million (0.16%) at 1994 year-end.

Total deposits of $12.5 billion at year-end 1995 were divided: demand and other noninterest-bearing 23%, savings and money market 27%, savings certificates 17%, other time 3%, and foreign 30%.

Important Developments

Nov. '96—Directors declared a two-for-one stock split, effective in December. They also increased the quarterly dividend by 16%, to $0.18 a share, payable January 2, 1997, to shareholders of record December 10, 1996. In addition, directors boosted the stock buy-back authorization to approximately 5 million shares (as adjusted).

Capitalization

Notes Payable: $732,800,000 (12/96).
Ser. C Auction Rate Cum. Pfd. Stk.: 600 shs.
Ser. D Flex. Auction Rate Cum. Pfd. Stk.: 600 shs.
Ser. E 6.25% Cum. Conv. Pfd. Stk.: 50,000 shs., ea. conv. into 1.2048 com. shs.

Per Share Data ($) (Year Ended Dec. 31)	1996	1995	1994	1993	1992	1991	1990	1989	1988	1987
Tangible Bk. Val.	NA	10.56	10.26	8.51	7.19	6.41	5.52	4.84	4.28	3.33
Earnings	2.21	1.88	1.58	1.48	1.32	1.14	1.03	1.04	1.11	-0.79
Dividends	0.65	0.54	0.46	0.39	0.33	0.29	0.26	0.22	0.18	0.16
Payout Ratio	29%	29%	29%	26%	25%	25%	25%	21%	16%	NM
Prices - High	37¾	28	21⅝	25¼	21⅝	17½	11¼	11⅞	8	8½
- Low	24⅝	15⅞	16⅛	18½	16⅜	9	6½	7⅜	6⅛	5
P/E Ratio - High	17	15	14	17	16	15	11	11	7	NM
- Low	11	8	10	13	12	8	6	7	6	NM
Income Statement Analysis (Million $)										
Net Int. Inc.	NA	358	338	329	311	282	249	237	232	209
Tax Equiv. Adj.	NA	37.6	33.4	34.1	32.5	36.0	38.1	36.0	23.8	28.0
Non Int. Inc.	NA	677	630	551	506	409	367	330	307	242
Loan Loss Prov.	NA	6.0	6.0	20.0	30.0	31.0	14.0	16.0	20.0	179
% Exp/Op Revs.	NA	66	70	69	69	69	71	71	69	72
Pretax Inc.	NA	321	262	234	207	164	140	125	131	-68.0
Eff. Tax Rate	NA	31%	30%	28%	28%	22%	17%	9.40%	17%	NM
Net Inc.	NA	220	182	168	150	127	115	113	109	-65.0
% Net Int. Marg.	NA	2.30	2.36	2.65	2.96	3.00	2.80	2.95	3.20	3.25
Balance Sheet & Other Fin. Data (Million $)										
Earning Assets:										
Money Mkt	NA	1,784	2,642	2,705	2,318	1,710	1,397	970	1,290	1,654
Inv. Securities	NA	5,760	5,053	4,002	3,180	3,115	2,194	2,244	2,185	1,936
Com'l Loans	NA	3,708	3,107	2,809	2,881	3,176	2,831	2,924	2,660	2,160
Other Loans	NA	6,288	5,484	4,814	4,055	3,104	2,706	2,736	2,006	1,803
Total Assets	NA	19,934	18,562	16,903	14,960	13,193	11,789	10,938	9,904	9,326
Demand Deposits	NA	3,313	2,830	2,762	2,712	1,824	2,021	1,803	1,965	2,001
Time Deposits	NA	9,175	8,904	7,572	7,159	6,737	6,088	5,236	4,788	4,846
LT Debt	NA	352	792	1,144	545	266	172	241	175	175
Common Eqty.	NA	1,282	1,111	982	841	701	589	531	410	324
% Ret. on Assets	NA	1.1	1.0	1.1	1.1	1.0	1.0	1.1	1.2	NM
% Ret. on Equity	NA	17.7	16.7	17.9	18.3	19.0	19.8	22.8	28.9	NM
% Loan Loss Resv.	NA	1.5	1.7	1.9	2.1	2.3	2.7	2.7	3.2	5.9
% Loans/Deposits	NA	79.3	73.2	73.8	70.3	73.4	68.3	80.4	69.1	57.9
% Equity to Assets	NA	6.2	5.9	5.8	5.8	5.2	4.7	4.4	3.9	4.6

Data as orig. reptd.; bef. results of disc opers. and/or spec. items. Per share data adj. for stk. divs. as of ex-div. date. E-Estimated. NA-Not Available. NM-Not Meaningful. NR-Not Ranked.

Office—50 S. LaSalle St., Chicago, IL 60675. **Tel**—(312) 630-6000. **Chrmn & CEO**—W. A Osborn. **Pres & COO**—B. G. Hastings. **SEVP & CFO**—P. R. Pero. **EVP & Secy**—P. L. Rossiter. **Investor Contact**—Laurie K. McMahon (312-444-7811). **Dirs**—D. E. Cross, R. S. Hamada, B. G. Hastings, R. A. Helman, A. L. Kelly, A. Krainik, R. D. Krebs, F. A. Krehbiel, W. G. Mitchell, W. A. Osborn, H. B. Smith, W. D. Smithburg, B. L. Thomas. **Transfer Agent & Registrar**—Harris Trust & Savings Bank, Chicago. **Incorporated**—in Delaware in 1971; bank chartered in Illinois in 1889. **Empl**— 6,531. **S&P Analyst:** Brendan McGovern

Old Kent Financial

4869

Nasdaq Symbol **OKEN**

16-FEB-97

Industry: Banking

Summary: This bank holding company, with $12.6 billion in assets, owns six non-bank subsidiaries and operates more than 200 branches in Michigan and Illinois.

| S&P Opinion: Accumulate (★★★★) | Recent Price • 50 | Yield • 2.7% |
| | 52 Wk Range • 50⅝-35⅝ | 12-Mo. P/E • 14.7 |

Quantitative Evaluations

Outlook (1 Lowest—5 Highest)
• **1+**

Fair Value
• **39⅜**

Risk
• **Low**

Earn./Div. Rank
• **A+**

Technical Eval.
• **Bullish** since 8/96

Rel. Strength Rank (1 Lowest—99 Highest)
• **70**

Insider Activity
• **NA**

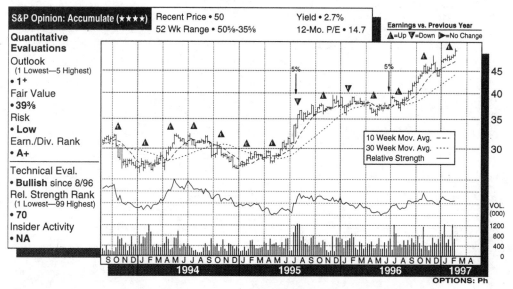

Earnings vs. Previous Year
▲=Up ▼=Down ▶=No Change

10 Week Mov. Avg. - - -
30 Week Mov. Avg. ·····
Relative Strength —

VOL. (000)
OPTIONS: Ph

Overview - 28-JAN-97

Earnings should continue to grow in 1997, but more slowly than in the past. In the absence of acquisitions, loan growth may moderate as the bank reduces credit in specific markets and adjusts its loan portfolio. In 1996, total loans increased over $600 million, to $8.1 billion, outweighing narrowing net interest margins (4.41% versus 4.46%). Credit quality weakened, but nonperforming asset levels are manageable at 0.39% of total assets (0.45% a year earlier), and the bank has traditionally provisioned in excess of net chargeoffs. After expanding mortgage banking activities (up 78% over 1995), OKEN may benefit from any increase in refinancing volume. Despite a SAIF assessment in the third quarter, net income in 1996 rose 12%, to $158.7 million ($3.39 a share) from $141.8 million ($2.96, including $0.26 in restructuring charges). Because of its conservative balance sheet, highly concentrated banking network, and reasonable price/book value ratio of 2.2, the bank may be an attractive acquisition target.

Valuation - 28-JAN-97

In 1996, OKEN derived over 80% of total revenues from interest sources. A drop in loan volume would put pressure on interest income growth. To counter this possibility, the bank is trying to increase noninterest income sources, and acquisitions of specialized financial services companies should continue. For the long term, the shares remain attractive, reflecting the company's emphasis on operating efficiency, an increasing focus on fee-based income sources, possible acquisitions of traditional banking institutions, conservative lending practices, and consistent profitability. The stock, with a 2.8% yield, and recently trading at about 12X our 1997 EPS estimate of $3.80, is recommended for conservative growth investors.

Key Stock Statistics

S&P EPS Est. 1997	3.80	Tang. Bk. Value/Share	21.68
P/E on S&P Est. 1997	13.2	Beta	0.77
Dividend Rate/Share	1.36	Shareholders	13,200
Shs. outstg. (M)	45.2	Market cap. (B)	$ 2.3
Avg. daily vol. (M)	0.152	Inst. holdings	30%

Value of $10,000 invested 5 years ago: $ 28,080

Fiscal Year Ending Dec. 31

	1996	1995	1994	1993	1992	1991
Revenues (Million $)						
1Q	282.5	255.8	197.5	199.2	208.4	214.5
2Q	286.7	274.9	217.0	204.2	204.0	213.2
3Q	293.0	281.4	225.3	202.0	202.5	213.7
4Q	303.2	275.4	235.1	196.4	200.4	221.0
Yr.	1,165	1,088	874.8	801.8	815.2	862.5
Earnings Per Share ($)						
1Q	0.82	0.73	0.72	0.67	0.55	0.51
2Q	0.79	0.78	0.79	0.74	0.64	0.53
3Q	0.87	0.80	0.79	0.75	0.64	0.54
4Q	0.91	0.66	0.74	0.68	0.65	0.54
Yr.	3.39	2.96	3.04	2.85	2.49	2.10

Next earnings report expected: late April

Dividend Data (Dividends have been paid since 1937.)

Amount ($)	Date Decl.	Ex-Div. Date	Stock of Record	Payment Date
5%	Jun. 17	Jun. 21	Jun. 25	Jul. 25 '96
0.320	Aug. 19	Aug. 28	Aug. 30	Sep. 13 '96
0.340	Oct. 21	Nov. 13	Nov. 15	Dec. 13 '96
0.340	Jan. 20	Feb. 12	Feb. 14	Mar. 14 '97

Business Summary - 28-JAN-97

Old Kent Financial is a multibank holding company that as of 1995 year-end was operating 16 regional offices and six non-banking subsidiaries. The bank's principal markets, Michigan and Illinois, are served by 216 full-service banking offices.

Gross loans outstanding totaled $7.43 billion at the end of 1995 and were divided:

	1995
Commercial loans and leases	56%
Consumer	29%
Credit card	4%
Residential mortgages	11%

The allowance for loan losses was $174,248,000 (2.35% of loans outstanding) at the end of 1995, versus $167,253,000 (2.44%) a year earlier. Net loan charge-offs in 1995 amounted to $13,409,000 (0.19% of average loans), versus $9,771,000 (0.16%) in 1994. At 1995 year-end, nonperforming assets (including nonaccrual loans, restructured loans and other real estate owned) were $54,535,000 (0.58% of loans outstanding), down from $72,780,000 (0.88%) a year earlier.

Deposits averaged $9.36 billion in 1995 and were apportioned: 73% time and savings, 16% noninterest-bearing, and 11% negotiable and foreign.

Interest and fees on loans provided 61% of total income for 1995, other interest income 22%, trust income 4%, service charges on deposit accounts 4%, and other noninterest income 9%.

On a tax-equivalent basis, the average yield on total earning assets was 8.44% in 1995 (7.66% in 1994), while the average rate paid on interest-bearing liabilities was 4.71% (3.57%), for a net spread of 3.73% (4.09%).

During 1996, OKEN acquired Republic Mortgage Corp. (20 offices, $39 million in assets) of Utah, a mortgage originator with a residential servicing portfolio of $130 million. Old Kent also acquired National Pacific Mortgage Corp., with a residential servicing portfolio of $1.8 billion in California and Oregon.

Important Developments

Dec. '96—OKEN completed its acquisition of Seaway Financial Corp. ($362 million in assets) via an exchange of stock valued at approximately $72 million, expanding its presence in the Detroit and Port Huron markets. Separately, OKEN reported that it had repurchased 2.5 million of its common shares during the second half of 1996, with the intention of future reissuance.

Capitalization

Subord. Debt: $100,000,000 (12/96).
Other Borrowings: $753,000,000.

Per Share Data ($)

(Year Ended Dec. 31)	1996	1995	1994	1993	1992	1991	1990	1989	1988	1987
Tangible Bk. Val.	NA	19.33	16.91	17.08	15.18	15.19	13.80	13.68	12.48	11.70
Earnings	3.39	2.96	3.04	2.85	2.49	2.10	1.99	1.95	1.79	1.70
Dividends	1.27	1.16	1.07	0.97	0.82	0.71	0.66	0.58	0.53	0.49
Payout Ratio	37%	39%	35%	34%	33%	34%	33%	30%	30%	29%
Prices - High	48⅞	39⅝	32⅜	34	31⅛	21⅜	17½	17⅞	15¼	16¼
- Low	35⅝	27¼	26⅜	27	20⅜	12⅞	11	13½	11¼	10⅞
P/E Ratio - High	14	13	11	12	12	10	9	9	9	10
- Low	11	9	9	9	8	6	6	7	6	6

Income Statement Analysis (Million $)

	1996	1995	1994	1993	1992	1991	1990	1989	1988	1987
Net Int. Inc.	NA	477	432	407	386	339	311	290	266	205
Tax Equiv. Adj.	NA	7.8	7.3	7.4	8.2	9.7	11.7	13.6	17.2	22.7
Non Int. Inc.	NA	187	150	145	122	106	99	90.0	76.0	53.0
Loan Loss Prov.	NA	21.7	21.2	34.0	57.7	39.8	32.1	24.1	17.3	17.0
% Exp/Op Revs.	NA	64	61	58	57	61	61	60	62	56
Pretax Inc.	NA	215	205	194	164	133	123	118	103	85.0
Eff. Tax Rate	NA	34%	34%	34%	32%	30%	29%	28%	26%	26%
Net Inc.	NA	142	136	128	111	93.0	87.5	85.4	77.1	63.4
% Net Int. Marg.	NA	4.40	4.60	4.80	4.80	4.47	4.36	4.10	4.15	4.31

Balance Sheet & Other Fin. Data (Million $)

	1996	1995	1994	1993	1992	1991	1990	1989	1988	1987
Earning Assets:										
Money Mkt	NA	237	45.0	164	139	379	248	562	683	770
Inv. Securities	NA	3,117	3,412	3,567	3,007	2,692	1,951	1,818	1,767	1,287
Com'l Loans	NA	2,009	1,719	1,407	1,257	1,268	1,644	1,950	1,749	1,779
Other Loans	NA	5,422	4,969	4,085	3,651	3,843	3,674	3,120	2,937	2,031
Total Assets	NA	12,003	10,946	9,856	8,699	8,826	8,205	8,127	7,854	6,455
Demand Deposits	NA	1,506	1,364	1,145	1,036	978	908	975	1,025	925
Time Deposits	NA	7,851	7,593	6,826	6,218	6,336	6,053	5,805	5,480	4,488
LT Debt	NA	100	1.1	1.2	16.2	74.7	80.9	87.6	93.4	63.4
Common Eqty.	NA	1,016	859	813	•726	673	608	575	511	406
% Ret. on Assets	NA	1.2	1.3	1.4	1.3	1.1	1.1	1.1	1.0	1.1
% Ret. on Equity	NA	14.8	16.1	16.7	16.3	14.6	15.1	15.1	15.2	15.4
% Loan Loss Resv.	NA	2.3	2.4	2.6	2.5	1.7	1.4	1.3	1.2	1.2
% Loans/Deposits	NA	79.4	74.7	68.9	67.7	69.9	76.4	74.8	72.0	70.4
% Equity to Assets	NA	8.1	8.3	8.3	7.8	7.6	7.2	6.8	6.5	6.7

Data as orig. reptd.; bef. results of disc. opers. and/or spec. items. Per share data adj. for stk. divs. as of ex-div. date. E-Estimated. NA-Not Available. NM-Not Meaningful. NR-Not Ranked.

Office—One Vandenberg Center, Grand Rapids, MI 49503. **Tel**—(616) 771-5000. **Chrmn, Pres & CEO**—D. J. Wagner. **Vice Chrmn**—R. L. Sadler. **Vice Chrmn & Treas**—B. P. Sherwood III. **EVP, CFO**—Richard W. Wroten. **SVP & Secy**—M. J. Allen Jr. **SVP & Investor Contact**—Albert T. Potas (616-771-1931). **Dirs**—J. M. Bissell, J. D. Boyles, J. C. Canepa, R. M. DeVos Jr., J. P. Hackett, E. Hanka, E. D. Holton, M. J. Jandernoa, J. P. Keller, W. U. Parfet, P. A. Pierre, R. L. Sadler, P. F. Secchia, B. P. Sherwood III, D. J. Wagner. **Transfer Agent**—Old Kent Bank, Grand Rapids. **Incorporated**—in Michigan in 1972. **Empl**—5,649. **S&P Analyst:** E. Fitzpatrick

Pfizer Inc.

1810
NYSE Symbol **PFE**

In S&P 500

18-FEB-97   Industry:
Drugs

Summary: This company is a leading producer of ethical drugs, hospital products, animal health items and nonprescription medications.

S&P Opinion: Buy (★★★★★)	Recent Price • 96½	Yield • 1.4%
	52 Wk Range • 96¾-61½	12-Mo. P/E • 32.3

Earnings vs. Previous Year
▲=Up ▼=Down ▶=No Change

Quantitative Evaluations

Outlook
  (1 Lowest—5 Highest)
• **1⁻**

Fair Value
• **81⅝**

Risk
• **Average**

Earn./Div. Rank
• **A-**

Technical Eval.
• **Bullish** since 5/95

Rel. Strength Rank
  (1 Lowest—99 Highest)
• **84**

Insider Activity
• **Neutral**

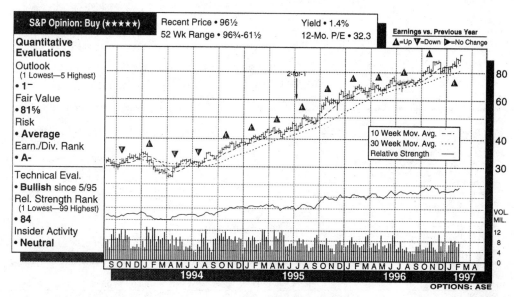

10 Week Mov. Avg. - - - -
30 Week Mov. Avg. - - -
Relative Strength ——

2-for-1

VOL. MIL.

OPTIONS: ASE

Overview - 14-FEB-97

Pfizer should again post strong double-digit earnings growth in 1997, fueled primarily by a strong lineup of new drugs. Key products exhibiting impressive gains include Norvasc and Cardura cardiovasculars (up 42% and 29%, respectively, in 1996), Zithromax anti-infective (up 53%), Zoloft antidepressant (up 29%), and Glucotrol XL treatment for diabetes (up 57%). Volume should also be augmented by new drugs such as Zyrtec low-sedating antihistamine, Aricept for Alzheimer's, and Lipitor cholesterol-lowering agent. Gains in these drugs should more than outweigh declining sales in older lines such as Procardia XL cardiovascular, Glucotrol anti-diabetic, and Feldene antiarthritic. Gains are also seen for hospital products, consumer items and animal health products.

Valuation - 14-FEB-97

The shares moved higher in recent months, buoyed by strength in pharmaceutical issues in general and Pfizer's impressive 20% earnings gain in 1996. Earnings growth is being driven by a strong portfolio of new drugs, which account for over two thirds of Pfizer's drug sales. PFE has also achieved significant growth overseas, rising from 17th place in the international drug market in 1992 to its present No. 9 position. The worldwide sales force has recently been increased by about 17%, to about 11,000. During 1997, the company plans to file new drug applications for ziprasidone antipsychotic, Viagra for male erectile dysfunction, and dofetilide for cardiac arrhythmias. The R&D pipeline also includes promising treatments for migraine, cancer, diabetic neuropathy, fungal infections and other conditions. We continue to recommend purchase of the shares, which are to be split two for one in April.

Key Stock Statistics

S&P EPS Est. 1997	3.50	Tang. Bk. Value/Share	6.69
P/E on S&P Est. 1997	27.6	Beta	1.16
Dividend Rate/Share	1.36	Shareholders	62,900
Shs. outstg. (M)	644.6	Market cap. (B)	$ 62.2
Avg. daily vol. (M)	1.454	Inst. holdings	62%

Value of $10,000 invested 5 years ago: $ 25,457

Fiscal Year Ending Dec. 31

	1996	1995	1994	1993	1992	1991
Revenues (Million $)						
1Q	2,682	2,338	1,983	2,338	1,761	1,696
2Q	2,661	2,401	1,923	2,401	1,694	1,631
3Q	2,803	2,539	2,075	1,873	1,828	1,773
4Q	3,160	2,744	2,300	1,989	1,947	1,850
Yr.	11,306	10,021	8,281	7,478	7,230	6,950
Earnings Per Share ($)						
1Q	0.81	0.68	0.59	0.68	0.44	0.39
2Q	0.61	0.49	0.42	0.49	0.33	0.26
3Q	0.80	0.66	0.54	-0.32	0.44	0.40
4Q	0.77	0.64	0.54	0.45	0.42	Nil
Yr.	2.99	2.47	2.09	1.02	1.63	1.07

Next earnings report expected: mid April

Dividend Data (Dividends have been paid since 1901.)

Amount ($)	Date Decl.	Ex-Div. Date	Stock of Record	Payment Date
0.300	Apr. 25	May. 08	May. 10	Jun. 13 '96
0.300	Jun. 27	Jul. 31	Aug. 02	Sep. 12 '96
0.300	Oct. 24	Nov. 06	Nov. 08	Dec. 12 '96
0.340	Jan. 23	Feb. 05	Feb. 07	Mar. 13 '97

A Division of The McGraw·Hill Companies

Pfizer Inc.

Business Summary - 14-FEB-97

Pfizer (PFE) traces its history back to 1849 when it was founded by Charles Pfizer and Charles Erhart as a chemical products firm. Today it is a leading global pharmaceutical concern, manufacturing and marketing a wide range of prescription drugs. It also holds important interests in hospital products, animal health items and consumer products. PFE's growth over the past half century was paced by strategic acquisitions, new drug discoveries and vigorous foreign expansion. PFE derived 49% of sales and 40% of profits from non-U.S. business in 1995.

Segment contributions from continuing businesses in 1995 were:

	Sales	Profits
Health care	84%	95%
Animal health	12%	4%
Consumer	4%	1%

Representing 72% of total 1996 sales, prescription pharmaceuticals are the chief engine of PFE's growth. Principal drugs include Norvasc calcium channel blocker heart drug (sales of $1.8 billion in 1996), Zoloft treatment for depression and obsessive/compulsive disorder ($1.3 billion), Procardia XL cardiovascular ($1.0 billion), Diflucan antifungal ($910 million), Zithromax broad-spectrum quinolone antibiotic ($619 million), and Cardura for hypertension and enlarged prostates ($533 million). Other important drugs are Glucotrol and Glucotrol XL for diabetes, Feldene anti-arthritic, and Zyrtec/Reactine antihistamine. In February 1997, PFE launched Aricept for Alzheimer's disease and Lipitor cholesterol-lowering agent.

PFE plans to spend some $2 billion on R&D in 1997, up from $1.7 billion in 1996. Key compounds in the pipeline include Trovan broad-spectrum quinolone antibiotic, ziprasidone antipsychotic, Viagra for male erectile dysfunction, dofetilide for cardiac arrhythmias, eletriptan for migraine, several cancer treatments, and other drugs for diabetic neuropathy, fungal infections and other ailments.

Hospital products (13% of sales) should continue to show single-digit sales growth in the years ahead. This business segment includes Howmedica, a leading maker of reconstructive hip, knee and bone cement products and other implantable items; Schneider angioplasty catheters; Valleylab electrosurgical and ultrasound surgical equipment; and various other items.

The animal health product line (13%) includes feed additives, vaccines, antibiotics, antihelmintics and other veterinary products. The animal health business has been impacted by a depressed livestock market in recent years. Consumer products (4%) include Ben-Gay ointment, Visine eye drops, Desitin ointment, Pacquin hand cream, Plax dental rinse, and Barbasol shave cream.

Capitalization

Long Term Debt: $553,000,000 (9/96).
Minority Interest: $52,000,000.

Per Share Data ($) (Year Ended Dec. 31)	1996	1995	1994	1993	1992	1991	1990	1989	1988	1987
Tangible Bk. Val.	NA	6.69	6.88	6.02	7.26	7.63	7.71	6.86	6.50	5.54
Cash Flow	NA	3.06	2.56	1.42	2.01	1.42	1.51	1.30	1.45	1.27
Earnings	2.99	2.47	2.09	1.02	1.63	1.07	1.20	1.01	1.17	1.02
Dividends	1.20	1.04	0.94	0.84	0.74	0.66	0.60	0.55	0.50	0.45
Payout Ratio	40%	42%	45%	82%	46%	60%	49%	53%	42%	43%
Prices - High	91¼	66⅞	39¾	37⅞	43½	43⅛	20½	19	15⅛	19¼
- Low	60¼	37¼	26⅝	26¼	32⅝	18⅜	13⅝	13½	11⅞	10⅜
P/E Ratio - High	31	27	19	37	27	40	17	19	13	19
- Low	20	15	13	26	20	17	11	13	10	10
Income Statement Analysis (Million $)										
Revs.	NA	10,021	8,281	7,478	7,230	6,950	6,406	5,671	5,385	4,920
Oper. Inc.	NA	2,527	2,248	1,906	1,686	1,471	1,254	1,153	1,189	1,103
Depr.	NA	374	289	254	260	238	217	201	187	172
Int. Exp.	NA	205	142	121	116	138	142	131	87.0	66.0
Pretax Inc.	NA	2,299	1,862	851	1,535	944	1,103	917	1,104	1,011
Eff. Tax Rate	NA	32%	30%	23%	29%	23%	27%	25%	28%	31%
Net Inc.	NA	1,554	1,298	658	1,094	722	801	681	791	690
Balance Sheet & Other Fin. Data (Million $)										
Cash	NA	1,512	2,019	1,177	1,704	1,548	1,068	1,058	808	1,031
Curr. Assets	NA	6,152	5,788	4,733	5,385	4,808	4,436	4,505	4,095	4,101
Total Assets	NA	12,729	11,099	9,331	9,590	9,635	9,052	8,325	7,638	6,923
Curr. Liab.	NA	5,187	4,826	3,444	3,217	3,421	3,117	2,912	2,344	1,957
LT Debt	NA	833	604	571	571	397	193	191	227	249
Common Eqty.	NA	5,507	4,324	3,865	4,719	5,026	5,092	4,536	4,301	3,882
Total Cap.	NA	6,553	5,179	4,665	5,472	5,742	5,666	5,062	4,866	4,471
Cap. Exp.	NA	696	672	634	674	594	548	457	344	258
Cash Flow	NA	1,928	1,588	912	1,353	960	1,019	882	978	862
Curr. Ratio	NA	1.2	1.2	1.4	1.7	1.4	1.4	1.5	1.7	2.1
% LT Debt of Cap.	NA	12.7	11.7	12.2	10.4	6.9	3.4	3.8	4.7	5.6
% Net Inc.of Revs.	NA	15.5	15.7	8.8	15.1	10.4	12.5	12.0	14.7	14.0
% Ret. on Assets	NA	13.0	12.8	7.0	11.5	7.7	9.2	8.5	10.8	11.4
% Ret. on Equity	NA	31.6	32.0	15.4	22.6	14.3	16.7	15.4	19.3	18.9

Data as orig. reptd.; bef. results of disc. opers. and/or spec. items. Per share data adj. for stk. divs. as of ex-div. date. E-Estimated. NA-Not Available. NM-Not Meaningful. NR-Not Ranked.

Office—235 E. 42nd St., New York, NY 10017. **Tel**—(212) 573-2323. **Website**—http://www.pfizer.com **Chrmn & CEO**—W. C. Steere, Jr. **EVP & CFO**—D. L. Shedlarz. **SVP & Secy**—C. L. Clemente. **Investor Contact**—J. R. Gardner. **Dirs**—M. S. Brown, M. A. Burns, G. B. Harvey, C. J. Horner, S. O. Ikenberry, H. P. Kamen, T. G. Labrecque, F. G. Rohatyn, R. J. Simmons, W. C. Steere, Jr., J.-P. Valles. **Transfer Agent**—Co. office. **Registrar**—Mellon Securities Trust Co., NYC. **Incorporated**—in Delaware in 1942. **Empl**— 43,800. **S&P Analyst:** H.B. Saftlas

Procter & Gamble

1868

NYSE Symbol **PG**

In S&P 500

16-FEB-97 Industry: Household Products

Summary: This leading consumer products company markets household and personal care products in more than 140 countries.

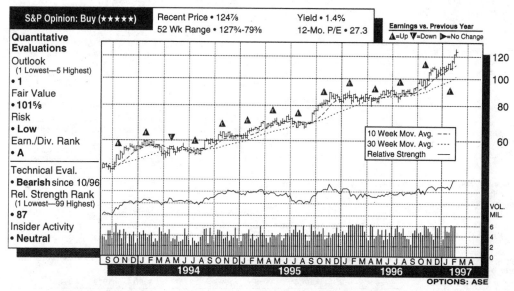

S&P Opinion: Buy (★★★★)	Recent Price • 124⅞	Yield • 1.4%
	52 Wk Range • 127¾-79⅜	12-Mo. P/E • 27.3

Earnings vs. Previous Year ▲=Up ▼=Down ▶=No Change

Quantitative Evaluations

Outlook (1 Lowest—5 Highest)
• **1**

Fair Value
• **101⅝**

Risk
• **Low**

Earn./Div. Rank
• **A**

Technical Eval.
• **Bearish** since 10/96

Rel. Strength Rank (1 Lowest—99 Highest)
• **87**

Insider Activity
• **Neutral**

10 Week Mov. Avg. – – –
30 Week Mov. Avg. ·······
Relative Strength —

OPTIONS: ASE

Overview - 30-JAN-97

Sales should remain in a solid uptrend for the second half of FY 97 (Jun.), fueled by international volume growth, acquisitions, joint ventures, penetration into emerging growth markets, and new products. Despite pricing pressures in Europe where PG is introducing its everyday low price strategy, and higher marketing and advertising costs aimed at supporting new products and increasing or maintaining share, margins should widen on a lower overall cost structure. Lower raw material prices and more efficient distribution should also boost margins, as should an ongoing shift in the sales mix to higher-margin personal, beauty and health care products. Over the next few years, earnings growth should outpace sales growth. Net profits are expected to rise about 12% - 14% annually. Long-term results could be enhanced by widespread use of Olean (Olestra), a calorie-free fat replacement food product that was approved for use in snack foods by the U.S. Food and Drug Administration in 1996.

Valuation - 30-JAN-97

Over the years, PG's shares have trended upward on steady, fairly predictable earnings growth. The shares are now trading at 20 times our estimated earnings per share of $5.30 for FY 98. This price-earnings multiple is toward the high end of PG's historical annual price earnings multiple range. However, given PG's impressive track record, we recommend that the shares be purhased by risk-averse investors who are focused on a longer-term, buy-and-hold strategy and are looking for above-average appreciation potential. A history of annual dividend increases lends additional appeal to the stock, as does the company's increased penetration in fast-growing emerging growth markets. An aggressive share buyback program also lends support to the shares.

Key Stock Statistics

S&P EPS Est. 1997	4.80	Tang. Bk. Value/Share	8.10
P/E on S&P Est. 1997	26.0	Beta	1.15
S&P EPS Est. 1998	5.30	Shareholders	216,300
Dividend Rate/Share	1.80	Market cap. (B)	$ 85.2
Shs. outstg. (M)	682.0	Inst. holdings	46%
Avg. daily vol. (M)	1.355		

Value of $10,000 invested 5 years ago: $ 29,355

Fiscal Year Ending Jun. 30

	1997	1996	1995	1994	1993	1992
Revenues (Million $)						
1Q	8,903	9,027	8,161	7,564	7,880	7,210
2Q	9,142	9,090	8,467	7,788	7,840	7,510
3Q	—	8,587	8,312	7,441	7,350	7,480
4Q	—	8,580	8,494	7,503	7,365	7,170
Yr.	—	35,284	33,434	30,296	30,433	29,360
Earnings Per Share ($)						
1Q	1.39	1.27	1.12	0.95	0.57	0.76
2Q	1.35	1.18	1.06	0.92	0.81	0.73
3Q	E1.15	1.07	0.88	0.66	0.73	0.67
4Q	E0.91	0.77	0.65	0.56	-1.83	0.46
Yr.	E4.80	4.29	3.71	3.09	0.25	2.62

Next earnings report expected: late April

Dividend Data (Dividends have been paid since 1891.)

Amount ($)	Date Decl.	Ex-Div. Date	Stock of Record	Payment Date
0.400	Apr. 09	Apr. 17	Apr. 19	May. 15 '96
0.450	Jul. 10	Jul. 17	Jul. 19	Aug. 15 '96
0.450	Oct. 08	Oct. 16	Oct. 18	Nov. 15 '96
0.450	Jan. 14	Jan. 22	Jan. 24	Feb. 14 '97

A Division of The McGraw·Hill Companies

The Procter & Gamble Company

Business Summary - 30-JAN-97

Procter & Gamble markets a wide range of laundry, cleaning, paper, beauty care, health care, and food and beverage products in more than 140 countries around the world. In July 1991, it acquired Revlon Inc.'s worldwide Max Factor and Betrix lines of cosmetics and fragrances, and in FY 95 (Jun.) it acquired Giorgio of Beverly Hills from Avon and the European tissue business of Vereinigte Papierwerke Schickedanz AG. In early 1993, the company sold its commercial pulp business and exited the 100%-juice business. Contributions by business segment in FY 96 were:

	Sales	Profits
Laundry/cleaning products	31%	37%
Beauty care products	20%	19%
Food & beverage products	12%	11%
Paper	29%	25%
Health care	8%	8%

North America contributed 49% of sales and 65% of net income in FY 96; Europe, the Middle East and Africa, 34% and 22%; Asia, 11% and 7%; and Latin America, 6% and 6%.

Among the more popular laundry and cleaning brands are Ariel, Tide, Cascade, Dawn, Mr. Proper, and Downy. Net sales increased 4.4% in FY 96, year to year.

Beauty care products include Pantene, Vidal Sassoon, Secret, Safeguard, Olay, Cover Girl and Giorgio Beverly Hills. Net sales increased 6.3% in FY 96.

Food and beverage products include Folgers, Jif, Sunny Delight, Pringles, Crisco and Duncan Hines. Net sales increased 2.0% in FY 96.

Paper products include Bounty, Charmin, Always, Whisper, Pampers and Attends. Net sales increased 9.7% in FY 96.

Health care products include Crest, Scope, Metamucil, Vicks and Aleve. Net sales declined 2.3% in FY 96.

Important Developments

Jan. '97—Commenting on results in its FY 97 second quarter, PG said the 14% year-to-year rise in share earnings reflected higher sales from all of the company's categories and substantially wider margins on higher volume and cost savings arising from restructuring efforts. The company said its results reflected building successful brands throughout the world with focus on innovation and consumer value.

Capitalization

Long Term Debt: $4,629,000,000 (9/96).
Preferred Stock: $1,879,000,000.

Per Share Data ($) (Year Ended Jun. 30)	1996	1995	1994	1993	1992	1991	1990	1989	1988	1987
Tangible Bk. Val.	8.10	5.97	7.19	5.20	4.75	4.23	5.67	4.49	6.48	6.00
Cash Flow	6.27	5.53	4.75	1.92	3.97	3.39	3.36	2.81	2.42	1.31
Earnings	4.29	3.71	3.09	0.25	2.62	2.46	2.25	1.78	1.49	0.47
Dividends	1.60	1.40	1.32	1.10	1.02	0.98	0.88	0.75	0.69	0.68
Payout Ratio	37%	38%	43%	449%	39%	39%	39%	41%	46%	144%
Prices - High	111	89½	64⅝	58⅞	55¾	47¾	45⅝	35⅛	22	25⅞
- Low	79⅜	60⅝	51¼	45¼	45⅛	38	30⅞	21⅛	17⅝	15
P/E Ratio - High	26	24	21	NM	21	19	20	20	15	55
- Low	19	16	17	NM	17	15	14	12	12	32
Income Statement Analysis (Million $)										
Revs.	35,284	33,434	30,296	30,433	29,362	27,026	24,081	21,398	19,336	17,000
Oper. Inc.	6,173	5,432	5,432	4,301	3,777	3,549	3,072	2,727	2,429	2,177
Depr.	1,358	1,253	1,134	1,140	910	847	770	688	633	565
Int. Exp.	484	488	482	577	535	412	445	398	332	361
Pretax Inc.	4,669	4,000	3,346	349	349	2,687	2,421	1,939	1,630	617
Eff. Tax Rate	35%	34%	34%	23%	35%	34%	34%	38%	37%	47%
Net Inc.	3,046	2,645	2,211	269	1,872	1,773	1,602	1,206	1,020	327
Balance Sheet & Other Fin. Data (Million $)										
Cash	2,520	2,178	2,656	2,322	1,776	1,384	1,407	1,587	1,065	741
Curr. Assets	10,807	10,842	9,988	9,975	9,366	8,435	7,644	6,578	5,593	4,981
Total Assets	27,730	28,125	25,535	24,935	24,025	20,468	18,487	16,351	14,820	13,715
Curr. Liab.	7,825	8,648	8,040	8,287	7,642	6,733	5,417	4,656	4,224	3,458
LT Debt	4,670	5,161	4,980	5,174	5,223	4,111	3,588	3,698	2,462	2,524
Common Eqty.	9,836	8,676	8,677	7,308	7,085	5,741	6,518	5,215	6,337	5,740
Total Cap.	17,030	16,281	14,159	12,798	15,777	13,157	12,364	11,248	10,121	9,670
Cap. Exp.	2,179	2,146	1,841	1,911	1,911	1,979	1,300	1,029	1,018	990
Cash Flow	4,301	3,796	3,243	1,307	2,688	2,542	2,325	1,878	1,642	881
Curr. Ratio	1.4	1.3	1.2	1.2	1.2	1.3	1.4	1.4	1.3	1.4
% LT Debt of Cap.	27.4	31.7	35.2	40.4	33.1	31.2	29.0	32.9	24.3	26.1
% Net Inc.of Revs.	8.6	7.9	7.3	0.9	6.4	6.6	6.7	5.6	5.3	1.9
% Ret. on Assets	10.9	9.9	8.7	1.1	8.5	9.2	8.9	7.9	7.1	2.4
% Ret. on Equity	31.8	32.7	26.3	2.0	27.7	28.0	25.7	21.1	16.7	5.5

Data as orig. reptd.; bef. results of disc. opers. and/or spec. items. Per share data adj. for stk. divs. as of ex-div. date. E-Estimated. NA-Not Available. NM-Not Meaningful. NR-Not Ranked.

Office—1 Procter & Gamble Plaza, Cincinnati, OH 45202. **Registrar**—PNC Bank, Ohio, Cincinnati. **Tel**—(513) 983-1100. **Chrmn & CEO**—J. E. Pepper. **Pres & COO**—D. I. Jager. **SVP & CFO**—E. G. Nelson. **Secy**—T. L. Overbey. **Treas**—C. C. Daley, Jr. **Investor Contact**—G. A. Dowdell. **Dirs**—E. L. Artzt, N. R. Augustine, D. R. Beall, G. F. Brunner, R. B. Cheney, H. Einsmann, R. J. Ferris, J. T. Gorman, D. I. Jager, C. R. Lee, L. Martin, J. E. Pepper, J. C. Sawhill, J. F. Smith, Jr., R. Snyderman, R. D. Storey, M. v.N. Whitman. **Transfer Agent**—Co. itself. **Incorporated**—in Ohio in 1905. **Empl**— 103,000. **S&P Analyst:** Maureen C. Carini

STANDARD &POOR'S
STOCK REPORTS

Schering-Plough

1985J

NYSE Symbol **SGP**

In S&P 500

18-FEB-97

Industry: Drugs

Summary: This company is a leading producer of prescription and OTC pharmaceuticals and has important interests in sun care, animal health and foot care products.

S&P Opinion: Accumulate (★★★★)	Recent Price • 78⅝	Yield • 1.7%
	52 Wk Range • 80-52½	12-Mo. P/E • 23.8

Quantitative Evaluations

Outlook
(1 Lowest—5 Highest)
• 3

Fair Value
• 75⅜

Risk
• **Low**

Earn./Div. Rank
• **A+**

Technical Eval.
• **Bullish** since 5/96

Rel. Strength Rank
(1 Lowest—99 Highest)
• 85

Insider Activity
• **Neutral**

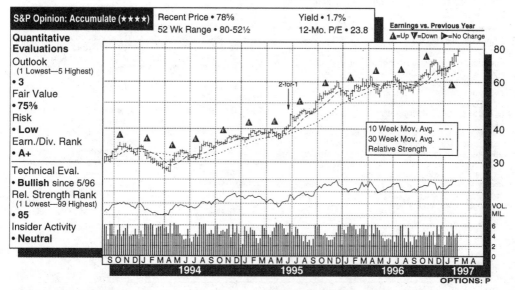

Earnings vs. Previous Year
▲=Up ▼=Down ▶=No Change

10 Week Mov. Avg. ---
30 Week Mov. Avg. ·····
Relative Strength —

OPTIONS: P

Overview - 18-FEB-97

Sales should post another healthy gain in 1997. Despite expected further generic erosion in the important Proventil anti-asthma line (sales of $316 million in 1996), volume should benefit from strong gains in Claritin and Claritin-D nonsedating antihistamine agents ($1.15 billion), Intron A anticancer and anti-infective agent ($524 million) and cardiovascular drugs ($533 million). New products such as Cedax antibiotic, Nasonex allergy drug and Fareston breast cancer treatment should also make meaningful contributions to sales. Modest gains are forecast for the company's dermatological products, animal health items and consumer products. Margins should be well maintained, on improved volume and cost efficiencies. With fewer shares outstanding, EPS should reach $3.70, up from the $3.30 reported for 1996.

Valuation - 18-FEB-97

The shares appreciated with the rest of the drug group in recent months, buoyed by strong earnings momentum and investor preference for recession-resistant drug stocks. Near term results should continue to benefit from growth in Claritin, the No. 1 worldwide antihistamine with 1996 sales of $1.15 billion; Intron A, an important antiviral/anticancer agent; and Vancenase, an inhaled steroid for allergies. New drugs such as Cedax, Nasonex and Fareston should also boost sales. The company's mix of popular prescription drugs and OTC medications, its highly productive R&D program and strict controls on operating costs should provide the basis for continued strong earnings growth in the years ahead. The R&D pipeline includes new treatments for allergies, asthma, cancer, infections and heart disease. The shares merit accumulation for above-average long-term total return.

Key Stock Statistics

S&P EPS Est. 1997	3.70	Tang. Bk. Value/Share	6.07
P/E on S&P Est. 1997	21.3	Beta	1.16
Dividend Rate/Share	1.32	Shareholders	34,100
Shs. outstg. (M)	369.4	Market cap. (B)	$ 29.0
Avg. daily vol. (M)	0.892	Inst. holdings	61%

Value of $10,000 invested 5 years ago: $ 26,935

Fiscal Year Ending Dec. 31

	1996	1995	1994	1993	1992	1991
Revenues (Million $)						
1Q	1,383	1,224	1,162	1,090	1,022	949.0
2Q	1,477	1,333	1,190	1,123	1,020	913.0
3Q	1,382	1,257	1,126	1,062	1,020	888.0
4Q	1,414	1,291	1,180	1,066	994.4	866.0
Yr.	5,656	5,104	4,657	4,341	4,056	3,616
Earnings Per Share ($)						
1Q	0.89	0.77	0.65	0.57	0.48	0.39
2Q	0.86	0.74	0.63	0.54	0.46	0.39
3Q	0.79	0.68	0.59	0.51	0.44	0.37
4Q	0.76	0.66	0.54	0.49	0.42	0.36
Yr.	3.30	2.85	2.41	2.11	1.80	1.51

Next earnings report expected: late April

Dividend Data (Dividends have been paid since 1952.)

Amount ($)	Date Decl.	Ex-Div. Date	Stock of Record	Payment Date
0.330	Apr. 23	May. 01	May. 03	May. 28 '96
0.330	Jun. 17	Jul. 31	Aug. 02	Aug. 27 '96
0.330	Oct. 22	Oct. 30	Nov. 01	Nov. 26 '96
0.330	Jan. 28	Feb. 05	Feb. 07	Feb. 28 '97

Business Summary - 18-FEB-97

Schering-Plough is a leading manufacturer of prescription and over-the-counter (OTC) pharmaceuticals and has interests in sun care, animal health and foot care products. Contributions by business segment in 1995 were:

	Sales	Profits
Pharmaceutical products	88%	90%
Health care products	12%	10%

International operations accounted for 45% of sales and 32% of profits in 1995. R&D equaled 14.1% of sales in 1996 versus 12.9% in 1995.

Respiratory drugs (accounting for 36% of 1995 sales) include Claritin nonsedating antihistamine and Claritin-D, a combination decongestant; Theo-Dur, Proventil and Uni-Dur asthma treatments; and Vancenase allergy nasal products and Vanceril asthma inhaler.

Anti-infectives and anticancer products (20%) consist of Intron-A (alpha-2 interferon), which is marketed for various anticancer and antiviral indications; Cedax, a third-generation cephalosporin antibiotic; Eulexin, a treatment for prostatic cancer; Leucomax, a granulocyte macrophage colony stimulating factor; and Netromycin, an aminoglycoside antibiotic.

Dermatological products (10%) include high-potency steroids such as Diprolene and Diprosone; Elocon, a topical steroid cream and ointment; and Lotrisone, a topical antifungal and anti-inflammatory cream. Cardi-

ovasculars (8%) consist of Imdur, an oral nitrate; Nitro-Dur, a transdermal nitroglycerin patch for angina pectoris; Normodyne, an anti-hypertensive; and K-Dur, a potassium supplement. Other products (13%) include Losec anti-ulcer drug (marketed overseas), Fibre Trim diet aid products, animal health items and other drugs.

Health care products encompass OTC medicines (5%) such as Afrin nasal spray, Chlor-Trimeton allergy tablets, Coricidin and Drixoral cold medications, Correctal laxative and Gyne-Lotrimin for vaginal yeast infections; foot care items (5%) sold under Dr. Scholl's and other names; and Coppertone and other sun care products (3%).

Important Developments

Feb. '97—SGP submitted a New Drug Application to the FDA seeking clearance to market mometasone furoate ointment for the twice-daily treatment of psoriasis. Mometasone furoate is an anti-inflammatory corticosteroid. Sales of SGP's prescription pharmaceuticals rose 13% in 1996, driven by growth in the respiratory, cardiovascular, anti-infective and anticancer categories. Worldwide sales of Claritin expanded 46%, while sales of Intron A increased 21%. Animal health sales rose 3%, but volume in over-the-counter and consumer lines declined 4%.

Capitalization

Long Term Debt: $42,000,000 (9/96).

Per Share Data ($)

(Year Ended Dec. 31)	1996	1995	1994	1993	1992	1991	1990	1989	1988	1987
Tangible Bk. Val.	NA	4.46	3.78	3.61	3.53	2.86	4.31	3.94	3.30	2.95
Cash Flow	NA	3.27	2.82	2.44	2.10	1.77	1.49	1.27	1.08	0.88
Earnings	3.30	2.85	2.41	2.11	1.80	1.51	1.25	1.05	0.87	0.68
Dividends	1.28	1.16	0.99	0.87	0.75	0.63	0.53	0.44	0.35	0.26
Payout Ratio	39%	41%	41%	41%	42%	40%	42%	43%	40%	36%
Prices - High	$73^1/_8$	$60^3/_4$	38	$35^1/_2$	$35^1/_8$	$33^5/_8$	$25^3/_8$	$21^1/_2$	$14^7/_8$	$13^7/_8$
- Low	$50^1/_8$	$35^1/_2$	$27^1/_4$	$25^7/_8$	25	$20^3/_8$	$18^1/_2$	$13^7/_8$	$11^3/_8$	$7^7/_8$
P/E Ratio - High	22	21	16	17	19	22	20	21	17	20
- Low	15	12	11	12	14	14	15	13	13	11

Income Statement Analysis (Million $)

	1996	1995	1994	1993	1992	1991	1990	1989	1988	1987
Revs.	NA	5,104	4,657	4,341	4,056	3,616	3,323	3,158	2,969	2,699
Oper. Inc.	NA	1,609	1,407	1,234	1,124	1,003	832	767	684	590
Depr.	NA	157	158	127	120	115	109	99	95.0	90.0
Int. Exp.	NA	69.0	68.0	61.0	71.0	77.0	89.0	100	124	92.0
Pretax Inc.	NA	1,395	1,213	1,078	954	861	769	646	534	455
Eff. Tax Rate	NA	25%	24%	24%	25%	25%	27%	27%	27%	31%
Net Inc.	NA	1,053	922	825	720	646	565	471	390	316

Balance Sheet & Other Fin. Data (Million $)

	1996	1995	1994	1993	1992	1991	1990	1989	1988	1987
Cash	NA	322	161	429	529	927	920	935	808	786
Curr. Assets	NA	1,956	1,739	1,901	2,013	2,102	2,000	2,047	1,914	1,784
Total Assets	NA	4,665	4,326	4,317	4,157	4,013	4,103	3,614	3,426	3,180
Curr. Liab.	NA	2,362	2,029	2,132	1,969	1,528	1,530	1,214	1,336	1,333
LT Debt	NA	87.0	186	182	184	754	183	186	190	190
Common Eqty.	NA	1,623	1,574	1,582	1,597	1,346	2,081	1,955	1,677	1,443
Total Cap.	NA	1,965	2,006	1,940	1,980	2,286	2,436	2,271	1,988	1,746
Cap. Exp.	NA	294	272	365	403	339	243	186	156	118
Cash Flow	NA	1,210	1,080	952	840	760	674	571	485	406
Curr. Ratio	NA	0.8	0.9	0.9	1.0	1.4	1.3	1.7	1.4	1.3
% LT Debt of Cap.	NA	4.4	9.3	9.4	9.3	33.0	7.5	8.2	9.5	10.9
% Net Inc.of Revs.	NA	20.6	19.8	19.0	17.8	17.9	17.0	14.9	13.1	11.7
% Ret. on Assets	NA	23.4	21.8	19.8	17.7	16.7	14.8	13.4	11.8	10.5
% Ret. on Equity	NA	65.9	59.6	52.7	49.2	39.9	28.3	25.9	24.9	22.3

Data as orig. reptd.; bef. results of disc. opers. and/or spec. items. Per share data adj. for stk. divs. as of ex-div. date. E-Estimated. NA-Not Available. NM-Not Meaningful. NR-Not Ranked.

Office—One Giralda Farms, Madison, NJ 07940-1000. **Tel**—(201) 822-7000.**Fax**—(201) 822-7048. **Chrmn**—R. P. Luciano. **Pres & CEO**—R. J. Kogan. **Sr VP & Investor Contact**—Geraldine U. Foster. **VP & Secy**—W. J. Silbey. **VP-Fin**—J. L. Wyszomierski. **VP-Treas**—E. K. Moore. **Dirs**—H. W. Becherer, H. A. D'Andrade, D. C. Garfield, R. E. Herzlinger, R. J. Kogan, R. P. Luciano, H. B. Morley, C. E. Mundy, Jr., R. de J. Osborne, P. F. Russo, W. A. Schreyer, R. F. W. van Oordt, R. J. Ventres, J. Wood. **Transfer Agent & Registrar**—Bank of New York, NYC. **Incorporated**—in New Jersey in 1970. **Empl**— 20,100. **S&P Analyst:** H. B. Saftlas

16-FEB-97 **Industry:** Conglomerate/diversified

Summary: This company is a diversified manufacturer of institutional, graphics/mail order, industrial and other products.

Quantitative Evaluations

Outlook
(1 Lowest—5 Highest)
• **2+**

Fair Value
• **28⅛**

Risk
• **Low**

Earn./Div. Rank
• **A**

Technical Eval.
• **Bearish** since 2/97

Rel. Strength Rank
(1 Lowest—99 Highest)
• **31**

Insider Activity
• **NA**

Recent Price • 29⅛
52 Wk Range • 32⅛-25⅜

Yield • 2.6%
12-Mo. P/E • 14.1

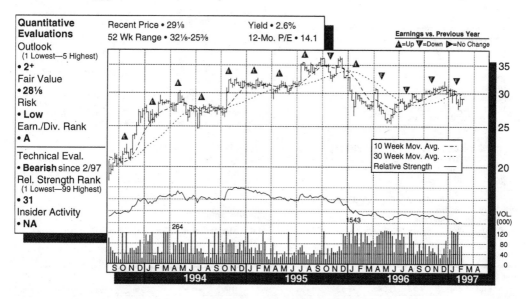

Earnings vs. Previous Year
▲=Up ▼=Down ▶=No Change

10 Week Mov. Avg. ---
30 Week Mov. Avg. ····
Relative Strength ──

Business Profile - 23-JAN-97

Standex seeks growth by acquiring companies that complement and expand current operations. Although results overall have not returned to the high level of the first half of FY 96 (Jun.), they have rebounded considerably from the disappointing second half of FY 96. While SXI continues to face slowness in its European operations and softness in certain higher margin seasonal product lines, management still expects FY 97 to be another good year for the company. A 5.6% dividend hike in October 1996 marked the 33rd dividend increase in 32 years.

Operational Review - 23-JAN-97

Based on a brief report, net sales in the six months ended December 31, 1996, declined 1.3%, as SXI's European divisions continued to be impacted by slow economic conditions, and growth in the food service group was slower than anticipated. Pretax income decreased 13%. Following taxes at 37.9%, versus 36.3%, net income was off 15%, to $15,669,000 ($1.16 a share, on 4.2% fewer shares), from $18,486,000 ($1.31).

Stock Performance - 14-FEB-97

In the past 30 trading days, SXI's shares have declined 2%, compared to a 8% rise in the S&P 500. Average trading volume for the past five days was 14,060 shares, compared with the 40-day moving average of 24,244 shares.

Key Stock Statistics

Dividend Rate/Share	0.76	Shareholders	4,400
Shs. outstg. (M)	13.4	Market cap. (B)	$0.390
Avg. daily vol. (M)	0.022	Inst. holdings	48%
Tang. Bk. Value/Share	8.93		
Beta	0.01		

Value of $10,000 invested 5 years ago: $ 28,017

Fiscal Year Ending Jun. 30

	1997	1996	1995	1994	1993	1992
Revenues (Million $)						
1Q	140.2	142.2	140.6	127.3	127.0	113.0
2Q	152.3	154.1	143.9	133.5	136.0	127.0
3Q	—	130.3	141.6	130.9	118.0	118.0
4Q	—	136.0	143.2	137.7	125.6	120.0
Yr.	—	562.7	569.3	529.4	506.3	477.0
Earnings Per Share ($)						
1Q	0.56	0.66	0.80	0.41	0.33	0.25
2Q	0.60	0.65	0.62	0.46	0.40	0.33
3Q	—	0.41	0.56	0.41	0.32	0.28
4Q	—	0.49	0.66	0.50	0.42	0.36
Yr.	—	2.21	2.64	1.78	1.47	1.23

Next earnings report expected: mid April

Dividend Data (Dividends have been paid since 1964.)

Amount ($)	Date Decl.	Ex-Div. Date	Stock of Record	Payment Date
0.180	Apr. 24	May. 02	May. 06	May. 25 '96
0.180	Jul. 31	Aug. 08	Aug. 12	Aug. 24 '96
0.190	Oct. 29	Nov. 05	Nov. 08	Nov. 25 '96
0.190	Jan. 29	Feb. 06	Feb. 10	Feb. 25 '97

A Division of The **McGraw-Hill** Companies

STANDARD
&POOR'S
STOCK REPORTS

Standex International Corporation

2122
16-FEB-97

Business Summary - 23-JAN-97

Standex International Corporation is a diversified manufacturer, producing and marketing a wide variety of products. Contributions by industry segment in FY 96 (Jun.) were:

	Sales	Profits
Institutional products	45%	41%
Graphics/mail order	28%	24%
Industrial products	27%	35%

The institutional products segment custom-designs and manufactures casters and wheels, chiropractic and traction tables, HVAC pipe duct and fittings, feeding systems for hospitals, schools and correctional institutions; makes or distributes a variety of electric slicing, meat grinding and vegetable cutting machines for commercial use, as well as heavy-duty food waste disposers mainly for the fast food industry; manufactures refrigerated and non-refrigerated storage and display cabinets; fabricates and installs walk-in coolers and freezers, as well as large refrigerated warehouses; and makes commercial barbecue ovens, china and cookware for restaurants; and a wide variety of metal fabricated products and specialty hardware.

The graphics/mail order segment manufactures mechanical binding systems; designs and builds punch-ing and binding equipment; and produces a broad range of custom continuous forms for business, as well as specialized forms and election supplies for municipal governments. It also publishes nondenominational religious curricula and Vacation Bible School (VBS) material; and mail order markets grapefruit and other food items.

The industrial products segment manufactures hydraulic cylinders and metal spinning components, engraved embossing rolls and plates for the texturization of paper, plastics, metals, rubber and other materials; makes electronic components and assemblies; produces machinery used to emboss ferrous and nonferrous metals; and makes other machinery.

In August 1995, Standex acquired DSC Technologies, Inc. The Crystal Lakes, Ill., company develops monitoring, data-acquisition and radio frequency identification systems for the transportation industry.

Important Developments

Oct. '96—Standex acquired Fellowship Bookstores, Inc., a chain of three Christian bookstores located in the Fresno, CA area with annual sales of about $4.8 million, for an undisclosed sum of cash and stock.

Capitalization

Long Term Debt: $122,724,000 (9/96).

Per Share Data ($)

(Year Ended Jun. 30)	1996	1995	1994	1993	1992	1991	1990	1989	1988	1987
Tangible Bk. Val.	8.93	8.36	7.04	6.85	7.11	6.69	6.44	5.90	6.30	6.02
Cash Flow	3.10	3.49	2.54	2.25	1.89	1.62	1.62	1.46	0.98	1.07
Earnings	2.21	2.64	1.78	1.47	1.23	1.05	1.07	1.01	0.55	0.71
Dividends	0.71	0.63	0.52	0.43	0.38	0.36	0.33	0.30	0.28	0.26
Payout Ratio	32%	24%	29%	29%	28%	32%	30%	28%	48%	37%
Prices - High	32⅞	36¾	32⅝	27¾	19	13⅝	13⅞	13¼	12	10⅝
- Low	25⅜	29	24⅝	18½	11	10⅛	10⅜	10¼	7⅛	6¼
P/E Ratio - High	15	14	18	19	15	13	13	13	22	15
- Low	11	11	14	13	9	10	10	10	13	9

Income Statement Analysis (Million $)

	1996	1995	1994	1993	1992	1991	1990	1989	1988	1987
Revs.	563	569	529	506	477	482	460	444	430	409
Oper. Inc.	69.0	72.0	58.1	55.3	49.2	51.1	50.7	50.4	47.7	42.4
Depr.	12.5	12.4	11.8	12.9	11.9	12.0	11.3	10.3	10.2	9.1
Int. Exp.	9.0	8.4	6.9	5.6	6.6	7.9	8.3	6.8	5.4	4.6
Pretax Inc.	48.1	57.8	42.2	37.5	33.7	32.6	34.8	35.6	22.4	29.7
Eff. Tax Rate	36%	34%	36%	36%	35%	38%	38%	37%	42%	42%
Net Inc.	30.7	38.3	27.1	24.0	21.9	20.2	21.7	22.3	13.1	17.4

Balance Sheet & Other Fin. Data (Million $)

	1996	1995	1994	1993	1992	1991	1990	1989	1988	1987
Cash	5.1	9.0	5.0	7.5	10.9	7.3	8.0	7.9	12.2	9.4
Curr. Assets	207	220	197	182	186	177	182	170	165	159
Total Assets	335	343	324	309	317	297	298	277	276	267
Curr. Liab.	68.5	77.2	70.2	73.2	74.5	72.9	66.8	61.8	57.0	49.4
LT Debt	114	112	113	94.4	86.7	70.1	73.0	65.0	48.8	45.9
Common Eqty.	135	132	119	122	137	139	142	137	156	160
Total Cap.	261	256	246	229	236	220	225	211	217	215
Cap. Exp.	15.3	12.0	13.2	10.7	15.7	13.8	12.7	12.7	15.0	15.2
Cash Flow	43.2	50.7	38.9	36.9	33.8	32.2	33.1	32.6	23.3	26.5
Curr. Ratio	3.0	2.8	2.8	2.5	2.5	2.4	2.7	2.7	2.9	3.2
% LT Debt of Cap.	43.6	43.7	46.0	41.2	36.7	31.9	32.4	30.8	22.5	21.3
% Net Inc.of Revs.	5.5	6.8	5.1	4.7	4.6	4.2	4.7	5.0	3.0	4.2
% Ret. on Assets	9.1	11.5	8.8	8.0	7.4	7.0	7.8	8.5	5.0	6.9
% Ret. on Equity	23.0	30.5	23.1	19.4	16.6	14.9	16.0	16.0	8.6	11.4

Data as orig. reptd.; bef. results of disc. opers. and/or spec. items. Per share data adj. for stk. divs. as of ex-div. date. E-Estimated. NA-Not Available. NM-Not Meaningful. NR-Not Ranked.

Office—6 Manor Parkway, Salem, NH 03079. **Tel**—(603) 893-9701. **Chrmn**—T. L. King. **Pres & CEO**—E. J. Trainor. **SVP, CFO & Investor Contact**—Lindsay M. Sedwick. **Secy**—R. H. Booth. **Dirs**—J. Bolten, Jr., W. L. Brown, D. R. Crichton, S. S. Dennis III, T. H. DeWitt, W. F. Greeley, D. B. Hogan, T. L. King, C. K. Landry, H. N. Muller III, S. Sackel, L. M. Sedwick. E. J. Trainor. **Transfer Agent & Registrar**—Boston EquiServe, Boston. **Incorporated**—in Ohio in 1955; reincorporated in Delaware in 1975.**Empl**— 4,800. **S&P Analyst:** D.P.B.

16-FEB-97

Industry: Banking

Summary: This multi-state bank holding company, with approximately $9.9 billion in assets, operates 263 offices in Ohio, Kentucky and Indiana.

S&P Opinion: Hold (★★★)		
Recent Price • 39⅞	Yield • 1.6%	
52 Wk Range • 40-20⅜	12-Mo. P/E • 22.3	

Quantitative Evaluations

Outlook
(1 Lowest—5 Highest)
• 1+

Fair Value
• 32½

Risk
• Low

Earn./Div. Rank
• A+

Technical Eval.
• **Bullish** since 2/95

Rel. Strength Rank
(1 Lowest—99 Highest)
• 95

Insider Activity
• **Favorable**

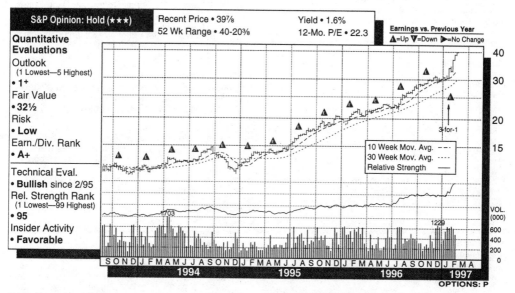

Earnings vs. Previous Year
▲=Up ▼=Down ▶=No Change

10 Week Mov. Avg. - - -
30 Week Mov. Avg. ·······
Relative Strength ——

3-for-1

VOL. (000)

1994   1995   1996   1997

OPTIONS: P

Overview - 29-JAN-97

Star Banc's EPS increased 19% in 1996, meeting our estimate of $1.79 (as adjusted). The strong results reflected growth in net interest and noninterest income, together with diligent expense control. We expect similar results for this well managed organization in 1997. While loan growth of 8.8% was good, the contribution to earnings from this growth was more pronounced, as STB's net interest margin expanded to 4.78%, from 4.44% in 1995. Loans should continue to grow at a high single digit pace in 1997, funded by growth in low cost demand deposits and the sale of investment securities. Star Banc is fostering a more aggressive sales culture in areas such as cash management and trust businesses, in an effort to boost fee-based revenues. As a result, we expect noninterest income, which was up 24% in 1996, to continue to increase over grow 20% in coming quarters. Directors recently increased the company's stock repurchase plan to 9 million shares (10% of the shares outstanding, as adjusted) over the next three years.

Valuation - 29-JAN-97

Star Banc's shares enjoyed a banner year in 1996, rising over 56%, more than twice as much as the S&P 500 Index. As a result, the shares were recently trading at over 15X our 1997 EPS estimate of $2.07 (as adjusted), at the high end of the historical range and significantly above regional bank multiples. Given Star's record of outstanding performance and its prospects for continued strength in 1997, we believe that the stock deserves a premium valuation. However, after the run-up in price in 1996, the shares are fully valued at current levels, and we expect the stock to be only a market performer over the next six to 12 months.

Key Stock Statistics

S&P EPS Est. 1997	2.07	Tang. Bk. Value/Share	6.59
P/E on S&P Est. 1997	19.3	Beta	0.91
Dividend Rate/Share	0.63	Shareholders	7,900
Shs. outstg. (M)	87.4	Market cap. (B)	$ 3.5
Avg. daily vol. (M)	0.146	Inst. holdings	36%

Value of $10,000 invested 5 years ago: $ 55,333

Fiscal Year Ending Dec. 31

	1996	1995	1994	1993	1992	1991
Revenues (Million $)						
1Q	218.5	204.4	156.0	157.5	159.7	161.5
2Q	223.0	208.5	162.8	157.5	155.9	160.5
3Q	230.6	213.7	172.4	157.4	164.3	171.2
4Q	—	221.9	195.5	158.6	162.0	166.0
Yr.	—	848.5	686.7	631.1	641.9	659.2
Earnings Per Share ($)						
1Q	0.43	0.36	0.31	0.28	0.20	0.17
2Q	0.45	0.37	0.32	0.28	0.22	0.19
3Q	0.43	0.38	0.33	0.26	0.23	0.18
4Q	0.48	0.40	0.34	0.30	0.21	0.20
Yr.	1.79	1.52	1.30	1.12	0.86	0.75

Next earnings report expected: early April

Dividend Data (Dividends have been paid since 1863.)

Amount ($)	Date Decl.	Ex-Div. Date	Stock of Record	Payment Date
0.470	Jun. 11	Jun. 26	Jun. 28	Jul. 15 '96
0.470	Sep. 10	Sep. 26	Sep. 30	Oct. 15 '96
0.470	Dec. 10	Dec. 27	Dec. 31	Jan. 15 '97
3-for-1	Dec. 10	Jan. 16	Dec. 31	Jan. 15 '97

A Division of The McGraw·Hill Companies

Business Summary - 29-JAN-97

Star Banc Corporation is a bank holding company that operates 263 branches in central, southern and northern Ohio, northern Kentucky and eastern Indiana. Total loans outstanding, net of unearned interest, were $6.93 billion at year-end 1995, versus $6.25 billion a year earlier. Loans were divided as follows:

	1995	1994
Retail	35%	32%
Commercial	28%	30%
Residential mortgage	18%	19%
Commercial mortgage	16%	16%
Real estate construction	4%	4%

The reserve for loan losses at December 31, 1995, was $106,909,000 ($95,979,000 a year earlier), equal to 1.54% (1.54%) of loans outstanding (net of unearned income). Net chargeoffs in 1995 were $14,171,000 ($11,549,000 in 1994), or 0.21% (0.20%) of average loans. Nonperforming assets (including loans on nonaccrual status, past due 90 days or more or renegotiated, plus other real estate owned) totaled $39,968,000 at the end of 1995 ($38,044,000 a year earlier), equal to 0.58% (0.61%) of loans (net of unearned interest) and other real estate owned.

Total deposits of $7.69 billion at the end of 1995 were apportioned: noninterest-bearing 18%, savings and NOW 26%, money market 12%, time deposits of $100,000 and over 5%, and all other time deposits 39%.

The company has four wholly owned nonbank subsidiaries: First National Cincinnati Corp.; Star Banc Center Company, which owns and operates Star Banc Center, an office complex in downtown Cincinnati; Star Banc Finance, Inc., which offers consumer finance products and services; and Miami Valley Insurance Co., which issues credit life and accident and health insurance.

Important Developments

Jan. '97—The bank said net chargeoffs were $9.0 million (0.48% of average loans) in the 1996 fourth quarter, up from $4.8 million (0.27%) in the 1995 period, continuing a two-year uptrend. STB added that it expects the level to continue to rise, because of an increased proportion of consumer loans in its portfolio.

Dec. '96—Directors approved a three-for-one stock split, effective in January 1997. Directors also increased the company's stock repurchase plan to 9 million shares (10% of the shares outstanding, as adjusted) over the next three years.

Capitalization

Long Term Debt: $148,556,000 (9/96).

Per Share Data ($)

(Year Ended Dec. 31)	1996	1995	1994	1993	1992	1991	1990	1989	1988	1987
Tangible Bk. Val.	NA	6.57	6.07	6.77	5.99	5.69	5.44	5.34	4.98	4.75
Earnings	1.79	1.52	1.30	1.12	0.86	0.75	0.74	0.67	0.64	0.56
Dividends	0.63	0.53	0.47	0.39	0.35	0.33	0.32	0.29	0.27	0.26
Payout Ratio	35%	35%	36%	35%	40%	45%	43%	44%	43%	46%
Prices - High	31⅜	20¾	14⅞	13⅛	13⅛	9⅛	7¾	9	7¼	8⅜
- Low	18¾	12⅛	11⅛	11	8⅛	5	4⅞	6⅛	5⅞	5⅝
P/E Ratio - High	18	14	12	12	15	12	10	13	11	15
- Low	10	8	9	10	9	7	7	9	9	10

Income Statement Analysis (Million $)

	1996	1995	1994	1993	1992	1991	1990	1989	1988	1987
Net Int. Inc.	NA	378	346	323	308	269	247	228	206	156
Tax Equiv. Adj.	NA	4.0	3.1	3.3	4.5	5.9	7.3	8.8	10.0	13.8
Non Int. Inc.	NA	136	117	113	100	84.1	76.4	71.3	63.7	58.5
Loan Loss Prov.	NA	25.1	24.4	33.0	40.9	39.9	40.4	35.4	25.9	21.8
% Exp/Op Revs.	NA	55	56	57	62	60	58	60	61	60
Pretax Inc.	NA	205	178	153	114	96.0	92.7	80.2	73.7	57.4
Eff. Tax Rate	NA	33%	35%	34%	33%	31%	30%	28%	25%	28%
Net Inc.	NA	137	117	100	76.1	65.8	64.9	58.0	55.4	41.5
% Net Int. Marg.	NA	4.44	4.56	4.67	4.70	4.69	4.58	4.52	4.53	4.48

Balance Sheet & Other Fin. Data (Million $)

	1996	1995	1994	1993	1992	1991	1990	1989	1988	1987
Earning Assets:										
Money Mkt	NA	22.5	56.7	173	448	298	338	271	416	366
Inv. Securities	NA	1,703	2,328	1,600	1,647	959	821	820	872	643
Com'l Loans	NA	2,235	2,332	1,790	1,731	1,685	1,799	1,753	1,659	1,299
Other Loans	NA	4,789	3,917	3,550	3,308	3,227	2,826	2,592	2,291	1,802
Total Assets	NA	9,573	9,391	7,637	7,715	6,646	6,295	5,949	5,657	4,533
Demand Deposits	NA	1,372	1,215	1,201	1,137	936	880	846	825	832
Time Deposits	NA	6,322	6,149	4,815	5,266	4,493	4,250	4,127	3,898	2,832
LT Debt	NA	161	166	51.7	56.8	62.9	31.9	35.4	36.9	21.6
Common Eqty.	NA	820	716	661	587	537	500	463	430	349
% Ret. on Assets	NA	1.4	1.4	1.3	1.1	1.0	1.1	1.0	1.1	1.0
% Ret. on Equity	NA	17.8	16.8	15.9	13.3	12.5	13.4	13.0	13.4	12.3
% Loan Loss Resv.	NA	1.5	1.5	1.6	1.6	1.5	1.5	1.4	1.3	1.3
% Loans/Deposits	NA	90.0	84.9	88.0	78.0	89.5	88.9	85.8	82.3	83.2
% Equity to Assets	NA	8.1	8.4	8.3	7.8	8.2	8.0	7.9	8.0	7.9

Data as orig. reptd.; bef. results of disc opers. and/or spec. items. Per share data adj. for stk. divs. as of ex-div. date. E-Estimated. NA-Not Available. NM-Not Meaningful. NR-Not Ranked.

Office—425 Walnut St., Cincinnati, OH 45202. **Tel**—(513) 632-4000. **Chrmn, Pres & CEO**—J. A. Grundhofer. **EVP & CFO**—D. M. Moffett. **EVP & Secy**—T. J. Lakin. **VP & Investor Contact**—Steve Dale (513-632-4524). **Dirs**—J. R. Bridgeland Jr., L. L. Browning Jr., V. B. Buyniski, S. M. Cassidy, R. R. Clark, V. A. Coombe, J. C. Dannemiller, J. A. Grundhofer, J. P. Hayden Jr., R. L. Howe, T. J. Klinedinst, C. S. Mechem Jr., D. J. Meyer, D. B. O'Maley, O. M. Owens, T. E. Petry, W. C. Portman, O. W. Waddell. **Transfer Agent**—Star Bank, N.A., Cincinnati. **Incorporated**—in Delaware in 1973; lead bank chartered in 1863. **Empl**—3,920. **S&P Analyst:** Brendan McGovern

16-FEB-97 Industry: Finance

Summary: This major financial intermediary serves the education credit market, buying and servicing student loans.

S&P Opinion: Hold (★★★)	Recent Price • 108¾	Yield • 1.6%
	52 Wk Range • 113¼-66	12-Mo. P/E • 14.7

Quantitative Evaluations

Outlook (1 Lowest—5 Highest)
• **5+**

Fair Value
• **132¾**

Risk
• **Average**

Earn./Div. Rank
• **A**

Technical Eval.
• **Bullish** since 10/96

Rel. Strength Rank (1 Lowest—99 Highest)
• **81**

Insider Activity
• **NA**

Earnings vs. Previous Year
▲=Up ▼=Down ▶=No Change

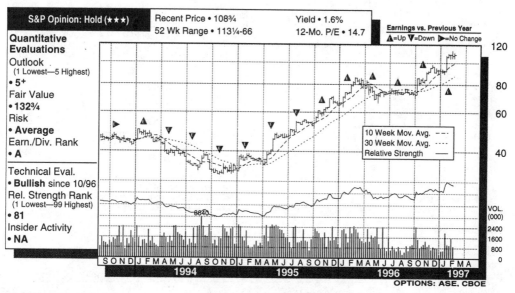

10 Week Mov. Avg. ---
30 Week Mov. Avg. .....
Relative Strength ——

OPTIONS: ASE, CBOE

Overview - 22-JAN-97

Earnings are expected to improve in 1997. Student loan purchases could grow to $10.3 billion, from 1996's $9.9 billion, reflecting greater penetration of the school market and growth in the size of the overall market resulting from more liberal eligibility requirements. Margins on student loans have been reduced. In a higher interest rate environment, floor income, or income SLM realizes on certain loans in a low rate environment, will be virtually nil. Warehousing advances should decline, as the company has chosen to deemphasize this low-margin business. Cost savings are anticipated from staff reductions in virtually all areas, and from the outsourcing of certain data processing functions. Credit losses should remain negligible, because nearly all of SLM's student loans are backed directly or indirectly by the government. EPS should continue to benefit from large but declining share repurchases.

Valuation - 22-JAN-97

The stock of this government-sponsored enterprise is expected to be an average performer for the foreseeable future. The stock was recently trading at about 13X estimated 1996 EPS, about average for a financial stock. Although this multiple may appear low, since the company has virtually no credit or interest rate risk and typically generates a high return on shareholders' equity, we hesitate to recommend the shares for several reasons. First, if shareholders approve a change to recharter SLM as a private corporation, it is not clear whether the company would be successful in any new lines of business it chose to enter. In addition, the threat of direct lending by the U.S. government, although less than it was several years ago, still represents a considerable challenge.

Key Stock Statistics

S&P EPS Est. 1997	7.70	Tang. Bk. Value/Share	15.03
P/E on S&P Est. 1997	14.1	Beta	1.40
Dividend Rate/Share	1.76	Shareholders	25,000
Shs. outstg. (M)	57.7	Market cap. (B)	$ 6.3
Avg. daily vol. (M)	0.224	Inst. holdings	85%

Value of $10,000 invested 5 years ago: $ 16,727

Fiscal Year Ending Dec. 31

	1996	1995	1994	1993	1992	1991
Revenues (Million $)						
1Q	840.6	915.8	595.0	624.6	676.7	837.2
2Q	821.1	924.0	660.7	591.2	674.8	784.4
3Q	820.5	926.7	753.1	588.6	648.6	783.4
4Q	905.3	927.1	842.8	613.1	614.7	716.7
Yr.	3,590	3,694	2,852	2,417	2,615	3,122
Earnings Per Share ($)						
1Q	1.82	1.17	1.42	1.62	1.01	0.83
2Q	1.79	1.20	1.30	1.56	1.30	0.87
3Q	1.79	1.28	1.19	1.53	1.53	0.90
4Q	2.01	1.76	1.10	1.70	1.41	0.95
Yr.	7.41	5.34	5.03	6.41	5.24	3.55

Next earnings report expected: late April

Dividend Data (Dividends have been paid since 1983.)

Amount ($)	Date Decl.	Ex-Div. Date	Stock of Record	Payment Date
0.400	May. 17	Jun. 04	Jun. 06	Jun. 20 '96
0.400	Jul. 19	Sep. 03	Sep. 05	Sep. 19 '96
0.440	Nov. 22	Dec. 03	Dec. 05	Dec. 19 '96
0.440	Jan. 24	Feb. 24	Feb. 26	Mar. 13 '97

Business Summary - 22-JAN-97

Student Loan Marketing Association (Sallie Mae) is a corporation established by Congress in 1972 to purchase student loans insured under federally sponsored programs and to make secured loans to providers of education credit. The company also finances academic plant and equipment. In essence, the company's mission is to promote higher education and improve the skill levels of American workers.

The company makes a secondary market for student loans by buying such loans from various lenders. Student loans consist principally of loans originated under the Federal Family Education Loan Program (FFELP) and the Health Education Assistance Loan Program (HEAL). On most FFELP loans, the U.S. pays interest on loans while the student is in school, including a special allowance. This allowance, together with stated interest on the loans, provides for an interest rate of 3.25% to 3.50% over the 91-day treasury bill rate. SLM buys most loans after borrowers graduate. In 1996, Sallie Mae purchased $9.9 billion of student loans, versus $9.4 billion the year before.

Warehousing advances are secured loans made by Sallie Mae to financial and educational institutions to fund certain student loans and other forms of education-related credit. Warehousing advances totaled $2.8 billion at December 31, 1996, down from $3.9 billion a year earlier.

In August 1993, Congress passed the Administration's Budget Reconciliation package. The bill provides for a phase-in of direct student loan lending over a period of several years, which could have a material adverse effect on Sallie Mae. One goal of the legislation was for the government to make 60% of guaranteed student loans by the 1998-99 school year.

Important Developments

Jan. '97—Sallie Mae attributed strong earnings for the 1996 fourth quarter and full year, nothwithstanding the increased impact of direct lending, to the following: strong growth in managed student loans, higher income related to student loan securitization and lower servicing costs, offset somewhat by additions to reserves.

Capitalization

Short Term Debt: $22,156,548,000 (12/96).
Long Term Debt: $22,606,226,000. (12/96).
Adj. Rate Cum. Pfd.: 4,277,650 shs. ($50 par).

Per Share Data ($) (Year Ended Dec. 31)	1996	1995	1994	1993	1992	1991	1990	1989	1988	1987
Tangible Bk. Val.	NA	15.03	17.10	12.69	11.25	10.09	9.35	8.35	6.45	4.96
Earnings	7.41	5.34	5.03	6.41	5.24	3.55	2.96	2.53	2.14	1.66
Dividends	1.70	1.51	1.42	1.25	1.05	0.85	0.59	0.41	0.24	0.16
Payout Ratio	23%	28%	28%	20%	20%	24%	20%	16%	11%	10%
Prices - High	98 1/4	70 7/8	49 7/8	75 1/4	76	76	56 1/2	53 1/2	34 1/2	35 7/8
- Low	63 1/4	32 7/8	31 1/4	39 7/8	59	43 5/8	32 3/4	33 3/8	28	24 3/8
P/E Ratio - High	13	13	10	12	15	21	19	22	16	22
- Low	9	6	6	6	11	12	11	13	13	15
Income Statement Analysis (Million $)										
Int. Mtgs.	NA	2,974	2,351	2,031	2,072	2,268	3,503	2,275	1,729	1,324
Int. Invest.	NA	719	500	387	543	854	922	894	443	259
Int. Exp.	NA	3,021	2,142	1,481	1,812	2,562	3,024	2,751	1,799	1,269
Guaranty Fees	NA	Nil	Nil	Nil	Nil	Nil	Nil	Nil	Nil	Nil
Loan Loss Prov.	NA	Nil	17.0	16.5	36.2	53.2	31.1	16.9	NA	NA
Admin. Exp.	NA	161	130	109	101	31.1	79.0	70.0	62.0	50.0
Pretax Inc.	NA	512	579	827	701	469	400	348	310	262
Eff. Tax Rate	NA	28%	29%	31%	31%	27%	25%	26%	27%	31%
Net Inc.	NA	371	412	567	487	345	301	258	225	181
Balance Sheet & Other Fin. Data (Million $)										
Mtges.	NA	39,514	38,951	35,197	33,447	31,801	28,770	24,630	21,191	18,400
Inv.	NA	7,614	10,435	9,157	10,094	6,337	4,221	2,522	3,104	NA
Cash & Equiv.	NA	1,253	2,262	1,113	1,974	6,040	7,030	7,317	3,464	NA
Total Assets	NA	50,002	52,961	46,509	46,621	45,320	41,124	35,488	28,628	22,864
ST Debt	NA	17,447	16,016	13,619	13,716	11,986	14,801	14,965	9,820	NA
LT Debt	NA	30,083	34,319	30,925	30,724	31,153	24,243	18,623	17,163	21,443
Equity	NA	867	1,257	1,066	1,006	936	879	823	581	460
% Ret. on Assets	NA	0.8	0.8	1.2	1.1	0.8	0.8	0.8	0.9	0.9
% Ret. on Equity	NA	35.0	35.5	53.7	49.1	36.5	32.9	31.7	41.0	38.9
Equity/Assets Ratio	NA	2.1	2.7	2.2	2.1	2.1	2.2	2.2	NA	NA
Price Times Book Value:										
Hi	NA	4.7	2.9	5.9	6.8	7.5	6.0	6.4	5.3	7.2
Low	NA	2.2	1.8	3.1	5.2	4.3	3.5	4.0	4.3	4.9

Data as orig. reptd.; bef. results of disc opers. and/or spec. items. Per share data adj. for stk. divs. as of ex-div. date. EPS for 3Q 1995 are for 9 mos. E-Estimated. NA-Not Available. NM-Not Meaningful. NR-Not Ranked.

Established—in 1972 by a 1965 Act of Congress, as amended. **Office**—1050 Thomas Jefferson St., N.W., Washington, DC 20007. **Tel**—(202) 333-8000. **Pres & CEO**—L. A. Hough. **VP & Secy**—A. M. Plubell. **EVP & CFO**—D. B. McGlone. **VP & Investor Contact**—Leeny Oberg (202-298-3144). **Dirs-Representing General Public:**— M. N. Berger, K. E. Durmer, D. S. Gilleland, R. T. Montoya, J. E. Moore, I. Natividad, R. J. Thayer. **Representing Financial Institutions:**—D. A. Daberko, C. L. Daley, T. H. Jacobsen, A. L. Lord, J. E. Rohr, J. W. Spiegel, D. J. Vitale. **Representing Educational Institutions:**— W. Arceneaux (Chrmn), J. E. Brandon, R. F. Hunt, B. J. Lambert III, A. A. Porter, Jr., S. L. Shapiro, R. H. Waterfield. **Transfer Agent & Registrar**—Chemical Bank, NYC. **Empl**— 4,863. **S&P Analyst:** Paul L. Huberman, CFA

STANDARD
&POOR'S
STOCK REPORTS

SunTrust Banks

2168M

NYSE Symbol **STI**

In S&P 500

16-FEB-97 Industry: Banking

Summary: This bank holding company, the 19th largest in the U.S., operates more than 700 full-service branch offices in Florida, Georgia, Tennessee and Alabama.

| S&P Opinion: Hold (★★★) | Recent Price • 53⅝ | Yield • 1.7% |
| | 52 Wk Range • 54¾-33¼ | 12-Mo. P/E • 19.4 |

Quantitative Evaluations

Outlook
(1 Lowest—5 Highest)
• **1+**

Fair Value
• **45**

Risk
• **Low**

Earn./Div. Rank
• **A+**

Technical Eval.
• **Bullish** since 1/95

Rel. Strength Rank
(1 Lowest—99 Highest)
• **79**

Insider Activity
• **Neutral**

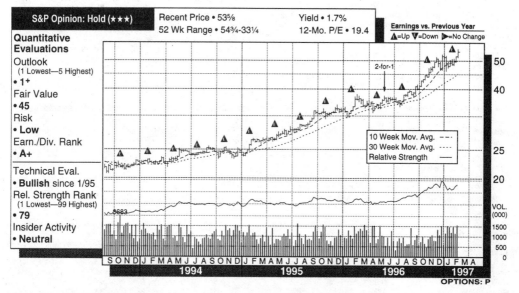

Earnings vs. Previous Year
▲=Up ▼=Down ▶=No Change

10 Week Mov. Avg. - - -
30 Week Mov. Avg. · · · ·
Relative Strength —

OPTIONS: P

Overview - 20-JAN-97

Loan growth recently accelerated slightly into the low double-digits and is expected to continue at that pace into 1997, as STI's regional service territory remains among the healthiest in the nation. The net interest margin narrowed somewhat in 1996, reflecting a shift to more expensive sources of funds. A stabilizing margin entering 1997 should lead to a more pronounced contribution from loan growth. Credit quality remains strong, with the allowance for loan losses at 342% of nonperforming loans at December 31, 1996. Demonstrating STI's conservative loss reserve posture, the loan loss provision in 1996 continued to exceed the level of net chargeoffs by a wide margin, leading to a further build-up of loss reserves. Growth in noninterest income, led by trust income and service charges, reflects further success of the company's growth initiatives, although expenses to support such initiatives will also rise. Overall, earnings are expected to rise about 11% in 1997.

Valuation - 20-JAN-97

Earnings should continue to benefit from above average loan growth from an attractive service territory and stabilizing margins, although expenses to support growth initiatives will limit the overall earnings improvement. Based on projected earnings growth and an average dividend yield, the shares appear adequately valued at 16 times our 1997 earnings estimate of $3.05 a share. Due to its significant stake in Coca-Cola Co., which provides hefty dividend income, the shares typically trade at a premium valuation to other regional banks.

Key Stock Statistics

S&P EPS Est. 1997	3.05	Tang. Bk. Value/Share	20.18
P/E on S&P Est. 1997	17.6	Beta	0.96
Dividend Rate/Share	0.90	Shareholders	29,000
Shs. outstg. (M)	223.0	Market cap. (B)	$ 12.0
Avg. daily vol. (M)	0.286	Inst. holdings	47%

Value of $10,000 invested 5 years ago: $ 30,270

Fiscal Year Ending Dec. 31

	1996	1995	1994	1993	1992	1991
Revenues (Million $)						
1Q	994.2	903.4	767.2	774.4	802.0	853.4
2Q	998.6	932.7	798.3	770.8	786.2	853.2
3Q	1,018	942.5	825.8	772.8	764.8	832.6
4Q	1,054	961.8	860.9	770.7	757.2	821.4
Yr.	4,064	3,740	3,252	3,089	3,110	3,361
Earnings Per Share ($)						
1Q	0.66	0.59	0.52	0.45	0.39	0.35
2Q	0.68	0.61	0.54	0.47	0.41	0.36
3Q	0.70	0.63	0.55	0.48	0.42	0.36
4Q	0.72	0.64	0.57	0.49	0.43	0.38
Yr.	2.76	2.47	2.18	1.89	1.64	1.45

Next earnings report expected: early April

Dividend Data (Dividends have been paid since 1985.)

Amount ($)	Date Decl.	Ex-Div. Date	Stock of Record	Payment Date
0.200	Apr. 16	May. 29	Jun. 01	Jun. 15 '96
0.200	Aug. 13	Aug. 28	Sep. 01	Sep. 15 '96
0.225	Nov. 12	Nov. 27	Dec. 02	Dec. 16 '96
0.225	Feb. 12	Feb. 26	Feb. 28	Mar. 14 '97

A Division of The McGraw-Hill Companies

Business Summary - 20-JAN-97

SunTrust Banks, formed through the 1985 merger of SunBanks (Florida) and Trust Co. of Georgia, operates more than 700 full-service banking offices in Florida, Georgia, Tennessee and Alabama. Primary businesses include traditional deposit and credit services as well as trust and investment services. The company also provides mortgage banking, corporate finance, credit cards, factoring, discount brokerage, credit-related insurance, and data processing and information services. At 1995 year-end, it had discretionary trust assets of $47 billion and a mortgage servicing portfolio of $10.6 billion.

Contributions of the subsidiary banks ($ million) in 1995 were:

	Net Inc.	Return on Assets
SunTrust Banks of Florida	$300.5	1.41%
SunTrust Banks of Georgia	266.3	1.67%
SunTrust Banks of Tennessee	88.5	1.35%

Average earning assets during 1995 of $38.4 billion (up from $36.1 billion in 1994) were divided: loans 77%, investment securities 21% and other short-term investments 2%. Average sources of funds were noninterest-bearing deposits 16%, NOW/money market 22%, savings deposits 8%, time deposits 28% (average deposits of $31.8 billion were up 3.0%), short-term borrowings 12%, long-term debt 2%, equity 7% and other 5%.

At year-end 1995, nonperforming assets were $251 million (0.80% of loans and other real estate owned), down from $275 million (0.96%) a year earlier. The reserve for loan losses was 2.23% of loans, versus 2.27%. Domestic net chargeoffs during 1995 were 0.22% of average loans, against 0.23% in 1994.

The company owns 48,266,496 (adjusted) shares of common stock of Coca-Cola Co., which had a market value of about $2.54 billion at 1996 year-end.

Important Developments

Nov. '96—STI's SunTrust Capital Markets subsidiary said it was continuing to expand its corporate and institutional sales activities by opening an office in Pittsburgh, Pa. The new office will market and sell fixed-income securities to corporate and institutional clients throughout the North and Midwest.

Capitalization

Long Term Debt: $1,565,000,000 (9/96).

Per Share Data ($) (Year Ended Dec. 31)	1996	1995	1994	1993	1992	1991	1990	1989	1988	1987
Tangible Bk. Val.	NA	17.66	13.90	13.90	10.08	9.24	8.36	7.42	6.52	5.82
Earnings	2.76	2.47	2.18	1.89	1.64	1.45	1.38	1.30	1.19	1.08
Dividends	0.82	0.74	0.66	0.58	0.51	0.47	0.43	0.39	0.35	0.32
Payout Ratio	30%	29%	30%	31%	31%	32%	31%	30%	29%	30%
Prices - High	52½	35½	25¾	24⅞	22⅞	20	12⅛	13½	12¼	13⅞
- Low	32	23⅝	21¾	20¾	16¾	10¼	8¼	9⅞	9¼	8½
P/E Ratio - High	19	14	12	13	14	14	9	10	10	13
- Low	12	10	10	11	10	7	6	8	8	8
Income Statement Analysis (Million $)										
Net Int. Inc.	NA	1,676	1,620	1,572	1,515	1,352	1,265	1,216	1,146	1,052
Tax Equiv. Adj.	NA	49.6	55.7	62.7	68.6	76.0	88.0	93.0	96.0	132
Non Int. Inc.	NA	720	703	726	658	601	548	510	464	396
Loan Loss Prov.	NA	112	138	189	220	206	197	178	186	143
% Exp/Op Revs.	NA	60	59	60	61	61	62	61	62	61
Pretax Inc.	NA	826	782	701	589	503	444	441	372	348
Eff. Tax Rate	NA	32%	33%	32%	30%	26%	21%	24%	17%	19%
Net Inc.	NA	565	523	474	413	371	350	337	309	283
% Net Int. Marg.	NA	4.50	4.60	4.80	5.11	4.83	4.88	5.05	5.13	5.26
Balance Sheet & Other Fin. Data (Million $)										
Earning Assets:										
Money Mkt	NA	1,425	1,095	1,204	1,920	1,987	1,165	1,642	1,225	1,492
Inv. Securities	NA	9,677	9,319	10,644	8,384	7,257	6,012	4,643	4,051	3,845
Com'l Loans	NA	10,560	9,552	8,570	8,158	7,570	7,907	7,322	7,037	7,250
Other Loans	NA	20,741	18,996	16,722	14,740	14,144	14,404	14,058	13,399	11,525
Total Assets	NA	46,471	42,709	40,728	36,649	34,554	33,411	31,044	29,177	27,188
Demand Deposits	NA	7,821	7,654	7,611	6,935	5,944	5,848	5,529	5,531	5,619
Time Deposits	NA	25,362	24,565	22,875	21,909	22,044	20,978	19,433	18,413	16,875
LT Debt	NA	1,002	930	630	545	475	480	485	491	426
Common Eqty.	NA	4,270	3,453	3,610	2,704	2,546	2,305	2,089	1,880	1,674
% Ret. on Assets	NA	1.3	1.3	1.3	1.2	1.1	1.1	1.2	1.1	1.1
% Ret. on Equity	NA	14.6	14.8	16.5	15.8	15.2	16.0	16.9	17.4	17.8
% Loan Loss Resv.	NA	2.2	2.3	2.2	2.0	1.7	1.6	1.6	1.5	1.6
% Loans/Deposits	NA	94.3	88.6	83.0	79.0	77.1	82.4	84.6	84.0	81.9
% Equity to Assets	NA	8.7	8.5	8.9	7.7	7.4	7.1	6.7	6.5	6.2

Data as orig. reptd.; bef. results of disc. opers. and/or spec. items. Per share data adj. for stk. divs. as of ex-div. date. E-Estimated. NA-Not Available. NM-Not Meaningful. NR-Not Ranked.

Office—303 Peachtree St., Atlanta, GA 30303; P.O. Box 4418, Atlanta, GA 30302. **Tel**—(404) 588-7711. **Website**—http://www.SunTrust.com **Chrmn & CEO**—J. B. Williams. **Pres**—L. P. Humann. **Exec VP & CFO**—J. W. Spiegel. **Investor Contact**—James C. Armstrong. **Dirs**—J. H. Brown, J. D. Camp Jr., R. C. Goizueta, J. T. Glover, T. M. Hahn Jr., D. H. Hughes, L. P. Humann, J. L. Lanier Jr., H. G. Pattillo, S. L. Probasco Jr., R. R. Rollins, R. W. Scherer, J. W. Tucker Jr., J. B. Williams, J. H. Williams. **Transfer Agent**—SunTrust Bank, Atlanta. **Incorporated**—in Georgia in 1984. **Empl**— 19,415. **S&P Analyst:** Stephen R. Biggar

STANDARD & POOR'S
STOCK REPORTS

TCA Cable TV

5356T
Nasdaq Symbol **TCAT**

In S&P MidCap 400

16-FEB-97 Industry: Broadcasting

Summary: This company's cable systems, located primarily in smaller markets in nine southern and western states, serve about 670,000 subscribers.

S&P Opinion: Hold (★★★)	Recent Price • 31¾	Yield • 2.0%
	52 Wk Range • 35-23¾	12-Mo. P/E • 22.5

Quantitative Evaluations

Outlook (1 Lowest—5 Highest)
• 5

Fair Value
• 37½

Risk
• **Low**

Earn./Div. Rank
• **A-**

Technical Eval.
• **Bearish** since 12/96

Rel. Strength Rank (1 Lowest—99 Highest)
• 75

Insider Activity
• **Neutral**

Earnings vs. Previous Year
▲=Up ▼=Down ▶=No Change

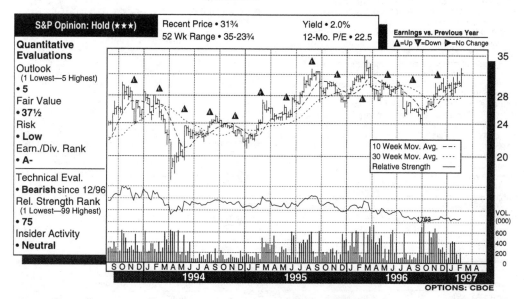

10 Week Mov. Avg. – – –
30 Week Mov. Avg. ·······
Relative Strength ——

OPTIONS: CBOE

Overview - 30-JAN-97

The company's recently reported FY 96 (Oct.) earnings were right on target, at $1.41 a share. Double-digit advances in revenues and cash flow are expected through FY 97, boosted by acquisitions, as well as rate increases allowed on regulated services under new FCC guidelines. Subscriber growth and healthy demand for premium and other fee-based services will also contribute to the improvement. Profit comparisons should benefit from the revenue gains and increased efficiencies. A new joint venture with Donrey Media Group will aid profitability through economies of scale. Profitability will also benefit from growth in higher-margin businesses and services. Interest expense will be higher, reflecting borrowings for acquisitions.

Valuation - 30-JAN-97

The stock, recovering from its recent low reached in the summer of 1996, continues to outperform its peers, reflecting no doubt on the company's history of paying dividends and reporting steadily rising earnings. The long-term attractiveness of the company stems from its strategy of remaining a viable player in cable TV, despite its relatively small size. TCA has carved out a lucrative niche, serving small markets in the South and West, and is strengthening its position through strategic acquisitions and partnerships. The company is in the fourth year of a five-year system upgrade to increase channel capacity and provide state-of-the-art telecommunications and data transmission capabilities. The $100 million project, funded internally, bodes well for TCA's competitive stance and is providing new revenue streams. The company is unusual among cable system operators in that it is consistently profitable and pays quarterly cash dividends.

Key Stock Statistics

S&P EPS Est. 1997	1.65	Tang. Bk. Value/Share	NM
P/E on S&P Est. 1997	19.2	Beta	1.07
Dividend Rate/Share	0.64	Shareholders	3,600
Shs. outstg. (M)	24.8	Market cap. (B)	$0.788
Avg. daily vol. (M)	0.043	Inst. holdings	42%

Value of $10,000 invested 5 years ago: $ 19,306

Fiscal Year Ending Oct. 31

	1996	1995	1994	1993	1992	1991
Revenues (Million $)						
1Q	55.00	43.30	39.28	36.65	33.60	30.30
2Q	57.58	43.95	39.85	37.84	34.60	31.80
3Q	69.40	49.13	41.08	38.31	35.10	32.20
4Q	71.33	52.79	42.10	39.49	35.60	32.80
Yr.	253.3	189.2	162.3	152.3	138.8	127.1
Earnings Per Share ($)						
1Q	0.34	0.31	0.23	0.19	0.14	0.08
2Q	0.36	0.31	0.24	0.21	0.16	0.08
3Q	0.35	0.31	0.21	0.20	0.16	0.09
4Q	0.36	0.34	0.25	0.23	0.15	0.10
Yr.	1.41	1.27	0.93	0.83	0.61	0.35

Next earnings report expected: mid March

Dividend Data (Dividends have been paid since 1982.)

Amount ($)	Date Decl.	Ex-Div. Date	Stock of Record	Payment Date
0.140	Mar. 28	Apr. 08	Apr. 10	Apr. 24 '96
0.140	Jun. 25	Jul. 05	Jul. 09	Jul. 23 '96
0.140	Sep. 19	Sep. 30	Oct. 02	Oct. 16 '96
0.160	Dec. 12	Jan. 06	Jan. 08	Jan. 22 '97

A Division of The McGraw-Hill Companies

STANDARD
&POOR'S
STOCK REPORTS

TCA Cable TV, Inc.

5356T
16-FEB-97

Business Summary - 30-JAN-97

TCA Cable TV develops, operates and manages cable television systems. At December 31, 1996, it owned or managed cable systems serving more than 670,000 subscribers primarily in Arkansas, Louisiana, Texas, Missouri, New Mexico, Mississippi and Idaho, where over-the-air television reception is unsatisfactory.

Basic service includes signals of nearby over-the-air TV stations and additional satellite programming such as signals of distant independent stations and continuous time, news and weather information. Expanded basic service includes a variety of packaged programming, purchased from independent suppliers and combined in different formats to appeal to different tastes. TCA also offers premium services such as HBO, Showtime and The Disney Channel. In FY 95 (Oct.), the company derived 67.4% of revenues from basic or expanded basic subscriptions, 17.5% from premium subscriptions, 9.4% from advertising and 5.7% from other sources such as home shopping channels and pay-per-view services.

TCA's operating plan calls for geographically clustered cable systems in medium-density markets. Clustering allows for lower costs through operating efficiencies, as well as future potential for connected markets large enough to offer pay-per-view and other nonregulated ancillary services.

Important Developments

Oct. '96—The company reported that advertising revenues during the third quarter increased to $10.6 million, representing 15% of total revenues. TCAT's Cable-Time subsidiary has become the largest third-party cable advertising insertion firm in the U.S.

Mar. '96—The company agreed to be the U.S. advertising sales representative for 24 Televisa-owned TV stations along the Texas border, from Brownsville to El Paso, and in northern Mexico, including Monterrey, Nuevo Leon.

Dec. '95—TCA purchased a cable system in Alexandria, LA, serving 29,000 subscribers. Separately, the company formed a partnership with Donrey Media Group, consisting of all 22 of TCA's systems in Arkansas and Mississippi and of Donrey's five systems in Arkansas, Oklahoma and California. The partnership, TCA Cable Partners, is owned 75% by TCA and serves more than 224,000 customers. It was designed to aid the company's clustering strategy.

Capitalization

Long Term Debt: $310,824,385 (7/96).

Per Share Data ($)

(Year Ended Oct. 31)	1996	1995	1994	1993	1992	1991	1990	1989	1988	1987
Tangible Bk. Val.	NM	NM	-2.62	-3.41	-4.15	-4.91	-5.57	-5.66	0.56	2.22
Cash Flow	2.93	2.43	2.30	2.18	1.95	1.27	1.06	1.19	0.97	0.78
Earnings	1.41	1.27	0.93	0.83	0.61	0.35	0.20	0.45	0.40	0.23
Dividends	0.56	0.48	0.44	0.40	0.34	0.28	0.24	0.20	0.16	0.12
Payout Ratio	40%	38%	47%	48%	56%	80%	120%	44%	40%	57%
Prices - High	35	32¹/₂	28³/₈	30¹/₈	23¹/₄	19	17¹/₂	21³/₈	17³/₄	15¹/₈
- Low	23³/₄	20⁷/₈	17¹/₂	18¹/₂	17	13¹/₂	9⁷/₈	15³/₈	13¹/₄	8¹/₂
P/E Ratio - High	25	26	31	36	38	54	88	48	45	66
- Low	17	16	19	22	28	39	49	34	34	37

Income Statement Analysis (Million $)

	1996	1995	1994	1993	1992	1991	1990	1989	1988	1987
Revs.	253	189	162	152	139	127	114	79.0	69.0	60.0
Oper. Inc.	120	94.2	79.6	77.7	70.4	53.9	49.4	41.1	33.1	28.6
Depr.	37.5	28.4	33.6	33.3	32.8	22.5	20.8	18.0	13.8	12.2
Int. Exp.	21.9	13.8	9.7	11.0	13.2	17.9	20.7	5.4	4.6	6.4
Pretax Inc.	60.4	52.3	37.9	33.7	24.7	13.9	8.2	18.0	15.7	10.2
Eff. Tax Rate	37%	40%	39%	39%	39%	39%	42%	40%	39%	50%
Net Inc.	34.9	31.3	23.0	20.4	15.0	8.5	4.8	10.8	9.6	5.1

Balance Sheet & Other Fin. Data (Million $)

	1996	1995	1994	1993	1992	1991	1990	1989	1988	1987
Cash	3.5	1.3	2.5	1.5	0.8	1.0	0.7	1.0	0.8	0.7
Curr. Assets	NA	NA	NA	NA	NA	NA	NA	NA	NA	NA
Total Assets	664	454	286	288	290	306	325	328	135	138
Curr. Liab.	NA	NA	48.3	45.3	48.8	40.5	27.9	22.2	18.5	15.8
LT Debt	314	220	99	118	130	165	205	216	37.0	52.0
Common Eqty.	146	118	99	90.3	78.0	70.8	64.9	65.8	59.5	53.7
Total Cap.	573	338	238	243	241	265	297	305	117	122
Cap. Exp.	45.9	39.8	28.5	23.4	16.5	11.9	20.2	49.9	12.1	26.5
Cash Flow	72.5	59.6	56.6	53.8	47.8	31.0	25.6	28.9	23.4	17.3
Curr. Ratio	NA	NA	NA	NA	NA	NA	NA	NA	NA	NA
% LT Debt of Cap.	54.8	65.1	41.6	48.4	54.0	62.0	69.1	70.8	31.8	42.3
% Net Inc.of Revs.	13.8	16.5	14.2	13.4	10.8	6.7	4.2	13.7	13.9	8.4
% Ret. on Assets	6.2	8.5	8.0	7.1	5.0	2.7	1.5	4.7	7.0	4.2
% Ret. on Equity	26.4	28.8	24.3	24.3	20.1	12.4	7.3	17.3	16.9	12.2

Data as orig. reptd.; bef. results of disc. opers. and/or spec. items. Per share data adj. for stk. divs. as of ex-div. date. E-Estimated. NA-Not Available. NM-Not Meaningful. NR-Not Ranked.

Office—3015 SSE Loop 323, Tyler, TX 75701. **Tel**—(903) 595-3701. **Chrmn & CEO**—R. M. Rogers. **Pres & COO**—F. R. Nichols. **VP, CFO, Treas & Investor Contact**—Jimmie F. Taylor. **Secy**—Karen L. Garrett. **Dirs**—J. F. Ackerman, B. R. Fisch, K. S. Gunter, W. J. McKinney, F. R. Nichols, A. W. Riter Jr., R. K. Rogers, R. M. Rogers, F. W. Smith. **Transfer Agent & Registrar**—ChaseMellon Shareholder Services, Ridgefield Park, NJ. **Incorporated**—in Texas in 1981. **Empl**— 1,080. **S&P Analyst:** William H. Donald

STANDARD &POOR'S
STOCK REPORTS

U.S. Bancorp
Nasdaq Symbol **USBC**

5488
In S&P 500

16-FEB-97

Industry:
Banking

Summary: This bank holding company operates more than 600 branches in Oregon, Washington, Idaho, Nevada, northern California and Utah.

S&P Opinion: Hold (★★★)	Recent Price • 49⅝	Yield • 2.5%
	52 Wk Range • 50⅝-29¼	12-Mo. P/E • 16.1

Quantitative Evaluations

Outlook
(1 Lowest—5 Highest)
• **2⁻**

Fair Value
• **44⅝**

Risk
• **Average**

Earn./Div. Rank
• **A**

Technical Eval.
• **Neutral** since 12/96

Rel. Strength Rank
(1 Lowest—99 Highest)
• **85**

Insider Activity
• **NA**

Earnings vs. Previous Year
▲=Up ▼=Down ▷=No Change

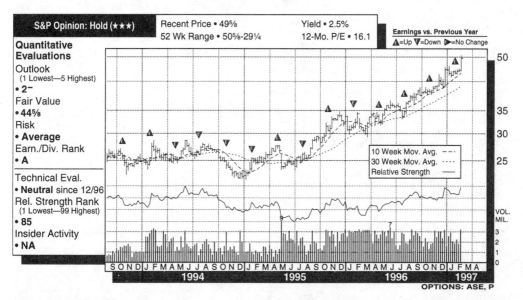

10 Week Mov. Avg. - - -
30 Week Mov. Avg. ......
Relative Strength ——

OPTIONS: ASE, P

Overview - 06-FEB-97

Loan growth is expected to continue in the 5% to 7% range in 1997, reflecting recent acquisitions and the company's presence in states with good economic growth. Margins are not expected to stray much from the current 5.3% to 5.4% level, as declining yields on assets are offset by lower cost of funds, leading to modest net interest income gains. Noninterest expense has been well controlled, benefiting from a restructuring program designed to reduce the overhead ratio, which was 55% in the fourth quarter of 1996, down from 79% in the 1995 period. Long-range goals of increasing return on assets to 1.50% and return on equity to 19% by 1997 have largely been met on a core basis ahead of schedule.

Valuation - 06-FEB-97

The shares rose about 34% in 1996, easily beating the S&P 500 but in line with the gain for the average major regional bank. For much of 1996, investors remained concerned about dilution of earnings from recent acquisitions. The recent purchase of California Bancshares strengthened the company's presence in the growing and densely populated northern California region, while economic growth throughout the company's service territory remains strong. USBC has made great strides in improving its efficiency ratio and can now turn its attention to building revenues. The company plans to place particular emphasis on growing noninterest income and active capital management in 1997. The shares, recently trading at 13.6X estimated 1997 EPS of $3.35, appear fairly valued for now based on expected growth rates.

Key Stock Statistics

S&P EPS Est. 1997	3.35	Tang. Bk. Value/Share	14.90
P/E on S&P Est. 1997	14.8	Beta	0.90
Dividend Rate/Share	1.24	Shareholders	15,500
Shs. outstg. (M)	151.1	Market cap. (B)	$ 7.5
Avg. daily vol. (M)	0.542	Inst. holdings	49%

Value of $10,000 invested 5 years ago: $ 26,073

Fiscal Year Ending Dec. 31

	1996	1995	1994	1993	1992	1991
Revenues (Million $)						
1Q	730.9	705.2	451.2	472.9	485.3	504.7
2Q	910.4	735.5	473.8	484.9	480.6	502.9
3Q	772.7	745.3	518.2	504.3	469.0	503.1
4Q	776.2	731.2	493.0	503.4	500.1	503.2
Yr.	3,069	2,917	1,936	1,966	1,935	2,014
Earnings Per Share ($)						
1Q	0.73	0.60	-0.32	0.59	0.48	0.51
2Q	0.82	0.43	0.49	0.61	0.54	0.43
3Q	0.75	0.73	0.60	0.63	0.40	0.53
4Q	0.79	0.13	0.63	0.64	0.63	0.54
Yr.	3.08	2.09	1.40	2.47	2.05	2.01

Next earnings report expected: late April

Dividend Data (Dividends have been paid since 1899.)

Amount ($)	Date Decl.	Ex-Div. Date	Stock of Record	Payment Date
0.280	Feb. 15	Mar. 06	Mar. 08	Apr. 01 '96
0.280	Apr. 17	Jun. 05	Jun. 07	Jul. 01 '96
0.310	Aug. 15	Sep. 04	Sep. 06	Oct. 01 '96
0.310	Nov. 21	Dec. 04	Dec. 06	Jan. 02 '97

Business Summary - 06-FEB-97

U.S. Bancorp is a regional multibank holding company headquartered in Portland, OR. Activities are concentrated in the Pacific Northwest, but there are operations throughout the Far West and the rest of the U.S. Following the December 1995 acquisition of West One Bancorp, the company holds the largest deposit share position in Oregon and Idaho and third largest in Washington. Other financial services businesses include lease financing, consumer and commercial finance including credit cards, discount brokerage, investment advisory services, and insurance agency and credit life insurance services.

Average earning assets of $26.9 billion in 1995 ($25.9 billion in 1994) consisted of loans 82%, investment securities 16%, money market investments 1%, and other 1%. Average sources of funds were noninterest-bearing deposits 17%, interest-bearing deposits 56%, short-term borrowings 12%, long-term debt 4%, equity 8% and other 3%.

At 1995 year-end, the allowance for loan losses was $434.5 million (1.91% of loans and leases), up from $387.6 million (1.79%) a year earlier. Net chargeoffs in 1995 were $74.0 million (0.33% of average loans), versus $80.3 million (0.39%) in 1994. Nonperforming assets totaled $166.6 million (0.73% of loans and related assets), down from $230.6 million (1.06%) in 1994.

On a tax-equivalent basis, the yield on average interest-earning assets in 1995 was 9.07% (8.20% in 1994), while the average rate on interest-bearing liabilities was 4.58% (3.51%), for a net spread of 4.49% (4.69%).

Important Developments

Jan. '97—The company noted that it repurchased four million of its common shares during the fourth quarter of 1996 under an October 1996 authorization to buyback up to 7.5 million shares, or about 5% of those outstanding.

Dec. '96—USBC said it completed the acquisition of Sun Capital Bancorp and its Sun Capital Bank subsidiary, including three branch offices in Utah and $70 million in assets.

Capitalization

Long Term Debt: $1,811,472,000 (12/96).
Preferred Stock: $150,000,000.
Redeem. Capital Securities: $300,000,000.

Per Share Data ($)

(Year Ended Dec. 31)	1996	1995	1994	1993	1992	1991	1990	1989	1988	1987
Tangible Bk. Val.	NA	16.38	16.58	16.77	14.95	14.38	13.22	11.80	10.63	9.70
Earnings	3.08	2.09	1.40	2.47	2.05	2.01	2.04	1.69	1.40	1.12
Dividends	1.18	1.06	0.94	0.85	0.76	0.71	0.61	0.51	0.46	0.37
Payout Ratio	38%	51%	67%	34%	37%	35%	30%	30%	33%	33%
Prices - High	47	36	28⅝	28⅞	26⅝	23¾	18⅛	18¼	12	14½
- Low	29¼	22	22⅛	22	19⅞	11¾	9⅞	10½	9⅜	8¾
P/E Ratio - High	15	17	20	12	13	12	9	11	9	13
- Low	9	11	16	9	10	6	5	6	7	8

Income Statement Analysis (Million $)

	1996	1995	1994	1993	1992	1991	1990	1989	1988	1987
Net Int. Inc.	NA	1,399	962	928	860	768	659	604	527	447
Tax Equiv. Adj.	NA	50.1	32.9	34.9	36.7	46.6	46.1	33.9	29.5	43.0
Non Int. Inc.	NA	522	464	532	443	367	292	233	215	176
Loan Loss Prov.	NA	124	107	93.0	134	125	103	84.0	69.0	57.0
% Exp/Op Revs.	NA	66	75	66	65	63	60	63	65	64
Pretax Inc.	NA	509	216	384	300	275	252	211	173	138
Eff. Tax Rate	NA	35%	30%	33%	31%	29%	28%	29%	28%	28%
Net Inc.	NA	329	152	258	208	196	183	151	124	100
% Net Int. Marg.	NA	5.38	5.34	5.29	5.18	4.93	4.61	4.96	4.87	4.79

Balance Sheet & Other Fin. Data (Million $)

	1996	1995	1994	1993	1992	1991	1990	1989	1988	1987
Earning Assets:										
Money Mkt	NA	787	568	512	916	586	434	585	635	1,109
Inv. Securities	NA	4,142	2,774	3,413	3,015	1,680	1,602	2,212	1,566	1,441
Com'l Loans	NA	11,746	8,204	7,371	7,039	7,392	7,484	6,727	5,516	4,968
Other Loans	NA	11,039	7,550	7,648	7,230	6,984	5,881	4,897	4,239	3,743
Total Assets	NA	31,794	21,816	21,415	20,741	18,875	17,613	16,975	14,383	13,353
Demand Deposits	NA	6,010	4,022	3,910	3,479	2,617	2,431	2,429	2,323	2,105
Time Deposits	NA	17,255	11,027	11,601	11,947	10,699	10,103	9,003	7,845	7,417
LT Debt	NA	1,377	995	1,052	1,329	1,221	673	610	633	484
Common Eqty.	NA	2,467	1,627	1,668	1,481	1,412	1,197	1,054	944	858
% Ret. on Assets	NA	1.1	0.7	1.3	1.1	1.1	1.0	1.0	0.9	0.8
% Ret. on Equity	NA	12.9	8.6	15.8	14.5	14.7	16.3	15.1	13.8	12.3
% Loan Loss Resv.	NA	1.9	1.9	1.8	1.8	1.6	1.5	1.3	1.3	1.3
% Loans/Deposits	NA	97.9	104.7	96.8	92.5	108.0	106.6	101.7	95.9	91.5
% Equity to Assets	NA	8.6	7.7	7.6	7.2	7.3	6.4	6.6	6.7	6.7

Data as orig. reptd.; bef. results of disc. opers. and/or spec. items. Per share data adj. for stk. divs. as of ex-div. date. E-Estimated. NA-Not Available. NM-Not Meaningful. NR-Not Ranked.

Office—111 S.W. Fifth Ave., P.O. Box 8837, Portland, OR 97204. **Organized**—in Oregon in 1968; U.S. National Bank of Oregon chartered in 1891. **Tel**—(503) 275-6111. **Website**—http://www.usbancorp.com **Chrmn & CEO**—G. B. Cameron. **Exec VP & CFO**—S. P. Erwin. **Secy**—J. J. Demott. **Sr VP & Investor Contact**—Donald F. Bowler (503) 275-5702. **Dirs**—H. L. Bettis, G. B. Cameron, C. S. Chambers, F. G. Drake, R. L. Dryden, J. B. Fery, J. Green III, D. R. Nelson, A. T. Noble, P. A. Redmond, N. S. Rogers, B. R. Whiteley. **Transfer Agent & Registrar**—U.S. Bancorp c/o First Chicago Trust Co. of New York, Jersey City, NJ. **Empl**— 14,081. **S&P Analyst:** Stephen R. Biggar

16-FEB-97   Industry: Services

Summary: This holding company was formed to acquire and own firms engaged primarily in institutional investment management.

S&P Opinion: Accumulate (★★★★)	Recent Price • 28¾	Yield • 2.4%
	52 Wk Range • 29⅜-21⅛	12-Mo. P/E • 21.3

Quantitative Evaluations

Outlook (1 Lowest—5 Highest)
• **1⁻**

Fair Value
• **20**

Risk
• **Low**

Earn./Div. Rank
• **A+**

Technical Eval.
• **Bullish** since 10/96

Rel. Strength Rank (1 Lowest—99 Highest)
• **71**

Insider Activity
• **Neutral**

Earnings vs. Previous Year
▲=Up ▼=Down ▶=No Change

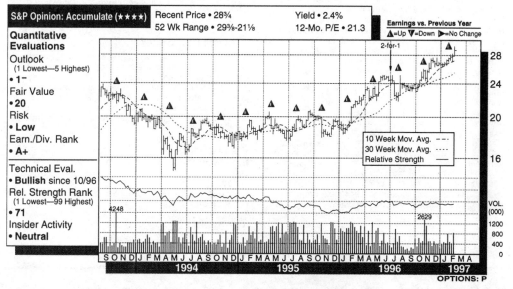

10 Week Mov. Avg. - - -
30 Week Mov. Avg. · · · ·
Relative Strength —

OPTIONS: P

Overview - 14-FEB-97

EPS and cash flow per share are likely to grow in low double-digits over the next several years. We expect continued acquisitions of asset management and real estate firms. For 1997, we anticipate five to seven transactions. The pace of transactions appears to be accelerating, possibly because more managers may be willing sellers after the long bull market. Transactions are structured to be immediately accretive to cash flow. Asset management is a long-term growth industry, reflecting a need to fund pension plans for a large and growing U.S. retirement-age population. Prospects are further enhanced by the attractive economics of the investment management business, UAM's substantial free cash flow, and large share repurchases. The company is able to use its acquisition-related charges as a tax shield. Net client cash flows were -$3.3 billion in 1996.

Valuation - 14-FEB-97

The shares are ranked "accumulate." UAM is attractively valued at about 8X projected 1997 cash flow per share, a discount to the market, to mutual fund management companies and to its expected growth rate. However, there is a major concern: continued negative client cash flows at the company's affiliates. For some time, this has been a persistent problem which management must address. Cash flow is the most relevant valuation measure for the company, because earnings are depressed by large non-cash amortization charges for costs assigned to contracts acquired. In a typical quarter, the company's cash flow is about twice its net income. We expect low double-digit cash flow growth over the long term, based on continued acquisitions, share buybacks, and growth in retirement fund assets.

Key Stock Statistics

S&P EPS Est. 1997	1.55	Tang. Bk. Value/Share	7.76
P/E on S&P Est. 1997	18.5	Beta	1.24
Dividend Rate/Share	0.68	Shareholders	400
Shs. outstg. (M)	60.9	Market cap. (B)	$ 1.8
Avg. daily vol. (M)	0.124	Inst. holdings	67%

Value of $10,000 invested 5 years ago: $ 21,272

Fiscal Year Ending Dec. 31

	1996	1995	1994	1993	1992	1991
Revenues (Million $)						
1Q	208.5	151.1	121.3	110.0	67.30	49.60
2Q	206.7	171.0	115.5	109.7	68.30	52.70
3Q	219.6	175.9	118.9	111.4	73.50	59.30
4Q	248.5	200.5	136.5	118.8	85.90	65.00
Yr.	883.3	698.5	492.3	449.9	295.0	226.6
Earnings Per Share ($)						
1Q	0.28	0.25	0.25	0.22	0.18	0.15
2Q	0.29	0.26	0.24	0.22	0.19	0.15
3Q	0.32	0.26	0.25	0.23	0.19	0.17
4Q	0.47	0.29	0.25	0.25	0.22	0.18
Yr.	1.35	1.08	1.00	0.93	0.78	0.65

Next earnings report expected: late April

Dividend Data (Dividends have been paid since 1986.)

Amount ($)	Date Decl.	Ex-Div. Date	Stock of Record	Payment Date
2-for-1	May. 16	Jun. 24	Jun. 07	Jun. 21 '96
0.160	Jun. 17	Jun. 26	Jun. 28	Jul. 15 '96
0.170	Sep. 13	Sep. 26	Sep. 30	Oct. 15 '96
0.170	Dec. 13	Dec. 27	Dec. 31	Jan. 15 '97

Business Summary - 02-AUG-96

United Asset Management is a holding company organized to acquire and own firms engaged primarily in institutional investment management. To its knowledge, it is the only such holding company in the U.S. At December 31, 1995, UAM had 45 wholly owned subsidiaries (affiliated firms) registered as investment advisers with some $142 billion under management. At December 31, 1995, the affiliated firms served nearly 6,000 clients.

The mix of assets under management for clients of UAM firms was 59% U. S. equities, 18% U. S. bonds and cash, 10% real estate, 8% international securities and 5% stable value assets. The client list includes many of the largest corporate, government, charitable, and union funds in the U. S. and abroad along with the funds of several mutual fund organizations, many individuals and a number of professional groups.

Revenues of UAM's affiliated firms are derived from fees for investment advisory services provided to institutional and other clients. Investment advisory fees are generally a function of the overall fee rate charged to each account and the level of assets under mangement by the affiliated firms. Assets under management can be affected by the addition of new client accounts or client contributions, withdrawals of assets from or terminations of clients accounts and investment performance, which may depend on general market conditions.

Each affiliated firm operates under its own name with its own investment philosophy and approach. Each conducts its own investment analysis, portfolio selection, marketing and client service.

Important Developments

Feb. '97—UAM said that during periods of strong market growth such as that experienced for the last two years, industry data show that net withdrawals are common in defined benefit retirement plans, which represent nearly 45% of the company's client assets. When market performance is strong, plan sponsors reduce cash contributions to their funds even as they pay benefits.

Capitalization

Long Term Debt: $607,486,000 (12/96).
Options: To buy 3,606,211 com. shs. at an avg. price of $30.47 a sh.
Warrants: To buy 5,624,790 shs. at an avg. price of $38.99 a sh.

Per Share Data ($)

(Year Ended Dec. 31)	1996	1995	1994	1993	1992	1991	1990	1989	1988	1987
Tangible Bk. Val.	NA	7.76	6.73	6.18	5.48	4.85	4.30	NA	NA	NA
Cash Flow	NA	2.78	2.03	2.16	1.60	1.33	1.07	0.96	0.85	0.76
Earnings	1.35	1.08	1.00	0.93	0.78	0.65	0.53	0.47	0.41	0.39
Dividends	0.66	0.58	0.50	0.42	0.34	0.28	0.22	0.17	0.13	0.09
Payout Ratio	49%	53%	50%	45%	41%	38%	37%	33%	32%	22%
Prices - High	27⅝	20¾	20⅞	23⅞	16⅜	15⅜	10½	10⅝	7⅞	11½
- Low	18¼	17⅜	14⅞	14¼	11	7¼	6⅛	6¾	4¾	4½
P/E Ratio - High	20	19	21	26	21	24	20	22	19	29
- Low	13	16	15	15	14	11	11	14	12	11

Income Statement Analysis (Million $)

	1996	1995	1994	1993	1992	1991	1990	1989	1988	1987
Revs.	NA	698	492	450	295	227	170	148	122	110
Oper. Inc.	NA	263	176	164	117	91.0	72.0	63.0	55.0	46.0
Depr.	NA	101	61.0	54.1	39.6	32.4	28.4	24.8	22.6	15.1
Int. Exp.	NA	42.3	13.3	15.1	15.5	17.0	14.2	13.8	13.2	7.3
Pretax·Inc.	NA	118	103	94.5	62.5	43.0	30.9	25.6	20.2	24.3
Eff. Tax Rate	NA	43%	43%	44%	44%	43%	41%	40%	40%	46%
Net Inc.	NA	67.0	59.0	53.3	35.0	24.6	18.2	15.4	12.1	13.1

Balance Sheet & Other Fin. Data (Million $)

	1996	1995	1994	1993	1992	1991	1990	1989	1988	1987
Cash	NA	124	89.1	62.8	21.8	21.1	17.5	17.8	11.2	41.4
Curr. Assets	NA	261	179	143	75.9	63.6	45.9	41.9	28.7	57.0
Total Assets	NA	1,385	916	676	581	447	390	343	292	250
Curr. Liab.	NA	181	114	78.5	46.8	46.2	39.5	28.5	17.9	35.8
LT Debt	NA	673	364	211	258	189	174	150	125	64.0
Common Eqty.	NA	486	400	353	250	186	153	146	135	140
Total Cap.	NA	1,204	764	597	535	401	351	315	274	214
Cap. Exp.	NA	13.6	8.8	4.5	4.7	2.1	1.4	2.0	1.0	1.2
Cash Flow	NA	168	120	107	74.6	57.0	46.6	40.2	34.7	28.5
Curr. Ratio	NA	1.4	1.6	1.8	1.6	1.4	1.2	1.5	1.6	1.6
% LT Debt of Cap.	NA	55.9	47.6	35.3	48.3	47.2	49.6	47.8	45.5	29.6
% Net Inc.of Revs.	NA	9.6	12.0	11.8	11.9	10.8	10.7	10.4	9.9	11.9
% Ret. on Assets	NA	5.9	7.4	8.0	6.2	5.6	4.8	4.8	4.6	5.1
% Ret. on Equity	NA	15.2	15.7	16.7	14.7	13.9	11.9	10.9	9.0	9.2

Data as orig. reptd.; bef. results of disc. opers. and/or spec. items. Per share data adj. for stk. divs. as of ex-div. date. E-Estimated. NA-Not Available. NM-Not Meaningful. NR-Not Ranked.

Office—One International Place, Boston, MA 02110. **Tel**—(617) 330-8900. **Pres & CEO**—N. H. Reamer. **EVP & COO**—J. F. McNamara. **EVP, CFO & Investor Contact**—William H. Park. **Secy**—J. C. Vincent, Jr. **Dirs**—R. A. Englander, R. J. Greenebaum, C. E. Haldeman, Jr., R. M. Kommerstad, M. T. Lardner, J. O. Light, J. F. McNamara, N. H. Reamer, D. I. Russell, P. Scaturro, J. A. Shane, B. S.Thomas. **Transfer Agent & Registrar**—First National Bank of Boston. **Incorporated**—in Delaware in 1980. **Empl**— 45. **S&P Analyst:** Paul L. Huberman,CFA

STANDARD &POOR'S
STOCK REPORTS
Wachovia Corp.
2407D
NYSE Symbol **WB**
In S&P 500

16-FEB-97 Industry: Banking

Summary: This bank holding company, the 20th largest in the U.S., operates 490 branches in North Carolina, South Carolina and Georgia.

S&P Opinion: Hold (★★★)		
Recent Price • 63	Yield • 2.5%	
52 Wk Range • 63½-39⅝	12-Mo. P/E • 16.5	

Quantitative Evaluations

Outlook (1 Lowest—5 Highest)
• **2+**

Fair Value
• **58⅝**

Risk
• **Low**

Earn./Div. Rank
• **A**

Technical Eval.
• **Bearish** since 10/96

Rel. Strength Rank (1 Lowest—99 Highest)
• **84**

Insider Activity
• **Favorable**

Earnings vs. Previous Year
▲=Up ▼=Down ▶=No Change

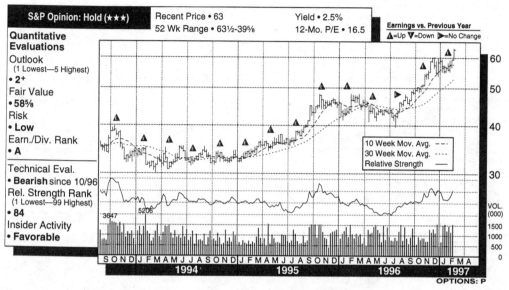

10 Week Mov. Avg. – – –
30 Week Mov. Avg. ·····
Relative Strength ——

OPTIONS: P

Overview - 10-FEB-97

Healthy loan demand in both the commercial and consumer categories in WB's service territory should boost the level of average earning assets about 10% in 1997. A relatively stable net interest margin on similar assets yields and funding costs will likely lead to net interest income gains in the high single-digits. Double-digit growth in noninterest income is expected, led by gains in service charges, credit card income and investment fees. Asset quality remains among the best of the major regional banks, with the reserve for loan losses at 6.8 times the level of nonperforming loans at December 31, 1996. A focus on cost containment and an ongoing reorganization of the delivery network to more closely align services with customers should favorably affect results in future quarters.

Valuation - 10-FEB-97

The shares rose about 24% in 1996, outperforming the S&P 500 but well under the average gain for major regional banks. The outpacing of the broader market reflects a generally favorable environment for banks, namely stable interest rates and moderate inflation, while the peer group underperformance most likely reflects the shares' relatively high valuation of nearly 2.5 times book value and 14 times estimated 1997 earnings of $4.15 a share. While the shares remain a good long-term holding, we would expect only average appreciation from current levels over the next nine to 12 months.

Key Stock Statistics

S&P EPS Est. 1997	4.15	Tang. Bk. Value/Share	22.57
P/E on S&P Est. 1997	15.2	Beta	0.99
Dividend Rate/Share	1.60	Shareholders	28,000
Shs. outstg. (M)	165.2	Market cap. (B)	$ 10.4
Avg. daily vol. (M)	0.287	Inst. holdings	51%

Value of $10,000 invested 5 years ago: $ 25,476

Fiscal Year Ending Dec. 31

	1996	1995	1994	1993	1992	1991
Revenues (Million $)						
1Q	968.0	848.9	679.3	689.5	720.1	806.0
2Q	991.1	995.4	723.3	674.9	713.8	794.0
3Q	1,023	956.9	759.4	682.4	692.6	785.0
4Q	1,030	977.7	808.0	703.7	651.9	753.2
Yr.	4,011	3,779	2,970	2,750	2,778	3,138
Earnings Per Share ($)						
1Q	0.87	0.83	0.72	0.70	0.62	0.50
2Q	0.94	0.94	0.78	0.71	0.63	0.56
3Q	0.98	0.88	0.80	0.71	0.63	0.52
4Q	1.02	0.85	0.83	0.71	0.64	-0.24
Yr.	3.81	3.50	3.13	2.83	2.51	1.34

Next earnings report expected: mid April

Dividend Data (Dividends have been paid since 1936.)

Amount ($)	Date Decl.	Ex-Div. Date	Stock of Record	Payment Date
0.360	Apr. 26	May. 02	May. 06	Jun. 03 '96
0.400	Jul. 25	Aug. 02	Aug. 06	Sep. 03 '96
0.400	Oct. 25	Nov. 04	Nov. 06	Dec. 02 '96
0.400	Jan. 24	Feb. 04	Feb. 06	Mar. 03 '97

A Division of The McGraw·Hill Companies

STANDARD
&POOR'S
STOCK REPORTS

Wachovia Corporation

2407D

16-FEB-97

Business Summary - 10-FEB-97

Wachovia Corp. (formerly First Wachovia) was formed in 1985 through the merger of Wachovia Corp. and First Atlanta Corp., parent of the second largest bank in Georgia. In December 1991, South Carolina National Corp., the largest bank in South Carolina, was acquired. Based on total assets of $47.5 billion at September 30, 1996, WB was the 20th largest U.S. bank holding company. It has 220 banking offices in North Carolina, 125 in Georgia and 145 in South Carolina. Among important business areas are trust services ($20.2 billion of assets under management), which includes fiduciary, investment management and related financial services; discount brokerage and investment advisory services; and residential mortgage origination, government securities underwriting, sales and trading, foreign exchange, corporate finance and other money-market services.

In 1995, average earning assets of $37.0 billion (up from $32.8 billion in 1994) consisted of: commercial loans 30%, commercial mortgages 10%, residential mortgages 11%, retail loans 20%, construction loans 2%, investment securities 23%, trading assets 3%, and other 1%. Average sources of funds were: interest-free deposits 13%, demand deposits 8%, savings,

money-market deposits and CDs 36%, foreign time deposits 2%, short-term borrowings 19%, long-term debt 12%, equity 8%, and other 2%.

At year-end 1995, nonperforming assets were $69 million (0.24% of loans and related assets), down from $101 million (0.39%) a year earlier. The reserve for loan losses was 1.40% of loans, versus 1.57%. Net chargeoffs during 1995 of $101.1 million were 0.37% of average loans, versus $70.4 million (0.29%) in 1994.

As of December 31, 1996, the Tier 1 capital ratio was 9.1%, versus 9.4% a year earlier; the total capital ratio was 13.4%, down from 13.6%.

Important Developments

Jan. '97—The company said it signed a definitive agreement to acquire a majority interest in Banco Portugues do Atlantico-Brasil S.A., a $100 million-asset bank based in Sao Paulo, Brazil, that is engagedmainly in corporate trade finance. WB intends to continue the bank's focus on trade finance and to expand its services to include other commercial, merchant and investment banking services. The acquisition is expected to be completed by mid-1997.

Capitalization

Long Term Debt: $6,171,070,000 (9/96).

Per Share Data ($)

(Year Ended Dec. 31)	1996	1995	1994	1993	1992	1991	1990	1989	1988	1987
Tangible Bk. Val.	NA	22.11	18.77	17.61	15.58	13.84	13.23	12.12	10.94	9.58
Earnings	3.81	3.49	3.13	2.83	2.51	1.34	2.13	1.94	1.81	1.35
Dividends	1.52	1.38	1.23	1.11	1.00	0.92	0.82	0.70	0.58	0.50
Payout Ratio	40%	40%	39%	39%	40%	69%	39%	36%	32%	37%
Prices - High	60¹/₄	48¹/₄	35³/₈	40¹/₂	34³/₄	30	22³/₈	22³/₄	17	19³/₈
- Low	39⁵/₈	32	30¹/₈	31⁷/₈	28¹/₄	20¹/₄	16¹/₄	15¹/₂	13⁷/₈	12³/₄
P/E Ratio - High	16	14	11	14	14	22	11	12	9	14
- Low	10	9	10	11	11	15	8	8	8	9

Income Statement Analysis (Million $)

	1996	1995	1994	1993	1992	1991	1990	1989	1988	1987
Net Int. Inc.	NA	1,441	1,324	1,284	1,255	1,169	817	771	736	683
Tax Equiv. Adj.	NA	99	100	99	79.0	95.0	93.0	85.0	75.0	99
Non Int. Inc.	NA	759	604	628	555	490	375	335	297	279
Loan Loss Prov.	NA	104	72.0	93.0	119	293	86.0	62.0	61.0	150
% Exp/Op Revs.	NA	52	54	57	58	63	58	60	60	58
Pretax Inc.	NA	869	761	688	596	281	371	338	315	212
Eff. Tax Rate	NA	31%	29%	28%	27%	18%	20%	21%	23%	17%
Net Inc.	NA	602	539	492	433	230	297	269	244	177
% Net Int. Marg.	NA	4.16	4.34	4.64	4.75	4.50	4.33	4.39	4.72	4.98

Balance Sheet & Other Fin. Data (Million $)

	1996	1995	1994	1993	1992	1991	1990	1989	1988	1987
Earning Assets:										
Money Mkt	NA	1,710	1,098	1,492	1,565	2,399	1,663	1,692	1,352	1,182
Inv. Securities	NA	9,029	7,723	7,879	6,486	6,265	3,779	3,598	3,309	3,062
Com'l Loans	NA	12,486	10,376	8,843	8,442	8,505	7,307	6,703	5,934	5,328
Other Loans	NA	16,366	15,515	14,134	12,644	12,112	9,329	8,594	7,819	7,013
Total Assets	NA	44,981	39,188	36,526	33,367	33,158	26,271	24,050	21,815	19,342
Demand Deposits	NA	9,329	5,663	6,144	5,627	4,758	4,988	4,377	4,276	4,060
Time Deposits	NA	17,040	17,406	17,209	17,749	18,248	13,225	13,010	12,216	10,282
LT Debt	NA	5,430	4,790	590	439	171	113	171	179	284
Common Eqty.	NA	3,774	3,287	3,018	2,775	2,484	1,929	1,740	1,557	1,298
% Ret. on Assets	NA	1.4	1.5	1.5	1.4	0.7	1.2	1.2	1.2	1.0
% Ret. on Equity	NA	17.1	17.4	17.1	16.7	9.3	16.4	16.5	17.2	14.3
% Loan Loss Resv.	NA	1.4	1.6	1.8	1.8	1.8	1.1	1.1	1.1	1.5
% Loans/Deposits	NA	114.3	112.2	98.4	90.2	89.6	91.3	87.8	83.2	85.8
% Equity to Assets	NA	8.4	8.4	8.5	8.2	7.7	7.6	7.3	7.1	6.8

Data as orig. reptd.; bef. results of disc. opers. and/or spec. items. Per share data adj. for stk. divs. as of ex-div. date. E-Estimated. NA-Not Available. NM-Not Meaningful. NR-Not Ranked.

Offices—301 N. Main St., Winston-Salem, NC 27150; 191 Peachtree St., N.E., Atlanta, GA 30303. **Tels**—(910) 770-5000; (404) 332-5000. **Chrmn**—J. G. Medlin Jr. **Pres & CEO**—L. M. Baker Jr. **EVP & CFO**—R. S. McCoy Jr. **EVP & Treas**—R. B. Roberts. **Investor Contact**—James C. Mabry (910-732-5788). **Dirs**—L. M. Baker Jr., R. C. Barkley Jr., C. C. Bowles, J. L. Clendenin, L. M. Gressette Jr., T. K. Hearn Jr., W. H. Hipp, R. M. Holder Jr., D. R. Hughes, F. K. Iverson, J. W. Johnston, J. G. Medlin Jr., W. Robertson, H. J. Russell, S. H. Smith Jr., C. M. Taylor, J. C. Whitaker, Jr. **Transfer Agent**—Wachovia Bank of North Carolina, Winston-Salem. **Incorporated**—in North Carolina in 1985. **Empl**— 16,185. **S&P Analyst:** Stephen R. Biggar

Wilmington Trust

5660F

Nasdaq Symbol **WILM**

In S&P MidCap 400

16-FEB-97

Industry:
Banking

Summary: This bank holding company, through its Wilmington Trust Co. subsidiary, operates more than 60 branches offering a broad variety of financial services, mainly in Delaware.

S&P Opinion: Accumulate (★★★★)

Recent Price • 45	Yield • 2.9%	
52 Wk Range • 45-30¾	12-Mo. P/E • 15.9	

Quantitative Evaluations

Outlook
  (1 Lowest—5 Highest)
• **2+**

Fair Value
• **39¼**

Risk
• **Low**

Earn./Div. Rank
• **A+**

Technical Eval.
• **Bearish** since 11/95

Rel. Strength Rank
  (1 Lowest—99 Highest)
• **84**

Insider Activity
• **Neutral**

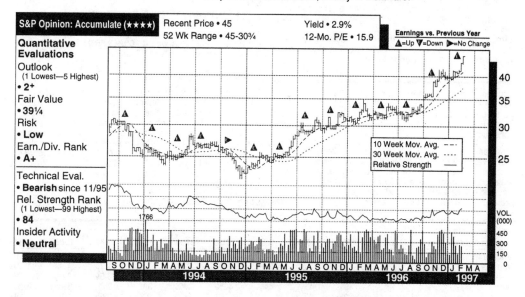

Earnings vs. Previous Year
▲=Up ▼=Down ▶=No Change

10 Week Mov. Avg. – –
30 Week Mov. Avg. ······
Relative Strength ——

Overview - 23-JAN-97

Earnings per share rose 11% in 1996, reflecting steady growth in net interest income, higher fees on trust and asset management services and expense control. The net interest margin was relatively flat in 1996, and should remain stable in the coming quarters as WILM continues to employ a similar mix of earning assets and liabilities. In 1997, we expect loan volume to advance at a pace similar to the 7.1% increase seen in 1996, driven by growth in the commercial loan and residential mortgage portfolios. Wilmington should also benefit from continued growth in noninterest income, with new fee schedules on deposit accounts and higher trust and asset management fees expanding revenues. Noninterest expense growth, which had been moderate for the first half of 1996, accelerated in the third and fourth quarters on higher personnel and other operating expenses. We expect provisioning levels to be moderately higher in the coming year.

Valuation - 23-JAN-97

Wilmington Trust continues to be an outstanding performer in the key areas of profitability, posting exceptional returns on assets and equity of 1.83% and 21.38%, respectively, in 1996. The shares outperformed the broader market during the year, posting a 32% gain. While it is improbable that WILM will match that gain in 1997, we do expect the stock to be an above-average performer, based on continued advances in net interest and fee income, coupled with expense control and share repurchases. Trading at 13 times our 1997 earnings estimate of $3.10, and with a 3.2% yield, the shares are an attractive long-term investment.

Key Stock Statistics

S&P EPS Est. 1997	3.10	Tang. Bk. Value/Share	13.42
P/E on S&P Est. 1997	14.5	Beta	0.83
Dividend Rate/Share	1.32	Shareholders	9,100
Shs. outstg. (M)	34.0	Market cap. (B)	$ 1.5
Avg. daily vol. (M)	0.045	Inst. holdings	35%

Value of $10,000 invested 5 years ago: $ 18,788

Fiscal Year Ending Dec. 31

	1996	1995	1994	1993	1992	1991
Revenues (Million $)						
1Q	131.2	116.5	101.1	100.6	110.9	107.5
2Q	133.2	126.0	104.7	100.2	106.1	106.6
3Q	135.4	127.5	104.3	100.5	104.6	107.8
4Q	141.2	95.31	110.8	103.3	104.2	107.6
Yr.	541.1	505.0	465.3	404.6	425.8	429.5
Earnings Per Share ($)						
1Q	0.66	0.60	0.58	0.53	0.47	0.44
2Q	0.70	0.64	0.60	0.55	0.51	0.48
3Q	0.73	0.66	0.59	0.59	0.55	0.54
4Q	0.74	0.66	0.60	0.57	0.56	0.55
Yr.	2.83	2.56	2.37	2.24	2.09	2.04

Next earnings report expected: late April

Dividend Data (Dividends have been paid since 1914.)

Amount ($)	Date Decl.	Ex-Div. Date	Stock of Record	Payment Date
0.330	Apr. 18	Apr. 29	May. 01	May. 15 '96
0.330	Jul. 18	Jul. 30	Aug. 01	Aug. 15 '96
0.330	Oct. 17	Oct. 30	Nov. 01	Nov. 15 '96
0.330	Jan. 16	Jan. 30	Feb. 03	Feb. 17 '97

A Division of The McGraw-Hill Companies

STANDARD
&POOR'S
STOCK REPORTS

Wilmington Trust Corporation

5660F
16-FEB-97

Business Summary - 23-JAN-97

Wilmington Trust Corporation conducts commercial banking, savings, trust, investment management and other financial activities through its Wilmington Trust Co. subsidiary. At March 20, 1996, WILM operated 65 full-service branches, mainly in Delaware. The company also has offices in Maryland, Pennsylvania, Florida and Nevada.

Gross loans outstanding amounted to $3.53 billion at year-end 1995, compared with $3.29 billion a year earlier. Loans were divided as follows:

	1995	1994
Commercial, financial & agricultural	33%	31%
Mortgage--commercial	22%	22%
Mortgage--residential	19%	19%
Consumer	23%	25%
Construction	3%	3%

The reserve for possible loan losses at December 31, 1995, was $49,867,000 ($48,669,000 a year earlier), equal to 1.47% (1.56%) of average loans outstanding. Nonaccruing loans totaled $33,576,000 (0.99% of loans outstanding) at 1995 year end, compared with $28,851,000 (0.93%) a year earlier.

Total deposits at 1995 year end amounted to $3.59 billion, of which noninterest-bearing demand deposits represented about 20%, savings 9%, interest checking 14%, money market 15%, certificates of under $100,000 34%, and certificates of $100,000 and more 8%.

On a tax-equivalent basis, the average yield on total interest-earning assets was 8.46% in 1995 (7.58% in 1994), while the average rate paid on total interest-bearing liabilities was 4.70% (3.55%), for a net interest spread of 3.76% (4.03%).

Important Developments

Nov. '96—Wilmington Trust said it had repurchased 546,412 shares of its common stock through the first nine months of 1996. The company is authorized to buy back 3,453,588 additional shares under a 4,000,000 share repurchase program originally announced in April 1996. This most recent buyback plan follows the completion of a 3,000,000 share repurchase program that began in October 1993.

Capitalization

Long Term Debt: $28,000,000 (9/96).

Per Share Data ($) (Year Ended Dec. 31)	1996	1995	1994	1993	1992	1991	1990	1989	1988	1987
Tangible Bk. Val.	NA	13.09	11.80	10.87	10.12	9.72	8.41	7.45	6.53	5.56
Earnings	2.83	2.56	2.37	2.24	2.09	2.04	1.90	1.70	1.49	1.23
Dividends	1.29	1.17	1.06	0.98	0.88	0.79	0.72	0.59	0.46	0.39
Payout Ratio	46%	46%	45%	44%	42%	39%	38%	35%	31%	32%
Prices - High	41¾	32½	28½	31	29	29⅜	22½	23⅛	15¾	18
- Low	30¼	22¾	22	24¾	22⅝	18	15⅛	13¼	11½	10
P/E Ratio - High	15	13	12	14	14	14	12	14	11	15
- Low	11	9	9	11	11	9	8	8	8	8

Income Statement Analysis (Million $)										
Net Int. Inc.	NA	197	184	175	165	142	126	114	99	86.0
Tax Equiv. Adj.	NA	11.0	10.5	11.3	12.1	16.1	18.5	18.9	16.4	21.4
Non Int. Inc.	NA	125	115	113	108	96.0	90.0	75.0	71.0	69.0
Loan Loss Prov.	NA	12.3	4.6	9.5	13.0	13.3	10.5	10.3	10.3	10.7
% Exp/Op Revs.	NA	55	55	54	54	51	52	52	53	52
Pretax Inc.	NA	132	121	117	109	94.0	84.0	73.0	64.0	55.0
Eff. Tax Rate	NA	32%	30%	29%	28%	24%	20%	18%	19%	21%
Net Inc.	NA	90.0	85.2	82.8	78.8	71.9	67.0	59.4	51.8	43.4
% Net Int. Marg.	NA	4.54	4.64	4.76	4.62	4.47	4.32	4.62	4.54	4.33

Balance Sheet & Other Fin. Data (Million $)										
Earning Assets:										
Money Mkt	NA	78.9	132	190	147	141	117	237	191	361
Inv. Securities	NA	1,361	985	1,093	802	828	835	793	482	528
Com'l Loans	NA	1,159	1,006	923	867	842	791	739	676	659
Other Loans	NA	2,363	2,277	2,117	2,142	1,932	1,824	1,642	1,369	1,112
Total Assets	NA	5,372	4,742	4,638	4,285	4,061	3,834	3,703	2,982	2,891
Demand Deposits	NA	721	696	587	528	424	392	452	421	543
Time Deposits	NA	2,864	2,613	2,804	2,746	2,623	2,461	2,162	1,871	1,851
LT Debt	NA	28.0	Nil	Nil	Nil	Nil	Nil	Nil	3.3	3.5
Common Eqty.	NA	459	418	395	377	346	296	258	228	193
% Ret. on Assets	NA	1.8	1.9	2.0	1.9	1.9	1.9	1.9	1.9	1.6
% Ret. on Equity	NA	20.7	20.8	21.1	21.5	22.7	24.5	24.4	25.2	23.7
% Loan Loss Resv.	NA	1.4	1.5	1.7	1.6	1.5	1.5	1.5	1.5	1.5
% Loans/Deposits	NA	98.2	99.1	89.6	91.5	90.7	91.3	90.8	89.3	74.0
% Equity to Assets	NA	9.7	9.0	9.3	8.9	8.4	7.7	7.8	7.4	6.8

Data as orig. reptd.; bef. results of disc. opers. and/or spec. items. Per share data adj. for stk. divs. as of ex-div. date. E-Estimated. NA-Not Available. NM-Not Meaningful. NR-Not Ranked.

Office—1100 N. Market St., Wilmington, DE 19890-0001. **Tel**—(302) 651-1000. **Chrmn & CEO**—T. T. Cecala. **Pres & COO**—R. V. A. Harra Jr. **VP & Investor Contact**—Charles W. King (302-651-8069). **VP & Secy**—T. P. Collins. **Dirs**—R. H. Bolling Jr., C. S. Burger, T. T. Cecala, R. R. Collins Jr., C. S. Crompton Jr., H. S. Dunn Jr., E. B. duPont, R.K. Elliot, E. P. Fairman, R. C. Forney, T. L. Gossage, R. V. A. Harra Jr.,—A. B. Kirkpatrick Jr., R. L. Mears, W. D. Mertz, H. E. Miller, S. J. Mobley, G. B. Pearson Jr., L. W. Quill, D. P. Roselle, T. P. Sweeney, B. J. Taylor II, M. J. Theisen, R. W. Tunell Jr. **Transfer Agent & Registrar**—Co. itself. **Incorporated**—in Delaware in 1901; reincorporated in 1985. **Empl**— 2,332. **S&P Analyst:** Brendan McGovern

STOCKS WITH HIGHER YIELDS

ALLTEL Corp.

69

NYSE Symbol **AT**

In S&P 500

15-FEB-97

Industry: Telecommunications

Summary: This company operates one of the largest U.S. telephone systems, serving 1.6 million subscriber lines in 14 states.

S&P Opinion: Accumulate (★★★★)

Recent Price • 33⅞	Yield • 3.2%
52 Wk Range • 34⅛-26⅝	12-Mo. P/E • 22.1

Quantitative Evaluations

Outlook
(1 Lowest—5 Highest)
• **3**

Fair Value
• **33⅛**

Risk
• **Low**

Earn./Div. Rank
• **A**

Technical Eval.
• **Bearish** since 11/96

Rel. Strength Rank
(1 Lowest—99 Highest)
• **72**

Insider Activity
• **NA**

Earnings vs. Previous Year
▲=Up ▼=Down ▶=No Change

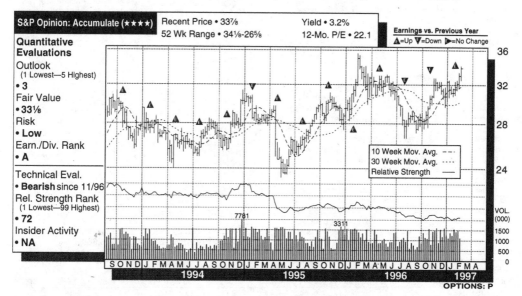

10 Week Mov. Avg. ---
30 Week Mov. Avg. ····
Relative Strength —

OPTIONS: P

Overview - 06-FEB-97

ALLTEL should continue to post earnings gains above the industry average, reflecting its successful growth strategy. AT's strategy focuses on diversification into nonregulated businesses, such as information services (IS) and wireless communications, while also maximizing growth prospects for core telephone businesses. The reorganization of IS into more product/service-focus profit centers should allow AT to take advantage of growing demand for information processing services. The wireless unit's customer base continues to grow rapidly, despite heightened competition, and recently increased its potential wireless customer base by almost 300% through a successful bid in a federal auction. Meanwhile, telephone operations remain an integral part of AT's strategy. We expect AT to continue to pursue wireline opportunities in markets where it can leverage the existing presence of its wireless operations.

Valuation - 06-FEB-97

The shares have gained following a decline after the enactment of federal telecommunications legislation on investor concerns regarding the prospect of increasing competition. While the new law opens local markets to competition, the company will not be impacted as much because it operates in many smaller markets. New competitors will likely concentrate initially on the larger metropolitan markets. Meanwhile, future results at the information services unit should benefit from a continuing transition to a broader customer base. EPS is expected to reach $2.15 in 1997, up from the $1.53 (including nonrecurring charges of $0.39) reported in 1996. With earnings expected to advance over 10% (before charges) in 1997, the shares, which also provide a healthy dividend yield, are expected to provide above-average total return.

Key Stock Statistics

S&P EPS Est. 1997	2.15	Tang. Bk. Value/Share	8.45
P/E on S&P Est. 1997	15.8	Beta	0.46
S&P EPS Est. 1998	2.35	Shareholders	92,000
Dividend Rate/Share	1.10	Market cap. (B)	$ 6.4
Shs. outstg. (M)	189.6	Inst. holdings	37%
Avg. daily vol. (M)	0.297		

Value of $10,000 invested 5 years ago: $ 20,003

Fiscal Year Ending Dec. 31

	1996	1995	1994	1993	1992	1991
Revenues (Million $)						
1Q	774.3	763.6	709.4	546.7	507.0	412.0
2Q	804.5	786.5	734.6	568.9	521.0	440.0
3Q	807.4	785.8	745.3	571.7	525.0	439.0
4Q	806.3	773.9	772.4	654.8	538.0	457.0
Yr.	3,192	3,110	2,962	2,342	2,092	1,748
Earnings Per Share ($)						
1Q	0.44	0.41	0.38	0.33	0.26	0.29
2Q	0.48	0.52	0.40	0.34	0.31	0.29
3Q	0.10	0.45	0.42	0.35	0.32	0.29
4Q	0.51	0.48	0.23	0.36	0.33	0.30
Yr.	1.53	1.86	1.43	1.39	1.22	1.17

Next earnings report expected: mid April

Dividend Data (Dividends have been paid since 1961.)

Amount ($)	Date Decl.	Ex-Div. Date	Stock of Record	Payment Date
0.260	Apr. 25	Jun. 05	Jun. 07	Jul. 03 '96
0.260	Jul. 25	Sep. 05	Sep. 09	Oct. 03 '96
0.275	Oct. 24	Dec. 04	Dec. 06	Jan. 03 '97
0.275	Jan. 31	Feb. 20	Feb. 24	Apr. 03 '97

A Division of The **McGraw-Hill** Companies

Business Summary - 06-FEB-97

ALLTEL Corp. is a diversified telecommunications company. Business segment contributions in 1995 were:

	Revenue	Profits
Telephone operations	39%	59%
Information services	30%	19%
Product distribution	14%	4%
Cellular	13%	17%
Other	4%	1%

At December 31, 1996, the company provided local telephone service to over 1,681,395 access lines in 14 states. In November 1994, ALLTEL signed definitive agreements to sell certain telephone properties serving approximately 117,000 access lines, primarily in the western U.S., to Citizens Utilities Company. Compensation totalled about $292 million, consisting of cash, assumed debt and 3,600 access lines in Pennsylvania. The final sale was completed in April 1996.

The information services unit provides outsourcing, software and information processing services to telecommunications, health care and banking companies. AT's cellular operations serve 8.2 million POPs (population adjusted for percent ownership) in 18 states concentrated in the Sun Belt region. Cellular subscribers numbered 795,136 at December 31, 1996. Distribution operations include ALLTEL Supply, a leading supplier of telecom equipment, and HWC Distribution, which distributes specialty wire and cable products. Other operations include the publication of telephone directories, paging services and a 7% interest in WorldCom Inc., a long distance carrier.

In October 1996, ALLTEL announced it will invest up to $12.5 million and become a minority investor in Apex Global Information Services, Inc., one of only six global providers of Internet access.

Important Developments

Jan. '97—ALLTEL said it successfully bid for 73 markets in 12 states in a federal Personal Communications Services (PCS) auction. When issued by the FCC, the "D" and "E" spectrum blocks licenses will enable the company to increase the size of its potential wireless customer base from 8.4 million to 31.4 million. AT also believes that the licenses will dramatically increase the overlap of its system-wide wireline and wireless territories from 25% to 55%. ALLTEL will pay about $144 million for the licenses, or approximately $5 per potential customer.

Jan. '97—The company said it has repurchased 2.9 million of its shares under a 3.5 million common share buyback program authorized by its directors in October 1996.

Capitalization

Long Term Debt: $1,756,142,000 (12/96).
Red. Cum. Preferred Stock: $6,455,000.
Cum. Preferred Stock: $9,198,000.

Per Share Data ($)

(Year Ended Dec. 31)	1996	1995	1994	1993	1992	1991	1990	1989	1988	1987
Tangible Bk. Val.	NA	7.64	5.96	5.53	4.86	4.58	4.60	4.85	5.15	4.95
Cash Flow	NA	4.02	3.34	2.84	2.54	2.50	2.34	2.40	2.15	NA
Earnings	1.53	1.86	1.43	1.39	1.22	1.17	1.17	1.16	0.97	1.02
Dividends	1.05	0.98	0.90	0.82	0.76	0.71	0.65	0.59	0.52	0.47
Payout Ratio	69%	53%	63%	59%	62%	61%	56%	51%	54%	46%
Prices - High	35⅝	31⅛	31⅜	31¼	25	21⅝	19⅝	21	12⅝	11⅜
- Low	26⅝	23¼	24	22⅞	17⅝	15⅞	12⅜	11¾	8⅝	7¾
P/E Ratio - High	23	17	22	22	20	18	17	18	13	11
- Low	17	12	17	16	14	14	11	10	9	7

Income Statement Analysis (Million $)

	1996	1995	1994	1993	1992	1991	1990	1989	1988	1987
Revs.	NA	3,110	2,962	2,342	2,092	1,748	1,574	1,226	1,068	736
Depr.	NA	410	362	272	245	217	192	165	155	125
Maint.	NA	148	151	131	122	109	104	106	101	96.0
Constr. Credits	NA	Nil	NA	2.0	2.0	1.9	1.4	1.2	1.4	1.8
Eff. Tax Rate	NA	38%	38%	42%	36%	33%	32%	30%	35%	34%
Net Inc.	NA	355	272	262	229	189	193	154	125	104

Balance Sheet & Other Fin. Data (Million $)

	1996	1995	1994	1993	1992	1991	1990	1989	1988	1987
Gross Prop.	NA	4,842	4,697	4,235	3,297	2,913	2,759	2,486	2,395	1,991
Net Prop.	NA	2,973	2,963	2,676	2,062	1,825	1,755	1,615	1,553	1,311
Cap. Exp.	NA	523	596	426	367	308	272	231	201	162
Total Cap.	NA	4,270	3,896	3,575	2,643	2,405	2,265	2,057	1,839	1,457
Fxd. Chgs. Cov.	NA	4.5	4.1	5.4	4.8	4.0	4.5	3.9	3.8	3.8
Capitalization:										
LT Debt	NA	1,762	1,846	1,596	1,018	992	905	799	675	554
Pfd.	NA	16.3	17.1	18.0	19.1	21.3	23.5	36.1	37.9	40.8
Common	NA	1,926	1,616	1,545	1,295	1,072	1,005	884	779	572
% Ret. on Revs.	NA	11.4	9.2	11.2	10.9	10.8	12.3	12.6	11.7	14.2
% Ret. On Invest.Cap	NA	16.6	10.9	11.6	12.7	11.4	12.2	11.5	10.4	10.6
% Return On Com.Eqty	NA	20.0	17.1	18.3	18.8	18.0	19.3	18.2	16.3	18.8
% Earn. on Net Prop.	NA	23.0	16.6	14.0	15.8	14.3	15.2	14.0	11.7	10.4
% LT Debt of Cap.	NA	47.6	53.1	50.5	43.7	47.6	46.8	46.5	45.2	47.5
Capital. % Pfd.	NA	0.4	0.5	0.6	0.8	1.0	1.2	2.1	2.6	3.5
Capital. % Common	NA	52.0	46.4	48.9	55.5	51.4	52.0	51.4	52.2	49.0

Data as orig. reptd.; bef. results of disc. opers and/or spec. items. Per share data adj. for stk. divs. as of ex-div. date. E-Estimated. NA-Not Available. NM-Not Meaningful. NR-Not Ranked.

Office—One Allied Drive, Little Rock, AR 72202.**Tel**—(501) 661-8000. **Chrmn, Pres & CEO**—J. T. Ford. **SVP & CFO**—D. J. Ferra. **SVP & Secy**—F. X. Frantz. **Treas**—J. M. Green. **VP & Investor Contact**—Shawne S. Leach.**Dirs**—B. W. Agee, M. D. Andreas, J. R. Belk, J. T. Ford, S. T. Ford, L. L. Gellerstedt III, W. W. Johnson, E. A. Mahony, Jr., J. P. McConnell, J. Natori, J. E. Steuri, C. H. Tiedemann, R. Townsend, W. H. Zimmer, Jr. **Transfer Agent & Registrar**—KeyCorp Shareholder Services Inc. **Incorporated**—in Delaware. **Empl**— 15,685. **S&P Analyst:** Philip D. Wohl

19-FEB-97 Industry: Banking

Summary: This state-chartered savings bank operates in and around Waterbury, CT.

Quantitative Evaluations

Outlook
(1 Lowest—5 Highest)
• NA

Fair Value
• NA

Risk
• **Low**

Earn./Div. Rank
• **B+**

Technical Eval.
• **Bearish** since 11/96

Rel. Strength Rank
(1 Lowest—99 Highest)
• **40**

Insider Activity
• NA

Recent Price • 28	Yield • 4.9%
52 Wk Range • 29⅞-24	12-Mo. P/E • 9.9

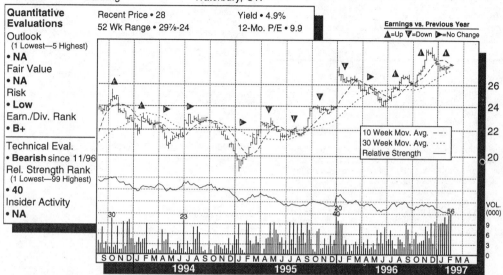

Earnings vs. Previous Year
▲=Up ▼=Down ▶=No Change

10 Week Mov. Avg. – – –
30 Week Mov. Avg. ·······
Relative Strength ——

Business Profile - 19-FEB-97

This Connecticut-chartered savings bank, with total assets of $559.1 million, is headquartered in Waterbury, with offices in that city, as well as in Torrington and neighboring towns. During 1995, the lending department expanded its origination capabilities for both mortgages and business loans, and the data systems area completed a major technology project. In November 1996, BKC's directors declared a special dividend of $0.14 per share in addition to the regular quarterly dividend of $0.34 per share; the combined dividend was payable December 20, 1996, to stockholders of record on December 6, 1996. At December 31, 1996, mortgage loans, which account for 97% of the bank's net loan portfolio, were 5.8% higher than at the previous year end, while commercial loans dropped 21% year to year. Officers and directors own about 20% of the slightly more than two million common shares outstanding.

Operational Review - 19-FEB-97

Net interest income in 1996 rose 9.9%, year to year, reflecting a 5.8% rise in mortgage loans as well as a greater amount of securities held for sale. The provision for loan losses fell 38%, to $1,525,000, as asset quality improved. Noninterest income was up 8.7%, as higher stock option premiums and other income outweighed the 48% drop in gain on the sale of securities. With significantly lower losses and lower losses on real estate, pretax income advanced 56%. After taxes at 32.4%, against 27.0%, net income was up 45%, to $6,629,000 ($2.83 a share), from $4,588,000 ($1.99).

Stock Performance - 14-FEB-97

In the past 30 trading days, BKC's shares have increased 0.90%, compared to a 8% rise in the S&P 500. Average trading volume for the past five days was 11,100 shares, compared with the 40-day moving average of 4,951 shares.

Key Stock Statistics

Dividend Rate/Share	1.36	Shareholders	NA
Shs. outstg. (M)	2.3	Market cap. (B)	$0.064
Avg. daily vol. (M)	0.008	Inst. holdings	13%
Tang. Bk. Value/Share	18.48		
Beta	0.25		

Value of $10,000 invested 5 years ago: $ 23,244

Fiscal Year Ending Dec. 31

	1996	1995	1994	1993	1992	1991
Revenues (Million $)						
1Q	9.75	8.61	7.41	8.92	7.43	8.03
2Q	10.27	9.09	7.60	8.70	8.82	8.09
3Q	10.47	9.15	7.79	9.23	8.29	7.95
4Q	11.64	10.99	7.97	9.19	8.08	7.77
Yr.	42.13	37.83	30.77	36.04	32.62	31.84
Earnings Per Share ($)						
1Q	0.67	0.67	0.69	0.69	0.55	0.51
2Q	0.71	0.09	0.69	0.69	0.55	0.49
3Q	0.72	0.61	0.69	0.69	0.55	0.47
4Q	0.74	0.62	0.69	0.69	0.18	0.47
Yr.	2.83	1.99	2.76	2.76	1.83	1.94

Next earnings report expected: mid April

Dividend Data (Dividends have been paid since 1982.)

Amount ($)	Date Decl.	Ex-Div. Date	Stock of Record	Payment Date
0.340	May. 16	Jun. 12	Jun. 14	Jun. 28 '96
0.340	Aug. 21	Sep. 11	Sep. 13	Sep. 27 '96
0.14 Spl.	Nov. 29	Dec. 04	Dec. 06	Dec. 20 '96
0.340	Nov. 29	Dec. 04	Dec. 06	Dec. 20 '96

A Division of The McGraw-Hill Companies

Business Summary - 19-FEB-97

American Bank of Connecticut is a state-chartered savings bank, headquartered in Waterbury. The bank is primarily a home mortgage lender. Deposits are insured by the Federal Deposit Insurance Corp. (FDIC).
The loan portfolio broke down as follows in recent years:

	12/95	12/94
Mortgage loans:		
1- to 4-family residences	66%	69%
Commercial real estate	20%	16%
Multifamily residences	5%	6%
Construction	4%	4%
Commercial loans	5%	4%
Consumer loans	1%	1%

The bank's market area is comprised of the cities of Waterbury and Torrington and contiguous towns. Its main office and seven other offices are located in Waterbury, with other branch offices in Middlebury, Seymour, Torrington, Watertown, Winsted and Woodbury. American Bank originates loans almost exclusively for retention in its own portfolio. In addition to retail banking, the bank engages in commercial credit, commercial real estate and consumer credit.

American Bank competes for business not only with other financial institutions in its market area, but also with credit unions, insurance companies and nationally offered money-market mutual funds. BKC believes that its competitive advantage lies in the convenience of its office locations and the attractiveness of its products.
During 1995, the loan portfolio grew by $19.4 million, versus $6.0 million in 1994. Nonaccrual loans, generally loans over 90 days delinquent, amounted to $4.6 million at year-end 1995, down from $6.9 million at year-end 1994. Loans categorized as troubled debt restructures due to deterioration of the financial condition of the borrower increased to $8.6 million at December 31, 1995, from $3.2 million a year earlier.

Important Developments

Nov. '96—BKC's directors declared a special dividend of $0.14 per share in addition to the regular quarterly dividend of $0.34 per share; the combined dividend was payable December 20, 1996, to stockholders of record on December 6, 1996.

Capitalization

Total Borrowings: $108,376,000 (12/96).

Per Share Data ($)

(Year Ended Dec. 31)	1996	1995	1994	1993	1992	1991	1990	1989	1988	1987
Tangible Bk. Val.	NA	18.48	16.05	15.39	14.19	15.15	14.07	13.33	11.73	10.30
Earnings	2.83	1.99	2.72	2.76	1.83	1.94	2.59	2.80	2.55	2.31
Dividends	1.50	1.32	1.32	1.39	1.32	1.32	1.32	1.20	1.10	0.95
Payout Ratio	53%	65%	48%	50%	72%	68%	51%	43%	43%	41%
Prices - High	29⅞	27¼	23¼	25½	20¼	16⅞	19⅞	20⅝	20⅞	21¾
- Low	24	18⅞	20⅛	18⅜	15⅜	11⅞	10¾	18⅝	17⅛	12½
P/E Ratio - High	11	13	8	9	11	9	8	7	8	9
- Low	8	9	7	7	8	6	4	7	7	5

Income Statement Analysis (Million $)

	1996	1995	1994	1993	1992	1991	1990	1989	1988	1987
Net Int. Inc.	NA	16.0	17.0	16.6	15.8	12.8	10.8	9.1	9.1	9.1
Loan Loss Prov.	NA	2.5	0.8	0.9	4.6	4.1	2.2	0.2	0.1	-0.2
Non Int. Inc.	NA	4.9	2.4	4.8	6.0	2.8	4.9	5.1	3.4	NA
Non Int. Exp.	NA	12.1	10.0	11.5	11.9	6.0	5.8	5.2	5.0	NA
Pretax Inc.	NA	6.3	8.6	8.9	5.2	5.6	7.7	8.8	7.5	6.8
Eff. Tax Rate	NA	27%	28%	32%	23%	24%	27%	31%	26%	27%
Net Inc.	NA	4.6	6.3	6.1	4.0	4.2	5.6	6.1	5.5	5.0
% Net Int. Marg.	NA	Nil	4.30	4.30	4.40	4.10	3.40	3.40	3.40	3.40

Balance Sheet & Other Fin. Data (Million $)

	1996	1995	1994	1993	1992	1991	1990	1989	1988	1987
Total Assets	NA	476	471	458	453	351	334	327	280	246
Loans	NA	341	322	317	275	258	270	251	215	182
Deposits	NA	371	371	380	376	252	243	238	207	198
Capitalization:										
Debt	NA	59.4	59.7	40.0	40.0	62.6	55.6	54.1	40.9	20.0
Equity	NA	44.6	39.0	37.6	34.4	33.1	30.6	29.0	25.5	22.3
Total	NA	104	99	77.6	74.4	95.7	86.2	83.1	66.3	42.3
% Ret. on Assets	NA	1.0	1.3	1.4	0.9	1.2	1.7	2.0	2.1	2.1
% Ret. on Equity	NA	11.0	16.3	16.6	11.5	13.3	18.9	22.3	23.1	24.1
% Loan Loss Resv.	NA	1.6	1.6	2.1	2.2	1.5	0.8	0.1	0.1	NA
% Risk Based Capital	NA	NA	NA	12.7	12.3	14.1	NA	NA	NA	NA
Price Times Book Value:										
Hi	NA	1.5	1.4	1.7	1.3	1.1	1.4	1.5	1.8	2.1
Low	NA	1.0	1.3	1.2	1.0	0.8	0.8	1.4	1.5	1.2

Data as orig. reptd.; bef. results of disc. opers. and/or spec. items. Per share data adj. for stk. divs. as of ex-div. date. E-Estimated. NA-Not Available. NM-Not Meaningful. NR-Not Ranked.

Chartered—in Connecticut in 1985. **Office**—Two West Main St. (P.O. Box 2589), Waterbury, CT 06723. **Tel**—(203) 757-9401. **Pres**—G. C. Guilbert. **VP-Treas**—R. M. Donohoe. **VP-CFO**—F. G. Champagne. **VP-Secy & Investor Contact**—Betty Ann Veillette. **Dirs**—R. H. Caulfield, N. S. Drubner, G. C. Guilbert, C. T. Kellogg, G. S. Oneglia, P. A. Sirop, A. Y. Smith, R. W. Wesson. **Transfer Agent**—American Stock Transfer and Trust Co., NYC. **Empl**— 107. **S&P Analyst:** E. Fitzpatrick.

15-FEB-97 Industry: Services

Summary: This company compiles and computerizes lists of pre-school children, and elementary, junior high school, high school and college students, to rent for use in direct marketing.

Quantitative Evaluations

Outlook (1 Lowest—5 Highest)
• 2

Fair Value
• 21⅝

Risk
• Average

Earn./Div. Rank
• B+

Technical Eval.
• **Bearish** since 1/97

Rel. Strength Rank (1 Lowest—99 Highest)
• 13

Insider Activity
• Neutral

Recent Price • 23½
52 Wk Range • 37½-20¼

Yield • 5.1%
12-Mo. P/E • 14.2

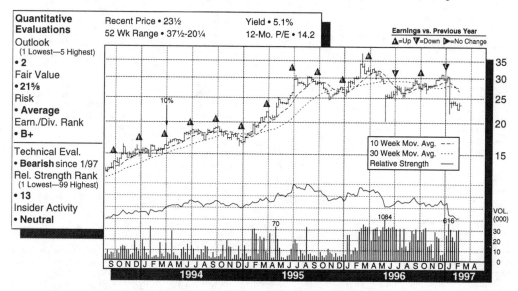

Earnings vs. Previous Year
▲=Up ▼=Down ▶=No Change

10 Week Mov. Avg. – – –
30 Week Mov. Avg. ·······
Relative Strength ——

Business Profile - 13-FEB-97

The company is continuing to increase its penetration into new markets for its lists, which are rented to colleges, universities, record and publishing companies, and other educational and financial institutions, as well as to branches of the armed services for recruitment purposes. After announcing a shortfall in revenues and earnings for the third quarter of FY 97 (Feb.), which it attributed to a small reduction in sales to certain major customers, the company indicated that it will aggressively promote its services so that its growth will "continue with the same vigor and momentum that it has experienced during the past five years."

Operational Review - 13-FEB-97

Revenues in the nine months ended November 30, 1996, edged up 1.7%, year to year, despite a third quarter shortfall reflecting a small reduction in sales to certain major customers. With expenses associated with the opening of a branch sales office, as well as professional fees and lobbying costs, and lower investment income, net income fell 3.8%, to $4,921,892 ($1.10 a share, on 1.5% fewer shares outstanding), from $5,118,653 ($1.13).

Stock Performance - 14-FEB-97

In the past 30 trading days, AMZ's shares have declined 23%, compared to a 8% rise in the S&P 500. Average trading volume for the past five days was 6,720 shares, compared with the 40-day moving average of 20,321 shares.

Key Stock Statistics

Dividend Rate/Share	1.20	Shareholders	300
Shs. outstg. (M)	4.5	Market cap. (B)	$0.105
Avg. daily vol. (M)	0.005	Inst. holdings	50%
Tang. Bk. Value/Share	3.88		
Beta	-0.34		

Value of $10,000 invested 5 years ago: $ 30,023

Fiscal Year Ending Feb. 28

	1997	1996	1995	1994	1993	1992
Revenues (Million $)						
1Q	5.10	5.33	4.29	3.56	2.96	2.83
2Q	3.74	3.12	2.78	2.31	1.89	1.80
3Q	4.60	4.77	3.53	2.99	2.37	1.78
4Q	—	5.67	4.89	3.78	2.89	2.37
Yr.	—	18.89	15.49	12.63	10.11	8.79
Earnings Per Share ($)						
1Q	0.44	0.51	0.40	0.32	0.26	0.25
2Q	0.26	0.20	0.18	0.14	0.11	0.11
3Q	0.41	0.42	0.29	0.24	0.16	0.12
4Q	—	0.55	0.49	0.31	0.24	0.16
Yr.	—	1.68	1.36	1.00	0.77	0.65

Next earnings report expected: early April

Dividend Data (Dividends have been paid since 1989.)

Amount ($)	Date Decl.	Ex-Div. Date	Stock of Record	Payment Date
0.300	Apr. 19	Apr. 29	May. 01	May. 14 '96
0.300	Jul. 03	Jul. 29	Jul. 31	Aug. 09 '96
0.300	Oct. 02	Oct. 16	Oct. 18	Nov. 08 '96
0.300	Jan. 07	Jan. 28	Jan. 30	Feb. 06 '97

A Division of The McGraw·Hill Companies

STANDARD
&POOR'S
STOCK REPORTS

American List Corporation

7122

15-FEB-97

Business Summary - 24-JUL-96

American List Corporation, together with wholly owned American Student List Co. Inc., is a leading provider of direct marketing information of pre-school children and students from elementary school, high school, college and post-graduate schools throughout the U.S, primarily used for direct mail and telemarketing programs. In FY 96 (Feb.), the company rented its lists to about 3,600 customers, including brokers and advertising agencies, financial institutions, retailers and educational institutions whose objective was to provide students and their parents with information pertaining to their products and services.

The company believes that its database is one of the most comprehensive and accurate currently available in the U.S. Lists contain information such as name, address, sex, date of birth, and telephone number of the individuals included. The database is continually updated and verified from numerous sources. Based on customer requirements, AMZ can format its information on mailing labels, magnetic tapes, computer diskettes, 3x5 index cards, or other media.

Most of AMZ's business focuses on lists of students who are, or are about to become, high school seniors (55% of total FY 96 revenues). Customers are marketers of credit cards, scholarships, catalogue items, formal wear, magazines, computers, software and accessories, as well as colleges, universities, business schools, trade and technical schools and other educa-

tional institutions that use direct mailings to encourage enrollment. The U.S. government also uses lists for direct mail, encouraging high school graduates to enlist in the armed services.

The process of renting a list is intended by the company as a one-time use, for which the renting party is charged a flat fee. There is an additional charge for any subsequent use of the list.

AMZ's competitors include large and small list compilers, managers and brokers, and marketing consultants and advertising agencies. Its closest competitor in the high school list business is Educational Testing Services of Princeton, NJ, which provides lists solely for non-profit institution.

In FY 94, the company entered into a 10-year exclusive licensing agreement with Metromail Corp., a major competitor. AMZ can reproduce and distribute Metromail's college student list, and use its sources and customer list to compile its own college student list. In exchange, Metromail received $4.2 million and the right to broker company lists to third parties.

Through the June 1995 acquisition of GeoDemX Corp., AMZ entered the emerging market of geodemographic software, which permits an organization to selectively target a prospective customer base that is similar to that organization's existing customer base.

Capitalization

Long Term Debt: $1,546,817 (11/96).

Per Share Data ($)

(Year Ended Feb. 28)	1996	1995	1994	1993	1992	1991	1990	1989	1988	1987
Tangible Bk. Val.	3.51	3.45	2.65	2.39	2.21	2.22	1.89	2.04	1.62	1.30
Cash Flow	1.79	1.37	1.02	0.79	0.67	0.72	0.89	0.47	0.42	0.34
Earnings	1.68	1.36	1.00	0.77	0.65	0.70	0.88	0.46	0.41	0.33
Dividends	0.95	0.80	0.79	0.61	0.61	0.27	1.03	Nil	Nil	Nil
Payout Ratio	57%	59%	79%	79%	93%	39%	117%	Nil	Nil	Nil
Cal. Yrs.	1995	1994	1993	1992	1991	1990	1989	1988	1987	1986
Prices - High	30¾	19¼	16⅜	12¾	16¾	14¾	10½	8⅜	7⅜	11¼
- Low	16⅝	14½	11	9	8⅝	9⅜	6	4⅝	3⅜	4½
P/E Ratio - High	18	14	16	17	26	21	12	18	18	34
- Low	10	NA	11	12	13	13	7	9	8	14

Income Statement Analysis (Million $)

Revs.	18.9	15.5	12.6	10.1	8.8	8.8	7.1	5.8	7.2	4.9
Oper. Inc.	12.2	9.8	7.3	5.5	4.6	4.8	3.9	3.0	3.0	2.6
Depr.	0.5	0.1	0.1	0.1	0.1	0.1	0.1	0.1	0.1	0.0
Int. Exp.	0.2	0.1	Nil	Nil	Nil	Nil	Nil	Nil	NA	Nil
Pretax Inc.	12.0	9.9	7.4	5.7	4.9	5.2	6.4	3.3	3.1	2.9
Eff. Tax Rate	37%	38%	39%	38%	39%	38%	37%	37%	41%	48%
Net Inc.	7.6	6.2	4.6	3.5	3.0	3.2	4.0	2.1	1.9	1.5

Balance Sheet & Other Fin. Data (Million $)

Cash	3.6	10.5	10.4	7.3	6.6	7.5	6.8	7.6	5.8	4.6
Curr. Assets	18.3	15.9	14.3	11.2	10.3	10.5	9.0	9.9	8.1	6.2
Total Assets	22.5	20.1	15.5	12.6	11.8	11.6	9.9	10.3	8.7	6.4
Curr. Liab.	1.4	1.4	2.6	0.7	0.6	0.6	0.8	1.0	0.8	0.4
LT Debt	1.9	2.3	Nil	Nil	Nil	Nil	Nil	Nil	0.2	Nil
Common Eqty.	19.2	16.4	12.9	11.9	11.2	11.0	9.0	9.3	7.8	6.0
Total Cap.	21.1	18.7	12.9	11.9	11.2	11.0	9.0	9.3	8.0	6.0
Cap. Exp.	0.2	0.1	0.1	0.0	0.3	0.1	0.1	0.0	0.1	0.1
Cash Flow	8.1	6.3	4.7	3.6	3.1	3.3	4.1	2.2	2.0	1.5
Curr. Ratio	13.1	11.2	5.5	16.1	16.1	16.9	10.9	10.0	10.8	15.6
% LT Debt of Cap.	8.9	12.4	Nil	Nil	Nil	Nil	Nil	Nil	2.6	Nil
% Net Inc.of Revs.	40.2	39.9	36.2	34.7	33.5	36.4	56.1	36.4	25.6	31.0
% Ret. on Assets	35.7	34.6	32.5	28.7	25.1	29.7	39.8	22.0	24.5	27.3
% Ret. on Equity	42.8	42.2	36.8	30.4	26.6	31.8	43.7	24.5	27.0	29.0

Data as orig. reptd.; bef. results of disc. opers. and/or spec. items. Per share data adj. for stk. divs. as of ex-div. date. E-Estimated. NA-Not Available. NM-Not Meaningful. NR-Not Ranked.

Office—330 Old Country Rd., Mineola, NY 11501. **Tel**—(516) 248-6100. **Fax**—(516) 248-6364. **Chrmn, Pres, Treas & Investor Contact**—Martin Lerner. **VPs**—D. Damore, T. J. Rolla, J. Stumacher. **Dirs**—J. M. Davis, B. Ermini, M. Lerner, P. Lubitz, K. Wood. **Transfer Agent & Registrar**—Continental Stock Transfer & Trust Co., NYC. **Incorporated**—in Delaware in 1970. **Empl**—38. **S&P Analyst:** C.F.B.

STANDARD &POOR'S
STOCK REPORTS

Ameritech

184T
NYSE Symbol **AIT**

In S&P 500

15-FEB-97 | Industry: Telecommunications

Summary: Ameritech is the third largest telephone holding company in the U.S., based on 1995 access lines. It provides service in parts of five upper-midwestern states.

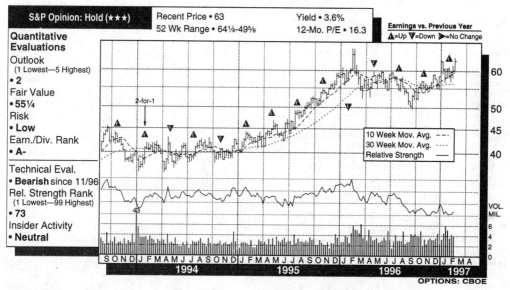

S&P Opinion: Hold (★★★)	Recent Price • 63	Yield • 3.6%
	52 Wk Range • 64⅛-49⅝	12-Mo. P/E • 16.3

Quantitative Evaluations

Outlook (1 Lowest—5 Highest)
• 2

Fair Value
• 55¼

Risk
• **Low**

Earn./Div. Rank
• **A-**

Technical Eval.
• **Bearish** since 11/96

Rel. Strength Rank (1 Lowest—99 Highest)
• 73

Insider Activity
• **Neutral**

Earnings vs. Previous Year
▲=Up ▼=Down ▷=No Change

2-for-1

- 10 Week Mov. Avg. — · —
- 30 Week Mov. Avg. ·····
- Relative Strength ——

60
50
45
40

VOL. MIL.
6
4
2
0

S O N D | J F M A M J J A S O N D | J F M A M J J A S O N D | J F M A M J J A S O N D | J F M A
1994 | **1995** | **1996** | **1997**

OPTIONS: CBOE

Overview - 13-JAN-97

Ameritech is moving to position itself for a competitive telephone market; its strategy focuses on entering complementary lines of business such as cable television and long-distance services, while upgrading its network. Although the Telecommunications Act of 1996 (Feb.) opened AIT's local markets to competition, it also allows the company to offer long-distance service to its cellular customers. In early 1997, AIT applied to offer wireline long distance service in Michigan. Although we are doubtful the company will receive regulatory approval at this time, AIT intends to begin offering long distance service sometime in the Spring. Meanwhile, the company has worked with state regulators to increase its pricing flexibility, while restructuring its operations to better position telephone operations for competition. These actions should result in continued revenue growth and margin expansion in the core business, despite heightened competition.

Valuation - 13-JAN-97

After rising sharply in 1995, the shares rose only 3.0% during 1996 compared to a 20% gain in the S&P 500, primarily due to investor concern over increased competition resulting from the enactment of federal telecommunications legislation. Over the long-term, we believe that the company is very well positioned to meet any competitive threats, while simultaneously taking advantage of opportunities to enter new lines of business. We expect the stock's performance to continue to benefit from AIT's successful efforts to prepare itself to operate in a rapidly changing market. But, although the shares, which yield an above-average 3.9%, are trading at only 13 times our 1997 EPS estimate of $4.20, we believe current regulatory uncertainty will limit appreciation over the near term.

Key Stock Statistics

S&P EPS Est. 1997	4.20	Tang. Bk. Value/Share	13.51
P/E on S&P Est. 1997	15.0	Beta	0.86
S&P EPS Est. 1998	4.55	Shareholders	956,300
Dividend Rate/Share	2.26	Market cap. (B)	$ 34.6
Shs. outstg. (M)	549.4	Inst. holdings	45%
Avg. daily vol. (M)	0.833		

Value of $10,000 invested 5 years ago: $ 23,565

Fiscal Year Ending Dec. 31

	1996	1995	1994	1993	1992	1991
Revenues (Million $)						
1Q	3,567	3,146	3,034	2,797	2,690	2,630
2Q	3,744	3,369	3,184	2,951	2,810	2,740
3Q	3,722	3,381	3,170	2,947	2,810	2,710
4Q	3,884	3,532	3,182	3,016	2,840	2,740
Yr.	14,917	13,427	12,570	11,710	11,150	10,820
Earnings Per Share ($)						
1Q	0.86	1.05	0.08	0.55	0.63	0.54
2Q	1.02	0.91	0.81	0.71	0.64	0.57
3Q	0.94	0.92	0.46	0.78	0.62	0.71
4Q	1.04	0.74	0.78	0.73	0.63	0.38
Yr.	3.87	3.63	2.13	2.78	2.51	2.20

Next earnings report expected: mid April

Dividend Data (Dividends have been paid since 1984.)

Amount ($)	Date Decl.	Ex-Div. Date	Stock of Record	Payment Date
0.530	Mar. 20	Mar. 27	Mar. 29	May. 01 '96
0.530	Jun. 19	Jun. 26	Jun. 28	Aug. 01 '96
0.530	Sep. 18	Sep. 26	Sep. 30	Nov. 01 '96
0.565	Dec. 18	Dec. 27	Dec. 31	Feb. 01 '97

A Division of The **McGraw·Hill** *Companies*

Business Summary - 13-JAN-97

Ameritech is the third largest U.S. telephone holding company, based on 1995 U.S. access lines. Its telephone subsidiaries provide local service in five midwestern states to 19.4 million customer access lines.

During 1995, the company received approval from the Federal Communications Commission (FCC) to implement pure price regulation without sharing of earnings, effective January 1, 1995. Under price regulation, regulators place limits on prices, not on profits as they once did under rate-of-return regulation. As a result, no limits exist on Ameritech's earnings in any federal or state regulatory jurisdiction.

Ameritech cellular provides wireless communications services. At June 30, 1996, 2,185,000 cellular lines and over 944,000 pagers were in service.

Other units provide directory advertising and publishing; sell, install and maintain business customer premises equipment (CPE) and sell network and central office-based services; arrange financing and leasing of computer and communications products; develop and invest in new products and technology; and develop international business opportunities.

A consortium led by AIT and Bell Atlantic acquired Telecom Corp. of New Zealand for US$2.45 billion in 1990. The companies sold 31% of Telecom Corp.'s share capital in an international public offering in July 1991. During 1993, AIT reduced its stake to 24.9%. AIT also owns 34.5% of MATAV, the telephone company of Hungary, and led a consortium that won the privatization bid for Belgacom, the telephone company of Belgium.

AIT is also a partner in a venture with BellSouth, GTE, SBC Communications and Walt Disney. The venture, known as Americast, will provide video programming and interactive services.

Important Developments

Jan. '97—Ameritech became the first major communications company to apply to the Federal Communications Commission (FCC) for permission to provide long distance service under terms spelled out in the federal Telecommunications Act of 1996. Upon FCC approval, the company plans to enter the long distance market in Michigan this Spring.

Dec. '96— Ameritech International, AIT's global business unit, announced that it has sold its interest in the Polish cellular joint venture PTK Centertel Sp. z.o.o. The two remaining partners, Telekomunikacja Polska SA (TPSA) and France Telecom Mobiles International, have purchased all of Ameritech International's shares.

Capitalization

Long Term Debt: $4,309,000,000 (9/96).

Per Share Data ($)

(Year Ended Dec. 31)	1996	1995	1994	1993	1992	1991	1990	1989	1988	1987
Tangible Bk. Val.	NA	12.67	10.98	14.25	12.82	15.06	14.50	14.09	14.44	13.73
Cash Flow	NA	7.56	6.15	6.75	6.30	5.79	5.81	5.70	5.63	NA
Earnings	3.87	3.63	2.13	2.78	2.51	2.20	2.36	2.29	2.28	2.12
Dividends	2.16	2.03	1.94	1.86	1.78	1.71	1.61	1.49	1.38	1.27
Payout Ratio	56%	56%	91%	67%	71%	78%	68%	65%	61%	60%
Prices - High	66⅞	59⅜	43⅛	45½	37	34⅞	34⅞	34⅛	24½	25
- Low	49⅝	39⅞	36¼	35	28⅛	27⅞	26¼	23½	20½	18½
P/E Ratio - High	17	16	20	16	15	16	15	15	11	12
- Low	13	11	17	13	11	13	11	10	9	9

Income Statement Analysis (Million $)

	1996	1995	1994	1993	1992	1991	1990	1989	1988	1987
Revs.	NA	13,428	12,570	11,710	11,153	10,818	10,663	10,211	9,903	9,536
Depr.	NA	2,177	2,205	2,162	2,031	1,915	1,825	1,797	1,757	1,793
Maint.	NA	NA	NA	1,729	1,737	1,647	1,662	1,590	1,601	1,636
Constr. Credits	NA	19.7	13.3	11.3	7.6	22.9	20.6	17.8	18.1	28.9
Eff. Tax Rate	NA	35%	33%	32%	32%	30%	31%	31%	32%	38%
Net Inc.	NA	2,008	1,170	1,513	1,346	1,166	1,254	1,238	1,237	1,188

Balance Sheet & Other Fin. Data (Million $)

	1996	1995	1994	1993	1992	1991	1990	1989	1988	1987
Gross Prop.	NA	30,874	29,546	29,117	28,370	27,158	26,370	25,092	24,224	24,034
Net Prop.	NA	13,457	13,455	17,366	17,335	16,986	16,652	16,296	16,078	15,933
Cap. Exp.	NA	3,015	2,466	2,564	2,267	2,200	2,154	2,015	1,895	1,956
Total Cap.	NA	12,518	11,370	14,179	14,460	16,187	15,912	16,458	16,058	15,741
Fxd. Chgs. Cov.	NA	7.6	5.0	5.7	4.9	3.9	4.8	5.4	5.7	6.1
Capitalization:										
LT Debt	NA	4,513	4,448	4,090	4,586	4,964	5,074	5,069	4,487	4,389
Pfd.	NA	Nil	Nil	Nil	Nil	Nil	Nil	Nil	Nil	Nil
Common	NA	7,015	6,055	7,845	6,992	8,097	7,732	7,686	7,844	7,610
% Ret. on Revs.	NA	15.0	9.3	12.9	12.1	10.8	11.8	12.1	12.5	12.5
% Ret. On Invest.Cap	NA	29.8	12.6	14.1	12.1	10.8	10.7	10.1	10.2	9.9
% Return On Com.Eqty	NA	30.7	14.4	20.4	19.8	14.5	16.3	15.8	15.8	15.5
% Earn. on Net Prop.	NA	17.5	9.5	11.0	10.0	8.9	9.9	9.9	9.7	9.7
% LT Debt of Cap.	NA	39.2	42.3	34.3	39.6	38.0	39.6	39.7	36.4	36.6
Capital. % Pfd.	NA	Nil	Nil	Nil	Nil	Nil	Nil	Nil	Nil	Nil
Capital. % Common	NA	60.8	57.7	65.7	60.4	62.0	60.4	60.3	63.6	63.4

Data as orig. reptd.; bef. results of disc. opers. and/or spec. items. Per share data adj. for stk. divs. as of ex-div. date. E-Estimated. NA-Not Available. NM-Not Meaningful. NR-Not Ranked.

Office—30 South Wacker Drive, Chicago, IL 60606. **Tel**—(800) 257-0902. **E-mail**—share.owners@ameritech.com **Website**—http://www.ameritech.com **Chrmn, Pres & CEO**—R. C. Notebaert. **EVP & CFO**—Oren G. Shaffer. **Secy**—B. B. Howat. **VP & Investor Contact**—Sari L. Macrie. **Dirs**—D. C. Clark, M. R. Goodes, H. H. Gray, J. A. Henderson, S. B. Lubar, L. M. Martin, A. C. Martinez, J. B. McCoy, R. C. Notebaert, J. D. Ong, A. B. Rand, J. A. Unruh. **Transfer Agent & Registrar**—First Chicago Trust Co. of New York, NYC. **Incorporated**—in Delaware in 1983. **Empl**—65,345. **S&P Analyst:** Brad Ohlmuller

15-FEB-97

Industry: Chemicals

Summary: This company (83%-owned by Atlantic Richfield) is a leading producer of propylene oxide, styrene monomer and polymers, and oxygenated chemicals.

Quantitative Evaluations

Outlook (1 Lowest—5 Highest)
• **1**

Fair Value
• **42⅞**

Risk
• **Low**

Earn./Div. Rank
• **B**

Technical Eval.
• **Bullish** since 10/95

Rel. Strength Rank (1 Lowest—99 Highest)
• **34**

Insider Activity
• **NA**

Recent Price • 48¼
52 Wk Range • 54-47⅛

Yield • 5.8%
12-Mo. P/E • 13.4

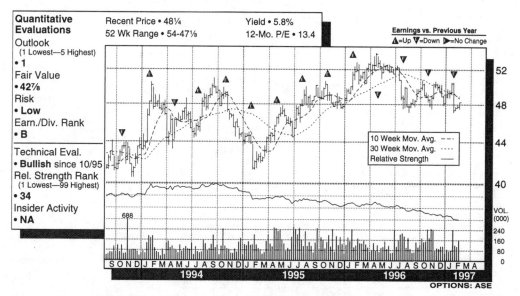

Earnings vs. Previous Year
▲=Up ▼=Down ▶=No Change

10 Week Mov. Avg. – – –
30 Week Mov. Avg. · · · · ·
Relative Strength ——

OPTIONS: ASE

Business Profile - 04-FEB-97

To reduce the impact of economic cycles on its earnings, RCM is pursuing strategic alternatives that include equity agreements and long-term contracts for styrene, as well as expansion of its core propylene oxide (PO) and derivatives business. In September 1996, the company sold its plastics business, which will enable it to focus entirely on its core businesses. A five-year, $2.6 billion capital spending program is targeted primarily for growth projects in those core businesses. The December 1996 acquisition of Olin Corp.'s toluene diisocyanate (TDI) business made RCM the second largest marketer of TDI in the world. The dividend has provided a yield that is among the highest among major chemical equities.

Operational Review - 04-FEB-97

Based on a preliminary report, revenues in 1996 fell 7.6% from those of 1995, primarily reflecting lower styrene monomer prices. Operating income fell 34%, as margins narrowed due to the lower selling prices and higher raw materials costs. Net income was down 31%, to $348,000 ($3.60 a share), from $508,000 ($5.28). The company expects raw material cost pressures to continue to squeeze product margins during the first quarter of 1997.

Stock Performance - 14-FEB-97

In the past 30 trading days, RCM's shares have declined 2%, compared to a 8% rise in the S&P 500. Average trading volume for the past five days was 17,950 shares, compared with the 40-day moving average of 22,264 shares.

Key Stock Statistics

Dividend Rate/Share	2.80	Shareholders	1,600
Shs. outstg. (M)	96.8	Market cap. (B)	$ 4.7
Avg. daily vol. (M)	0.031	Inst. holdings	7%
Tang. Bk. Value/Share	20.91		
Beta	0.92		

Value of $10,000 invested 5 years ago: $ 16,054

Fiscal Year Ending Dec. 31

	1996	1995	1994	1993	1992	1991
Revenues (Million $)						
1Q	982.0	1,141	757.0	767.0	762.0	682.0
2Q	959.0	1,149	824.0	803.0	769.0	703.0
3Q	1,035	999	895.0	782.0	787.0	705.0
4Q	979.0	993.0	947.0	840.0	780.0	747.0
Yr.	3,955	4,282	3,423	3,192	3,100	2,837
Earnings Per Share ($)						
1Q	1.10	1.31	0.47	0.54	0.62	0.54
2Q	0.84	1.56	0.71	0.49	0.19	0.34
3Q	1.00	1.21	0.84	0.49	0.73	0.36
4Q	0.66	1.19	0.78	0.71	0.50	0.71
Yr.	3.60	5.28	2.80	2.23	2.05	1.96

Next earnings report expected: mid April

Dividend Data (Dividends have been paid since 1987.)

Amount ($)	Date Decl.	Ex-Div. Date	Stock of Record	Payment Date
0.700	Apr. 18	May. 01	May. 03	Jun. 07 '96
0.700	Jul. 18	Aug. 07	Aug. 09	Sep. 06 '96
0.700	Oct. 17	Nov. 06	Nov. 08	Dec. 06 '96
0.700	Jan. 23	Feb. 12	Feb. 14	Mar. 07 '97

A Division of The McGraw-Hill Companies

Business Summary - 04-FEB-97

ARCO Chemical Co. is a leading producer of intermediate and specialty chemicals. Contributions by geographic segment in 1995 were:

	Sales	Profits
U.S.	61%	89%
Europe	32%	9%
Asia Pacific	7%	2%

The company's major products are propylene oxide (PO) and derivatives, tertiary butyl alcohol (TBA) and its derivative methyl tertiary butyl ether (MTBE), and styrene monomer (SM) and derivatives. RCM's process technologies enable it to manufacture PO and, depending on the facility, either TBA or SM as co-products. The company is the world's largest PO producer (annual capacity of 3.7 billion lbs.). PO derivatives include polyols (1.30 billion lbs.) used to produce urethane chemicals; propylene glycols (910 million lbs.) for unsaturated polyester resins, coolants, de-icers, and food, drug and cosmetics uses; glycol ethers and acetates for coatings and solvents; and butanediol used in resins and urethanes. RCM itself consumed 54% of its 1995 PO production.

RCM is the world's largest producer of TBA (annual capacity of 5.3 billion lbs.) and MTBE (70,500 bbl./day, including third party producers), used mainly as blending components and octane enhancers in gasoline. Styrene (annual capacity of 3.4 billion lbs.) is used in plastics and rubbers. Polystyrenics (515 million lbs.) consist of Dylite expandable polystyrene (PS) for insulation, packaging and consumer products, and Dylark engineering resins for the automotive market. RCM consumed 12% of its 1995 styrene output in the manufacture of polystyrenics products.

Important Developments

Dec. '96—RCM completed the previously announced acquisition of Olin Corporation's toluene diisocyanate (TDI) and aliphatic diisocyanate (ADI) businesses for $565 million. Revenues for the two businesses totaled $298 million for the twelve months ended June 30, 1996. The acquisition makes RCM the second largest marketer of TDI worldwide with a market share of 19%.
Sep. '96—The company sold its plastics business to NOVA Corp for approximately $160 million. The business, including polystyrene and engineering resins, had 1995 revenues of $310 million. Proceeds will be invested in the expansion of RCM's core PO and derivatives business.

Capitalization

Long Term Debt: $855,000,000 (9/96).
Minority Interest: $184,000,000.

Per Share Data ($)

(Year Ended Dec. 31)	1996	1995	1994	1993	1992	1991	1990	1989	1988	1987
Tangible Bk. Val.	NA	20.41	17.27	16.35	16.99	17.69	18.34	16.59	14.32	11.21
Cash Flow	NA	7.70	4.81	4.19	3.76	3.36	4.43	5.19	5.85	NA
Earnings	3.60	5.28	2.80	2.23	2.05	1.96	3.21	4.22	5.00	2.58
Dividends	2.80	2.65	2.50	2.50	2.50	2.50	2.50	2.13	0.85	0.20
Payout Ratio	78%	50%	89%	112%	122%	128%	78%	50%	17%	8%
Prices - High	54	50⅝	51	47¼	47¼	44¼	44¼	40⅜	38	38¾
- Low	47⅛	41¼	43⅛	39¼	36½	33⅛	29¾	28¾	23¼	17
P/E Ratio - High	15	10	18	21	23	23	14	10	8	15
- Low	13	8	15	18	18	17	9	7	5	7

Income Statement Analysis (Million $)

	1996	1995	1994	1993	1992	1991	1990	1989	1988	1987
Revs.	NA	4,282	3,423	3,192	3,098	2,837	2,830	2,663	2,700	1,952
Oper. Inc.	NA	1,056	698	613	625	399	556	676	805	482
Depr.	NA	233	193	188	164	134	117	93.0	83.0	84.0
Int. Exp.	NA	89.0	88.0	105	116	118	75.0	37.0	51.0	32.0
Pretax Inc.	NA	756	416	311	322	319	467	599	763	421
Eff. Tax Rate	NA	33%	35%	31%	39%	41%	34%	32%	35%	39%
Net Inc.	NA	508	269	214	197	188	308	405	494	257

Balance Sheet & Other Fin. Data (Million $)

	1996	1995	1994	1993	1992	1991	1990	1989	1988	1987
Cash	NA	260	144	42.0	144	200	486	144	410	709
Curr. Assets	NA	1,382	1,124	943	1,012	1,124	1,406	852	1,170	1,291
Total Assets	NA	4,135	3,737	3,502	3,599	3,676	3,739	2,655	2,548	2,534
Curr. Liab.	NA	589	545	487	509	533	541	414	637	976
LT Debt	NA	887	898	888	1,044	1,119	1,181	390	271	166
Common Eqty.	NA	1,969	1,659	1,576	1,630	1,696	1,758	1,591	1,375	1,116
Total Cap.	NA	3,388	3,050	2,912	2,934	3,030	3,147	2,202	1,863	1,521
Cap. Exp.	NA	195	186	181	295	557	539	262	230	295
Cash Flow	NA	741	462	402	361	322	425	498	577	324
Curr. Ratio	NA	2.3	2.1	1.9	2.0	2.1	2.6	2.1	1.8	1.3
% LT Debt of Cap.	NA	26.2	29.4	30.5	35.6	36.9	37.5	17.7	14.5	10.9
% Net Inc.of Revs.	NA	11.9	7.9	6.7	6.4	6.6	10.9	15.2	18.3	13.2
% Ret. on Assets	NA	12.9	7.4	6.0	5.4	5.1	9.6	15.6	19.8	12.9
% Ret. on Equity	NA	28.0	16.6	13.3	11.8	10.9	18.4	27.3	40.3	24.9

Data as orig. reptd.; bef. results of disc. opers. and/or spec. items. Per share data adj. for stk. divs. as of ex-div. date. E-Estimated. NA-Not Available. NM-Not Meaningful. NR-Not Ranked.

Office—3801 West Chester Pike, Newtown Square, PA 19073-2387. **Tel**—(610) 359-2000. **Chrmn**—M. R. Bowlin. **Pres & CEO**—A. L. Hirsig. **SVP & CFO**—W. J. Tusinski. **Secy**—R. J. Millstone. **Investor Contact**—Patricia Bartlett. **Dirs**—R. J. Arnault, W. F. Beran, M. R. Bowlin, E. K. Damon, Jr., A. G. Fernandes, A. R. Hirsig, J. A. Middleton, S. R. Mut, F. Savage, M. O. Schlanger, R. H. Stewart III, W. J. Tusinski. **Transfer Agent & Registrar**—First Chicago Trust Co. of New York, Jersey City, NJ. **Incorporated**—in Delaware in 1965. **Empl**—4,460. **S&P Analyst:** Adam Penn

STANDARD &POOR'S
STOCK REPORTS

Bankers Trust

284

NYSE Symbol **BT**

In S&P 500

15-FEB-97

Industry:
Banking

Summary: This bank holding company, the seventh largest in the U.S., focuses on client finance, advisory, risk management, transaction processing, and trading and positioning activities.

S&P Opinion: Hold (★★★)	Recent Price • 92¾	Yield • 4.3%
	52 Wk Range • 93⅜-63	12-Mo. P/E • 13.7

Quantitative Evaluations

Outlook
(1 Lowest—5 Highest)
• **3⁻**

Fair Value
• **89⅞**

Risk
• **Low**

Earn./Div. Rank
• **B**

Technical Eval.
• **Bullish** since 3/96

Rel. Strength Rank
(1 Lowest—99 Highest)
• **76**

Insider Activity
• **Neutral**

Earnings vs. Previous Year
▲=Up ▼=Down ▶=No Change

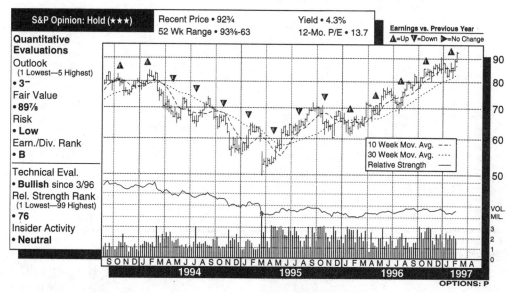

10 Week Mov. Avg. — —
30 Week Mov. Avg. ·····
Relative Strength ——

VOL.
MIL.

1994   1995   1996   1997

OPTIONS: P

Overview - 11-FEB-97

Hampered in the past three years by a drop off in demand for derivatives products, the company has more recently focused on investing in businesses with long-term profit potential, particularly trust activities, such as securities processing, investment and cash management and employee benefit plan administration, which will provide a more stable source of earnings for the future. In particular, the investment banking business, aided by higher corporate finance fees, has shown improvement. Expense growth has been hurt by higher salary, incentive and employee benefit costs, a trend not expected to abate in the near term given competitive market conditions. In the absence of a non-recurring gain in 1996, earnings are expected to rise about 9% in 1997.

Valuation - 11-FEB-97

The shares were recently upgraded to hold from avoid based on an improvement in earnings quality as BT shifts to more predictable business lines with longer-term profit potential, such as trust activities, while other more volatile business segments are having less of an impact. The $4.00 annual dividend, which was once thought at risk due to weak earnings that resulted in an abnormally high payout ratio, now appears secure. After lagging the performance of major banks in 1996, the shares are expected to track market averages in the year ahead.

Key Stock Statistics

S&P EPS Est. 1997	7.40	Tang. Bk. Value/Share	55.32
P/E on S&P Est. 1997	12.5	Beta	1.14
Dividend Rate/Share	4.00	Shareholders	22,000
Shs. outstg. (M)	81.7	Market cap. (B)	$ 7.6
Avg. daily vol. (M)	0.419	Inst. holdings	60%

Value of $10,000 invested 5 years ago: $ 18,045

Fiscal Year Ending Dec. 31

	1996	1995	1994	1993	1992	1991
Revenues (Million $)						
1Q	2,340	1,695	1,716	1,755	1,592	1,845
2Q	2,257	2,107	1,892	1,899	1,738	1,700
3Q	2,480	2,311	1,914	2,106	1,662	1,643
4Q	2,561	2,196	1,981	2,040	1,559	1,656
Yr.	9,638	8,309	7,503	7,800	6,550	6,844
Earnings Per Share ($)						
1Q	1.52	-2.11	1.90	2.64	2.02	1.85
2Q	1.67	0.98	2.09	2.90	2.39	2.16
3Q	1.99	1.72	1.98	3.60	2.45	2.17
4Q	1.59	1.36	1.19	3.26	1.97	1.57
Yr.	6.78	2.03	7.17	12.40	8.82	7.75

Next earnings report expected: mid April

Dividend Data (Dividends have been paid since 1904.)

Amount ($)	Date Decl.	Ex-Div. Date	Stock of Record	Payment Date
1.000	Mar. 19	Mar. 27	Mar. 29	Apr. 25 '96
1.000	Jun. 18	Jun. 26	Jun. 28	Jul. 25 '96
1.000	Sep. 17	Sep. 25	Sep. 27	Oct. 25 '96
1.000	Dec. 17	Dec. 24	Dec. 27	Jan. 25 '97

Business Summary - 11-FEB-97

Bankers Trust New York is the parent of Bankers Trust Co., the seventh largest bank in the U.S. BT concentrates on wholesale banking. Core businesses and their contribution to net income (in $ millions) in recent years were as follows:

	1995	1994
Client finance	$141	$140
Client advisory	67	87
Client financial risk management	-202	259
Client transaction processing	76	99
Trading and positioning	250	71

Core businesses focus on meeting the credit and capital needs of clients (client finance), providing advice and structuring transactions designed to implement client financial strategies (client advisory), helping clients manage their financial exposure (client financial risk management), and providing operating and administrative services (client transaction processing). Trading and positioning consists of proprietary activity involving securities, derivatives, currency, commodity and funding transactions.

During 1995, average earning assets of $82.1 billion (up from $76.3 billion in 1994) were divided: trading account assets 37%, investment securities 8%, domestic loans 8%, foreign loans 6% and other temporary investments 41%. Average sources of funds were noninterest-bearing deposits 3%, other domestic deposits 5%, foreign deposits 15%, short-term borrowings 45%, long-term debt 7%, equity 4% and other 21%.

At year-end 1995, nonperforming assets were $1.17 billion (9.3% of total loans outstanding), down from $1.43 billion (11.4%) a year earlier. The reserve for loan losses was $992 million (7.9% of loans), against $1.25 billion (10.0%). Net chargeoffs were 2.48% of average loans during 1995, against 0.78% in 1994.

At December 31, 1996, Tier 1 capital was estimated at 8.5% of risk-adjusted assets, equal with the year-earlier level. Total capital at December 31 was estimated at 13.4% of risk-adjusted assets, down from 13.9%.

Important Developments

Jan. '97—The company said it was exercising its option to redeem all of its 8.55% cumulative preferred stock, Series I, effective March 1, 1997.

Capitalization

Long Term Debt: $11,109,000,000 (12/96).
Preferred Stock: $810,000,000.
Redeem. Capital Securities: $730,000,000.

Per Share Data ($)

(Year Ended Dec. 31)	1996	1995	1994	1993	1992	1991	1990	1989	1988	1987
Tangible Bk. Val.	NA	52.09	55.14	53.10	39.90	35.33	31.19	26.29	43.14	37.39
Earnings	6.78	2.03	7.17	12.40	8.82	7.75	7.80	-12.10	8.09	0.02
Dividends	4.00	4.00	3.70	3.24	2.88	2.60	2.38	2.14	1.92	1.71
Payout Ratio	59%	197%	52%	26%	33%	34%	31%	NM	24%	NM
Prices - High	90⅞	72	84⅝	83½	70⅛	68	46¾	58¼	41¼	55¼
- Low	61	49¾	54¾	65¾	50	39½	28½	34½	29⅝	26¼
P/E Ratio - High	13	35	12	7	8	9	6	NM	5	NM
- Low	9	25	8	5	6	5	4	NM	4	NM

Income Statement Analysis (Million $)

	1996	1995	1994	1993	1992	1991	1990	1989	1988	1987
Net Int. Inc.	NA	817	1,172	1,314	1,147	737	793	859	926	1,006
Tax Equiv. Adj.	NA	41.0	83.0	82.0	52.0	32.0	55.0	89.0	94.0	121
Non Int. Inc.	NA	2,243	2,401	3,351	2,335	2,476	2,307	1,963	1,649	1,621
Loan Loss Prov.	NA	31.0	25.0	93.0	225	238	194	1,877	50.0	862
% Exp/Op Revs.	NA	93	75	64	66	67	67	60	61	54
Pretax Inc.	NA	311	869	1,550	906	834	815	-821	914	296
Eff. Tax Rate	NA	31%	29%	31%	16%	20%	18%	NM	29%	100%
Net Inc.	NA	215	615	1,070	761	667	665	-979	648	1.0
% Net Int. Marg.	NA	1.05	1.64	1.82	1.81	1.46	1.48	1.79	2.07	2.28

Balance Sheet & Other Fin. Data (Million $)

	1996	1995	1994	1993	1992	1991	1990	1989	1988	1987
Earning Assets:										
Money Mkt	NA	68,728	63,391	59,842	40,233	35,768	26,466	22,326	19,312	16,608
Inv. Securities	NA	6,283	7,475	7,073	6,215	6,516	7,030	6,204	4,328	4,294
Com'l Loans	NA	4,298	4,439	6,004	8,271	7,094	8,316	7,219	9,921	10,813
Other Loans	NA	8,455	8,164	9,296	9,144	10,043	13,264	14,040	14,314	15,556
Total Assets	NA	104,002	97,016	92,082	72,448	63,959	63,596	55,658	57,942	56,521
Demand Deposits	NA	3,292	3,826	3,892	4,206	4,042	7,085	6,262	7,688	6,668
Time Deposits	NA	22,416	21,113	18,884	20,865	18,792	21,503	19,958	24,803	23,552
LT Debt	NA	9,294	6,455	5,597	3,992	3,081	2,650	2,435	2,450	2,571
Common Eqty.	NA	4,119	4,309	4,284	3,309	2,912	2,524	2,136	3,499	2,889
% Ret. on Assets	NA	0.2	0.6	1.3	1.0	1.1	1.0	NM	1.1	NM
% Ret. on Equity	NA	3.9	14.6	29.7	27.4	28.3	31.8	NM	20.3	NM
% Loan Loss Resv.	NA	7.9	10.0	8.7	9.4	10.6	10.1	12.9	5.4	5.0
% Loans/Deposits	NA	49.1	50.1	66.7	69.1	74.7	75.1	80.7	74.2	86.6
% Equity to Assets	NA	4.2	3.8	4.1	3.6	3.7	3.1	5.0	5.6	4.6

Data as orig. reptd.; bef. results of disc opers. and/or spec. items. Per share data adj. for stk. divs. as of ex-div. date. E-Estimated. NA-Not Available. NM-Not Meaningful. NR-Not Ranked.

Office—280 Park Ave., New York, NY 10017.**Tel**—(212) 250-2500. **Website**—http://www.bankerstrust.com **Chrmn, Pres & CEO**—F. N. Newman. **EVP-CFO & Contr**—R. H. Daniel.**Secy**—J. T. Byrne Jr.**VP-Investor Contact**—Mary M. Flournoy (212) 454-3201.**Dirs**—G. B. Beitzel, P. A. Griffiths, W. R. Howell, J. M. Huntsman, V. E. Jordan Jr., H. Maxwell, F. N. Newman, N. J. Nicholas Jr., R. E. Palmer, P. C. Stewart,D. L. Staheli, G. J. Vojta, P. Volcker. **Transfer Agent & Registrar**—Harris Trust Co. of New York, Chicago.**Incorporated**—in New York in 1966. **Empl**— 14,069. **S&P Analyst:** Stephen R. Biggar

STANDARD &POOR'S
STOCK REPORTS

Bell Atlantic

311

NYSE Symbol **BEL**

In S&P 500

15-FEB-97 | **Industry:** Telecommunications

Summary: This major telephone company, which also provides cellular services and has investments in international telecommunications ventures, plans to merge with NYNEX.

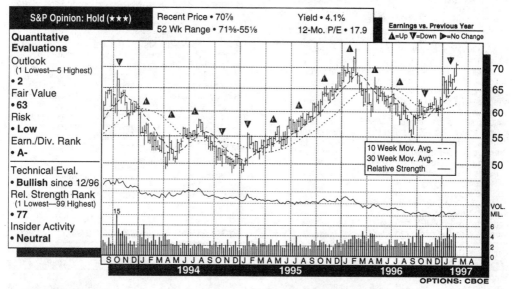

| S&P Opinion: Hold (★★★) | Recent Price • 70⅞ | Yield • 4.1% |
| | 52 Wk Range • 71⅜-55⅛ | 12-Mo. P/E • 17.9 |

Quantitative Evaluations

Outlook
(1 Lowest—5 Highest)
• 2

Fair Value
• 63

Risk
• Low

Earn./Div. Rank
• A-

Technical Eval.
• Bullish since 12/96

Rel. Strength Rank
(1 Lowest—99 Highest)
• 77

Insider Activity
• Neutral

Earnings vs. Previous Year
▲=Up ▼=Down ▶=No Change

10 Week Mov. Avg. ---
30 Week Mov. Avg. ....
Relative Strength —

OPTIONS: CBOE

Overview - 27-JAN-97

In April 1996, the company announced plans to acquire NYNEX (NYN) by exchanging 0.768 of a BEL share for each NYN share. The merger would create a global powerhouse, with about $30 billion in annual revenues. The combined territories would cover 25% of the U.S. population; international operations would include Europe, Mexico, Asia and the Czech Republic. BEL/NYN's region accounts for nearly 30% of U.S. long-distance market, and 5% of international long-distance traffic originating in the U.S. The merger is expected to produce annual savings of $600 million, and capital savings of an additional $250 million. Federal telecommunications legislation will eventually open up BEL's local market to competition, but, as with all Bells, BEL/NYN's ubiquitous networks mean that competitors, likely to operate initially as resellers, will still use Bell networks.

Valuation - 27-JAN-97

The shares, which had been restricted by uncertainty regarding the impact of federal telecom legislation, have risen recently, on solid earnings growth. The shares also yield a well above average 4.3%. As a result of an extremely competitive telecommunications environment, BEL is likely only to track the market near term. Long-term prospects, however, are bright. The combined company should prosper as it enters long-distance and video markets, and should be able to deal effectively with new competition. Once allowed to offer long-distance service within its territory, the new company will exploit the fact that 45% of all long-distance calls made by BEL/NYN customers terminate in their combined region. Results should also benefit from strong growth of the wireless and international units. We recommend holding the stock for long-term total return.

Key Stock Statistics

S&P EPS Est. 1997	4.65	Tang. Bk. Value/Share	16.65
P/E on S&P Est. 1997	15.2	Beta	0.69
S&P EPS Est. 1998	5.30	Shareholders	990,600
Dividend Rate/Share	2.88	Market cap. (B)	$ 31.0
Shs. outstg. (M)	437.8	Inst. holdings	33%
Avg. daily vol. (M)	0.845		

Value of $10,000 invested 5 years ago: $ 17,971

Fiscal Year Ending Dec. 31

	1996	1995	1994	1993	1992	1991
Revenues (Million $)						
1Q	3,208	3,450	3,420	3,163	3,077	3,000
2Q	3,260	3,565	3,430	3,220	3,150	3,080
3Q	3,298	3,261	3,455	3,290	3,170	3,100
4Q	3,371	3,154	3,487	3,317	3,250	3,100
Yr.	13,081	13,430	13,791	12,990	12,650	12,280
Earnings Per Share ($)						
1Q	1.07	0.95	0.91	0.85	0.81	0.88
2Q	1.12	1.02	0.95	0.88	0.74	0.89
3Q	1.10	1.38	0.63	0.89	0.91	0.96
4Q	0.79	0.90	0.72	0.77	0.76	0.68
Yr.	3.96	4.25	3.21	3.39	3.23	3.41

Next earnings report expected: late April

Dividend Data (Dividends have been paid since 1984.)

Amount ($)	Date Decl.	Ex-Div. Date	Stock of Record	Payment Date
0.720	Mar. 26	Apr. 08	Apr. 01	May. 01 '96
0.720	Jun. 25	Jul. 08	Jul. 10	Aug. 01 '96
0.720	Sep. 24	Oct. 08	Oct. 10	Nov. 01 '96
0.720	Nov. 26	Jan. 08	Jan. 10	Feb. 03 '97

Business Summary - 27-JAN-97

Bell Atlantic is the second largest U.S. provider of local exchange telephone service, based on 1996 U.S. access lines, serving over 20.5 million customer access lines in six East Coast states and Washington, DC. The telephone units also publish telephone directories and engage in other related activities.

In July 1995, the company and NYNEX merged their cellular operations. BEL owns 63% of the venture, Bell Atlantic NYNEX Mobile (BANM), and NYNEX owns 37%. However, the venture is managed as an equal partnership. The company and NYNEX also formed a national wireless partnership, known as PrimeCo Personnal Communications L.P., with AirTouch Communications (ATI) and U S WEST (USW). The partnership, 50%-owned by BANM, builds on BEL's merger of its cellular assets with those of NYNEX. In an earlier transaction, USW and ATI agreed to form a cellular joint venture that will have operations in 21 states. In 1995, PrimeCo successfully bid for 11 licenses in the FCC's auction of personal communications services (PCS) licenses. The licenses will complement the partners' existing cellular assets.

BEL is a partner, together with NYNEX and Pacific Telesis, in Tele-TV, which will develop video programming and other products and services. In late 1995, the company and NYNEX completed a $100 million investment in wireless cable provider CAI Wireless. BEL also owns a minority interest in Bell Communications Research, which provides technical assistance and consulting services to telephone companies. However, in December 1996, Bell Atlantic, NYNEX and CAI Wireless Systems, Inc. (Nasdaq: CAWS) said they were suspending a 1995 business agreement for one year, and were providing CAI with an option to repurchase a $100 million investment in CAI securities by BEL and NYN. BEL and NYN said they were re-evaluating their decision to use CAI's MMDS (Multichannel Multipoint Distribution Service) transport systems as an early-to-market video strategy, because of a number of factors, including changing market conditions for entertainment services, the technical availability of fiber-based full service networks, and CAI's desire to expand its use of spectrum beyond video transport.

International operations include a 24.9% interest in Telecom Corp. of New Zealand; a 42% interest in a Mexican cellular company; and interests in cellular ventures in Italy, Slovakia and the Czech Republic.

Important Developments

Nov. '96—Shareholders overwhelmingly approved Bell Atlantic's merger with NYNEX Corp. The companies remained confident that the merger would close in the first quarter of 1997.

Capitalization

Long Term Debt: $6,135,200,000 (12/96).

Per Share Data ($) (Year Ended Dec. 31)	1996	1995	1994	1993	1992	1991	1990	1989	1988	1987
Tangible Bk. Val.	NA	15.27	13.87	18.60	17.74	19.48	22.40	21.46	22.95	21.70
Cash Flow	NA	10.27	NA	NA	NA	NA	NA	NA	NA	NA
Earnings	3.96	4.25	3.21	3.39	3.23	3.41	3.38	2.72	3.33	3.12
Dividends	2.86	2.79	2.74	2.68	2.58	2.48	2.36	2.20	2.04	1.92
Payout Ratio	72%	66%	85%	79%	80%	73%	69%	81%	61%	62%
Prices - High	74 7/8	68 7/8	59 5/8	69 1/8	53 7/8	54 1/8	57 1/8	56 1/8	37 1/4	39 7/8
- Low	55 1/8	48 3/8	48 3/8	49 5/8	40 1/4	43	39 1/2	34 3/4	31 1/8	30 1/4
P/E Ratio - High	19	16	19	20	17	16	17	21	11	13
- Low	14	11	15	15	12	13	12	13	9	10
Income Statement Analysis (Million $)										
Revs.	NA	13,430	13,791	12,900	12,647	12,280	12,298	11,449	10,880	10,298
Depr.	NA	2,627	2,652	2,545	2,417	2,299	2,377	2,420	2,354	2,117
Maint.	NA	NA	NA	NA	1,875	1,791	1,768	1,718	1,612	1,725
Constr. Credits	NA	NA	NA	NA	NA	20.6	24.4	28.5	32.5	30.6
Eff. Tax Rate	NA	38%	39%	35%	32%	33%	34%	31%	29%	37%
Net Inc.	NA	1,862	1,402	1,482	1,382	1,332	1,313	1,075	1,317	1,240
Balance Sheet & Other Fin. Data (Million $)										
Gross Prop.	NA	33,554	33,746	32,330	31,046	31,848	30,784	29,312	27,570	25,321
Net Prop.	NA	15,921	16,938	20,366	20,330	19,962	19,447	18,874	18,174	17,245
Cap. Exp.	NA	2,627	2,699	2,449	2,547	2,545	2,747	3,008	2,889	2,364
Total Cap.	NA	14,597	18,228	22,187	21,830	19,444	21,781	20,905	20,121	17,976
Fxd. Chgs. Cov.	NA	6.0	4.9	4.7	3.9	3.8	4.0	3.8	4.6	4.8
Capitalization:										
LT Debt	NA	6,407	6,806	7,206	7,348	7,960	8,171	7,721	6,557	5,199
Pfd.	NA	145	85.0	Nil	Nil	Nil	Nil	Nil	Nil	Nil
Common	NA	6,685	6,081	8,224	7,816	7,831	8,930	8,591	9,177	8,742
% Ret. on Revs.	NA	13.9	10.2	11.4	10.9	10.8	10.7	9.4	12.1	12.0
% Ret. On Invest.Cap	NA	21.0	9.8	9.5	9.5	9.9	9.2	7.9	9.1	9.9
% Return On Com.Eqty	NA	29.2	19.6	17.3	17.4	15.9	14.8	11.7	14.5	14.4
% Earn. on Net Prop.	NA	18.8	10.2	9.9	9.2	9.4	10.1	8.3	9.6	9.6
% LT Debt of Cap.	NA	48.4	52.5	46.7	48.5	50.4	47.8	47.3	41.7	37.3
Capital. % Pfd.	NA	1.1	0.6	Nil	Nil	Nil	Nil	Nil	Nil	Nil
Capital. % Common	NA	50.5	46.9	53.3	51.5	49.6	52.2	52.7	58.3	62.7

Data as orig. reptd; bef. results of disc. opers. and/or spec. items. Per share data adj. for stk. divs. as of ex-div date. E-Estimated. NA-Not Available. NM-Not Meaningful. NR-Not Ranked.

Office—1717 Arch St., Philadelphia, PA 19103. **Tel**—(215) 963-6000. **Website**—http://www.bel-atl.com **Chrmn & CEO**—R. W. Smith. **Vice Chmn**—L. T. Babbio, Jr., J. G. Cullen. **EVP & CFO**—W. O. Albertini. **VP & Secy**—P. A. Bulliner. **Investor Contact**—Peter D. Crawford. **Dirs**—W. W. Adams, W. O. Albertini, L. T. Babbio, T. E. Bolger, F. C. Carlucci, W. G. Copeland, J. G. Cullen, J. H. Gilliam, Jr., T. H. Kean, J. C. Marous, Jr., J. F. Maypole, J. Neubauer, T. H. O'Brien, E. Pfeiffer, R. L. Ridgway, R. W. Smith, S. Young. **Transfer Agent**—Bank of New York, NYC. **Incorporated**—in Delaware in 1983. **Empl**— 61,800. **S&P Analyst:** Philip D. Wohl

15-FEB-97   **Industry:** Utilities-Electric

Summary: This utility supplies electricity to a population of 1.5 million in Boston and 39 surrounding cities and towns. BSE owns the 670-mw Pilgrim nuclear plant.

S&P Opinion: Hold (★★★)	Recent Price • 26½	Yield • 7.1%
	52 Wk Range • 28¾-21¾	12-Mo. P/E • 10.2

Quantitative Evaluations

Outlook
(1 Lowest—5 Highest)
• **2⁻**

Fair Value
• **26⅜**

Risk
• **Low**

Earn./Div. Rank
• **B+**

Technical Eval.
• **Bullish** since 11/96

Rel. Strength Rank
(1 Lowest—99 Highest)
• **47**

Insider Activity
• **NA**

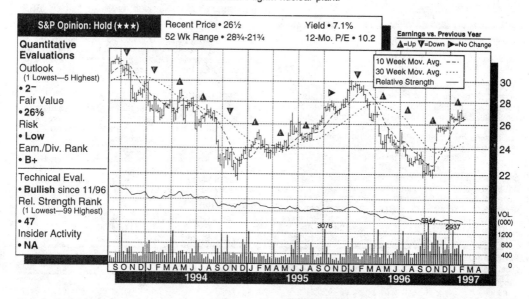

Earnings vs. Previous Year
▲=Up ▼=Down ▶=No Change

- 10 Week Mov. Avg. – – –
- 30 Week Mov. Avg. ·····
- Relative Strength ——

Overview - 10-FEB-97

Higher kilowatt-hour sales, combined with rate hikes in each of the past two years, helped to boost revenues in recent periods. BSE's nuclear plant, Pilgrim, achieved its highest-ever capacity, rising from 76.4% utilization in 1995 to 90.5% in 1996. The high operating rate and a solid Boston economy should help maintain earnings strength in 1997. However, gains are likely to be restricted by discounts to a few large customers under a manufacturing retention rate structure approved by Massachusetts regulators and charges to accelerate amortization of three nuclear assets. A low industrial load, as well as rates that are near the low end for the region, insulate the company from growing electric utility competition. An aggressive but reasonable state regulatory environment is a long-term plus for BSE, as is the company's ability to gradually reduce its comparatively high debt leverage.

Valuation - 10-FEB-97

We continue to recommend holding the stock. Following a 23% gain in 1995, the shares fell 8.9% in 1996, compared to a 5% decline for the S&P Electric Companies index. As with most utilities, BSE's share price is sensitive to shifts in the interest rate environment. Excess power generating capacity in the service region remains a threat to pricing, although it is somewhat mitigated by regulatory assurance of a reasonable opportunity to recover net stranded costs over a period of five to ten years. Given reasonable growth in earnings as well, BSE's dividend payout rate, now at about 71% of projected 1997 earnings of $2.65 a share, should be secured by growing cash flows.

Key Stock Statistics

S&P EPS Est. 1997	2.65	Tang. Bk. Value/Share		21.14
P/E on S&P Est. 1997	10.0	Beta		0.58
Dividend Rate/Share	1.88	Shareholders		38,200
Shs. outstg. (M)	48.5	Market cap. (B)		$ 1.3
Avg. daily vol. (M)	0.119	Inst. holdings		34%

Value of $10,000 invested 5 years ago: $ 14,952

Fiscal Year Ending Dec. 31

	1996	1995	1994	1993	1992	1991
Revenues (Million $)						
1Q	387.9	379.7	377.5	354.8	344.0	308.0
2Q	389.8	380.8	368.7	346.1	301.0	290.0
3Q	498.0	498.5	449.1	436.0	408.0	392.0
4Q	390.7	369.4	353.4	345.4	359.4	330.0
Yr.	1,666	1,629	1,549	1,482	1,412	1,320
Earnings Per Share ($)						
1Q	0.44	0.36	0.35	0.25	0.23	0.10
2Q	0.50	0.48	0.43	0.43	0.02	0.01
3Q	1.58	1.46	1.46	1.47	1.60	1.64
4Q	0.09	-0.21	0.16	0.13	0.24	0.21
Yr.	2.61	2.08	2.41	2.28	2.10	1.96

Next earnings report expected: late April

Dividend Data (Dividends have been paid since 1890.)

Amount ($)	Date Decl.	Ex-Div. Date	Stock of Record	Payment Date
0.470	Mar. 28	Apr. 08	Apr. 10	May. 01 '96
0.470	Jun. 27	Jul. 08	Jul. 10	Aug. 01 '96
0.470	Sep. 26	Oct. 08	Oct. 10	Nov. 01 '96
0.470	Dec. 19	Jan. 08	Jan. 10	Feb. 03 '97

A Division of The McGraw·Hill Companies

STANDARD
&POOR'S
STOCK REPORTS

Boston Edison Company

354

15-FEB-97

Business Summary - 10-FEB-97

Boston Edison supplies electricity to about 654,000 retail customers in the city of Boston and 39 surrounding cities and towns. Revenue contributions by customer class in recent years:

	1995	1994	1993	1992
Residential	28%	28%	27%	26%
Commercial	50%	50%	49%	47%
Industrial	9%	9%	10%	10%
Other	13%	13%	14%	17%

Fuel sources for internal generation in 1995 were nuclear 43%, natural gas 40% and oil 17%. Purchased power came to 25% of total capability. Peak load in 1995 was 2,785 mw, and capability at time of peak totaled 3,466 mw, for a capacity margin of 20%.

BSE owns the 670-mw Pilgrim nuclear station, which resumed full-power operation in October 1989 after an outage for equipment modification that began in April 1986. In 1989, a net charge of $106 million ($2.78 a share) was recorded for customer settlement agreements and other costs related to Pilgrim.

The company sees no need to build new capacity to meet demand growth until after 2000. Capital projects, largely to maintain and improve existing facilities, were $181 million in 1995. Spending is expected to decrease to $160 million in 1996, $140 million in 1997,

$130 million in 1998, $120 million in 1999 and $110 million in 2000.

In September 1995, BSE sold one million common shares to Merrill Lynch & Co.; it used net proceeds of $26 million to lower short-term debt.

In a corporate reorganization November 1, 1995, BSE separated its business units into customer, generating-fossil, generating-nuclear and corporate services to reduce operating costs, simplify decision-making and expedite response to customers. As part of the reorganization, the company initiated an early retirement program to reduce the workforce by 450 employees by the end of 1996.

Important Developments

Jan. '97—The company filed for Massachusetts Dept. of Public Utilities (DPU) approval of an initial investment in the formation of a holding company. Following expected DPU approval, the company would file a registration statement with the SEC in March and seek shareholder approval in May. Earlier, in October, BSE and Williams Energy Group signed a letter of intent to form a joint venture to market electricity, natural gas and energy services in all six New England states.

Capitalization

Long Term Debt: $1,058,676,000 (9/96).
Red. Cum. Pfd. Stock: $88,000,000.
Cum. Pfd. Stock: $123,000,000.

Per Share Data ($)

(Year Ended Dec. 31)	1996	1995	1994	1993	1992	1991	1990	1989	1988	1987
Tangible Bk. Val.	NA	20.04	20.11	19.42	18.77	17.92	17.22	16.73	19.38	18.37
Earnings	2.61	2.08	2.41	2.28	2.10	1.96	1.60	-0.88	1.86	1.97
Dividends	1.88	1.82	1.76	1.70	1.64	1.58	1.52	1.82	1.82	1.79
Payout Ratio	72%	87%	73%	75%	78%	81%	95%	NM	98%	91%
Prices - High	30⅛	29½	29⅞	32⅝	28¼	24⅞	20¼	22⅛	18¾	28
- Low	21¾	23⅛	21½	26⅜	22⅛	18¼	16½	15⅜	12½	16¾
P/E Ratio - High	12	14	12	14	13	13	13	NM	10	14
- Low	8	11	9	12	10	9	10	NM	7	9

Income Statement Analysis (Million $)

	1996	1995	1994	1993	1992	1991	1990	1989	1988	1987
Revs.	NA	1,629	1,549	1,482	1,412	1,320	1,259	1,269	1,203	1,181
Depr.	NA	153	149	138	129	126	122	121	105	90.0
Maint.	NA	NA	NA	NA	NA	99	102	91.0	107	123
Fxd. Chgs. Cov.	NA	2.4	2.3	2.1	1.8	1.7	1.7	0.3	2.0	2.4
Constr. Credits	NA	4.8	7.5	6.5	7.8	9.0	8.8	10.5	22.9	17.6
Eff. Tax Rate	NA	37%	30%	23%	8.70%	17%	30%	NM	27%	38%
Net Inc.	NA	112	125	118	107	95.0	80.0	-16.0	84.0	87.0

Balance Sheet & Other Fin. Data (Million $)

	1996	1995	1994	1993	1992	1991	1990	1989	1988	1987
Gross Prop.	NA	4,648	4,511	4,324	4,082	3,889	3,709	3,492	3,271	3,017
Cap. Exp.	NA	194	221	254	231	214	256	236	245	309
Net Prop.	NA	2,956	2,930	2,854	2,720	2,611	2,529	2,400	2,275	2,107
Capitalization:										
LT Debt	NA	1,160	1,137	1,272	1,091	1,137	1,074	949	967	823
% LT Debt	NA	49	50	54	51	54	55	52	50	48
Pfd.	NA	215	217	219	221	221	221	221	221	171
% Pfd.	NA	9.10	9.50	9.30	10	11	11	12	12	10
Common	NA	989	916	876	840	753	671	645	734	725
% Common	NA	42	40	37	39	36	34	36	38	42
Total Cap.	NA	2,925	2,852	2,924	2,676	2,626	2,462	2,287	2,475	2,289
Oper. Ratio	NA	86.0	85.4	84.8	84.4	84.4	85.7	85.9	86.7	87.9
% Earn. on Net Prop.	NA	7.7	7.8	8.1	8.3	8.0	7.3	7.6	7.3	7.2
% Ret. on Revs.	NA	6.9	8.1	8.0	7.6	7.2	6.3	NM	7.0	7.3
% Ret. On Invest.Cap	NA	7.9	8.0	8.1	8.3	8.3	7.8	3.6	7.0	7.2
% Return On Com.Eqty	NA	10.2	12.1	11.9	11.5	11.3	11.8	NM	9.6	11.9

Data as orig. reptd.; bef. results of disc. opers. and/or spec. items. Per share data adj. for stk. divs. as of ex-div. date. E-Estimated. NA-Not Available. NM-Not Meaningful. NR-Not Ranked.

Office—800 Boylston St., Boston, MA 02199-8003. **Tel**—(617) 424-2000. **E-mail**—ir@bedison.com **Chrmn, Pres & CEO**—T. J. May. **SVP-Fin & CFO**—C. E. Peters Jr. **Clerk**—Theodora S. Convisser. **Investor Contact**—Philip J. Lembo. **Dirs**—W. F. Connell, G. L. Countryman, T. G. Dignan Jr., C. K. Gifford, N. S. Gifford, K. I. Guscott, M. S. Horner, T. J. May, S. H. Penney, B. W. Reznicek, H. Roth Jr., S. J. Sweeney, P. E. Tsongas. **Transfer Agent & Registrar**—First National Bank of Boston. **Incorporated**—in Massachusetts in 1886. **Empl**—4,026. **S&P Analyst:** Justin McCann

CFX Corp.

7397
ASE Symbol **CFX**

19-FEB-97

Industry: Banking

Summary: This multibank holding company provides a wide range of banking services in New Hampshire and Massachusetts.

Quantitative Evaluations

Outlook
(1 Lowest—5 Highest)
• **NA**

Fair Value
• **NA**

Risk
• **Average**

Earn./Div. Rank
• **B+**

Technical Eval.
• **Neutral** since 2/97

Rel. Strength Rank
(1 Lowest—99 Highest)
• **80**

Insider Activity
• **Neutral**

Recent Price • 17¾
52 Wk Range • 18⅝-11⅝

Yield • 4.7%
12-Mo. P/E • 17.9

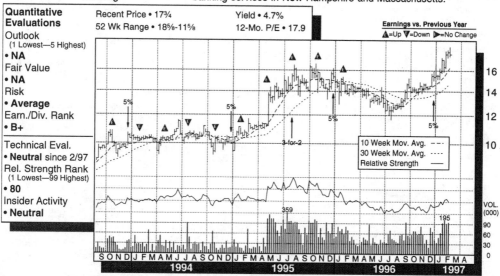

Earnings vs. Previous Year
▲=Up ▼=Down ▶=No Change

10 Week Mov. Avg. — - —
30 Week Mov. Avg. ·······
Relative Strength ———

Business Profile - 18-FEB-97

This multibank holding company, the largest financial institution in southwestern New Hampshire, has grown significantly through recent acquisitions. Following the purchases of Safety Fund Corp. and Milford Co/Operative Bank, CFX has $1.6 billion in assets with 42 full service branches, two loan production offices and 68 ATM and remote locations in New Hampshire and Massachusetts. In February 1997, CFX signed an agreement to acquire Portsmouth Bank Shares Inc. for about $106 million in stock. Excluding acquisition-related costs, the efficiency ratio improved to 61.47% in the fourth quarter of 1996 from 67.21% a year earlier. The dividend was reinstated in the third quarter.

Operational Review - 18-FEB-97

Based on a preliminary report, net interest and dividend income for 1996 rose 13%, year to year (1995 restated for acquisitions), as greater loan volumes outweighed a decline in the net interest margin (4.24% versus 4.36%). The provision for loan and lease losses was down 3.4% to $2,935,000. Other income advanced 18%, aided by increased service charges, almost double the amount of net gains on loan sales, and an $877,000 pension settlement gain. Other expense rose 11%, penalized by $4,522,000 ($0.28 a share, after tax) of acquisition-related expenses and a $700,000 SAIF assessment; pretax income advanced 13%. After taxes at 34.8%, versus 33.7%, net income climbed 12%, to $12,641,000 ($0.99 a share), from $11,249,000 ($0.89, after preferred dividends).

Stock Performance - 14-FEB-97

In the past 30 trading days, CFX's shares have increased 15%, compared to a 8% rise in the S&P 500. Average trading volume for the past five days was 26,820 shares, compared with the 40-day moving average of 18,492 shares.

Key Stock Statistics

Dividend Rate/Share	0.84	Shareholders	3,300
Shs. outstg. (M)	12.9	Market cap. (B)	$0.226
Avg. daily vol. (M)	0.026	Inst. holdings	5%
Tang. Bk. Value/Share	10.05		
Beta	0.81		

Value of $10,000 invested 5 years ago: $ 45,746

Fiscal Year Ending Dec. 31

	1996	1995	1994	1993	1992	1991
Revenues (Million $)						
1Q	—	17.33	12.89	13.07	14.35	15.24
2Q	60.46	18.64	13.35	12.77	14.09	14.91
3Q	31.83	18.89	13.82	12.83	13.73	15.09
4Q	—	19.14	15.85	12.42	13.40	15.01
Yr.	—	74.00	55.91	48.78	55.58	60.25
Earnings Per Share ($)						
1Q	—	0.20	0.17	0.13	0.10	0.11
2Q	0.59	0.26	0.21	0.22	0.14	0.08
3Q	0.04	0.27	0.20	0.24	0.15	0.01
4Q	0.36	0.28	0.24	0.16	0.17	-0.19
Yr.	0.99	0.99	0.82	0.75	0.56	0.04

Next earnings report expected: mid April

Dividend Data (Dividends have been paid since 1987.)

Amount ($)	Date Decl.	Ex-Div. Date	Stock of Record	Payment Date
0.200	Sep. 10	Sep. 18	Sep. 20	Oct. 18 '96
5%	Dec. 10	Dec. 18	Dec. 20	Jan. 17 '97
0.220	Dec. 10	Dec. 18	Dec. 20	Jan. 17 '97
Div Omitted	—			Apr. 26 '96

Business Summary - 18-FEB-97

CFX Corporation (formerly Cheshire Financial Corporation), the largest financial institution in southwestern New Hampshire, is a holding company for three banking subsidiaries: CFX Bank, headquartered in Keene, New Hampshire, Orange Savings Bank, headquartered in Orange, Mass., and The Safety Fund National Bank, headquartered in Fitchburg, Mass.

A wide range of banking services is provided through 42 full-service offices and 67 automated teller and remote service banking locations in New Hampshire and central Massachusetts.

Total loans and leases totaled $699 million as of December 31, 1995, up from $640.4 million a year earlier, divided as follows:

	1995	1994
Real estate		
Residential	68%	70%
Construction	1%	1%
Commercial	12%	13%
Commercial, financial & agricultural	8%	8%
Consumer & other	11%	8%

The allowance for loan losses at December 31, 1995, totaled $7,689,000 (equal to 1.10% of total loans), up from $7,558,000 (1.18%) a year earlier. Net chargeoffs in 1995 totaled $1,493,000 ($831,000 in 1994), or 0.2% of average loans (0.1%). At December 31, 1995, nonperforming loans amounted to $7,844,000 (1.1% of total loans), up from $7,134,000 (1.1%) a year earlier, and nonperforming assets totaled $8,973,000 (1.00% of total assets), versus $9,119,000 (1.09%).

The CFX Mortgage subsidiary provides mortgages through two loan production offices and throughout the branch network.

CFX Funding L.L.C. (51% owned) engages in the facilitation of lease financing and securitization nationwide.

Important Developments

Feb. '97—CFX signed a definitive agreement to acquire Portsmouth Bank Shares Inc. (POBS), a savings and loan with $269 million in assets, in a stock swap transaction valued at about $106 million.

Jul. '96—The company completed the acquisitions of The Safety Fund Corp. (SFC) and Milford Co/operative Bank as of July 1, 1996. CFX acquired SFC ($297 million in assets; 12 branches in Worcester County, MA) for about $43.4 million in stock. CFX bought The Milford Co/Operative Bank ($160 million in assets; six branches in New Hampshire) for $26.5 million in stock.

Capitalization

Total Debt: $203,955,000 (12/96).

Per Share Data ($)

(Year Ended Dec. 31)	1996	1995	1994	1993	1992	1991	1990	1989	1988	1987
Tangible Bk. Val.	NA	10.15	10.52	11.36	9.60	9.78	9.74	9.95	9.77	NA
Earnings	0.99	0.99	0.82	0.75	0.56	0.04	-0.13	0.67	0.55	0.43
Dividends	0.57	0.76	0.51	0.39	0.33	0.38	0.55	0.55	0.55	0.09
Payout Ratio	58%	76%	62%	53%	59%	NM	NM	81%	100%	21%
Prices - High	16⅝	16⅝	11⅝	10⅞	7¼	5⅞	7	8⅜	8⅞	13⅜
- Low	11⅝	9½	9¼	6⅞	4½	3⅝	3¼	6	5⅜	5⅛
P/E Ratio - High	17	17	14	15	13	NM	NM	12	16	31
- Low	12	10	11	9	8	NM	NM	9	9	12

Income Statement Analysis (Million $)

	1996	1995	1994	1993	1992	1991	1990	1989	1988	1987
Net Int. Inc.	NA	32.9	28.0	26.5	25.3	22.9	21.7	18.6	15.1	9.6
Loan Loss Prov.	NA	1.6	0.4	3.0	2.9	3.8	4.0	1.0	0.3	0.3
Non Int. Inc.	NA	9.4	6.2	6.3	3.2	1.7	-1.1	1.6	0.9	0.6
Non Int. Exp.	NA	28.4	25.2	23.5	19.8	10.9	15.3	12.6	9.6	5.0
Pretax Inc.	NA	12.3	8.7	6.3	5.8	0.8	1.3	6.7	5.9	5.0
Eff. Tax Rate	NA	35%	37%	20%	35%	33%	153%	34%	34%	38%
Net Inc.	NA	7.9	5.5	5.0	3.8	0.6	-0.7	4.4	3.9	3.1
% Net Int. Marg.	NA	4.14	4.10	4.30	4.10	3.90	4.00	3.80	3.70	NA

Balance Sheet & Other Fin. Data (Million $)

	1996	1995	1994	1993	1992	1991	1990	1989	1988	1987
Total Assets	NA	901	756	735	661	662	614	541	506	335
Loans	NA	691	562	458	470	472	482	437	411	270
Deposits	NA	666	551	551	576	564	508	435	392	240
Capitalization:										
Debt	NA	101	92.2	47.0	Nil	19.0	26.0	26.0	27.0	13.0
Equity	NA	90.0	77.9	75.6	73.1	71.3	71.3	72.4	75.4	77.9
Total	NA	191	170	123	73.3	90.5	139	98.0	102	91.0
% Ret. on Assets	NA	1.0	0.7	0.7	0.5	0.3	NM	0.8	0.9	1.3
% Ret. on Equity	NA	9.0	7.1	6.7	5.2	2.8	NM	5.9	5.1	5.2
% Loan Loss Resv.	NA	1.1	1.2	1.6	1.7	1.5	1.0	0.6	0.6	NA
% Risk Based Capital	NA	14.7	17.0	NA	16.0	NA	15.9	19.0	NA	NA
Price Times Book Value:										
Hi	NA	1.6	1.1	1.0	0.8	0.6	0.7	0.8	0.9	NA
Low	NA	0.9	0.9	0.6	0.5	0.4	0.3	0.6	0.6	NA

Data as orig. reptd.; bef. results of disc opers. and/or spec. items. Per share data adj. for stk. divs. as of ex-div. date. Rev. & EPS figures for 1996 2Q are for 6 mos. end. Jun. E-Estimated. NA-Not Available. NM-Not Meaningful. NR-Not Ranked.

Office—102 Main St., Keene, NH 03431. **Tel**—(603) 352-2502. **Chrmn**—E. E. Gaffey. **Pres & CEO**—P. J. Baxter. **EVP & COO**—M. A. Gavin. **Secy**—C. V. Bean. **CFO & Investor Contact**—G. R. Tewksbury. **Treas**—W. H. Dennison. **Dirs**—R. F. Astrella, P. J. Baxter, R. B. Baybutt, C. V. Bean, C. L. Frink, E. E. Gaffey, E. S. Hager, D. S. Hatfield, Jr., P. A. Mason, W. R. Peterson, L. W. Slanetz. **Transfer Agent & Registrar**—Chase Mellon Shareholder Services, Ridgefield Park, NJ. **Incorporated**—in New Hampshire in 1986. **Empl**— 342. **S&P Analyst:** E. Fitzpatrick.

CRIIMI MAE

415K

NYSE Symbol **CMM**

15-FEB-97

Industry: Real Estate Investment Trust

Summary: This self-administered REIT invests in government insured and guaranteed mortgages, as well as uninsured mortgage and mortgage-related products.

Quantitative Evaluations

Recent Price • 17
52 Wk Range • 17¼-10

Yield • 7.5%
12-Mo. P/E • 18.3

Outlook
(1 Lowest—5 Highest)
• **NA**

Fair Value
• **NA**

Risk
• **Low**

Earn./Div. Rank
• **NR**

Technical Eval.
• **Bullish** since 10/95

Rel. Strength Rank
(1 Lowest—99 Highest)
• **95**

Insider Activity
• **Neutral**

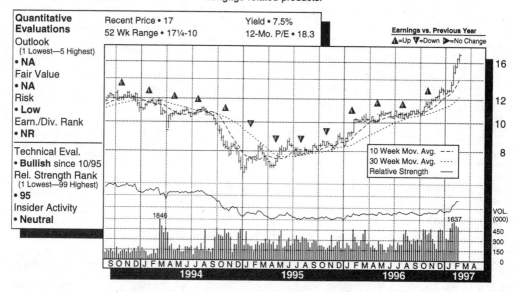

Earnings vs. Previous Year
▲=Up ▼=Down ▶=No Change

10 Week Mov. Avg. – – –
30 Week Mov. Avg. ·······
Relative Strength ——

Business Profile - 13-FEB-97

CRIIMI MAE's long-term strategy has been to increase recurring earnings while reducing exposure to rising borrowing costs, by expanding its lines of business to include mortgage servicing, underwriting, originating and advisory services. The trust relies on these capabilities when investing in mortgage and mortgage-related products that are backed by a range of income producing real estate. Recent results were bolstered by the ongoing expansion of CMM's commercial mortgage operations, and future performance should benefit from the acquisition of $228 million of subordinated commercial mortgage-backed securities during the fourth quarter of 1996.

Operational Review - 13-FEB-97

Gross revenues in the nine months ended September 30, 1996, rose 28%, year to year, principally reflecting higher income from subordinated investments in commercial mortgage-backed securities, equity in earnings from investments, and other investment income. Total expenses were up 23%, fueled by a 29% increase in interest costs and higher amortization, general and administrative expenses. After a net gain on mortgage dispositions of $9,268,010, versus $1,624,870, and minority interests, net income increased 92%, to $24,447,802 ($0.74 a share, on 10% more shares), from $12,762,168 ($0.43).

Stock Performance - 14-FEB-97

In the past 30 trading days, CMM's shares have increased 32%, compared to a 8% rise in the S&P 500. Average trading volume for the past five days was 197,700 shares, compared with the 40-day moving average of 180,190 shares.

Key Stock Statistics

Dividend Rate/Share	1.28	Shareholders	22,000
Shs. outstg. (M)	31.2	Market cap. (B)	$0.530
Avg. daily vol. (M)	0.265	Inst. holdings	9%
Tang. Bk. Value/Share	10.83		
Beta	1.25		

Value of $10,000 invested 5 years ago: $ 32,799

Fiscal Year Ending Dec. 31

	1996	1995	1994	1993	1992	1991
Revenues (Million $)						
1Q	24.94	21.07	27.55	12.89	12.60	14.04
2Q	25.41	19.38	17.63	12.91	12.15	13.92
3Q	25.35	20.42	19.16	15.20	13.12	12.92
4Q	—	20.41	19.17	15.45	12.83	13.43
Yr.	—	22.64	71.44	56.45	50.70	54.32
Earnings Per Share ($)						
1Q	0.38	0.19	0.45	0.22	0.34	0.32
2Q	0.21	0.17	0.24	0.17	0.14	0.17
3Q	0.16	0.11	0.22	0.19	0.17	0.12
4Q	—	0.19	0.18	0.20	0.14	0.16
Yr.	—	0.65	1.07	0.78	0.79	0.78

Next earnings report expected: late February

Dividend Data (Dividends have been paid since 1989.)

Amount ($)	Date Decl.	Ex-Div. Date	Stock of Record	Payment Date
0.300	Mar. 08	Mar. 14	Mar. 18	Mar. 29 '96
0.300	Jun. 07	Jun. 13	Jun. 17	Jun. 28 '96
0.300	Sep. 10	Sep. 18	Sep. 20	Sep. 30 '96
0.320	Dec. 09	Dec. 17	Dec. 19	Dec. 31 '96

A Division of The McGraw·Hill Companies

STANDARD
&POOR'S
STOCK REPORTS

CRIIMI MAE Inc.

415K

15-FEB-97

Business Summary - 13-FEB-97

CRIIMI MAE is a full-service commercial mortgage company, structured as a self-administered REIT. It invests in government insured and guaranteed mortgages secured by multifamily housing complexes located throughout the U.S., and in uninsured mortgage and mortgage-related investments backed by multifamily and other commercial mortgages, such as subordinated ownership interests in bonds issued in commercial loan securitizations. The trust's business plan contemplates further expansion in investments in uninsured assets backed by multifamily and other commercial mortgages, and building its servicing business as it originates, acquires and securitizes assets. Insured mortgage investments continue to decline as a percentage of total assets.

At December 31, 1995, total assets of $1.2 billion were distributed as follows:

	1995
Government insured multifamily mortgages	58%
Uninsured mortgage investments	23%
Investment in CRI Liquidating REIT, Inc.	10%
Other assets	7%
Investment in AIM Funds	2%

As of December 31, 1995, CMM held 190 federally insured mortgage investments with an aggregate carry-ing value of $807.1 million, down from 217 mortgages with a carrying value of $857.6 million a year earlier.

The trust's principal objectives are to provide increasing dividends to its shareholders and to enhance the value of CRIMMI MAE's stock.

Through mid-1994, CMM invested almost exclusively in government insured multifamily mortgage investments. In late 1994 and 1995, it expanded its operations and began investing in uninsured mortgage and mortgage-related assets backed by multifamily and other commercial mortgages, using a combination of debt and equity. These uninsured mortgage investments include higher yielding, higher risk, subordinated ownership interests in bonds issued in commercial mortgage loan securitizations.

Important Developments

Dec. '96—With the Dec. 31, 1996, payment, CMM raised its quarterly common stock dividend to $0.32 a share, from $0.30, paid for each of the first three quarters of 1996. Separately, the trust sold 75,000 shares of Series A cumulative convertible preferred stock at $100 a share, for gross proceeds of $7.5 million. The net proceeds were combined with other equity and debt to acquire $79.9 million of subordinated commercial mortgage-backed securities.

Capitalization

Bank Term Loans: $9,547,880 (9/96).

Per Share Data ($)

(Year Ended Dec. 31)	1995	1994	1993	1992	1991	1990	1989	1988	1987	1986
Tangible Bk. Val.	8.87	9.38	10.67	9.24	9.35	10.25	10.37	13.15	NA	NA
Earnings	0.65	1.07	0.78	0.79	0.78	0.91	0.95	2.00	1.65	1.94
Dividends	0.92	1.16	1.12	1.08	1.08	1.08	2.44	NM	NM	NM
Payout Ratio	142%	108%	144%	137%	138%	119%	257%	NM	NM	NM
Prices - High	9¼	12	12¾	10	9½	9¼	9⅞	NA	NA	NA
- Low	6¾	6½	9¾	8⅝	6⅝	6¼	7⅞	NA	NA	NA
P/E Ratio - High	14	11	16	13	12	10	10	NA	NA	NA
- Low	10	6	13	11	8	7	8	NA	NA	NA

Income Statement Analysis (Million $)

	1995	1994	1993	1992	1991	1990	1989	1988	1987	1986
Income Rental	2.1	1.1	3.7	2.2	3.4	4.5	2.1	2.4	3.6	1.6
Income Mortg.	66.1	67.0	50.3	45.9	49.3	50.0	40.0	44.3	43.8	35.3
Income Total	82.1	71.4	56.5	50.7	54.3	55.0	42.7	47.1	47.5	37.0
Expenses Gen.	4.6	7.5	13.7	5.7	6.1	5.7	14.0	5.9	4.0	3.3
Expenses Int.	49.9	39.2	28.0	24.4	25.8	22.3	1.1	Nil	Nil	Nil
Prov. for Losses	Nil	Nil	Nil	Nil	Nil	Nil	Nil	Nil	Nil	Nil
Depr.	0.7	Nil	Nil	0.4	0.5	0.5	0.5	0.6	0.4	NA
Net Inc.	18.5	26.0	15.8	16.0	15.6	18.4	19.5	41.2	31.7	24.1

Balance Sheet & Other Fin. Data (Million $)

	1995	1994	1993	1992	1991	1990	1989	1988	1987	1986
Cash	16.6	5.1	13.6	6.6	1.7	14.9	19.1	12.9	NA	NA
Total Assets	1,203	955	809	527	546	603	503	431	NA	NA
Real Estate Invest.	1,123	926	773	505	523	549	460	407	NA	NA
Loss Reserve	Nil	Nil	Nil	Nil	Nil	Nil	Nil	Nil	NA	NA
Net Invest.	1,123	926	773	505	523	549	460	407	NA	NA
ST Debt	Nil	Nil	95.0	186	161	148	10.0	Nil	NA	NA
Capitalization:										
Debt	854	627	384	62.0	85.0	116	129	Nil	NA	NA
Equity	286	250	215	193	198	211	223	278	NA	NA
Total	1,140	877	707	339	383	448	487	417	NA	NA
% Earn & Depr/Assets	1.8	2.9	2.4	3.1	2.8	3.4	4.3	9.0	7.7	NA
Price Times Book Value:										
Hi	1.0	1.3	1.2	1.1	1.0	0.9	1.0	NA	NA	NA
Low	0.8	0.7	0.9	0.9	0.7	0.6	0.8	NA	NA	NA

Data as orig. reptd.; bef. results of disc. opers. and/or spec. items. Per share data adj. for stk. divs. as of ex-div. date. E-Estimated. NA-Not Available. NM-Not Meaningful. NR-Not Ranked.

Office—11200 Rockville Pike, Rockville, MD 20852. **Tel**—(301) 816-2300. **Chrmn**—W. B. Dockser. **Pres & Secy**—H. W. Willoughby. **SVP & CFO**—Cynthia O. Azzara. **EVP & Treas**—J. R. Cohen.**Investor Contact**—Susan B. Railey (301- 468-3120). **Dirs**—G. G. Carlson, L. H. Dale, W. B. Dockser, G. R. Dunnells, R. F. Tardio, H. W. Willoughby. **Transfer Agent & Registrar**—Registrar & Transfer Co., Cranford, NJ. **Incorporated**—in Delaware in 1989; reincorporated in Maryland in 1993.**Empl**— 85. **S&P Analyst:** Thomas C. Ferguson

15-FEB-97

Industry: Real Estate Investment Trust

Summary: This real estate investment trust earns income from servicing mortgage loans, investing in mortgage-backed securities and other investment strategies.

S&P Opinion: Hold (★★★)

Recent Price • 24½
52 Wk Range • 25-14⅜

Yield • 9.2%
12-Mo. P/E • 10.6

Quantitative Evaluations

Outlook
(1 Lowest—5 Highest)
• **2⁻**

Fair Value
• **23⅞**

Risk
• **Average**

Earn./Div. Rank
• **NR**

Technical Eval.
• **Bullish** since 2/95

Rel. Strength Rank
(1 Lowest—99 Highest)
• **58**

Insider Activity
• **Neutral**

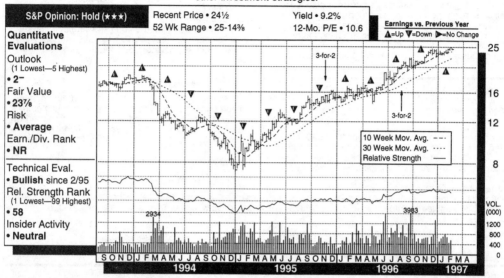

Earnings vs. Previous Year
▲=Up ▼=Down ▷=No Change

10 Week Mov. Avg. - - - -
30 Week Mov. Avg. - - - -
Relative Strength ———

Overview - 31-JAN-97

Profits are expected to improve further in 1997. A greater contribution from mortgage servicing is expected, as the company is purchasing servicing, and prepayments are expected to remain low. A subservicing contract with a major mortgage originator also aids prospects for higher fees in this segment. Modestly higher net interest income is expected, based primarily on greater purchases of interest-only securities (I/O) and the upward adjustment of rates on the company's ARMs, partially offset by a modest rise in funding costs associated with a projected increase in short-term interest rates. Considerably higher gains are expected, due mainly to the fact that the company's I/O securities, which provide stable cash flows, tend to increase in value in a higher rate environment. Administrative costs are expected to be slightly higher. Share buybacks could bolster comparisons.

Valuation - 31-JAN-97

The shares are expected to perform in line with market averages. Annualizing the last dividend, Capstead boasts a yield of some 9.6%. This is quite rich compared to the yield on the S&P 500. But the stock's risks must also be understood. Capstead is highly interest rate sensitive. Should the yield curve (rates on long term bonds less rates on short-term bonds) narrow, its interest rate spread and thus earnings would fall. The fact that most of the businesses the company is in are intensely competitive is another cause for concern. In addition, the stock has outpaced the market since early 1996, in part because of two large dividend increases. Thus, we believe that much of the good news is already reflected in the stock price. Given these considerations, the shares appear fully valued. However, management owns a large block of stock, giving it an incentive to act in shareholders' best interests.

Key Stock Statistics

S&P EPS Est. 1997	2.55	Tang. Bk. Value/Share	5.26
P/E on S&P Est. 1997	9.6	Beta	1.53
Dividend Rate/Share	2.26	Shareholders	2,500
Shs. outstg. (M)	41.8	Market cap. (B)	$ 1.0
Avg. daily vol. (M)	0.121	Inst. holdings	29%

Value of $10,000 invested 5 years ago: $ 31,392

Fiscal Year Ending Dec. 31

	1996	1995	1994	1993	1992	1991
Revenues (Million $)						
1Q	198.8	171.9	131.3	159.3	101.9	48.30
2Q	204.1	177.3	143.3	159.4	123.9	50.80
3Q	201.7	186.0	161.1	162.7	134.4	61.10
4Q	208.4	165.6	168.3	159.5	144.2	78.00
Yr.	813.1	727.8	604.1	640.8	504.4	238.2
Earnings Per Share ($)						
1Q	0.47	0.16	0.40	0.39	0.36	0.28
2Q	0.60	0.23	0.30	0.40	0.37	0.29
3Q	0.60	0.33	0.36	0.41	0.39	0.33
4Q	0.64	0.37	0.29	0.43	0.39	0.39
Yr.	2.31	1.09	1.36	1.63	1.50	1.30

Next earnings report expected: late April

Dividend Data (Dividends have been paid since 1985.)

Amount ($)	Date Decl.	Ex-Div. Date	Stock of Record	Payment Date
0.800	Jun. 10	Jun. 18	Jun. 20	Jun. 28 '96
3-for-2	Jul. 22	Aug. 16	Jul. 31	Aug. 15 '96
0.550	Sep. 09	Sep. 17	Sep. 19	Sep. 30 '96
0.565	Dec. 09	Dec. 17	Dec. 19	Dec. 31 '96

A Division of The McGraw·Hill Companies

Business Summary - 31-JAN-97

Capstead Mortgage Corp., a real estate investment trust, earns income from servicing mortgage loans, investing in mortgage-backed securities and other investment strategies. The company's business plan is to build its mortgage servicing and mortgage securities portfolios with the goal of producing reasonably balanced operating results in a rising or falling interest rate environment.

Contributions to income in recent years were:

	1995	1994
Mortgage investments	23%	57%
CMO investments	15%	9%
Mortgage servicing	45%	20%
Other	17%	14%

Mortgage investments at December 31, 1995, totaled $4.5 billion, up from $3.3 billion a year earlier, and were divided: 66% adjustable-rate agency securities, 12% adjustable-rate AAA-rated mortgages, 11% fixed-rate agency securities and 11% other.

The company's mortgage servicing portfolio (excluding pending transfers) increased during 1995 to $25.6 billion with a weighted average interest rate of 7.37% and earning an average annual service fee of 30.4 basis points. Annualized portfolio run-off, consisting of prepayments and scheduled payments on mortgages serviced, was 9.44% in 1995, up from 7.22% in 1994, due primarily to lower prevailing interest rates.

In November 1995, the company exited the jumbo mortgage loan conduit business after concluding that accepting the associated credit risk was not in its shareholders' best interest. During 1995, the company did not issue any collateralized mortgage obligations (CMOs).

Important Developments

Jan. '97—Capstead said that its decision during the second quarter of 1996 to modestly reduce its commitment to adjustable-rate mortgage securities and to increase its investments in interest-only mortgage securities helped improve profitability in the fourth quarter.

Capitalization

Debt: $3,861,892,000 of collateralized mortgage securities (12/96).
$1.60 Cum. Pfd. Stk.: $6,567,000.
$1.26 Cum. Conv. Pfd. Stk.: $259,829,000.

Per Share Data ($)

(Year Ended Dec. 31)	1996	1995	1994	1993	1992	1991	1990	1989	1988	1987
Tangible Bk. Val.	NA	5.26	6.07	8.42	6.37	6.53	6.07	6.10	7.48	9.05
Earnings	2.31	1.09	1.36	1.64	1.50	1.30	1.04	0.77	1.08	1.13
Dividends	2.11	1.09	1.43	1.63	1.45	1.14	1.01	0.93	1.09	1.12
Payout Ratio	92%	100%	105%	99%	97%	88%	97%	121%	101%	99%
Prices - High	24⅝	16⅜	18¾	19	17½	13⅛	7¼	9	10½	12⅝
- Low	14⅜	7½	7⅜	15¾	12¼	6	5¼	6¼	7	7⅛
P/E Ratio - High	11	15	14	12	12	10	7	12	10	11
- Low	6	7	5	10	8	5	5	8	6	6

Income Statement Analysis (Million $)

	1996	1995	1994	1993	1992	1991	1990	1989	1988	1987
Income Rental	NA	105	47.1	66.7	3.9	2.7	2.2	1.9	2.0	0.4
Income Mortg.	NA	623	557	575	501	236	180	132	123	91.0
Income Total	NA	728	604	642	504	238	182	134	125	91.0
Expenses Gen.	NA	73.4	43.7	56.2	35.8	14.7	8.4	7.7	4.3	4.2
Expenses Int.	NA	577	475	491	415	190	144	110	100	67.0
Prov. for Losses	NA	2.2	3.5	2.8	7.8	1.7	1.4	0.7	0.7	0.3
Depr.	NA	Nil	Nil	Nil	Nil	Nil	Nil	Nil	Nil	Nil
Net Inc.	NA	77.4	85.6	94.3	53.2	33.7	29.1	16.4	21.1	19.9

Balance Sheet & Other Fin. Data (Million $)

	1996	1995	1994	1993	1992	1991	1990	1989	1988	1987
Cash	NA	18.7	21.7	87.8	30.3	25.7	1.2	10.2	1.2	11.6
Total Assets	NA	9,904	8,944	6,980	7,230	3,825	1,829	1,736	1,247	1,126
Real Estate Invest.	NA	9,353	8,576	6,838	7,174	3,790	1,828	1,722	1,236	1,112
Loss Reserve	NA	5.9	7.3	6.9	8.2	3.5	2.9	2.1	0.7	0.7
Net Invest.	NA	9,347	8,569	6,831	7,166	3,786	1,825	1,720	1,236	1,111
ST Debt	NA	4,629	3,191	2,444	1,449	856	85.0	41.0	142	96.0
Capitalization:										
Debt	NA	4,539	5,102	3,891	5,143	2,709	1,490	1,440	928	852
Equity	NA	327	230	308	303	221	174	174	176	177
Total	NA	5,204	5,666	4,529	5,775	2,962	1,741	1,691	1,105	1,029
% Earn & Depr/Assets	NA	0.8	1.1	1.3	1.0	1.2	1.6	1.1	1.8	2.2
Price Times Book Value:										
Hi	NA	3.1	2.1	2.3	2.7	2.0	1.2	1.5	1.4	1.4
Low	NA	1.4	1.2	1.9	1.9	0.9	0.9	1.0	0.9	0.8

Data as orig. reptd.; bef. results of disc opers. and/or spec. items. Per share data adj. for stk. divs. as of ex-div. date. E-Estimated. NA-Not Available. NM-Not Meaningful. NR-Not Ranked.

Office—2711 N. Haskell Ave., Dallas, TX 75204. **Tel**—(214) 874-2323.**Website**—http://www.capstead.com **Chrmn & CEO**—R. K. Lytle. **Sr VP, Treas, Secy & Investor Contact**—Andrew F. Jacobs (214) 874-2350. **Dirs**—B. Longstreth, P. M. Low, R. K. Lytle, H. E. Miers, W. R. Smith, J. Tolleson.**Transfer Agent & Registrar**—KeyCorp Shareholder Services, Dallas.**Incorporated**—in Maryland in 1985. **Empl**— 172. **S&P Analyst:** Paul L. Huberman, CFA

15-FEB-97 Industry:
Util.-Diversified

Summary: This medium-sized utility provides electric and, to a lesser extent, gas service to a large area of New York's mid-Hudson River Valley.

Quantitative Evaluations	
Outlook (1 Lowest—5 Highest) • **1⁻**	
Fair Value • **28⅝**	
Risk • **Low**	
Earn./Div. Rank • **B+**	
Technical Eval. • **Bullish** since 5/96	
Rel. Strength Rank (1 Lowest—99 Highest) • **62**	
Insider Activity • **Neutral**	

Recent Price • 32½   Yield • 6.5%
52 Wk Range • 32¾-28¾   12-Mo. P/E • 10.9

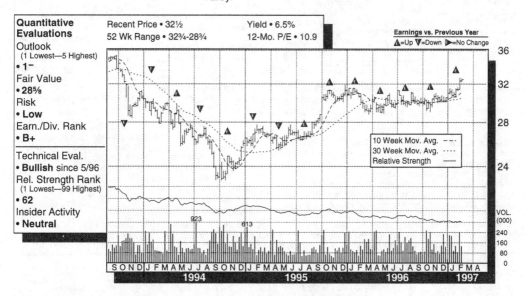

Earnings vs. Previous Year
▲=Up ▼=Down ▷=No Change

10 Week Mov. Avg. ‒·‒
30 Week Mov. Avg. ·····
Relative Strength ——

VOL. (000)

Business Profile - 06-FEB-97

CNH's Hudson River Valley territory in New York reflects a diversified economy, but one that has been adversely affected by the downsizing of its largest electricity customer, IBM. Electric power is mainly supplied by oil and coal and, to a lesser extent, nuclear (about 12%), gas and hydro facilities, and through purchases. The company plans $293 million in construction spending over the next five years, to improve its generating facilities and expand distribution capabilities. Tariffs were recently filed to comply with regulatory directives opening the natural gas market to competition.

Operational Review - 06-FEB-97

Revenues in the year ended December 31, 1996, rose fractionally, from the previous year, reflecting increased total electric sales, while colder winter weather contributed to increased firm sales of natural gas. Somewhat offsetting greater sales were higher operating and maintenance expenses, a non-recurring gain on the sale of long term investments in 1995, increased depreciation expenses, and other items. Net income advanced 6.4%, to $56,082,000 ($2.99 per share, after preferred dividends), from $52,722,000 ($2.74). Earnings benefited from a decrease in the amount of preferred dividend stock dividends paid following the redemption of two series of preferred stock.

Stock Performance - 14-FEB-97

In the past 30 trading days, CNH's shares have increased 4%, compared to a 8% rise in the S&P 500. Average trading volume for the past five days was 25,820 shares, compared with the 40-day moving average of 28,926 shares.

Key Stock Statistics

Dividend Rate/Share	2.12	Shareholders	25,400
Shs. outstg. (M)	17.6	Market cap. (B)	$0.571
Avg. daily vol. (M)	0.029	Inst. holdings	30%
Tang. Bk. Value/Share	24.82		
Beta	0.26		

Value of $10,000 invested 5 years ago: $ 15,948

Fiscal Year Ending Dec. 31

	1996	1995	1994	1993	1992	1991
Revenues (Million $)						
1Q	153.9	144.7	162.8	153.4	147.0	145.0
2Q	117.0	118.6	117.2	117.7	126.0	116.0
3Q	117.7	127.6	116.1	120.1	119.0	115.0
4Q	125.4	121.4	·119.5	126.2	132.0	119.0
Yr.	514.0	512.2	515.7	517.4	524.0	495.0
Earnings Per Share ($)						
1Q	1.20	1.06	1.22	1.15	0.92	0.92
2Q	0.58	0.55	0.45	0.59	0.55	0.55
3Q	0.73	0.70	0.65	0.55	0.63	0.60
4Q	0.48	0.43	0.36	0.41	0.55	0.34
Yr.	2.99	2.74	2.68	2.68	2.65	2.40

Next earnings report expected: late April

Dividend Data (Dividends have been paid since 1903.)

Amount ($)	Date Decl.	Ex-Div. Date	Stock of Record	Payment Date
0.525	Mar. 22	Apr. 08	Apr. 10	May. 01 '96
0.530	Jul. 01	Jul. 08	Jul. 19	Aug. 01 '96
0.530	Sep. 27	Oct. 08	Oct. 10	Nov. 01 '96
0.530	Dec. 20	Jan. 08	Jan. 10	Feb. 01 '97

Business Summary - 06-FEB-97

Central Hudson Gas & Electric supplies electricity to 261,876 customers and natural gas to 59,895 customers in a 2,600 sq. mi. area in the Hudson River Valley of New York. The company's territory has a diversified economy, including manufacturing and research concerns, farms, governmental agencies, public and private institutions, resorts, and wholesale and retail trade operations. Electric sales accounted for 80% of revenues and 90% of operating earnings in 1995. Contributions to electric revenues by customer class in recent years were:

	1995	1994	1993	1992
Residential	43%	44%	42%	39%
Commercial	32%	32%	30%	28%
Industrial	18%	20%	22%	25%
Other	7%	4%	6%	8%

The fuel mix in 1995 was oil 3%, coal 32%, gas 14%, purchased power 37%, nuclear 12% and hydro 2%. The company's maximum net capability in summer is 1,087 mw, and in winter 1,102 mw; maximum one-hour demand was 902 mw in August 1995. During 1995, the average price of electricity to customers was $0.0861 per kwh, representing an increase of about 1.8% over the $0.0846 per kwh charge in 1994. CNH's largest customer is IBM, which accounted for 10%, 12% and 14% of total electric revenues in 1995, 1994 and 1993, respectively. Downsizing at IBM facilities was the main contributor to a decline of 18% in 1995 industrial electric sales.

CNH's gas system consists of 159 mi. of transmission pipelines and 949 mi. of distribution pipelines. The company has in place five firm contracts for the supply of 10,497,708 Mcf of natural gas, all of which are with third party suppliers. Firm retail sales of natural gas increased 3.2% from those of 1994, reflecting an increase in the number of customers. IBM accounted for 6.0% of total 1995 gas revenues.

Construction spending for 1996 through 2000 was projected at $293 million, including $61.3 million for 1996. The company expected all 1996 capital spending to be financed internally. The construction program amounted to $49.3 million in 1995, a $7.9 million decrease from $57.2 million expended in 1994.

Important Developments

Jan. '97—CNH has established a plan to repurchase its common stock. The company has received regulatory approval to repurchase 2.5 million shares, or 14% of shares oustanding, over a three year period, 1997 through 1999. The target level for 1997 is 250,000 shares, with J.P. Morgan Securties acting as repurchase agent.

Capitalization

Long Term Debt: $361,552,000 (9/96).
Red. Preferred Stock: $35,000,000.
Cum. Preferred Stock: $21,030,000.

Per Share Data ($)

(Year Ended Dec. 31)	1996	1995	1994	1993	1992	1991	1990	1989	1988	1987
Tangible Bk. Val.	NA	24.82	22.46	21.91	22.69	21.96	21.76	21.11	20.59	19.54
Earnings	2.99	2.74	2.68	2.68	2.65	2.40	2.38	2.28	2.63	-0.99
Dividends	2.11	2.10	2.07	2.03	1.96	1.88	1.80	1.76	1.71	2.96
Payout Ratio	71%	77%	77%	77%	74%	78%	76%	77%	65%	NM
Prices - High	31½	31⅞	30⅜	35¾	31¼	29	24⅞	24⅛	21⅞	31⅞
- Low	28¾	25⅜	22⅞	28⅜	25⅞	22⅝	20	20⅜	16⅞	16½
P/E Ratio - High	11	12	11	13	12	12	10	11	8	NM
- Low	10	9	9	11	10	9	8	9	6	NM

Income Statement Analysis (Million $)

	1996	1995	1994	1993	1992	1991	1990	1989	1988	1987
Revs.	NA	512	516	517	524	495	504	470	438	429
Depr.	NA	41.5	40.4	39.7	39.6	37.2	36.1	35.3	31.9	28.2
Maint.	NA	29.4	32.7	34.5	34.2	31.5	30.4	23.9	23.8	20.6
Fxd. Chgs. Cov.	NA	3.2	3.6	3.3	2.7	2.4	2.2	2.1	2.3	1.4
Constr. Credits	NA	1.5	1.4	1.5	1.5	2.2	1.7	0.9	1.0	5.0
Eff. Tax Rate	NA	35%	35%	35%	34%	33%	33%	33%	33%	NM
Net Inc.	NA	52.7	50.9	50.4	47.7	42.9	41.0	39.1	43.8	-8.5

Balance Sheet & Other Fin. Data (Million $)

	1996	1995	1994	1993	1992	1991	1990	1989	1988	1987
Gross Prop.	NA	1,405	1,359	1,329	1,302	1,272	1,212	1,173	1,131	1,094
Cap. Exp.	NA	50.3	58.0	54.0	62.0	71.0	51.0	42.0	53.0	101
Net Prop.	NA	937	931	915	905	885	855	848	845	830
Capitalization:										
LT Debt	NA	389	389	392	441	416	408	447	449	430
% LT Debt	NA	43	43	44	49	49	50	53	54	54
Pfd.	NA	56.0	81.0	81.0	80.2	81.0	81.0	81.0	81.0	81.0
% Pfd.	NA	6.20	8.90	7.20	8.90	9.50	9.90	9.50	9.70	10
Common	NA	454	437	418	378	360	334	321	309	292
% Common	NA	51	48	37	42	42	41	38	37	36
Total Cap.	NA	1,089	1,146	1,122	1,012	962	913	931	908	848
Oper. Ratio	NA	86.2	85.8	85.6	85.8	84.7	84.5	83.7	81.6	81.2
% Earn. on Net Prop.	NA	7.6	7.9	8.2	8.3	8.7	9.1	9.0	9.6	9.1
% Ret. on Revs.	NA	10.3	9.9	9.7	9.1	8.7	8.1	8.3	10.0	NM
% Ret. On Invest.Cap	NA	7.5	7.2	7.5	8.1	8.4	8.9	8.8	9.6	NM
% Return On Com.Eqty	NA	10.7	10.7	11.3	10.8	10.6	10.8	10.1	12.4	NM

Data as orig. reptd.; bef. results of disc opers. and/or spec. items. Per share data adj. for stk. divs. as of ex-div. date. E-Estimated. NA-Not Available. NM-Not Meaningful. NR-Not Ranked.

Office—284 South Ave, Poughkeepsie, NY 12601-4879. **Tel**—(914) 452-2000. **Chrmn & CEO**—J. E. Mack III. **Pres & COO**—P. J. Ganci. **Contr**—D. S. Doyle. **Treas & Investor Contact**—Steven V. Lant (914-486-5254). **Dirs**—L. W. Cross, J. Effron, R. H. Eyman, F. D. Fergusson, H. K. Fridrich, E. F. X. Gallagher, P. J. Ganci, C. LaForge, J. E. Mack III, H. C. St. John, E. P. Swyer. **Transfer Agent & Registrar**—First Chicago Trust Co. of New York, Jersey City, NJ. **Incorporated**—in New York in 1926. **Empl**— 1,288. **S&P Analyst:** Michael C. Barr

15-FEB-97 | **Industry:** Utilities-Electric | **Summary:** This Dallas-based utility holding company has four utility units serving customers in Texas, Oklahoma, Louisiana and Arkansas.

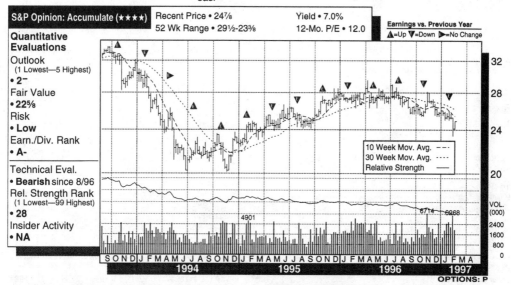

| **S&P Opinion: Accumulate (★★★)** | Recent Price • 24⅞ | Yield • 7.0% |
| | 52 Wk Range • 29½-23⅜ | 12-Mo. P/E • 12.0 |

Earnings vs. Previous Year
▲=Up ▼=Down ▶=No Change

Quantitative Evaluations

Outlook
(1 Lowest—5 Highest)
• **2⁻**

Fair Value
• **22⅝**

Risk
• **Low**

Earn./Div. Rank
• **A-**

Technical Eval.
• **Bearish** since 8/96

Rel. Strength Rank
(1 Lowest—99 Highest)
• **28**

Insider Activity
• **NA**

10 Week Mov. Avg. - - -
30 Week Mov. Avg. - - - -
Relative Strength ———

OPTIONS: P

Overview - 12-FEB-97

After acquisition-driven growth in 1996, operating revenues should remain strong in 1997, fueled by higher retail kilowatt-hour sales (up 4.9% in 1996) resulting from continued growth in demand from all customer classes within CSR's service territory. Although 1996 EPS was adversely impacted by $0.29 a share in domestic non-recurring factors (net), we expect results in 1997 will continue to benefit from CSR's well-controlled expenses. However, it appears that CSR's Central Power & Light subsidiary will only see a $7.2 million retail base rate increase, compared to the $71 million that was requested. Since the requested increase was put into effect under bond in May 1996, the difference between the bonded rates collected and the rate ultimately approved (in March) is subject to customer refund with interest. On the positive side, we expect to see continued strength from the highly efficient U.K. electric utility, SEEBOARD plc, which contributed $0.50 to 1996 results.

Valuation - 12-FEB-97

Despite recent weakness, we continue to recommend holding the stock. The shares were down 8% in 1996, compared to a 5% decline in the S&P Index of Electric Companies, and have more recently suffered from CSR's announcement that its Central Power & Light subsidiary is expected to receive rate relief substantially below the level that was requested. We expect this weakness to be transitory, however, as benefits from the SEEBOARD acquisition become more apparent, as does CSR's continued growth in related non-utility businesses. The balance sheet is strong, with long term debt estimated at roughly 52% of total capital. Good cash flow supports the relatively high dividend payout ratio (77% of projected 1997 earnings). We believe that CSR remains a good total-return investment.

Key Stock Statistics

S&P EPS Est. 1997	2.25	Tang. Bk. Value/Share	9.87
P/E on S&P Est. 1997	11.1	Beta	0.59
Dividend Rate/Share	1.74	Shareholders	74,000
Shs. outstg. (M)	210.9	Market cap. (B)	$ 5.2
Avg. daily vol. (M)	0.716	Inst. holdings	47%

Value of $10,000 invested 5 years ago: $ 12,299

Fiscal Year Ending Dec. 31

	1996	1995	1994	1993	1992	1991
Revenues (Million $)						
1Q	1,215	659.0	850.0	810.0	685.0	648.0
2Q	1,267	920.0	908.0	892.0	763.0	717.0
3Q	1,438	1,087	1,070	1,140	989.0	899.0
4Q	1,234	1,069	795.0	843.0	852.0	783.0
Yr.	5,464	3,735	3,623	3,688	3,289	3,047
Earnings Per Share ($)						
1Q	0.22	0.20	0.23	0.23	0.30	0.30
2Q	0.61	0.54	0.55	0.48	0.39	0.46
3Q	0.90	1.04	0.97	0.93	0.91	0.93
4Q	0.28	0.32	0.33	-0.25	0.43	0.30
Yr.	2.07	2.10	2.08	1.39	2.03	1.99

Next earnings report expected: mid April

Dividend Data (Dividends have been paid since 1947.)

Amount ($)	Date Decl.	Ex-Div. Date	Stock of Record	Payment Date
0.435	Apr. 18	May. 06	May. 08	May. 31 '96
0.435	Jul. 16	Aug. 06	Aug. 08	Aug. 30 '96
0.435	Oct. 24	Nov. 06	Nov. 08	Nov. 29 '96
0.435	Jan. 23	Feb. 05	Feb. 07	Feb. 28 '97

A Division of The McGraw·Hill Companies

Business Summary - 12-FEB-97

Central and South West Corporation is a public utility holding company. Its subsidiaries, Central Power & Light, Public Service of Oklahoma, Southwestern Electric Power and West Texas Utilities, provide electric (83% of 1995 revenues) and gas (17%) service to nearly 1.7 million customers (4.4 million people) in a widely diversified area covering 152,000 sq. mi. in Texas (61% of 1995 electric revenues), Oklahoma (9%), Louisiana (9%) and Arkansas (6%). Electric revenues in recent years were derived as follows:

	1995	1994	1993	1992
Residential	40%	38%	38%	38%
Commercial	28%	27%	27%	28%
Industrial	24%	24%	24%	24%
Other	8%	11%	11%	10%

Sources of electric generation in 1995 were natural gas (44%), coal (34%), lignite (9)%, purchased power (5%) and nuclear (8%). Peak demand in 1995 was 12,314 mw, and system capability at time of peak totaled 14,168 mw, for a capacity margin of 13%.

Capital outlays for construction in 1995 were $398 million. Based on growth projections, CSR does not plan to add significant generating capability through the end of the decade, and outlays budgeted for construction projects for 1996, 1997 and 1998, totaled $332 million,

$356 million and $343 million, respectively, mostly to improve and expand distribution facilities.

SEEBOARD plc, a regional U.K. electric company, was acquired in early 1996, for $2.12 billion. SEEBOARD serves some two million customers in an affluent suburban and rural area of southeastern England with above-average economic growth. It is also involved in gas supply, electricity generation, electrical contracting and retailing.

Other nonutility operations include CSW Energy, a developer of cogeneration projects; CSW Credit, which buys electric utilities' accounts receivable; CSW Leasing, an investor in leveraged leases; Central and South West Services, which provides professional services for the CSR system; and EnerShop, a cost-control consulting subsidiary.

Important Developments

Jan. '97—The company formed a limited partnership with ICG Communications to market telecommunication services in the four-state region of Texas, Oklahoma, Louisiana and Arkansas. Earlier, in December, CSR's CSW International subsidiary made an equity investment in Empresa De Electricidade Vale Paranapanema S.A., a Brazilian electric distribution company,

Capitalization

Long Term Debt: $4,315,000,000 (9/96).
Red. Cum. Pfd. Stock: $32,000,000.
Cum. Pfd. Stock: $293,000,000.

Per Share Data ($)

(Year Ended Dec. 31)	1996	1995	1994	1993	1992	1991	1990	1989	1988	1987
Tangible Bk. Val.	NA	9.87	15.90	14.45	14.71	14.30	13.80	13.28	13.75	13.11
Earnings	2.07	2.10	2.08	1.39	2.03	1.99	1.89	1.63	1.72	1.96
Dividends	1.74	1.72	1.70	1.62	1.54	1.46	1.38	1.30	1.22	1.14
Payout Ratio	84%	82%	82%	117%	76%	73%	73%	80%	71%	58%
Prices - High	29¹/₂	28¹/₂	30⁷/₈	34¹/₄	30	27¹/₈	23	20¹/₈	17³/₈	20¹/₄
- Low	25³/₈	22³/₈	20¹/₈	28¹/₄	24¹/₄	20³/₄	18³/₈	14⁷/₈	14³/₄	13¹/₂
P/E Ratio - High	14	14	15	25	15	14	12	12	10	10
- Low	12	11	10	20	12	10	10	9	9	7

Income Statement Analysis (Million $)

	1996	1995	1994	1993	1992	1991	1990	1989	1988	1987
Revs.	NA	3,735	3,623	3,687	3,289	3,047	2,744	2,549	2,512	2,436
Depr.	NA	384	356	330	308	291	284	277	254	248
Maint.	NA	161	176	197	170	181	164	155	133	124
Fxd. Chgs. Cov.	NA	2.3	2.8	2.5	2.8	2.8	2.5	2.5	2.7	3.6
Constr. Credits	NA	NA	NA	NA	2.0	5.0	4.0	42.0	158	172
Eff. Tax Rate	NA	20%	28%	29%	26%	28%	31%	29%	24%	29%
Net Inc.	NA	421	412	281	404	401	386	337	356	402

Balance Sheet & Other Fin. Data (Million $)

	1996	1995	1994	1993	1992	1991	1990	1989	1988	1987
Gross Prop.	NA	13,778	11,868	11,357	11,190	10,788	10,251	9,634	9,370	8,961
Cap. Exp.	NA	474	578	508	425	327	329	331	463	562
Net Prop.	NA	9,017	7,998	7,807	7,903	7,802	7,550	7,186	7,151	6,946
Capitalization:										
LT Debt	NA	3,914	2,940	2,749	2,647	2,518	2,513	2,537	2,514	2,410
% LT Debt	NA	53	47	46	45	44	45	46	46	46
Pfd.	NA	326	327	350	367	389	394	397	396	365
% Pfd.	NA	4.40	5.20	5.80	6.20	6.80	7.00	7.10	7.20	6.90
Common	NA	3,178	3,052	2,930	2,927	2,834	2,743	2,647	2,594	2,514
% Common	NA	43	48	49	49	49	49	47	47	48
Total Cap.	NA	10,232	8,687	8,299	7,951	7,677	7,528	7,366	7,196	6,931
Oper. Ratio	NA	82.4	83.6	87.6	82.0	81.4	82.0	80.7	81.7	82.1
% Earn. on Net Prop.	NA	4.9	7.5	5.9	7.5	7.4	6.7	6.9	6.5	6.4
% Ret. on Revs.	NA	11.3	11.4	7.6	12.3	13.2	14.1	13.2	14.2	16.5
% Ret. On Invest.Cap	NA	4.5	8.3	6.8	8.6	8.8	9.5	8.4	8.2	8.6
% Return On Com.Eqty	NA	12.9	13.2	10.6	13.3	13.4	13.2	11.7	12.7	15.3

Data as orig. reptd.; bef. results of disc opers. and/or spec. items. Per share data adj. for stk. divs. as of ex-div. date. E-Estimated. NA-Not Available. NM-Not Meaningful. NR-Not Ranked.

Office—1616 Woodall Rodgers Freeway, Dallas, TX 75202,1234. **Tel**—(214) 777-1000. **Website**—http://www.csw.com **Chrmn, Pres & CEO**—E. R. Brooks. **SVP & CFO**—G. D. Rosilier. **Secy**—F. L. Frawley. **Investor Contact**—Sharon R. Peavy. **Dirs**—G. Biggs, M. S. Boren, E. R. Brooks, D. M. Carlton, T. H. Cruikshank, J. Ellis, J. H. Foy, R. W. Lawless, H. D. Mattison, J. L. Powell, T. V. Shockley III, J. C. Templeton, L. D. Ward. **Transfer Agent & Registrar**—Co.'s office. **Incorporated**—in Delaware in 1925. **Empl**— 12,064. **S&P Analyst:** Justin McCann

Chemed Corp.

503D

NYSE Symbol **CHE**

In S&P SmallCap 600

15-FEB-97

Industry:
Chemicals

Summary: This company has positions in medical and dental supplies, home healthcare services and hospice care, sanitary maintenance products and services, and cleaning and appliance repair.

Quantitative Evaluations

Recent Price • 36¾
52 Wk Range • 39¼-34⅝

Yield • 5.7%
12-Mo. P/E • 11.2

Outlook
(1 Lowest—5 Highest)
• **NA**

Fair Value
• **NA**

Risk
• **Low**

Earn./Div. Rank
• **B+**

Technical Eval.
• **Bearish** since 11/95

Rel. Strength Rank
(1 Lowest—99 Highest)
• **39**

Insider Activity
• **Favorable**

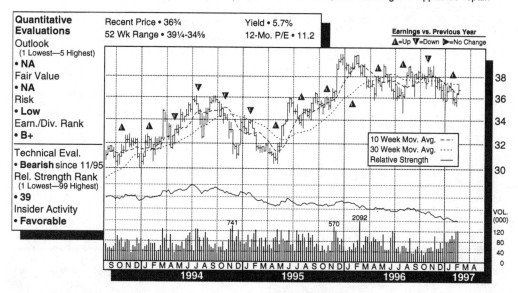

Earnings vs. Previous Year
▲=Up ▼=Down ▶=No Change

10 Week Mov. Avg. ---
30 Week Mov. Avg. ·····
Relative Strength —

Business Profile - 12-FEB-97

Chemed is optimistic about 1997 prospects for its four core operations. Moreover, it believes that its portfolio holdings, especially Omnicare Inc. and EXEL Ltd., continue to provide opportunities for capital gains which augment core earnings. Aftertax capital gains from the sales of investments rose to $1.81 a share in 1996 from $0.59 the year before. In August 1996, CHE completed a $41 a share cash tender offer for the 42% of Roto-Rooter, Inc. it did not already own; the offer was valued at about $88.6 million.

Operational Review - 12-FEB-97

Revenues from continuing operations for 1996 (preliminary) declined 2.2% from those of 1995, reflecting lower sales at National Sanitary Supply and at the Omnia Group. Despite excellent results from the Roto-Rooter Group and Patient Care Inc., Chemed's core earnings (which exclude investment gains, nonrecurring expenses and discontinued operations) were down 5%, to $1.42 a share from $1.50 the year before. However, with aftertax capital gains increasing to $17,731,000 ($1.81) from $5,882,000 ($0.59), income from continued operations advanced 55%, to $31,728,000 ($3.23) from $20,439,000 ($2.07). Results exclude income from discontinued operations of $0.06 and $0.28 a share, respectively.

Stock Performance - 14-FEB-97

In the past 30 trading days, CHE's shares have increased 0.34%, compared to a 8% rise in the S&P 500. Average trading volume for the past five days was 26,480 shares, compared with the 40-day moving average of 20,582 shares.

Key Stock Statistics

Dividend Rate/Share	2.08	Shareholders	6,000
Shs. outstg. (M)	9.8	Market cap. (B)	$0.360
Avg. daily vol. (M)	0.022	Inst. holdings	31%
Tang. Bk. Value/Share	0.88		
Beta	0.51		

Value of $10,000 invested 5 years ago: $ 17,805

Fiscal Year Ending Dec. 31

	1996	1995	1994	1993	1992	1991
Revenues (Million $)						
1Q	167.5	169.9	152.1	120.5	92.50	81.70
2Q	170.5	177.3	161.4	127.2	98.30	85.80
3Q	173.7	177.6	166.1	139.8	102.7	91.40
4Q	172.2	174.4	165.5	137.5	107.6	93.30
Yr.	683.8	699.2	645.0	525.1	401.0	352.3
Earnings Per Share ($)						
1Q	1.24	0.55	0.33	0.42	0.32	0.04
2Q	0.58	0.54	0.45	0.50	0.44	0.21
3Q	0.39	0.58	0.33	0.43	0.37	0.41
4Q	1.01	0.41	0.37	0.41	0.33	0.45
Yr.	3.23	2.35	1.47	1.75	1.45	1.10

Next earnings report expected: mid April

Dividend Data (Dividends have been paid since 1971.)

Amount ($)	Date Decl.	Ex-Div. Date	Stock of Record	Payment Date
0.520	May. 20	May. 23	May. 28	Jun. 07 '96
0.520	Aug. 08	Aug. 20	Aug. 22	Sep. 06 '96
0.520	Nov. 07	Nov. 20	Nov. 22	Dec. 10 '96
0.520	Feb. 06	Feb. 19	Feb. 21	Mar. 10 '97

A Division of The McGraw-Hill Companies

STANDARD
&POOR'S
STOCK REPORTS

Chemed Corporation

503D

15-FEB-97

Business Summary - 12-FEB-97

Chemed Corp. manufactures and distributes medical and dental disposable-product supplies; provides home healthcare services and supportive services for the primary, acute and long-term care markets; performs plumbing, drain cleaning and residential appliance and air conditioning repair; and provides sanitary-maintenance-product-distribution services. Segment contributions in 1995 were:

	Sales	Profits
National Sanitary Supply	49%	31%
Roto-Rooter	26%	41%
Omnia	12%	15%
Patient Care	13%	13%

National Sanitary Supply Co. (83% owned) is a leading U.S. distributor of sanitary maintenance products. It offers a broad line of janitorial products such as cleaning chemicals, paper goods, floor finishes, hand soaps, plastic products, waste handling products, cleaning equipment, packaging supplies and other janitorial supplies used by commercial, institutional and industrial businesses located primarily in the West, Southwest and Midwest. Sonic Corp. accounted for 15% of 1995 sales, consisting of low-margin food-service products.

Roto-Rooter, Inc. (wholly owned) provides sewer, drain and pipe cleaning services and appliance and plumbing repair and maintenance services and consumer prod-

ucts and equipment to residential and commercial clients, through both independent franchisees and company-owned operations.

The Omnia Group (formerly Veratex) manufactures medical and dental supplies and distributes them to dealers throughout the U.S.

Patient Care (acquired in January 1994) provides complete home healthcare services for patients in the New York/New Jersey/Connecticut area. Services include nursing, physical, speech, respiratory and occupational therapy, nutrition consulting, and other specialized services.

In 1995, the company's medical and dental products group, renamed the Omnia Group, divested its Veratex Retail telemarketing operation and strengthened its remaining manufacturing operations by acquiring the medical division of Central States Diversified Inc. The division manufactures and distributes disposable paper products marketed under the Pro-Tex-Mor brand.

Important Developments

Feb. '97—Chemed said that during 1996, it took pretax gains from its portfolio holdings amounting to about $25 million on sales of Omnicare Inc. shares and $3 million on EXEL Ltd. shares.

Capitalization

Long Term Debt: $80,563,000 (9/96).
Minority Interest: $10,718,000.

Per Share Data ($)

(Year Ended Dec. 31)	1996	1995	1994	1993	1992	1991	1990	1989	1988	1987
Tangible Bk. Val.	NA	7.21	5.24	2.05	5.65	7.58	11.04	11.77	11.86	12.86
Cash Flow	NA	3.91	2.56	2.65	2.10	1.68	2.51	3.45	2.98	2.97
Earnings	3.23	2.07	1.47	1.75	1.45	1.10	1.60	2.61	2.23	2.28
Dividends	2.08	2.06	2.04	2.01	2.00	1.97	1.96	1.84	1.72	1.60
Payout Ratio	64%	100%	139%	115%	137%	177%	121%	72%	78%	69%
Prices - High	40⅛	40¼	36⅛	32¾	32⅜	28¼	36¾	38¾	38½	44⅝
- Low	34⅝	30⅜	30¼	25½	24¼	17¼	18	32½	29½	25¾
P/E Ratio - High	12	19	25	19	22	26	23	15	17	20
- Low	11	15	21	15	17	16	11	12	13	11

Income Statement Analysis (Million $)

	1996	1995	1994	1993	1992	1991	1990	1989	1988	1987
Revs.	NA	699	645	525	401	352	599	592	501	391
Oper. Inc.	NA	51.2	39.8	32.0	21.5	16.4	44.1	57.9	50.5	48.9
Depr.	NA	18.2	10.7	8.8	6.3	5.9	9.5	8.4	7.1	6.2
Int. Exp.	NA	8.5	8.8	8.9	5.7	5.7	7.6	8.9	8.2	6.6
Pretax Inc.	NA	41.0	29.8	30.2	23.9	19.2	29.7	44.3	37.1	39.3
Eff. Tax Rate	NA	38%	37%	31%	27%	28%	35%	34%	37%	43%
Net Inc.	NA	20.4	14.5	17.1	14.3	11.0	16.6	26.2	20.6	20.4

Balance Sheet & Other Fin. Data (Million $)

	1996	1995	1994	1993	1992	1991	1990	1989	1988	1987
Cash	NA	19.2	24.2	15.8	47.7	83.0	1.4	6.5	4.4	4.7
Curr. Assets	NA	219	183	145	162	163	144	150	143	110
Total Assets	NA	532	505	430	405	364	328	335	323	264
Curr. Liab.	NA	145	143	128	104	85.0	94.0	88.0	83.0	67.0
LT Debt	NA	85.4	92.0	98.0	104	78.0	82.0	86.0	90.0	47.0
Common Eqty.	NA	209	186	137	134	139	113	121	111	113
Total Cap.	NA	310	322	267	266	245	227	242	235	191
Cap. Exp.	NA	15.4	18.4	13.9	8.2	11.4	13.0	14.1	14.6	8.9
Cash Flow	NA	38.6	25.2	26.0	20.6	16.9	26.0	34.6	27.7	26.5
Curr. Ratio	NA	1.5	1.3	1.1	1.6	1.9	1.5	1.7	1.7	1.6
% LT Debt of Cap.	NA	27.5	28.6	36.7	39.0	31.8	36.2	35.5	38.5	24.3
% Net Inc.of Revs.	NA	2.9	2.3	3.3	3.6	3.1	2.8	4.4	4.1	5.2
% Ret. on Assets	NA	3.9	3.1	4.1	3.4	3.5	5.0	7.6	6.8	7.7
% Ret. on Equity	NA	10.3	9.0	12.6	10.5	9.0	14.2	21.6	17.8	17.7

Data as orig. reptd.; bef. results of disc. opers. and/or spec. items. Per share data adj. for stk. divs. as of ex-div. date. E-Estimated. NA-Not Available. NM-Not Meaningful. NR-Not Ranked.

Office—2600 Chemed Center, 255 E. Fifth St, Cincinnati, OH 45202. **Tel**—(513) 762-6900. **Fax**—(513) 762-6919. **Chrmn & CEO**—E. L. Hutton. **Pres**—K. J. McNamara. **EVP, Treas & Investor Contact**—Timothy S. O'Toole. **VP & Secy**—Naomi C. Dallob. **Dirs**—J. A. Cunningham, J. H. Devlin, C. H. Erhart Jr., J. F. Gemunder, L. J. Gillis, P. P. Grace, W. R. Griffin, E. L. Hutton, T. C. Hutton, W. L. Krebs, S. E. Laney, K. J. McNamara, J. M. Mount, T. S. O'Toole, D. W. Robbins Jr., P. C. Voet, G. J. Walsh, III.**Transfer Agent & Registrar**—ChaseMellon Shareholder Services, Ridgefield Park, NJ. **Incorporated**—in Delaware in 1970. **Empl**— 7,335. **S&P Analyst:** J.J.S.

15-FEB-97

Industry:
Utilities-Gas

Summary: This retail pipeline distributor of natural gas serves about 145,000 customers in the Merrimack Valley region northwest of Boston and on Cape Cod.

Quantitative Evaluations

Recent Price • 21½
52 Wk Range • 24¼-20

Yield • 6.0%
12-Mo. P/E • 11.0

Outlook
(1 Lowest—5 Highest)
• **3⁻**

Fair Value
• **21⅜**

Risk
• **Low**

Earn./Div. Rank
• **B+**

Technical Eval.
• **Bearish** since 1/97

Rel. Strength Rank
(1 Lowest—99 Highest)
• **33**

Insider Activity
• **Neutral**

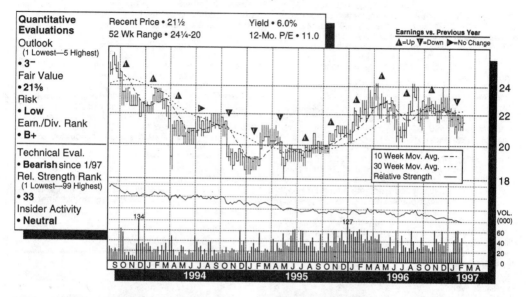

Earnings vs. Previous Year
▲=Up ▼=Down ▶=No Change

10 Week Mov. Avg. ― ―
30 Week Mov. Avg. ----
Relative Strength ―

Business Profile - 13-FEB-97

This retail pipeline distributor of natural gas serves some 145,000 customers in 24 municipalities located in the greater Lowell and Cape Cod areas of Massachusetts. Through its Transgas Inc. subsidiary, the company also provides over-the-road transportation of liquefied natural gas, propane, and other commodities. In 1996, CGES's earnings, dividend, and customers served continued to reach new highs. The company's objective continues to be to decrease O&M costs by 6%, grow its customer base 3% annually through 2004, maintain its current staffing levels and avoid a rate increase until 2000. In addition, the company believes that sales and marketing will play an increasingly crucial role in light of the opportunities resulting from deregulation of the utilities industry.

Operational Review - 13-FEB-97

Based on a preliminary report, revenues in 1996 increased 38%, due primarily to colder weather, a larger customer base and an increase in liquefied natural gas hauls at Transgas, Colonial's energy trucking subsidiary. Margins narrowed, reflecting warmer weather in the fourth quarter. Net income advanced 20%, to $16,478,000 ($1.95 per share), from $13,764,000 ($1.66).

Stock Performance - 14-FEB-97

In the past 30 trading days, CGES's shares have declined 1%, compared to a 8% rise in the S&P 500. Average trading volume for the past five days was 9,580 shares, compared with the 40-day moving average of 9,023 shares.

Key Stock Statistics

Dividend Rate/Share	1.30	Shareholders	5,600
Shs. outstg. (M)	8.5	Market cap. (B)	$0.182
Avg. daily vol. (M)	0.012	Inst. holdings	18%
Tang. Bk. Value/Share	12.22		
Beta	0.24		

Value of $10,000 invested 5 years ago: $ 16,514

Fiscal Year Ending Dec. 31

	1996	1995	1994	1993	1992	1991
Revenues (Million $)						
1Q	77.58	70.35	86.10	78.10	64.10	64.90
2Q	24.24	22.76	19.07	20.60	18.20	17.40
3Q	15.25	14.91	13.03	12.30	12.50	12.30
4Q	53.87	56.63	48.08	55.30	50.30	43.20
Yr.	170.9	164.6	166.3	166.3	145.1	137.7
Earnings Per Share ($)						
1Q	1.82	1.51	1.79	1.53	1.65	1.33
2Q	-0.26	-0.40	-0.41	-0.41	-0.47	-0.58
3Q	-0.42	-0.47	-0.59	-0.47	-0.51	-0.50
4Q	0.83	1.02	0.58	0.87	0.71	0.85
Yr.	1.95	1.66	1.36	1.52	1.38	1.11

Next earnings report expected: late April

Dividend Data (Dividends have been paid since 1937.)

Amount ($)	Date Decl.	Ex-Div. Date	Stock of Record	Payment Date
0.325	Apr. 17	May. 29	May. 31	Jun. 14 '96
0.325	Jul. 17	Aug. 28	Aug. 30	Sep. 13 '96
0.325	Oct. 16	Nov. 26	Nov. 29	Dec. 13 '96
0.325	Jan. 15	Feb. 26	Feb. 28	Mar. 14 '97

Colonial Gas Company

Business Summary - 13-FEB-97

Colonial Gas is a Massachusetts gas distribution utility engaged primarily in the retail pipeline distribution of natural gas in the Merrimack Valley and Cape Cod areas of that state. The service area covers about 622 square miles with a year-round population of about 500,000, which increases by about 350,000 during the summer tourist season on Cape Cod. CGES serves 141,399 utility customers in 24 municipalities. Through its Transgas Inc. subsidiary, CGES is engaged in the transportation of liquefied natural gas, propane and other products.

Gas sales amounted to 19,708,000 Mcf in 1995, up 1.4% from 19,445,000 Mcf in 1994. Peak daily sendout in 1995 was 199,275 Mcf, down 2.7% from 204,896 in 1994. Sales to residential customers accounted for 65% of gas sales in 1995 (57% in 1994), commercial and industrial customers 29% (39%) and interruptible (non-firm) customers 6% (4%). At the end of 1995, customers totaled 141,399, up 3.5% from 136,667 a year earlier, and were 90% residential and 10% commercial and industrial.

CGES meets its supply requirements through a combination of firm and spot purchases of pipeline-transported supply, supply from underground storage, liquefied natural gas and propane. The company maintains three firm contracts with the Tennessee Gas Pipeline Co. for the transportation of supply to the Merrimack Valley service area, and also contracts for underground storage service in conjunction with two Tennessee firm transportation contracts. CGES' portfolio of firm pipeline-transported supply for the Merrimack Valley area consists of four purchase contracts for domestically-produced gas and one purchase contract for Canadian-produced gas. Pipeline natural gas for Cape Cod is obtained under 14 firm contracts with Algonquin Gas Transmission Co. CGES portfolio of pipeline-transported supplies for the Cape Cod area consists of three purchase contracts for domestically-produced gas. Also, CGES has five storage contracts to service the Cape Cod area.

Colonial plans to sell a 50% interest in Transgas to Cabot LNG Corp. as part of a joint venture between CGES and Cabot Corp. The sale is expected to be completed by the middle of 1997, subject to regulatory approvals. The company expects to recognize a one-time gain of about $0.35 per share from the sale.

Important Developments

Jan. '97—CGES reported a net gain for the fourth quarter of 1996, of $0.83 per share, versus a gain of $1.02 in the eary-earlier period. Colonial said the decrease was due primarily to 5.8% warmer weather than the same period in 1995.

Capitalization

Long Term Debt: $85,305,000 (9/96).

Per Share Data ($) (Year Ended Dec. 31)	1996	1995	1994	1993	1992	1991	1990	1989	1988	1987
Tangible Bk. Val.	NA	12.22	11.71	11.39	10.83	10.42	10.38	10.17	9.81	9.23
Cash Flow	NA	2.93	2.49	2.38	2.14	1.83	1.55	2.20	1.93	2.01
Earnings	1.95	1.66	1.36	1.52	1.38	1.11	0.82	1.44	1.20	1.35
Dividends	1.30	1.28	1.26	1.23	1.21	1.19	1.17	1.14	1.11	1.09
Payout Ratio	66%	77%	92%	81%	88%	109%	142%	79%	94%	82%
Prices - High	24¼	21½	23¾	26½	23½	17⅞	15⅝	15⅜	14	17⅛
- Low	20	18	18¼	20	16⅝	14½	13⅞	12	11⅝	11⅜
P/E Ratio - High	12	13	17	17	17	16	19	11	12	13
- Low	10	11	13	13	12	13	17	8	10	8
Income Statement Analysis (Million $)										
Revs.	NA	165	166	166	145	138	134	140	116	118
Oper. Inc.	NA	21.6	32.6	33.1	29.6	26.7	19.7	24.2	21.9	23.8
Depr.	NA	10.2	9.2	6.8	5.9	5.5	5.1	4.7	4.4	4.0
Int. Exp.	NA	9.3	8.4	8.1	7.5	8.1	8.4	8.2	7.4	6.7
Pretax Inc.	NA	22.2	16.9	18.9	17.2	13.1	7.7	12.2	11.2	13.3
Eff. Tax Rate	NA	38%	35%	36%	38%	36%	26%	27%	35%	40%
Net Inc.	NA	13.8	11.0	12.0	10.6	8.3	5.7	8.9	7.3	8.0
Balance Sheet & Other Fin. Data (Million $)										
Cash	NA	7.5	9.0	5.5	4.4	2.3	4.6	5.4	6.4	4.6
Curr. Assets	NA	61.0	65.6	67.7	71.8	53.5	46.4	56.8	50.4	36.8
Total Assets	NA	342	331	312	303	264	238	234	212	188
Curr. Liab.	NA	102	91.4	73.4	64.6	74.0	47.7	54.6	53.4	34.8
LT Debt	NA	76.8	80.2	90.6	94.3	54.2	68.8	74.2	60.6	64.1
Common Eqty.	NA	105	99	94.3	87.8	82.2	80.1	66.6	63.0	58.2
Total Cap.	NA	225	225	227	220	174	185	174	157	152
Cap. Exp.	NA	24.1	28.2	26.2	27.1	16.8	16.6	13.1	15.5	15.0
Cash Flow	NA	24.0	20.2	18.9	16.5	13.8	10.8	13.6	11.7	12.0
Curr. Ratio	NA	0.6	0.7	0.9	1.1	0.7	1.0	1.0	0.9	1.1
% LT Debt of Cap.	NA	34.2	35.7	39.9	42.9	31.1	37.1	42.6	38.6	42.2
% Net Inc.of Revs.	NA	8.4	6.6	7.2	7.3	6.0	4.2	6.4	6.3	6.8
% Ret. on Assets	NA	4.1	3.4	3.9	3.8	3.3	2.2	4.0	3.6	4.6
% Ret. on Equity	NA	13.5	11.2	13.2	12.5	10.1	7.2	13.6	11.9	14.0

Data as orig. reptd.; bef. results of disc. opers. and/or spec. items. Per share data adj. for stk. divs. as of ex-div. date. E-Estimated. NA-Not Available. NM-Not Meaningful. NR-Not Ranked.

Formed—in Massachusetts in 1849. **Office**—40 Market St., Lowell, MA 01852.**Tel**—(508) 458-3171. **Chrmn**—F. L. Putnam Jr. **Pres & CEO**—F. L. Putnam III. **EVP & COO**—C. W. Sawyer. **EVP-Fin, CFO & Investor Contact**—Nickolas Stavropoulos. **VP & Treas**—D. W. Carroll. **Clerk**—Carol E. Elden. **Dirs**—V. W. Baur, J. P. Harrington, H. C. Homeyer, R. L. Hull, D. H. LeVan Jr., F. L. Putnam Jr., F. L. Putnam III, J. F. Reilly Jr., A. B. Sides Jr., M. M. Stapleton, N. Stravropoulos, C. O. Swanson. **Transfer Agent & Registrar**—First National Bank of Boston. **Empl**— 478. **S&P Analyst:** J. Robert Cho

15-FEB-97

Industry: Util.-Diversified

Summary: This electric and gas utility serves the commercial and residential economy of New York City. Purchased power is a significant source of energy for the company.

S&P Opinion: Hold (★★★)	Recent Price • 31⅛	Yield • 6.7%
	52 Wk Range • 33⅞-25⅞	12-Mo. P/E • 10.6

Quantitative Evaluations

Outlook
(1 Lowest—5 Highest)
• **1**

Fair Value
• **24½**

Risk
• **Low**

Earn./Div. Rank
• **A**

Technical Eval.
• **Bullish** since 11/96

Rel. Strength Rank
(1 Lowest—99 Highest)
• **57**

Insider Activity
• **NA**

Earnings vs. Previous Year
▲=Up ▼=Down ▶=No Change

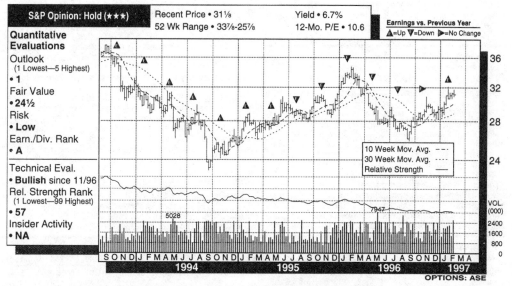

```
10 Week Mov. Avg. - - -
30 Week Mov. Avg. ·····
Relative Strength ——
```

OPTIONS: ASE

Overview - 04-FEB-97

We expect earnings growth in 1997 to be limited by the ongoing effects of a three-year adjustable rate agreement that went into effect April 1, 1995. The agreement provides for a rate freeze, a lower level of incentive opportunities, and a modest reduction in the allowed return on common equity. Although ED's rates are among the highest in the U.S., it remains fairly well insulated from increasing competition within the electric utility industry because of the absence of an industrial customer base. In addition, ED has joined East Coast Natural Gas Cooperative L.L.C., a natural gas distribution company serving the Eastern Seaboard; this should help to reduce the company's gas costs, particularly during high-demand, high-cost winter peak periods. In addition, ED is seeking other unregulated growth opportunities, such as energy marketing and enhanced customer service. The balance sheet is strong; long term debt, equal to 40.3% of total capital as of September 30, 1996, is below the industry average.

Valuation - 04-FEB-97

We continue to recommend holding the stock. The shares were down 8.3% in 1996, versus a 5% decline for the index of S&P Electric companies and a 20% gain for the S&P 500. Earnings growth, and consequently share price appreciation, is limited by subpar growth in the local economy and comparatively high costs. We believe that the stock is fairly valued in a range of 10X to 11X our 1997 EPS projection. The dividend yield of nearly 7% is above average for investor-owned utilities, but the relatively modest payout of about 71% is supported by strong cash generation. Although we expect limited upside for the shares in the next six to 12 months, we continue to see them as an attractive portfolio holding for income.

Key Stock Statistics

S&P EPS Est. 1997	2.90	Tang. Bk. Value/Share	22.81
P/E on S&P Est. 1997	10.7	Beta	0.65
Dividend Rate/Share	2.10	Shareholders	151,300
Shs. outstg. (M)	235.0	Market cap. (B)	$ 7.3
Avg. daily vol. (M)	0.519	Inst. holdings	33%

Value of $10,000 invested 5 years ago: $ 15,306

Fiscal Year Ending Dec. 31

	1996	1995	1994	1993	1992	1991
Revenues (Million $)						
1Q	1,867	1,669	1,698	1,586	1,456	1,479
2Q	1,540	1,460	1,392	1,396	1,280	1,331
3Q	1,920	1,880	1,822	1,800	1,718	1,720
4Q	1,632	1,528	1,461	1,484	1,479	1,343
Yr.	6,960	6,537	6,373	6,265	5,933	5,873
Earnings Per Share ($)						
1Q	0.78	0.82	0.77	0.62	0.47	0.43
2Q	0.28	0.29	0.33	0.23	0.30	0.24
3Q	1.38	1.38	1.41	1.35	1.30	1.29
4Q	0.49	0.44	0.47	0.46	0.39	0.36
Yr.	2.93	2.93	2.98	2.66	2.46	2.32

Next earnings report expected: late April

Dividend Data (Dividends have been paid since 1885.)

Amount ($)	Date Decl.	Ex-Div. Date	Stock of Record	Payment Date
0.520	Apr. 23	May. 13	May. 15	Jun. 15 '96
0.520	Jul. 23	Aug. 12	Aug. 14	Sep. 15 '96
0.520	Oct. 22	Nov. 08	Nov. 11	Dec. 15 '96
0.525	Jan. 28	Feb. 14	Feb. 19	Mar. 15 '97

A Division of The McGraw·Hill Companies

Business Summary - 04-FEB-97

Consolidated Edison supplies electricity to all of New York City (except part of Queens) and most of Westchester County. Gas and steam services are provided in certain parts of the service area. In 1995, electric sales accounted for 83% of revenues, gas 12% and steam 5%. Electric revenues in recent years by customer class were:

	1995	1994	1993	1992
Residential	33%	34%	34%	33%
Commercial-industrial	61%	62%	64%	66%
Other	6%	4%	2%	1%

Electric energy sources in 1995 were natural gas 54%, nuclear 11%, oil 5% and hydro and other 7%. Some 23% of 1995's energy requirements were met with purchased power. ED's nuclear capacity is derived from its Indian Point 2 plant in Westchester County. Peak demand in 1995 was 10,805 mw, and capability at peak totaled 14,115 mw, for a capacity margin of 23%. Gas sales in 1995 totaled 106,197,138 dekatherms, down 2.2% from 1994.

The company's near-term generating strategy is to develop conservation programs including demand-side management, implement plant life extension projects and continue to explore economic power purchases. Based on current demand growth projections, the company does not expect to add any new capacity resources to its system over the next 20 years. ED estimated construction expenditures of $678 million for 1996, down from $693 million in 1995, largely for electric facilities.

Important Developments

Oct. '96—In response to an order by the N.Y.S. Public Service Commission in its "Competitive Opportunities" proceeding, ED provided a plan outlining its transition to a competitive electricity marketplace. The proposal included a five-year rate freeze to be effective April 1997, the full recovery of stranded costs, a corporate reorganization into a holding company structure, and tax and regulatory reform. The company's plan also calls for the establishment of a state "System Security Operator" to ensure reliability, a power exchange with visible pricing for electricity, and increased wholesale competition as early as 1997. A retail access energy pilot program would begin April 1, 1998, and ED expects that all customers could participate in the program by 2003.

Capitalization

Long Term Debt: $4,090,810,000 (9/96), excl. $43,3321,000 of lease obligs. (9/96).
Red. Cum. Preferred Stock: $84,550,000.
Cum. Preferred Stock: $238,189,000.

Per Share Data ($)

(Year Ended Dec. 31)	1996	1995	1994	1993	1992	1991	1990	1989	1988	1987
Tangible Bk. Val.	NA	22.81	21.90	20.89	20.58	20.00	19.56	19.07	18.35	17.49
Earnings	2.93	2.93	2.98	2.66	2.46	2.32	2.34	2.49	2.47	2.21
Dividends	2.08	2.04	2.00	1.94	1.90	1.86	1.82	1.72	1.60	1.48
Payout Ratio	71%	70%	67%	73%	77%	80%	78%	69%	65%	67%
Prices - High	34¾	32¼	32⅜	37¾	32⅞	28¾	29¼	29⅞	23¾	26
- Low	25⅞	25½	23	30¼	25	22½	19¾	22¼	20½	18¾
P/E Ratio - High	12	11	11	14	13	12	13	12	10	12
- Low	9	9	8	11	10	10	8	9	8	8

Income Statement Analysis (Million $)

	1996	1995	1994	1993	1992	1991	1990	1989	1988	1987
Revs.	NA	6,537	6,373	6,265	5,933	5,873	5,739	5,551	5,109	5,094
Depr.	NA	456	422	404	381	360	343	325	308	229
Maint.	NA	512	506	571	529	521	510	483	447	447
Fxd. Chgs. Cov.	NA	4.0	4.3	3.9	3.6	3.5	3.8	4.2	4.4	4.5
Constr. Credits	NA	5.6	18.9	10.6	13.8	14.4	9.0	13.1	12.1	15.3
Eff. Tax Rate	NA	35%	37%	36%	35%	34%	34%	34%	33%	40%
Net Inc.	NA	724	734	659	604	567	571	606	599	550

Balance Sheet & Other Fin. Data (Million $)

	1996	1995	1994	1993	1992	1991	1990	1989	1988	1987
Gross Prop.	NA	14,851	14,390	13,750	13,191	12,521	11,922	11,366	10,868	10,408
Cap. Exp.	NA	706	805	803	830	784	736	630	629	544
Net Prop.	NA	10,814	10,561	10,156	9,730	9,263	8,815	8,411	8,071	7,743
Capitalization:										
LT Debt	NA	3,962	4,078	3,694	3,494	3,420	3,371	3,150	2,890	2,907
% LT Debt	NA	39	41	39	39	40	40	39	37	39
Pfd.	NA	640	640	641	641	633	636	639	642	645
% Pfd.	NA	6.30	6.40	6.80	7.10	7.30	7.50	7.80	8.30	8.50
Common	NA	5,523	5,313	5,069	4,887	4,608	4,502	4,382	4,205	4,007
% Common	NA	55	53	54	54	53	53	54	54	53
Total Cap.	NA	12,603	12,562	11,965	10,252	9,751	9,517	9,116	8,626	8,447
Oper. Ratio	NA	84.1	83.7	84.8	85.2	86.2	86.0	85.9	84.9	85.8
% Earn. on Net Prop.	NA	51.4	10.0	9.6	9.3	9.0	9.3	9.5	9.8	9.5
% Ret. on Revs.	NA	11.1	11.5	10.5	10.2	9.7	10.0	10.9	11.7	10.8
% Ret. On Invest.Cap	NA	11.5	8.5	8.5	9.0	8.9	8.9	9.5	9.6	9.0
% Return On Com.Eqty	NA	12.7	13.5	12.5	12.0	11.6	12.0	13.2	13.7	12.7

Data as orig. reptd.; bef. results of disc. opers. and/or spec. items. Per share data adj. for stk. divs. as of ex-div. date. E-Estimated. NA-Not Available. NM-Not Meaningful. NR-Not Ranked.

Registrar—ChaseMellon Shareholder Services, Ridgefield Park, NJ. **Office**—4 Irving Place, New York, NY 10003. **Tel**—(212) 460-4600. **Website**—http://www.coned.com **Chrmn, Pres & CEO**—E. R. McGrath. **SVP & CFO**—Joan S. Freilich. **Secy**—A. M. Bankston. **VP & Treas**—G. R. Rajani. **Investor Contact**—William J. Clifford. **Trustees**—E. V. Conway, G. J. Davis, R. M. Davis, E. V. Futter, A. Hauspurg, S. Hernandez-Pinero, P. W. Likins, R. J. McCann, E. R. McGrath, F. P. Rose, D. K. Ross, R. G. Schwartz, R. A. Voell, M. V. Whalen Jr. **Transfer Agent**—Co.'s office. **Incorporated**—in New York in 1884. **Empl**—17,097. **S&P Analyst:** Justin McCann

15-FEB-97

Industry: Utilities-Water

Summary: This utility holding company owns eight water utilities, in Ohio, Illinois, Pennsylvania, New Jersey, New Hampshire and Maine, and also provides technical services.

Quantitative Evaluations

Outlook (1 Lowest—5 Highest)
• **1⁻**

Fair Value
• **13¾**

Risk
• **Low**

Earn./Div. Rank
• **B**

Technical Eval.
• **Bearish** since 10/96

Rel. Strength Rank (1 Lowest—99 Highest)
• **49**

Insider Activity
• **NA**

Recent Price • 18¼
52 Wk Range • 19¼-14½

Yield • 6.6%
12-Mo. P/E • 25.3

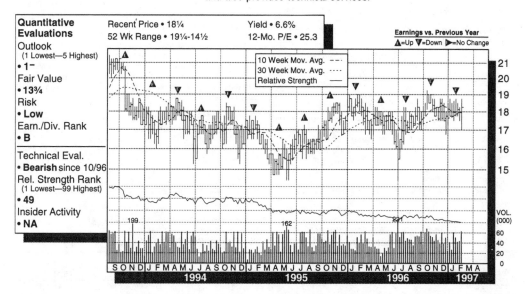

Earnings vs. Previous Year
▲=Up ▼=Down ▶=No Change

10 Week Mov. Avg. ---
30 Week Mov. Avg. ····
Relative Strength —

Business Profile - 13-FEB-97

Consumers Water is a utility holding company with eight water utilities in six states. It has acquired eight water systems over the past five years and intends to continue its acquisition program. In the first nine months of 1996, CONW settled six rate requests allowing for total revenues of $2.9 million. An additional two rate cases, in which $2.1 million of revenues were sought, were pending. Due to a large capital expenditure program, as well as higher equity ratios required to maintain favorable debt ratings, the company expects that it will return to the equity market again in the next few years. Cash flow not provided by a stock offering would be financed with short-term debt.

Operational Review - 13-FEB-97

Based on a preliminary report, revenues for 1996 advanced 5.5% from those of 1995, due primarily to rate increases. Profitability was adversely affected by greater operating expenses associated with the new Roaring Creek, PA, treatment plant, which was placed in service in June 1995, as well as higher costs at Consumer Applied Technologies due to new contracts. Following a loss on the sale of properties (reflecting a reversal of a gain recorded in 1994), versus a prior-year gain, net income fell 45%, to $6,251,000 ($0.72 a share), from $11,303,000 ($1.34).

Stock Performance - 14-FEB-97

In the past 30 trading days, CONW's shares have increased 3%, compared to a 8% rise in the S&P 500. Average trading volume for the past five days was 16,400 shares, compared with the 40-day moving average of 9,408 shares.

Key Stock Statistics

Dividend Rate/Share	1.20	Shareholders	6,400
Shs. outstg. (M)	8.7	Market cap. (B)	$0.158
Avg. daily vol. (M)	0.011	Inst. holdings	14%
Tang. Bk. Value/Share	20.36		
Beta	0.13		

Value of $10,000 invested 5 years ago: $ 14,164

Fiscal Year Ending Dec. 31

	1996	1995	1994	1993	1992	1991
Revenues (Million $)						
1Q	25.06	22.53	20.82	20.94	20.10	19.40
2Q	26.68	25.52	23.45	22.50	22.80	21.70
3Q	29.35	28.48	25.17	24.50	24.20	23.40
4Q	26.30	25.25	23.90	21.12	22.50	20.70
Yr.	107.4	101.8	93.34	89.08	89.60	85.20
Earnings Per Share ($)						
1Q	0.21	0.19	0.14	0.29	0.16	0.20
2Q	0.19	0.35	0.31	0.24	0.32	0.82
3Q	0.42	0.53	0.40	0.50	0.39	0.39
4Q	-0.10	0.28	0.37	0.60	0.27	0.08
Yr.	0.72	1.34	1.22	1.63	1.14	1.46

Next earnings report expected: late April

Dividend Data (Dividends have been paid since 1951.)

Amount ($)	Date Decl.	Ex-Div. Date	Stock of Record	Payment Date
0.300	Mar. 06	May. 08	May. 10	May. 24 '96
0.300	Jun. 06	Aug. 07	Aug. 09	Aug. 26 '96
0.300	Sep. 06	Nov. 06	Nov. 11	Nov. 25 '96
0.300	Dec. 11	Feb. 06	Feb. 10	Feb. 25 '97

A Division of The McGraw-Hill Companies

STANDARD
&POOR'S
STOCK REPORTS

Consumers Water Company

3612

15-FEB-97

Business Summary - 13-FEB-97

Consumers Water Company supplies water from 27 separate systems to 223,000 industrial, commercial and residential customers in six states. The company also owns 100% of Consumers Applied Technologies, Inc. (formerly C/P Utility Services), a provider of technical services to utilities.

Contributions to water revenues by class of customer in recent years were:

	1995	1994	1993
Residential	65%	65%	65%
Commercial	13%	13%	13%
Fire protection	13%	13%	13%
Industrial	9%	9%	9%

The company owned 3,297 miles of mains at year-end 1995. Consumers owns directly or indirectly at least 90% of the voting stock of eight water companies, the largest of which, Ohio Water Service Co., accounted for 32% of water utility revenues in 1995. Other subsidiaries operate in Illinois, Pennsylvania, New Jersey, New Hampshire and Maine.

Of the 27 primary water systems, 13 have surface supplies (lakes, ponds and streams) as their source of supply; 12 obtain water principally or entirely from wells; two obtain their water supplies from adjacent systems, one of which is an affiliated utility. Less than 5% of CONW subsidiaries' water usage is purchased from other systems. In general, the company considers the surface and well supplies at its subsidiaries to be adequate for anticipating average daily demand and normal peak demand.

During 1994, Maine Water Co. and Wanakah Water Co. merged into Camden & Rockland Water Co. The name of the surviving corporation was then changed to Consumers Maine Water Co. In October 1994, the Damariscotta & Newcastle division of its Consumer Maine Water Co. subsidiary was taken by local communities by eminent domain for $600,000.

Consumers Applied Technologies, Inc. offers utility services, primarily in the areas of corrosion control, meter services, contract operations, water conservation and environmental engineering services.

Important Developments

Nov. '96—The company said that it started planning a major plant upgrade at Consumers Pennsylvania Water Co.-Shenango Valley Division. The project is expected to cost about $30 million when it is completed in 2000. The upgrade of one of the company's older water treatment plants is required to keep in compliance with regulations and to meet expected increases in demand.

Capitalization

Long Term Debt: $161,388,000 (9/96).
Minority Interest: $2,345,000.
$5.25 Cum. Pfd. Stk.: 10,542 shs. ($100 par).

Per Share Data ($) (Year Ended Dec. 31)	1996	1995	1994	1993	1992	1991	1990	1989	1988	1987
Tangible Bk. Val.	NA	20.42	19.67	12.05	11.82	11.62	10.56	11.95	11.81	11.16
Earnings	0.72	1.34	1.22	1.63	1.14	1.46	1.21	1.15	1.59	1.51
Dividends	1.20	1.18	1.17	1.14	1.13	1.11	1.09	1.05	0.98	0.92
Payout Ratio	167%	88%	96%	70%	99%	76%	90%	91%	62%	61%
Prices - High	19¼	19	18¾	21½	19¾	18½	18¼	20½	21¼	22½
- Low	14½	14½	15¼	17	14¼	13¾	10	14¾	15¾	15
P/E Ratio - High	27	14	15	13	17	13	15	18	13	15
- Low	20	11	12	10	13	9	6	13	10	10

Income Statement Analysis (Million $)

	1996	1995	1994	1993	1992	1991	1990	1989	1988	1987
Revs.	NA	102	93.3	89.1	89.6	85.2	81.6	87.1	87.9	80.5
Depr.	NA	10.5	9.0	8.0	7.7	6.4	6.0	6.0	5.8	4.9
Maint.	NA	NA	NA	NA	5.3	5.7	5.3	5.4	NA	4.9
Fxd. Chgs. Cov.	NA	2.1	2.1	2.0	1.7	1.5	1.5	1.5	1.9	2.0
Constr. Credits	NA	1.0	1.4	0.8	0.4	1.1	0.3	0.8	1.4	0.9
Eff. Tax Rate	NA	36%	34%	33%	34%	34%	32%	32%	30%	37%
Net Inc.	NA	11.3	10.0	12.0	8.0	9.4	7.3	6.9	9.4	8.9

Balance Sheet & Other Fin. Data (Million $)

	1996	1995	1994	1993	1992	1991	1990	1989	1988	1987
Gross Prop.	NA	436	396	360	349	313	303	287	263	236
Cap. Exp.	NA	40.5	39.3	34.7	26.3	30.7	24.3	26.1	30.3	28.0
Net Prop.	NA	362	327	297	289	258	251	237	217	194
Capitalization:										
LT Debt	NA	162	130	124	120	101	105	100	89.0	83.0
% LT Debt	NA	60	56	55	58	55	61	57	55	55
Pfd.	NA	3.4	3.3	3.3	3.3	3.3	3.3	3.4	3.5	3.6
% Pfd.	NA	1.30	1.40	1.50	1.60	1.80	1.90	1.90	2.20	2.30
Common	NA	106	101	96.9	84.2	80.1	64.0	71.5	69.8	65.2
% Common	NA	39	43	43	41	43	37	41	43	43
Total Cap.	NA	366	322	303	276	244	228	226	212	199
Oper. Ratio	NA	77.6	78.8	79.0	78.8	79.5	78.9	79.4	80.5	80.2
% Earn. on Net Prop.	NA	6.6	6.3	6.4	6.9	6.9	7.0	7.9	8.3	8.7
% Ret. on Revs.	NA	11.1	10.7	13.5	9.0	11.1	9.0	7.9	10.7	11.0
% Ret. On Invest.Cap	NA	7.1	7.1	6.7	7.6	8.0	8.8	8.7	9.5	9.0
% Return On Com.Eqty	NA	10.9	10.1	13.2	9.8	13.1	10.8	9.7	14.0	14.1

Data as orig. reptd.; bef. results of disc. opers. and/or spec. items. Per share data adj. for stk. divs. as of ex-div. date. E-Estimated. NA-Not Available. NM-Not Meaningful. NR-Not Ranked.

Office—Three Canal Plaza, Portland, ME 04101. **Tel**—(207) 773-6438. **Website**—http://www.consumerswater.com **Chrmn**—D. R. Hastings II. **Pres & CEO**—P. L. Haynes. **VP & Secy**—B. R. Mullany. **Sr VP-CFO**—J. F. Isacke. **VP & Treas**—R. E. Ervin. **Dirs**—C. Elia, D. R. Hastings II, P. L. Haynes, J. S. Ketchum, J. E. Menario, J. E. Newman, J. E. Palmer Jr., E. D. Rosen, W. B. Russell, J. H. Schiavi. **Transfer Agent**—Continental Stock Transfer & Trust Co., NYC. **Incorporated**—in Maine in 1926. **Empl**—618. **S&P Analyst:** J.J.S.

CoreStates Financial   669F

NYSE Symbol **CFL**

In S&P 500

15-FEB-97   Industry: Banking

Summary: This bank holding company delivers financial services primarily in Pennsylvania, Delaware and New Jersey, as well as selected services worldwide.

S&P Opinion: Hold (★★★)	Recent Price • 53¾	Yield • 3.6%
	52 Wk Range • 55⅜-35½	12-Mo. P/E • 17.8

Quantitative Evaluations

Outlook
(1 Lowest—5 Highest)
• **4⁻**

Fair Value
• **58⅛**

Risk
• **Average**

Earn./Div. Rank
• **B+**

Technical Eval.
• **Bearish** since 12/96

Rel. Strength Rank
(1 Lowest—99 Highest)
• **63**

Insider Activity
• **Neutral**

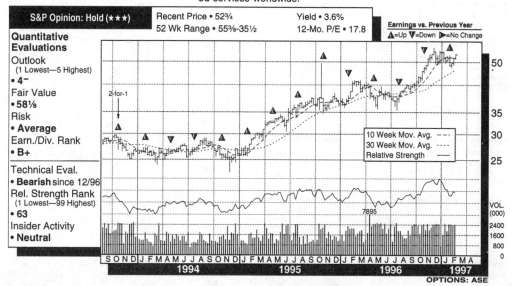

Earnings vs. Previous Year
▲=Up ▼=Down ▶=No Change

10 Week Mov. Avg. – – -
30 Week Mov. Avg. ·····
Relative Strength —

7895

VOL. (000)

OPTIONS: ASE

Overview - 10-JAN-97

Much of the earnings gain projected for 1997 is expected to come from efficiency improvements following a process redesign and merger-related cost savings. The redesign program, aimed at reducing expenses by $180 million and enhancing revenues by $30 million, includes a strategy to organize around customers and markets, rather than products. The in-market acquisition of Meridian Bancorp in April 1996, while dilutive to 1996 earnings, is expected to produce pretax savings of about $186 million and to be accretive in 1997. Loan growth is expected in the mid single-digits. The net interest margin was stable in the third quarter of 1996; at 5.58%, it is still well above peer levels on a high proportion of loans to assets. Loss reserves are adequate, and only modestly higher provisions are expected. Reported earnings comparisons in 1996 were penalized by Meridian merger integration expenses of about $0.52 a share.

Valuation - 10-JAN-97

The company's focus on integrating acquired operations has hampered earnings progress in recent quarters. However, with the integration process substantially complete, CFL can now turn its attention toward growing loans and fee revenue. Loan growth has been sluggish, reflecting a generally slow Northeast economy and competitive factors. CFL continues to make significant strides in reducing noninterest expense with its process redesign program and merger cost savings, and has emerged as one of the most efficient among the large banks. The acquisition of Meridian Bancorp has diversified the company's geographic reach, broadened its product mix, and better positioned it for the long term. With a better than average dividend yield and favorable long-term prospects, the shares remain a worthwhile hold.

Key Stock Statistics

S&P EPS Est. 1997	4.45	Tang. Bk. Value/Share	18.06
P/E on S&P Est. 1997	11.9	Beta	0.91
Dividend Rate/Share	1.88	Shareholders	43,300
Shs. outstg. (M)	223.6	Market cap. (B)	$ 11.8
Avg. daily vol. (M)	0.496	Inst. holdings	47%

Value of $10,000 invested 5 years ago: $ 26,035

Fiscal Year Ending Dec. 31

	1996	1995	1994	1993	1992	1991
Revenues (Million $)						
1Q	689.1	713.3	600.8	487.8	523.0	624.2
2Q	1,044	721.8	621.5	500.0	510.9	601.1
3Q	1,060	711.3	621.7	516.3	515.2	608.9
4Q	—	721.7	712.8	509.5	584.8	638.8
Yr.	—	2,868	2,497	2,014	2,134	2,473
Earnings Per Share ($)						
1Q	0.96	0.38	-0.21	0.63	0.51	0.47
2Q	0.36	0.89	0.44	0.71	0.57	0.51
3Q	0.89	0.96	0.74	0.73	0.59	0.55
4Q	0.91	0.44	0.78	0.73	0.60	0.55
Yr.	2.97	3.22	1.75	2.80	2.27	2.09

Next earnings report expected: late April

Dividend Data (Dividends have been paid since 1844.)

Amount ($)	Date Decl.	Ex-Div. Date	Stock of Record	Payment Date
0.420	Feb. 20	Mar. 05	Mar. 07	Apr. 01 '96
0.420	May. 21	Jun. 06	Jun. 10	Jul. 01 '96
0.420	Jul. 16	Sep. 04	Sep. 06	Oct. 01 '96
0.470	Oct. 16	Dec. 05	Dec. 09	Jan. 01 '97

Business Summary - 28-JUN-96

CoreStates Financial Corp, following its April 1996 acquisition of Meridian Bancorp., is the 21st largest bank holding company in the U.S. The company provides wholesale banking services, consumer financial services, including retail banking, and trust and investment management services through 334 full service branch offices in eastern and central Pennsylvania and New Jersey and one office in Delaware. Nonbank affiliates include Congress Financial Corp., a commercial financing and factoring business, and Electronic Payment Services, a consumer electronic transaction processing joint venture. CFL also engages in discount brokerage, investment advisory and lease financing. Net income contributions and return on assets from core lines of business in 1995 were as follows:

	Net Inc.	Return on assets
Wholesale banking	54%	1.58%
Consumer finance	37%	2.24%
Trust & investment management	3%	2.03%
Electronic Payment Services	6%	37.33%

Average earning assets in 1995 of $25.2 billion (up from $24.3 billion in 1994) were divided: commercial loans 37%, real estate loans 23%, consumer loans 11%, other loans 11%, investment securities 9% and temporary investments 9%. Average sources of funds were: noninterest-bearing demand deposits 21%, domestic deposits 49%, foreign deposits 3%, short-term borrowings 7%, long-term debt 7%, equity 8% and other 5%.

At the end of 1995, nonperforming assets totaled $171.5 million (0.81% of loans and related assets), down from $310.9 million (1.51%) a year earlier. The reserve for loan losses was 2.35% of loans, versus 2.44%. Net chargeoffs were 0.53% of average loans in 1995 and 1.13% in 1994.

Important Developments

Oct. '96—Directors authorized the repurchase of up to 22 million CFL common shares, or about 10% of those outstanding, through December 1997. Directors also increased the quarterly common stock dividend 12%, to $0.47 a share.

Capitalization

Long Term Debt: $2,518,080,000 (9/96).

Per Share Data ($)

(Year Ended Dec. 31)	1996	1995	1994	1993	1992	1991	1990	1989	1988	1987
Tangible Bk. Val.	NA	17.23	16.22	16.68	14.58	14.03	12.71	15.79	14.21	12.78
Earnings	2.97	3.22	1.75	2.80	2.27	2.09	1.03	2.52	2.25	1.95
Dividends	1.73	1.36	1.24	1.14	1.02	0.97	0.96	0.87	0.77	0.70
Payout Ratio	58%	42%	71%	41%	45%	46%	93%	35%	34%	36%
Prices - High	55⅜	49½	29⅛	30¼	29	24⅜	22⅝	25¼	21	21⅜
- Low	35½	25⅝	22⅞	25⅛	21	12	11⅜	19⅛	16¾	14⅝
P/E Ratio - High	19	15	17	11	13	12	22	10	9	11
- Low	12	8	13	9	9	6	11	8	7	7

Income Statement Analysis (Million $)

Net Int. Inc.	NA	1,489	1,389	1,118	1,057	1,048	1,020	731	674	608
Tax Equiv. Adj.	NA	16.8	21.3	24.0	28.0	34.0	41.0	46.0	45.0	69.0
Non Int. Inc.	NA	594	549	503	533	554	400	288	234	208
Loan Loss Prov.	NA	105	247	100	119	188	321	85.0	77.0	69.0
% Exp/Op Revs.	NA	61	67	63	68	65	65	63	64	61
Pretax Inc.	NA	715	392	488	390	331	158	270	236	212
Eff. Tax Rate	NA	37%	37%	33%	33%	31%	28%	26%	24%	24%
Net Inc.	NA	452	249	328	262	228	114	199	179	162
% Net Int. Marg.	NA	5.97	5.80	5.82	5.61	5.58	5.35	5.50	5.39	5.37

Balance Sheet & Other Fin. Data (Million $)

Earning Assets:										
Money Mkt	NA	2,437	2,483	1,282	1,875	1,718	1,261	493	1,367	1,242
Inv. Securities	NA	1,990	2,881	2,732	2,610	2,091	1,914	1,580	1,615	1,606
Com'l Loans	NA	9,441	10,690	10,252	8,412	8,044	8,685	6,062	5,720	5,364
Other Loans	NA	11,110	9,837	5,420	7,057	6,984	8,181	6,030	5,246	4,767
Total Assets	NA	29,621	29,325	23,666	23,699	21,624	23,520	16,849	16,431	15,036
Demand Deposits	NA	6,701	6,362	6,008	5,820	5,077	4,937	3,594	3,482	3,271
Time Deposits	NA	14,801	15,678	10,945	11,442	10,964	11,645	7,847	7,633	7,030
LT Debt	NA	1,698	1,791	1,455	1,243	1,143	787	602	614	629
Common Eqty.	NA	2,379	2,350	1,959	1,704	1,539	1,380	1,246	1,118	1,001
% Ret. on Assets	NA	1.6	0.9	1.4	1.2	1.0	0.5	1.2	1.2	1.1
% Ret. on Equity	NA	19.6	11.0	18.3	16.3	15.6	7.6	16.8	16.9	16.0
% Loan Loss Resv.	NA	2.3	2.4	2.1	2.1	2.3	2.4	1.5	1.4	1.4
% Loans/Deposits	NA	97.9	93.1	96.5	89.6	93.7	101.7	105.7	98.7	98.4
% Equity to Assets	NA	8.1	8.2	7.9	7.2	6.6	6.5	7.2	6.7	6.5

Data as orig. reptd.; bef. results of disc opers. and/or spec. items. Per share data adj. for stk. divs. as of ex-div. date. E-Estimated. NA-Not Available. NM-Not Meaningful. NR-Not Ranked.

Main Office—Broad and Chestnut Sts., P.O. Box 7618, Philadelphia, PA 19101-7618. **Tel**—(215) 973-3827. **Website**—http://www.corestates.com **Chrmn & CEO**—T. A. Larsen. **Vice Chrmn**—C. L. Coltman, III. **Pres**—Rosemarie B. Greco. **Secy**—M. R. O'Leary. **Investor Contact**—Gary Brooten. **Dirs**—G. A. Butler, R. W. Cardy, N. G. Harris, C. E. Hughes, S. A. Jackson, E. E. Jones, T. A. Larsen, H. Lotman, G. Lynett, S. A. McCullough, P. A. McFate, J. A. Miller, M. Miller, Jr., S. W. Naidoff, S. S. Preston III, L. R. Pugh, J. M. Seabrook, J. L. Shane, R. W. Smith, H. A. Sorgenti, G. Strawbridge, Jr., P. S. Strawbridge, J. M. von Seldeneck. **Transfer Agent & Registrar**—First Chicago Trust Co. of New York, Jersey City, NJ. **Empl**— 13,639. **S&P Analyst:** Stephen R. Biggar

15-FEB-97 | **Industry:** Utilities-Electric | **Summary:** This electric utility holding company is the parent of Duquesne Light Co., which supplies electricity in Pittsburgh and southwestern Pennsylvania.

S&P Opinion: Accumulate (★★★★)	

Recent Price • 29⅝   Yield • 4.6%
52 Wk Range • 30⅞-25¾   12-Mo. P/E • 12.8

Quantitative Evaluations

Outlook
(1 Lowest—5 Highest)
• **3**

Fair Value
• **28¾**

Risk
• **Low**

Earn./Div. Rank
• **A-**

Technical Eval.
• **Bullish** since 7/96

Rel. Strength Rank
(1 Lowest—99 Highest)
• **55**

Insider Activity
• **Neutral**

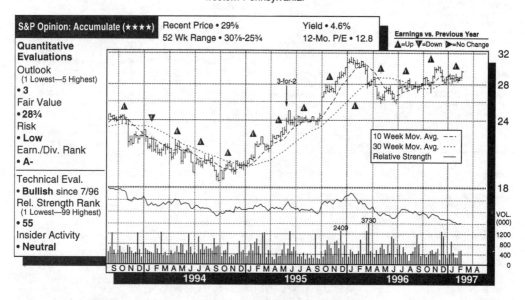

Earnings vs. Previous Year
▲=Up ▼=Down ▶=No Change

10 Week Mov. Avg. ---
30 Week Mov. Avg. ....
Relative Strength —

Overview - 13-FEB-97

Retail electric sales growth, lower production costs, efficient capacity utilization, low capital requirements and a robust market-driven segment should help DQE's earnings grow 5%-7% in 1997. While revenue at Duquesne Light will most likely grow only slightly, revenue from DQE's market-driven subsidiaries should continue to grow at a brisk rate and help offset the effects of accelerated depreciation on utility earnings. Accelerated depreciation and decommissioning of nuclear assets will negatively impact earnings in the near term but will provide the company with an improved asset base. As the non-utility segment has provided the majority of growth, DQE will accelerate its efforts in seeking additional opportunities in this area. The acquisition of GSF Energy, Inc. (a leader in landfill gas recovery), an investment in H-Power (a leading fuel cell development company), and an agreement with Heinz to provide energy services are some of the projects DQE is counting on to provide growth.

Valuation - 13-FEB-97

DQE stock declined slightly in 1996, but the company remained sound fundamentally while increasing earnings and dividends. DQE has one of the strongest cash flows in the industry and has a relatively low price/cash flow ratio. The dividend yield is a little below average, but with a good cash position, a hike of 5% or more is likely in late 1997. Although DQE's mitigation measures for its utility segment will keep net earnings percentage increases in the single digits, most of the major ratios, including price/book, P/E and price/sales indicate that DQE is undervalued. Given DQE's strong fundamentals and the likelihood of further dividend increases, we recommend accumulating the shares for total return.

Key Stock Statistics

S&P EPS Est. 1997	2.45	Tang. Bk. Value/Share	17.76
P/E on S&P Est. 1997	12.1	Beta	0.61
Dividend Rate/Share	1.36	Shareholders	78,000
Shs. outstg. (M)	77.2	Market cap. (B)	$ 2.3
Avg. daily vol. (M)	0.080	Inst. holdings	36%

Value of $10,000 invested 5 years ago: $ 17,797

Fiscal Year Ending Dec. 31

	1996	1995	1994	1993	1992	1991
Revenues (Million $)						
1Q	300.5	298.3	310.0	286.7	298.0	288.0
2Q	293.4	283.4	296.6	278.7	290.0	288.6
3Q	335.4	347.3	338.3	336.5	314.0	333.4
4Q	295.9	291.3	290.8	293.6	282.0	289.0
Yr.	1,225	1,220	1,236	1,196	1,185	1,199
Earnings Per Share ($)						
1Q	0.55	0.53	0.47	0.40	0.43	0.41
2Q	0.50	0.46	0.42	0.41	0.39	0.37
3Q	0.74	0.72	0.61	0.61	0.57	0.53
4Q	0.53	0.50	0.49	0.35	0.39	0.36
Yr.	2.32	2.20	1.99	1.78	1.78	1.67

Next earnings report expected: early May

Dividend Data (Dividends have been paid since 1913.)

Amount ($)	Date Decl.	Ex-Div. Date	Stock of Record	Payment Date
0.320	Feb. 27	Mar. 08	Mar. 12	Apr. 01 '96
0.320	May. 28	Jun. 07	Jun. 11	Jul. 01 '96
0.320	Aug. 27	Sep. 06	Sep. 10	Oct. 01 '96
0.340	Nov. 26	Dec. 06	Dec. 10	Jan. 01 '97

A Division of The McGraw-Hill Companies

Business Summary - 13-FEB-97

DQE Inc. is the holding company for Duquesne Light Co., which supplies electricity to an area of about 800 sq. mi., with a population of about 1.5 million, in Pittsburgh and southwestern Pennsylvania. DQE's diversified operations, which include Duquesne Enterprises, Montauk, and DQE Energy Services, Inc., contributed 18.5% of 1996 earnings. Duquesne Enterprises owns Allegheny Development Corporation, Property Ventures, Ltd., Exide Electronics Group and Chester Environmental, Inc. These companies are involved in energy and utility services, environmental services, power quality, non-interruptible power products and real estate. Montauk serves DQE's financial needs, and DQE Energy Services provides customers with energy management services, in an effort to keep up with increasing competition in the energy market. Contributions to retail electricity sales in recent years were:

	1996	1995	1994	1993
Residential	27%	27%	27%	27%
Commercial	46%	46%	46%	46%
Industrial	26%	26%	27%	26%

Sources of electric generation in 1995 were 69% coal and 31% nuclear. Peak demand in 1995 was 2,666 mw and generating capability at time of peak was 2,834 mw, for a capacity margin of 5.9%. The average cost of generation per kilowatt-hour in 1995 was $0.0222 compared to $0.0223 in 1994.

In 1995, the company spent $78.7 million for utility construction, down from $94.3 million in 1994. Annual spending of about $95 million for utility construction is seen for 1996-8.

Important Developments

Jan. '97—Duquesne Energy, a DQE affiliate, entered into an alliance and exclusive licensing arrangement with CQ Inc., a fuel technology company. Duquesne Energy will build plants to produce a pelletized fuel product, which combines coal and by-products of the manufacture of paper and plastic. This product, to be sold under the trademark E-Fuel, can be used as an alternative to coal. CQ Inc. is currently producing E-Fuel for industrial use. DQE believes that E-Fuel will be very competitive in the marketplace and will provide environmental advantages to customers.
Jan. '97—DQE signed an agreement to provide energy services to Heinz U.S.A.'s Northside Complex in Pittsburgh, PA. Under the 15-year agreement, DQE will operate and maintain the energy facility, including fuel procurement and the production of electricity, steam and compressed air services. According to the company, this project is a natural extension of its ability to operate and maintain power production facilities.

Capitalization

Long Term Debt: $1,439,746,000 (12/96).
Subsid. Pfd. Stock: $223,072,000.

Per Share Data ($)

(Year Ended Dec. 31)	1996	1995	1994	1993	1992	1991	1990	1989	1988	1987
Tangible Bk. Val.	NA	17.13	16.27	15.41	14.70	13.95	13.33	12.77	12.27	11.66
Earnings	2.32	2.20	1.99	1.78	1.78	1.67	1.49	1.35	1.24	1.21
Dividends	1.30	1.21	1.13	1.07	1.03	0.97	0.92	0.87	0.81	0.80
Payout Ratio	56%	55%	57%	60%	58%	58%	62%	64%	66%	66%
Prices - High	31½	30¾	23	24⅝	21⅝	20⅝	16⅞	15⅞	12⅝	9½
- Low	25¾	19⅝	18⅜	20⅞	17⅞	15¾	13⅝	11⅝	7⅞	7⅛
P/E Ratio - High	14	14	12	14	12	12	11	12	10	8
- Low	11	9	9	12	10	9	9	9	6	6

Income Statement Analysis (Million $)

	1996	1995	1994	1993	1992	1991	1990	1989	1988	1987
Revs.	NA	1,220	1,236	1,196	1,185	1,199	1,134	1,121	1,063	888
Depr.	NA	192	161	143	128	119	122	119	111	82.0
Maint.	NA	81.5	79.5	80.3	79.1	83.8	97.8	83.3	73.2	66.4
Fxd. Chgs. Cov.	NA	3.5	3.3	3.0	2.9	2.7	2.3	2.1	2.0	2.2
Constr. Credits	NA	Nil	NA	2.0	5.0	4.0	3.0	3.0	3.0	104
Eff. Tax Rate	NA	36%	38%	38%	42%	41%	39%	37%	31%	NM
Net Inc.	NA	171	157	141	142	134	122	113	137	151

Balance Sheet & Other Fin. Data (Million $)

	1996	1995	1994	1993	1992	1991	1990	1989	1988	1987
Gross Prop.	NA	4,746	4,710	4,555	4,357	4,268	4,182	4,199	4,103	4,008
Cap. Exp.	NA	94.2	121	101	115	128	110	88.0	93.0	155
Net Prop.	NA	3,060	3,140	3,119	3,016	3,035	3,046	3,055	3,066	3,099
Capitalization:										
LT Debt	NA	1,436	1,419	1,473	1,485	1,509	1,610	1,660	1,672	1,831
% LT Debt	NA	51	51	52	53	55	56	56	56	55
Pfd.	NA	71.0	95.0	133	132	137	189	220	245	261
% Pfd.	NA	2.50	3.40	4.70	4.70	5.00	6.60	7.50	8.20	7.80
Common	NA	1,329	1,277	1,231	1,171	1,111	1,079	1,066	1,071	1,234
% Common	NA	47	46	43	42	40	38	36	36	37
Total Cap.	NA	3,753	3,884	4,135	3,474	3,429	3,518	3,564	3,549	3,862
Oper. Ratio	NA	73.6	74.9	78.8	78.6	77.7	76.2	75.9	77.0	79.1
% Earn. on Net Prop.	NA	10.4	7.1	8.3	8.4	8.4	8.9	8.8	7.9	5.6
% Ret. on Revs.	NA	14.0	12.7	11.8	11.9	11.1	10.7	10.1	12.9	17.0
% Ret. On Invest.Cap	NA	9.8	6.7	6.9	8.0	7.9	7.9	7.8	8.2	7.6
% Return On Com.Eqty	NA	13.1	12.5	11.8	12.4	12.2	11.3	10.6	10.4	10.7

Data as orig. reptd.; bef. results of disc opers. and/or spec. items. Per share data adj. for stk. divs. as of ex-div. date. E-Estimated. NA-Not Available. NM-Not Meaningful. NR-Not Ranked.

Office—Cherrington Corporate Center, Suite 100, 500 Cherrington Parkway, Coraopolis, PA 15108. **Tel**—(412) 262-4700. **Website**—http:// www.dqe.com **Interim CEO**—D. D. Marshall. **EVP, CFO & Treas**—G. L. Schwass. **Secy**—D. S. Eismont. **Dirs**—D. Berg, D. E. Boyce, R. P. Bozzone, S. Falk, W. H. Knoell, D. D. Marshall, R. Mehrabian, T. J. Murrin, R. B. Pease, E. W. Springer. **Transfer Agent & Registrar**—Bank of Boston, Canton, MA. **Incorporated**—in Pennsylvania in 1912. **Empl**—3,875. **S&P Analyst:** J. Robert Cho

15-FEB-97 Industry: Graphic Arts

Summary: This major printer of bank checks also produces computer forms, provides software and services to financial institutions, and is a direct marketer of consumer products.

S&P Opinion: Accumulate (★★★★)

Recent Price • 31⅜	Yield • 4.7%
52 Wk Range • 39¾-29¾	12-Mo. P/E • 39.2

Quantitative Evaluations

Outlook
(1 Lowest—5 Highest)
• 3

Fair Value
• 31½

Risk
• Average

Earn./Div. Rank
• B+

Technical Eval.
• **Bullish** since 1/97

Rel. Strength Rank
(1 Lowest—99 Highest)
• 33

Insider Activity
• NA

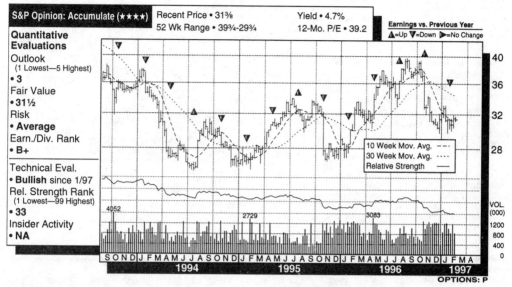

Earnings vs. Previous Year
▲=Up ▼=Down ▶=No Change

10 Week Mov. Avg. ---
30 Week Mov. Avg. ·····
Relative Strength ——

OPTIONS: P

Overview - 30-JAN-97

As part of a major effort to reposition itself from being largely a check printing company into an electronic payments and information services concern, DLX has completed the first year of a major two-year restructuring program that involves closing and consolidating 26 of its 41 printing and warehousing facilities, consolidating other operations, and divesting a number of slow-growth, low-margin businesses. DLX plans to boost the revenue generating capabilities of its ongoing business through a number of measures. Although it expects to eliminate $150 million in annual operating costs by the end of 1997, it will also incur unspecified charges in the effort. DLX's growth programs will require a sharp rise in internal financing capability, only part of which will come from the sale of nonessential assets. Nevertheless, the net impact of these initiatives on 1997 EPS will be positive.

Valuation - 30-JAN-97

Spurred by a massive ongoing restructuring, operating earnings are recovering from a three-year downturn. DLX is selling at a relatively low P/E of only 14X the $2.15 a share that management has targeted for 1997, which is a 13% improvement over last year's $1.90 (before special charges). The gain for 1997 is impressive given that DLX will have divested units representing some $380 million in revenues. The company's dominance in the check printing market, its strong cash flow, and its aggressive new management leadership place it in a favorable position to profitably serve the financial institutions market. Although DLX's significantly higher need for internal financing, continuing consolidation in the financial institutions sector and fierce competition are cautionary factors, the longer term operating outlook is favorable.

Key Stock Statistics

S&P EPS Est. 1997	2.15	Tang. Bk. Value/Share	4.85
P/E on S&P Est. 1997	14.6	Beta	0.53
Dividend Rate/Share	1.48	Shareholders	20,800
Shs. outstg. (M)	82.4	Market cap. (B)	$ 2.6
Avg. daily vol. (M)	0.195	Inst. holdings	64%

Value of $10,000 invested 5 years ago: $ 9,971

Fiscal Year Ending Dec. 31

	1996	1995	1994	1993	1992	1991
Revenues (Million $)						
1Q	488.1	465.4	430.0	406.0	385.0	369.0
2Q	446.6	442.3	412.3	362.9	364.0	348.0
3Q	460.5	449.2	478.9	372.0	373.0	362.0
4Q	480.5	501.1	478.9	441.2	413.0	396.0
Yr.	1,896	1,858	1,748	1,582	1,534	1,475
Earnings Per Share ($)						
1Q	0.23	0.42	0.46	0.62	0.58	0.49
2Q	0.46	0.37	0.36	0.03	0.57	0.52
3Q	0.41	0.37	0.40	0.45	0.60	0.54
4Q	-0.30	-0.01	0.49	0.61	0.67	0.63
Yr.	0.80	1.15	1.71	1.71	2.42	2.18

Next earnings report expected: late April

Dividend Data (Dividends have been paid since 1921.)

Amount ($)	Date Decl.	Ex-Div. Date	Stock of Record	Payment Date
0.370	May. 06	May. 16	May. 20	Jun. 03 '96
0.370	Aug. 09	Aug. 15	Aug. 19	Sep. 03 '96
0.370	Nov. 08	Nov. 14	Nov. 18	Dec. 02 '96
0.370	Jan. 31	Feb. 13	Feb. 18	Mar. 03 '97

A Division of The **McGraw-Hill** *Companies*

STANDARD
&POOR'S
STOCK REPORTS

Deluxe Corporation

735

15-FEB-97

Business Summary - 30-JAN-97

Deluxe Corp. (formerly Deluxe Check Printers) accounts for nearly 55% of the U.S. check printing market; is the largest U.S. third-party processor of automated teller machine (ATM) transactions; the leading processor of interchange transactions for shared ATM networks; and the nation's largest check authorization service for retailers. Segment contributions (profits in million $) in 1995 were:

	Revs.	Profits
Payment systems	64%	$208.5
Business systems	19%	-39.1
Consumer specialty products	17%	14.4

Effective January 1, 1996, DLX reorganized its business units into two market-serving segments -- Financial Services and Deluxe Direct. Deluxe Financial Services provides check printing, electronic funds transfer and related services to financial institutions in the U.S., Canada and the U.K.; payment systems protection services including check authorization, account verification and collection services to financial institutions and retailers; and electronic benefit transfer services to state governments. Deluxe Direct provides direct mail checks and specialty papers to households and small businesses; tax forms and electronic tax filing services to tax preparers; and direct mail greeting cards, gift wrap and related products to households.

Important Developments

Jan. '97—DLX reported that its fourth-quarter 1996 results included net pretax charges totaling $107.4 million, or $0.95 a share after tax, for goodwill impairment, restructuring costs, gains and losses on sales of businesses, and other costs. Excluding these one-time charges, earnings were $0.55, up from $0.46 on a comparable basis in the like 1995 quarter. DLX said its planned divestiture program will be substantially complete by the end of the first quarter. The program of writeoffs and sales removes a total of $240 million in purchase-related goodwill from the company's balance sheet, as well as a number of slow-growth and low-margin businesses.

Aug. '96—DLX sold its Colwell health care forms business. Separately, DLX sold its T/Maker subsidiary, which markets electronic artwork and graphics. Earlier, the company sold its ink division and its internal bank forms business.

Capitalization

Long Term Debt: $109,100,000 (12/96).

Per Share Data ($)										
(Year Ended Dec. 31)	**1996**	**1995**	**1994**	**1993**	**1992**	**1991**	**1990**	**1989**	**1988**	**1987**
Tangible Bk. Val.	NA	4.96	5.90	6.15	7.77	6.93	5.88	5.47	4.61	3.77
Cash Flow	NA	2.40	2.76	2.58	3.21	3.08	2.64	2.31	2.13	2.10
Earnings	0.80	1.15	1.71	1.71	2.42	2.18	2.03	1.79	1.68	1.74
Dividends	1.48	1.48	1.46	1.42	1.34	1.22	1.10	0.98	0.86	0.76
Payout Ratio	185%	129%	85%	83%	55%	56%	54%	54%	51%	44%
Prices - High	39¾	34	38	47⅞	49	48½	35⅞	35¾	28⅜	42¼
- Low	27	25¾	25⅝	31¾	38⅛	32⅝	26⅝	24	21	20
P/E Ratio - High	50	30	22	28	20	22	18	20	17	24
- Low	34	22	15	19	16	15	13	13	13	11

Income Statement Analysis (Million $)										
Revs.	NA	1,858	1,748	1,582	1,534	1,474	1,414	1,316	1,196	948
Oper. Inc.	NA	287	320	353	389	364	.326	289	265	240
Depr.	NA	103	86.4	72.3	66.6	76.0	74.1	44.9	38.1	30.4
Int. Exp.	NA	13.1	11.3	10.3	15.4	8.2	1.4	2.2	5.1	0.6
Pretax Inc.	NA	169	241	236	325	295	283	246	227	237
Eff. Tax Rate	NA	44%	42%	40%	38%	38%	39%	38%	37%	37%
Net Inc.	NA	94.4	141	142	203	183	172	153	143	149

Balance Sheet & Other Fin. Data (Million $)										
Cash	NA	19.9	78.0	222	381	317	114	45.0	22.0	159
Curr. Assets	NA	381	421	522	611	539	344	263	220	337
Total Assets	NA	1,295	1,256	1,252	1,200	1,099	924	847	786	866
Curr. Liab.	NA	369	290	298	224	208	199	168	167	315
LT Debt	NA	111	111	111	116	111	12.0	10.0	11.0	13.0
Common Eqty.	NA	780	814	801	830	748	676	631	568	491
Total Cap.	NA	926	966	954	975	891	725	679	619	551
Cap. Exp.	NA	125	126	62.1	71.6	76.0	64.0	88.4	78.9	96.1
Cash Flow	NA	198	227	214	269	259	223	198	182	179
Curr. Ratio	NA	1.0	1.4	1.8	2.7	2.6	1.7	1.6	1.3	1.1
% LT Debt of Cap.	NA	12.0	11.5	11.6	11.8	12.4	1.6	1.5	1.8	2.3
% Net Inc.of Revs.	NA	5.1	8.1	9.0	13.2	12.4	12.2	11.6	12.0	15.7
% Ret. on Assets	NA	7.4	11.2	11.7	17.7	18.1	19.6	18.7	17.3	19.5
% Ret. on Equity	NA	11.8	17.5	17.5	25.7	25.7	26.5	25.5	27.0	32.9

Data as orig. reptd.; bef. results of disc. opers. and/or spec. items. Per share data adj. for stk. divs. as of ex-div. date. E-Estimated. NA-Not Available. NM-Not Meaningful. NR-Not Ranked.

Office—3680 Victoria St. N., Shoreview, MN 55126-2966. **Tel**—(612) 483-7111. **Chrmn**—H. V. Haverty.**Pres & CEO**—J. A. Blanchard III. **EVP & COO**—J. K. Twogood. **SVP & Secy**—J. H. LeFevre. **SVP, CFO & Investor Contact**—Charles M. Osborne (612-483-7355). **Dirs**—J. A. Blanchard III, B. B. Grogan, H. V. Haverty, A. F. Jacobson, W. MacMillan, S. Nachtsheim, J. J. Renier, J. K. Twogood. **Transfer Agent & Registrar**—Norwest Bank Minnesota, South St. Paul. **Incorporated**—in Minnesota in 1920. **Empl**— 19,300. **S&P Analyst:** William H. Donald

15-FEB-97   Industry:
Utilities-Electric

Summary: Dominion Resources is a utility holding company whose main unit, Virginia Electric & Power Co., provides electric service in Virginia and, to a lesser extent, in North Carolina.

S&P Opinion: Hold (★★★)	Recent Price • 40¼	Yield • 6.4%
	52 Wk Range • 43⅛-36⅞	12-Mo. P/E • 15.2

Quantitative Evaluations

Outlook
(1 Lowest—5 Highest)
• **1⁻**

Fair Value
• **34½**

Risk
• **Low**

Earn./Div. Rank
• **B+**

Technical Eval.
• **Bullish** since 1/97

Rel. Strength Rank
(1 Lowest—99 Highest)
• **54**

Insider Activity
• **NA**

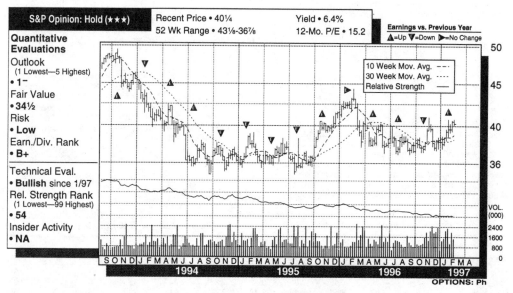

Earnings vs. Previous Year
▲=Up ▼=Down ▶=No Change

10 Week Mov. Avg. ---
30 Week Mov. Avg. .....
Relative Strength —

VOL.
(000)
2400
1600
800
0

1994 1995 1996 1997

OPTIONS: Ph

Overview - 04-FEB-97

Control of both operating costs and capital outlays has helped Virginia Power reduce generating costs in recent years. D is among the lowest cost U.S. generators; ongoing restructuring and cost cutting activities are expected to yield annual savings in the range of $55 million to $65 million through the end of the century. We expect the company to improve its competitive position through price concessions under longer term contracts for its large industrial customers, and through unregulated ventures such as building, owning and operating self-generation facilities for new, large energy intensive customers moving into its service region. The acquisition of U.K.-based East Midlands Electricity plc will also add to future prospects.

Valuation - 04-FEB-97

We continue to recommend holding the stock. The shares were down 6.7% in 1996, versus a 2% decline for the S&P Electric Utilities Index and a 20% advance for the S&P 500. Although D's fundamentals improved in 1996, the shares were restricted by a rising interest rate environment and $92 million ($0.33 a share) of restructuring charges. We expect fundamentals to improve further, as D continues to reduce high cost power purchases, and new, more profitable business activities take hold. Although the dividend payout is above the industry average, as is the yield, growing cash flows from a high plant utilization rate, and reduced construction outlays, should allow the dividend to be supported at current levels. However, we do not anticipate any increase until earnings growth reduces the payout ratio to 60% to 70%.

Key Stock Statistics

S&P EPS Est. 1997	3.15	Tang. Bk. Value/Share	26.73
P/E on S&P Est. 1997	12.8	Beta	0.41
Dividend Rate/Share	2.58	Shareholders	233,500
Shs. outstg. (M)	180.2	Market cap. (B)	$ 7.3
Avg. daily vol. (M)	0.331	Inst. holdings	36%

Value of $10,000 invested 5 years ago: $ 14,475

Fiscal Year Ending Dec. 31

	1996	1995	1994	1993	1992	1991
Revenues (Million $)						
1Q	1,239	1,129	1,167	1,106	944.0	904.0
2Q	1,121	1,043	1,110	1,005	875.0	901.0
3Q	1,287	1,345	1,210	1,287	1,077	1,064
4Q	1,195	1,135	1,005	1,036	895.0	917.0
Yr.	4,842	4,652	4,491	4,434	3,791	3,786
Earnings Per Share ($)						
1Q	0.85	0.63	0.84	0.74	0.59	0.67
2Q	0.53	0.45	0.80	0.63	0.38	0.57
3Q	0.91	1.14	0.94	1.20	0.92	1.16
4Q	0.36	0.23	0.23	0.55	0.77	0.54
Yr.	2.65	2.45	2.81	3.12	2.66	2.94

Next earnings report expected: late April

Dividend Data (Dividends have been paid since 1925.)

Amount ($)	Date Decl.	Ex-Div. Date	Stock of Record	Payment Date
0.645	Feb. 16	Feb. 28	Mar. 01	Mar. 20 '96
0.645	Apr. 19	May. 29	May. 31	Jun. 20 '96
0.645	Jul. 18	Aug. 28	Aug. 30	Sep. 20 '96
0.645	Oct. 18	Nov. 26	Nov. 29	Dec. 20 '96

A Division of The McGraw-Hill Companies

STANDARD
&POOR'S
STOCK REPORTS

Dominion Resources, Inc.

766J
15-FEB-97

Business Summary - 04-FEB-97

Dominion Resources is a utility holding company whose main subsidiary, Virginia Electric & Power Co., provides electric service in Virginia and to a lesser extent in North Carolina. The company's Virginia and North Carolina service territory, characterized by government installations, high-technology centers and financial services businesses, has one of the strongest economies in the nation. Electric revenues by customer class in recent years were:

	1995	1994	1993	1992
Residential	46%	44%	43%	42%
Commercial	30%	27%	28%	29%
Industrial	12%	11%	11%	11%
Other	12%	18%	18%	18%

Sources of electric generation in 1995 were 39% coal, 32% nuclear, 25% purchased and interchanged, and 4% oil, gas and other. Peak demand in 1995 was 14,003 mw and capability at peak totaled 17,318 mw for a capacity margin of 19%. Dominion purchases power from cogenerators and independent power producers. It plans to meet future load through the construction of generating units and additional purchases from nonutility generators. The company may need new peaking power generation by 2000, but does not expect to require new base load generation until the middle of

the next decade. Projected construction and nuclear fuel expenditures for 1996-98 were expected to total $1.6 billion, including allowance for funds used during construction.

Through three non-utility subsidiaries, the company is also involved in the development of non-utility power projects, the acquisition and development of natural gas reserves, residential real estate development, and investment management. In 1995, non-utility operations accounted for 6.4% of revenues and 8.6% of EPS.

Important Developments

Jan. '97—The company said it either owned or had received valid acceptances for about 86% of the common stock of East Midlands Electricity plc, a regional electricity company that serves 2.3 million customers in the U.K. D expects to finance the acquisition, which is estimated to cost approximately $2.2 billion, through a combination of debt, issued by its newly created U.K. subsidiary, DR Investments, and equity provided by the parent. The transaction is expected to be completed by the first quarter of 1997.

Capitalization

Long Term Debt: $4,920,300,000 (9/96).
Subsid. Red. Preferred Stock: $180,000,000.
Subsid. Preferred Stock: $509,000,000.

Per Share Data ($)

(Year Ended Dec. 31)	1996	1995	1994	1993	1992	1991	1990	1989	1988	1987
Tangible Bk. Val.	NA	26.73	26.51	26.38	25.21	24.41	23.41	22.67	21.91	20.96
Earnings	2.65	2.45	2.81	3.12	2.66	2.94	2.92	2.76	3.01	3.03
Dividends	2.58	2.58	2.55	2.48	2.40	2.31	2.23	2.15	2.07	1.99
Payout Ratio	97%	105%	91%	79%	92%	79%	78%	79%	70%	67%
Prices - High	44⅜	41⅝	45⅜	49½	41	38⅛	32⅝	32	31½	33¼
- Low	36⅞	34⅞	34⅞	38¼	34⅛	29⅞	27⅝	27	27¼	24½
P/E Ratio - High	17	17	16	16	15	13	11	12	10	11
- Low	14	14	12	12	13	10	9	10	9	8

Income Statement Analysis (Million $)

	1996	1995	1994	1993	1992	1991	1990	1989	1988	1987
Revs.	NA	4,652	4,491	4,434	3,791	3,786	3,533	3,700	3,344	NA
Depr.	NA	551	533	510	450	450	423	463	492	NA
Maint.	NA	261	263	279	281	305	281	295	272	NA
Fxd. Chgs. Cov.	NA	2.3	2.6	2.8	2.5	2.4	2.3	2.2	2.4	NA
Constr. Credits	NA	6.7	6.4	5.1	9.5	11.8	5.1	6.2	3.5	NA
Eff. Tax Rate	NA	30%	26%	29%	32%	31%	31%	29%	22%	NA
Net Inc.	NA	425	478	559	475	511	504	470	491	NA

Balance Sheet & Other Fin. Data (Million $)

	1996	1995	1994	1993	1992	1991	1990	1989	1988	1987
Gross Prop.	NA	15,977	15,415	15,009	14,147	13,388	12,684	12,148	11,360	NA
Cap. Exp.	NA	578	721	1,127	941	815	827	938	827	NA
Net Prop.	NA	10,322	10,245	10,207	9,687	9,278	8,959	8,733	8,218	NA
Capitalization:										
LT Debt	NA	4,612	4,711	4,751	4,404	4,393	4,396	4,547	4,177	NA
% LT Debt	NA	45	47	48	47	49	50	52	51	NA
Pfd.	NA	824	816	829	829	735	758	782	750	NA
% Pfd.	NA	8.10	8.10	8.20	8.90	8.20	8.60	9.00	9.20	NA
Common	NA	4,742	4,586	4,436	4,131	3,878	3,624	3,421	3,224	NA
% Common	NA	47	45	44	44	43	41	39	40	NA
Total Cap.	NA	12,111	12,016	11,897	11,173	10,237	10,013	10,023	9,376	NA
Oper. Ratio	NA	80.0	76.9	79.3	78.2	76.6	75.8	77.1	76.2	NA
% Earn. on Net Prop.	NA	11.2	10.2	9.2	8.8	9.7	9.7	9.9	9.7	NA
% Ret. on Revs.	NA	9.1	10.6	12.6	12.5	13.5	14.3	12.7	14.8	NA
% Ret. On Invest.Cap	NA	8.6	8.8	9.9	9.8	11.2	11.3	10.8	10.9	NA
% Return On Com.Eqty	NA	9.1	10.6	11.9	10.5	12.1	12.5	12.2	13.9	NA

Data as orig. reptd.; bef. results of disc opers. and/or spec. items. Per share data adj. for stk. divs. as of ex-div. date. E-Estimated. NA-Not Available. NM-Not Meaningful. NR-Not Ranked.

Office—901 East Byrd St. (P.O. Box 26532), Richmond, VA 23261-6532. Tel—(804) 775-5700. Chrmn, President & CEO—T. E. Capps.VP & Treas—L. R. Robertson. VP & Secy—J. K. Davis, Jr. Investor Contact—William C. Hall, Jr. (804-775-5813). Dirs—J. B. Adams, Jr., T. L. Baucom, J. B. Bernhardt, J. F. Betts, T. E. Capps, J. W. Harris, B. J. Lambert III, R. L. Leatherwood, H. L. Lindsay, Jr., K. A. Randall, J. T Rhodes, W. T. Roos, F. S. Royal, J. B. Sack, S. D. Simmons, J. W. Snow, R. H. Spilman, W. G. Thomas, D. A. Wollard. Transfer Agent & Registrar—ChaseMellon Shareholder Services, Ridgefield, NJ. Incorporated—in Virginia in 1909. Empl—10,592. S&P Analyst: Justin McCann

STANDARD &POOR'S
STOCK REPORTS

Duke Power

779

NYSE Symbol **DUK**

In S&P 500

15-FEB-97

Industry: Utilities-Electric

Summary: One of the nation's largest investor-owned electric utilities, DUK serves the Piedmont region of North and South Carolina. It also conducts a variety of diversified operations.

S&P Opinion: Accumulate (★★★★)	Recent Price • 46	Yield • 4.6%
	52 Wk Range • 51½-43⅜	12-Mo. P/E • 13.6

Quantitative Evaluations

Outlook (1 Lowest—5 Highest)
• **3+**

Fair Value
• **45⅛**

Risk
• **Low**

Earn./Div. Rank
• **A-**

Technical Eval.
• **Bearish** since 11/96

Rel. Strength Rank (1 Lowest—99 Highest)
• **34**

Insider Activity
• **NA**

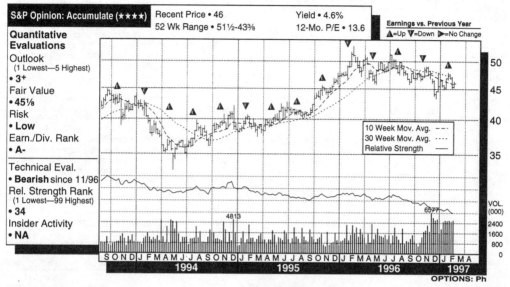

Earnings vs. Previous Year
▲=Up ▼=Down ▶=No Change

10 Week Mov. Avg. ‐ ‐ ‐
30 Week Mov. Avg. ·······
Relative Strength ——

VOL. (000)

OPTIONS: Ph

Overview - 13-FEB-97

The planned merger between Duke Power and PanEnergy Corp. (PEL) would result in a company (Duke Energy Corp.) that would be the third largest marketer of natural gas in North America; the fourth largest natural gas liquids producer in the U.S.; the owner of a network of more than 37,000 miles of interstate natural gas pipeline; as well as one of the largest and lowest-cost electric utilities in the country. Although the merger would not become accretive until nearly two years after its completion (expected by year-end 1997), it should bring an additional $225 million in pretax income by 2000. On its own, Duke will continue to benefit from a dominant position in one of the more vibrant utility markets in the U.S., ongoing cost cutting activities, and its expansion into high-growth ventures that include power marketing to wholesale distributors of electricity.

Valuation - 13-FEB-97

We continue to recommend the accumulation of the stock. The shares were down 2.4% in 1996, versus a 5% decline for the S&P Index of Electric Companies, in part due to the uncertainty surrounding the direction of interest rates, but also to concerns over the dilutive impact of its planned merger with PanEnergy Corp. (PEL). While the stock has recovered from the sharp decline that followed the November 1996 announcement of the merger, it remains well below its 1996 high. To complete the transaction, Duke will issue about $7.7 billion in stock to PEL shareholders and there will be an approximate $200 million increase in annual dividends. While the merger will not become accretive until around the turn of the century, we believe it will provide significant competitive advantages in a rapidly changing and increasingly integrated energy market.

Key Stock Statistics

S&P EPS Est. 1997	3.60	Tang. Bk. Value/Share	23.40
P/E on S&P Est. 1997	12.8	Beta	0.38
Dividend Rate/Share	2.12	Shareholders	29,300
Shs. outstg. (M)	201.6	Market cap. (B)	$ 9.3
Avg. daily vol. (M)	0.828	Inst. holdings	39%

Value of $10,000 invested 5 years ago: $ 16,417

Fiscal Year Ending Dec. 31

	1996	1995	1994	1993	1992	1991
Revenues (Million $)						
1Q	1,162	1,111	1,099	1,008	981.0	894.0
2Q	1,120	1,052	1,083	987.0	899.0	899.0
3Q	1,292	1,380	1,273	1,290	1,140	1,101
4Q	1,184	1,133	1,034	996.9	941.0	923.0
Yr.	4,758	4,677	4,489	4,282	3,961	3,817
Earnings Per Share ($)						
1Q	0.88	0.92	0.79	0.63	0.45	0.61
2Q	0.71	0.61	0.56	0.53	0.36	0.61
3Q	1.25	1.33	1.13	1.12	0.85	0.96
4Q	0.53	0.39	0.40	0.52	0.55	0.42
Yr.	3.37	3.25	2.88	2.80	2.21	2.60

Next earnings report expected: mid April

Dividend Data (Dividends have been paid since 1926.)

Amount ($)	Date Decl.	Ex-Div. Date	Stock of Record	Payment Date
0.510	Apr. 25	May. 15	May. 17	Jun. 17 '96
0.530	Jul. 29	Aug. 14	Aug. 16	Sep. 16 '96
0.530	Oct. 29	Nov. 13	Nov. 15	Dec. 16 '96
0.530	Jan. 28	Feb. 12	Feb. 14	Mar. 17 '97

A Division of The McGraw·Hill Companies

STANDARD
&POOR'S
STOCK REPORTS

Duke Power Company

779

15-FEB-97

Business Summary - 13-FEB-97

Duke Power supplies electricity to nearly 1.8 million customers in the Piedmont region of North Carolina and South Carolina. The company's largest customer is the textile industry, which accounted for 11% of electric revenues in 1995. Electric revenues by customer class in recent years were:

	1995	1994	1993	1992
Residential	33%	32%	33%	33%
Commercial	24%	24%	24%	24%
Industrial	28%	29%	28%	30%
Other	15%	15%	15%	13%

Power sources in 1995 were nuclear 54%, coal 43% and hydro and other 3%. Peak demand was 15,542 mw in 1995; capability totaled 17,000 mw, for a capacity margin of 8.6%. DUK projects demand growth of 1.8% a year through 2010.

Plant construction cost $281 million in 1995, primarily to complete the Lincoln Turbine Station, which added 1,200 mw of generating capacity, and to replace steam generators. Two of Lincoln's 16 facilities began operating in May 1995, 10 were completed in late 1995 and the remaining four were put into service in March 1996. Construction expenditures are projected at $2.3 billion for 1996 through 2000, mainly for distribution and production related activities. Funding is to come largely from internally generated funds.

Diversified operations, reorganized as Associated Enterprises Group (AEG), contributed 7.6% of net income in 1995 and consist of Church Street Capital Corp., internal investment managers; Duke Fluor Daniel and Duke Engineering, which design and build coal-fired and other generating plants in the U.S. and abroad; Crescent Resources, a real estate developer; Nantahala Power and Light Co., a small, franchised utility; and Duke Energy, which develops, owns and operates advanced fossil-fuel generating plants in the U.S. and abroad. DUK also markets power with Louis Dreyfus Electric Power, the largest power marketer in the U.S.

Important Developments

Feb. '97—Duke Power and PanEnergy (PEL) filed with the Federal Energy Regulatory Commision to approve the proposed merger of the two companies. Earlier, in November, the companies agreed to merge in a tax-free stock swap in which PanEnergy shareholders would receive 1.0444 shares of Duke's common stock for each PEL share. Duke would issue about $7.7 billion in new stock to PEL shareholders and would own a 56% interest in the new company, which would be named Duke Energy Corp.

Capitalization

Long Term Debt: $3,603,847,000 (9/96).
Preferred Stock: $684,000,000.

Per Share Data ($)

(Year Ended Dec. 31)	1996	1995	1994	1993	1992	1991	1990	1989	1988	1987
Tangible Bk. Val.	NA	22.17	20.91	19.91	19.52	19.30	18.35	17.60	15.63	14.25
Earnings	3.37	3.25	2.88	2.80	2.21	2.60	2.40	2.56	1.95	2.20
Dividends	2.08	2.00	1.92	1.84	1.76	1.68	1.60	1.52	1.44	1.37
Payout Ratio	62%	62%	67%	66%	80%	65%	67%	59%	74%	62%
Prices - High	53	47⅞	43	44⅞	37½	35	32⅜	28¼	24½	25⅞
- Low	43⅜	37⅜	32⅞	35⅜	31⅜	26¾	25½	21⅜	21⅛	19¾
P/E Ratio - High	16	15	15	16	17	13	13	11	13	12
- Low	13	11	11	12	14	10	11	8	11	9

Income Statement Analysis (Million $)

	1996	1995	1994	1993	1992	1991	1990	1989	1988	1987
Revs.	NA	4,677	4,489	4,282	3,961	3,817	3,681	3,639	3,627	3,706
Depr.	NA	458	460	488	491	432	406	411	418	411
Maint.	NA	NA	NA	375	403	355	404	349	383	375
Fxd. Chgs. Cov.	NA	4.3	4.1	4.2	3.1	3.5	3.4	3.8	3.2	3.9
Constr. Credits	NA	23.1	27.4	27.1	21.2	70.0	109	80.0	68.0	47.0
Eff. Tax Rate	NA	40%	38%	40%	37%	34%	32%	34%	32%	43%
Net Inc.	NA	715	639	626	508	584	538	572	448	500

Balance Sheet & Other Fin. Data (Million $)

	1996	1995	1994	1993	1992	1991	1990	1989	1988	1987
Gross Prop.	NA	14,937	14,489	13,760	14,953	14,337	13,617	12,689	11,698	10,777
Cap. Exp.	NA	713	772	655	588	807	1,052	1,060	949	790
Net Prop.	NA	9,361	9,264	8,924	8,882	8,699	8,450	7,917	7,374	6,917
Capitalization:										
LT Debt	NA	3,711	3,567	3,285	3,202	3,160	3,103	2,822	2,729	2,723
% LT Debt	NA	40	40	39	39	40	41	40	40	41
Pfd.	NA	684	780	781	780	731	742	675	684	692
% Pfd.	NA	7.50	8.80	9.30	9.60	9.20	9.70	9.40	10	10
Common	NA	4,785	4,533	4,338	4,151	4,066	3,817	3,657	3,444	3,236
% Common	NA	51	52	51	51	51	50	51	50	49
Total Cap.	NA	11,824	11,501	10,895	9,798	9,558	9,241	8,685	8,306	8,016
Oper. Ratio	NA	91.1	82.6	81.0	81.7	81.5	82.5	80.6	82.6	82.2
% Earn. on Net Prop.	NA	14.5	8.6	9.2	8.2	8.2	7.9	9.2	8.8	9.7
% Ret. on Revs.	NA	15.3	14.2	14.6	12.8	15.3	14.6	15.7	12.4	13.5
% Ret. On Invest.Cap	NA	12.6	7.9	8.5	8.4	9.1	8.8	9.5	8.3	9.3
% Return On Com.Eqty	NA	14.3	13.3	12.5	11.1	13.5	13.1	14.7	13.4	14.2

Data as orig. reptd.; bef. results of disc opers. and/or spec. items. Per share data adj. for stk. divs. as of ex-div. date. E-Estimated. NA-Not Available. NM-Not Meaningful. NR-Not Ranked.

Office—422 South Church St., Charlotte, NC 28242. **Registrar**—First Union National Bank of North Carolina, Charlotte. **Tel**—(704) 594-0887. **Chrmn & CEO**—W. H. Grigg. **Vice Chrmn**—S. C. Griffith, Jr. **Pres & COO**—R. B. Priory. **SVP & CFO**—R. J. Osborne. **Secy**—E. T. Ruff.**Treas & Investor Contact**—S. A. Becht.**Dirs**—G. A. Bernhardt, C. C. Bowles, R. J. Brown, W. A. Coley, S. C. Griffith Jr., W. H. Grigg, P. H. Henson, G. D. Johnson Jr., J. V. Johnson, W. W. Johnson, M. Lennon, J. G. Martin, B. Mickel, R. B. Priory, R. M. Robinson II.**Transfer Agent**—Co.'s office. **Incorporated**—in New Jersey in 1917; reincorporated in North Carolina in 1964. **Empl**— 17,121. **S&P Analyst:** Justin McCann

EastGroup Properties
800M

NYSE Symbol **EGP**

15-FEB-97

Industry:
Real Estate Investment Trust

Summary: This REIT owns a portfolio consisting primarily of garden apartment complexes, industrial/warehouse properties and office buildings.

Quantitative Evaluations

Recent Price • 28⅝   Yield • 6.8%
52 Wk Range • 29-20¾   12-Mo. P/E • 14.1

Outlook
(1 Lowest—5 Highest)
• **NA**

Fair Value
• **NA**

Risk
• **Low**

Earn./Div. Rank
• **NR**

Technical Eval.
• **Bullish** since 8/96

Rel. Strength Rank
(1 Lowest—99 Highest)
• **67**

Insider Activity
• **NA**

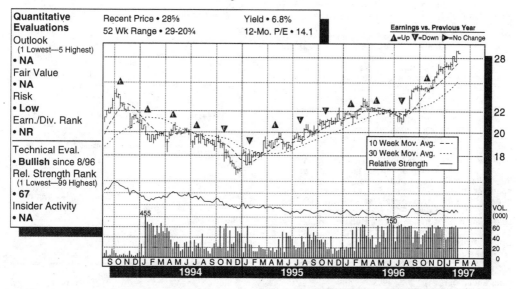

Business Profile - 14-JAN-97

In mid-1996, this REIT merged with two other REITS, Copley Properties, Inc. and LNH REIT, adding $117.2 million and $6.2 million, respectively, in real estate properties, consisting of 12 industrial and office properties with 2,151,000 sq. ft. of leasable space. As a result, EGP shares outstanding increased 65%, and total assets spurted 83%. The inclusion of Copley and LNH operations was reflected in the quarter ending September 30, 1996. The dividend was raised 4.3% with the September 1996 payment, reflecting the trust's stated goal of raising its dividend at a rate that outpaces inflation but is lower than the rate of growth in funds from operations.

Operational Review - 14-JAN-97

Total revenues were up 21% year to year in the nine months ended June 30, 1996, reflecting a 20% increase in income from real estate operations, as well as sharply higher interest and other income. Total expenses grew less rapidly, as operating expenses were well controlled. After a sharp rise in real estate investment gains, net income advanced 51%, to $7,250,000 ($1.35 a share, on 27% more shares), from $4,816,000 ($1.14). Funds from operations were up 38%, to $10.2 million ($1.90 a share), from $7.4 million ($1.75), reflecting the benefits of the LNH and Copley mergers, completed in the 1996 second quarter.

Stock Performance - 14-FEB-97

In the past 30 trading days, EGP's shares have increased 6%, compared to a 8% rise in the S&P 500. Average trading volume for the past five days was 12,120 shares, compared with the 40-day moving average of 11,813 shares.

Key Stock Statistics

Dividend Rate/Share	1.96	Shareholders	800
Shs. outstg. (M)	7.0	Market cap. (B)	$0.201
Avg. daily vol. (M)	0.015	Inst. holdings	20%
Tang. Bk. Value/Share	20.40		
Beta	0.63		

Value of $10,000 invested 5 years ago: $ 33,126

Fiscal Year Ending Dec. 31

	1996	1995	1994	1993	1992	1991
Revenues (Million $)						
1Q	7.41	7.28	5.40	3.74	—	—
2Q	8.11	7.78	5.97	3.86	—	—
3Q	12.10	7.73	6.37	3.85	—	—
4Q	—	7.47	7.16	4.64	3.68	—
Yr.	—	30.26	24.90	16.09	13.70	—
Earnings Per Share ($)						
1Q	0.60	0.36	0.34	0.19	0.13	0.28
2Q	0.42	0.53	0.91	0.32	0.19	0.17
3Q	0.38	0.25	0.28	1.48	0.16	0.25
4Q	—	0.68	0.20	0.62	-1.97	1.58
Yr.	—	1.82	1.74	2.61	-1.49	2.28

Next earnings report expected: mid March

Dividend Data (Dividends have been paid since 1978.)

Amount ($)	Date Decl.	Ex-Div. Date	Stock of Record	Payment Date
0.470	Feb. 28	Mar. 13	Mar. 15	Mar. 29 '96
0.470	Jun. 05	Jun. 14	Jun. 18	Jun. 28 '96
0.490	Sep. 11	Sep. 18	Sep. 21	Sep. 27 '96
0.490	Dec. 05	Dec. 12	Dec. 16	Dec. 27 '96

A Division of The McGraw·Hill Companies

Business Summary - 14-JAN-97

EastGroup Properties is an equity-oriented REIT that holds a balanced portfolio of apartment complexes and industrial/warehouse properties, as well as selected office buildings. Geographically, it is concentrated in major market areas of the Southeast and Southwest, with emphasis on Florida, Texas, Arizona and California.

In June 1996, EGP acquired Copley Properties, Inc., for 2,159,155 beneficial shares. The merger increased EastGroup's ownership of industrial and office propreties to over 5,000,000 sq. ft., and extended EGP's Sunbelt presence in Arizona and California. In May 1996, LNH REIT, Inc. was acquired in exchange for 618,244 shares.

At June 30, 1996, real estate investments totaled $292.9 million (before accumulated depreciation of $20.9 million), of which real estate properties accounted for 96% and mortgage loans 4%; land purchase-leasebacks and land were less than 1%. The trust owned 33 properties in 16 states, including 20 industrial properties, nine apartment complexes, and three office buildings as of 1995 year-end. One of the apartment buildings, Garden Villa Apartments, was sold in early 1996 for approximately $4.1 million, including the assumption of debt. EGP recorded a gain on the sale of about $1.4 million ($0.34 a share). In July 1996, EGP sold 33 acres of non-earning land (acquired in the Copley merger) for $3.5 million.

EGP seeks to buy well located, undermanaged and undervalued properties at attractive initial yields and to improve the operation and cash flow performance of such properties through hands-on management techniques, operating efficiencies and, where appropriate, renovation and expansion. The trust seeks diversification, but only in the areas and three property types in which it has particular experience.

Important Developments

Dec. '96—The trust sold its Plantations at Killearn Apartments (184 units) in Tallahassee, FL, for about $7.4 million, resulting in a gain of approximately $470,000. Separately, it sold its Pin Oaks Apartments (142 units) in Houston, TX, and Eastgate Apartments (108 units) in Wichita, KS, for a total price of $6.2 million, generating a $2.9 million gain ($0.42 a share). The sales reflected the trust's strategy of disposing of non-core assets and concentrating on the Sunbelt markets, including California, Florida, Texas and Arizona.
Sep. '96—The trust acquired a two-building industrial complex (259,352 sq. ft.) located in Tulsa, OK, for $5,675,000.
Aug. '96—The trust acquired the 234,000 sq. ft. Walnut Business Center in Fullerton, CA, for $8,141,000. The property is a two-building warehouse complex that is 100% leased to four tenants.

Capitalization

Total Debt: $138,665,000 (9/96).
Minority Interest: $3,059,000 (9/96).
Shares of Beneficial Interest: 7,026,864 ($1 par).

Per Share Data ($) (Year Ended Dec. 31)	1995	1994	1993	1992	1991	1990	1989	1988	1987	1986
Tangible Bk. Val.	19.58	19.46	19.83	19.14	22.03	21.32	22.24	19.41	18.76	19.62
Earnings	1.82	1.74	2.61	-1.49	2.28	1.19	5.56	3.48	2.51	3.10
Dividends	1.84	1.74	1.55	1.14	1.88	2.15	2.60	2.60	2.60	4.17
Payout Ratio	101%	100%	59%	NM	82%	181%	47%	75%	104%	135%
Prices - High	22 3/8	21 1/8	24 1/4	17 3/8	17 7/8	21 1/4	25	24 1/4	31 3/4	33 1/4
- Low	17 1/4	16 1/2	16 1/2	11 3/4	11 3/4	9 3/8	19 3/4	20 1/4	19 5/8	27 1/4
P/E Ratio - High	12	12	9	NM	8	18	4	7	13	11
- Low	9	9	6	NM	5	8	4	6	8	9
Income Statement Analysis (Million $)										
Income Rental	28.4	23.2	13.8	11.1	9.9	11.1	10.6	3.9	4.2	4.0
Income Mortg.	1.0	1.0	1.2	1.3	1.9	1.8	1.0	1.6	2.0	2.1
Income Total	30.3	24.9	16.1	13.7	16.8	14.8	25.6	10.9	7.7	9.1
Expenses Gen.	19.6	16.3	11.1	11.0	8.2	9.1	8.6	2.0	1.1	0.8
Expenses Int.	6.3	3.8	3.1	2.8	2.8	2.6	2.5	0.9	NA	NA
Prov. for Losses	Nil	Nil	NM	1.7	Nil	Nil	Nil	0.8	Nil	Nil
Depr.	5.6	4.5	3.1	2.4	2.0	1.9	1.7	0.6	0.3	0.3
Net Inc.	7.7	7.2	6.4	-3.7	5.7	3.0	14.0	8.9	6.7	8.3
Balance Sheet & Other Fin. Data (Million $)										
Cash	0.0	0.3	2.7	0.2	3.1	0.4	0.2	0.1	6.3	11.7
Total Assets	158	155	108	86.0	87.0	84.0	88.0	71.0	50.0	55.0
Real Estate Invest.	163	168	117	97.0	90.0	84.0	88.0	71.0	46.0	46.0
Loss Reserve	Nil	Nil	0.5	1.7	Nil	2.7	2.7	4.3	3.5	4.2
Net Invest.	144	151	103	84.0	81.0	81.0	85.0	66.0	41.0	42.0
ST Debt	6.8	5.6	24.7	3.0	3.5	0.6	0.9	0.3	0.1	1.1
Capitalization:										
Debt	60.5	62.6	28.5	32.6	26.5	28.9	28.2	19.0	0.3	1.2
Equity	82.9	82.2	48.8	47.0	54.8	53.4	55.7	49.3	48.9	52.1
Total	144	145	78.6	79.7	81.3	82.3	83.9	68.3	49.2	53.3
% Earn & Depr/Assets	8.5	8.9	9.9	NM	8.8	5.7	19.7	15.7	13.3	14.9
Price Times Book Value:										
Hi	1.1	1.1	1.2	0.9	0.8	1.0	1.1	1.2	1.7	1.7
Low	0.9	0.8	0.8	0.6	0.5	0.4	0.9	1.0	1.0	1.4

Data as orig. reptd.; bef. results of disc opers. and/or spec. items. Per share data adj. for stk. divs. as of ex-div. date. E-Estimated. NA-Not Available. NM-Not Meaningful. NR-Not Ranked.

Registrar & Transfer Agent—Keycorp Shareholders Services, Inc., Cleveland. **Office**—300 One Jackson Place, 188 East Capitol St., Jackson, MS 39201-2195. **Organized**—in Maryland in 1969. **Tel**—(601) 354-3555. **Chmn**—L. R. Speed. **Pres**—D. H. Hoster II. **EVP, CFO & Secy & Investor Contact**—N. K. McKey. **Trustees**—A. G. Anagnos, H. C. Bailey, Jr., D. H. Hoster II, H. B. Judell, J. N. Palmer, D. Osnos, L. R. Speed. **Empl**— 29. **S&P Analyst:** C.C.P.

Enova Corp.

830B
NYSE Symbol **ENA**

15-FEB-97 Industry: Util.-Diversified

Summary: This holding company for San Diego Gas & Electric Co. recently agreed to merge with Pacific Enterprises.

S&P Opinion: Accumulate (★★★★)	Recent Price • 22½	Yield • 6.9%
	52 Wk Range • 24⅜-20⅜	12-Mo. P/E • 11.4

Quantitative Evaluations

Outlook (1 Lowest—5 Highest)
• **2**

Fair Value
• **20⅜**

Risk
• **NA**

Earn./Div. Rank
• **A-**

Technical Eval.
• **NA**

Rel. Strength Rank (1 Lowest—99 Highest)
• **42**

Insider Activity
• **NA**

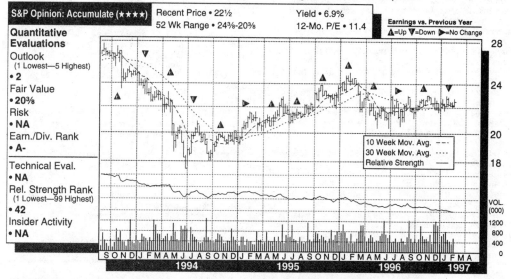

Earnings vs. Previous Year
▲=Up ▼=Down ▶=No Change

10 Week Mov. Avg. ---
30 Week Mov. Avg. ·····
Relative Strength —

VOL. (000)

Overview - 04-FEB-97

On October 14, 1996, ENA agreed to merge with Pacific Enterprises (PET), the parent of Southern California Gas. With a combined customer base of nearly six million -- the largest number of any investor-owned utility -- the new entity should be well positioned to compete in California's rapidly deregulating energy market. The merger is expected to be completed by the end of 1997, and should provide $1.2 billion in cost savings over 10 years. After 2.1% growth in 1996, we see EPS growing about 3.5% in 1997, aided by an improving service economy and the availability of low-cost purchased power. For the longer term, we expect earnings of the combined company to grow 5% to 6% annually, fueled by significant operating synergies, a greater percentage of earnings from higher growth gas operations, and increasing contributions from unregulated businesses. Enova should also benefit from the utilization of performance-based ratemaking.

Valuation - 04-FEB-97

We continue to recommend accumulation of the shares, reflecting the positive implications of the proposed merger with PET, as well as the favorable terms of California's recent comprehensive restructuring legislation. Although SDG&E enjoys the lowest electric rates of the state's three major IOUs, and is somewhat insulated from competition due to its small concentration of industrial customers and low level of stranded assets, the uncertainty surrounding the pace and outcome of regulatory reform had been a drag on the shares. With legislative concerns now mitigated, we believe investors will begin to focus on the higher EPS growth expected from the merger, resulting in a gradual expansion of the P/E multiple. With natural gas companies historically commanding higher multiples that electric utilities, we expect the P/E to also reflect the higher gas component of the new entity.

Key Stock Statistics

S&P EPS Est. 1997	2.05	Tang. Bk. Value/Share	13.28
P/E on S&P Est. 1997	11.0	Beta	0.51
Dividend Rate/Share	1.56	Shareholders	84,200
Shs. outstg. (M)	116.6	Market cap. (B)	$ 2.6
Avg. daily vol. (M)	0.089	Inst. holdings	20%

Value of $10,000 invested 5 years ago: $ 13,185

Fiscal Year Ending Dec. 31

	1996	1995	1994	1993	1992	1991
Revenues (Million $)						
1Q	465.9	478.0	504.4	492.3	471.0	448.0
2Q	471.0	445.2	463.0	467.3	437.0	407.0
3Q	507.6	478.7	491.5	495.0	488.0	452.0
4Q	549.0	468.8	523.2	525.5	475.0	482.0
Yr.	1,993	1,871	1,982	1,980	1,871	1,789
Earnings Per Share ($)						
1Q	0.57	0.56	0.50	0.49	0.46	0.45
2Q	0.41	0.41	-0.30	0.36	0.34	0.46
3Q	0.54	0.51	0.50	0.49	0.46	0.45
4Q	0.47	0.50	0.47	0.47	0.51	0.40
Yr.	1.98	1.94	1.17	1.81	1.77	1.76

Next earnings report expected: early May

Dividend Data (Dividends have been paid since 1909.)

Amount ($)	Date Decl.	Ex-Div. Date	Stock of Record	Payment Date
0.390	May. 28	Jun. 06	Jun. 10	Jul. 15 '96
0.390	Aug. 27	Sep. 06	Sep. 10	Oct. 15 '96
0.390	Nov. 25	Dec. 06	Dec. 10	Jan. 15 '97
0.390	Jan. 27	Mar. 06	Mar. 10	Apr. 15 '97

A Division of The McGraw-Hill Companies

Business Summary - 21-NOV-96

Enova Corp., the holding company for San Diego Gas & Electric, provides electric services to 1.2 million customers and gas services to 700,000 customers in Southern California. Non-regulated subsidiaries are engaged in energy management, energy products and services development, equipment leasing and real estate investments. In 1995, electricity accounted for 80% of operating revenues, gas 17%, and diversified businesses 3%. Contributions to electric revenues in 1995 were residential 40%, commercial 39%, industrial 17%, and other 4%.

Sources of generation in 1995 were natural gas 22%, oil less than 1%, nuclear 16%, and purchased 61%. Peak load in 1995 was 3,260 mw, and capability at peak was 3,857 mw, for a capacity margin of 15%. Gas sales in 1995 were 517 million therms, down from 547 million therms in 1994.

ENA has a 20% stake in the San Onofre nuclear generating plants (SONGS), which began operating in 1984. In late 1992, regulators ordered SONGS 1 permanently shut down. ENA has already fully recovered the unit's costs and it will be eventually decommissioned. ENA's Southwest Powerlink accesses power from the Palo Verde nuclear station in Arizona. Construction capital outlays were $221 million in 1995, and are projected at $220 million annually through 2000.

In late September 1996, Governor Wilson signed Assembly Bill 1890 which, consistent with the CPUC's December 1995 policy decision, opens up the California market to full retail competition, allowing customers' direct access to generation over a five-year period beginning in 1998. As part of the restructuring, California utilities must bid their generators into a wholesale power exchange and must purchase power from this pool over the transition period. The bill includes a utility rate cap at June 10, 1996 system average rates, but provides fuel-cost protection for SDG&E and provides financing for a portion of its competitive transition charge. Residential and small commercial customers will receive a 10% rate reduction secured by revenue bonds.

Important Developments

Oct. '96—Enova Corp. and Pacific Enterprises (PET), the parent of Southern California Gas Co., agreed to merge in a tax-free, stock-for-stock transaction valued at $2.8 billion. ENA shareholders will receive one common share of the new holding company, while each PET common share will be exchanged for 1.5038 shares. Subject to various approvals, the merger is expected to be completed by the end of 1997. In the interim, the two companies will form a joint venture to provide integrated energy and energy-related products and services to select marketing segments.

Capitalization

Long Term Debt: $1,443,344,000 (9/96).
Preferred Stock: $103,475,000.

Per Share Data ($)

(Year Ended Dec. 31)	1996	1995	1994	1993	1992	1991	1990	1989	1988	1987
Tangible Bk. Val.	NA	13.28	12.65	12.48	11.99	11.40	11.08	10.73	10.51	10.63
Earnings	1.98	1.94	1.17	1.81	1.77	1.76	1.76	1.58	1.59	1.48
Dividends	1.56	1.56	1.52	1.48	1.44	1.39	1.35	1.35	1.30	1.25
Payout Ratio	79%	80%	130%	82%	81%	79%	77%	86%	82%	84%
Prices - High	25	23⅞	25	27¾	25	23⅛	23⅛	22⅞	19¾	19
- Low	20⅜	19⅛	17½	23¼	21⅛	18⅝	19½	18¼	15	14⅛
P/E Ratio - High	13	12	21	15	14	13	13	14	12	13
- Low	10	10	15	13	12	11	11	12	9	10

Income Statement Analysis (Million $)

	1996	1995	1994	1993	1992	1991	1990	1989	1988	1987
Revs.	NA	1,871	1,982	1,980	1,871	1,789	1,772	2,082	2,076	1,904
Depr.	NA	278	265	251	214	195	186	177	173	152
Maint.	NA	92.0	71.0	82.0	73.0	68.1	62.9	67.6	66.5	66.0
Fxd. Chgs. Cov.	NA	3.8	3.5	4.3	4.0	3.8	4.0	3.9	3.6	3.7
Constr. Credits	NA	9.3	8.9	22.2	11.1	9.3	9.0	10.3	13.2	14.7
Eff. Tax Rate	NA	37%	35%	35%	38%	33%	37%	37%	33%	39%
Net Inc.	NA	31.2	143	219	211	208	208	187	189	179

Balance Sheet & Other Fin. Data (Million $)

	1996	1995	1994	1993	1992	1991	1990	1989	1988	1987
Gross Prop.	NA	5,534	5,329	5,134	4,819	4,823	4,594	4,384	4,159	4,052
Cap. Exp.	NA	221	264	354	277	252	235	237	196	224
Net Prop.	NA	3,100	3,149	3,118	2,979	3,032	2,988	2,950	2,938	2,917
Capitalization:										
LT Debt	NA	1,350	1,340	1,412	1,496	1,164	1,167	1,113	1,179	1,205
% LT Debt	NA	452	46	46	49	44	45	44	46	46
Pfd.	NA	118	118	118	131	139	142	147	150	156
% Pfd.	NA	4.00	4.00	3.90	4.30	5.30	5.40	5.90	5.90	6.00
Common	NA	1,520	1,474	1,516	1,449	1,358	1,303	1,256	1,230	1,243
% Common	NA	51	50	50	47	51	50	50	48	48
Total Cap.	NA	3,651	3,566	3,567	3,420	3,037	2,969	2,857	2,893	2,951
Oper. Ratio	NA	81.5	83.8	85.2	84.2	82.4	83.0	86.6	86.9	86.3
% Earn. on Net Prop.	NA	11.1	10.3	9.6	9.9	10.5	10.1	9.6	9.4	9.1
% Ret. on Revs.	NA	12.5	7.2	11.0	11.3	11.6	11.7	9.0	9.1	9.4
% Ret. On Invest.Cap	NA	13.1	7.0	9.0	9.8	10.5	10.9	10.0	10.1	9.6
% Return On Com.Eqty	NA	15.1	9.1	14.2	14.3	14.8	15.4	14.2	14.6	13.5

Data as orig. reptd.; bef. results of disc opers. and/or spec. items. Per share data adj. for stk. divs. as of ex-div. date. E-Estimated. NA-Not Available. NM-Not Meaningful. NR-Not Ranked.

Office—101 Ash St., San Diego, CA 92101. Tel—(619) 239-7700. Website—http://www.enova.com Chrmn—T. A. Page. Pres & CEO—S. L. Baum. SVP, CFO & Treas—D. R. Kuzma. Investor Contact—Mark Fisher. Dirs—R. C. Atkinson, S. L. Baum, A. Burr, R. A. Collato, D. W. Derbes, D. Felsinger, R. H. Goldsmith, W. D. Jones, R. R. Ocampo, T. A. Page, T. C. Stickel. Transfer Agent & Registrar—First Chicago Trust, NYC. Incorporated—in California in 1905. Empl—3,880. S&P Analyst: Justin McCann

STANDARD &POOR'S
STOCK REPORTS

Entergy Corp.

831M

NYSE Symbol **ETR**

In S&P 500

15-FEB-97

Industry: Utilities-Electric

Summary: This electric utility holding company provides service to about 2.4 million retail customers in Arkansas, Texas, Louisiana and Mississippi.

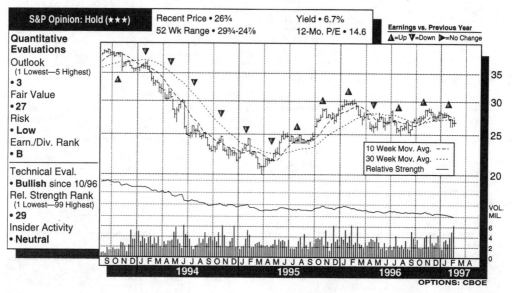

S&P Opinion: Hold (★★★)	Recent Price • 26¾ Yield • 6.7%
	52 Wk Range • 29¾-24⅞ 12-Mo. P/E • 14.6

Quantitative Evaluations

Outlook
(1 Lowest—5 Highest)
• **3**

Fair Value
• **27**

Risk
• **Low**

Earn./Div. Rank
• **B**

Technical Eval.
• **Bullish** since 10/96

Rel. Strength Rank
(1 Lowest—99 Highest)
• **29**

Insider Activity
• **Neutral**

Earnings vs. Previous Year
▲=Up ▼=Down ►=No Change

10 Week Mov. Avg. - - - -
30 Week Mov. Avg. ·····
Relative Strength ———

S O N D J F M A M J J A S O N D J F M A M J J A S O N D J F M A M J J A S O N D J F M A
1994   1995   1996   1997

OPTIONS: CBOE

Overview - 11-DEC-96

We expect ETR to achieve annual EPS growth from continuing operations of about 5% over the next couple of years. Retail electricity sales should advance about 3%, on average, aided by a higher customer count reflecting a more active service area economy. In addition, greater operating efficiencies and a reduction in headcount will reduce operating and maintenance costs about 2% during 1997. Other positive factors include lower debt service costs and reduced preferred dividend requirements contributions from Latin American and offshore generation projects. For the longer-term, EPS gains will be driven by the company's expansion of domestic energy related retail services and nonregulated ventures, such as its security monitoring business.

Valuation - 11-DEC-96

The shares of this major Texas utility are down about 6% so far in 1996, about in line with the performance of the S&P Electric Utilities Index. The decline primarily reflects investor concerns about rising interest rates. For the next six to 12 months, however, the shares are likely to outperform the average of ETR's peers, reflecting the settlement of certain regulatory issues, including the disposition of a lawsuit related to the River Bend Nuclear plant. Although we expect comparatively modest earnings growth for the next several years, ETR's commitment to use cash to repay debt and expand its growing investment in non-regulated businesses will add to returns in the long term. Management has indicated that it will pursue a conservative long-term dividend payout ratio goal of 65% to 70% of earnings. With the current payout closer to 72% of estimated 1997 EPS, an increase is unlikely for the foreseeable future.

Key Stock Statistics

S&P EPS Est. 1997	2.50	Tang. Bk. Value/Share	28.80
P/E on S&P Est. 1997	10.7	Beta	0.75
Dividend Rate/Share	1.80	Shareholders	103,100
Shs. outstg. (M)	230.9	Market cap. (B)	$ 6.2
Avg. daily vol. (M)	1.005	Inst. holdings	68%

Value of $10,000 invested 5 years ago: $ 12,267

Fiscal Year Ending Dec. 31

	1996	1995	1994	1993	1992	1991
Revenues (Million $)						
1Q	1,599	1,346	1,406	926.4	916.0	893.0
2Q	2,138	1,572	1,586	1,070	958.0	981.0
3Q	1,858	1,937	1,806	1,411	1,237	1,255
4Q	1,569	1,426	1,165	1,078	1,004	922.0
Yr.	7,164	6,274	5,963	4,485	4,117	4,051
Earnings Per Share ($)						
1Q	-0.38	0.25	0.31	0.33	0.54	0.46
2Q	0.83	0.71	0.63	0.75	0.46	0.45
3Q	1.22	1.16	0.63	1.34	1.16	1.12
4Q	0.17	0.02	-0.07	0.21	0.32	0.61
Yr.	1.83	2.13	1.49	2.62	2.48	2.64

Next earnings report expected: early March

Dividend Data (Dividends have been paid since 1988.)

Amount ($)	Date Decl.	Ex-Div. Date	Stock of Record	Payment Date
0.450	Mar. 25	May. 08	May. 10	Jun. 01 '96
0.450	Jul. 26	Aug. 05	Aug. 07	Sep. 01 '96
0.450	Oct. 25	Nov. 04	Nov. 06	Dec. 01 '96
0.450	Jan. 31	Feb. 10	Feb. 12	Mar. 01 '97

A Division of The McGraw·Hill Companies

Business Summary - 11-DEC-96

Entergy Corp. (formerly Middle South Utilities) is the holding company for Entergy Arkansas, Entergy Louisiana, Entergy Mississippi and Entergy New Orleans, which provide electricity to more than 2.4 million retail customers. On December 31, 1993, ETR acquired Entergy Gulf States (formerly Gulf States Utilities (GSU)), which serves parts of Louisiana and Texas and owns 70% of the River Bend nuclear plant, for $2.3 billion. The company also owns System Energy Resources, which has a 90% interest in the Grand Gulf 1 nuclear plant. Revenues in 1995 were 98% electric and 2% gas/steam. Electric revenue sources in recent years were:

	1995	1994	1993	1992
Residential	36%	37%	36%	36%
Commercial	24%	26%	24%	25%
Industrial	30%	32%	27%	27%
Other	10%	5%	13%	12%

Power sources in 1995 were nuclear 30%, gas 42%, coal 13%, and purchased power 15%. Peak demand in 1995 was 19,590 mw.

In 1994, ETR's total outlays to expand its business were $472 million, largely for investments in power generation abroad and to expand its energy services unit, and it plans to invest up to $150 million a year through 1997 to expand nonregulated businesses. ETR has no plans to construct new generating capacity, but outlays to upgrade existing facilities are projected to total $571 million, $510 million and $507 million, respectively, for 1996, 1997 and 1998.

In January 1996, ETR acquired CitiPower, an electric distribution utility serving Melbourne, Australia, for approximately $1.2 billion.

In April 1996, in a move to streamline its business to serve customers better and operate more efficiently, ETR reorganized its five operating subsidiaries under a single corporate identity, adopting the Entergy name and logo.

Important Developments

Nov. '96—ETR acquired Sentry Alarms Systems of America, Inc., a Clearwater, FL-based full service security monitoring company with $22 million in annual revenues, for approximately $41 million. In September, ETR signed a letter of intent to acquire National Security Service of Raleigh, NC, a full-service security monitoring company with $25 million in annual revenues.

Capitalization

Long Term Debt: $7,642,768,000 (9/96).
Subsidiary Preference Stock: $150,000,000.
Subsidiary Preferred Stock: $712,941,000.

Per Share Data ($)

(Year Ended Dec. 31)	1996	1995	1994	1993	1992	1991	1990	1989	1988	1987
Tangible Bk. Val.	NA	28.25	27.74	27.16	24.23	23.31	22.01	20.50	23.70	21.86
Earnings	1.83	2.13	1.49	2.62	2.48	2.64	2.44	-2.31	2.01	1.74
Dividends	1.80	1.80	1.80	1.65	1.45	1.25	1.05	0.90	0.20	Nil
Payout Ratio	98%	85%	121%	63%	58%	47%	43%	NM	10%	Nil
Prices - High	30³/₈	29¹/₄	37⁷/₈	39⁷/₈	33⁵/₈	29⁷/₈	23⁵/₈	23¹/₈	16¹/₈	16¹/₄
- Low	24⁷/₈	20	21¹/₄	32¹/₂	26¹/₈	21⁷/₈	18	15¹/₂	8¹/₂	7³/₄
P/E Ratio - High	17	14	25	15	14	11	10	NM	8	9
- Low	14	9	14	12	11	8	7	NM	4	4

Income Statement Analysis (Million $)

	1996	1995	1994	1993	1992	1991	1990	1989	1988	1987
Revs.	NA	6,274	5,963	4,485	4,116	4,051	3,982	3,724	3,565	3,455
Depr.	NA	691	657	444	425	399	393	406	391	384
Maint.	NA	NA	NA	307	302	283	278	279	238	256
Fxd. Chgs. Cov.	NA	2.3	1.6	2.4	2.1	2.1	2.2	0.4	1.8	1.8
Constr. Credits	NA	18.0	21.8	14.0	12.0	15.0	11.0	11.0	16.0	9.0
Eff. Tax Rate	NA	41%	24%	36%	34%	34%	37%	NM	32%	38%
Net Inc.	NA	485	342	458	438	482	478	-472	411	357

Balance Sheet & Other Fin. Data (Million $)

	1996	1995	1994	1993	1992	1991	1990	1989	1988	1987
Gross Prop.	NA	24,080	23,557	23,180	15,051	14,813	14,591	14,297	14,101	13,955
Cap. Exp.	NA	618	676	512	427	397	400	370	346	417
Net Prop.	NA	15,821	15,917	16,022	10,736	10,812	10,928	10,998	11,111	11,240
Capitalization:										
LT Debt	NA	7,081	7,367	7,679	5,326	5,493	6,072	6,347	6,448	6,190
% LT Debt	NA	49	49	50	52	53	56	56	53	54
Pfd.	NA	954	1,001	900	705	690	642	681	794	827
% Pfd.	NA	6.60	6.90	5.90	6.80	6.60	5.90	6.10	6.50	7.20
Common	NA	6,472	6,351	6,536	4,279	4,208	4,121	4,220	4,901	4,528
% Common	NA	45	44	43	42	41	38	38	40	39
Total Cap.	NA	18,897	19,959	19,917	12,088	12,348	12,677	12,893	13,808	12,929
Oper. Ratio	NA	80.6	82.1	77.9	76.7	73.7	73.7	73.1	70.0	70.8
% Earn. on Net Prop.	NA	7.7	6.7	7.4	8.9	9.8	9.6	9.0	9.6	9.2
% Ret. on Revs.	NA	7.7	5.7	10.2	10.6	11.9	12.0	NM	11.5	10.3
% Ret. On Invest.Cap	NA	6.3	5.5	6.3	8.7	9.3	9.2	1.9	9.0	9.0
% Return On Com.Eqty	NA	7.6	5.3	12.6	10.3	11.6	11.5	NM	8.7	8.2

Data as orig. reptd.; bef. results of disc opers. and/or spec. items. Per share data adj. for stk. divs. as of ex-div. date. E-Estimated. NA-Not Available. NM-Not Meaningful. NR-Not Ranked.

Office—1039 Loyola Ave., New Orleans, LA 70113. **Tel**—(504) 529-5262. **Website**—http://www.entergy.com **Chrmn, Pres & CEO**—E. Lupberger. **Vice Chrmn**—J. L. Maulden. **SVP & CFO**—G. D. McInvale. **Investor Contact**—M. Stuart Ball. **VP & Treas**—W. J. Regan, Jr., **VP & Secy**—M. G. Thompson. **Dirs**—W. F. Blount, J. A. Cooper, Jr., L. J. Fjeldstad, N. C. Francis, K. Hodges, Jr., R. v.d. Luft, E. Lupberger, K. R. McKee, P. W. Murrill, J. R. Nichols, E. H. Owen, J. N. Palmer, R. D. Pugh, H. D. Shackelford, W. C. Smith,— B. A. Steinhagen. **Transfer Agent & Registrar**—ChaseMellon Securities Trust Co., Ridgefield Park, NJ. **Incorporated**—in Delaware in 1994; in Florida in 1949. **Empl**— 11,915. **S&P Analyst:** Maureen C. Carini

Essex County Gas

3815B

NASDAQ Symbol **ECGC**

15-FEB-97

Industry: Utilities-Gas

Summary: This Massachusetts utility purchases, distributes and sells natural gas in the northeastern part of the state to nearly 42,000 customers.

Quantitative Evaluations

Outlook (1 Lowest—5 Highest)
• **NA**

Fair Value
• **NA**

Risk
• **Low**

Earn./Div. Rank
• **A**

Technical Eval.
• **Bullish** since 2/97

Rel. Strength Rank (1 Lowest—99 Highest)
• **29**

Insider Activity
• **NA**

Recent Price • 24¼
52 Wk Range • 27-23

Yield • 6.8%
12-Mo. P/E • 10.5

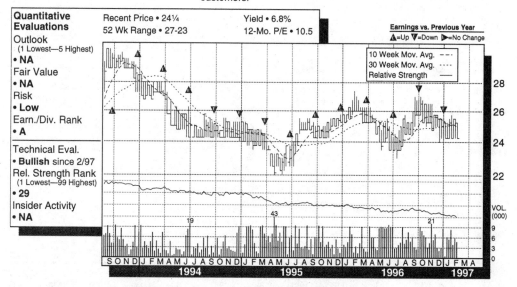

Earnings vs. Previous Year
▲=Up ▼=Down ▶=No Change

10 Week Mov. Avg. - - -
30 Week Mov. Avg. ┄┄
Relative Strength ─

Business Profile - 21-JAN-97

This natural gas utility serves primarily residential customers in the northeastern part of Massachusetts. As a result of the implementation of FERC Order No. 636 in 1993, the company's pipeline supplier, Tennessee Gas Pipeline Co., is now providing transportation services only. ECGC now contracts for its own gas supply through the Mansfield Consortium, a group of gas companies that pool interests and benefit from economies of scale in procuring gas supplies. Since most customers use natural gas for space heating purposes, colder weather in FY 96 (Aug.) had a positive impact on revenues; coupled with slightly higher prices and a larger customer base, revenues and earnings advanced 11% and 21%, respectively. The dividend was raised 2.5% with the January 1997 payment (the ninth consecutive year the dividend has been increased), and an approved rate increase of about $2.1 million (4.0%) went into effect December 1, 1996.

Operational Review - 21-JAN-97

Based on a brief report, operating revenues in the three months ended November 30, 1996, rose 17%, year to year, reflecting higher firm gas volumes due to more favorable weather and customer growth. Total degree days in the company's service area rose 7.8%, to 978 days, from 907 days. However, the net loss widened to $260,669 ($0.16 a share, based on 2.2% more shares), from $208,087 ($0.13).

Stock Performance - 14-FEB-97

In the past 30 trading days, ECGC's shares were unchanged, compared to a 8% rise in the S&P 500. Average trading volume for the past five days was 940 shares, compared with the 40-day moving average of 1,105 shares.

Key Stock Statistics

Dividend Rate/Share	1.64	Shareholders	1,300
Shs. outstg. (M)	1.7	Market cap. (B)	$0.040
Avg. daily vol. (M)	0.001	Inst. holdings	6%
Tang. Bk. Value/Share	20.10		
Beta	0.28		

Value of $10,000 invested 5 years ago: $ 14,593

Fiscal Year Ending Aug. 31

	1997	1996	1995	1994	1993	1992
Revenues (Million $)						
1Q	8.14	6.96	6.70	6.60	7.45	5.34
2Q	—	22.63	20.16	23.70	20.56	19.67
3Q	—	15.55	14.10	13.99	13.89	13.41
4Q	—	4.79	4.09	4.25	3.12	4.35
Yr.	—	49.93	45.05	48.54	45.02	42.78
Earnings Per Share ($)						
1Q	-0.16	-0.13	-0.18	-0.16	-0.20	-0.33
2Q	—	1.83	1.33	1.48	1.28	1.39
3Q	—	0.65	0.61	0.58	0.56	0.51
4Q	—	0.01	0.24	0.22	0.31	0.22
Yr.	—	2.36	2.00	2.12	1.95	1.79

Next earnings report expected: early April

Dividend Data (Dividends have been paid since 1915.)

Amount ($)	Date Decl.	Ex-Div. Date	Stock of Record	Payment Date
0.400	Mar. 05	Mar. 13	Mar. 15	Apr. 01 '96
0.400	Jun. 04	Jun. 12	Jun. 14	Jul. 01 '96
0.400	Sep. 06	Sep. 12	Sep. 16	Oct. 01 '96
0.410	Dec. 10	Dec. 18	Dec. 20	Jan. 01 '97

A Division of The McGraw·Hill Companies

Business Summary - 21-JAN-97

With nearly 42,000 customers, Essex County Gas Co. (ECGC) purchases, distributes and sells natural gas to residential, commercial and light-industrial users in the most northeastern part of Massachusetts. In FY 96 (Aug.), residential heating customers accounted for 64% of total operating revenues, commercial and industrial customers 30%, interruptible customers 4% and other sources 2%.

In the past several years customer growth has been bolstered by a significant increase in new residential construction in ECGC's local economy, where natural gas is the fuel of choice. Total sales of gas (000 Mcf) in FY 96, FY 95 and FY 94 rose 10%, 1.2% and 4.9%, respectively. About 78% of all natural gas used by ECGC's customers in FY 96 was delivered to Essex through a pipeline owned by Tennessee Gas Pipeline Co. Total gas sendout in FY 96 was up 10%, to 6,648,866 Mcf, versus 6,037,442 in FY 95. Essex owns a propane plant with a storage capacity of 40,000 Mcf, and its wholly owned LNG Storage owns a liquid natural gas facility with a storage capacity of 400,000 Mcf. In addition to gas sales, Essex rents water heaters and conversion burners and performs service work. These businesses contributed less than 2% of total revenues in FY 96.

During the past few years, Essex has been pursuing a portfolio approach for securing and transporting its firm gas supplies. To accomplish this, the company joined a buying cooperative called the Mansfield Consortium. By pooling resources, Essex will benefit from improved pricing terms, as well as economies of scale. The company has secured long-term gas supply contracts with several gas suppliers at market-sensitive prices.

ECGC's gas business competes primarily with oil for industrial boiler uses and oil and electricity for residential and commercial space heating. Natural gas may be the choice fuel in the future for its significant environmental and operational and maintenance advantages over oil, plus significant price advantage over electricity.

Results in FY 96 benefited from colder weather as the majority of ECGC's customers use natural gas for space heating purposes. Total degree days in the company's service area rose 11%, to 6,947 days, from 6,258 days in the year-earlier period. The colder weather, coupled with slightly higher prices and a nearly 3.0% rise in ECGC's customer base, resulted in an 11% rise in revenues and 21% rise in net income.

A rate increase of about $2.1 million (4.0%) was approved by regulators, effective December 1, 1996. ECGC's original rate increase request was for $3.4 million.

Capitalization

Long Term Debt: $19,765,000 (8/96).

Per Share Data ($)

(Year Ended Aug. 31)	1996	1995	1994	1993	1992	1991	1990	1989	1988	1987
Tangible Bk. Val.	20.14	19.11	18.37	17.48	15.92	15.31	15.02	14.01	13.09	12.25
Cash Flow	4.03	3.58	3.62	3.43	3.32	2.94	3.48	3.21	2.96	2.62
Earnings	2.36	2.00	2.12	1.95	1.79	1.48	2.10	1.94	1.80	1.56
Dividends	1.59	1.55	1.51	1.47	1.43	1.40	1.30	1.24	1.19	1.16
Payout Ratio	67%	77%	72%	75%	80%	95%	63%	65%	67%	76%
Prices - High	27⅜	25¾	28½	30½	25½	23½	19	18¾	18¼	19½
- Low	23	22	24	24	20	18	17	16¾	14	13¾
P/E Ratio - High	12	13	13	16	14	16	9	10	10	13
- Low	10	11	11	12	11	12	8	9	8	9

Income Statement Analysis (Million $)

	1996	1995	1994	1993	1992	1991	1990	1989	1988	1987
Revs.	49.9	45.1	48.5	45.0	42.8	38.4	39.3	34.3	33.9	31.2
Oper. Inc.	6.7	5.9	10.0	9.5	8.1	7.6	8.3	7.3	6.6	6.2
Depr.	2.7	2.5	2.3	2.2	2.0	1.9	1.7	1.6	1.4	1.3
Int. Exp.	2.8	2.8	2.5	2.7	2.8	2.8	2.6	2.3	2.0	1.8
Pretax Inc.	5.6	4.6	5.2	4.5	3.5	2.9	4.0	3.5	3.4	3.2
Eff. Tax Rate	32%	30%	36%	35%	34%	33%	34%	32%	36%	41%
Net Inc.	3.8	3.2	3.3	2.9	2.3	1.9	2.7	2.4	2.2	1.9

Balance Sheet & Other Fin. Data (Million $)

	1996	1995	1994	1993	1992	1991	1990	1989	1988	1987
Cash	0.3	0.1	0.1	0.1	0.5	0.0	0.0	0.5	0.0	0.3
Curr. Assets	9.0	10.9	11.4	10.5	11.8	7.3	7.9	8.1	6.9	7.6
Total Assets	89.8	86.6	83.5	76.3	73.2	65.2	62.4	58.1	51.8	47.2
Curr. Liab.	22.6	21.5	19.9	15.7	20.4	12.3	16.7	12.1	12.3	8.4
LT Debt	20.4	21.3	22.4	22.9	21.8	23.8	17.5	19.8	15.3	15.6
Common Eqty.	33.0	30.7	28.9	27.0	21.0	19.8	19.0	17.4	15.9	14.5
Total Cap.	64.6	62.8	61.4	59.5	51.8	52.0	44.7	45.0	38.6	38.1
Cap. Exp.	8.0	7.0	6.2	6.7	6.1	5.2	6.3	6.9	6.1	4.6
Cash Flow	6.5	5.7	5.6	5.1	4.3	3.8	4.4	3.9	3.5	3.1
Curr. Ratio	0.4	0.5	0.6	0.7	0.6	0.6	0.5	0.7	0.6	0.9
% LT Debt of Cap.	31.6	34.0	36.5	38.5	40.6	45.8	39.1	44.0	39.6	41.0
% Net Inc.of Revs.	7.7	7.1	6.8	6.4	5.5	5.0	6.8	7.0	6.5	5.9
% Ret. on Assets	4.4	3.7	4.1	3.6	3.4	3.0	4.4	4.3	4.4	3.8
% Ret. on Equity	12.1	10.7	11.7	11.2	11.4	9.7	14.3	14.2	14.1	12.4

Data as orig. reptd.; bef. results of disc. opers. and/or spec. items. Per share data adj. for stk. divs. as of ex-div. date. E-Estimated. NA-Not Available. NM-Not Meaningful. NR-Not Ranked.

Office—7 North Hunt Rd., Amesbury, MA 01913. **Tel**—(508) 388-4000. **Chrmn**—C. E. Billups. **Pres & CEO**—P. H. Reardon. **VP, Treas & Investor Contact**—James H. Hastings. **Clerk**—Cathy E. Brown. **Dirs**—C. E. Billups, B. C. Bixby, D. A. Burkhardt, E. J. Curtis, D. J. Dotson, R. P. Hamel, R. S. Jackson, E. H. Jostrom, R. L. Meade, K. L. Paul, P. H. Reardon, B. S. Wellman. **Transfer Agent & Registrar**—American Stock Transfer & Trust Co., NYC. **Incorporated**—in Massachusetts in 1853. **Empl**—127. **S&P Analyst:** Jennifer B. Kelly

Federal Realty Investment   870M

NYSE Symbol **FRT**

14-FEB-97

Industry:
Real Estate Investment Trust

Summary: This equity real estate investment trust specializes in the ownership, management and redevelopment of prime community and neighborhood shopping centers.

Quantitative Evaluations		
Outlook (1 Lowest—5 Highest) • **NA**		
Fair Value • **NA**		
Risk • **Low**		
Earn./Div. Rank • **NR**		
Technical Eval. • **Bearish** since 11/96		
Rel. Strength Rank (1 Lowest—99 Highest) • **57**		
Insider Activity • **NA**		

Recent Price • 27¾
52 Wk Range • 28¾-20¼

Yield • 6.1%
12-Mo. P/E • 35.1

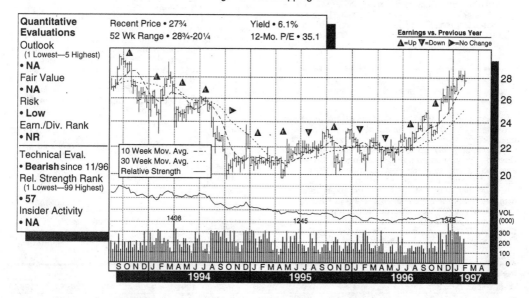

Earnings vs. Previous Year
▲=Up ▼=Down ▶=No Change

10 Week Mov. Avg. ---
30 Week Mov. Avg. ····
Relative Strength —

Business Profile - 14-FEB-97

Federal Realty's core strategy involves making long-term investments in prime shopping center properties, renovating the properties when necessary, and attracting quality specialty retailers as tenants. In recent periods, overall occupancy rates for the trust's portfolio have slipped fractionally; however, this has been outweighed by sizeable increases in weighted average rent per sq. ft. for re-leased space. Federal Realty has paid dividends to its shareholders continuously since its founding in 1962, and has increased its dividend rate in each of the past 29 years.

Operational Review - 14-FEB-97

Based on a preliminary report, total revenues in 1996 climbed 16% from those of the previous year, due principally to a 15% increase in rental income and a 32% rise in other income. Total expenses were up 14%, with 16% higher rental and interest costs, and a 9.3% rise in depreciation and amortization charges. Following losses on the sale of real estate and other charges, net income advanced 24%, to $28,742,000 ($0.86 a share, on 5.4% more shares), from $23,110,000 ($0.72). Funds from operations rose 14%, to $65,254,000 ($1.94), from $57,034,000 ($1.79).

Stock Performance - 07-FEB-97

In the past 30 trading days, FRT's shares have increased 2%, compared to a 4% rise in the S&P 500. Average trading volume for the past five days was 39,483 shares, compared with the 40-day moving average of 65,315 shares.

Key Stock Statistics

Dividend Rate/Share	1.68	Shareholders	5,300
Shs. outstg. (M)	35.8	Market cap. (B)	$0.975
Avg. daily vol. (M)	0.046	Inst. holdings	52%
Tang. Bk. Value/Share	10.15		
Beta	0.31		

Value of $10,000 invested 5 years ago: $ 20,535

Fiscal Year Ending Dec. 31

	1996	1995	1994	1993	1992	1991
Revenues (Million $)						
1Q	43.77	36.93	33.69	26.64	—	—
2Q	43.57	36.99	32.79	28.44	—	—
3Q	44.34	38.97	34.80	28.90	—	—
4Q	43.33	41.50	36.48	31.35	26.48	—
Yr.	164.9	154.4	137.8	115.3	100.2	—
Earnings Per Share ($)						
1Q	0.19	0.21	0.15	0.10	0.08	0.08
2Q	0.21	0.16	0.17	0.14	0.10	0.07
3Q	0.24	0.19	0.16	0.16	0.15	0.04
4Q	0.22	0.16	0.20	0.19	0.08	0.09
Yr.	0.86	0.72	0.67	0.60	0.41	0.25

Next earnings report expected: mid February

Dividend Data (Dividends have been paid since 1962.)

Amount ($)	Date Decl.	Ex-Div. Date	Stock of Record	Payment Date
0.410	Feb. 16	Mar. 21	Mar. 25	Apr. 15 '96
0.410	Jun. 12	Jun. 26	Jun. 28	Jul. 15 '96
0.420	Sep. 11	Sep. 24	Sep. 26	Oct. 15 '96
0.420	Nov. 21	Dec. 30	Jan. 02	Jan. 15 '97

A Division of The McGraw·Hill Companies

STANDARD
&POOR'S
STOCK REPORTS

Federal Realty Investment Trust

870M
14-FEB-97

Business Summary - 14-FEB-97

Federal Realty Investment Trust is a real estate investment trust that invests substantially all of its assets in income-producing real estate, with primary emphasis on shopping centers. Real estate investments (at cost) totaled $1,009.7 million at December 31, 1995 (before accumulated depreciation of $190.8 million); the trust also held mortgage notes receivable of $13.6 million. Real estate investments at year end were divided as follows:

	1995	1994
Shopping centers	77%	77%
Shopping centers under capital leases	22%	22%
Apartments	1%	1%

At December 31, 1995, the trust's 61 retail properties consisted of 52 shopping centers and 9 main street retail buildings, located in 13 states and the District of Columbia, primarily along the East Coast, between the Boston metropolitan area and Richmond, VA. The trust also owned one apartment development in Silver Spring, MD, with 282 units. The shopping centers, which usually feature stores of supermarket, drug or discount department store chains, were in Pennsylvania (10), Maryland (9), Virginia (10), New Jersey (9), Illinois (5), Massachusetts (2), Connecticut, North Carolina, Michigan, Georgia, New York, Tennessee and Louisiana (one each).

Properties are purchased for long-term investment and income, rather than resale. A fundamental element of the trust's strategy is to acquire and upgrade older community and neighborhood shopping centers in major metropolitan locations and to enhance their revenue potential through a program of renovation, re-leasing and re-merchandising. It also seeks to execute tenant leases that provide for additional rent based on tenant sales revenue and annual rent escalations. Property acquisitions are financed with first mortgages and, in certain cases, second mortgages or long-term leases.

In 1995, the trust acquired 1.3 million sq. ft. of retail properties at a cost of approximately $124 million. The trust has more than 1,700 tenants, ranging from sole proprietors to major national retailers. No one tenant accounts for over 5% of revenues.

Important Developments

Feb. '97—Federal Realty completed the direct sale of 3,000,000 common shares at $28 per share to a large equity mutual fund. Net proceeds of approximately $83.9 million will be used principally to repay borrowing on the Trust's revolving credit facilities.

Capitalization

Long Term Debt: $290,289,000 (9/96), incl. $75,289,000 of conv. debs.
Common Shares of Beneficial Interest: : 34,148,894.

Per Share Data ($)

(Year Ended Dec. 31)	1996	1995	1994	1993	1992	1991	1990	1989	1988	1987
Tangible Bk. Val.	NA	10.06	11.09	10.03	8.95	7.58	7.61	8.62	6.68	7.12
Earnings	0.86	0.72	0.67	0.60	0.41	0.25	0.35	0.82	0.68	0.47
Dividends	1.66	1.61	1.57	1.55	1.53	1.50	1.44	1.38	1.26	1.14
Payout Ratio	193%	234%	234%	231%	373%	600%	411%	168%	185%	243%
Prices - High	28¾	23⅝	29½	30¼	25¼	21	22	26	22¼	25¾
- Low	20¼	19¾	19⅝	23⅞	18¾	13⅝	12½	20¾	19	17¼
P/E Ratio - High	33	33	44	45	62	84	63	32	33	55
- Low	24	27	29	36	46	55	36	25	28	37

Income Statement Analysis (Million $)

	1996	1995	1994	1993	1992	1991	1990	1989	1988	1987
Income Rental	NA	143	128	106	90.0	88.4	80.7	72.8	58.3	50.9
Income Mortg.	NA	4.1	3.9	3.9	5.5	4.7	6.6	6.6	6.2	6.9
Income Total	NA	154	138	115	100	98.0	91.0	83.0	68.0	60.0
Expenses Gen.	NA	91.8	85.4	66.9	57.6	54.5	50.8	44.6	36.4	30.5
Expenses Int.	NA	39.3	31.5	31.6	35.2	38.1	34.7	33.1	25.8	23.6
Prov. for Losses	NA	Nil	Nil	Nil	Nil	Nil	Nil	Nil	Nil	Nil
Depr.	NA	34.9	29.8	25.4	23.0	21.9	19.1	16.2	12.1	9.5
Net Inc.	NA	23.1	20.5	16.1	9.5	4.4	5.8	12.0	9.3	6.0

Balance Sheet & Other Fin. Data (Million $)

	1996	1995	1994	1993	1992	1991	1990	1989	1988	1987
Cash	NA	10.8	7.6	13.6	71.9	51.6	33.8	65.1	46.3	87.2
Total Assets	NA	886	754	691	604	563	551	564	476	402
Real Estate Invest.	NA	1,023	866	772	616	583	573	537	458	326
Loss Reserve	NA	Nil	Nil	Nil	Nil	Nil	Nil	Nil	Nil	Nil
Net Invest.	NA	832	705	637	502	487	494	476	410	287
ST Debt	NA	NA	13.7	15.0	14.4	24.5	45.1	42.2	13.2	7.9
Capitalization:										
Debt	NA	348	359	349	334	355	344	347	343	274
Equity	NA	327	345	284	223	151	129	146	96.0	100
Total	NA	675	704	633	557	506	473	494	439	374
% Earn & Depr/Assets	NA	7.1	7.0	6.4	5.6	4.7	4.5	5.4	4.9	4.4
Price Times Book Value:										
Hi	NA	2.3	2.7	3.0	2.8	2.8	2.9	3.0	3.3	3.6
Low	NA	2.0	1.8	2.4	2.1	1.8	1.6	2.4	2.8	2.4

Data as orig. reptd.; bef. results of disc opers. and/or spec. items. Per share data adj. for stk. divs. as of ex-div. date. E-Estimated. NA-Not Available. NM-Not Meaningful. NR-Not Ranked.

Office—4800 Hampden Lane, Suite 500, Bethesda, MD 20814. **Organized**—in the District of Columbia in 1962. **Tel**—(301) 652-3360. **Pres & CEO**—S. J. Guttman. **SVP-Fin, Treas & Investor Contact**—Mary Jane Morrow. **VP & Secy**—Catherine R. Mack. **Trustees**—D. L. Berman, A. Cornet de Ways Ruart, K. Gamble, S. J. Gorlitz, S. J. Guttman, M. S. Lerner, W. F. Loeb, D. H. Misner, G. Perry.**Transfer Agent & Registrar**—American Stock Transfer & Trust Co., NYC. **Empl**— 195. **S&P Analyst:** Thomas C. Ferguson

15-FEB-97

Industry: Utilities-Electric

Summary: Florida Progress is the holding company for Florida Power, which provides electric utility services to central, northern and Gulf Coast Florida.

S&P Opinion: Hold (★★★)	Recent Price • 30¾	Yield • 6.7%
	52 Wk Range • 36¼-30⅜	12-Mo. P/E • 13.8

Quantitative Evaluations

Outlook
(1 Lowest—5 Highest)
• 1

Fair Value
• 27¼

Risk
• **Low**

Earn./Div. Rank
• **A-**

Technical Eval.
• **Bearish** since 11/96

Rel. Strength Rank
(1 Lowest—99 Highest)
• 24

Insider Activity
• **NA**

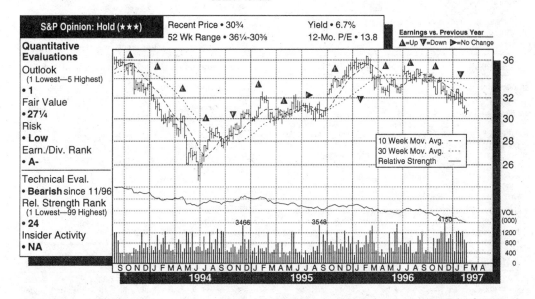

Earnings vs. Previous Year
▲=Up ▼=Down ▶=No Change

10 Week Mov. Avg. - - -
30 Week Mov. Avg. ·····
Relative Strength ——

Overview - 13-FEB-97

Before non-recurring items, Florida Progress increased its earnings by 4.4% in 1996, reflecting the favorable demographics in Florida. The state has a good economy, and the customer base is expected to continue to grow at about 2% per year. Florida Power, which earned $2.40 a share, compared to $2.27 in 1995, has one of the lowest electricity prices in western Florida and should be able to successfully compete against independent power producers and other utilities, if deregulation in Florida were to speed up. Although the Crystal River nuclear plant was placed on the Nuclear Regulatory Commission's Watch List, management should be able to restart the plant in the near future. Management also seems to be committed to cutting costs and divesting from its remaining non-energy related segment, Mid-Continent Life. Regardless of the outcome of these issues, the company should be able to boost revenue another 3%-5% in 1997.

Valuation - 13-FEB-97

Population growth and the bright economic outlook in Florida should keep revenues on a steady climb. The dividend is secure and should grow another 2% in 1997, which makes the yield attractive. The stock price relative to revenue and cash flow is low enough to limit the downside risk. On the upside, restructuring and refinancing activity will continue to be a drag on earnings, which should rise 3%-5%, with a comparable move in the stock price. We see a total return of 10%-15% in 1997 and recommend holding the shares for income and growth.

Key Stock Statistics

S&P EPS Est. 1997	2.70	Tang. Bk. Value/Share	21.86
P/E on S&P Est. 1997	11.4	Beta	0.29
Dividend Rate/Share	2.06	Shareholders	40,100
Shs. outstg. (M)	97.0	Market cap. (B)	$ 3.0
Avg. daily vol. (M)	0.222	Inst. holdings	38%

Value of $10,000 invested 5 years ago: NA

Fiscal Year Ending Dec. 31

	1996	1995	1994	1993	1992	1991
Revenues (Million $)						
1Q	739.5	703.2	639.2	493.0	464.0	457.0
2Q	773.6	742.9	693.2	553.3	512.0	528.0
3Q	879.0	862.6	756.2	768.9	627.0	589.0
4Q	774.9	746.9	682.9	633.5	494.0	501.0
Yr.	3,158	3,056	2,772	2,449	2,095	2,075
Earnings Per Share ($)						
1Q	0.50	0.49	0.41	0.38	0.36	0.43
2Q	0.61	0.58	0.58	0.49	0.41	0.54
3Q	1.01	0.95	0.80	0.93	0.86	0.87
4Q	0.47	0.48	0.49	0.42	0.41	0.32
Yr.	2.59	2.50	2.28	2.22	2.06	2.16

Next earnings report expected: mid April

Dividend Data (Dividends have been paid since 1937.)

Amount ($)	Date Decl.	Ex-Div. Date	Stock of Record	Payment Date
0.515	Feb. 08	Mar. 01	Mar. 05	Mar. 20 '96
0.515	May. 20	Jun. 03	Jun. 05	Jun. 20 '96
0.515	Aug. 16	Sep. 03	Sep. 05	Sep. 20 '96
0.515	Nov. 21	Nov. 27	Dec. 02	Dec. 20 '96

A Division of The McGraw·Hill Companies

Business Summary - 13-FEB-97

This holding company owns Florida Power Corp., which provides electric service to about 1.3 million customers in 32 of Florida's 67 counties. In 1996, Florida Power accounted for 76% of total revenues and 92% of earnings. Diversified operations include coal mining, marine operations, rail services and life insurance. Electric sales in recent years were derived as follows:

	1996	1995	1994	1993
Residential	46%	46%	46%	47%
Commercial	26%	27%	28%	28%
Industrial	13%	12%	12%	12%
Other	15%	15%	14%	13%

The fuel mix in 1995 was 39% coal, 19% nuclear, 12% oil, 4% gas and 26% purchased power. Peak load in 1995 (winter) was 7,722 mw, and system capability (including purchased power sources) was 8,526 mw, for a 10.4% capacity margin. Retail electric kwh sales increased an average of 3.1% annually during the past 10-year period. FPC's customer base grew 2% in 1996.

Important Developments

Jan. '97—FPC signed an agreement to acquire the 220-megawatt Tiger Bay cogeneration facility near Ft. Meade, FL, for $445 million. By buying this facility and terminating the purchased power obligations, FPC and its customers are expected to realize substantial long-term savings. This was part of an ongoing strategy to reduce and restructure the financial impact of long-term purchase power contracts that became disadvantageous in the midst of lower-than-predicted fuel costs, lower construction costs and more efficient plant technology. Separately, the company accounced that the Nuclear Regulatory Commission (NRC) placed FPC's Crystal River nuclear plant on the NRC's Watch List as a category two plant, which is a plant that is authorized to operate but will be closely monitored by the NRC. The NRC cited the plant's 1996 decline in engineering performance as one of the main reasons for placing it on the list. Management believes that the NRC's action will not significantly affect Florida Power's plans to restart the nuclear unit.

Dec. '96—FPC announced that it completed the spin-off of Echelon International (NYSE: EIN), the company's real estate lending and leasing unit, under which FPC shareholders received one EIN share for each 15 shares of FLorida Progress held. The spin-off was part of FPC's continuing plan to focus on its core utility and coal and transportation businesses.

Capitalization

Long Term Debt: $1,776,900,000 (12/96).
Subsid. Cum. Pfd. Stk.: $33,500,000.

Per Share Data ($)

(Year Ended Dec. 31)	1996	1995	1994	1993	1992	1991	1990	1989	1988	1987
Tangible Bk. Val.	NA	21.55	20.85	20.40	19.83	19.15	18.37	17.92	17.20	16.51
Earnings	2.59	2.50	2.28	2.22	2.06	2.16	2.33	2.45	2.35	2.49
Dividends	2.05	2.02	1.99	1.95	1.90	1.84	1.78	1.72	1.67	1.61
Payout Ratio	79%	81%	87%	88%	92%	88%	77%	70%	71%	65%
Prices - High	36½	35¾	33⅝	36⅜	33¼	31½	27	26⅞	25¼	29¼
- Low	31½	29⅜	24¾	31¼	27⅞	24½	22⅜	22¼	21⅜	19⅝
P/E Ratio - High	14	14	15	16	16	15	12	11	11	12
- Low	12	12	11	14	14	11	10	9	9	8

Income Statement Analysis (Million $)

	1996	1995	1994	1993	1992	1991	1990	1989	1988	1987
Revs.	NA	2,272	2,081	1,958	1,774	1,719	1,709	1,627	1,469	1,472
Depr.	NA	294	262	240	210	206	161	155	137	134
Maint.	NA	114	123	137	140	135	126	138	118	113
Fxd. Chgs. Cov.	NA	3.5	3.2	3.2	3.0	2.7	2.8	2.9	2.9	3.3
Constr. Credits	NA	7.3	10.9	15.6	18.7	9.4	4.2	5.2	4.1	4.3
Eff. Tax Rate	NA	35%	33%	35%	32%	33%	36%	30%	24%	37%
Net Inc.	NA	239	212	196	176	175	180	187	180	188

Balance Sheet & Other Fin. Data (Million $)

	1996	1995	1994	1993	1992	1991	1990	1989	1988	1987
Gross Prop.	NA	6,058	5,878	5,674	5,252	4,851	4,581	4,382	4,183	4,049
Cap. Exp.	NA	335	368	462	494	360	277	261	207	199
Net Prop.	NA	3,609	3,669	3,641	3,442	3,193	3,077	2,998	2,930	2,907
Capitalization:										
LT Debt	NA	1,685	1,860	1,867	1,656	1,581	1,326	1,127	1,050	1,117
% LT Debt	NA	43	47	49	46	47	45	41	40	43
Pfd.	NA	139	144	149	216	231	234	234	234	234
% Pfd.	NA	3.50	3.60	3.90	6.00	6.80	7.80	8.60	9.00	8.90
Common	NA	2,078	1,984	1,821	1,738	1,588	1,424	1,372	1,317	1,265
% Common	NA	53	50	48	48	47	48	50	51	48
Total Cap.	NA	4,698	4,842	4,712	4,556	4,367	3,955	3,690	3,538	3,485
Oper. Ratio	NA	85.9	59.9	63.9	67.2	65.5	66.2	66.5	65.2	NA
% Earn. on Net Prop.	NA	14.4	13.0	12.5	12.2	13.3	14.3	NA	NA	NA
% Ret. on Revs.	NA	10.5	10.1	10.0	9.9	10.2	10.5	11.5	12.2	12.8
% Ret. On Invest.Cap	NA	8.0	10.0	7.1	6.8	7.9	8.8	9.1	8.8	9.3
% Return On Com.Eqty	NA	11.8	11.1	11.0	10.6	11.6	12.9	13.9	13.9	15.5

Data as orig. reptd.; bef. results of disc. opers. and/or spec. items. Per share data adj. for stk. divs. as of ex-div. date. E-Estimated. NA-Not Available. NM-Not Meaningful. NR-Not Ranked.

Office—Barnett Tower, One Progress Plaza, St. Petersburg, FL 33701 (Mail: Box 33028, St. Petersburg, FL 33733-8028). **Tel**—(813) 824-6400. **Chrmn & CEO**—J. R. Critchfield. **Pres & COO**—R. Korpan. **Sr VP & CFO**—J. R. Heinicka. **VP & Secy**—K. E. Armstrong. **Investor Contact**—Mark A. Myers (813) 866-4245. **Dirs**—J. B. Critchfield, W. D. Frederick, M. P. Graney, A. J. Keesler Jr., R. Korpan, C. V. McKee, V. J. Naimoli, R. A. Nunis, C. B. Reed, J. D. Ruffier, R. T. Stuart Jr., J. G. Wittner. **Transfer Agent & Registrar**—ChaseMellon Shareholder Services, Ridgefield Park, NJ. **Incorporated**—in Florida in 1899; reincorporated in Florida in 1982. **Empl**—7,174. **S&P Analyst:** J. Robert Cho

STANDARD &POOR'S
STOCK REPORTS

GTE Corp.

934P

NYSE Symbol **GTE**

In S&P 500

15-FEB-97

Industry: Telecommunications

Summary: GTE is the largest U.S.-based local telephone holding company and one of the largest cellular carriers.

S&P Opinion: Accumulate (★★★★)	Recent Price • 48⅛	Yield • 3.9%
	52 Wk Range • 49¼-37¾	12-Mo. P/E • 16.7

Quantitative Evaluations

Outlook
(1 Lowest—5 Highest)
• **1**

Fair Value
• **41¾**

Risk
• **Low**

Earn./Div. Rank
• **B+**

Technical Eval.
• **Bullish** since 11/96

Rel. Strength Rank
(1 Lowest—99 Highest)
• **73**

Insider Activity
• **NA**

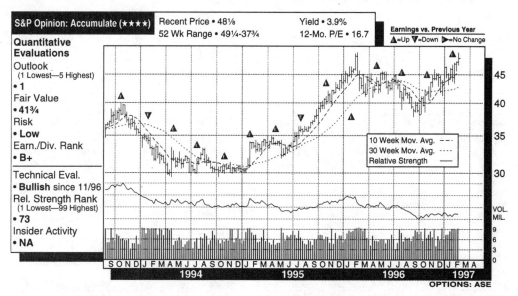

Earnings vs. Previous Year
▲=Up ▼=Down ▶=No Change

10 Week Mov. Avg. – –
30 Week Mov. Avg. - - - -
Relative Strength —

OPTIONS: ASE

Overview - 06-FEB-97

Revenues are expected to grow 6% to 8% in 1997, driven by growth in the company's core local telephone and wireless businesses, as well as gains in new initiatives such as long-distance, internet and video services. Unlike the regional Bell companies, GTE is free to offer long-distance services in its own regions. GTE expects to double its long-distance customer base in 1997, and increase long-distance revenues about seven times. The company continues to develop its overseas business, and seeks to double income from international operations by 2000. Underdeveloped telecommunications networks in GTE's international markets offer an excellent opportunity for the company to develop new sources of revenue.

Valuation - 06-FEB-97

The shares have recovered following unwarranted worries about increased competition since the enactment of the telecommunications bill last February. The shares should continue to climb, for two reasons. First, GTE's regions are typically less densely populated than others. New competition is therefore not expected to be as intense as that faced by the Bell companies. Second, unlike the Bells, GTE may immediately offer long-distance service in its own regions. This should help offset new local competition. Long-term results will benefit from strong demand from new and enhanced services, such as long distance, voice messaging, caller ID and the Internet, as well as rapid cellular growth. In addition to the company's promising long-term prospects, the stock offers a healthy dividend yield. GTE is trading at 14 times our 1997 EPS estimate of $3.20, at the lower end of its historical P/E range and above our projected high single-digit long-term growth rate. We recommend the shares for above-average total return.

Key Stock Statistics

S&P EPS Est. 1997	3.20	Tang. Bk. Value/Share	4.63
P/E on S&P Est. 1997	15.0	Beta	0.77
S&P EPS Est. 1998	3.50	Shareholders	538,000
Dividend Rate/Share	1.88	Market cap. (B)	$ 46.3
Shs. outstg. (M)	961.8	Inst. holdings	41%
Avg. daily vol. (M)	1.933		

Value of $10,000 invested 5 years ago: $ 17,782

Fiscal Year Ending Dec. 31

	1996	1995	1994	1993	1992	1991
Revenues (Million $)						
1Q	4,951	4,665	4,750	4,830	4,820	4,690
2Q	5,293	4,932	4,960	4,920	5,060	4,850
3Q	5,344	4,996	5,000	4,940	4,970	4,850
4Q	5,751	5,364	5,250	5,060	5,130	5,230
Yr.	21,339	19,957	19,940	19,750	19,980	19,620
Earnings Per Share ($)						
1Q	0.63	0.56	0.52	0.48	0.43	0.21
2Q	0.66	0.60	0.62	0.46	0.45	0.44
3Q	0.78	0.72	0.69	0.59	0.52	0.51
4Q	0.82	0.74	0.72	-0.50	0.55	0.53
Yr.	2.89	2.62	2.55	1.03	1.95	1.69

Next earnings report expected: mid April

Dividend Data (Dividends have been paid since 1936.)

Amount ($)	Date Decl.	Ex-Div. Date	Stock of Record	Payment Date
0.470	Apr. 17	May. 20	May. 22	Jul. 01 '96
0.470	Aug. 01	Aug. 20	Aug. 22	Oct. 01 '96
0.470	Nov. 07	Nov. 20	Nov. 22	Jan. 01 '97
0.470	Jan. 16	Feb. 18	Feb. 20	Apr. 01 '97

STANDARD
&POOR'S
STOCK REPORTS

GTE Corporation

934P

15-FEB-97

Business Summary - 06-FEB-97

GTE is the largest U.S.-based telephone holding company, and engages in unregulated telecom and other businesses. Recent segment contributions were:

	1995	1994
Local services	29%	27%
Network access services	22%	22%
Toll services	13%	17%
Cellular services	11%	8%
Directory services	7%	7%
Other services and sales	18%	19%

In the U.S., GTE provides local exchange telephone service through over 20.0 million access lines in portions of 28 states. It is selling or trading non-strategic operations. Through a 20% interest in the Venezuelan national telephone company, it provides local, national and international long-distance services in that country. Subsidiaries also provide telephone service through about 3.1 million access lines in Canada, Argentina and the Dominican Republic.

The telecommunications products and services segment provides directory advertising; intelligence and electronic defense systems; specialized telecommunications services and systems; aircraft-passenger telecommunications; and cellular telephone service in the U.S., Canada, Venezuela, Argentina and the Dominican Republic. At December 31, 1996, GTE provided cellular service to about 3,749,000 subscribers in the U.S.

In August 1995, GTE agreed to join the Walt Disney Co., Ameritech, BellSouth and SBC Communications as an equal partner in Americast, a video programming and interactive services venture.

Important Developments

Dec. '96—The company announced the start-up of cellular service in Sapporo, Japan, and expects the number of cellular subscribers to reach 310,000 by the year 2000, up from 25,000 at the operation's inception.

Nov. '96—GTE was awarded the General Services Administration's Federal Wireless Telecommunications Services contract, valued at an estimated $300 million over eight years. Under the contract, the GTE/Bell Atlantic NYNEX Mobile team will provide wireless and data telecommunications services to a potential customer base of over three million federal government employees nationwide.

Nov. '96—GTE announced the commercial launch of its digital wireless service in Austin, TX. The launch was the first in a series of GTE digital wireless deployments in company's markets nationwide. GTE plans to deploy wireless digital technologies in its San Jose, CA, market in December, and in most of its other major markets over the next 15 months.

Capitalization

Long Term Debt: $13,578,000,000 (9/96).
Minority Interest: $2,301,000,000.

Per Share Data ($)

(Year Ended Dec. 31)	1996	1995	1994	1993	1992	1991	1990	1989	1988	1987
Tangible Bk. Val.	NA	4.21	8.63	7.75	8.30	9.75	11.52	12.01	12.46	11.92
Cash Flow	NA	6.41	6.13	4.65	5.58	5.38	6.40	6.04	5.68	5.40
Earnings	2.89	2.62	2.55	1.03	1.95	1.69	2.26	2.08	1.79	1.65
Dividends	1.88	1.88	1.88	1.83	1.76	1.64	1.52	1.40	1.30	1.24
Payout Ratio	65%	72%	74%	178%	94%	98%	68%	68%	72%	75%
Prices - High	49¼	45⅛	35¼	39⅞	35¾	35	36	35⅝	23	22⅜
- Low	37¾	30	29½	34⅛	28⅞	27½	23½	21½	16⅞	14¾
P/E Ratio - High	17	17	14	39	18	21	16	17	13	14
- Low	13	11	12	33	15	16	10	10	9	9

Income Statement Analysis (Million $)

	1996	1995	1994	1993	1992	1991	1990	1989	1988	1987
Revs.	NA	19,957	19,944	19,748	19,984	19,621	18,374	17,424	16,460	15,421
Depr.	NA	3,675	3,432	3,419	3,289	3,254	2,753	2,621	2,559	2,474
Maint.	NA	NA	NA	2,136	2,097	2,206	NA	NA	NA	NA
Constr. Credits	NA	Nil	28.0	40.0	43.0	56.0	59.0	NA	NA	NA
Eff. Tax Rate	NA	37%	37%	34%	34%	29%	29%	30%	32%	34%
Net Inc.	NA	2,538	2,451	990	1,787	1,529	1,541	1,417	1,225	1,119

Balance Sheet & Other Fin. Data (Million $)

	1996	1995	1994	1993	1992	1991	1990	1989	1988	1987
Gross Prop.	NA	50,947	44,287	43,099	43,354	41,846	34,890	NA	NA	NA
Net Prop.	NA	22,437	26,631	26,362	27,300	26,969	22,327	NA	NA	NA
Cap. Exp.	NA	4,034	4,192	3,893	3,909	3,965	3,453	NA	NA	NA
Total Cap.	NA	23,048	27,899	27,002	28,994	33,807	26,787	24,986	23,904	23,303
Fxd. Chgs. Cov.	NA	4.3	4.4	3.4	2.8	2.5	2.7	NA	NA	NA
Capitalization:										
LT Debt	NA	12,744	12,163	13,019	14,182	16,049	NA	NA	NA	NA
Pfd.	NA	Nil	1,741	1,373	1,363	1,785	1,818	NA	NA	NA
Common	NA	6,871	10,473	9,482	9,964	10,854	8,647	NA	NA	NA
% Ret. on Revs.	NA	12.7	12.3	5.0	8.9	7.8	8.4	8.1	7.4	7.3
% Ret. On Invest.Cap	NA	14.1	13.9	8.2	10.4	9.6	10.5	NA	NA	NA
% Return On Com.Eqty	NA	29.2	23.3	10.0	16.9	14.5	18.1	NA	NA	NA
% Earn. on Net Prop.	NA	33.7	12.5	7.4	12.0	11.5	12.5	NA	NA	NA
% LT Debt of Cap.	NA	65.0	37.4	54.5	55.6	56.0	53.4	NA	NA	NA
Capital. % Pfd.	NA	Nil	5.3	5.8	5.3	6.2	8.1	NA	NA	NA
Capital. % Common	NA	35.0	32.1	39.7	39.1	37.8	38.5	NA	NA	NA

Data as orig. reptd.; bef. results of disc. opers. and/or spec. items. Per share data adj. for stk. divs. as of ex-div. date. E-Estimated. NA-Not Available. NM-Not Meaningful. NR-Not Ranked.

Office—One Stamford Forum, Stamford, CT 06904. **Tel**—(203) 965-2000. **Chrmn & CEO**—C. R. Lee. **Pres**—K. B. Foster. **SVP-Fin & CFO**—J. M. Kelly. **Secy**—M. Drost. **VP & Treas**—D. J. Cohrs. **Dirs**—E. L. Artzt, J. R. Barker, E. H. Budd, K. B. Foster, J. L. Johnson, R. W. Jones, J. L. Ketelson, C. R. Lee, M. T. Masin, S. O. Moose, R. E. Palmer, H. Sloan, R. D. Storey. **Transfer Agents & Registrars**—First National Bank of Boston. **Incorporated**—in New York in 1935. **Empl**—106,000. **S&P Analyst:** Philip D. Wohl

STANDARD &POOR'S
STOCK REPORTS

Health & Retirement Prop. Trust 1112M
NYSE Symbol **HRP**

14-FEB-97

Industry: Real Estate Investment Trust

Summary: This real estate investment trust invests primarily in senior housing and health care-related real estate. It has $1.2 billion invested in 175 properties, in 30 states.

S&P Opinion: Accumulate (★★★★)	Recent Price • 19¼	Yield • 7.5%
	52 Wk Range • 20-16¼	12-Mo. P/E • 17.2

Quantitative Evaluations

Outlook (1 Lowest—5 Highest)
• **NA**

Fair Value
• **NA**

Risk
• **Low**

Earn./Div. Rank
• **NR**

Technical Eval.
• **Bullish** since 5/96

Rel. Strength Rank (1 Lowest—99 Highest)
• **51**

Insider Activity
• **NA**

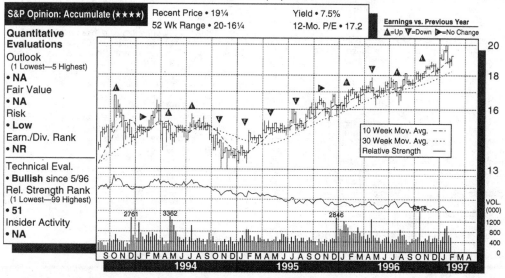

Earnings vs. Previous Year ▲=Up ▼=Down ▶=No Change

10 Week Mov. Avg. – – –
30 Week Mov. Avg. · · · · ·
Relative Strength —

Overview - 14-FEB-97

During 1996, funds from operations rose 17%, year to year, to $99.1 million ($1.50 a share, on 12% more shares), from $84.6 million ($1.43), largely the result of additional real estate investments. HRP invested a total of $241 million in new properties during the year, expanding its portfolio 25%, however, with more than half of this amount occurring in the fourth quarter, the real impact will be felt in 1997 and beyond. Interest expense has declined 7.1%, year to year, after an equity offering in late 1995 reduced debt levels for most of the year. The company continues to look for additional properties which are not dependent on Medicare or Medicaid funding; it has budgeted $200 million for new real estate investments in 1997. At December 31, 1996, the portfolio totaled $928.8 million, after depreciation, versus $722.4 million at 1995 year end. Looking into 1997, earnings should rise as HRP continues to expand its portfolio; HRP's April shelf filing to offer up to $750 million ($510 million remaining) in debt and/or equity securities will help support this growth.

Valuation - 14-FEB-97

Earnings in 1997 should benefit from the addition of more properties, improved credit terms, continued high quality tenants and contributions from fast growing (and more cyclical) Hospitality Properties Trust (NYSE: HPT), a hotel REIT that is 15% owned by HRP. However, HRP is not without risk, as the trust's reliance on floating rate medium and shorter-term debt can significantly raise funding costs in a rising interest rate environment. The substitution of such debt with the subordinated debt, as well as HRP's use of interest rate caps to offset risk, should decrease exposure. HRP's shares, yielding almost 7.4% and trading at 12 times our 1997 FFO estimate of $1.60 a share, are attractive for tax-deferred retirement accounts and income investors.

Key Stock Statistics

S&P EPS Est. 1997	1.45	Tang. Bk. Value/Share	10.27
P/E on S&P Est. 1997	13.3	Beta	0.70
Dividend Rate/Share	1.44	Shareholders	3,800
Shs. outstg. (M)	66.3	Market cap. (B)	$ 1.3
Avg. daily vol. (M)	0.140	Inst. holdings	18%

Value of $10,000 invested 5 years ago: $ 20,883

Fiscal Year Ending Dec. 31

	1996	1995	1994	1993	1992	1991
Revenues (Million $)						
1Q	27.74	25.99	17.55	12.70	11.50	10.40
2Q	28.83	30.50	19.92	13.80	11.90	10.90
3Q	29.04	28.97	23.82	14.70	12.40	11.00
4Q	30.81	27.23	25.40	15.35	12.90	11.50
Yr.	116.4	112.7	86.68	56.49	48.70	43.80
Earnings Per Share ($)						
1Q	0.28	0.31	0.37	0.27	0.24	0.26
2Q	0.34	0.26	0.28	0.27	0.25	0.26
3Q	0.28	0.27	0.27	0.28	0.25	0.26
4Q	0.27	0.24	0.09	0.28	0.28	0.24
Yr.	1.17	1.08	0.98	1.10	1.02	1.01

Next earnings report expected: late April

Dividend Data (Dividends have been paid since 1987.)

Amount ($)	Date Decl.	Ex-Div. Date	Stock of Record	Payment Date
0.350	Apr. 10	Apr. 23	Apr. 25	May. 21 '96
0.350	Jul. 01	Jul. 23	Jul. 25	Aug. 22 '96
0.360	Sep. 18	Oct. 15	Oct. 17	Nov. 22 '96
0.360	Jan. 10	Jan. 22	Jan. 24	Feb. 20 '97

A Division of The McGraw·Hill Companies

STANDARD
&POOR'S
STOCK REPORTS

Health and Retirement Properties Trust

1112M

14-FEB-97

Business Summary - 14-FEB-97

This real estate investment trust primarily invests in income-producing nursing homes and other long-term care facilities, assisted living facilities, retirement complexes, and facilities that provide subacute and specialty rehabilitation services. In August 1995, HRP sold a majority of its interest in Hospitality Properties Trust (HPT), a REIT specializing in hotel properties, to the public. At December 31, 1995, HRP held a 32% equity stake in HPT. In April, HPT's public stock offering of 14.5 million shares caused HRP's ownership to drop to 15%.

At year-end 1995, HRP owned 102 properties with 13,741 beds, acquired for a total of $778.2 million, and had mortgage investments in 57 properties with 5,968 beds totaling $141.3 million, for a total portfolio of $919.5 million and 19,709 beds. The investment portfolio composition was 50% in long term care facilities, including 17% in nursing homes; 34% in retirement and assisted living centers; 10% in HPT, and 6% in other health care. The facilities were in Nebraska (16), California (15), Iowa (13), Colorado (11), North Carolina (11), Connecticut (9), Wisconsin (9), Ohio (7), Massachusetts (8), Texas (6), Vermont (8), Kansas (9), Florida (6), Arizona (5), Wyoming (4), South Dakota (3), Virginia (3), Missouri (3), Pennsylvania (2), Illinois (2), Michigan (2), Kentucky, Georgia, Louisiana, New Jersey, New Hampshire, Maryland and Washington (7). The investment in Hospitality Properties Trust included 37 properties.

HRP aims to provide income for distribution to shareholders and capital growth resulting from appreciation in the residual value of owned properties.

HRPT Advisors acts as adviser to the trust and provides management services and investment advice. The adviser receives an annual fee equal to 0.7% of the average invested capital of the trust (as defined) up to $250 million, and 0.5% of amounts over $250 million, plus incentive compensation. The 1995 fee was $5,183,000, up from $3,839,000 in 1994.

In January 1996, HRP sold approximately 7.0 million common shares to the public at $16 a share, raising over $105 million. Proceeds from the sale were used to paydown about $100 million in revolving debt.

Important Developments

Feb. '97—HRP said that in 1996 it spent $241 million on new investments, which included 10 medical office buildings, four retirement facilities, five nusing homes, and two medical clinics.

Oct. '96—HRP closed on its $240 million convertible subordinated debenture offer, with the proceeds used to repay a $147 million balance on its credit facility and for general business purposes. In addition, it announced it will take a $1.5 million charge in the fourth quarter ($3.9 million for the year), related to the early extinguishment of debt.

Capitalization

Total Debt: $492,175,000 (12/96).

Per Share Data ($)

(Year Ended Dec. 31)	1996	1995	1994	1993	1992	1991	1990	1989	1988	1987
Tangible Bk. Val.	NA	10.39	10.49	10.00	8.53	8.76	7.78	8.24	8.30	8.36
Earnings	1.17	1.08	0.98	1.10	1.02	1.01	0.89	0.76	0.77	0.85
Dividends	1.41	1.37	1.32	1.29	1.25	0.99	1.39	1.13	1.12	1.08
Payout Ratio	121%	127%	135%	117%	123%	98%	156%	149%	145%	128%
Prices - High	19⅜	16⅞	16½	16¾	14¾	14⅜	9⅞	10½	9⅜	10⅛
- Low	15⅞	13¼	13	11¼	8⅞	7⅝	7	7½	7⅜	6¾
P/E Ratio - High	17	16	17	15	14	14	11	14	12	12
- Low	14	12	13	10	9	8	8	10	10	8

Income Statement Analysis (Million $)

	1996	1995	1994	1993	1992	1991	1990	1989	1988	1987
Income Rental	NA	89.6	63.9	46.1	43.0	36.8	20.3	18.6	14.7	7.0
Income Mortg.	NA	23.1	22.8	10.4	5.7	7.0	10.1	4.6	4.2	3.8
Income Total	NA	113	86.7	56.5	48.7	43.8	32.9	23.2	18.9	10.8
Expenses Gen.	NA	29.8	19.8	12.5	12.0	10.0	9.1	5.8	4.7	2.6
Expenses Int.	NA	24.3	9.0	6.2	9.5	11.7	9.5	9.6	6.5	2.2
Prov. for Losses	NA	Nil	6.0	Nil	Nil	Nil	Nil	Nil	Nil	Nil
Depr.	NA	22.8	14.7	9.1	9.1	7.3	4.5	4.1	3.4	1.6
Net Inc.	NA	64.2	51.9	37.7	27.2	22.1	14.3	7.9	7.7	6.1

Balance Sheet & Other Fin. Data (Million $)

	1996	1995	1994	1993	1992	1991	1990	1989	1988	1987
Cash	NA	18.6	59.8	13.9	14.1	42.1	9.7	11.6	2.2	3.7
Total Assets	NA	1,000	840	528	374	341	290	206	155	155
Real Estate Invest.	NA	920	806	542	384	314	288	198	154	151
Loss Reserve	NA	Nil	Nil	Nil	Nil	Nil	Nil	Nil	Nil	Nil
Net Invest.	NA	864	767	507	358	294	275	190	149	150
ST Debt	NA	Nil	1.5	40.0	70.2	0.7	0.5	0.4	0.3	0.2
Capitalization:										
Debt	NA	270	217	33.0	69.0	103	126	70.0	70.0	62.0
Equity	NA	686	602	441	228	234	148	132	83.0	84.0
Total	NA	956	819	474	297	337	273	202	153	145
% Earn & Depr/Assets	NA	9.5	9.7	10.4	10.2	9.3	7.6	6.7	7.2	7.0
Price Times Book Value:										
Hi	NA	1.6	1.6	1.7	1.7	1.6	1.3	1.3	1.1	1.2
Low	NA	1.3	1.2	1.1	1.0	0.9	0.9	0.9	0.9	0.8

Data as orig. reptd.; bef. results of disc opers. and/or spec. items. Per share data adj. for stk. divs. as of ex-div. date. E-Estimated. NA-Not Available. NM-Not Meaningful. NR-Not Ranked.

Office—400 Centre St., Newton, MA 02158. **Tel**—(617) 332-3990. **Pres & COO**—David J. Hegarty. **Treas, CFO & Investor Contact**—Ajay Saini. **Trustees**—B. M. Gans, J. Manning, G. M. Martin, B. M. Portnoy, R. J. Watts. **Transfer Agent & Registrar**—State Street Bank & Trust Co., Quincy, MA. **Incorporated**—in Maryland in 1986. **Empl**— 0. **S&P Analyst:** E. Fitzpatrick

Landauer, Inc.

8349

ASE Symbol **LDR**

15-FEB-97

Industry:
Pollution Control

Summary: LDR provides radiation monitoring and radon gas detection services.

Quantitative Evaluations

Outlook
(1 Lowest—5 Highest)
• **2⁻**

Fair Value
• **21⅝**

Risk
• **Low**

Earn./Div. Rank
• **B+**

Technical Eval.
• **Bearish** since 7/96

Rel. Strength Rank
(1 Lowest—99 Highest)
• **39**

Insider Activity
• **NA**

Recent Price • 22⅛
52 Wk Range • 24⅞-19

Yield • 5.4%
12-Mo. P/E • 16.8

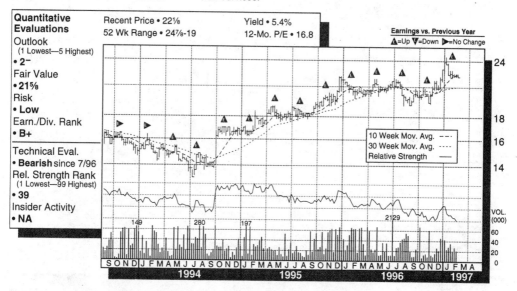

Earnings vs. Previous Year
▲=Up ▼=Down ▶=No Change

10 Week Mov. Avg. – – –
30 Week Mov. Avg. • • • •
Relative Strength ——

Business Profile - 13-FEB-97

Landauer recently said it was continuing its operational and market development of a new radiation measurement technology based on the principal of optically stimulated luminescence. The company also noted that it completed during the second half of FY 96 (Sep.) the development of RadPro, an integrated software package designed to enable users to perform a variety of analytical and administrative functions from the costumer's own database of dosimetry information. In international operations, LDR has entered into a joint marketing agreement in the UK whereby the newly privatized Atomic Energy Authority is to begin using and selling Landauer's complete range of dosimetry services, primarily to the nuclear power industry and to defense and industrial customers. In November 1996 LDR increased its cash dividend by 9.1% to $0.30 quarterly. Officers and directors own about 13% of the less than nine million shares outstanding.

Operational Review - 13-FEB-97

Net sales and operating profit for the three months ended December 31, 1996, advanced 5.3% and 8.2%, respectively, year to year, reflecting contributions from radiation dosimetry services and higher radon service agreement sales. After 5.3% lower other income and taxes at 35.6%, versus 37.6% (increased foreign business activities provided higher tax credits), net income was up 10%, to $0.33 a share from $0.30.

Stock Performance - 14-FEB-97

In the past 30 trading days, LDR's shares have declined 6%, compared to a 8% rise in the S&P 500. Average trading volume for the past five days was 4,060 shares, compared with the 40-day moving average of 6,051 shares.

Key Stock Statistics

Dividend Rate/Share	1.20	Shareholders	600
Shs. outstg. (M)	8.5	Market cap. (B)	$0.188
Avg. daily vol. (M)	0.005	Inst. holdings	52%
Tang. Bk. Value/Share	2.60		
Beta	0.08		

Value of $10,000 invested 5 years ago: $ 16,541

Fiscal Year Ending Sep. 30

	1997	1996	1995	1994	1993	1992
Revenues (Million $)						
1Q	9.15	8.69	8.01	7.46	7.14	6.50
2Q	—	9.49	8.67	8.32	7.64	6.95
3Q	—	9.01	8.57	7.82	7.16	7.17
4Q	—	9.33	8.78	7.96	7.33	7.20
Yr.	—	36.52	34.03	31.65	29.27	27.82
Earnings Per Share ($)						
1Q	0.33	0.30	0.27	0.24	0.24	0.23
2Q	—	0.34	0.31	0.28	0.25	0.24
3Q	—	0.31	0.29	0.26	0.22	0.22
4Q	—	0.34	0.32	0.27	0.24	0.24
Yr.	—	1.29	1.19	1.05	0.95	0.93

Next earnings report expected: late April

Dividend Data (Dividends have been paid since 1990.)

Amount ($)	Date Decl.	Ex-Div. Date	Stock of Record	Payment Date
0.275	Mar. 13	Mar. 26	Mar. 28	Apr. 11 '96
0.275	Jun. 12	Jun. 25	Jun. 27	Jul. 11 '96
0.275	Sep. 18	Sep. 30	Oct. 02	Oct. 10 '96
0.300	Nov. 07	Dec. 24	Dec. 27	Jan. 09 '97

Business Summary - 13-FEB-97

Landauer (formerly Tech/Ops Landauer) offers a service for measuring, primarily through film and thermoluminescent badges worn by client personnel, the dosages of x-ray, gamma radiation, and other penetrating ionizing radiations to which the wearer has been exposed. While most revenues are derived from U.S. customers, these services are marketed in the UK and Canada as well.

Operations also include a service for detecting radon gas. Personnel dosimetry services are also offered for monitoring nitrous oxide anesthetic gases. As of the end of FY 96 (Sep.), these services constituted a small part of revenues.

The HomeBuyer's Preferred subsidiary offers a radon monitoring service, and when warranted, remediation to purchasers of personal residences. This service is targeted to corporate employee relocation programs, which have generally regarded radon as a serious environmental hazard.

Tokyo-based Nagase-Landauer (50%-owned) provides radiation monitoring services in Japan.

Marketing is carried on primarily by full-time company personnel located in Illinois, Michigan, California, New Hampshire, New Jersey, Georgia, Texas, and the UK. U.S. sales personnel also market these services in Canada. In addition, other firms and individuals market the company's services on a commission basis, primarily to small customers.

Landauer has more than 45,000 customers, representing almost 900,000 individuals who use the company's services. Typically, a client will contract for a year's service in advance, representing 12 monthly readings and reports.

Radon gas detection kits are marketed primarily to institutional customers and retail customers through certain major retail chains. LDR markets to wholesale distributors that in turn sell to smaller retailers.

The company holds exclusive world-wide licenses to patent rights for certain technologies which measure radiation exposure to crystalline materials when stimulated with light. These licenses were acquired by Landauer from Battelle Memorial Institute in 1994 as part of a collaborative effort to develop a new generation of radiation dosimetry technology. In addition, Landauer holds certain patent rights which relate to various designs of alpha-track radon detection devices. These patents expire from the years 2000 through 2010.

Research and development expenses, which are charged to selling, general, and administrative expenses as incurred, amounted to $1.53 million in FY 96 (4.2% of total revenues).

Capitalization

Long Term Debt: None (12/96).

Per Share Data ($)

(Year Ended Sep. 30)	1996	1995	1994	1993	1992	1991	1990	1989	1988	1987
Tangible Bk. Val.	2.60	2.46	2.29	2.00	1.83	2.03	1.65	1.66	0.93	0.90
Cash Flow	1.58	1.47	1.30	1.17	1.12	1.06	0.94	0.85	0.67	0.54
Earnings	1.29	1.19	1.05	0.95	0.93	0.88	0.77	0.76	0.60	0.49
Dividends	1.10	1.00	0.88	0.80	1.15	0.50	0.80	Nil	Nil	Nil
Payout Ratio	85%	84%	84%	85%	123%	57%	104%	Nil	Nil	Nil
Prices - High	24⅞	20⅜	17	17¼	21⅜	17⅞	15⅛	17⅛	12¼	4⅞
- Low	19	16¼	13⅛	14⅝	14½	14¼	10¾	9⅛	4⅞	4⅝
P/E Ratio - High	19	17	16	18	23	20	20	23	21	10
- Low	15	14	13	15	16	16	14	12	8	9

Income Statement Analysis (Million $)

	1996	1995	1994	1993	1992	1991	1990	1989	1988	1987
Revs.	36.5	34.0	31.7	29.3	27.8	26.9	24.7	25.9	19.8	17.2
Oper. Inc.	18.3	17.0	15.4	14.0	13.2	12.6	10.8	10.4	8.4	7.4
Depr.	2.5	2.4	2.1	1.9	1.6	1.6	1.4	0.8	0.6	0.5
Int. Exp.	Nil	Nil	Nil	Nil	Nil	Nil	0.0	0.0	0.0	0.0
Pretax Inc.	17.4	16.0	14.2	12.8	12.2	11.8	10.3	10.2	8.0	7.2
Eff. Tax Rate	38%	37%	38%	37%	36%	37%	37%	38%	37%	45%
Net Inc.	10.9	10.1	8.9	8.0	7.9	7.4	6.5	6.4	5.0	4.0

Balance Sheet & Other Fin. Data (Million $)

	1996	1995	1994	1993	1992	1991	1990	1989	1988	1987
Cash	11.2	8.4	6.2	4.3	10.9	12.3	7.8	8.3	2.0	0.2
Curr. Assets	21.3	17.3	14.1	11.9	17.0	19.0	13.9	14.6	7.9	4.5
Total Assets	41.6	38.7	35.6	32.1	29.6	30.4	24.9	25.0	17.3	12.7
Curr. Liab.	16.7	15.0	13.1	11.9	10.7	9.6	7.3	6.8	5.4	4.4
LT Debt	Nil	Nil	Nil	Nil	Nil	Nil	Nil	0.3	0.3	0.3
Common Eqty.	24.9	23.8	22.5	20.2	18.9	20.7	17.5	17.7	11.3	7.8
Total Cap.	24.9	23.8	22.5	20.2	18.9	20.8	17.6	18.1	11.9	8.4
Cap. Exp.	1.8	2.1	1.5	2.7	1.7	0.9	1.2	1.0	1.1	0.9
Cash Flow	13.4	12.4	11.0	9.9	9.5	9.0	7.9	7.2	5.7	4.4
Curr. Ratio	1.3	1.2	1.1	1.0	1.6	2.0	1.9	2.1	1.5	1.0
% LT Debt of Cap.	Nil	Nil	Nil	Nil	Nil	Nil	Nil	1.6	2.6	3.9
% Net Inc.of Revs.	16.7	29.6	28.1	27.4	28.3	27.6	26.3	24.7	25.4	23.1
% Ret. on Assets	27.1	27.0	26.3	26.0	26.3	26.9	26.1	30.2	33.6	33.2
% Ret. on Equity	40.3	43.4	41.7	41.0	39.7	38.9	37.0	44.1	52.8	55.5

Data as orig. reptd.; bef. results of disc. opers. and/or spec. items. Per share data adj. for stk. divs. as of ex-div. date. E-Estimated. NA-Not Available. NM-Not Meaningful. NR-Not Ranked.

Office—2 Science Rd., Glenwood, IL 60425-1586. **Tel**—(708) 755-7000. **Chrmn**—M. G. Schorr. **Pres & CEO**—T. M. Fulton. **VP-CFO, Treas, Secy & Investor Contact**—James M. O'Connell. **Dirs**—R. J. Cronin, G. D. Eppen, T. M. Fulton, R. R. Risk, P. B. Rosenberg, H. Roth, Jr., M. G. Schorr, M. D. Winfield. **Transfer Agent & Registrar**—American Stock Transfer, NYC. **Incorporated**—in Delaware in 1988. **Empl**— 260. **S&P Analyst:** N.J. DeVita

18-FEB-97

Industry:
Real Estate Investment Trust

Summary: The largest healthcare REIT in the U.S., Meditrust specializes in nursing homes and other long-term care investments.

S&P Opinion: Accumulate (★★★★)

Recent Price • 38¼	Yield • 7.3%
52 Wk Range • 40⅝-31¾	12-Mo. P/E • 14.4

Quantitative Evaluations

Outlook
(1 Lowest—5 Highest)
• **NA**

Fair Value
• **NA**

Risk
• **Low**

Earn./Div. Rank
• **NR**

Technical Eval.
• **Bearish** since 11/96

Rel. Strength Rank
(1 Lowest—99 Highest)
• **37**

Insider Activity
• **Neutral**

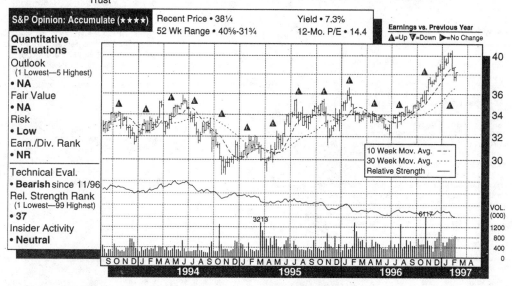

Earnings vs. Previous Year
▲=Up ▼=Down ▶=No Change

10 Week Mov. Avg. – – –
30 Week Mov. Avg. ·······
Relative Strength —

Overview - 19-FEB-97

Funds from operations (an important measure of operating performance for a REIT, because depreciation and amortization, which are non-cash charges, typically comprise an appreciable component of net income) is expected to increase in 1997 to $3.15 a share from 1996's $3.01(1995 FFO was $2.86 a share). The primary engine driving profits is new property investments. In 1996, new property investments totaled $606 million. For 1997, acquisitions should total about $500 million. MT generally realizes a positive spread of about 3.5% over its financing costs on new property additions. The great majority of investments will be concentrated in nursing homes and assisted living centers, although the medical office portfolio should also grow. Rental revenues could benefit in the long term from escalator clauses specified in certain contracts.

Valuation - 19-FEB-97

The shares are rated accumulate. Meditrust enjoys a favorable long-term growth outlook, primarily due to continued new property investments. Each year the company reviews proposals requesting billions in financing, but only selects the most creditworthy applicants. MT realizes attractive spreads on its investments, partly because its long operating history allows it to issue debt at competitive rates. For example, in September 1996, the trust sold $175 million of long-term debt at less than a 1% spread over comparable treasury securities. The favorable fundamentals of the retirement housing market are another reason for our positive stance. With a growing elderly population, the demand for nursing homes and assisted living facilities is anticipated to increase steadily well into the next century. Finally, the shares offer an attractive yield (recently about 7.3%), higher than both the REIT industry average and yields on long-term government bonds.

Key Stock Statistics

S&P EPS Est. 1997	2.85	Tang. Bk. Value/Share	22.51
P/E on S&P Est. 1997	13.4	Beta	0.11
Dividend Rate/Share	2.80	Shareholders	5,200
Shs. outstg. (M)	60.9	Market cap. (B)	$ 2.3
Avg. daily vol. (M)	0.153	Inst. holdings	48%

Value of $10,000 invested 5 years ago: $ 18,781

Fiscal Year Ending Dec. 31

	1996	1995	1994	1993	1992	1991
Revenues (Million $)						
1Q	59.33	48.93	41.00	36.60	30.90	26.50
2Q	62.17	52.44	42.38	37.30	33.20	28.00
3Q	64.80	52.75	43.16	38.60	34.80	29.10
4Q	67.72	55.25	46.46	38.27	33.40	29.30
Yr.	254.0	209.4	173.0	150.8	132.4	112.9
Earnings Per Share ($)						
1Q	0.64	0.60	0.53	0.50	0.49	0.42
2Q	0.66	0.63	0.56	0.51	0.49	0.43
3Q	0.67	0.64	0.57	0.51	0.49	0.44
4Q	0.68	0.65	0.62	0.51	0.49	0.44
Yr.	2.66	2.52	2.28	2.03	1.95	1.75

Next earnings report expected: late April

Dividend Data (Dividends have been paid since 1986.)

Amount ($)	Date Decl.	Ex-Div. Date	Stock of Record	Payment Date
0.693	Apr. 09	Apr. 26	Apr. 30	May. 15 '96
0.697	Jul. 09	Jul. 29	Jul. 31	Aug. 15 '96
0.702	Oct. 08	Oct. 29	Oct. 31	Nov. 15 '96
0.708	Jan. 10	Jan. 29	Jan. 31	Feb. 14 '97

A Division of The **McGraw·Hill** Companies

STANDARD
&POOR'S
STOCK REPORTS

Meditrust

1466

18-FEB-97

Business Summary - 19-FEB-97

Meditrust is the largest dedicated healthcare real estate investment trust in the U.S. At December 31, 1995, property investments, based on purchase price or mortgage amount, were divided as follows:

	1995
Nursing homes	70%
Rehabilitation	14%
Medical office buildings	5%
Acute-care hospitals	4%
Other	7%

At December 31, 1995, the portfolio consisted of 41% sale/leaseback transactions, 53% mortgage loans and 6% development financing. A typical transaction has an initial lease or first mortgage term of 10 years, and the first mortgage amortizes over 25 years. After reviewing about $3 billion of investment opportunities in 1995, MT made new investments of about $358 million.

Long-term care facilities (nursing homes) offer restorative, rehabilitative and custodial nursing care for patients not requiring more extensive and sophisticated treatment available at acute-care hospitals. The facilities are designed to provide custodial care and to supplement hospital care. Rehabilitation hospitals provide treatment to restore physical, psycho-social, educational, vocational and economic usefulness and independence to disabled persons. Psychiatric hospitals offer comprehensive, multidisciplinary adult, adolescent and substance-abuse psychiatric programs. Retirement living facilities offer residential units for active and ambulatory elderly residents.

Many of the operators with which the trust does business with rely on governmental reimbursement, primarily Medicare and Medicaid, for a significant portion of their operating revenues. Congress has considered replacing the Medicaid program with block grants to the states, and has also considered other limitations on spending.

Important Developments

Jan. '97—Management said that the trust had acquired $606 million of real estate investments in 1996, with $276 million related to retirement and assisted living facilities, $265 million to nursing homes, and $65 million to medical office buildings. Separately, Meditrust said that 0.1% of its leases and mortgages would expire or mature in 1997.

Capitalization

Debt: $859,890,000 (12/96).

Per Share Data ($)

(Year Ended Dec. 31)	1996	1995	1994	1993	1992	1991	1990	1989	1988	1987
Tangible Bk. Val.	NA	20.75	19.44	17.84	16.12	16.48	14.60	14.11	14.92	14.37
Earnings	2.66	2.52	2.28	2.03	1.95	1.75	1.57	1.37	1.17	1.24
Dividends	2.78	2.70	2.62	2.54	2.46	2.38	2.33	2.09	1.93	1.73
Payout Ratio	105%	107%	115%	125%	126%	136%	148%	153%	165%	140%
Prices - High	40	35½	37⅞	34⅝	31⅜	30⅞	21¾	21½	21⅜	20½
- Low	31¾	29	28¾	29⅛	25⅜	18½	16¼	15¾	15⅝	14
P/E Ratio - High	15	14	16	17	16	18	14	16	18	17
- Low	12	12	13	14	13	11	10	11	13	11

Income Statement Analysis (Million $)

	1996	1995	1994	1993	1992	1991	1990	1989	1988	1987
Income Rental	NA	85.6	82.1	80.5	69.7	67.0	58.1	50.8	40.9	24.4
Income Mortg.	NA	124	90.9	70.4	62.7	42.6	28.8	19.0	3.8	0.5
Income Total	NA	209	173	151	132	113	89.0	72.0	46.0	26.0
Expenses Gen.	NA	25.2	25.1	24.0	22.9	18.1	16.6	15.5	11.3	7.0
Expenses Int.	NA	64.2	67.4	62.2	58.2	56.9	43.5	34.6	17.8	5.2
Prov. for Losses	NA	Nil	Nil	Nil	Nil	Nil	Nil	Nil	Nil	Nil
Depr.	NA	18.2	17.2	16.3	14.0	13.2	10.8	9.6	7.9	5.0
Net Inc.	NA	120	80.5	63.6	51.4	37.9	29.0	21.5	16.8	13.3

Balance Sheet & Other Fin. Data (Million $)

	1996	1995	1994	1993	1992	1991	1990	1989	1988	1987
Cash	NA	44.2	39.9	16.3	24.9	16.9	13.6	15.2	17.2	4.6
Total Assets	NA	1,892	1,595	1,310	1,095	928	822	682	514	309
Real Estate Invest.	NA	1,855	1,550	1,288	1,081	889	782	672	506	298
Loss Reserve	NA	Nil	Nil	Nil	Nil	Nil	Nil	Nil	Nil	Nil
Net Invest.	NA	1,778	1,484	1,214	1,022	843	747	647	490	290
ST Debt	NA	0.8	64.2	48.7	74.9	11.4	0.5	0.4	0.2	NM
Capitalization:										
Debt	NA	761	702	610	525	452	512	417	250	141
Equity	NA	1,062	770	586	431	428	273	222	235	156
Total	NA	1,823	1,472	1,195	957	880	785	638	484	297
% Earn & Depr/Assets	NA	7.9	6.7	6.6	6.5	5.8	5.3	5.2	7.0	7.0
Price Times Book Value:										
Hi	NA	1.7	1.8	1.9	1.9	1.9	1.5	1.4	1.4	1.4
Low	NA	1.4	0.8	1.6	1.6	1.1	1.1	1.0	1.0	1.0

Data as orig. reptd.; bef. results of disc opers. and/or spec. items. Per share data adj. for stk. divs. as of ex-div. date. E-Estimated. NA-Not Available. NM-Not Meaningful. NR-Not Ranked.

Office—197 First Ave., Needham Heights, MA 02194-9127. **Organized**—in Massachusetts in 1985. **Tel**—(617) 433-6000. **Fax**—(617) 433-1290. **E-mail**—meditrust@reit.com **Website**—http://www.reit.com **Chrmn & CEO**—A. D. Gosman. **Pres**—D. F. Benson. **COO**—M. F. Bushee. **Investor Contact**—Elaine Quinlan. **SVP & Secy**—M. S. Benjamin. **Trustees**—D. F. Benson, E. W. Brooke, H. L. Carey, R. Cataldo, A. D. Gosman, P. L. Lowe, T. J. Magovern, G. Tsai Jr., F. W. Zuckerman. **Transfer Agent & Registrar**—Fleet Bank, Providence, RI. **Empl**—37. **S&P Analyst:** Paul L. Huberman, CFA

Merchants New York Bancorp 4580M
NASDAQ Symbol **MBNY**

15-FEB-97 **Industry:** Banking

Summary: MBNY is a $1.1 billion bank holding company that provides commercial and retail banking services through its branch system in Manhattan.

Quantitative Evaluations

Outlook (1 Lowest—5 Highest)
• **NA**

Fair Value
• **NA**

Risk
• **Low**

Earn./Div. Rank
• **A-**

Technical Eval.
• **Bearish** since 12/96

Rel. Strength Rank (1 Lowest—99 Highest)
• **63**

Insider Activity
• **Favorable**

Recent Price • 33½
52 Wk Range • 34¼-26

Yield • 4.2%
12-Mo. P/E • 13.3

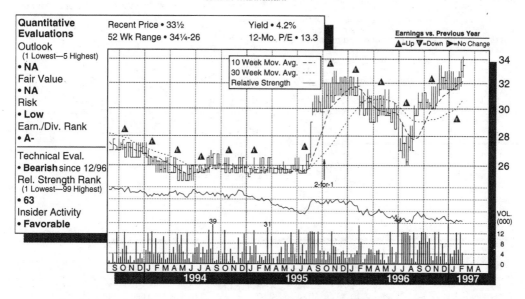

Business Profile - 13-FEB-97

Through its Merchants Bank of New York subsidiary, this holding company offers conventional banking services to small and medium-size businesses and to individuals in New York City. Results for the quarter ended December 30, 1996, marked the 17th consecutive quarter of year-to-year earnings gains. Merchants has paid 254 consecutive quarterly cash dividends, and, during 1996, it raised the dividend by almost 17%, representing the 44th increase in its payout since 1950. The company's risk-based capital ratio stands at approximately 22%, well above the required 8%, and MBNY maintains a debt-free balance sheet.

Operational Review - 13-FEB-97

Based on a brief preliminary report, net interest income in 1996 rose 5.2% from that of the prior year, on wider interest rate spreads and higher levels of earning assets. Securities gains nearly doubled. Pretax income was up 11%. After taxes at 36.9%, versus 36.3%, net income climbed 10%, to $12,670,771 ($2.52) from $11,465,430 ($2.29).

Stock Performance - 14-FEB-97

In the past 30 trading days, MBNY's shares have increased 6%, compared to a 8% rise in the S&P 500. Average trading volume for the past five days was 860 shares, compared with the 40-day moving average of 2,377 shares.

Key Stock Statistics

Dividend Rate/Share	1.40	Shareholders	1,500
Shs. outstg. (M)	5.0	Market cap. (B)	$0.167
Avg. daily vol. (M)	0.002	Inst. holdings	3%
Tang. Bk. Value/Share	20.22		
Beta	0.09		

Value of $10,000 invested 5 years ago: $ 18,503

Fiscal Year Ending Dec. 31

	1996	1995	1994	1993	1992	1991
Revenues (Million $)						
1Q	18.45	17.95	15.27	—	12.92	14.57
2Q	18.76	18.44	16.26	—	12.79	14.48
3Q	20.28	18.76	17.06	—	13.82	14.53
4Q	—	19.57	16.07	—	16.22	14.64
Yr.	—	74.72	·64.66	68.71	55.75	58.22
Earnings Per Share ($)						
1Q	0.61	0.60	0.55	0.48	0.41	0.45
2Q	0.64	0.59	0.58	0.46	0.39	0.43
3Q	0.75	0.63	0.60	0.28	0.23	0.22
4Q	0.51	0.46	0.43	0.36	0.29	0.21
Yr.	2.52	2.28	2.15	1.59	1.32	1.31

Next earnings report expected: early May

Dividend Data (Dividends have been paid since 1932.)

Amount ($)	Date Decl.	Ex-Div. Date	Stock of Record	Payment Date
0.300	Feb. 21	Mar. 12	Mar. 14	Mar. 26 '96
0.300	May. 21	Jun. 12	Jun. 14	Jun. 25 '96
0.350	Aug. 20	Sep. 10	Sep. 12	Sep. 25 '96
0.350	Nov. 19	Dec. 04	Dec. 06	Dec. 18 '96

STANDARD
&POOR'S
STOCK REPORTS

Merchants New York Bancorp, Inc.

4580M

15-FEB-97

Business Summary - 13-FEB-97

Through its Merchants Bank of New York subsidiary, Merchants New York Bancorp is a one-bank holding company that operates seven branches in New York City, offering conventional retail and commercial banking, in addition to trust services, to small and medium-size businesses and to individuals. The bank's international department provides letters of credit and foreign collections to finance import and export transactions through its network of correspondent banks worldwide. In recent years, growth in the loan portfolio has come from various industries, thereby reducing MBNY's concentration of loans related to the diamond, jewelry and allied industries.

Gross loans outstanding at December 31, 1995, totaled $271.0 million, versus $268.2 million a year earlier, and were divided:

	1995	1994
Commercial & industrial	94.7%	94.7%
Mortgage	4.2%	4.2%
Installment	1.1%	1.1%

The allowance for loan losses at year-end 1995 was $6.48 million (2.39% of total loans outstanding), versus $6.19 million (2.30%) a year earlier. Net loan chargeoffs in 1995 amounted to $1.78 million (0.65% of net average loans), down from $2.62 million (0.96%) in 1994. At December 31, 1995, nonaccrual, past-due and restructured loans totaled $2.45 million (0.90% of gross loans), up from $1.62 million (0.60%) at 1994 year-end.

Average deposits of $831.6 million during 1995 were apportioned: demand 25%, NOW 5%, money market 15%, savings 4% and time 51%.

Interest and fees on loans contributed 36% of total income for 1995, interest on investment securities 57%, service fees 5% and other income 2%.

The average yield on interest-earning assets in 1995 was 7.82% (6.80% in 1994), and the average rate paid on interest-bearing liabilities was 4.88% (3.74%), for a net interest spread of 2.94% (3.06%).

Capitalization

Long Term Debt: None (12/96).

Per Share Data ($)

(Year Ended Dec. 31)	1996	1995	1994	1993	1992	1991	1990	1989	1988	1987
Tangible Bk. Val.	NA	20.11	15.65	15.67	14.88	14.36	13.85	12.92	11.51	9.74
Earnings	2.52	2.28	2.16	1.59	1.32	1.31	1.63	2.11	2.09	1.86
Dividends	1.30	1.10	0.90	0.80	0.80	0.80	0.68	0.72	0.32	0.26
Payout Ratio	52%	48%	42%	50%	61%	61%	42%	34%	15%	14%
Prices - High	33½	33	27½	31	23¾	24½	34⅜	55	68	53⅞
- Low	26	25¼	25	23¼	21½	19	21	31⅜	45⅜	33⅝
P/E Ratio - High	13	14	13	19	18	19	21	26	33	29
- Low	10	11	12	15	16	15	13	15	22	18

Income Statement Analysis (Million $)

	1996	1995	1994	1993	1992	1991	1990	1989	1988	1987
Net Int. Inc.	NA	37.7	36.2	35.3	31.0	29.1	27.4	27.4	25.8	21.8
Tax Equiv. Adj.	NA	NA	NA	NA	NA	NA	NA	NA	NA	NA
Non Int. Inc.	NA	5.2	3.3	8.4	6.6	4.9	4.4	4.7	3.8	NA
Loan Loss Prov.	NA	2.1	1.9	9.8	8.4	7.4	2.2	0.7	0.3	0.1
% Exp/Op Revs.	NA	53	56	47	50	52	52	50	48	NA
Pretax Inc.	NA	18.0	15.7	13.0	10.5	9.1	13.3	16.1	15.2	12.7
Eff. Tax Rate	NA	36%	32%	40%	38%	28%	39%	35%	32%	27%
Net Inc.	NA	11.5	10.7	7.9	6.5	6.5	8.1	10.5	10.4	9.2
% Net Int. Marg.	NA	4.23	4.02	3.76	4.69	4.87	4.75	4.83	4.96	4.81

Balance Sheet & Other Fin. Data (Million $)

	1996	1995	1994	1993	1992	1991	1990	1989	1988	1987
Earning Assets:										
Money Mkt	NA	52.0	47.0	23.0	13.0	30.3	46.6	42.0	37.0	NA
Inv. Securities	NA	630	606	600	587	309	266	245	251	NA
Com'l Loans	NA	257	254	273	284	276	288	278	240	NA
Other Loans	NA	14.3	14.1	10.2	10.8	12.3	14.5	17.1	16.5	NA
Total Assets	NA	1,027	1,001	1,006	1,086	714	671	668	668	565
Demand Deposits	NA	268	271	259	252	223	198	208	213	NA
Time Deposits	NA	524	561	587	708	370	366	377	381	NA
LT Debt	NA	Nil	Nil	Nil	Nil	Nil	Nil	Nil	Nil	Nil
Common Eqty.	NA	100	77.7	77.8	73.9	71.3	68.7	64.1	57.1	48.3
% Ret. on Assets	NA	1.2	1.1	0.8	0.9	1.0	1.3	1.6	1.8	1.8
% Ret. on Equity	NA	12.6	13.3	10.4	8.9	9.2	12.0	17.1	19.6	21.0
% Loan Loss Resv.	NA	2.4	2.3	2.3	1.5	1.1	1.3	1.1	1.0	NA
% Loans/Deposits	NA	34.2	32.2	33.4	30.6	48.4	53.2	50.1	42.9	NA
% Equity to Assets	NA	9.4	8.4	7.5	9.9	10.8	10.4	9.6	9.0	8.3

Data as orig. reptd.; bef. results of disc opers. and/or spec. items. Per share data adj. for stk. divs. as of ex-div. date. E-Estimated. NA-Not Available. NM-Not Meaningful. NR-Not Ranked.

Office—275 Madison Ave., New York, NY 10016. **Tel**—(212) 973-6600. **Chrmn**—S. B. Witty. **Vice Chrmn**—R. H. Hertz. **Pres & CEO**—J. G. Lawrence. **Exec VP & COO**—W. J. Cardew. **Acting Secy**—Karen L. Deitz. **Dirs**—C. J. Baum, W. J. Cardew, R. H. Hertz, I. Karten, J. G. Lawrence, R. Markel, P. Meyrowitz, A. Mirken, M. J. Nelson, L. Schlussel, C. I. Silberman, S. B. Witty. **Transfer Agent & Registrar**—American Stock Transfer & Trust Co., NYC. **Incorporated**—in Delaware in 1992; bank subsidiary incorporated in 1926. **Empl**— 246. **S&P Analyst:** Thomas C. Ferguson

15-FEB-97

Industry:
Real Estate Investment Trust

Summary: This self-administered real estate investment trust (REIT) acquires, develops and operates upscale garden apartments in the South Atlantic region of the U.S.

Quantitative Evaluations

Recent Price • 22¼	Yield • 7.0%
52 Wk Range • 23¼-18¼	12-Mo. P/E • 18.1

Outlook (1 Lowest—5 Highest)
• **NA**

Fair Value
• **NA**

Risk
• **Low**

Earn./Div. Rank
• **NR**

Technical Eval.
• **Bullish** since 1/97

Rel. Strength Rank (1 Lowest—99 Highest)
• **55**

Insider Activity
• **Favorable**

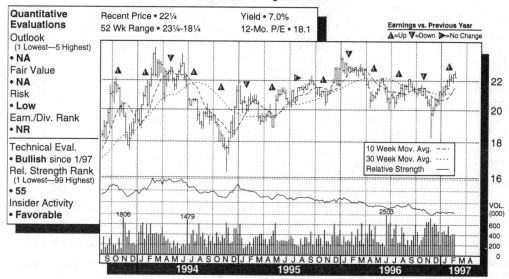

Earnings vs. Previous Year
▲=Up ▼=Down ▷=No Change

10 Week Mov. Avg. ‑ ‑ ‑
30 Week Mov. Avg. ‑‑‑‑
Relative Strength ——

Business Profile - 13-FEB-97

This real estate investment trust (REIT) has continued to expand its investments in apartments both through acquisitions and development, and cash flows produced by its communities have risen accordingly. In 1996, MRY bought 11 apartment communities, containing 2,475 units, for a cost of $137.6 million. It also placed in service 414 units of new development at a cost of $28.4 million. Together, this represented a 16% expansion of its holdings at cost. At the end of 1996, MRY operated 24,936 apartment units in 91 communities in 27 cities in 10 states. Directors have raised the quarterly cash dividend 5.4%, to $0.39 a share from $0.37, with the March 31, 1997, payment.

Operational Review - 13-FEB-97

Net income for 1996 (preliminary) advanced 20%, to $64,006,000 ($1.23 a share) from $53,537,000 ($1.06) the year before. Funds from operations increased 19%, to $94,047,000 ($2.02 a share) from $79,359,000 ($1.84). In 1996's fourth quarter, total apartment revenues increased 17%, year to year; total apartment revenues for the full year were up 22%. For the 18,410 units that MRY owned for all of 1996 and 1995, revenues for 1996 rose only 2.1%, as a result of the construction of new units which led to weakening markets. Management anticipates an improvement in the company's markets later in 1997 and a return to good earnings growth in 1998.

Stock Performance - 14-FEB-97

In the past 30 trading days, MRY's shares have increased 5%, compared to a 8% rise in the S&P 500. Average trading volume for the past five days was 83,460 shares, compared with the 40-day moving average of 85,849 shares.

Key Stock Statistics

Dividend Rate/Share	1.56	Shareholders	3,700
Shs. outstg. (M)	37.6	Market cap. (B)	$0.836
Avg. daily vol. (M)	0.090	Inst. holdings	37%
Tang. Bk. Value/Share	13.96		
Beta	0.14		

Value of $10,000 invested 5 years ago: $ 36,953

Fiscal Year Ending Dec. 31

	1996	1995	1994	1993	1992	1991
Revenues (Million $)						
1Q	44.53	33.76	23.77	15.79	10.56	—
2Q	46.31	35.37	24.44	11.82	—	—
3Q	48.39	41.47	26.60	16.71	4.05	—
4Q	—	46.00	30.82	14.33	7.88	—
Yr.	—	156.6	105.6	58.65	29.59	—
Earnings Per Share ($)						
1Q	0.28	0.27	0.26	0.59	0.52	0.25
2Q	0.32	0.27	0.27	0.22	0.26	0.19
3Q	0.30	0.31	0.29	0.19	0.13	0.29
4Q	0.32	0.21	0.28	0.33	0.16	0.21
Yr.	1.23	1.06	1.10	1.30	1.07	0.94

Next earnings report expected: NA

Dividend Data (Dividends have been paid since 1987.)

Amount ($)	Date Decl.	Ex-Div. Date	Stock of Record	Payment Date
0.370	Apr. 15	Jun. 12	Jun. 14	Jun. 28 '96
0.370	Jul. 15	Sep. 12	Sep. 16	Sep. 30 '96
0.370	Oct. 21	Dec. 12	Dec. 16	Dec. 31 '96
0.390	Jan. 20	Mar. 12	Mar. 14	Mar. 31 '97

A Division of The **McGraw-Hill** *Companies*

Business Summary - 13-FEB-97

Merry Land & Investment Co. is a self-managed real estate investment trust (REIT) that owns and operates upscale apartments in the South Atlantic region of the U.S. The trust seeks real estate investments with good capital appreciation prospects and in which it can increase cash flow and minimize corporate taxation.

At December 31, 1995, MRY had real estate investments of about $1.1 billion and owned 80 suburban apartment projects containing a total of 22,296 units in Maryland, Virginia, Ohio, Tennessee, Florida, Georgia, North Carolina, South Carolina and Texas. As of December 31, 1995, the average monthly rent was $639, with an occupancy rate of 95.2%. The projects are generally newer garden apartments of about seven years of age, in wood frame, two- or three-story buildings without elevators, and command rental rates in the upper range of their markets.

In 1989, the trust began a long-term plan to increase its real estate holdings in relation to total assets. With favorable supply and demand characteristics for multifamily properties in the Southeast, MRY accelerated its acquisition program in 1993, purchasing 25 apartment communities with 7,452 units at a total cost of $335.2 million. A major portion of the acquisitions was in Florida, because of that state's large population and high growth rate. In 1994, 4,872 units were acquired at an aggregate cost of $226.2 million. In 1995, a total of 3,444 units were acquired at a total cost of $196.3 mil-

lion. The trust intends to continue to focus on acquiring communities throughout the South.

In eairly 1996, the trust began a program of apartment development in order to provide an additional means of expanding its apartment holdings. At December 31, 1995, MRY had 1,174 units under construction in Georgia, 1,316 units under development in Tennessee, Virginia, Georgia and North Carolina and 200 units under future development in North Carolina.

Important Developments

Jan. '97—MRY sold Hunters Chase Apartments, a 244 unit apartment community in Cleveland, Ohio, for $15 million. It said that it will recognize a gain of $1.5 million on the transaction.
Dec. '96—The trust purchased a 194-unit luxury apartment community in Orlando, FL for $10 million.
Nov. '96—MRY acquired The Regency, a 178-unit luxury apartment community in Charlotte, NC, for $11.2 million.
Oct. '96—The trust purchased a 79.6 acre tract of land in Southern Davidson County, GA for $3.1 million. The trust is planning development of 360 luxury apartment units on 36 acres of the tract in the spring of 1997.

Capitalization

Total Debt: $387,546,000 of mortgage debt and senior notes. (12/96).
Conv. Pref. Stock: $273,965,000 (12/96) (Series A, B, C and D).

Per Share Data ($)

(Year Ended Dec. 31)	1996	1995	1994	1993	1992	1991	1990	1989	1988	1987
Tangible Bk. Val.	NA	13.70	13.72	12.38	8.50	7.87	7.17	7.05	6.44	6.27
Earnings	1.23	1.06	1.10	1.30	1.07	0.94	0.62	0.93	0.90	0.90
Dividends	1.48	1.40	1.25	0.90	0.66	0.44	0.40	0.30	0.80	0.80
Payout Ratio	120%	132%	114%	69%	73%	47%	65%	32%	90%	94%
Prices - High	23¾	24	24½	22⅛	15¼	8¼	5⅛	7½	8¾	12¼
- Low	18¼	18⅞	16¼	14¼	7¼	4	3⅝	4¾	7	6¼
P/E Ratio - High	19	23	22	17	14	9	8	8	10	14
- Low	15	18	15	11	7	4	6	5	8	7

Income Statement Analysis (Million $)

	1996	1995	1994	1993	1992	1991	1990	1989	1988	1987
Income Rental	NA	145	103	56.2	23.5	16.5	13.8	8.0	6.6	6.3
Income Mortg.	NA	6.9	2.4	2.5	5.9	14.5	21.8	21.9	20.4	17.1
Income Total	NA	158	106	66.6	32.3	33.1	37.4	37.5	31.5	25.6
Expenses Gen.	NA	89.2	58.7	33.3	15.1	11.5	8.8	5.8	5.0	5.0
Expenses Int.	NA	15.6	10.4	5.6	5.8	12.8	22.7	22.5	17.9	14.1
Prov. for Losses	NA	Nil	Nil	Nil	Nil	Nil	Nil	Nil	Nil	Nil
Depr.	NA	26.9	18.4	9.3	4.2	3.1	2.3	1.5	1.4	1.3
Net Inc.	NA	53.5	37.0	26.4	11.4	8.8	5.9	9.1	8.6	7.9

Balance Sheet & Other Fin. Data (Million $)

	1996	1995	1994	1993	1992	1991	1990	1989	1988	1987
Cash	NA	92.3	28.4	16.4	10.9	11.8	11.2	13.9	26.7	42.5
Total Assets	NA	1,073	807	562	236	263	319	334	301	283
Real Estate Invest.	NA	1,040	815	565	221	248	301	310	265	240
Loss Reserve	NA	Nil	Nil	Nil	Nil	Nil	Nil	Nil	Nil	Nil
Net Invest.	NA	973	773	541	206	238	293	304	258	233
ST Debt	NA	Nil	75.0	NM	64.0	120	195	219	190	190
Capitalization:										
Debt	NA	360	138	157	53.8	64.9	52.9	42.2	43.3	31.5
Equity	NA	696	585	398	107	74.0	66.0	68.0	62.0	58.0
Total	NA	1,056	723	555	161	139	119	110	106	89.0
% Earn & Depr/Assets	NA	8.6	8.1	8.9	6.3	4.1	2.5	3.3	3.4	4.1
Price Times Book Value:										
Hi	NA	1.8	1.8	1.8	1.8	1.0	0.7	1.1	1.4	1.9
Low	NA	1.4	1.2	1.2	0.9	0.5	0.5	0.7	1.1	1.0

Data as orig. reptd.; bef. results of disc opers. and/or spec. items. Per share data adj. for stk. divs. as of ex-div. date. E-Estimated. NA-Not Available. NM-Not Meaningful. NR-Not Ranked.

Office—624 Ellis St., P.O. Box 1417, Augusta, GA 30903. **Tel**—(706) 722-6756. **Fax**—(706) 722-4681. **Chrmn**—B. A. Knox.**Pres & CEO**—W. T. Houston. **EVP & COO**—M. N. Thompson.**Secy**—W. H. Barrett. **Investor Contact**—Linda H. Randolph. **Dirs**—W. H. Barrett, W. T. Houston, R. P. Kirby, B. A. Knox, P. S. Simon, M. N. Thompson, H. C. Long II, P. Merry Jr. **Transfer Agent**—First Union National Bank of North Carolina, Charlotte.**Incorporated**—in Georgia in 1966. **Empl**— 718. **S&P Analyst:** J.J.S.

15-FEB-97

Industry:
Utilities-Electric

Summary: This utility holding company, serving more than 1.3 million customers throughout Massachusetts, Rhode Island and New Hampshire, is New England's second largest utility system.

| S&P Opinion: Hold (★★★) | Recent Price • 35⅛ | Yield • 6.7% |
| | 52 Wk Range • 39⅞-31 | 12-Mo. P/E • 10.9 |

Quantitative Evaluations

Outlook
(1 Lowest—5 Highest)
• 1

Fair Value
• 31⅛

Risk
• **Low**

Earn./Div. Rank
• **A-**

Technical Eval.
• **Bullish** since 11/96

Rel. Strength Rank
(1 Lowest—99 Highest)
• 52

Insider Activity
• **NA**

Earnings vs. Previous Year
▲=Up ▼=Down ▶=No Change

10 Week Mov. Avg. — —
30 Week Mov. Avg. ·····
Relative Strength ——

Overview - 16-DEC-96

Revenue growth for 1997 will continue to be restricted by discounted prices for at-risk industrial customers. EPS are likely to be hurt by the effects of higher depreciation rates approved in recent rate settlements, as well as increased charges for dismantling a retired generating facility. In one of the first big breakups of the electric utility industry under deregulation, NES has agreed to sell or spin off most of its power generating assets. The assets, which include 15 hydroelectric and five fossil fuel plants, are valued at $1.1 billion. After the sale, the NES retail companies will become "wires only companies," responsible for the transmission and distribution of electricity to customers and the provision of related services. For the longer term, the anticipated lower rates could also give NES a competitive advantage. However there is great risk that NES will not realize book value for its generating assets in the currently depressed generation market, particularly if other utilities follow this route. Being first has its advantages, though, and NES hopes for a sale by the end of 1997.

Valuation - 16-DEC-96

After falling over 20% through the first nine months of 1996, the shares have begun to rebound in recent weeks, as investors give their thumbs up to NES's plans to divest its generating assets. However, the outcome of the sale and the impact of future regulatory action and competition add significant risk to future earnings, and we expect the stock to continue to underperform its peers and the general market. We regard the dividend as secure, reflecting the company's ample cash flow and below average ratio of debt to equity. Although we do not expect NES to increase the dividend for the foreseeable future, the above-average yield continues to make NES shares a worthwhile holding for income.

Key Stock Statistics

S&P EPS Est. 1997	3.30	Tang. Bk. Value/Share	25.86
P/E on S&P Est. 1997	10.6	Beta	0.56
Dividend Rate/Share	2.36	Shareholders	51,100
Shs. outstg. (M)	64.9	Market cap. (B)	$ 2.3
Avg. daily vol. (M)	0.117	Inst. holdings	36%

Value of $10,000 invested 5 years ago: $ 14,995

Fiscal Year Ending Dec. 31

	1996	1995	1994	1993	1992	1991
Revenues (Million $)						
1Q	586.2	558.3	577.0	579.0	575.0	574.0
2Q	551.1	533.5	517.0	518.0	499.0	475.0
3Q	616.9	599.1	592.0	577.0	541.0	521.0
4Q	586.5	580.7	557.4	560.0	567.0	524.0
Yr.	2,351	2,272	2,243	2,234	2,182	2,094
Earnings Per Share ($)						
1Q	0.95	0.73	1.07	0.82	0.99	1.14
2Q	0.54	0.52	0.51	0.30	0.47	0.29
3Q	0.99	1.14	0.91	0.85	0.74	0.69
4Q	0.74	0.76	0.58	0.96	0.65	0.65
Yr.	3.22	3.15	3.07	2.93	2.85	2.77

Next earnings report expected: late April

Dividend Data (Dividends have been paid since 1947.)

Amount ($)	Date Decl.	Ex-Div. Date	Stock of Record	Payment Date
0.590	Feb. 27	Mar. 07	Mar. 11	Apr. 01 '96
0.590	May. 28	Jun. 06	Jun. 10	Jul. 01 '96
0.590	Aug. 27	Sep. 06	Sep. 10	Oct. 01 '96
0.590	Nov. 26	Dec. 06	Dec. 10	Jan. 02 '97

A Division of The McGraw·Hill Companies

STANDARD
&POOR'S
STOCK REPORTS

New England Electric System

1646

15-FEB-97

Business Summary - 16-DEC-96

New England Electric System is a utility holding company that provides electric service to 1.3 million customers in Massachusetts, Rhode Island and New Hampshire. The second largest electric utility in New England, it generates, transmits, distributes and sells electric energy and provides related services. It also operates several related companies, including an oil and gas exploration company.

In 1995, 41% of revenues from electricity sales was derived from residential customers, 38% from commercial, 15% from industrial and 2% from other customers. Approximately 80% of NES's large municipal, commercial and industrial customers have contracts providing a 5% discount in exchange for giving three to five years notice before changing suppliers.

In 1995, coal accounted for 38% of power generation, nuclear 14%, gas 22%, hydro 10%, oil 10%, and other 6%. Peak load in 1995 was 4,381 mw, and capability totaled 5,482 mw, for a capacity margin of 20%.

Utility plant expenditures for 1996 are estimated at $245 million, substantially all of which will be funded by internal resources. About 50% of 1996 spending will be for construction of generating and transmission facilities, with the remainder largely for distribution facilities.

Closely mirroring the comprehensive restructuring legislation passed in August 1996 in Rhode Island, in September, Massachusetts Electric and New England

Power (NEP) reached an agreement with The Attorney General on a "Consumers First" plan which would allow all Massachusetts residential and business consumers to choose their electricity supplier on January 1, 1998. A "standard offer" option would guarantee customers a minimum of 10% savings even if they choose not to enter the competitive market right away.

Important Developments

Sep. '96—As part of a settlement with the Massachusetts Department of Public Utilities, the NES subsidiaries agreed to sell or spin off ownership of their fossil and hydroelectric power plants to a non-affiliated entity or entities, in exchange for the ability to recover sunk costs during the transition to a competitive electricity market. Sunk costs will be recovered through a 12-year nonbypassable access charge on retail distribution rates, initially set at 2.8 cents per kilowatt for the first three years. NES also intends to divest its regulated oil and gas business, and potentially its minority interest in five operating nuclear plants in four New England states. Full divestiture is expected to be completed by 1998.

Capitalization

Long Term Debt: $1,608,386,000 (9/96).
Minority Interest: $48,005,000.
Subsid. Red. Preferred Stock: $126,166,000.

Per Share Data ($)

(Year Ended Dec. 31)	1996	1995	1994	1993	1992	1991	1990	1989	1988	1987
Tangible Bk. Val.	NA	25.13	24.17	23.46	22.88	22.05	21.30	19.09	18.17	21.25
Earnings	3.22	3.15	3.07	2.93	2.85	2.77	4.11	2.36	-0.94	3.05
Dividends	2.36	2.34	2.28	2.22	2.14	2.07	2.04	2.04	2.04	2.01
Payout Ratio	73%	74%	74%	76%	75%	75%	50%	86%	NM	66%
Prices - High	40⅝	40	39	43⅜	39	32⅝	28⅝	28⅞	25½	32⅞
- Low	31	29⅝	28⅞	36⅞	29¼	24	22½	22¼	20	20
P/E Ratio - High	13	13	13	15	14	12	7	12	NM	11
- Low	10	9	9	13	10	9	5	9	NM	7

Income Statement Analysis (Million $)

	1996	1995	1994	1993	1992	1991	1990	1989	1988	1987
Revs.	NA	2,272	2,243	2,234	2,182	2,094	1,855	1,643	1,520	1,448
Depr.	NA	265	301	297	302	278	259	257	229	179
Maint.	NA	136	161	146	163	148	137	122	120	101
Fxd. Chgs. Cov.	NA	3.3	4.2	3.7	3.4	3.2	3.8	2.5	1.6	3.4
Constr. Credits	NA	22.0	18.0	6.6	4.9	4.3	31.9	29.7	3.8	34.9
Eff. Tax Rate	NA	37%	39%	38%	37%	36%	21%	19%	NM	31%
Net Inc.	NA	205	199	190	191	180	262	139	-54.0	169

Balance Sheet & Other Fin. Data (Million $)

	1996	1995	1994	1993	1992	1991	1990	1989	1988	1987
Gross Prop.	NA	5,567	5,327	4,994	4,790	4,666	4,548	4,222	3,733	3,871
Cap. Exp.	NA	329	438	305	242	193	218	532	192	165
Net Prop.	NA	3,856	3,717	3,483	3,375	3,321	3,302	3,073	2,661	2,863
Capitalization:										
LT Debt	NA	1,675	1,520	1,512	1,533	1,548	1,679	1,638	1,434	1,387
% LT Debt	NA	48	46	47	47	48	51	53	54	51
Pfd.	NA	196	202	203	223	226	225	217	163	163
% Pfd.	NA	5.60	6.10	6.30	6.90	7.00	6.90	7.10	6.10	5.90
Common	NA	1,632	1,581	1,530	1,486	1,440	1,380	1,212	1,056	1,200
% Common	NA	47	48	47	46	45	42	40	40	44
Total Cap.	NA	4,377	4,150	4,049	3,969	3,930	3,991	3,764	3,370	3,573
Oper. Ratio	NA	85.8	86.8	86.4	86.0	86.1	86.3	85.3	85.4	84.3
% Earn. on Net Prop.	NA	8.5	8.2	8.8	9.1	8.8	8.0	8.4	8.0	8.2
% Ret. on Revs.	NA	9.0	8.9	8.5	8.5	8.6	14.1	8.4	NM	11.7
% Ret. On Invest.Cap	NA	7.9	7.6	7.9	8.2	7.8	9.8	7.1	1.5	7.6
% Return On Com.Eqty	NA	12.7	12.7	12.6	12.6	12.6	20.5	12.6	NM	14.6

Data as orig. reptd.; bef. results of disc opers. and/or spec. items. Per share data adj. for stk. divs. as of ex-div. date. E-Estimated. NA-Not Available. NM-Not Meaningful. NR-Not Ranked.

Office—25 Research Drive, Westborough, MA 01582. **Organized**—in Massachusetts in 1926. **Tel**—(508) 389-2000. **Chrmn**—J. T. Bok. **Pres & CEO**—J. W. Rowe. **VP & Secy**—F. E. Greenman. **VP & CFO**—A. D. Houston. **Investor Contact**—Robert G. Seega. **Dirs**—J. T. Bok, P. L. Joskow, J. M. Kucharski, J. A. McClure, J. W. Rowe, G. M. Sage, C. E. Soule, A. Wexler, J. Q. Wilson, J. R. Winoker. **Transfer Agent & Registrar**—Boston EquiServe. **Empl**— 5,000. **S&P Analyst:** Maureen C. Carini

ONEOK Inc.

1717R

NYSE Symbol **OKE**

In S&P 500

20-FEB-97

Industry: Utilities-Gas

Summary: OKE operates a natural gas utility in Oklahoma and also engages in nonutility energy-related activities, including oil and gas exploration and natural gas liquids extraction.

S&P Opinion: Hold (★★★)		
Recent Price • 29¾		Yield • 4.0%
52 Wk Range • 30⅞-20⅞		12-Mo. P/E • 14.4

Quantitative Evaluations

Outlook
(1 Lowest—5 Highest)
• 1⁻

Fair Value
• 25½

Risk
• **Low**

Earn./Div. Rank
• **B+**

Technical Eval.
• **Bullish** since 12/96

Rel. Strength Rank
(1 Lowest—99 Highest)
• 56

Insider Activity
• **NA**

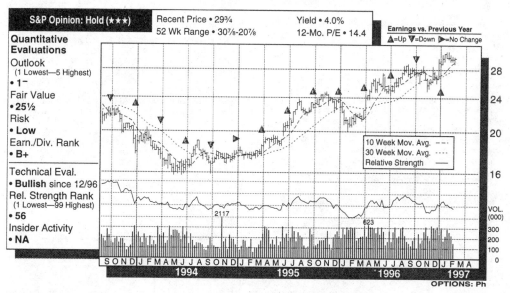

Earnings vs. Previous Year
▲=Up ▼=Down ▷=No Change

10 Week Mov. Avg. - - -
30 Week Mov. Avg. ----
Relative Strength ——

VOL. (000)

OPTIONS: Ph

Overview - 17-FEB-97

The pending agreement to acquire the natural gas assets of Western Resources (WR) would increase OKE's customer base by nearly 90% and make it the ninth largest gas distribution company in the U.S. The acquisition, which would increase consolidated revenues by approximately 50%, would be realized through the issuance to WR of 3 million new shares of common stock (resulting in an 11% increase in shares outstanding), along with 19.3 million shares of preferred stock with a dividend of 1.5 times (or a minimum of $1.80 a share) that of the common. It is also expected that upon the anticipated repeal of the Public Utility Holding Company Act (PUHCA), the preferred shares would be converted (one to one) into common shares. The acquisition should be accretive to earnings during the first year following its completion. On its own, we expect OKE to achieve modest gains for the remainder of the year, aided by continued cost cutting.

Valuation - 17-FEB-97

We continue to recommend holding the stock. OKE's shares advanced 31% in calendar 1996, compared to a 26% increase for the S&P Natural Gas Index, and were recently trading at about 14x our FY 97 EPS estimate of $2.05. With nonregulated businesses, most notably the gas marketing unit, expected to make increased contributions to earnings in coming years, some expansion of earnings and cash flow multiples is possible in the long term. The dividend was raised 3.4% with the May 1996 payment. However, over the next several years, the dividend growth rate is expected to significantly trail EPS increases. Nevertheless, the stock, with a current yield of 4.1%, remains an attractive holding for total return.

Key Stock Statistics

S&P EPS Est. 1997	2.05	Tang. Bk. Value/Share	15.19
P/E on S&P Est. 1997	14.5	Beta	0.10
Dividend Rate/Share	1.20	Shareholders	13,300
Shs. outstg. (M)	27.3	Market cap. (B)	$0.809
Avg. daily vol. (M)	0.044	Inst. holdings	48%

Value of $10,000 invested 5 years ago: $ 23,005

Fiscal Year Ending Aug. 31

	1997	1996	1995	1994	1993	1992
Revenues (Million $)						
1Q	248.8	238.5	166.3	177.2	159.4	155.0
2Q	—	464.7	287.4	295.4	314.0	265.0
3Q	—	289.7	304.5	190.5	188.0	151.0
4Q	—	231.5	191.8	129.3	128.2	107.0
Yr.	—	1,224	949.9	792.4	789.1	677.0
Earnings Per Share ($)						
1Q	0.44	0.31	0.29	0.29	0.22	0.21
2Q	E1.43	1.42	1.05	0.98	1.17	0.87
3Q	E0.41	0.42	0.33	0.21	0.10	0.10
4Q	E-0.23	-0.22	-0.09	-0.14	-0.06	0.03
Yr.	E2.05	1.93	1.58	1.34	1.43	1.21

Next earnings report expected: late March

Dividend Data (Dividends have been paid since 1939.)

Amount ($)	Date Decl.	Ex-Div. Date	Stock of Record	Payment Date
0.300	Apr. 18	Apr. 26	Apr. 30	May. 15 '96
0.300	Jul. 18	Jul. 29	Jul. 31	Aug. 15 '96
0.300	Oct. 17	Oct. 29	Oct. 31	Nov. 15 '96
0.300	Dec. 12	Jan. 29	Jan. 31	Feb. 14 '97

Business Summary - 17-FEB-97

ONEOK is a diversified energy company engaged in natural gas utility operations in Oklahoma and nonutility energy-related, marketing, processing and production activities. Segment contributions (profits in millions) in FY 96 (Aug.) were:

	Oper. Revs.	Oper. Profits
Distribution & Transmision	43.9%	$97.4
Marketing	48.9%	12.8
Processing	4.8%	9.0
Production	2.1%	2.8
Other	0.3%	-1.0

Gas utility operations are conducted principally by Oklahoma Natural Gas Co., which distributes gas to about 729,500 customers in 294 communities in Oklahoma, with Oklahoma City and Tulsa the largest markets, and at wholesale to other distributors serving 44 Oklahoma communities. Regulated (distribution and transmission) gas sales in FY 96 totaled $487,294,000 (compared to $502,427,000 in FY 95) with operating income of $97,341,000 ($91,570,000).

The company's marketing operations purchases and markets natural gas, primarily in the mid-continent area of the U.S. Although formed in 1992, marketing did not have significant operations until 1995. In FY 96, OKE established ONEOK Producer Services to bring gas marketing and other services to small producers.

ONEOK owns an interest in 15 gas processing plants. The operations include the extraction of natural gas liquids (NGLs) and the separation of mixed NGLs into such component products as ethane, butane, propane and isobutane. In its production activities, OKE has a working interest in 821 gas wells and 230 oil wells primarily in Oklahoma and Louisiana.

Important Developments

Jan. '97—The company agreed to acquire PSEC, Inc., a privately-held, Oklahoma-based producer of oil and gas, and PSPC, Ltd., the managing general partner of an Oklahoma gas gathering system, for an undisclosed combination of cash and stock. The transaction includes 180 wells with proven reserves of 21 billion cubic feet of natural gas and 168,000 barrels of oil.

Dec. '96—ONEOK agreed to acquire the natural gas assets of NYSE-listed Western Resources (WR) in exchange for 3 million new shares of OKE common stock and 19.3 million shares of convertible preferred stock. The $660 million transaction includes distribution properties serving 660,000 customers; a transmission and gathering system with 976 miles of pipeline; and a 42% interest in a New Mexico plant with a capacity of 200 million cubic feet per day.

Capitalization

Long Term Debt: $336,821,000 (11/96).
Cum. Preferred Stock: $9,000,000.

Per Share Data ($)

(Year Ended Aug. 31)	1996	1995	1994	1993	1992	1991	1990	1989	1988	1987
Tangible Bk. Val.	15.19	14.38	13.88	13.63	13.28	13.03	12.51	12.11	11.34	11.22
Earnings	1.93	1.58	1.34	1.43	1.21	1.33	1.21	1.29	0.24	0.68
Dividends	1.18	1.12	1.11	1.06	0.96	0.82	0.74	0.47	0.64	1.28
Payout Ratio	61%	71%	83%	74%	79%	62%	62%	37%	267%	188%
Prices - High	28⅞	24¾	20⅜	26¼	19	16⅞	16½	17	10	22
- Low	20	17⅛	15¾	17⅝	14	12½	11⅞	9¼	4⅞	7¼
P/E Ratio - High	15	16	15	18	16	13	14	13	41	32
- Low	10	11	12	12	12	9	10	7	20	11

Income Statement Analysis (Million $)

	1996	1995	1994	1993	1992	1991	1990	1989	1988	1987
Revs.	1,224	950	792	789	677	689	668	618	571	587
Depr.	72.9	50.4	50.8	48.0	46.8	38.2	34.3	31.2	79.5	42.1
Maint.	NA	NA	6.4	7.0	6.6	6.4	6.2	6.7	7.7	7.7
Fxd. Chgs. Cov.	3.4	2.8	2.7	2.6	2.5	3.1	3.1	3.4	1.3	1.9
Constr. Credits	0.3	0.4	0.6	0.5	0.5	0.4	0.3	0.2	0.3	0.4
Eff. Tax Rate	39%	37%	37%	35%	37%	38%	38%	39%	33%	49%
Net Inc.	52.8	42.8	36.2	38.4	32.6	35.9	33.0	36.6	7.1	19.4

Balance Sheet & Other Fin. Data (Million $)

	1996	1995	1994	1993	1992	1991	1990	1989	1988	1987
Gross Prop.	1,337	1,276	1,218	1,196	1,124	1,047	952	897	1,046	1,037
Cap. Exp.	542	81.0	74.0	86.0	70.0	111	69.0	43.0	32.0	33.0
Net Prop.	795	766	737	752	684	663	591	561	616	671
Capitalization:										
LT Debt	337	351	363	376	381	283	216	144	232	287
% LT Debt	44	47	49	50	51	44	39	30	42	47
Pfd.	9.0	9.0	9.0	9.0	9.0	9.0	9.0	9.0	9.0	9.0
% Pfd.	1.20	1.20	1.20	1.20	1.20	1.40	1.60	1.90	1.60	1.50
Common	415	389	370	363	354	347	333	334	318	315
% Common	55	52	50	49	48	54	60	69	57	52
Total Cap.	761	938	940	944	926	821	731	651	713	795
Oper. Ratio	92.8	91.6	91.0	90.4	90.4	90.9	91.4	90.1	92.4	89.9
% Earn. on Net Prop.	11.3	10.7	9.7	10.8	9.6	10.0	10.0	10.4	6.8	8.7
% Ret. on Revs.	4.3	4.5	4.6	4.9	4.8	5.2	4.9	5.9	1.2	3.3
% Ret. On Invest.Cap	16.0	8.6	7.5	8.1	7.4	8.0	8.3	9.0	5.8	7.3
% Return On Com.Eqty	12.6	11.2	9.7	10.6	9.2	10.4	9.8	11.1	2.1	5.8

Data as orig. reptd.; bef. results of disc. opers. and/or spec. items. Per share data adj. for stk. divs. as of ex-div. date. E-Estimated. NA-Not Available. NM-Not Meaningful. NR-Not Ranked.

Office—100 W. Fifth St., Tulsa, OK 74103. **Tel**—(918) 588-7000. **Website**—http://www.ONEOK.com **Chrmn, Pres & CEO**—L. W. Brummett. **VP, CFO & Treas**—J. D. Neal. **VP & Secy**—N.E. Duckworth. **Investor Contact**—Weldon Watson. **Dirs**—E. G. Anderson, W. M. Bell, L. W. Brummett, D. R. Cummings, W. L. Ford, J. M. Graves, S. J. Jatras, D. L. Kyle, B. H. Mackie, D. A. Newsom, G. D. Parker, J. D. Scott, G. R. Williams, S. L. Young. **Transfer Agent & Registrar**—Liberty National Bank & Trust Co. of Oklahoma City. **Incorporated**—in Delaware in 1933. **Empl**—1,884. **S&P Analyst:** Justin McCann

Pacific Enterprises

1735V

NYSE Symbol **PET**

In S&P 500

16-FEB-97

Industry: Utilities-Gas

Summary: This Los Angeles-based utility holding company for Southern California Gas recently agreed to merge with Enova Corp.

S&P Opinion: Accumulate (★★★★)	Recent Price • 30⅞ Yield • 4.7%
	52 Wk Range • 32½-24½ 12-Mo. P/E • 13.0

Quantitative Evaluations

Outlook
(1 Lowest—5 Highest)
• **2**

Fair Value
• **29¾**

Risk
• **Low**

Earn./Div. Rank
• **B**

Technical Eval.
• **Bullish** since 5/96

Rel. Strength Rank
(1 Lowest—99 Highest)
• **49**

Insider Activity
• **NA**

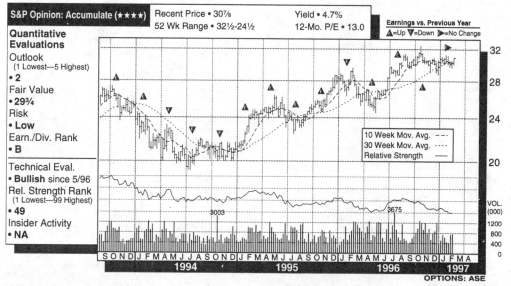

Earnings vs. Previous Year
▲=Up ▼=Down ▶=No Change

10 Week Mov. Avg. – – –
30 Week Mov. Avg. · · · ·
Relative Strength —

OPTIONS: ASE

Overview - 05-FEB-97

On October 14, 1996, PET agreed to merge with Enova Corp. (ENA), the parent of San Diego Gas & Electric. With a combined customer base of nearly six million -- the largest number of any investor-owned utility -- the new entity should be well positioned to compete in California's rapidly deregulating energy market. The merger is expected to be completed by the end of 1997, and should provide $1.2 billion in cost savings over 10 years. PET's revenues and earnings in 1997 should continue to benefit from expected improvement in the Southern California economy, which should result in increased earnings from SoCalGas, and efforts to reduce costs. The introduction of incentive based rate plans in California should also have a positive earnings impact. For the longer term, we expect earnings of the combined company to grow 5% to 6% annually, fueled by significant operating synergies and increasing contributions from unregulated businesses.

Valuation - 05-FEB-97

We continue to recommend accumulation of PET stock. Although the shares were up only 7.5% in 1996, underperforming both the S&P 500 (up 20%) and the S&P Index of natural gas companies (up 26%), they have gained more than 20% from their 1996 low. The future combination with Enova Corp. will insulate PET from fluctuations in natural gas demand and allow it to compete for electric utility customers as the industry deregulates. For now, the shares, trading at about 13 times our estimate of $2.30 for 1997, are valued in line with PET's peers. However, with dividends expected to be increased at an above-average rate, we continue to see the shares as a solid income-generating investment vehicle. Also adding to long-term appeal is the 3.3 million shares remaining to be purchased under PET's 4.25 million (5%) stock buyback program.

Key Stock Statistics

S&P EPS Est. 1997	2.30	Tang. Bk. Value/Share	15.47
P/E on S&P Est. 1997	13.4	Beta	0.49
Dividend Rate/Share	1.44	Shareholders	39,200
Shs. outstg. (M)	85.0	Market cap. (B)	$ 2.6
Avg. daily vol. (M)	0.116	Inst. holdings	50%

Value of $10,000 invested 5 years ago: $ 14,505

Fiscal Year Ending Dec. 31

	1996	1995	1994	1993	1992	1991
Revenues (Million $)						
1Q	631.0	618.0	705.0	618.0	747.0	1,703
2Q	560.0	599.0	651.0	652.0	648.0	1,562
3Q	596.0	528.0	591.0	649.0	630.0	1,553
4Q	776.0	598.0	717.0	825.0	875.0	1,781
Yr.	2,563	2,343	·2,664	2,899	2,900	6,599
Earnings Per Share ($)						
1Q	0.57	0.51	0.43	0.45	0.41	0.53
2Q	0.67	0.51	0.47	0.49	0.39	0.50
3Q	0.57	0.55	0.47	0.59	0.38	0.25
4Q	0.56	0.56	0.58	0.52	0.42	-2.68
Yr.	2.37	2.12	1.95	2.06	1.60	-1.45

Next earnings report expected: early May

Dividend Data (Dividends have been paid since 1909.)

Amount ($)	Date Decl.	Ex-Div. Date	Stock of Record	Payment Date
0.360	Apr. 02	Apr. 17	Apr. 19	May. 15 '96
0.360	Jun. 04	Jul. 17	Jul. 19	Aug. 15 '96
0.360	Oct. 01	Oct. 17	Oct. 21	Nov. 15 '96
0.360	Jan. 07	Jan. 16	Jan. 21	Feb. 14 '97

A Division of The McGraw-Hill Companies

STANDARD &POOR'S
STOCK REPORTS

Pacific Enterprises

1735V
16-FEB-97

Business Summary - 05-FEB-97

Pacific Enterprises (formerly Pacific Lighting) distributes natural gas in Southern California, including Los Angeles, and in parts of central California, through its Southern California Gas (SoCalGas) unit, the largest U.S. gas distributor. In January 1996, Pacific Enterprises entered into a preliminary agreement to acquire a 12.5% stake in two Argentine natural gas utility holding companies with distribution activities in the Argentine regions of Pampeana and Sur. Gas revenues by customer group in recent years were:

	1995	1994	1993
Residential	63%	63%	60%
Commercial/industrial	30%	29%	31%
Utility electric generation	4%	4%	5%
Wholesale & other	3%	4%	4%

Gas throughput of 937 Bcf in 1995, down from 1,020 Bcf in 1994, was divided: 38% commercial and industrial, 25% residential, 22% electric generation, 14% wholesale, and 1% exchange. About 63% of gas deliveries in 1995 were customer-owned gas, down from 64% in 1994. At 1995 year end, the population of the company's service area totaled 17,260,000, up from 17,070,000 a year earlier. Active meters were 4.73 million, versus 4.69 million. The weighted average rate base at March 31, 1996 was $2,726 million, down from $2,854 million the prior year. In 1996, SoCalGas is authorized to earn a 9.42% (9.67% in 1995) rate of return on rate base and a 11.6% (12.00%) rate of return on common equity. SoCalGas provides a gas storage service; as of December 31, 1995, SoCalGas stored about 42 Bcf of customer-owned gas.

Other activities include the operation of an interstate and offshore natural gas pipeline and building and operating electricity-generating plants fueled by renewable energy sources, including gas.

Important Developments

Oct. '96—Enova Corp. and Pacific Enterprises (PET), the parent of Southern California Gas Co., agreed to merge in a tax-free, stock-for-stock transaction valued at $2.8 billion. ENA shareholders will receive one common share of the new holding company, while each PET common share will be exchanged for 1.5038 shares. Subject to various approvals, the merger is expected to be completed by the end of 1997. In the interim, the two companies will form a joint venture to provide integrated energy and energy-related products and services to select marketing segments.

Capitalization

Long Term Debt: $1,225,000,000 (12/96).
Subsidiary Preferred Stock: $175,000,000.

Per Share Data ($) (Year Ended Dec. 31)	1996	1995	1994	1993	1992	1991	1990	1989	1988	1987
Tangible Bk. Val.	NA	15.53	14.31	12.19	9.44	19.74	23.76	27.55	28.40	27.11
Cash Flow	NA	5.22	4.87	5.08	4.76	4.02	4.49	8.47	8.55	7.61
Earnings	2.37	2.12	1.95	2.06	1.60	-1.45	-0.86	3.05	3.51	3.69
Dividends	1.42	1.34	1.26	0.60	0.44	2.62	3.48	3.48	3.48	3.48
Payout Ratio	60%	63%	65%	29%	28%	NM	NM	122%	103%	95%
Prices - High	32 1/2	28 5/8	24 1/2	27 3/8	27 3/8	43 3/8	52	53 3/4	52 7/8	61 1/4
- Low	24 1/2	21	19 1/4	18 1/2	17 3/8	23 1/4	34 1/4	37 1/8	35 5/8	45 3/4
P/E Ratio - High	14	14	13	13	17	NM	NM	18	15	17
- Low	10	10	10	9	11	NM	NM	12	10	12
Income Statement Analysis (Million $)										
Revs.	NA	2,377	2,664	2,899	2,900	6,599	6,923	6,762	5,932	5,339
Oper. Inc.	NA	422	650	671	649	509	995	924	887	765
Depr.	NA	243	239	243	236	393	374	352	311	233
Int. Exp.	NA	117	132	142	163	230	248	258	226	158
Pretax Inc.	NA	314	321	317	265	-35.0	-17.0	368	410	404
Eff. Tax Rate	NA	41%	43%	40%	46%	NM	NM	41%	44%	43%
Net Inc.	NA	185	182	191	143	-81.0	-35.0	218	229	232
Balance Sheet & Other Fin. Data (Million $)										
Cash	NA	351	287	152	432	103	187	309	158	60.0
Curr. Assets	NA	1,170	1,323	1,264	1,547	1,966	2,181	2,158	1,924	1,402
Total Assets	NA	5,259	5,445	5,596	5,414	6,701	7,291	7,326	6,866	5,027
Curr. Liab.	NA	965	1,146	1,463	1,165	1,526	2,213	2,122	2,074	1,388
LT Debt	NA	1,386	1,550	1,394	1,915	2,381	1,998	1,816	1,917	1,403
Common Eqty.	NA	1,295	1,210	1,026	711	1,441	1,680	1,911	1,814	1,612
Total Cap.	NA	3,377	3,400	3,127	3,245	4,793	4,665	4,789	4,566	3,547
Cap. Exp.	NA	240	249	327	329	537	654	640	1,076	521
Cash Flow	NA	428	399	409	356	289	314	550	527	451
Curr. Ratio	NA	1.2	1.2	0.9	1.3	1.3	1.0	1.0	0.9	1.0
% LT Debt of Cap.	NA	41.0	45.6	44.6	59.0	49.7	42.8	37.9	42.0	39.6
% Net Inc.of Revs.	NA	7.8	6.8	6.6	4.9	NM	NM	3.2	3.9	4.3
% Ret. on Assets	NA	3.5	3.3	3.3	2.3	NM	NM	2.9	3.7	4.6
% Ret. on Equity	NA	14.0	14.3	18.2	10.9	NM	NM	10.2	12.2	13.8

Data as orig. reptd.; bef. results of disc. opers. and/or spec. items. Per share data adj. for stk. divs. as of ex-div. date. E-Estimated. NA-Not Available. NM-Not Meaningful. NR-Not Ranked.

Office—555 West Fifth St., Los Angeles, CA 90013. **Tel**—(213) 895-5000. **Co-Chrmn**—W. B. Wood, Jr. **CEO**—W. B. Wood. **SVP & CFO**—L. J. Dagley. **Secy**—T. C. Sanger. **Treas**—D. V. Arriola. **Investor Contact**—Clem Teng. **Dirs**—H. H. Bertea, H. L. Carter, R. D. Farman, W. D. Godbold Jr., I. E. Lozano Jr., H. M. Messmer Jr., P. A. Miller, R. J. Stegemeier, D. L. Walker, W. B. Wood. **Transfer Agent & Registrar**—Chase Bank, NYC. **Incorporated**—in California in 1907. **Empl**— 7,900. **S&P Analyst:** Justin McCann

STANDARD &POOR'S
STOCK REPORTS

Penney (J.C.)

1780

NYSE Symbol **JCP**

In S&P 500

16-FEB-97

Industry:
Retail Stores

Summary: J.C. Penney is one of the largest U.S. retailers through its department stores and catalog operations. Penney also operates a chain of drug stores.

S&P Opinion: Hold (★★★)	Recent Price • 48⅝	Yield • 4.3%
	52 Wk Range • 57-46⅛	12-Mo. P/E • 14.5

Earnings vs. Previous Year
▲=Up ▼=Down ▶=No Change

Quantitative Evaluations

Outlook
(1 Lowest—5 Highest)
• **3⁻**

Fair Value
• **47½**

Risk
• **Low**

Earn./Div. Rank
• **B+**

Technical Eval.
• **Bearish** since 12/96

Rel. Strength Rank
(1 Lowest—99 Highest)
• **33**

Insider Activity
• **Neutral**

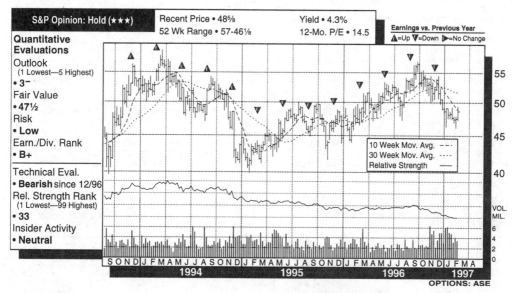

10 Week Mov. Avg. ---
30 Week Mov. Avg. ·····
Relative Strength —

VOL.
MIL.

OPTIONS: ASE

Overview - 06-JAN-97

Sales in FY 98 (Jan.) should show modest increases in comparable-store sales of some 3%; total sales should increase 8%, boosted by seven stores in Washington D.C., acquired from Woodward & Lothrop. Gross margins could widen somewhat as competitive pricing eases. SG&A expenses should remain well controlled. Operating income could increase some 6% to 7%. Interest expense will be higher, as the company uses debt financing to fund acquisition of drug store chains. The company's strong cash flow will be used for its $700 million annual capital expenditure program over the next three years. JCP plans to open more than 100 stores in that time. The company is testing a freestanding soft goods home furnishings store with a total of 21 locations planned in the near future. The freed up space in department stores would be replaced by expanded lines of apparel, which has higher margins.

Valuation - 06-JAN-97

The share price of this successful, well-managed, moderate-priced department store chain have fallen in tandem with the year-end selloff in retail stocks. However, we believe that the shares should be held for total return. The company should continue to gain marketshare as the retail landscape becomes less crowded. However, with growth in retailing limited, the company's acquisition of drug store chains provides an opportunity for growth and solid earnings gains. We anticipate more acquisitions of small drug chains and groups of stores over time. The company's strong cash flow and healthy dividend yield of about 4% limit the downside.

Key Stock Statistics

S&P EPS Est. 1997	3.25	Tang. Bk. Value/Share	25.32
P/E on S&P Est. 1997	15.0	Beta	0.64
S&P EPS Est. 1998	4.40	Shareholders	53,000
Dividend Rate/Share	2.08	Market cap. (B)	$ 11.0
Shs. outstg. (M)	226.0	Inst. holdings	74%
Avg. daily vol. (M)	0.760		

Value of $10,000 invested 5 years ago: $ 21,284

Fiscal Year Ending Jan. 31

	1997	1996	1995	1994	1993	1992
Revenues (Million $)						
1Q	4,452	4,367	4,350	3,964	3,790	3,430
2Q	4,507	4,435	4,242	3,963	3,790	3,460
3Q	5,537	5,128	5,149	4,735	4,340	3,940
4Q	—	6,632	6,639	6,321	6,090	5,380
Yr.	—	20,562	20,380	18,983	18,010	16,200

Earnings Per Share ($)						
1Q	0.58	0.63	0.88	0.68	0.54	0.31
2Q	0.37	0.46	0.52	0.43	0.31	0.09
3Q	0.98	1.00	1.11	0.88	0.75	0.46
4Q	E1.30	1.39	1.78	1.80	1.55	0.13
Yr.	E3.25	3.48	4.29	3.79	3.15	0.98

Next earnings report expected: mid February

Dividend Data (Dividends have been paid since 1922.)

Amount ($)	Date Decl.	Ex-Div. Date	Stock of Record	Payment Date
0.520	Mar. 13	Apr. 08	Apr. 10	May. 01 '96
0.520	May. 20	Jul. 08	Jul. 10	Aug. 01 '96
0.520	Sep. 11	Oct. 08	Oct. 10	Nov. 01 '96
0.520	Nov. 13	Jan. 08	Jan. 10	Feb. 01 '97

A Division of The McGraw·Hill Companies

J.C. Penney Company, Inc.

Business Summary - 20-JUN-96

J.C. Penney operates 1,238 department stores in 50 states, Puerto Rico, Mexico and Chile. The company also operates 548 freestanding sales centers and 526 drug stores.

At January 27, 1996, the company was operating 1,238 J.C. Penney stores with sales per square foot in of $156, down from $159 in FY 95. These stores are primarily in premier regional shopping centers in the suburbs. The company was also operating 548 freestanding sales centers and merchants. Catalog sales totaled $3.7 billion in FY 96, and accounted for 18% of total retail sales.

The company has created a merchandise development organization to build private label brands into a coordinated merchandising collection to compete with national brands. The strategy focuses on developing well-priced, fashionable, coordinated apparel and home lines. Private label names include, Worthington brand for career women, Original Arizona Jean Company, Stafford Executive suits and Classic Traditions, a home furnishings collection.

Drug stores, operating under the Thrift Drug Center names, averaged sales per gross square foot were $253. These units accounted for 9.0% of total retail sales in FY 96.

J.C. Penney Life Insurance Co. markets life, health and credit insurance through direct response. At the end of FY 96, there were 9.0 million policies and certificates in force. J.C. Penney National Bank offers Visa and MasterCard credit cards; about 470,000 credit cards were active at the end of FY 96.

Important Developments

Dec. '96—The company completed its cash tender offer for 50.1% of Eckerd Corp. (ECK) shares at $35 each; the remaining ECK shareholders will receive 0.6604 of a JCP share. The merger is expected to close in the first quarter of 1997. In October, JCP acquired Fay's Inc., a 272 store retail drug store chain, for 5.2 million common shares valued at about $278 million. Separately, management said that sales in the third quarter of FY 97 increased 8.0%. Gross margin as a percentage of sales narrowed, reflecting aggressive marketing programs but SG&A expenses declined to 22.5% of sales from 23.4% of sales a year ago. As of July 27, 1996, the company repurchased 7.5 million shares of its common stock.

Capitalization

Long Term Debt: $4,663,000,000 (10/26/96).
ESOP 7.9% Preferred Stock: $574,000,000. Conv. into 11.8 million com. shs.

Per Share Data ($) (Year Ended Jan. 31)	1996	1995	1994	1993	1992	1991	1990	1989	1988	1987
Tangible Bk. Val.	23.58	23.27	21.59	20.04	15.02	15.86	15.16	13.24	15.07	14.50
Cash Flow	5.15	5.65	5.10	4.46	2.33	3.56	4.28	3.99	2.87	2.53
Earnings	3.48	4.29	3.79	3.15	0.99	2.29	3.16	3.01	2.05	1.77
Dividends	1.92	1.68	1.80	1.32	1.32	1.32	1.12	1.00	0.74	0.62
Payout Ratio	55%	38%	47%	42%	134%	58%	35%	31%	34%	35%
Cal. Yrs.	1995	1994	1993	1992	1991	1990	1989	1988	1987	1986
Prices - High	50	59	56 3/8	40 1/4	29 1/8	37 7/8	36 5/8	27 7/8	33	22 1/8
- Low	39 7/8	41	35 3/8	25 3/8	21 1/4	18 3/4	25 1/4	19	17 7/8	13 1/4
P/E Ratio - High	14	14	15	13	30	16	12	9	16	13
- Low	11	10	9	8	22	8	8	6	9	7
Income Statement Analysis (Million $)										
Revs.	20,562	21,706	19,578	19,085	17,295	17,410	17,045	15,938	16,008	15,443
Oper. Inc.	1,200	2,292	1,943	1,825	1,485	1,432	1,780	1,535	1,638	1,504
Depr.	341	323	316	308	314	299	275	258	241	229
Int. Exp.	383	320	289	324	327	331	358	365	324	383
Pretax Inc.	1,341	1,699	1,554	1,259	468	832	1,170	1,192	964	958
Eff. Tax Rate	38%	38%	39%	38%	44%	31%	32%	32%	37%	45%
Net Inc.	838	1,057	944	777	264	577	802	807	608	530
Balance Sheet & Other Fin. Data (Million $)										
Cash	173	261	173	397	111	137	408	670	112	639
Curr. Assets	9,409	9,468	8,565	6,970	6,695	6,799	7,539	7,246	7,130	7,532
Total Assets	17,102	16,202	14,788	13,563	12,520	12,325	12,698	12,254	10,842	11,188
Curr. Liab.	4,020	4,481	3,883	3,077	2,409	2,662	3,400	2,785	2,686	2,712
LT Debt	4,080	3,335	2,929	3,171	3,354	3,135	2,755	3,064	2,608	2,655
Common Eqty.	5,509	5,292	5,096	4,486	3,504	3,697	3,649	3,251	4,173	4,340
Total Cap.	11,152	9,989	9,307	8,707	8,335	8,550	8,232	8,367	8,156	8,476
Cap. Exp.	717	550	480	453	515	637	519	487	376	350
Cash Flow	1,179	1,340	1,220	1,052	544	842	1,042	1,048	849	759
Curr. Ratio	2.3	2.1	2.2	2.3	2.8	2.6	2.2	2.6	2.7	2.8
% LT Debt of Cap.	36.6	33.4	31.5	36.4	40.2	36.7	33.5	36.6	32.0	31.3
% Net Inc.of Revs.	4.1	4.9	4.8	4.1	1.5	3.3	4.7	5.1	3.8	3.4
% Ret. on Assets	4.8	6.9	6.6	5.9	2.1	4.7	6.5	7.4	5.7	4.9
% Ret. on Equity	14.8	19.9	18.8	17.5	6.4	15.0	22.4	22.7	14.9	12.6

Data as orig. reptd.; bef. results of disc. opers. and/or spec. items. Per share data adj. for stk. divs. as of ex-div. date. E-Estimated. NA-Not Available. NM-Not Meaningful. NR-Not Ranked.

Office—6501 Legacy Dr., Plano, TX 75024-3698. **Registrar & Transfer Agent**—Chemical Bank, NYC. **Tel**—(214) 431-1000. **Website**—http://www.jcpenney.com **Chrmn**—W. R. Howell. **Vice Chrmn & CEO**—J. E. Oesterreicher. **Pres & COO**—W. B. Tygart. **EVP-CFO**—R. E. Northam. **Investor Contact**—Wynn C. Watkins. **Dirs**—M. A. Burns, C. H. Chandler, W. R. Howell, V. E. Jordan Jr., G. Nigh, J. E. Oesterreicher, J. C. Pfeiffer, A. W. Richards, C. S. Sanford, R. G. Turner, W. B. Tygart, J. D. Williams. **Incorporated**—in Delaware in 1924. **Empl**— 202,000. **S&P Analyst:** Karen J. Sack, CFA

Philip Morris
1822

NYSE Symbol **MO**

In S&P 500

16-FEB-97

Industry: Tobacco

Summary: Philip Morris is the world's largest cigarette producer, the largest U.S. food processor (Kraft Foods), and the second largest U.S. brewer (Miller Brewing).

S&P Opinion: Accumulate (★★★★)

Recent Price • 125½	Yield • 3.8%
52 Wk Range • 126¼-85⅝	12-Mo. P/E • 16.3

Quantitative Evaluations

Outlook
(1 Lowest—5 Highest)
• **2+**

Fair Value
• **117¼**

Risk
• **Low**

Earn./Div. Rank
• **A+**

Technical Eval.
• **Bullish** since 11/96

Rel. Strength Rank
(1 Lowest—99 Highest)
• **83**

Insider Activity
• **NA**

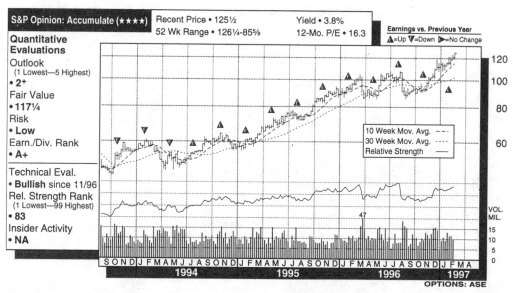

Earnings vs. Previous Year
▲=Up ▼=Down ▶=No Change

10 Week Mov. Avg. – – –
30 Week Mov. Avg. .....
Relative Strength ——

OPTIONS: ASE

Overview - 04-FEB-97

Total tobacco profits are expected to climb at a mid-teen annual pace in 1997, driven primarily by a continued high single-digit rise in worldwide cigarette volume, an improving product mix shift to full-priced, premium brands (principally Marlboro), and higher selling prices. Food and beer profits are expected to grow more modestly, led by an improved U.S. and international business mix. A stronger dollar relative to key foreign currencies may be a near-term restraining factor, but reduced interest expense and continued aggressive stock repurchases should allow earnings per share to advance by nearly 16%, to $8.90 in 1997. Further divestments of underperforming businesses are possible, which could enhance our near-term earnings estimates. A 2-for-1 stock split is likely by 1997 year-end.

Valuation - 04-FEB-97

Given our bullish earnings growth projections, MO's relatively modest P/E valuation (approximately 20% below that of the S&P 500), and an attractive 4% dividend yield, we believe MO offers investors above average total return prospects over the next six to 12 months. Although tobacco industry risks are above average, we believe that a recent development was very positive for the industry in this regard: in mid-1996, a federal court's decertification of class-action status of a lawsuit brought on behalf of smokers seeking damages established an important legal precedent influencing future federal and state class-action certification efforts. Although other hurdles remain (including possible FDA oversight of the tobacco industry), we believe that the stock's strong fundamentals and low relative valuation outweigh such potential risks.

Key Stock Statistics

S&P EPS Est. 1997	8.90	Tang. Bk. Value/Share	NM
P/E on S&P Est. 1997	14.1	Beta	1.27
Dividend Rate/Share	4.80	Shareholders	144,400
Shs. outstg. (M)	814.4	Market cap. (B)	$102.2
Avg. daily vol. (M)	2.272	Inst. holdings	59%

Value of $10,000 invested 5 years ago: $ 19,225

Fiscal Year Ending Dec. 31

	1996	1995	1994	1993	1992	1991
Revenues (Million $)						
1Q	13,734	13,300	12,727	12,570	11,850	11,950
2Q	13,760	13,763	13,532	13,160	12,940	12,530
3Q	13,688	13,329	13,673	12,580	12,660	11,790
4Q	13,371	12,747	13,844	12,320	12,650	11,790
Yr.	54,553	53,139	53,776	50,621	50,100	48,060
Earnings Per Share ($)						
1Q	1.89	1.60	1.34	1.38	1.20	0.99
2Q	1.97	1.67	1.42	1.20	1.48	1.22
3Q	2.01	1.71	1.42	1.11	1.44	1.20
4Q	1.81	1.53	1.27	0.38	1.34	0.83
Yr.	7.68	6.51	5.45	4.06	5.45	4.24

Next earnings report expected: mid April

Dividend Data (Dividends have been paid since 1928.)

Amount ($)	Date Decl.	Ex-Div. Date	Stock of Record	Payment Date
1.000	Feb. 28	Mar. 13	Mar. 15	Apr. 10 '96
1.000	May. 29	Jun. 12	Jun. 14	Jul. 10 '96
1.200	Aug. 28	Sep. 12	Sep. 16	Oct. 10 '96
1.200	Nov. 27	Dec. 12	Dec. 16	Jan. 10 '97

STANDARD
&POOR'S
STOCK REPORTS

Philip Morris Companies Inc.

1822

16-FEB-97

Business Summary - 04-FEB-97

Philip Morris is the largest cigarette company in the world and a major food and beer producer. Segment contributions in 1996:

	Revs.	Profits
Tobacco	53%	64%
Food	40%	31%
Brewing	6%	3%
Financial & real estate	1%	2%

International operations accounted for approximately 51% of sales (including U.S. exports) and 42% of operating profits in 1996.

Philip Morris U.S.A., with 48% of the U.S. cigarette market, accounted for 18% of total company sales and 33% of operating profits in 1996. Major brands include Marlboro, Benson & Hedges, Merit, Virginia Slims and Cambridge. MO is a defendant in a number of product-liability suits related to cigarettes. Philip Morris International's share of the world market in 1995 (excluding U.S.; latest available) was approximately 12%.

Kraft Foods is the largest processor and marketer in the U.S. of packaged grocery, coffee, cheese and processed meat products. Kraft Foods International produces a wide variety of similar products that are manufactured and marketed in Europe, Canada, Latin America and the Asia/Pacific region. Food products include Post cereals; Jell-O desserts; Maxwell House coffee; Velveeta, Cracker Barrel and Churny cheeses; Oscar Mayer meat products; and Claussen pickles.

Miller Brewing (No. 2 U.S. brewer) holds about 22% of the U.S. beer market. Brands include High Life, Lite, Genuine Draft, Lowenbrau, and Meister Brau. Miller also imports more than 20 brands from six countries, including Molson and Foster's Lager.

Important Developments

Jan. '97—During 1996, domestic tobacco profits increased 12%, year to year, primarily reflecting 4% greater cigarette shipments and a favorable product mix shift toward full-priced brands (principally Marlboro). International tobacco profits rose 18%, driven by 11% greater unit volume and increased prices, partially offset by unfavorable currency exchange translations. Food profits rose 4% (8% excluding divestments), aided by volume gains and cost reductions. Beer profits fell 1% on lower volumes. Separately, during the year, MO raised the annual dividend 20%, to $4.80 per share, and repurchased 28.6 million of its common shares for $2.8 billion; the share repurchases were part of a three-year, $6 billion program begun in the fourth quarter of 1994.

Capitalization

Long Term Debt: $11,827,000,000 (12/96).

Per Share Data ($)

(Year Ended Dec. 31)	1996	1995	1994	1993	1992	1991	1990	1989	1988	1987
Tangible Bk. Val.	NA	-6.42	-8.20	-9.30	-6.72	-6.69	-7.70	-6.58	-8.00	2.93
Cash Flow	NA	8.49	7.33	5.90	7.09	5.80	5.26	4.41	3.00	2.64
Earnings	7.68	6.51	5.45	4.06	5.45	4.24	3.83	3.18	2.22	1.94
Dividends	4.40	3.65	3.03	2.60	2.35	1.91	1.55	1.25	1.01	0.79
Payout Ratio	57%	56%	56%	64%	43%	45%	40%	39%	45%	40%
Prices - High	119	94³/₈	64¹/₂	77⁵/₈	86⁵/₈	81³/₄	52	45³/₄	25¹/₂	31¹/₈
- Low	85⁵/₈	55³/₄	47¹/₄	45	69¹/₂	48¹/₄	36	25	20¹/₈	18¹/₈
P/E Ratio - High	15	14	12	19	16	19	14	14	12	16
- Low	11	9	9	11	13	11	9	8	9	9

Income Statement Analysis (Million $)

	1996	1995	1994	1993	1992	1991	1990	1989	1988	1987
Revs.	NA	53,139	53,776	50,621	50,095	48,064	44,323	39,011	25,860	22,279
Oper. Inc.	NA	12,192	11,080	9,939	11,550	10,515	9,271	7,931	5,130	4,646
Depr.	NA	1,671	1,631	1,611	1,484	1,438	1,325	1,142	733	668
Int. Exp.	NA	1,259	1,288	1,478	1,513	1,696	1,746	1,789	739	727
Pretax Inc.	NA	9,347	8,216	6,196	8,608	6,971	6,311	5,058	3,727	3,348
Eff. Tax Rate	NA	41%	43%	42%	43%	44%	44%	42%	45%	45%
Net Inc.	NA	5,478	4,725	3,568	4,939	3,927	3,540	2,946	2,064	1,842

Balance Sheet & Other Fin. Data (Million $)

	1996	1995	1994	1993	1992	1991	1990	1989	1988	1987
Cash	NA	1,138	184	182	1,021	126	146	118	168	189
Curr. Assets	NA	14,879	NA	NA	NA	NA	NA	NA	NA	6,572
Total Assets	NA	53,811	52,649	51,205	50,014	47,384	46,569	38,528	36,960	19,145
Curr. Liab.	NA	14,273	NA	NA	NA	NA	NA	NA	NA	5,176
LT Debt	NA	13,107	14,975	15,021	14,265	14,200	16,108	14,685	17,102	5,222
Common Eqty.	NA	13,985	12,786	11,627	12,563	12,512	11,947	9,571	7,679	6,823
Total Cap.	NA	30,830	31,156	29,715	29,716	29,186	30,753	26,264	26,500	13,333
Cap. Exp.	NA	1,621	1,726	1,592	1,573	1,562	1,355	1,246	3,145	776
Cash Flow	NA	7,149	6,356	5,179	6,423	5,365	4,865	4,088	2,797	2,510
Curr. Ratio	NA	1.4	NA	NA	NA	NA	NA	NA	NA	1.3
% LT Debt of Cap.	NA	42.6	48.1	50.6	48.0	48.7	52.4	55.9	64.6	39.2
% Net Inc.of Revs.	NA	10.3	8.8	7.0	9.9	8.2	8.0	7.6	8.0	8.3
% Ret. on Assets	NA	10.3	9.2	7.1	10.3	8.4	8.3	7.8	7.4	10.0
% Ret. on Equity	NA	41.0	39.2	29.8	40.0	32.2	32.9	34.1	28.8	29.6

Data as orig. reptd.; bef. results of disc. opers. and/or spec. items. Per share data adj. for stk. divs. as of ex-div. date. E-Estimated. NA-Not Available. NM-Not Meaningful. NR-Not Ranked.

Office—120 Park Ave., New York, NY 10017. **Tel**—(212) 880-5000. **Chrmn & CEO**—G. C. Bible. **SVP-CFO**—H. G. Storr. **VP-Secy**—G. P. Holsenbeck. **Investor Contact**—Michael Kenny. **Dirs**—E. E. Bailey, G. C. Bible, M. H. Bring, H. Brown, W. H. Donaldson, J. Evans, R. E. R. Huntley, R. Murdoch, J. D. Nichols, R. D. Parsons, R. S. Penske, J. S. Reed, H. G. Storr, S. M. Wolf. **Transfer Agents & Registrars**—First Chicago Trust Co. of New York, NYC. **Incorporated**—in Virginia in 1919. **Empl**— 165,000. **S&P Analyst:** Kenneth A. Shea

Potomac Electric Power   1863S

NYSE Symbol **POM**

In S&P MidCap 400

16-FEB-97

Industry: Utilities-Electric

Summary: This electric utility, which serves customers in Washington D.C., including the Federal Government, and suburban Maryland is planning to merge with Baltimore Gas & Electric.

S&P Opinion: Hold (★★★)	Recent Price • 25⅝	Yield • 6.5%	Earnings vs. Previous Year
	52 Wk Range • 27⅜-23⅝	12-Mo. P/E • 13.8	▲=Up ▼=Down ▶=No Change

Quantitative Evaluations

Outlook (1 Lowest—5 Highest)
• **2**

Fair Value
• **24½**

Risk
• **Low**

Earn./Div. Rank
• **B**

Technical Eval.
• **Bearish** since 1/97

Rel. Strength Rank (1 Lowest—99 Highest)
• **45**

Insider Activity
• **NA**

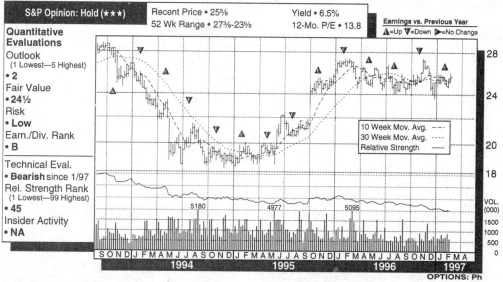

10 Week Mov. Avg. — ·—
30 Week Mov. Avg. ·····
Relative Strength ——

OPTIONS: Ph

Overview - 13-FEB-97

The pending merger with Baltimore Gas & Electric will result in a new company, Constellation Energy Corp., with assets totaling $15 billion and annual revenue of approximately $5 billion. The federal and state regulatory approval process is expected to be completed during the spring of 1997. The merger is expected to realize cost savings of roughly $1.3 billion over 10 years, with much of the savings (mainly from workforce reductions) to come soon after the completion of the merger, while the rest will be achieved through economies of scale and the elimination of duplicate functions. Results in 1996 were aided by the continuing effect of a 3.8% rate hike in the District of Columbia and the absence of one-time, non-cash charges of $1.04 in 1995. On its own, POM should see long-term benefit from the low level of price-sensitive industrial customers and steady growth in its service territory.

Valuation - 13-FEB-97

We continue to recommend holding the stock. After a 40% gain in 1995, the shares were down 1.9% in 1996 (compared to a 5% decline for the S&P Index of Electric Companies and a 20% advance for the S&P 500). However, we expect POM's shares to reflect the joint cost-savings ability of the new company being created through the proposed merger with Baltimore Gas & Electric (BGE), along with the combined company's greater insulation from a more deregulated and competitive environment. While the stock appears fully valued at a P/E multiple of 14X our EPS estimate for 1997, an above-average dividend yield makes POM shares an attractive holding for income. With the dividend payout at an above-average 89% of earnings, an increase is not expected prior to the completion of the merger. The dividend of the combined company, Constellation Energy, is expected to be $1.67 a share.

Key Stock Statistics

S&P EPS Est. 1997	1.86	Tang. Bk. Value/Share	16.25
P/E on S&P Est. 1997	13.8	Beta	0.60
Dividend Rate/Share	1.66	Shareholders	97,000
Shs. outstg. (M)	118.5	Market cap. (B)	$ 3.0
Avg. daily vol. (M)	0.141	Inst. holdings	25%

Value of $10,000 invested 5 years ago: $ 14,555

Fiscal Year Ending Dec. 31

	1996	1995	1994	1993	1992	1991
Revenues (Million $)						
1Q	436.6	364.9	393.0	339.5	326.0	290.0
2Q	501.8	445.4	467.5	419.7	390.5	361.0
3Q	658.2	663.6	607.5	614.3	553.6	563.0
4Q	413.7	402.3	355.1	351.8	331.5	339.0
Yr.	2,010	1,876	1,823	1,725	1,602	1,552
Earnings Per Share ($)						
1Q	0.09	-0.07	0.09	0.08	0.04	0.04
2Q	0.57	-0.52	0.51	0.63	0.41	0.38
3Q	1.14	1.20	1.11	1.21	1.06	1.21
4Q	0.06	0.04	0.08	0.02	0.15	0.22
Yr.	1.86	0.65	1.79	1.95	1.66	1.87

Next earnings report expected: late April

Dividend Data (Dividends have been paid since 1904.)

Amount ($)	Date Decl.	Ex-Div. Date	Stock of Record	Payment Date
0.415	Apr. 24	May. 28	May. 30	Jun. 28 '96
0.415	Jul. 25	Aug. 27	Aug. 29	Sep. 30 '96
0.415	Oct. 24	Nov. 25	Nov. 27	Dec. 31 '96
0.415	Jan. 23	Mar. 06	Mar. 10	Mar. 31 '97

Potomac Electric Power Company

STANDARD
&POOR'S
STOCK REPORTS

1863S
16-FEB-97

Business Summary - 13-FEB-97

Potomac Electric Power provides retail electric service in the Washington metropolitan area, including the District of Columbia (40% of revenues) and major portions of Montgomery and Prince Georges counties in Maryland (60%), with a population of some 1.9 million. Electricity is also sold at wholesale. POM's unique service territory, with virtually no heavy industry, benefits from economic stability and low unemployment. Electric revenues by customer class in recent years were:

	1995	1994	1993	1992
Residential	30%	30%	30%	28%
Commercial	47%	47%	47%	48%
Federal government	14%	14%	14%	15%
Other	9%	9%	9%	9%

Sources of electric generation in 1995 were coal 85%, oil and natural gas 15%. POM also sells and purchases power to and from outside suppliers. Peak demand in 1995 was 5,732 mw, and capability at peak totaled 6,846 mw, for a capacity margin of 16%.

POM expects annual growth in peak demand at a compound annual rate of roughly 1%. The company's ongoing strategies to meet increasing electric demand include conservation and energy use management programs designed to curtail growth in peak demand and defer construction of additional generating capacity. It also expects to rely more heavily on purchased power.

In July 1995, the District of Columbia Public Service Commission authorized a $27.9 million increase in POM's base rate revenues and a $29.2 million rate increase in 1994.

In September 1995, POM and Baltimore Gas & Electric (BGE) agreed to merge into a new company, Constellation Energy Corp. In the merger, POM common shareholders would receive 0.997 share of the new company for each POM common share held; BGE common shares would be exchanged for those of Constellation on a share-for-share basis. The companies anticipate the combined company will realize savings from workforce reductions and other cost saving activities of about $1.3 billion over ten years. As of the closing date, the annual dividend to be paid would be $1.67 a share. The company hopes to have all necessary approvals for the merger by the spring of 1997.

Capitalization

Long Term Debt: $1,767,598,000 (12/96).
Red. Preferred Stock: $142,500,000.
Cum. Preferred Stock: $125,298,000.

Per Share Data ($)

(Year Ended Dec. 31)	1996	1995	1994	1993	1992	1991	1990	1989	1988	1987
Tangible Bk. Val.	NA	15.79	16.27	16.33	15.68	15.31	14.26	14.11	13.11	12.53
Earnings	1.86	0.65	1.79	1.95	1.66	1.87	1.62	2.16	2.14	2.11
Dividends	1.66	1.66	1.66	1.64	1.60	1.56	1.52	1.46	1.38	1.30
Payout Ratio	89%	NM	93%	84%	96%	83%	94%	68%	64%	62%
Prices - High	27⅜	26¼	26⅝	28⅞	27½	25⅛	24	24¼	24	27⅜
- Low	23⅝	18⅜	18¼	23⅞	22⅝	19⅝	18	19¼	19¼	18
P/E Ratio - High	15	40	15	15	17	13	15	11	11	13
- Low	13	28	10	12	14	10	11	9	9	9

Income Statement Analysis (Million $)

	1996	1995	1994	1993	1992	1991	1990	1989	1988	1987
Revs.	NA	1,876	1,791	1,702	1,562	1,552	1,412	1,395	1,350	1,332
Depr.	NA	205	180	163	150	134	124	120	121	116
Maint.	NA	93.0	93.0	94.0	91.0	90.0	91.0	93.0	93.0	100
Fxd. Chgs. Cov.	NA	2.5	3.1	3.0	2.5	3.1	2.9	3.7	3.9	4.4
Constr. Credits	NA	9.1	19.0	23.0	29.7	32.9	27.2	15.5	8.7	5.3
Eff. Tax Rate	NA	58%	35%	31%	31%	28%	27%	32%	27%	38%
Net Inc.	NA	94.0	227	242	201	210	170	215	211	208

Balance Sheet & Other Fin. Data (Million $)

	1996	1995	1994	1993	1992	1991	1990	1989	1988	1987
Gross Prop.	NA	6,161	5,938	5,665	5,368	5,048	4,659	4,271	3,946	3,700
Cap. Exp.	NA	231	317	323	358	432	420	345	273	241
Net Prop.	NA	4,400	4,298	4,131	3,931	3,707	3,398	3,098	2,857	2,679
Capitalization:										
LT Debt	NA	3,029	3,001	2,617	2,468	2,483	2,117	1,639	1,531	1,104
% LT Debt	NA	59	57	54	54	56	57	52	52	45
Pfd.	NA	264	269	272	274	226	176	126	143	144
% Pfd.	NA	5.20	5.10	5.60	6.00	5.10	4.70	4.00	4.90	5.90
Common	NA	1,871	1,955	1,955	1,823	1,716	1,435	1,394	1,249	1,191
% Common	NA	36	37	54	40	39	39	44	43	49
Total Cap.	NA	5,169	6,005	5,698	5,164	4,982	4,270	3,691	3,433	2,941
Oper. Ratio	NA	81.5	82.2	81.2	84.6	81.3	81.9	80.3	79.8	80.3
% Earn. on Net Prop.	NA	8.0	7.7	8.1	6.3	8.2	7.9	9.2	9.9	10.0
% Ret. on Revs.	NA	5.0	13.0	14.0	12.9	13.5	12.1	15.4	15.6	15.6
% Ret. On Invest.Cap	NA	5.6	6.1	6.9	6.4	7.1	7.0	8.8	9.5	10.3
% Return On Com.Eqty	NA	4.9	10.8	11.9	11.4	12.6	11.3	15.5	16.5	17.3

Data as orig. reptd.; bef. results of disc. opers. and/or spec. items. Per share data adj. for stk. divs. as of ex-div. date. E-Estimated. NA-Not Available. NM-Not Meaningful. NR-Not Ranked.

Office—1900 Pennsylvania Ave, N.W., Washington, D.C. 20068. **Tel**—(202) 872-2000. **Chrmn & CEO**—E. F. Mitchell. **Pres**—J. M. Derrick, Jr. **Vice Chrmn**—H. L. Davis. **SVP & CFO**—D. R. Wraase. **Secy**—E. S. Rogers. **Investor Contact**—Peyton G. Middleton, Jr. **Dirs**—R. R. Blunt Sr., A. J. Clark, H. L. Davis, J. M. Derrick, Jr., R. E. Marriott, D. O. Maxwell, F. D. McKenzie, A. D. McLaughlin, E. F. Mitchell, P. F. O'Malley, L. A. Simpson, A. T. Young. **Transfer Agent & Registrar**—ChaseMellon Shareholder Services, Ridgefield Park, NJ.**Incorporated**—in District of Columbia in 1896. **Empl**— 4,863. **S&P Analyst:** Justin McCann

16-FEB-97

Industry:
Housewares

Summary: Premark makes commercial food equipment and consumer/decorative products, including West Bend small appliances. PMI spun off its Tupperware segment in mid-1996.

S&P Opinion: Hold (★★★)	Recent Price • 22	Yield • 5.5%
	52 Wk Range • 61¾-15	12-Mo. P/E • 12.0

Quantitative Evaluations

Outlook
(1 Lowest—5 Highest)
• **4**

Fair Value
• **27½**

Risk
• **High**

Earn./Div. Rank
• **B**

Technical Eval.
• **Bullish** since 10/96

Rel. Strength Rank
(1 Lowest—99 Highest)
• **30**

Insider Activity
• **Neutral**

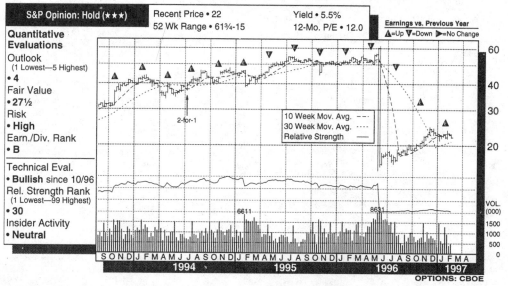

Earnings vs. Previous Year
▲=Up ▼=Down ▶=No Change

10 Week Mov. Avg. – –
30 Week Mov. Avg. ·····
Relative Strength —

OPTIONS: CBOE

Overview - 04-FEB-97

We expect sales from continuing operations to rise moderately in 1997, on continued demand for food equipment in domestic markets; a continuation of strong sales at Wilsonart, mainly reflecting new products and expanded distribution; and modest sales increases at Precor and West Bend. However, earnings at the food equipment group will be restricted by temporary disruptions in U.S. operations due to recent manufacturing realignments, as well as the impact of weak economies in several of the company's European markets. Over the longer term, margins should improve somewhat, on increased volume at the food equipment group in the U.S. and cost savings from the plant consolidation at this group; an improved cost structure at Florida Tile, and the absence of costs related to the roll-out of laminated floors. Interest and corporate expenses should also be lower reflecting the absence of Tupperware and Hartco Flooring.

Valuation - 04-FEB-97

PMI shares have traded in a narrow range since mid-1996 when the company spun off its Tupperware operations. Operating results for this company are extremely sensitive to economic cycles and/or competitive markets. Results at the food equipment division in Europe have been under pressure for several years, on economic weakness in certain markets, and PMI is currently undergoing a review of the division. On a positive note, the recent introduction of laminated flooring at the Wilsonart division has met with enormous success by flooring installers. Although our long-term outlook for this company's prospects are above-average, we believe the shares are adequately valued at 14 times our $1.65 EPS estimate for 1997, and would not add to our position at current levels.

Key Stock Statistics

S&P EPS Est. 1997	1.75	Tang. Bk. Value/Share	11.62
P/E on S&P Est. 1997	12.6	Beta	1.19
Dividend Rate/Share	1.20	Shareholders	25,000
Shs. outstg. (M)	62.5	Market cap. (B)	$ 1.4
Avg. daily vol. (M)	0.153	Inst. holdings	65%

Value of $10,000 invested 5 years ago: $ 12,128

Fiscal Year Ending Dec. 31

	1996	1995	1994	1993	1992	1991
Revenues (Million $)						
1Q	528.7	519.6	801.6	519.6	678.0	650.0
2Q	565.7	539.0	831.3	539.0	732.0	711.0
3Q	563.2	556.3	824.3	556.3	713.0	669.0
4Q	610.0	598.5	993.6	598.5	823.2	785.0
Yr.	2,268	2,213	3,451	2,213	2,946	2,816
Earnings Per Share ($)						
1Q	0.19	0.22	0.57	0.22	0.32	0.15
2Q	-0.27	0.27	0.86	0.27	0.47	0.44
3Q	0.46	0.41	0.62	0.41	-1.45	0.29
4Q	0.48	0.34	1.35	1.11	0.77	0.74
Yr.	0.87	1.24	3.39	2.57	0.07	1.63

Next earnings report expected: early May

Dividend Data (Dividends have been paid since 1987.)

Amount ($)	Date Decl.	Ex-Div. Date	Stock of Record	Payment Date
0.080	Aug. 07	Sep. 11	Sep. 13	Oct. 04 '96
0.001	Nov. 18	Dec. 12	Dec. 16	Jan. 06 '97
0.080	Nov. 06	Dec. 12	Dec. 16	Jan. 06 '97

A Division of The McGraw·Hill Companies

Premark International, Inc.

Business Summary - 04-FEB-97

Premark International manufactures and markets consumer and commercial products under well known brand names. The company spun off of its Tupperware (NYSE: TUP) segment (classified as a discontinued operation in 1995) in mid-1996. Business segment contributions from continuing operations in 1995:

	Sales	Profits
Food equipment	56%	55%
Decorative products	31%	30%
Consumer products	13%	15%

Approximately 57% of food equipment was sold in the U.S. in 1995, 36% in Europe, and the remainder un areas outside of Europe and the U.S. Practically all of the consumer/decorative products were sold in the U.S.

The food equipment group, which includes Hobart, Wolf and Vulcan-Hart, produces commercial food preparation equipment, including food mixers, slicers, cutters, meat saws and grinders; weighing and wrapping equipment and related systems; baking and cooking equipment such as ovens, ranges, fryers, griddles and broilers; refrigeration equipment; and warewashers.

The decorative products division consists of the Wilsonart division (decorative plastic laminates used on cabinetry, countertops, vanities, store fixtures and furniture); and Florida Tile (ceramic wall and floor tile). The consumer products division consists of West Bend (small electric appliances and stainless steel cookware) and Precor (home physical fitness equipment).

The spun-off Tupperware business manufactures and sells, directly to the consumer through independent distributors, molded plastic food storage and serving containers, educational toys and personal care and home products. Tupperware had net sales of $1.36 billion and operating income of $234.5 million in 1995.

Important Developments

Jan. '97—For the fourth quarter of 1996, PMI reported that income from continuing operations jumped 48%, to $32.0 million ($0.48 a share), from $21.6 million ($0.34), excluding $55.7 million ($0.88) income from the discontinued Tupperware operations in 1995. The company attributed the majority of the earnings increase to continued strong performance at Wilsonart, as well as significant improvements at Florida Tile and increases in the West Bend and Precor businesses.

Capitalization

Long Term Debt: $115,856,000 (12/96).

Per Share Data ($)

(Year Ended Dec. 31)	1996	1995	1994	1993	1992	1991	1990	1989	1988	1987
Tangible Bk. Val.	NA	13.74	12.44	9.86	8.17	10.21	9.19	10.06	9.56	9.31
Cash Flow	NA	2.35	5.34	4.09	2.62	3.25	2.22	2.13	2.73	1.98
Earnings	0.87	1.24	3.39	2.58	0.07	1.63	0.82	1.12	1.75	1.04
Dividends	0.73	1.01	0.64	0.54	0.48	0.42	0.42	0.39	0.26	0.15
Payout Ratio	84%	81%	19%	21%	NM	26%	50%	34%	15%	14%
Prices - High	61¾	54¾	48	41⅞	25⅝	20⅜	15½	21	18⅛	15⅞
- Low	15	38½	33⅝	19⅛	14⅞	8⅛	6⅜	14¾	11⅛	9¼
P/E Ratio - High	71	44	14	16	NM	13	19	19	10	15
- Low	17	31	10	7	NM	5	8	13	6	9

Income Statement Analysis (Million $)

	1996	1995	1994	1993	1992	1991	1990	1989	1988	1987
Revs.	NA	2,213	3,451	3,097	2,946	2,816	2,721	2,592	2,397	2,197
Oper. Inc.	NA	216	447	359	365	308	253	231	276	210
Depr.	NA	71.4	130	102	168	103	89.0	71.0	68.0	64.0
Int. Exp.	NA	26.6	23.8	32.1	35.1	55.7	49.6	30.5	26.1	24.2
Pretax Inc.	NA	120	311	230	34.0	160	99	142	197	126
Eff. Tax Rate	NA	34%	28%	25%	86%	36%	48%	45%	38%	43%
Net Inc.	NA	78.9	226	173	5.0	102	52.0	78.0	121	72.0

Balance Sheet & Other Fin. Data (Million $)

	1996	1995	1994	1993	1992	1991	1990	1989	1988	1987
Cash	NA	20.0	121	140	72.0	88.0	41.0	97.0	123	131
Curr. Assets	NA	880	1,274	1,139	1,001	1,037	1,026	1,046	994	1,037
Total Assets	NA	1,961	2,358	2,117	1,959	2,034	2,034	1,757	1,655	1,586
Curr. Liab.	NA	603	921	888	750	780	659	605	564	560
LT Debt	NA	122	122	168	274	279	496	254	238	236
Common Eqty.	NA	1,009	972	812	710	836	758	801	754	663
Total Cap.	NA	1,131	1,105	989	995	1,196	1,323	1,116	1,035	959
Cap. Exp.	NA	85.7	148	146	141	98.0	303	103	119	96.0
Cash Flow	NA	150	355	275	173	205	141	150	190	136
Curr. Ratio	NA	1.5	1.4	1.3	1.3	1.3	1.6	1.7	1.8	1.9
% LT Debt of Cap.	NA	10.8	11.1	17.0	27.6	23.3	37.5	22.8	23.0	24.6
% Net Inc.of Revs.	NA	3.6	6.5	5.6	0.2	3.6	1.9	3.0	5.1	3.3
% Ret. on Assets	NA	4.1	10.1	8.5	0.2	5.0	2.9	4.6	7.5	4.8
% Ret. on Equity	NA	8.0	25.3	22.6	0.6	12.8	7.0	10.1	17.1	11.6

Data as orig. reptd.; bef. results of disc. opers. and/or spec. items. Per share data adj. for stk. divs. as of ex-div. date. E-Estimated. NA-Not Available. NM-Not Meaningful. NR-Not Ranked.

Office—1717 Deerfield Rd., Deerfield, IL 60015. **Tel**—(847) 405-6000. **Chrmn & CEO**—W. L. Batts. **Pres**—J. M. Ringler. **Sr VP & CFO**—L. B. Skatoff. **Sr VP & Secy**—J. M. Costigan. **Investor Contact**—Christine Hanneman. **Dirs**—W. L. Batts, W. O. Bourke, R. M. Davis, L. C. Elam, W. J. Farrell, E. V. Goings, C. J. Grum, J. E. Luecke, B. Marbut, J. B. McKinnon, D. R. Parker, R. M. Price, J. M. Ringler, J. D. Stoney. **Transfer Agent & Registrar**—ChaseMellon Shareholder Services, NYC. **Incorporated**—in Delaware in 1986. **Empl**— 24,300. **S&P Analyst:** Maureen C. Carini

STANDARD &POOR'S
STOCK REPORTS

Southern Co.

2066

NYSE Symbol **SO**

In S&P 500

16-FEB-97

Industry:
Utilities-Electric

Summary: This major utility holding company, serving much of the southeastern U.S., has diversified its power sources through its 45.7% interest in the two-unit Vogtle nuclear project.

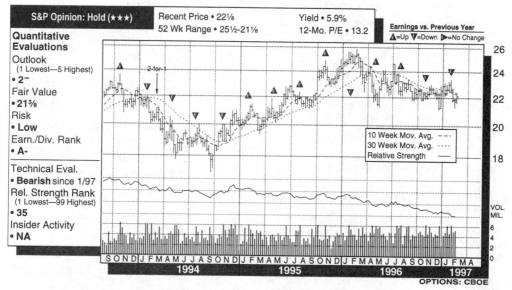

S&P Opinion: Hold (★★★)	Recent Price • 22⅛	Yield • 5.9%
	52 Wk Range • 25½-21⅛	12-Mo. P/E • 13.2

Quantitative Evaluations

Outlook
(1 Lowest—5 Highest)
• **2⁻**

Fair Value
• **21⅜**

Risk
• **Low**

Earn./Div. Rank
• **A-**

Technical Eval.
• **Bearish** since 1/97

Rel. Strength Rank
(1 Lowest—99 Highest)
• **35**

Insider Activity
• **NA**

Earnings vs. Previous Year
▲=Up ▼=Down ▶=No Change

10 Week Mov. Avg. ———
30 Week Mov. Avg. - - - -
Relative Strength ———

OPTIONS: CBOE

Overview - 13-FEB-97

Utility earnings in 1997 will benefit from continued 4%-5% growth in electricity demand from SO's service territory. An expanding manufacturing base, which includes the new Mercedes Benz plant in Alabama, should help sustain above-average demand. SO is well positioned within this increasingly competitive industry, due to its low rates for industrial customers. EPS should continue to benefit from cost cuts, lower interest expenses, nonregulated energy businesses, as well as a modest net contribution from its U.K.-based subsidiary, South Western Electricity plc. SO's cash flow should remain healthy and its comparatively modest long-term debt level is not likely to exceed 45% of total capitalization. However, the recent acquisition of 80% of Hong Kong-based Consolidated Electric Power Asia (CEPA) could dilute EPS gains by as much as $0.02 in 1997, $0.08 in 1998, and $0.02 in 1999.

Valuation - 13-FEB-97

We continue to recommend holding the stock. The shares were down 8.1% in 1996, compared to a 5% decline for the S&P Index of Electric Companies and a 20% gain for the S&P 500. The weakness reflects, in part, concern over an increase in interest rates and the impact of heightened competition in the industry. Although it will take three years until the CEPA acquisition becomes accretive, SO continues to enjoy a low-risk profile as opportunities from new nonregulated ventures accelerate earnings growth and equity returns. The dividend was raised 3.2% for the March 1997 payment, and the payout and yield are about average for the industry. Though SO shares are fairly valued at 12 times the $1.75 we see for 1997, we continue to view them as an attractive holding for total return.

Key Stock Statistics

S&P EPS Est. 1997	1.75	Tang. Bk. Value/Share	13.12
P/E on S&P Est. 1997	12.6	Beta	0.42
Dividend Rate/Share	1.30	Shareholders	225,700
Shs. outstg. (M)	673.7	Market cap. (B)	$ 14.9
Avg. daily vol. (M)	1.152	Inst. holdings	27%

Value of $10,000 invested 5 years ago: $ 17,039

Fiscal Year Ending Dec. 31

	1996	1995	1994	1993	1992	1991
Revenues (Million $)						
1Q	2,416	1,929	1,932	1,840	1,808	1,787
2Q	2,534	2,184	2,069	2,068	2,011	2,018
3Q	2,917	2,759	2,381	2,636	2,386	2,366
4Q	2,453	2,308	1,915	1,945	1,868	1,879
Yr.	10,324	9,180	8,297	8,489	8,073	8,050
Earnings Per Share ($)						
1Q	0.35	0.31	0.22	0.28	0.29	0.22
2Q	0.43	0.40	0.39	0.39	0.35	0.28
3Q	0.69	0.71	0.64	0.69	0.64	0.59
4Q	0.21	0.24	0.27	0.21	0.22	0.32
Yr.	1.68	1.66	1.52	0.09	1.51	1.39

Next earnings report expected: late April

Dividend Data (Dividends have been paid since 1948.)

Amount ($)	Date Decl.	Ex-Div. Date	Stock of Record	Payment Date
0.315	Apr. 15	May. 02	May. 06	Jun. 06 '96
0.315	Jul. 19	Aug. 01	Aug. 05	Sep. 06 '96
0.315	Oct. 21	Oct. 31	Nov. 04	Dec. 06 '96
0.325	Jan. 20	Jan. 30	Feb. 03	Mar. 06 '97

STANDARD
&POOR'S
STOCK REPORTS

The Southern Company

2066
16-FEB-97

Business Summary - 13-FEB-97

The Southern Company is a utility holding company whose subsidiaries, Alabama Power, Georgia Power, Gulf Power, Mississippi Power and Savannah Electric & Power, serve nearly 3.6 million retail customers in the Southeast. Electric revenues by customer class were:

	1995	1994	1993	1992
Residential	34%	32%	32%	30%
Commercial	30%	29%	27%	27%
Industrial	26%	27%	26%	26%
Other	10%	12%	15%	17%

The textiles, chemical and paper industries comprised roughly one-third of SO's industrial customer base, which accounted for 34% of total 1995 energy revenues. In 1995, SO system's peak load was 27,420 mw, and system capability at peak totaled 30,733 mw, for a capacity margin of 11%. Power requirements were derived from coal 73%, nuclear 16%, hydro 4%, oil/gas 2% and purchased power 5%.

The company estimates capital outlays for ongoing construction programs of $1.5 billion in 1996, $1.4 billion in 1997 and $1.3 billion in 1998. They include construction of combustion turbine peaking units, to add about 600 megawatts by 1998, and significant expenditures for transmission and distribution facilities, as well as to upgrade existing generating plants to extend their useful lives. Construction projects in 1994 totaled $1.5 billion. SO expects to continue to make significant investment related to its core business to provide sustainable earnings growth.

To comply with emissions limits set by the Clean Air Act Amendments of 1990, systemwide compliance-related construction expenditures totaled about $320 million through 1995. Additional compliance-related construction costs during the period 1996 through 2000 are estimated at about $150 million.

In October 1995, SO acquired South Western Electricity plc, one of the U.K.'s 12 electric distribution companies, for approximately $1.8 billion in cash.

In June 1996, SO received clearance from the Federal Communications Commission to enter the telecommunications business. Two holding companies will be formed to engage in businesses ranging from leasing its fiber optics network to selling long-distance services.

Important Developments

Jan. '97—SO acquired 80% of Hong Kong-based Consolidated Electric Power Asia (CEPA), the world's fifth largest independent power producer, for approximately $2.7 billion. CEPA builds, owns and operates electric power generating plants in China and the Philippines and has projects under development in Indonesia, Pakistan and India.

Capitalization

Long Term Debt: $7,356,378,000 (9/96).
Subsidiary Pfd. Stock: $1,153,056,000.
Red. Pfd. Stock: $422,000,000.

Per Share Data ($)

(Year Ended Dec. 31)	1996	1995	1994	1993	1992	1991	1990	1989	1988	1987
Tangible Bk. Val.	NA	11.99	12.46	NA	11.05	10.72	10.57	10.54	10.29	10.11
Earnings	1.68	1.66	1.52	1.57	1.51	1.39	0.96	1.34	1.36	0.96
Dividends	1.26	1.22	1.18	1.14	1.10	1.07	1.07	1.07	1.07	1.07
Payout Ratio	75%	73%	78%	73%	73%	77%	112%	80%	79%	111%
Prices - High	25⅞	25	22⅛	23⅝	19⅝	17⅜	14¾	14⅞	12⅛	14½
- Low	21⅛	19⅜	17	18½	15¼	12⅞	11½	11	10¼	9
P/E Ratio - High	15	15	15	15	13	13	15	11	9	15
- Low	13	12	11	12	10	9	12	8	7	9

Income Statement Analysis (Million $)

	1996	1995	1994	1993	1992	1991	1990	1989	1988	1987
Revs.	NA	9,180	8,297	8,489	8,073	8,050	7,975	7,492	7,235	7,010
Depr.	NA	904	821	793	768	763	749	698	632	545
Maint.	NA	683	660	653	613	637	602	542	547	560
Fxd. Chgs. Cov.	NA	3.3	3.3	4.0	2.9	2.6	2.1	2.5	2.5	2.4
Constr. Credits	NA	25.0	29.0	22.0	22.0	31.0	67.0	134	268	346
Eff. Tax Rate	NA	39%	39%	35%	37%	34%	34%	30%	26%	32%
Net Inc.	NA	1,103	989	1,002	953	876	604	846	846	554

Balance Sheet & Other Fin. Data (Million $)

	1996	1995	1994	1993	1992	1991	1990	1989	1988	1987
Gross Prop.	NA	33,093	30,694	28,947	27,955	27,313	26,809	26,532	25,579	23,697
Cap. Exp.	NA	1,401	1,536	1,441	1,105	1,123	1,185	1,346	1,754	1,821
Net Prop.	NA	23,026	21,117	20,013	16,489	16,609	16,811	16,998	16,849	15,896
Capitalization:										
LT Debt	NA	8,306	7,593	7,411	7,241	7,992	8,458	8,575	8,433	8,204
% LT Debt	NA	45	44	45	46	49	51	51	51	52
Pfd.	NA	1,432	1,432	1,333	1,359	1,333	1,358	1,400	1,465	1,351
% Pfd.	NA	7.70	8.30	8.10	8.60	8.20	8.20	8.30	8.80	8.60
Common	NA	8,772	8,186	7,684	7,234	6,976	6,783	6,861	6,686	6,170
% Common	NA	47	48	47	46	43	41	41	40	39
Total Cap.	NA	24,877	23,063	22,358	16,791	17,305	17,662	17,947	17,745	16,885
Oper. Ratio	NA	79.5	79.3	79.2	78.2	78.4	79.6	78.5	80.7	82.6
% Earn. on Net Prop.	NA	8.5	8.3	9.7	10.6	10.4	9.6	9.5	8.4	7.8
% Ret. on Revs.	NA	12.0	11.9	11.8	11.8	10.9	7.6	11.3	11.7	7.9
% Ret. On Invest.Cap	NA	7.9	7.6	9.3	10.5	10.2	8.6	9.7	9.6	8.0
% Return On Com.Eqty	NA	13.0	12.5	13.4	13.4	12.7	8.9	12.5	13.0	9.1

Data as orig. reptd.; bef. results of disc. opers. and/or spec. items. Per share data adj. for stk. divs. as of ex-div. date. E-Estimated. NA-Not Available. NM-Not Meaningful. NR-Not Ranked.

Office—270 Peachtree St. N.W., Atlanta, GA 30303.**Tel**—(404) 393-0650. **Chrmn, Pres & CEO**—A. W. Dahlberg. **Secy**—T. Chisholm. **VP-Fin, CFO & Treas**—W. L. Westbrook. **Investor Contact**—Carl West (212) 269-8842. **Dirs**—J. C. Adams, A. D. Correll, A. W. Dahlberg, P. J. DeNicola, J. Edwards, H. A. Franklin, B. S. Gordon, L. G. Hardman III, E. B. Harris, W. A. Parker Jr., G. J. St. Pe, W. J. Rushton III, G. M. Shatto, H. Stockham. **Transfer Agent & Registrar**—Company's office. **Incorporated**—in Delaware in 1945.**Empl**— 27,826. **S&P Analyst:** Justin McCann

STANDARD &POOR'S
STOCK REPORTS

TECO Energy

2194

NYSE Symbol **TE**

In S&P MidCap 400

16-FEB-97

Industry: Utilities-Electric

Summary: This company owns Tampa Electric Co., which serves the Tampa Bay region in west central Florida, and also has significant diversified operations related to its core business.

S&P Opinion: Hold (★★★)	Recent Price • 24½	Yield • 4.6%
	52 Wk Range • 26⅜-23	12-Mo. P/E • 14.3

Quantitative Evaluations

Outlook
(1 Lowest—5 Highest)
• **3**

Fair Value
• 24⅛

Risk
• **Low**

Earn./Div. Rank
• **A**

Technical Eval.
• **Bullish** since 11/96

Rel. Strength Rank
(1 Lowest—99 Highest)
• **43**

Insider Activity
• **NA**

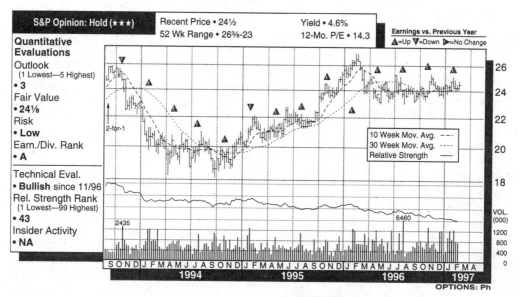

Earnings vs. Previous Year
▲=Up ▼=Down ▶=No Change

10 Week Mov. Avg. – – –
30 Week Mov. Avg. ·······
Relative Strength ——

OPTIONS: Ph

Overview - 13-FEB-97

Revenue growth for 1997 is expected to benefit from customer base growth at an above-average 2% rate and a strong local economy, partly offset by a customer base rate freeze. Ongoing cost savings should also aid results again in 1997. However, earnings for the next three years are likely to come under pressure as TE absorbs the costs of the new Polk generating unit without a rate increase. More significantly, in a move to strengthen its position as a diversified energy provider, Teco recently agreed to acquire Lykes Energy Inc., the parent of Peoples Gas System, Florida's largest natural gas distributor for about $300 million in stock. We expect the acquisition to dilute earnings by about $0.05 to $0.07 a share in 1997, but see accelerated growth prospects thereafter.

Valuation - 13-FEB-97

We continue to recommend holding the stock. The shares, which rose nearly 27% in 1995, were down nearly 6% in 1996, about in line with the 5% decline for the S&P Index of Electric Companies. Earnings are expected to be essentially flat in 1997. TE has little need for new plant and has no exposure to vulnerable, high-cost nuclear power generation or price-sensitive industrial customers. The company plans to maintain its dividend payout at 60%-70% of earnings. Despite a 5.7% boost in April, the payout was recently a below-average 66% of estimated 1997 EPS. With cash flow growing well above the industry average, the dividend is secure and is likely to be raised modestly in 1997. Though TE shares are fairly valued at 14 times estimated 1997 EPS of $1.70, we believe they are an attractive long-term holding for both capital appreciation and income.

Key Stock Statistics

S&P EPS Est. 1997	1.70	Tang. Bk. Value/Share	10.59
P/E on S&P Est. 1997	14.4	Beta	0.36
Dividend Rate/Share	1.12	Shareholders	31,600
Shs. outstg. (M)	117.4	Market cap. (B)	$ 2.9
Avg. daily vol. (M)	0.202	Inst. holdings	41%

Value of $10,000 invested 5 years ago: $ 14,735

Fiscal Year Ending Dec. 31

	1996	1995	1994	1993	1992	1991
Revenues (Million $)						
1Q	341.1	319.1	307.0	282.0	263.0	253.0
2Q	361.5	349.7	353.0	315.0	284.0	291.0
3Q	400.8	389.1	366.6	365.0	341.0	324.0
4Q	369.5	334.4	324.3	322.0	296.0	286.0
Yr.	1,474	1,392	1,351	1,284	1,183	1,154
Earnings Per Share ($)						
1Q	0.36	0.31	0.29	0.21	0.23	0.23
2Q	0.41	0.40	0.36	0.33	0.31	0.34
3Q	0.56	0.55	0.47	0.45	0.47	0.43
4Q	0.38	0.34	0.20	0.31	0.30	0.28
Yr.	1.71	1.60	1.32	1.30	1.30	1.28

Next earnings report expected: mid April

Dividend Data (Dividends have been paid since 1900.)

Amount ($)	Date Decl.	Ex-Div. Date	Stock of Record	Payment Date
0.280	Apr. 17	Apr. 29	May. 01	May. 15 '96
0.280	Jul. 17	Jul. 30	Aug. 01	Aug. 15 '96
0.280	Oct. 16	Oct. 30	Nov. 01	Nov. 15 '96
0.280	Jan. 15	Jan. 29	Jan. 31	Feb. 15 '97

Business Summary - 13-FEB-97

TECO Energy's principal subsidiary is Tampa Electric, which serves Tampa, Fla., and adjacent communities. The company has diversified extensively into nonregulated businesses, including transportation, energy production and real estate. Contributions to operating income in recent years were:

	1995	1994	1993	1992
Regulated utility	70%	74%	73%	77%
Energy services	29%	24%	25%	21%
Other	1%	2%	2%	2%

Tampa Electric serves over 501,000 customers in west central Florida, including Hillsborough, Polk, Pasco and Pinellas Counties. In 1995, the company sold 14.60 million megawatt hours (mwh) of power, versus 13.93 million mwh in 1994. TE's customer mix in 1995 (based on revenues) was 48% residential, 29% commercial, 10% industrial and 13% other, including bulk power for resale. The company derives about 99% of its power needs from coal. Total generating capability of TE's 19 power units at 1995 year-end was 3,404 mw.

Diversified operations include TECO Coal, whose subsidiaries sold about 30% of their 1995 production to Tampa Electric from properties in Kentucky and Tennessee; TECO Coalbed Methane, which participates in the production of natural gas from coalbeds located in Alabama's Black Warrior Basin; TECO Transport, which consists of four subsidiaries that transport, store and transfer coal and other bulk commodities to Tampa Electric (50%) and other customers (50%); and TECO Power Services, which seeks opportunities both in and outside Florida to develop, own and operate cogeneration and independent power projects.

The company introduced two new businesses in 1995: TECO Gas & Oil is involved in the exploration and development of conventional oil and gas in gulf waters off Texas and Louisiana; and TeCom is engaged in energy management and communications. TE also has interests in real estate development and financial investments.

Growth of unregulated businesses, including independent power production and cogeneration and coal transport, is a company goal, as are new sources of revenue and profit in closely related business areas.

Important Developments

Dec. '96—The company agreed to acquire Lykes Energy Inc., the parent of Peoples Gas System, Florida's largest natural gas distributor, in a tax-free stock-for-stock transaction valued at about $300 million. Subject to regulatory approvals, the merger is expected to be completed by mid-year 1997.

Capitalization

Long Term Debt: $950,835,000 (9/96).
Subsidiary Preferred Stock: $19,960,000.

Per Share Data ($)

(Year Ended Dec. 31)	1996	1995	1994	1993	1992	1991	1990	1989	1988	1987
Tangible Bk. Val.	NA	10.00	9.33	8.89	8.32	7.81	7.31	7.73	7.30	6.99
Earnings	1.71	1.60	1.32	1.30	1.30	1.28	1.23	1.18	1.07	0.98
Dividends	1.11	1.05	0.99	0.95	0.90	0.85	0.80	0.75	0.70	0.66
Payout Ratio	65%	66%	76%	73%	69%	67%	65%	63%	66%	68%
Prices - High	27	25¾	22⅝	25⅞	21⅛	20⅞	17	14¾	12½	14
- Low	23	20	18⅛	20¼	18	15¾	13⅛	11	10⅝	10⅛
P/E Ratio - High	16	16	17	20	16	16	14	13	12	14
- Low	13	12	14	16	14	12	11	9	10	10

Income Statement Analysis (Million $)

	1996	1995	1994	1993	1992	1991	1990	1989	1988	1987
Revs.	NA	1,392	1,351	1,284	1,183	1,154	1,097	1,060	1,034	970
Depr.	NA	175	174	165	142	133	121	112	106	101
Maint.	NA	101	101	99	94.3	89.4	79.2	78.6	NA	NA
Fxd. Chgs. Cov.	NA	3.4	3.5	3.6	4.0	3.9	4.2	4.3	NA	NA
Constr. Credits	NA	19.3	5.7	3.7	1.1	1.1	0.7	2.3	NA	NA
Eff. Tax Rate	NA	24%	23%	26%	27%	26%	31%	34%	32%	40%
Net Inc.	NA	186	153	150	149	145	139	134	126	117

Balance Sheet & Other Fin. Data (Million $)

	1996	1995	1994	1993	1992	1991	1990	1989	1988	1987
Gross Prop.	NA	4,491	4,096	3,846	3,639	3,286	2,881	2,669	NA	NA
Cap. Exp.	NA	433	309	271	255	410	253	157	NA	NA
Net Prop.	NA	2,874	2,620	2,483	2,382	2,219	1,945	1,815	NA	NA
Capitalization:										
LT Debt	NA	995	1,024	1,043	1,048	908	763	675	NA	NA
% LT Debt	NA	45	47	50	52	51	48	44	NA	NA
Pfd.	NA	55.0	55.0	NA	NA	NA	NA	NA	NA	NA
% Pfd.	NA	2.50	2.50	NA	NA	NA	NA	NA	NA	NA
Common	NA	1,167	1,084	1,028	956	891	831	877	NA	NA
% Common	NA	53	50	48	50	50	521	57	NA	NA
Total Cap.	NA	2,675	2,620	2,588	2,583	2,367	2,156	2,107	2,064	2,011
Oper. Ratio	NA	81.4	83.4	81.7	82.0	81.9	82.2	82.7	NA	NA
% Earn. on Net Prop.	NA	9.4	8.8	9.7	9.2	10.0	10.3	10.2	NA	NA
% Ret. on Revs.	NA	13.4	11.3	11.7	12.6	12.6	12.7	12.6	NA	NA
% Ret. On Invest.Cap	NA	10.2	8.9	8.8	8.6	9.3	9.3	9.2	NA	NA
% Return On Com.Eqty	NA	16.5	14.5	15.2	16.1	16.9	16.3	15.7	NA	NA

Data as orig. reptd.; bef. results of disc opers. and/or spec. items. Per share data adj. for stk. divs. as of ex-div. date. E-Estimated. NA-Not Available. NM-Not Meaningful. NR-Not Ranked.

Office—702 N. Franklin St., Tampa, FL 33602. **Tel**—(813) 228-4111. **Web site**—http://www.teco.net **Chrmn & CEO**—T. L. Guzzle. **Pres & COO**—G. F. Anderson. **Sr VP-Fin & CFO**—A. D. Oak. **Sr VP & Secy**—R. H. Kessel. **Treas & Investor Contact**—Sandra W. Callahan. **Dirs**—G. F. Anderson, C. D. Ausley, S. L. Baldwin, H. L. Culbreath, J. L. Ferman Jr., E. L. Flom, H. R. Guild Jr., T. L. Guzzle, D. Hendrix, R. L. Ryan, W. P. Sovey, J. T. Touchton, J. A. Urquhart, J. O. Welch Jr. **Transfer Agent & Registrar**—First National Bank of Boston. **Incorporated**—in Florida in 1899; reincorporated in 1949. **Empl**— 4,465. **S&P Analyst:** Justin McCann

STANDARD &POOR'S
STOCK REPORTS

Tenneco Inc.

2201

NYSE Symbol **TEN**

In S&P 500

16-FEB-97

Industry: Conglomerate/diversified

Summary: This holding company is focusing on its auto parts and packaging businesses following the divestiture of its natural gas pipeline and shipbuiding units.

S&P Opinion: Hold (★★★)	Recent Price • 40⅛	Yield • 4.5%
	52 Wk Range • 58½-38	12-Mo. P/E • 10.8

Quantitative Evaluations

Outlook (1 Lowest—5 Highest)
• **5+**

Fair Value
• **52½**

Risk
• **Low**

Earn./Div. Rank
• **B**

Technical Eval.
• **Bullish** since 12/96

Rel. Strength Rank (1 Lowest—99 Highest)
• **13**

Insider Activity
• **NA**

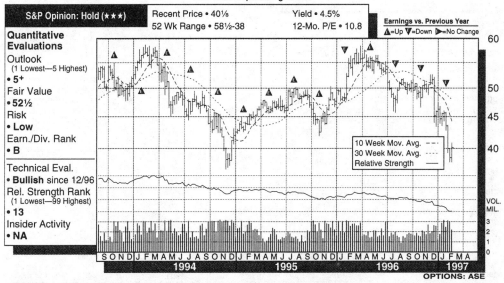

Earnings vs. Previous Year
▲=Up ▼=Down ▶=No Change

10 Week Mov. Avg. ---
30 Week Mov. Avg. ·····
Relative Strength —

OPTIONS: ASE

Overview - 14-JAN-97

Having divested its shipbuilding and energy units in December 1996, Tenneco is now focusing its efforts on packaging and auto parts. TEN substantially increased its packaging business with the 1995 acquisition of Mobil's packaging division, and the third quarter 1996 acquisition of Amoco's foam products unit. Additional acquisitions are likely to further diversify the group into less cyclical, faster-growing segments of packaging such as food containers and wrappings. Traditionally, packaging was centered on the more volatile linerboard and corrugated cardboard markets. Currently experiencing weak pricing, this segment now accounts for about 45% of its packaging revenues. Auto parts remains focused on exhaust and ride control products. Seeking global expansion in faster growing regions of the world such as India and East Asia, Tenneco Automotive has undertaken 15 acquisitions and joint ventures in the past two years.

Valuation - 16-JAN-97

Tenneco's focus on packaging and auto parts is intended to facilitate a valuation in line with comparable types of companies which sell at multiples of earnings ranging from 12 to 16. Presently, the stock trades at about 17 times projected 1997 earnings. TEN's valuation will probably remain unsettled until it is determined how fast this new enterprise can grow. In that context, and given that it is late in the economic cycle, it is prudent to recognize that both the auto parts and packaging industries are vulnerable to economic downturns (and multiple contractions). Also, TEN's numerous acquisitions in emerging markets have long-term appeal, but could result in near-term margin pressure. Based on these uncertainties, we rate TEN a near-term hold. But, the shares, with an above-average yield, could make for an attractive longer-term holding.

Key Stock Statistics

S&P EPS Est. 1997	2.65	Tang. Bk. Value/Share	17.93
P/E on S&P Est. 1997	15.1	Beta	0.97
Dividend Rate/Share	1.80	Shareholders	92,000
Shs. outstg. (M)	170.8	Market cap. (B)	$ 6.9
Avg. daily vol. (M)	0.572	Inst. holdings	1%

Value of $10,000 invested 5 years ago: NA

Fiscal Year Ending Dec. 31

	1996	1995	1994	1993	1992	1991
Revenues (Million $)						
1Q	2,725	2,163	3,049	3,250	3,210	3,330
2Q	2,792	2,198	3,258	3,482	3,440	3,510
3Q	2,803	2,136	3,049	3,150	3,180	3,180
4Q	1,686	2,402	2,818	3,376	3,310	3,640
Yr.	6,572	8,899	12,174	13,255	13,140	13,660
Earnings Per Share ($)						
1Q	0.90	0.84	0.66	0.46	0.22	-0.03
2Q	0.93	1.05	0.88	0.63	0.32	-0.15
3Q	0.67	1.23	0.81	0.64	0.28	-5.28
4Q	-0.21	1.05	1.14	0.83	-5.55	-0.17
Yr.	1.28	4.16	3.49	2.59	-4.85	-5.62

Next earnings report expected: early May

Dividend Data (Dividends have been paid since 1948.)

Amount ($)	Date Decl.	Ex-Div. Date	Stock of Record	Payment Date
0.450	Jul. 09	Aug. 22	Aug. 26	Sep. 10 '96
0.450	Oct. 08	Nov. 20	Nov. 22	Dec. 10 '96
0.300	Jan. 14	Feb. 26	Feb. 28	Mar. 11 '97
Stk.	Nov. 26		Dec. 11	Dec. 12 '96

A Division of The McGraw-Hill Companies

Business Summary - 16-JAN-97

Tenneco is streamlining its business interests to focus on packaging and auto parts. Segment contributions (profits in million $) in 1995 were:

	Revs.	Profits
Packaging	30.9%	$440
Automotive	27.8%	248
Energy	21.5%	286
Shipbuilding	19.7%	172

Tenneco is the fourth largest packaging company in the U.S. and eighth largest in the world. The segment includes the largest domestic producer of single-use food containers made from clear plastic, aluminum foil, pressed paperboard, and polystyrene foam, and the sixth largest domestic supplier of corrugated containers. Numerous other packaging and related products are also produced.

Automotive produces original equipment and aftermarket exhaust and ride-controls products. Walker Manufacturing produces mufflers, pipe, catalytic converters, tubular manifolds, headers and electronic noise control technology. Monroe Auto Equipment makes shock absorbers, struts, cartridges, load levelers and adjustable electronic suspensions. Plans call for expansion in India, China and other high growth Far East regions, and in Europe.

Energy (which was sold to El Paso Natural Gas Corp. in December 1996) operates 18,700 miles of interstate pipelines in the U.S. and Australia. Some 15% of total U.S. gas supplies are delivered to markets in 20 states.

The Newport News Shipbuilding business, which was spun off to TEN shareholders in December 1996, designs, builds, overhauls and repairs nuclear-powered and conventional military and commercial ships. The remaining 21% interest in Case Corp. was sold in March 1996 for $816 million, bringing financial benefits from the sale of Case to $4.4 billion.

Important Developments

Dec. '96—TEN successfully completed a major restructuring, by spinning off its Newport News Shipbuilding (NNS) unit to its shareholders (with an exchange ratio of one NNS share for every five TEN shares), and selling Tenneco Energy to El Paso Energy (NYSE: EPG); TEN shareholders received stock in El Paso worth a total of about $750 million. In addition, El Paso assumed TEN debt, liabilities and preferred stock worth $3.25 billion. Separately, Tenneco Automotive acquired approximately 94% of Fric-Rot S.A.I.C. for $52 million, making its fifteenth acquisition or joint venture in two years. With expected 1996 revenues of $45 million, Fric-Rot is Argentina's leading ride control manufacturer.

Capitalization

Long Term Debt: $2,100,000,000 (9/96).

Per Share Data ($)

(Year Ended Dec. 31)	1996	1995	1994	1993	1992	1991	1990	1989	1988	1987
Tangible Bk. Val.	NA	17.93	13.67	12.78	5.21	18.07	23.92	22.82	21.86	22.93
Cash Flow	NA	6.80	5.88	5.69	-0.83	-1.03	8.29	8.47	3.39	6.07
Earnings	1.28	4.16	3.49	2.59	-4.85	-5.62	4.37	4.46	-0.18	-1.22
Dividends	1.80	1.60	1.60	1.60	1.60	2.80	3.12	3.04	3.04	3.04
Payout Ratio	141%	38%	46%	62%	NM	NM	70%	68%	NM	NM
Prices - High	58½	50⅜	58¾	55	46	52	71	64¼	51	62½
- Low	43⅜	41⅞	37	39⅛	31¼	27⅜	40	46⅞	38¼	36⅛
P/E Ratio - High	46	12	17	21	NM	NM	16	14	NM	NM
- Low	34	10	11	15	NM	NM	9	11	NM	NM

Income Statement Analysis (Million $)

	1996	1995	1994	1993	1992	1991	1990	1989	1988	1987
Revs.	NA	8,899	12,174	13,255	13,139	13,662	14,511	14,083	13,234	14,790
Oper. Inc.	NA	1,403	1,681	1,455	1,348	696	1,728	1,761	1,236	1,552
Depr.	NA	449	429	509	579	563	488	509	519	1,074
Int. Exp.	NA	422	568	718	902	1,045	972	905	903	947
Pretax Inc.	NA	1,020	972	636	-606	-682	857	825	84.0	-156
Eff. Tax Rate	NA	26%	31%	23%	NM	NM	35%	29%	101%	NM
Net Inc.	NA	735	641	451	-682	-673	561	584	-1.0	-131

Balance Sheet & Other Fin. Data (Million $)

	1996	1995	1994	1993	1992	1991	1990	1989	1988	1987
Cash	NA	354	405	218	111	231	147	276	328	100
Curr. Assets	NA	3,582	3,895	5,417	6,283	6,968	7,945	7,523	7,454	4,620
Total Assets	NA	13,451	12,542	15,373	16,584	18,696	19,034	17,381	17,376	18,503
Curr. Liab.	NA	3,836	3,054	4,910	5,680	6,848	7,234	6,201	6,442	6,034
LT Debt	NA	3,751	3,570	4,799	6,400	6,837	5,976	5,573	5,612	6,167
Common Eqty.	NA	3,148	2,900	2,592	1,321	2,765	3,367	3,277	3,161	3,773
Total Cap.	NA	8,788	8,396	8,941	9,272	10,972	11,057	10,507	10,329	11,924
Cap. Exp.	NA	976	736	587	595	894	920	663	688	1,275
Cash Flow	NA	1,184	1,058	960	-119	-126	1,031	1,075	493	893
Curr. Ratio	NA	0.9	1.3	1.1	1.1	1.0	1.1	1.2	1.2	0.8
% LT Debt of Cap.	NA	42.7	42.5	54.0	69.0	62.3	54.0	53.0	54.3	51.7
% Net Inc.of Revs.	NA	8.3	5.3	3.4	NM	NM	3.9	4.1	NM	NM
% Ret. on Assets	NA	5.7	4.3	2.8	NM	NM	3.1	3.4	NM	NM
% Ret. on Equity	NA	24.3	21.8	22.3	NM	NM	16.6	17.6	NM	NM

Data as orig. reptd.; bef. results of disc. opers. and/or spec. items. Per share data adj. for stk. divs. as of ex-div. date. E-Estimated. NA-Not Available. NM-Not Meaningful. NR-Not Ranked.

Office—1275 King Street, Greenwich, CT 06831. **Tel**—(203) 863-1000. **Website**—http://www.tenneco.com **Chrmn & CEO**—D. G. Mead. **SVP & CFO**—R. T. Blakely. **VP & Secy**—K. A. Stewart. **Treas**—K. R. Osar. **Investor Contact**—Jack Lascar. **Dirs**—M. Andrews, W. M. Blumenthal, M. K. Eickhoff, P. T. Flawn, H. U. Harris, Jr., B. K. Johnson, J. B. McCoy, D. G. Mead, J. J. Sisco, W. L. Weiss, C. R. Wharton, Jr. **Transfer Agent & Registrar**—First Chicago Trust Co. of New York, Jersey City, NJ. **Incorporated**—in Delaware in 1947. **Empl**— 42,000. **S&P Analyst:** Robert Schpoont

STANDARD &POOR'S
STOCK REPORTS

UST Inc.

2269U

NYSE Symbol **UST**

In S&P 500

16-FEB-97

Industry: Tobacco

Summary: This company is a leading producer of moist smokeless tobacco products marketed under such leading brand names as Copenhagen and Skoal.

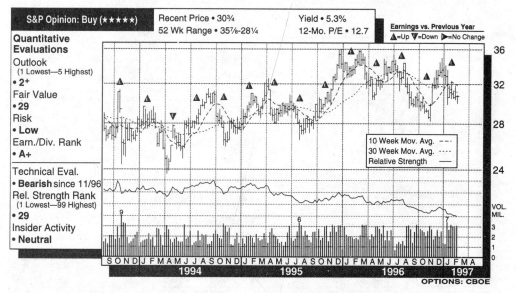

| S&P Opinion: Buy (★★★★★) | Recent Price • 30¾ | Yield • 5.3% |
| 52 Wk Range • 35⅞-28¼ | 12-Mo. P/E • 12.7 |

Earnings vs. Previous Year
▲=Up ▼=Down ▶=No Change

Quantitative Evaluations

Outlook
(1 Lowest—5 Highest)
• **2+**

Fair Value
• **29**

Risk
• **Low**

Earn./Div. Rank
• **A+**

Technical Eval.
• **Bearish** since 11/96

Rel. Strength Rank
(1 Lowest—99 Highest)
• **29**

Insider Activity
• **Neutral**

10 Week Mov. Avg. – – –
30 Week Mov. Avg. ·······
Relative Strength ——

OPTIONS: CBOE

Overview - 29-JAN-97

We project net sales to rise at a middle single-digit pace in 1997, driven by a mix of modest moist smokeless tobacco unit volume growth and modestly higher selling prices. In response to recent market share erosion in its important tobacco segment, UST has recently relaxed its past aggressive pricing policy somewhat. This could lead to modest operating margin contraction in the near term, but a projected easing in the effective tax rate, and fewer shares outstanding should allow earnings per share to rise at a near 10% clip, to $2.65. New products will be of greater importance to sustain unit sales growth in the future.

Valuation - 29-JAN-97

Despite a slowing in earnings growth over the past two years, this equity is very attractively valued for above-average total return potential. We believe that UST's already-dominant presence (80% share) and more aggressive new product initiatives in the highly profitabile moist smokeless tobacco market will help it to withstand recent inroads by price value brand competition, and allow it to achieve approximate 10% annual EPS growth over the next few years. This growth, together with the company's very strong balance sheet and a relatively high dividend yield, make the shares an attractive total return choice. As of mid-January, UST was trading at a discount of approximately 30% to the P/E ratio of the S&P 500. Although most tobacco-related equities also trade at sizable discounts to the overall market, we believe that this is unwarranted for UST, in part because of its much lower litigation risk; as a producer of moist smokeless tobacco, the company is not named as a defendant in many of the most important tobacco litigation cases.

Key Stock Statistics

S&P EPS Est. 1997	2.65	Tang. Bk. Value/Share	1.70
P/E on S&P Est. 1997	11.6	Beta	0.58
Dividend Rate/Share	1.62	Shareholders	13,100
Shs. outstg. (M)	186.2	Market cap. (B)	$ 5.7
Avg. daily vol. (M)	0.745	Inst. holdings	61%

Value of $10,000 invested 5 years ago: $ 11,400

Fiscal Year Ending Dec. 31

	1996	1995	1994	1993	1992	1991
Revenues (Million $)						
1Q	327.8	306.1	280.4	265.0	236.0	203.0
2Q	350.5	340.2	310.2	279.9	263.0	221.0
3Q	366.0	334.3	310.4	279.0	273.0	247.0
4Q	352.5	344.9	322.1	286.7	273.0	236.0
Yr.	1,397	1,325	1,223	1,110	1,044	907.0
Earnings Per Share ($)						
1Q	0.55	0.49	0.42	0.47	0.31	0.26
2Q	0.62	0.55	0.48	0.41	0.35	0.30
3Q	0.65	0.55	0.48	0.41	0.38	0.33
4Q	0.61	0.56	0.49	0.41	0.36	0.30
Yr.	2.42	2.16	1.87	1.71	1.41	1.18

Next earnings report expected: mid April

Dividend Data (Dividends have been paid since 1912.)

Amount ($)	Date Decl.	Ex-Div. Date	Stock of Record	Payment Date
0.370	May. 07	May. 31	Jun. 04	Jun. 14 '96
0.370	Jul. 25	Aug. 30	Sep. 04	Sep. 16 '96
0.370	Oct. 24	Dec. 02	Dec. 04	Dec. 16 '96
0.405	Dec. 12	Feb. 27	Mar. 03	Mar. 14 '97

A Division of The **McGraw·Hill** *Companies*

STANDARD
&POOR'S
STOCK REPORTS

UST Inc.

2269U
16-FEB-97

Business Summary - 29-JAN-97

UST Inc. (formerly U.S. Tobacco) is the leading U.S. manufacturer of smokeless tobacco (snuff and chewing tobacco), imports and sells other tobacco products, and produces and sells wine. Segment contributions (profits in millions) in 1995 were:

	Sales	Profits
Tobacco	87%	$720.9
Wine	8%	13.5
Other	5%	-5.3

Smokeless tobacco products include Copenhagen and Skoal, the world's two largest selling brands of moist smokeless tobacco. Moist brands also include Skoal Long Cut and Skoal Bandits. Other tobacco products carry the names Bruton, CC, Red Seal and WB Cut. The company sells tobacco products throughout the U.S., principally to chain stores and tobacco and grocery wholesalers. In 1986, federal legislation was enacted regulating smokeless tobacco products by requiring health warning notices on smokeless tobacco packages and advertising and by prohibiting the advertising of smokeless tobacco products on electronic media.

Wines consist of premium varietal and blended wines dominated by Washington State-produced Chateau Ste.

Michelle and Columbia Crest and two premium-quality California wines: Conn Creek and Villa Mt. Eden.

Other products include the company's international operations, video entertainment business, pipes, smokers' accessories, agricultural properties and a majority interest in a company that develops and markets equipment used in film-making.

Important Developments

Jan. '97—UST reported that domestic unit volume for moist smokeless tobacco products increased 2% in 1996, to 648 million cans, compared with the similar period for 1995; unit volume results for 1996 included the effects of an additional shipping day. On an equivalent shipping day basis, unit volume in 1996 approximated the 1995 level. Management believed that the principal factors for the flat volumes were increased growth of competitors' price value brands, a pricing policy change by the military in commissaries, less volume from its new product introductions than in the comparative period of the prior year, and wholesaler ordering patterns around the holidays. Management said its strategic plans for 1997 and beyond remain focused on expanding the market for moist smokeless tobacco while addressing the competitive situation in the marketplace.

Capitalization

Long Term Debt: $100,000,000 (9/96).

Per Share Data ($)

(Year Ended Dec. 31)	1996	1995	1994	1993	1992	1991	1990	1989	1988	1987
Tangible Bk. Val.	NA	1.53	1.79	2.20	2.38	2.22	2.19	2.19	2.05	1.79
Cash Flow	NA	2.30	2.00	1.83	1.51	1.28	1.07	0.89	0.78	0.64
Earnings	2.42	2.16	1.87	1.71	1.41	1.18	0.98	0.82	0.71	0.57
Dividends	1.48	1.30	1.12	0.96	0.80	0.66	0.55	0.46	0.37	0.30
Payout Ratio	61%	60%	60%	56%	54%	52%	52%	53%	50%	51%
Prices - High	35⅞	36	31½	32¾	35⅜	34	18¼	15⅜	10⅝	8⅛
- Low	28¼	26½	23⅝	24⅜	25¼	16⅜	12⅜	9¾	6⅛	4⅞
P/E Ratio - High	15	17	17	19	25	29	19	19	15	14
- Low	12	12	13	14	18	14	13	12	9	9

Income Statement Analysis (Million $)

	1996	1995	1994	1993	1992	1991	1990	1989	1988	1987
Revs.	NA	1,325	1,198	1,080	1,013	880	751	670	607	564
Oper. Inc.	NA	737	669	591	524	446	369	319	281	257
Depr.	NA	29.1	28.2	25.9	23.6	22.3	19.5	16.4	16.6	17.0
Int. Exp.	NA	4.8	4.6	1.2	0.7	0.7	1.6	3.1	4.4	5.3
Pretax Inc.	NA	705	641	602	503	426	352	302	261	235
Eff. Tax Rate	NA	39%	40%	39%	38%	38%	37%	37%	38%	44%
Net Inc.	NA	430	388	369	313	266	223	190	162	131

Balance Sheet & Other Fin. Data (Million $)

	1996	1995	1994	1993	1992	1991	1990	1989	1988	1987
Cash	NA	69.4	50.7	25.3	36.4	41.5	46.6	54.6	72.7	50.4
Curr. Assets	NA	426	382	335	330	305	266	280	291	261
Total Assets	NA	785	741	706	674	657	623	636	598	549
Curr. Liab.	NA	281	161	107	81.2	95.5	68.7	92.1	69.9	63.2
LT Debt	NA	100	125	40.0	Nil	Nil	3.1	6.8	21.8	37.1
Common Eqty.	NA	294	362	463	517	483	474	482	453	401
Total Cap.	NA	394	492	511	563	534	530	544	528	486
Cap. Exp.	NA	35.3	27.7	54.5	34.0	41.5	26.9	35.8	17.7	33.0
Cash Flow	NA	459	416	395	336	288	243	207	179	148
Curr. Ratio	NA	1.5	2.4	3.1	4.1	3.2	3.9	3.0	4.2	4.1
% LT Debt of Cap.	NA	25.4	25.4	7.8	Nil	Nil	0.6	1.2	4.1	7.6
% Net Inc.of Revs.	NA	32.4	32.4	34.1	30.9	30.2	29.7	28.4	26.7	23.2
% Ret. on Assets	NA	56.3	54.7	54.2	47.0	41.8	35.9	31.0	28.3	24.6
% Ret. on Equity	NA	131.0	96.3	76.5	62.5	55.8	47.3	40.9	38.0	34.1

Data as orig. reptd.; bef. results of disc. opers. and/or spec. items. Per share data adj. for stk. divs. as of ex-div. date. E-Estimated. NA-Not Available. NM-Not Meaningful. NR-Not Ranked.

Office—100 W. Putnam Ave., Greenwich, CT 06830. **Tel**—(203) 661-1100. **Chrmn, Pres & CEO**—V. A. Gierer Jr. **Exec VP & CFO**—J. J. Bucchignano. **Secy**—Debra A. Baker. **Investor Contact**—Mark A. Rozelle (203) 622-3520. **Dirs**—J. J. Bucchignano, J. W. Chapin, E. H. DeHority Jr., V. A. Gierer Jr., P. X. Kelley, R. L. Rossi, S. R. Stuart, J. P. Warwick, L. P. Weicker Jr. **Transfer Agent & Registrar**—First National Bank of Boston. **Incorporated**—in New Jersey in 1911; reincorporated in Delaware in 1986. **Empl**— 4,082. **S&P Analyst:** Kenneth A. Shea

United Dominion Realty Trust   2302
NYSE Symbol **UDR**

16-FEB-97 | **Industry:** Real Estate Investment Trust | **Summary:** This equity-oriented REIT invests in income-producing real estate, primarily apartments, in the mid-Atlantic and Southeast regions of the U.S.

Quantitative Evaluations

Outlook (1 Lowest—5 Highest)
• **NA**

Fair Value
• **NA**

Risk
• **Low**

Earn./Div. Rank
• **NR**

Technical Eval.
• **Bullish** since 12/96

Rel. Strength Rank (1 Lowest—99 Highest)
• **50**

Insider Activity
• **Neutral**

Recent Price • 15½   Yield • 6.2%
52 Wk Range • 16-13⅛   12-Mo. P/E • 31.6

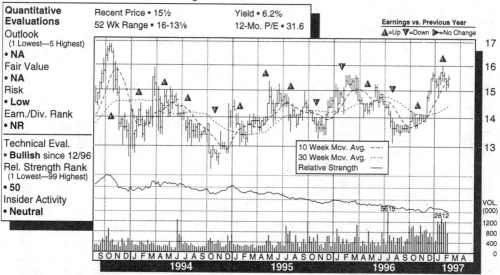

Earnings vs. Previous Year
▲=Up ▼=Down ▶=No Change

10 Week Mov. Avg. ---
30 Week Mov. Avg. ······
Relative Strength —

Business Profile - 03-FEB-97

United Dominion Realty, the largest REIT focusing on the ownership and operation of apartment communities in the mid-Atlantic and Southeast regions of the U.S., owned 41,344 apartment homes in 166 communities as of December 31, 1996. Its holdings were significantly increased by the January 1997 acquisition of South West Property Trust, a Dallas, TX-based REIT that owned more than 14,000 apartment units in 44 communities. In the transaction, UDR issued approximately $350 million of common stock, and assumed about $235 million of South West's debt. Also in January, the trust sold publicly 4,000,000 common shares at $15.75 each, and also sold $125 million of unsecured debt. Net proceeds of approximately $184 million will be used to repay short-term bank debt and to finance additional acquisitions.

Operational Review - 03-FEB-97

Based on a preliminary report, total revenues rose 24% in 1996, as gains from significant acquisitions outweighed a decline in occupancy rates. Expenses and charges also increased 24%, on higher rental and interest costs and depreciation charges. With a $4,346,000 gain on the sale of investments, versus a gain of $5,090,000, net income advanced 15%, to $37,991,000 ($0.49 a share, after preferred dividends, on 8.9% more shares), from $33,127,000 ($0.50). Funds from operations were also up 15%, to $71,713,000 ($1.25 a share), from $62,434,000 ($1.18).

Stock Performance - 14-FEB-97

In the past 30 trading days, UDR's shares have increased 2%, compared to a 8% rise in the S&P 500. Average trading volume for the past five days was 157,400 shares, compared with the 40-day moving average of 250,759 shares.

Key Stock Statistics

Dividend Rate/Share	0.96	Shareholders	5,900
Shs. outstg. (M)	85.5	Market cap. (B)	$ 1.3
Avg. daily vol. (M)	0.321	Inst. holdings	24%
Tang. Bk. Value/Share	7.21		
Beta	0.17		

Value of $10,000 invested 5 years ago: $ 19,893

Fiscal Year Ending Dec. 31

	1996	1995	1994	1993	1992	1991
Revenues (Million $)						
1Q	54.84	45.49	26.71	20.20	14.90	11.90
2Q	57.64	47.75	29.67	21.70	15.20	12.30
3Q	63.49	49.84	39.53	22.68	16.10	13.00
4Q	66.99	52.16	44.07	24.48	17.10	14.10
Yr.	242.1	195.2	140.0	89.08	63.20	51.30
Earnings Per Share ($)						
1Q	0.13	0.12	0.08	0.07	0.06	0.04
2Q	0.10	0.19	0.09	0.06	0.05	0.04
3Q	0.13	0.10	0.12	29.67	0.05	0.03
4Q	0.14	0.10	0.11	0.08	0.02	0.04
Yr.	0.49	0.50	0.41	0.29	0.19	0.15

Next earnings report expected: mid April

Dividend Data (Dividends have been paid since 1973.)

Amount ($)	Date Decl.	Ex-Div. Date	Stock of Record	Payment Date
0.240	Mar. 20	Apr. 10	Apr. 12	Apr. 30 '96
0.240	Jun. 25	Jul. 10	Jul. 12	Jul. 31 '96
0.240	Sep. 11	Oct. 09	Oct. 11	Oct. 31 '96
0.240	Dec. 10	Dec. 26	Dec. 30	Feb. 01 '97

A Division of The McGraw·Hill Companies

Business Summary - 03-FEB-97

United Dominion Realty Trust is a self-administered equity REIT that owns a diversified portfolio of income-producing real estate, primarily apartment communities, in the southeastern U.S. At December 31, 1995, real estate investments totaled $1.13 billion (before accumulated depreciation of $129.5 million), up from $1.01 million ($120.3 million) a year earlier.

Real estate investments by type of property at December 31, 1995, and 1994, were:

	1995	1994
Apartments	96%	92%
Shopping centers	4%	7%
Office & industrial buildings	Nil	1%

The trust's portfolio at 1995 year-end consisted of 152 income-producing properties: 141 apartment complexes (34,224 units), seven shopping centers (1.1 million sq. ft.) and four office and industrial properties (221,000 sq. ft.). The trust's apartment complexes were located in Virginia (21%), Florida (21%), North Carolina (20%), South Carolina (15%), Georgia, Maryland and Tennessee (7% each) and Delaware and Alabama (1% each). At year-end 1995, six of the trust's shopping centers were under contract to be sold.

UDR's core group of mature apartments, providing over 53% of the trust's rental income, was 94.8% occupied during 1995 (94.1% in 1994). Commercial properties were 82% occupied in 1995 (83%).

The trust's investment policy emphasizes the acquisition of apartments that are under-leased, under-managed or under-maintained, so that UDR can use its capital and management resources to upgrade the property, improve its maintenance, add new tenants and increase rental rates with the objective of creating value. The trust has concentrated its investments in the Southeast. During 1995, UDR purchased 5,142 apartments in 23 communities for about $195 million; it expected apartment acquisitions to remain its key strategy in 1996.

Important Developments

Jan. '97—The trust sold publicly 4,000,000 common shares at $15.75 a share. Concurrently, UDR sold $125 million of 7.25% debentures due January 2007. The two offerings raised a total of approximately $184 million in net proceeds, which was to be used to repay short-term bank debt and to fund the acquisition of additional apartment communities.

Capitalization

Notes Payable: $795,894,000 (9/96).

Per Share Data ($)

(Year Ended Dec. 31)	1996	1995	1994	1993	1992	1991	1990	1989	1988	1987
Tangible Bk. Val.	NA	7.30	7.09	6.24	5.60	5.02	5.10	5.51	4.83	4.26
Earnings	0.49	0.50	0.41	0.29	0.19	0.15	0.22	0.29	0.13	0.09
Dividends	1.18	0.87	0.78	0.70	0.66	0.63	0.62	0.61	0.56	0.51
Payout Ratio	NM	174%	190%	NM	347%	431%	288%	210%	431%	600%
Prices - High	15¾	15⅜	15⅞	16⅞	12¾	10½	9⅛	9⅝	9⅜	9⅜
- Low	13⅛	13	12¼	11⅞	9¾	7⅛	6¼	8½	7⅞	7⅛
P/E Ratio - High	32	31	39	58	67	72	43	33	72	NM
- Low	27	26	30	41	51	49	30	29	60	NM

Income Statement Analysis (Million $)

Income Rental	NA	195	140	89.1	63.2	51.3	44.0	37.2	32.1	25.4
Income Mortg.	NA	1.7	0.8	0.7	1.4	0.1	0.3	1.5	0.1	0.3
Income Total	NA	197	141	89.8	64.6	51.3	44.3	38.7	32.3	25.6
Expenses Gen.	NA	127	93.3	61.6	46.3	35.9	30.3	24.7	21.0	16.7
Expenses Int.	NA	40.6	28.3	16.9	11.7	11.9	9.4	9.9	9.4	7.9
Prov. for Losses	NA	Nil	Nil	Nil	1.6	Nil	Nil	Nil	Nil	Nil
Depr.	NA	40.0	29.6	20.4	16.0	13.1	10.6	9.0	7.5	5.9
Net Inc.	NA	33.1	19.2	11.2	6.6	3.6	5.0	5.6	1.9	1.0

Balance Sheet & Other Fin. Data (Million $)

Cash	NA	2.9	7.3	5.8	1.1	1.1	1.0	8.4	1.3	0.8
Total Assets	NA	1,081	912	506	390	314	260	232	192	161
Real Estate Invest.	NA	1,131	1,008	582	454	362	294	251	209	171
Loss Reserve	NA	Nil	Nil	Nil	Nil	Nil	Nil	NA	Nil	Nil
Net Invest.	NA	1,002	887	491	382	305	251	218	184	154
ST Debt	NA	350	368	157	105	95.0	48.0	21.0	31.0	32.0
Capitalization:										
Debt	NA	180	158	72.9	76.5	73.4	84.7	76.2	73.4	72.0
Equity	NA	411	357	260	198	136	118	128	80.0	51.0
Total	NA	696	515	333	274	210	203	204	153	123
% Earn & Depr/Assets	NA	7.3	6.9	7.0	6.4	5.8	6.4	6.9	5.3	4.5
Price Times Book Value:										
Hi	NA	2.1	3.9	2.7	2.3	2.1	1.8	1.7	1.9	2.2
Low	NA	1.8	1.7	1.9	1.7	1.4	1.2	1.5	1.6	1.7

Data as orig. reptd.; bef. results of disc. opers. and/or spec. items. Per share data adj. for stk. divs. as of ex-div. date. E-Estimated. NA-Not Available. NM-Not Meaningful. NR-Not Ranked.

Office—10 South Sixth St., Suite 203, Richmond, VA 23219-3802. **Tel**—(804) 780-2691. **E-mail**—udrt@ix.netcom.com **Chrmn**—C. H. Williams Jr. **Pres & CEO**—J. P. McCann. **SVP, CFO & Investor Contact**—James Dolphin. **VP & Secy**—K. E. Surface. **Dirs**—J. C. Bane, R. P. Buford, R. T. Dalton Jr., J. Dolphin, B. M. Kornblau, J. C. Lanford, J. P. McCann, H. F. Minor, C. H. Williams Jr. **Transfer Agent**—Mellon Securities Trust, Pittsburgh. **Incorporated**—in Virginia in 1972. **Empl**—1,159. **S&P Analyst:** Brendan McGovern

16-FEB-97

Industry:
Real Estate Investment Trust

Summary: UMH is a real estate investment trust that owns and operates mobile home parks in New Jersey, New York, Ohio, Pennsylvania and Tennessee.

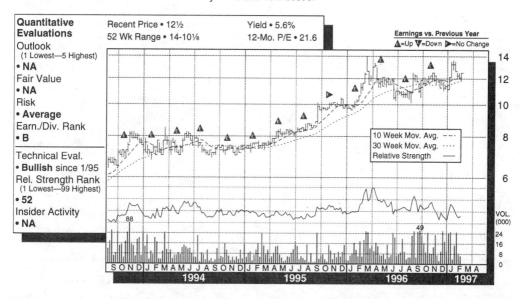

Quantitative Evaluations

Outlook
(1 Lowest—5 Highest)
• **NA**

Fair Value
• **NA**

Risk
• **Average**

Earn./Div. Rank
• **B**

Technical Eval.
• **Bullish** since 1/95

Rel. Strength Rank
(1 Lowest—99 Highest)
• **52**

Insider Activity
• **NA**

Recent Price • 12½   Yield • 5.6%
52 Wk Range • 14–10⅛   12-Mo. P/E • 21.6

Earnings vs. Previous Year
▲=Up ▼=Down ▶=No Change

10 Week Mov. Avg. – – –
30 Week Mov. Avg. ·······
Relative Strength —

Business Profile - 17-DEC-96

Earnings of this real estate investment trust, which owns and operates mobile home parks, have been in a long-term uptrend since profitability was restored in 1991. UMH's goal is to bring its market value to $100 million and to add 2,000 sites over the next five years. As of November 1996, the trust owned 23 mobile home parks with 5,200 sites. Based on a recent analysis, UMH had the best total return (stock appreciation plus dividends) of any equity REIT in the U.S. over the past 10 years. The dividend is being increased to $0.70 a share in 1997.

Operational Review - 17-DEC-96

Total revenues (rental and related income) in the nine months ended September 30, 1996, rose 8.9% year to year, reflecting higher rents, the addition of rental homes and the acquisition of Wood Valley in January 1996 and Spreading Oaks in August. Expenses rose less rapidly, with interest expense down 18%. After a $332,411 gain on the sale of assets, net income spurted 55%, to $2,764,197 ($0.45 a share, on 8.3% more shares), from $1,778,559 ($0.31).

Stock Performance - 14-FEB-97

In the past 30 trading days, UMH's shares have increased 3%, compared to a 8% rise in the S&P 500. Average trading volume for the past five days was 1,200 shares, compared with the 40-day moving average of 3,449 shares.

Key Stock Statistics

Dividend Rate/Share	0.70	Shareholders	900
Shs. outstg. (M)	6.2	Market cap. (B)	$0.078
Avg. daily vol. (M)	0.003	Inst. holdings	3%
Tang. Bk. Value/Share	2.30		
Beta	0.11		

Value of $10,000 invested 5 years ago: $ 52,080

Fiscal Year Ending Dec. 31

	1996	1995	1994	1993	1992	1991
Revenues (Million $)						
1Q	3.56	3.25	3.00	2.80	2.60	2.40
2Q	3.58	3.30	3.05	2.80	2.70	2.40
3Q	3.67	3.38	3.11	2.90	2.70	2.50
4Q	—	3.40	3.15	2.90	2.80	2.50
Yr.	—	13.33	12.32	11.50	10.90	9.70
Earnings Per Share ($)						
1Q	0.18	0.11	0.09	0.06	0.06	0.05
2Q	0.15	0.10	0.09	0.07	0.05	0.02
3Q	0.12	0.11	0.11	0.06	0.04	0.05
4Q	—	0.12	0.11	0.07	0.06	0.02
Yr.	—	0.44	0.40	0.26	0.21	0.14

Next earnings report expected: late February

Dividend Data (Dividends have been paid since 1990.)

Amount ($)	Date Decl.	Ex-Div. Date	Stock of Record	Payment Date
0.150	Apr. 11	May. 13	May. 15	Jun. 14 '96
0.150	Jul. 15	Aug. 13	Aug. 15	Sep. 16 '96
0.150	Sep. 27	Nov. 13	Nov. 15	Dec. 16 '96
0.175	Dec. 13	Feb. 12	Feb. 17	Mar. 17 '97

STANDARD
&POOR'S
STOCK REPORTS

United Mobile Homes, Inc.

9444M
16-FEB-97

Business Summary - 17-DEC-96

United Mobile Homes, Inc. is a real estate investment trust engaged in the ownership and operation of mobile home parks. It leases mobile home spaces (or sites) on a month-to-month basis to private mobile home owners and also leases mobile homes to tenants. As of year-end 1995, UMH was operating 21 mobile home parks which contained 4,920 sites.

The mobile home park communities are designed to accommodate detached, single-family manufactured housing units, which are produced off-site by manufacturers and delivered by truck to the site.

The number of sites at year end in recent years was:

	Sites
1995	4,920
1994	4,702
1993	4,686
1992	4,680
1991	4,680
1990	4,217

The five largest mobile home properties at year-end 1995 were: Port Royal Village located in Belle Vernon, PA (402 sites, 85% occupied); Sandy Valley Estates, Magnolia, OH (327, 94%); Cedarcrest, Vineland, NJ (283, 100%); Allentown Mobile Home Park, Memphis, TN (414, 73%); and Heather Highlands, Pittston, PA (457, 70%).

UMH's operating strategy includes efforts to increase its portfolio to improve efficiency by spreading its administrative costs over a larger base of properties. UMH's policy is to acquire manufactured housing communities that are above average in quality and command higher rents than other communities in the area. As of late 1996, the company said it was conducting an expansion program at a number of its communities; contracts had been signed totaling about $1.2 million for these expansions.

Important Developments

Oct. '96—UMH purchased 65 acres of vacant land adjacent to its Fairview Manor manufactured home community in Vineland, NJ, for $390,000.
Aug. '96—The trust acquired Spreading Oaks Village, a 153-space mobile home community located in Athens, Ohio, for $1,421,800, including closing costs.
Jan. '96—UMH acquired Wood Valley Mobile Home park, a 161-space manufactured home community located in Caledonia, Ohio, for $2,013,706, including closing costs.

Capitalization

Mortgages Payable: $17,441,871 (9/96).

Per Share Data ($)

(Year Ended Dec. 31)	1995	1994	1993	1992	1991	1990	1989	1988	1987	1986
Tangible Bk. Val.	1.73	1.41	1.18	0.93	0.77	0.67	0.65	0.66	0.74	0.78
Earnings	0.44	0.40	0.26	0.21	0.14	-0.02	-0.10	-0.07	-0.03	0.01
Dividends	0.52	0.43	0.32	0.22	0.20	0.05	Nil	Nil	Nil	Nil
Payout Ratio	118%	106%	127%	108%	147%	NM	Nil	Nil	Nil	Nil
Prices - High	10½	8½	8¼	5⅛	3¼	2⅝	3	2½	3⅜	2⅜
- Low	7⅛	6¾	4⅜	3	2⅜	1½	2¼	2⅛	1⅞	1⅜
P/E Ratio - High	24	21	32	24	23	NM	NM	NM	NM	NM
- Low	16	17	17	14	17	NM	NM	NM	NM	NM

Income Statement Analysis (Million $)

	1995	1994	1993	1992	1991	1990	1989	1988	1987	1986
Income Rental	NA	NA	NA	NA	NA	NA	NA	NA	NA	NA
Income Mortg.	NA	NA	NA	NA	NA	NA	NA	NA	NA	NA
Income Total	13.3	12.3	11.5	10.9	9.8	9.2	8.7	7.7	6.5	4.8
Expenses Gen.	NA	NA	NA	NA	NA	NA	NA	NA	NA	NA
Expenses Int.	NA	NA	NA	NA	NA	NA	NA	NA	NA	NA
Prov. for Losses	NA	NA	NA	NA	NA	NA	NA	NA	NA	NA
Depr.	2.1	NA	NA	NA	1.6	1.7	1.7	1.7	1.5	1.1
Net Inc.	2.5	2.1	1.4	1.0	0.6	-0.1	-0.4	-0.3	-0.1	0.0

Balance Sheet & Other Fin. Data (Million $)

	1995	1994	1993	1992	1991	1990	1989	1988	1987	1986
Cash	2.0	0.4	0.4	0.2	3.1	1.2	0.2	0.2	0.2	1.4
Total Assets	29.8	25.4	25.3	26.0	26.7	25.5	24.7	25.2	22.5	19.7
Real Estate Invest.	NA	NA	NA	NA	NA	NA	NA	NA	NA	NA
Loss Reserve	NA	NA	NA	NA	NA	NA	NA	NA	NA	NA
Net Invest.	NA	NA	NA	NA	NA	NA	NA	NA	NA	NA
ST Debt	NA	NA	NA	NA	NA	NA	NA	NA	NA	NA
Capitalization:										
Debt	NA	NA	NA	NA	NA	NA	NA	NA	NA	NA
Equity	NA	NA	NA	NA	NA	NA	NA	NA	NA	NA
Total	28.0	24.0	24.3	25.2	25.6	24.3	23.8	22.1	19.7	17.5
% Earn & Depr/Assets	NA	NA	NA	NA	NA	NA	NA	NA	NA	NA
Price Times Book Value:										
Hi	NA	NA	NA	NA	NA	NA	NA	NA	NA	NA
Low	NA	NA	NA	NA	NA	NA	NA	NA	NA	NA

Data as orig. reptd.; bef. results of disc. opers. and/or spec. items. Per share data adj. for stk. divs. as of ex-div. date. E-Estimated. NA-Not Available. NM-Not Meaningful. NR-Not Ranked.

Office—125 Wyckoff Rd., Eatontown, NJ 07724. **Tel**—(908) 389-3890. **Chrmn**—E. W. Landy. **Pres**—S. A. Landy. **VP-CFO**—Anna T. Chew. **Treas & Secy**—E. V. Bencivenga. **Investor Contact**—Rosemarie Faccone. **Dirs**—R. Anderson, E. V. Bencivenga, A. T. Chew, C. P. Kaempffer, E. W. Landy, S. A. Landy, R. H. Molke, E. Rothenberg, R. G. Sampson. **Transfer Agent & Registrar**—Mellon Securities Trust Co., NYC. **Incorporated**—in New Jersey 1968. **Empl**— 70. **S&P Analyst:** C.F.B.

WD-40 Company   5568

NASDAQ Symbol **WDFC**

In S&P SmallCap 600

16-FEB-97

Industry: Chemicals

Summary: This company, which is best known for its WD-40 product, also makes and markets 3-In-One oil.

Quantitative Evaluations		
Outlook (1 Lowest—5 Highest) • **NA**	Recent Price • 52½	Yield • 4.7%
Fair Value • **NA**	52 Wk Range • 53¼-41¾	12-Mo. P/E • 20.0

Risk • **Low**

Earn./Div. Rank • **B+**

Technical Eval. • **Bearish** since 10/96

Rel. Strength Rank (1 Lowest—99 Highest) • **55**

Insider Activity • **NA**

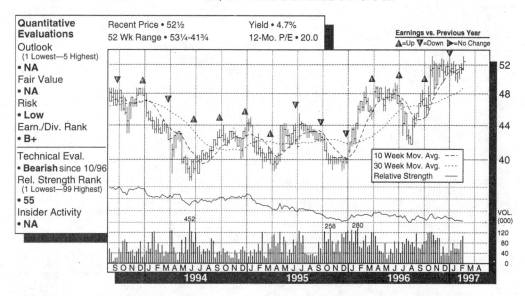

10 Week Mov. Avg. – – –
30 Week Mov. Avg. ·······
Relative Strength ——

Earnings vs. Previous Year
▲=Up ▼=Down ▷=No Change

Business Profile - 29-JAN-97

Net income was up 4.1% in FY 96 (Aug.), on a 12% increase in sales, as profitability was restricted by higher promotional expenses. WDFC sees the developing economies as an exceptional opportunity for future growth and plans to expand its presence in the international marketplace. In December 1995, the company acquired the 3-In-One Oil business (annual revenues of some $13 million) of Reckitt & Colman plc. WDFC has recently introduced T.A.L 5, an extra-strength lubricant that will be targeted for users in the manufacturing industries.

Operational Review - 29-JAN-97

Based on a brief report, revenues grew 2.4%, year to year, in the first quarter of FY 97 (Aug.). Margins narrowed, however, and pretax income dropped 21%, to $6,629,000, from $8,396,000. After taxes at 36.0%, versus 37.3%, net income fell 19%, to $4,240,000 ($0.55 a share) from $5.266,000 ($0.68).

Stock Performance - 14-FEB-97

In the past 30 trading days, WDFC's shares have increased 2%, compared to a 8% rise in the S&P 500. Average trading volume for the past five days was 21,200 shares, compared with the 40-day moving average of 13,246 shares.

Key Stock Statistics

Dividend Rate/Share	2.48	Shareholders	2,300
Shs. outstg. (M)	7.7	Market cap. (B)	$0.407
Avg. daily vol. (M)	0.015	Inst. holdings	32%
Tang. Bk. Value/Share	4.25		
Beta	0.53		

Value of $10,000 invested 5 years ago: $ 21,766

Fiscal Year Ending Aug. 31

	1997	1996	1995	1994	1993	1992
Revenues (Million $)						
1Q	28.27	27.61	29.77	28.88	24.60	21.90
2Q	—	35.08	29.39	27.56	29.37	28.00
3Q	—	34.23	29.92	29.46	29.31	21.60
4Q	—	33.99	27.70	26.27	25.70	28.50
Yr.	—	130.9	116.8	112.2	109.0	100.0
Earnings Per Share ($)						
1Q	0.55	0.68	0.72	0.68	0.64	0.47
2Q	—	0.77	0.73	-0.35	0.82	0.73
3Q	—	0.65	0.63	0.68	0.46	0.45
4Q	—	0.66	0.58	0.64	0.60	0.73
Yr.	—	2.76	2.66	1.65	2.52	2.38

Next earnings report expected: late March

Dividend Data (Dividends have been paid since 1973.)

Amount ($)	Date Decl.	Ex-Div. Date	Stock of Record	Payment Date
0.620	Mar. 25	Apr. 08	Apr. 10	Apr. 30 '96
0.620	Jun. 25	Jul. 08	Jul. 10	Jul. 30 '96
0.620	Sep. 24	Oct. 08	Oct. 10	Oct. 30 '96
0.620	Dec. 10	Jan. 08	Jan. 10	Jan. 30 '97

STANDARD
&POOR'S
STOCK REPORTS

WD-40 Company

5568

16-FEB-97

Business Summary - 29-JAN-97

After more than four decades of being identified with a single petroleum-based product, WD-40, this company has dramatically shifted its corporate identity and strategy.

With the acquisition of the 3-IN-ONE Oil brand in December 1995, and with the introduction of its new T.A.L 5 brand in early FY 97, WDFC has become a company that will be identified with three strong products.

The company's goal is to dominate the entire category of lubrication products by combining the smaller niche markets targeted by 3-IN-ONE Oil and T.A.L 5 with the broad-based market held by the WD-40 brand.

The product, WD-40, has five basic functions: acting as a cleaner, a lubricant, a rust preventative, a penetrant and a moisture displacer. It has a wide variety of uses in the home and in industrial applications, as well as in the protection of sporting goods, marine and automotive equipment. It is sold (primarily in aerosol cans) through chain stores, automotive parts outlets, hardware and sporting goods stores, and industrial distributors and suppliers.

3-IN-ONE Oil is a drip oil lubricant that is sold through the same distribution channels as the WD-40 brand. The key to its success is the lubrication control it gives consumers and industrial users, allowing precise application for small mechanisms and assemblies, tool maintenance and threads on screws and bolts. As a

low-cost, entry-level lubricant, it has excellent growth potential in the developing nations of Eastern Europe, Latin America and Asia.

The company developed T.A.L 5 (which stands for "Triple Additive Lubricant/ 5 functions) as an extra-strength synthetic spray lubricant for heavy-duty applications. The product resists breakdown due to corrosion, friction, temperature, load and motion. It can be applied to rubber, metal or plastic and will provide long-lasting strength and durability. WDFC will target T.A.L 5 at specialized users in the trades and general manufacturing industries.

The new product lineup gives the WD-40 Company the opportunity to pursue a comprehensive and targeted marketing strategy. The acquisition of the 3-IN-ONE Oil brand (which, along with T.A.L 5, will be introduced into the company's existing distribution system) provides WDFC with a built-in distribution network in 17 countries, including several markets in which the WD-40 product has not been sold.

With the ongoing consolidation in the marketplace, many of the major retailers are aggressively pursuing additional trade allowances. While these demands could produce a long-term negative impact on both sales and profits, the company believes that the new WDFC is in an excellent position to achieve future growth.

Capitalization

Long Term Debt: $2,427,000 (8/96).

Per Share Data ($)

(Year Ended Aug. 31)	1996	1995	1994	1993	1992	1991	1990	1989	1988	1987
Tangible Bk. Val.	4.25	5.78	5.47	5.96	5.91	5.38	5.16	5.01	4.84	4.36
Cash Flow	3.00	2.79	1.76	2.60	2.45	2.09	2.11	2.15	2.09	1.50
Earnings	2.76	2.66	1.65	2.52	2.38	2.02	2.05	2.08	2.06	1.46
Dividends	2.48	2.42	2.30	2.30	2.16	1.72	2.02	1.90	1.63	1.47
Payout Ratio	90%	91%	139%	91%	91%	85%	99%	91%	79%	100%
Prices - High	49½	45½	48	48¾	50	34	34½	38¼	33¼	46¼
- Low	40½	38¾	37¾	43	30¼	23¾	23½	30½	24½	22¾
P/E Ratio - High	18	17	29	19	21	17	17	18	16	32
- Low	15	15	23	17	13	12	11	15	12	16

Income Statement Analysis (Million $)

	1996	1995	1994	1993	1992	1991	1990	1989	1988	1987
Revs.	131	117	112	109	100	89.8	91.0	83.9	80.0	70.9
Oper. Inc.	34.4	32.5	33.2	33.6	28.8	24.2	23.8	24.3	23.4	20.9
Depr.	1.8	1.0	0.8	0.6	0.6	0.5	0.5	0.4	0.2	0.2
Int. Exp.	NA	NA	NA	Nil	Nil	Nil	Nil	Nil	Nil	Nil
Pretax Inc.	33.4	32.7	20.5	31.7	29.5	25.1	25.2	25.9	25.4	20.7
Eff. Tax Rate	36%	37%	38%	39%	39%	39%	39%	39%	39%	47%
Net Inc.	21.3	20.5	12.7	19.3	18.1	15.3	15.5	15.8	15.5	11.0

Balance Sheet & Other Fin. Data (Million $)

	1996	1995	1994	1993	1992	1991	1990	1989	1988	1987
Cash	6.5	24.3	22.7	21.9	19.1	24.9	21.6	22.4	21.6	18.0
Curr. Assets	37.6	49.6	45.5	43.2	41.4	43.9	43.2	41.1	40.7	36.7
Total Assets	61.7	59.6	54.9	58.8	53.5	47.8	46.8	44.6	43.3	39.1
Curr. Liab.	11.0	11.1	8.2	9.7	8.2	6.9	7.6	6.7	6.6	6.2
LT Debt	2.4	3.1	3.8	2.7	Nil	Nil	Nil	Nil	Nil	Nil
Common Eqty.	47.2	44.5	42.1	45.7	45.2	40.7	39.0	37.8	36.5	32.8
Total Cap.	49.7	47.6	45.9	48.3	45.3	40.8	39.2	38.0	36.7	33.0
Cap. Exp.	1.4	1.4	0.8	1.4	0.7	1.1	0.4	1.4	0.4	0.4
Cash Flow	23.1	21.4	13.5	19.9	18.6	15.8	16.0	16.2	15.7	11.3
Curr. Ratio	3.4	4.5	5.6	4.4	5.1	6.3	5.7	6.1	6.2	6.0
% LT Debt of Cap.	5.2	6.6	8.3	5.5	Nil	Nil	Nil	Nil	Nil	Nil
% Net Inc.of Revs.	16.3	17.5	11.3	17.7	18.1	17.0	17.0	18.8	19.4	15.5
% Ret. on Assets	35.1	35.7	22.3	34.4	35.5	32.4	33.9	35.8	37.7	28.3
% Ret. on Equity	46.5	47.2	28.9	42.5	41.8	38.4	40.4	42.4	44.8	33.7

Data as orig. reptd.; bef. results of disc. opers. and/or spec. items. Per share data adj. for stk. divs. as of ex-div. date. E-Estimated. NA-Not Available. NM-Not Meaningful. NR-Not Ranked.

Office—1061 Cudahy Place, San Diego, CA 92110. **Tel**—(619) 275-1400. **Chrmn**—J. S. Barry. **Pres, CEO & Investor Contact**—Gerald C. Schleif. **Secy**—H. F. Harmsen. **Treas**—P. E. Williams. **Dirs**—J. S. Barry, M. L. Crivello, D. W. Derbes, H. F. Harmsen, J. L. Heckel, M. L. Roulette, G. C. Schleif, C. F. Sehnert, E. J. Walsh. **Transfer Agent & Registrar**—Harris Trust Co. of California, Los Angeles. **Incorporated**—in California in 1953. **Empl**—149. **S&P Analyst:** Justin McCann

18-FEB-97

Industry: Real Estate Investment Trust

Summary: The portfolio of this real estate investment trust consists primarily of shopping centers, with most of the remainder industrial properties.

S&P Opinion: Accumulate (★★★★)

Recent Price • 42¾	Yield • 5.8%
52 Wk Range • 44¾-34¼	12-Mo. P/E • 21.5

Quantitative Evaluations

Outlook (1 Lowest—5 Highest)
• **NA**

Fair Value
• **NA**

Risk
• **Low**

Earn./Div. Rank
• **NR**

Technical Eval.
• **Bearish** since 1/97

Rel. Strength Rank (1 Lowest—99 Highest)
• **57**

Insider Activity
• **NA**

Earnings vs. Previous Year
▲=Up ▼=Down ▶=No Change

10 Week Mov. Avg. – – –
30 Week Mov. Avg. · · · ·
Relative Strength —

Overview - 18-FEB-97

Funds from operations (the most appropriate measure of a REIT's operating performance) is expected to grow in 1997 to about $3.25 a share versus the $3.05 expected for 1996 (FFO for 1995 was $2.82 a share). Weingarten should expand its shopping center portfolio by 1.5 million square feet, mainly through the acquisition of new centers in the Southwest. Many of these centers will be acquired at very attractive initial yields. To a lesser extent, square footage will be increased through expansion of existing centers, which were built in phases to reduce leasing risk. Rental revenues could be aided by a stronger economy in the Houston area, the rollover of old leases to market rates, and step-up clauses in certain leases. Occupancy levels will be flat to slightly improved from 92.5% at the end of September 1996. Higher interest costs are anticipated as a result of WRI's objective of extending the maturities on its borrowings.

Valuation - 18-FEB-97

The shares are an attractive total-return commitment for the next six to 12 months. The stock's dividend yield is more than twice that of the S&P 500, and small dividend increases are likely. Secondly, Weingarten is one of the nation's oldest and most distinguished REITs. It has steadily increased funds from operations since 1991. Continued modest but steady growth in earnings and cash flow over the long term is anticipated, based primarily on expansion of the shopping center portfolio and the trust's access to capital at attractive rates. Third, finances are extremely strong. Funds from operations cover interest costs by a factor of more than four to one. Finally, officers and trustees own a large block of the stock.

Key Stock Statistics

S&P EPS Est. 1996	2.10	Tang. Bk. Value/Share	15.24
P/E on S&P Est. 1996	20.4	Beta	0.18
S&P EPS Est. 1997	2.15	Shareholders	2,800
Dividend Rate/Share	2.48	Market cap. (B)	$ 1.1
Shs. outstg. (M)	26.6	Inst. holdings	42%
Avg. daily vol. (M)	0.037		

Value of $10,000 invested 5 years ago: $ 17,364

Fiscal Year Ending Dec. 31

	1996	1995	1994	1993	1992	1991
Revenues (Million $)						
1Q	36.76	32.09	28.89	24.21	21.58	19.92
2Q	37.18	32.66	29.42	25.01	22.50	20.45
3Q	37.96	33.89	31.13	26.84	22.77	21.00
4Q	—	35.56	31.36	27.23	23.12	21.27
Yr.	—	134.2	120.8	103.3	89.96	82.64
Earnings Per Share ($)						
1Q	0.48	0.43	0.41	0.38	0.28	0.26
2Q	0.48	0.41	0.39	0.34	0.37	0.26
3Q	0.61	0.42	0.45	0.37	0.28	0.28
4Q	E0.53	0.42	0.42	0.41	0.28	0.28
Yr.	E2.10	1.69	1.67	1.50	1.21	1.08

Next earnings report expected: late February

Dividend Data (Dividends have been paid since 1958.)

Amount ($)	Date Decl.	Ex-Div. Date	Stock of Record	Payment Date
0.620	Feb. 27	Mar. 04	Mar. 06	Mar. 15 '96
0.620	May. 03	May. 22	May. 24	Jun. 13 '96
0.620	Jul. 30	Aug. 27	Aug. 29	Sep. 13 '96
0.620	Oct. 30	Nov. 27	Dec. 02	Dec. 13 '96

A Division of The McGraw-Hill Companies

Business Summary - 18-FEB-97

Weingarten Realty is an equity-based real estate investment trust focused primarily on the development, acquisition and long-term ownership of anchored neighborhood and community shopping centers in the Southwest. At the end of 1995, the company's portfolio of 171 income-producing properties with 18.0 million square feet in 10 states was as follows:

	1995
Anchored shopping centers	151
Industrial properties	17
Multifamily residential	2
Office	1

Of the trust's 171 developed properties, 133 were in Texas (including 84 in Houston and Harris County). Remaining properties were in Louisiana (10), Arizona (six), Arkansas (six), New Mexico (five), Oklahoma (four), Nevada (four) and Kansas, Maine and Tennesee (one each). WRI has more than 2,900 leases and 2,200 different tenants.

Leases for WRI's properties range from less than a year for smaller spaces to more than 25 years for larger tenants; leases generally include minimum lease payments and contingent rentals for payment of taxes, insurance and maintenance and for an amount based on a percentage of the tenant's sales. Revenues and occupancy rates are affected by the square footage leased and the conditions of the markets in which the trust operates. Results of operations are also significantly affected by property operating expenses, cost of capital and acquisitions. Acquisitions and new developments at cost in 1995 totaled $115 million, up from $100.5 million in 1994.

The occupancy rate at year-end 1995 was 92%, unchanged from a year earlier. During 1995, the company completed 522 renewals on leases comprising over 1.5 million sq. ft. an an average rental rate increase of 7.4%. Net of capital costs for tenant improvements, the increase averaged 4.4%.

Important Developments

Oct. '96—Weingarten attributed its improved results for the three and nine months ended September 30, 1996, to property acquisitions, new development, and increases in rental rates on new leases or renewals. Funds from operations in the third quarter amounted to $0.78 a share, compared with $0.72 in the year-earlier quarter.

Capitalization

Total Debt: $326,410,000 (9/96).
Shares of Beneficial Interest: 26,545,424 shs. ($0.03 par).
Officers and trustees own or control 16%.

Per Share Data ($)

(Year Ended Dec. 31)	1995	1994	1993	1992	1991	1990	1989	1988	1987	1986
Tangible Bk. Val.	26.81	15.41	15.87	9.84	7.35	8.04	6.42	7.20	7.31	7.61
Earnings	1.69	1.67	1.50	1.21	1.08	1.01	0.97	1.53	1.28	1.27
Dividends	2.40	2.28	2.16	2.04	1.92	1.88	1.76	1.68	1.60	1.56
Payout Ratio	142%	137%	144%	169%	178%	186%	181%	110%	125%	123%
Prices - High	38½	40½	45¼	38	32⅞	31⅝	32½	28¼	28⅜	25
- Low	33⅜	32¾	36⅜	29½	24⅛	22½	25⅛	22⅜	18½	19½
P/E Ratio - High	23	24	30	31	30	31	34	4	22	20
- Low	20	20	24	24	22	22	26	3	14	15

Income Statement Analysis (Million $)

	1995	1994	1993	1992	1991	1990	1989	1988	1987	1986
Income Rental	125	112	94.2	83.2	74.5	65.4	59.6	54.0	50.8	46.3
Income Mortg.	Nil	Nil	Nil	Nil	NA	NA	NA	NA	NA	NA
Income Total	134	121	103	90.0	82.6	76.9	68.0	64.8	61.2	55.6
Expenses Gen.	72.7	66.1	58.6	51.8	45.1	40.8	37.0	34.7	31.6	28.5
Expenses Int.	16.7	10.7	10.0	18.7	20.2	19.9	17.4	13.2	12.3	9.7
Prov. for Losses	Nil	Nil	Nil	Nil	Nil	Nil	Nil	Nil	Nil	Nil
Depr.	30.1	26.8	23.4	21.3	19.0	17.7	15.9	14.0	12.7	10.9
Net Inc.	44.8	43.8	36.2	21.2	18.0	16.5	13.6	21.3	17.7	17.5

Balance Sheet & Other Fin. Data (Million $)

	1995	1994	1993	1992	1991	1990	1989	1988	1987	1986
Cash	3.4	3.3	3.2	1.1	2.1	1.5	0.6	0.5	5.1	6.7
Total Assets	735	682	602	472	440	416	365	350	333	301
Real Estate Invest.	859	783	679	587	520	470	438	415	391	351
Loss Reserve	Nil	Nil	Nil	Nil	Nil	Nil	Nil	Nil	Nil	Nil
Net Invest.	642	592	511	436	386	352	335	325	307	279
ST Debt	1.9	9.4	0.8	1.0	1.7	12.4	9.4	7.1	10.0	3.2
Capitalization:										
Debt	287	230	147	243	279	237	248	206	186	160
Equity	412	423	427	205	138	148	90.0	101	101	105
Total	699	653	574	448	417	385	338	307	287	265
% Earn & Depr/Assets	10.6	11.0	11.1	9.3	8.6	8.8	8.5	10.4	9.6	9.9
Price Times Book Value:										
Hi	1.4	2.6	2.9	3.9	4.5	3.9	5.1	3.9	3.9	3.3
Low	1.2	2.1	2.3	3.0	3.3	2.8	3.9	3.1	2.5	2.6

Data as orig. reptd.; bef. results of disc. opers. and/or spec. items. Per share data adj. for stk. divs. as of ex-div. date. E-Estimated. NA-Not Available. NM-Not Meaningful. NR-Not Ranked.

Office—2600 Citadel Plaza Drive, P.O. Box 924133, Houston, TX 77292-4133. **Tel**—(713) 866-6000. **Fax**—(713) 866-6049. **E-Mail**—ir@weingarten.com **Website**—http://www.weingarten.com **Chrmn & CEO**—S. Alexander. **Pres & COO**—M. Debrovner. **VP & CFO**—J. W. Robertson Jr. **VP, Secy & Investor Contact**—M. Candace DuFour. **Trustees**—A. M. Alexander, S. Alexander, M. Debrovner, M. A. Dow, S. A. Lasher, J. W. Robertson Jr., D. W. Schnitzer, M. J. Shapiro, J. T. Trotter. **Transfer Agent & Registrar**—Society National Bank, Houston. **Incorporated**—in Texas in 1984; reorganized as a REIT in 1988. **Empl**— 151. **S&P Analyst:** Paul L. Huberman, CFA

Wisconsin Energy 2492

NYSE Symbol **WEC**

In S&P MidCap 400

16-FEB-97

Industry: Util.-Diversified

Summary: A merger of this electric and gas utility holding company and Northern States Power Co., forming a new company, Primergy Corp., is expected to be completed in early 1997.

S&P Opinion: Hold (★★★)

Recent Price • 25½
52 Wk Range • 30¾-25⅛

Yield • 6.0%
12-Mo. P/E • 12.9

Quantitative Evaluations

Outlook
(1 Lowest—5 Highest)
• **2**

Fair Value
• **23⅜**

Risk
• **Low**

Earn./Div. Rank
• **A-**

Technical Eval.
• **Bullish** since 11/96

Rel. Strength Rank
(1 Lowest—99 Highest)
• **22**

Insider Activity
• **NA**

Earnings vs. Previous Year
▲=Up ▼=Down ▶=No Change

10 Week Mov. Avg. - - -
30 Week Mov. Avg. ....
Relative Strength —

VOL. (000)

2968   2556   3925

1200
800
400
0

S O N D J F M A M J J A S O N D J F M A M J J A S O N D J F M A M J J A S O N D J F M A
1994   1995   1996   1997

Overview - 12-FEB-97

Shareholders should benefit from a strengthened position in the industry after a planned merger with Northern States Power results in a new holding company, Primergy Corp. The merger, which is expected to be completed near the end of the first quarter of 1997, would create the nation's tenth largest investor-owned utility. Resulting cost savings are expected to reach $2 billion over 10 years, although much of that amount will be realized in the second five-year period. However, the savings are expected to be shared equally between shareholders and ratepayers. Excluding the planned merger, we expect earnings in 1997 and beyond to benefit from higher sales of electricity and gas, reflecting steady economic growth in WEC's service territory. As of September 30, 1996, long term debt was 41% of total capital, below the industry average.

Valuation - 12-FEB-97

Although the shares fell 12% in 1996, compared to a 5% decline for the S&P Index of Electric Companies, we continue to recommend holding the stock. While an uncertain interest rate environment has tempered investor enthusiasm for most electric utility shares, WEC was also impacted by the expected decline in 1996 earnings. More recently, the stock has been weakened by delays in the regulatory proceedings on the proposed merger with Northern States Power (NSP). Although the delay has created a degree of uncertainty, we still expect to see the merger completed by either the end of the first quarter or at some point in the second quarter. While we believe the combined company (Primergy) will benefit from a generally favorable regulatory climate and an improved competitive position, we see the shares producing only a modest total return over the near term.

Key Stock Statistics

S&P EPS Est. 1997	2.10	Tang. Bk. Value/Share	17.23
P/E on S&P Est. 1997	12.1	Beta	0.48
Dividend Rate/Share	1.52	Shareholders	300
Shs. outstg. (M)	111.3	Market cap. (B)	$ 2.8
Avg. daily vol. (M)	0.435	Inst. holdings	37%

Value of $10,000 invested 5 years ago: $ 12,680

Fiscal Year Ending Dec. 31

	1996	1995	1994	1993	1992	1991
Revenues (Million $)						
1Q	495.5	471.1	509.7	443.3	422.0	418.0
2Q	401.7	405.1	400.3	375.5	357.0	355.0
3Q	398.8	426.4	400.5	393.2	358.0	364.0
4Q	477.9	467.9	431.7	431.7	413.9	402.0
Yr.	1,774	1,770	1,742	1,644	1,552	1,539
Earnings Per Share ($)						
1Q	0.57	0.57	0.21	0.56	0.53	0.54
2Q	0.41	0.47	0.40	0.28	0.30	0.37
3Q	0.48	0.53	0.48	0.46	0.37	0.50
4Q	0.51	0.56	0.58	0.52	0.46	0.48
Yr.	1.97	2.13	1.67	1.81	1.67	1.87

Next earnings report expected: early May

Dividend Data (Dividends have been paid since 1939.)

Amount ($)	Date Decl.	Ex-Div. Date	Stock of Record	Payment Date
0.380	Apr. 25	May. 09	May. 13	Jun. 03 '96
0.380	Jul. 24	Aug. 09	Aug. 13	Sep. 03 '96
0.380	Nov. 30	Nov. 08	Nov. 13	Dec. 02 '96
0.380	Jan. 29	Feb. 11	Feb. 13	Mar. 03 '97

A Division of The McGraw·Hill Companies

Business Summary - 12-FEB-97

Wisconsin Energy is the holding company for Wisconsin Electric Power, which supplies electricity (81% of 1995 revenues), gas (18%) and steam service (1%) in Milwaukee, northern Wisconsin and the Upper Peninsula of Michigan. It also owns five nonregulated businesses. WEC's Wisconsin Natural Gas subsidiary was merged into Wisconsin Electric Power effective January 1, 1996. Electric revenues by customer class in recent years were:

	1995	1994	1993	1992
Residential	36%	36%	35%	34%
Small comm'l & ind'l	30%	30%	29%	29%
Large comm'l & ind'l	29%	29%	28%	30%
Other	5%	5%	8%	7%

During 1995, 70% of generating capability was derived from coal, 27% from nuclear, 2% hydro and 1% from other sources. WEC's nuclear capacity consists of the two-unit Point Beach nuclear station. Peak load in 1995 was 5,368 mw, and capability at peak totaled 5,619 mw, for a capacity margin of 4.4%. Gas deliveries in 1995 totaled 886,729,000 therms, versus 811,219,000 therms in 1994, as adjusted for the merger of Wisconsin Southern Gas Co. in early 1994. WEC anticipates electric kilowatt-hour sales growth at a compound annual rate of 1.1% over the next five years; growth in natural gas therm deliveries is put at about 2.1% compounded annually over the same period.

Capital outlays over the last three years were $1.1 billion, including $932 million of construction expenditures for new or improved facilities, including the completion of the Paris Generating Station, a four-unit, 300 mw combustion turbine facility in the summer of 1995. Conservation spending was $54 million; payments to a trust for eventual decommissioning of the Point Beach Nuclear Plant totaled $32 million.

In September 1995, shareholders approved a merger with NYSE-listed Northern States Power Co. (NSP) to form a new holding company, Primergy Corp. Company shareholders would receive one Primergy common share for each WEC share. The transaction is expected to be completed in January 1997, subject to regulatory approval.

Important Developments

Jan. '97—The company said the 7.5% decline in 1996 EPS reflected the $42.5 million rate decrease ordered by the Public Service Commission of Wisconsin, as well as a 36% drop in cooling degree days in the summer that was only partially offset by a 9.3% increase in heating degree days in the winter.

Capitalization

Long Term Debt: $1,330,600,000 (9/96).
Subsid. Preferred Stock: $30,450,000.

Per Share Data ($) (Year Ended Dec. 31)	1996	1995	1994	1993	1992	1991	1990	1989	1988	1987
Tangible Bk. Val.	NA	16.89	15.81	15.67	14.78	14.25	13.63	13.41	12.56	11.71
Earnings	1.97	2.13	1.67	1.81	1.67	1.87	1.85	1.92	1.82	1.70
Dividends	1.51	1.45	1.40	1.34	1.29	1.22	1.16	1.09	1.01	0.94
Payout Ratio	77%	68%	84%	74%	77%	65%	63%	57%	55%	55%
Prices - High	32	30⅞	27½	29⅜	28½	26½	21¾	21½	18⅝	19¼
- Low	26	25¾	23⅛	24¾	23¾	20	17¾	16¾	15	14
P/E Ratio - High	16	14	16	16	17	14	12	11	10	11
- Low	13	12	14	14	14	11	10	9	8	8
Income Statement Analysis (Million $)										
Revs.	NA	1,770	1,742	1,644	1,552	1,539	1,442	1,493	1,541	1,365
Depr.	NA	184	178	165	163	147	145	154	146	139
Maint.	NA	112	125	155	150	142	134	150	171	139
Fxd. Chgs. Cov.	NA	4.1	3.6	3.7	3.7	4.2	4.3	4.2	3.9	4.0
Constr. Credits	NA	8.9	10.1	14.7	12.1	13.4	12.2	9.1	5.4	3.4
Eff. Tax Rate	NA	37%	35%	34%	34%	34%	35%	34%	34%	41%
Net Inc.	NA	234	181	188	170	189	187	194	183	170
Balance Sheet & Other Fin. Data (Million $)										
Gross Prop.	NA	5,199	5,019	4,773	4,463	4,170	3,977	3,805	3,676	3,598
Cap. Exp.	NA	272	322	388	344	268	238	230	180	401
Net Prop.	NA	2,911	2,941	2,809	2,629	2,466	2,374	2,060	2,025	2,040
Capitalization:										
LT Debt	NA	1,368	1,284	1,286	1,210	1,094	990	1,004	1,044	849
% LT Debt	NA	42	42	43	42	41	40	41	44	41
Pfd.	NA	30.0	30.0	36.0	98.0	100	100	100	100	100
% Pfd.	NA	0.90	1.00	1.20	3.50	3.80	4.10	4.20	4.20	4.80
Common	NA	1,871	1,745	1,651	1,543	1,450	1,384	1,314	1,230	1,128
% Common	NA	57	57	56	54	55	56	54	52	54
Total Cap.	NA	3,843	3,628	3,547	3,402	3,180	3,003	2,585	2,545	2,227
Oper. Ratio	NA	81.4	85.0	84.0	84.6	83.7	83.3	82.3	83.1	81.5
% Earn. on Net Prop.	NA	11.2	9.1	9.7	9.4	10.4	10.3	12.9	12.8	13.1
% Ret. on Revs.	NA	13.2	10.4	11.5	10.9	12.3	12.9	13.0	11.9	12.4
% Ret. On Invest.Cap	NA	9.3	8.1	8.5	8.1	9.1	9.3	11.1	11.4	11.5
% Return On Com.Eqty	NA	12.9	10.6	11.8	11.3	13.4	13.8	15.2	15.5	15.5

Data as orig. reptd.; bef. results of disc opers. and/or spec. items. Per share data adj. for stk. divs. as of ex-div. date. E-Estimated. NA-Not Available. NM-Not Meaningful. NR-Not Ranked.

Office—231 West Michigan St. (P.O. Box 2949), Milwaukee, WI 53201. **Tel**—(414) 221-2345. **Website**—http://www.wisenergy.com **Chrmn, Pres & CEO**—R. A. Abdoo. **VP & Secy**—A. M. Brady. **Treas & CFO**—C. H. Baker. **Investor Contact**—Jim Schubilske (414-221-32596). **Dirs**—R. A. Abdoo, J. F. Ahearne, J. F. Bergstrom, J. W. Boston, R. A. Cornog, R. R. Grigg, Jr., G. B. Johnson, F. P. Stratton, Jr., J. G. Udell. **Transfer Agent & Registrar**—First National Bank of Boston. **Incorporated**—in Wisconsin in 1896; reincorporated in Wisconsin in 1986. **Empl**— 4,514. **S&P Analyst:** Justin McCann

To purchase the latest version of any report in this book, for delivery by fax or mail, call:

S&P Reports On-Demand at 1-800-292-0808

To purchase a report from the Internet, visit:

http://www.stockinfo.standardpoor.com.